The Tyndale Old Testament Commentaries

General Editor:
PROFESSOR D. J. WISEMAN, O.B.E., M.A., D. Lit., F.B.A., F.S.A.

ISAIAH

To

Ronald Inchley

Frank Entwistle

Donald Wiseman

G. T. Manley (*in memoriam*)

and to
Derek Kidner

with affection, respect
and gratitude

ISAIAH

AN INTRODUCTION AND COMMENTARY

by

ALEC MOTYER M.A., B.D., D.D.
formerly Principal of Trinity College, Bristol

INTER-VARSITY PRESS

InterVarsity Press, USA
P.O. Box 1400, Downers Grove, IL 60515, USA
World Wide Web: www.ivpress.com
E-mail: mail@ivpress.com
Inter-Varsity Press, England
38 De Montfort Street, Leicester LE1 7GP, England

InterVarsity Press®, U.S.A., is the book-publishing division of InterVarsity Christian Fellowship/USA®, a student movement active on campus at hundreds of universities, colleges and schools of nursing in the United States of America, and a member movement of the International Fellowship of Evangelical Students. For information about local and regional activities, write Public Relations Dept., InterVarsity Christian Fellowship/USA, 6400 Schroeder Rd., P.O. Box 7895, Madison, WI 53707-7895.

Inter-Varsity Press, England, is the book-publishing division of the Universities and Colleges Christian Fellowship (formerly the Inter-Varsity Fellowship), a student movement linking Christian Unions in universities and colleges throughout the United Kingdom and the Republic of Ireland, and a member movement of the International Fellowship of Evangelical Students. For information about local and national activities write to UCCF, 38 De Montfort Street, Leicester LE1 7GP.

UK ISBN 0-85111-973-5 (paperback)

USA ISBN 0-8308-1434-5 (hardback)

USA ISBN 0-87784-244-2 (paperback)

USA ISBN 0-87784-880-7 (set of Tyndale Old Testament Commentaries, hardback)

USA ISBN 0-87784-280-9 (set of Tyndale Old Testament Commentaries, paperback)

Text set in Great Britain

Printed in the United States of America

Library of Congress Cataloging-in-Publication Data

Motyer, J. A.
    Isaiah: an introduction :& commentary/ J. Alec Motyer.
        p.   cm.—(Tyndale Old Testament commentaries: 18)
    Includes bibliographical references.
    ISBN 0-8308-1434-5 (cloth: alk. paper).—ISBN (invalid)
083082442 (pbk.: alk. paper)
    1. Bible.   O.T. Isaiah—Commentaries.   I. Title.   II. Series.
    BS1515.3.M66   1999
    224'.107—dc21   *99-21941*

CIP

British Library Cataloguing in Publication Data

A catalogue record for this book is available from the British Library.

18	*17*	*16*	*15*	*14*	*13*	*12*	*11*	*10*	*9*	*8*	*7*	*6*	*5*	*4*	*3*	*2*	*1*
13	*12*	*11*	*10*	*09*	*08*	*07*	*06*	*05*	*04*	*03*	*02*	*01*	*00*	*99*			

GENERAL PREFACE

With this publication of *Isaiah*, the series of Tyndale Old Testament Commentaries draws to its conclusion. The aim throughout has been to provide the serious Bible reader with handy, up-to-date commentaries with the primary emphasis on the exegesis and meaning of the text. At the same time the series has sought to face major problems raised by critics of each book. Each author has been left to make his or her own contribution to the evangelical understanding and faith.

In 1993 Inter-Varsity Press published a major commentary, *The Prophecy of Isaiah*, by Dr Motyer. It was hailed as a major contribution, and the author's earlier invitation to contribute to the Tyndale series was renewed. The series rightly waited for this version. While it contains the essence of his earlier work and retains the earlier's structure and textual divisions, much is new and original in this concluding volume.

Isaiah is a book of soaring spiritual insight and stirring declaration of the promises of God. Indeed, it is sometimes known as 'the fifth gospel'. So perhaps it is appropriate that, despite his undoubted scholarship, it is Alec Motyer's preacher's heart that is most obviously at work in this commentary, bringing relevant application of the book to today's Christian church and reader.

In the Old Testament in particular no single English translation is adequate to reflect the original text. The version on which this commentary is based is the New International Version, but other translations are referred to as well, and on occasion the author supplies his own. Where necessary, words are transliterated in order to help the reader who is unfamiliar with Hebrew to identify the precise word under discussion. It is assumed throughout that the reader will have ready access to at least one reliable rendering of the Bible in English.

Interest in the meaning and message of the Old Testament continues undiminished, and it is hoped that this series will thus further the systematic study of the revelation of God and his will and ways as seen in these records. It is the prayer of the editor and publisher, as of the authors, that these books will help many to understand, and to respond to, the Word of God today.

D. J. WISEMAN

CONTENTS

AUTHOR'S PREFACE

I have set out to provide a 'reader's commentary' on Isaiah – a companion to daily Bible reading – and I believe that those who use it this way will reap the largest rewards from it. This is not to say that it cannot be used to look up 'spot' verses or passages, for I have done my best not to evade difficulties and, in every such place, to ask what a reader, Bible in hand, would find most useful to know.

In 1993 IVP were kind enough to publish my larger commentary, *The Prophecy of Isaiah*, and it is only fair to say how this present work compares with that. First, I have felt comfortable in using again the structured outline of Isaiah which I worked out for the earlier book. Some reviewers criticized this or that aspect of my analysis, but, while I promise them that I have pondered what they wrote, they have not persuaded me to change my mind. Isaiah does not always stop to put down markers for us, and we come to his precious text to do the best we can. I do not see, for example, that I have opted for anything outrageous in dividing the book after chapter 37 rather than 39. R. E. Clements, whose approach to Isaiah is very far from mine, notes that 'a redactor has quite consciously sought to use these narratives [*i.e.* chs. 36 – 39] to form a bridge between the "Assyrian" background of chs. 1 – 35 and the "Babylonian" background of chs. 40 – 66, with ch. 39 forming a key transition unit' (*Isaiah 1 – 39*, New Century Bible [Eerdmans/Marshalls, 1980], p. 277). I have simply made the 'bridge' into a 'border-crossing'.

Secondly, the majority of the explanatory and expository work in this commentary is certainly new in expression and quite considerably new in content. This is as it should be when we are dealing with the inexhaustible treasure of God's Word. I have only very occasionally consciously quoted from *The Prophecy of Isaiah*.

As ever, I owe a huge debt to Inter-Varsity Press and its ceaselessly kind director and editors. Even I cannot remember quite when it was that George Manley invited me to contribute an

Isaiah commentary to the Tyndale series, so long ago is it! I was both surprised and delighted when, having presented them with the larger commentary (for which they had not asked!), and thinking that surely my chance with the Tyndale series (sadly, like much else in life) had been frittered away, Frank Entwistle renewed the invitation. He, like Ronald Inchley before him, has been a gracious and more than patient friend. It is in order to enhance my book that I dedicate it to these three, and to the present editor of the Tyndale Old Testament Commentaries, men to whom we owe so much.

Originally, the plan was for a two-volume commentary and, to my delight, Derek Kidner had responded positively to my desire to dedicate volume two to him. I am certainly not going to allow the absorption of volume two (Is. 38 – 66) into volume one to deprive me of the pleasure and the honour of having his name associated with my book – even at the expense of overloading the now single dedicatory page! I count it a great privilege to forge this small link with one who is both a great friend and a far greater and more sensitive contributor than I to the art of Old Testament commentary.

The completion of the Old Testament Tyndale series, begun with Derek Kidner's delightful commentary on *Proverbs* in 1964, has been a long time coming and the fault is considerably mine. Just as God has been pleased to use individual volumes to his own glory in helping many readers to a fuller and deeper knowledge of his precious Word, may he now be pleased even more to use the completed series to that same supreme end!

Bishopsteignton   ALEC MOTYER
1998

CHIEF ABBREVIATIONS

AV	Authorized Version.
BDB	F. Brown, S. R. Driver and C. A. Briggs, *Hebrew and English Lexicon of the Old Testament* (OUP, 1929).
BHS	R. Elliger (ed.), *Biblia Hebraica Stuttgartensia* (Wurtembergische Bibelanstalt, 1968).
GKC	E. Kautzsch and A. E. Cowley (eds.), *Gesenius' Hebrew Grammar* (OUP, 1910).
KB	L. Koehler and W. Baumgartner, *Lexicon in Veteris Testamenti Libros* (Brill, 1958).
LXX	Septuagint (Greek version of the Old Testament).
MT	Masoretic Text (Hebrew Bible).
NASB	New American Standard Bible.
NBC	D. A. Carson, R. T. France, J. A. Motyer and G. J. Wenham (eds.), *New Bible Commentary, 21st Century Edition* (IVP, 1994).
NBCR	D. Guthrie, J. A. Motyer, A. M. Stibbs and D. J. Wiseman (eds.), *New Bible Commentary Revised* (IVP, 1970).
NBD	I. H. Marshall, A. R. Millard, J. I. Packer and D. J. Wiseman (eds.), *New Bible Dictionary*, 3rd ed. (IVP, 1996).
NIV	New International Version.
NKJV	New King James Version.
Q^a	The St Mark's Isaiah Scroll, Qumran.
RSV	Revised Standard Version.
RV	Revised Version.

NOTES

Bible references throughout are to the 1984 edition of the New International Version, unless indicated otherwise. The lower-case letters a, b, c, *etc.*, refer to the lines within the verse in question.

The Divine Name. In the Hebrew Old Testament, the personal name for the God of Israel was denoted by four Hebrew consonants, usually understood as expressing the form *Yahweh*. A strange scruple has, for the most part, prevented translators of the English Bible from using the Divine Name, adopting the convention of four upper-case letters, LORD, instead. The form 'Lord' represents a Hebrew noun (*ᵃḏōnāy*) meaning exactly that.

Inclusio. Developments in our understanding of the structures of Hebrew poetry (see, *e.g.*, E. R. Follis [ed.], *Directions in Biblical Hebrew Poetry* [Sheffield Academic Press, 1986]) have noted the feature called 'inclusio', meaning the 'bracketing' of a poem or stanza by identical words or matching thoughts.

The 'square root' sign ($\sqrt{}$) is used as a convenient way of expressing the root form of Hebrew verbs, *e.g.* on 4:1, p. 58.

FURTHER READING

P. Hacking, *Isaiah*, Crossway Bible Guides (Crossway, 1994) is good for group study.

B. Webb, *The Message of Isaiah*, The Bible Speaks Today (IVP, 1996) is full of insight and application, excellent for personal study.

D. Kidner, 'Isaiah', in *The New Bible Commentary, 21st Century Edition* (IVP, 1994). Brilliant for a 'first run through' of Isaiah. Full of perceptiveness.

J. N. Oswalt, *The Book of Isaiah 1 – 39* (Eerdmans, 1986) offers a very full treatment in the manner of a standard commentary, with discussion of contrasting opinions and patient unravelling of problems. Volume 2 is eagerly awaited.

J. A. Motyer, *The Prophecy of Isaiah* (IVP, 1993) is a more demanding 'read' than either the present commentary or Oswalt. Delves into literary and poetic structure as a tool for displaying meaning and message. Take it slowly!

David Stacey, *Isaiah 1 – 39* (Epworth, 1993). A gracious and helpful study, and a good introduction to the 'multiple-authorship' view of Isaiah.

P. D. Miscall, *Isaiah* (JSOT Press, 1993) is like reading from 1:1 – 66:24 in the company of a marvellously well-informed friend who knows how to stop over key words and phrases and to explain how they 'work' in their differing contexts in Isaiah. A gold-mine!

E. J. Young, *The Book of Isaiah* (Eerdmans, 1965) is massively conservative. Young's chief expertise was as a linguist, and especially in this area his commentary is of great value.

J. Skinner, *Isaiah*, 2 vols. (CUP, 1902, 1905) holds to 'three Isaiahs'. He rarely fails to say something illuminating and helpful in his careful verse-by-verse writing.

FURTHER READING

J. D. Smart, *History and Theology in Second Isaiah* (Epworth, 1967), and U. E. Simon, *A Theology of Salvation, Isaiah 40 – 55* (SPCK, 1953), adopt 'running commentary' styles with deep insights into the movement of the prophet's thought.

INTRODUCTION

ISAIAH'S MESSAGE

It is a daunting task for a reader to face sixty-six chapters in page after page of unbroken print. I offer here in this Introduction a 'reader's review', an attempt to survey the wood before examining the trees. Please read this before you begin to tackle the text, looking up the (by no means exhaustive) references provided *en route*.

(a) Isaiah 1 – 5
The account of Isaiah's call (6:1ff.) provides a convenient 'marker', suggesting that chapters 1 – 5 form an introductory unit. As the Commentary shows (pp. 41–66), this turns out to be a satisfactory observation. In these chapters Isaiah sketches the situation into which he was called. Their basic theme of disobedience (1:2–4, 15–16, 19–20; 2:5–9; 3:8–9; 5:7) is placed between the brackets of hope and no hope: on the one hand, the Lord has a future for his people (1:26–28; 2:2–4; 4:2–6), but on the other, sin must be judged (1:5–6, 24–25; 2:10–11; 3:11). This latter predominates: chapter 5 contains no note of hope and ends with a vision of unrelieved darkness (5:29–30).

(b) Isaiah 6 – 12
Opening with the story of a single sinner cleansed (6:5, 7), this section ends with the song of a saved community (12:1–6). Within these brackets the section does something characteristic of the whole Isaianic literature: it takes as its major theme a sub-topic from the section preceding. In 1:26 the coming glory of Zion is anticipated in Davidic terms: David was the first to occupy Jerusalem (2 Sa. 5:6–9) and things will yet be as they were 'at the beginning', *i.e.* the days of David come back again. This Davidic theme is central to chapters 7 – 11. Against the background of the apostate King Ahaz (7:10–12), the light of the coming perfect King shines out (7:14; 9:1–7; 11:1–9).

(c) Isaiah 13 – 27

Within the vision of the coming perfect King, a minor theme is the universal empire over which he would rule (9:7; 11:4, 6–9, 14–16). Is this wishful hyperbole or a solidly grounded hope? The worldwide, indeed cosmic, panorama of chapters 13 – 27 is designed to provide the answer. Isaiah 13:9–13, along with 14:1, sets out the philosophy of history which animates these chapters: the Lord is the world ruler and when his 'day' comes he will exert his rule alike over heaven and earth, but at the centre of all his operations lies his compassion for his own people. Zion has this sure place in the Lord's plans (14:32) and is a refuge for a troubled world (16:5); its ruler is sometimes David (16:5) and sometimes the Lord (24:23). The whole series comes to a dramatic climax in the contrast of two cities: the world's city – the human attempt to organize the world without God – which falls (24:10), and the strong city of salvation (26:1) which stands.

(d) Isaiah 28 – 37

Within the world panorama of chapters 13 – 27, the Lord's final purpose of 'one world, one people, one God' was set out in terms of the world map as Isaiah knew it: Israel sandwiched between the would-be superpower, Egypt, and the actual superpower, Assyria. At the End, the Lord will make them a united, co-equal whole (19:23–25; 27:11–13). In Isaiah's time the people of the tiny puppet kingdom of Judah could well have questioned the realism of such a hope! In answer to this spoken or unspoken query, Isaiah moves on into chapters 28 – 37, dealing with an actual history in which Judah, Egypt and Assyria – the very nations which formed his eschatological trio – became entangled. In chapter 28, Jerusalem seems rightly doomed (verse 11), but the Lord's cornerstone is there (verse 16) and it remains to be seen how the divine farmer will deal with his field (verses 23–29). In fact his purpose is an eleventh-hour deliverance (29:1–8). The people of Judah have sinfully involved themselves with Egypt (30:12) and invited the wrath of their overlord Assyria, the unnamed adversary of 30:17. But the supposed strength of Egypt is meaningless (30:7), and a divine purpose long since framed has determined that the Assyrian march against Zion is his funeral procession ending in his funeral pyre (30:33). Chapters 36 – 37 record how all this actually happened (37:36–38).

(e) Isaiah 38 – 55

Chapters 28 – 37 are dominated by the topic of the deliverance of Jerusalem from the Assyrian threat and the proof this offers historically of divine sovereignty in ordering earthly history. But there is a distinct sub-theme: this great deliverance is totally contrary to what Jerusalem's rulers and people deserve. The same could be said of chapters 7 – 11 where the coming King is an unmerited promise but, while that earlier section acknowledged national sinfulness (*e.g.* 8:11–12, 19), its major concern was the sin of the leadership. There is no passage quite like 30:8–17. Equally, while the great Isaianic title, the Holy One of Israel, occurs at 10:20, in chapters 28 – 35 it occurs more often than in the rest of Isaiah 1 – 37 taken together (29:19, 23; 30:11–12, 15; 31:1; 37:23): there has been a specific national rejection of the Holy God (30:11). There is thus a deeper problem than how Judah may or may not fare in the power politics of the day. What about sin and rebellion, rejection of the word of the Lord (28:11–12) and of the Lord of the word (30:10–11)? This situation receives pointed illustration in the sin of Hezekiah, detailed in chapters 38 and 39. To choose security in an alliance with Merodach-Baladan (39:1–4) was to throw the divine promise of security and deliverance (38:6) back in God's face and to abandon the way of faith. As a result the Lord of history would use the forces of history in the earthly chastisement of his people (39:5–7; 42:18–25). Nevertheless, mercy would triumph, and the comfort of God would come to his people as outlined in 40:1–2: the 'period of duress' (40:2a) would end; Cyrus the Restorer would send the exiles home and Jerusalem would rise again (44:28; 45:13; 48:20–22). But also, sin would be covered and cancelled (40:2b): the Lord's Servant, the Redeemer, would bring the people back to God (49: 5–6) by bearing their sins (53:8, 12).

(f) Isaiah 56 – 66

Isaiah foresees that the people will be less than happy to have Cyrus as their restorer (45:9–11) and it is easy to see why they felt like this. They were exiled from Jerusalem as a subject people, dominated by the imperial power of Babylon. To return home by permission of Cyrus the Persian left their situation unchanged; they were still subject, still under an imperial power. David had not returned; there was now not even a puppet king in Zion; national sovereignty seemed more of a dream than ever! So when will the Lord's people really be a free people, free of worldly influence and oppression? It is to this topic that Isaiah turns in chapters 56 – 66. The opening is significant: the people are still awaiting the Lord's salvation (56:1). But the Lord has his Agent at the ready: one who will dry his people's tears (61:1–3), put an end to their oppressors (62:8) and by himself execute the great double work of redemption and vengeance (63:1–6). At last, Jerusalem will be the centre of the New Earth (65:17–25).

ISAIAH'S THOUGHT

It is not an overstatement to say that today the pendulum of specialist opinion is swinging rapidly away from the older emphasis on differences within the Isaianic literature and more towards the great unities which bind it all together. This is not to say that the specialist world is any nearer to asserting one single author, Isaiah of Jerusalem: far from it. But the rigidity of a first, second and third Isaiah separated by hundreds of years is giving way to the thought of an ongoing 'Isaiah school', prolonging, enlarging and re-applying the teaching of the master-prophet.[1] For, after all, it will not do to impute silliness or carelessness to the ancient guardians of the written texts who in every other way give evidence of their extreme caution. We cannot, on the one hand, find them safeguarding the separate integrity of a fragment like Obadiah, or, as some would say, even inventing a name for the author of Malachi to guarantee its distinctness, and then, on the other hand, suppose that, querying what to do with the acme of Old Testament prophecy, Isaiah 40 – 55, they slotted it in with Isaiah 1 – 39 because they happened to have half a scroll, or whatever, to spare! It is a welcome thing to hail the scholarship which is steadily opening up the streams of unity in the Isaianic literature.

(a) History and faith
Isaiah is the Paul of the Old Testament in his teaching that faith in God's promises is the single most important reality for the Lord's people: this is the heart of chapters 1 – 37. He is the 'Hebrews' of the Old Testament in his proposal of faith as the sustaining strength of the Lord's people in life's dark days: this is the heart of chapters 38 – 55. He is also the James of the Old Testament in his insistence that 'faith works', proving itself in obedience: thus chapters 56 – 66. Behind all this lies the history through which he lived and future events as he envisaged them.

---

[1] A useful review of recent study is provided in the Society for Biblical Literature's Seminar Papers (Scholars Press, Atlanta, 1991), esp. R. Rendtorff, *The Book of Isaiah: A Complex Unity*. See also B. S. Childs, *Introduction to the Old Testament as Scripture* (SCM, 1979), pp. 311ff.; W. S. LaSor, D. A. Hubbard and F. W. Bush, *Old Testament Survey* (Eerdmans/Paternoster, 1982), pp. 365ff.; and R. B. Dillard and T. Longman, *An Introduction to the Old Testament* (Apollos, 1995), pp. 267ff.

i. God and history. In 10:5–15 Isaiah teaches how history 'works'. He sees two fundamental principles. The first is that the course of history is in the hand of God in the most direct, managerial sense. The Lord is neither like a boy launching his model yacht on one side of the pond, confident that the wind will bring it safely to the other side but uncertain what will happen in between, nor is he like a chess master patiently allowing the other player to make moves and then countering his opponent's intentions to secure his own victory. For Isaiah, even the superpowers of earth are but rods, axes and saws in the hands of a single divine Agent (10:5, 15). Secondly, within the divine programme, history is the outworking of moral purposes, the arena of choice and moral responsibility. Thus the Assyrian is held within the Lord's purpose to bring due punishment to Jerusalem (6, 12a): this is the moral government of the world which underlies the 'inanimate' models of rod, axe and saw. Yet the Assyrian is moved not by obedience to the perceived will of God but by the arrogance of his own imperialism (7–11, 13–14): he is out for self-advantage and the fulfilment of proud ambition, no matter at what expense to others. This makes him culpable before history's Ruler and he will be punished (12b). In this way Isaiah's view of history is consonant with the Bible's (especially the Old Testament's) fixed gaze beyond second causes to the First Cause, for preoccupation with second causes leads to living by our wits, working the system and making the right move, whereas concentration on the First Cause issues in a life of faith, trusting, 'cleaving to the Lord' (see Acts 11:23, AV), and living for his pleasure.

The nearest Isaiah comes to offering an illustration of this understanding of history is in his hint of the horse and the rider (37:29). All the violent strength lies in the horse; all the sovereign direction is the rider's. So it is in the show-jumping arena where the commentators move easily between congratulating the horse or the rider for a clear round – for there are two separate even though interlocking 'forces' at work. So it is in history. This is the 'theology of history' which made Isaiah the prophet of faith.

ii. The three crises. Crisis one: The unbelieving king. Isaiah ministered within the fifty-year period between the death of Uzziah (1:1; 6:1, probably 739 BC), and that of Hezekiah (1:1, 686 BC). This was also the great period of Assyrian imperialism initiated by Tiglath-Pileser III (Pul, 2 Ki. 15:19) in 745 BC. The Palestinian states almost immediately began to feel Assyrian pressure under which King Menaham accepted tributary status (2 Ki. 15:19). Pekah, however, who came to the throne by assassinating Menahem's son (2 Ki. 15:25), was not prepared to acquiesce in Assyrian overlordship without a struggle. He joined with Rezin of Aram in a defensive alliance and, for an undeclared reason, the two moved against Judah. Was this to pressurize Ahaz of Judah into joining the alliance, making it the cohesive strategy of all the west Palestinian states, or was it a punitive measure because Ahaz, foreseeing that Assyria would act against Aram and Ephraim, was already himself negotiating with Assyria[1] to secure his immunity when the attack came?[2] Whatever the truth about this matter, Isaiah's concern was how Ahaz proposed to react to the northern threat.

Isaiah 7:1–17 reviews the crisis, focusing on Isaiah's call to faith and Ahaz' refusal of that call. Faith meant taking no action in relation to the northern threat (7:4), simply resting on the word of divine promise (7:7), but the alternative to faith was made clear (7:9): there is no other way of security or of continuance. Ahaz, however, refused the way of faith (7:10–17), choosing rather to buy Assyrian protection (2 Ki. 16:5–9) and thereby, in J. N. Oswalt's memorable phrase, acting like a mouse asking a cat to help it against another cat! Short-term benefit was purchased (as Isaiah foresaw) dearly. In every real sense the Davidic monarchy ended with Ahaz, for the remaining kings reigned only as puppets by courtesy of either Assyria or Babylon, and with the exile (586 BC) the monarchy disappeared and no king ever again reigned in Zion. When the Lord makes promises, faith is the make-or-break decision of his people.

Crisis two: The faithful Lord. By the time of Hezekiah Palestine was in the Assyrian grip: Damascus fell to Tiglath-Pileser in 732 BC. Shalmaneser succeeded in 727 BC, made his eastern empire secure by 724 BC and turned his attention westward. He began the siege of Samaria, but its fall in 721 BC is accredited to Sargon. As always in those ancient conglomerate empires, Sargon's accession was greeted by widespread rebellion of subject peoples and he spent his first seven years quieting his eastern and northern dominions. This gave Hezekiah and the Jerusalem politicians a breathing-space in which to review their

[1] See J. N. Oswalt, *The Book of Isaiah, 1 – 39,* New International Commentary on the Old Testament (Eerdmans, 1986), pp. 6–7.

[2] There were two incursions from the north into Judah. In the first (2 Ch. 28:5–8; Is. 7:1), in spite of successes, the invaders did not proceed against Jerusalem itself. The second wave of invasion (2 Ch. 28:17–18, 'again') included Edomite and Philistine incursions.

policy *vis-à-vis* Assyria. And Egypt was at hand making encouraging pledges of support should the Palestinian states revolt. Some of them did so in 715 BC, and it is an interesting comment on Egyptian promises that, when Sargon took Ashdod (714 BC) and its king fled to Egypt, the Egyptians promptly handed him back to Assyria!

Hezekiah seems not to have been involved in this insurgence, since he was not included in Assyrian reprisals, but, sadly, his day was to come. 2 Kings 18:7 simply says he rebelled against the king of Assyria, but behind that bald statement lies a strange infatuation with Egypt, reviewed by Isaiah in chapters 28 – 35. The unreliability of Egypt fully justified Isaiah's irony (30:3–7), and he was absolutely right in deriding the politicians, jubilant over their 'coup', because in their Egyptian alliance they had succeeded only in signing their own death warrant (28:14–15)! He saw that the issue (as in the days of Ahaz) was not one of political astuteness but of faith. He had faced them with the word of God in such a simple form that they mocked it as kid's stuff (28:9); he reminded them of the solid rock of the Lord's promises to David, the foundation stone laid in Zion (28:16), but they would not build on it; he called them to repentance, rest, quietness and trust as the way of salvation and (warrior) strength (30:15) but they chose the world's militarism (30:16). The message is the same as to Ahaz, and the situation not vastly different, except that Ahaz chose to seek security in a contemporary killer, Assyria, while Hezekiah trusted the ancestral specialist in ethnic cleansing (Ex. 1:22). Only the Lord is the life-giver, and faith alone is the way of life; every other remedy is the way of death.

Sennacherib acceded in 705 BC, and by 701 BC he had all Palestine at his mercy and Hezekiah belatedly conscious of his folly (37:1–3).[1] Hezekiah, however, discovered the truth that 'if we are faithless, he will remain faithful' (2 Tim. 2:13). Faith is a potent force, not because of any reflex effect it has within the human psyche but because it reaches out to a trustworthy Object. Isaiah had long since known that Assyria would (so to speak) meet its Waterloo in Judah (14:24–27); in the thick of the crisis he reiterated the same message (37:21–29); and in the event so it was (37:36). Judah was delivered just as Isaiah forecast, by an eleventh-hour intervention (29:1–8), and, in fact, with this the zenith of Assyrian power passed.

Crisis three: The decisiveness of unbelief. The great

---

[1] For further details, see Commentary, pp. 183ff., 220–231.

deliverance (37:36) must have been a bitter-sweet experience for Hezekiah. It would have been very strange if he had not found himself saying, 'If only'! For within the series of events leading up to the Egyptian Alliance and Sennacherib's ferocious reaction, there had happened, within the secrecy of the palace, a personal crisis of faith for the king which was the hinge on which the national future turned. When we realize that before Sennacherib invaded – probably even before he came to the throne – Hezekiah had decisively turned from trusting the Lord to self-trust and worldly-trust, we appreciate how marvellous is the faithfulness of God who nevertheless intervened to shatter Assyria in the mountains of Judah (14:25) – not because the king trusted the promise, not because he merited deliverance, but simply because it is impossible for the Lord to pledge his word and then go back on it.

The tale of Hezekiah's crisis is simply told. Merodach-Baladan of Babylon was a superb 'freedom-fighter', determined to end Assyrian rule. He achieved this for the first time, ruling as king of Babylon from 722 BC until he was ousted by Sargon in 710 BC. The death of Sargon in 706 BC, however, gave him a second chance and once more he made Babylon an independent kingdom. It must have been at some point in relation to this second insurgency that he sent his fateful embassy to Hezekiah (39:1). The ostensible reason was a gesture to the convalescent king; the actual reason, in the letter which accompanied the gift, can be deduced from Hezekiah's reaction (39:2). Hezekiah may well have been already compromised by his negotiations with Egypt, and it was a small (but flattering) thing to be invited to a further alliance with the prince of freedom fighters! But in his illness Hezekiah had a specific promise from God: 'I will deliver you and this city from the hand of the king of Assyria' (38:6). From that point on it was surely simply a matter of trusting the promise and awaiting its fulfilment. To choose instead the way of alliances, armaments and resources (39:2) was as decisive a rejection of the way of faith as Isaiah recognized it to be (39:3-7).

There is no need to find anything difficult or strange in Isaiah's prediction of Babylonian captivity. Babylon was plainly a world power; Merodach-Baladan had already once achieved a balance of power in Mesopotamia. The prediction of Babylon was a sharply relevant message to the king to whom it was addressed: he had chosen Babylon and, like it or not, all his proud possessions would go there! But, of course, Isaiah could not leave it at that. In fact, he must either tear up all his earlier prophecies of the glories of the coming king (9:1–7; 11:1–16; 32:1ff.; 33:17) or else he must seek light from the Lord on how, notwithstanding the end of monarchy and kingdom in captivity, they would yet be fulfilled. When we remember that, like Hezekiah, Isaiah lived to experience the astounding faithfulness of the Lord to his word about shattering Assyria, it is no wonder that he set alongside his prediction of Babylonian captivity (39:5–7) his message of comfort that the days of duress would some day be over (40:1, 2a) and, alongside the king's great sin in abandoning faith, his forecast that sin would be exactly and abundantly dealt with (40:2b). In this way 39:5 – 40:12 can be compared with 8:21 – 9:7. When the dark day comes, then, for those with believing minds, there is a bright light beyond the darkness, a faith to sustain them in the grim realities of life.

(b) Faith waiting
The logic of his work as a prophet thus drove Isaiah to foresee a future for the Lord's people beyond Babylon. But, as we have seen above – and as chapters 56ff. elaborate – the return would be far from a fulfilment of the people's longings. They would come back still a subject people but now without even a semblance of a king (45:9–13). In fact neither they nor their circumstances would be vastly changed by the experience of exile, and chapters 56 – 66 include many evidences of mal-function – political (*e.g.* 56:9–12), religious (*e.g.* 57:3–8) and spiritual (*e.g.* 59:2–15). What then of the promises? Do the promises of the king in chapters 1 – 37 and of the Servant in chapters 38 – 55 still hold good? Yes, says the prophet, and you must exercise the patience of faith because my salvation is close at hand, and practise the obedience of faith as you 'maintain justice and do what is right' (56:1).

Isaiah was the prophet of faith, the faith that trusts the promises, perseveres through the darkness and obediently awaits the Lord's time.

i. Hope. The forward view, so prominent in the Isaianic literature, has two main foci: the city and the Messiah.
The city. Isaiah's vision (1:1) concerned Judah and Jerusalem, but to a major extent his preoccupation is the city, with the fate of the whole kingdom bound up with and settled by what happens in Jerusalem. Likewise the future is dominated by the prophet's expectations of restoration and renewal of the city. It is typical of the importance of this theme that references to the city, its trans-formation, international centrality and magnetism for pilgrims

should provide the brackets around the whole literature: 1:21–26; 2:2–4; 4:2–6 with 65:17–25; 66:7–13; 66:18–24.[1] Like all visionaries Isaiah largely furnished the future from the present. But his development of the 'city' theme shows that he was consciously thinking beyond the geographical Zion/Jerusalem to the ideal it embodied. Thus, for example, in 11:6–9 the Lord's 'holy mountain' has become the whole redeemed creation; also in 65:17–18 the easy way the prophet moves from the 'new earth' to the newly created Jerusalem speaks to the same point. In the Bible the 'city' began (Gn. 11:4) as humankind's attempt to achieve its own salvation without reference to God, and when Isaiah looks forward to the End, he sees the fall of the 'city' humankind has built (24:1–10), Babel on a worldwide scale. As we noted above, the fall of the human city was matched by the stability of the city of salvation (26:1–2). In a word, Isaiah's vision is of the Mount Zion to which the redeemed have already come (Heb. 12:22) and which is also yet to be revealed from heaven (Rev. 21:2).

The Messiah. The three sections of the Isaianic literature are each dominated by a messianic figure: in the context of inadequate Davidic kings – apostate Ahaz and gullible Hezekiah – Isaiah depicted the glorious King yet to come (chs. 1 – 37); in the aftermath of Hezekiah's great sin of unbelief and the judgment of exile on a sinful people, Isaiah foresaw the Servant of the Lord, the sinbearer, effectually the Saviour of the world (chs. 38 – 55); and finally, envisaging the post-exile people still in subjection, Isaiah promised the coming Conqueror, exacting vengeance, bringing salvation (chs. 56 – 66). An initial appreciation of these three messianic figures can be gained by reviewing the four passages in which Isaiah portrays each figure: 9:1–7; 11:1–16; 32:1–8; 33:17–24; 42:1–4; 49:1–6; 50:4–9; 52:13 – 53:12; 59:20–21; 61:1–3; 61:10 – 62:7; 63:1–6. The whole literature is thus a messianic panorama on a grand scale, as the diagram opposite illustrates.

The point at the base of the diagram is 'Isaiah's eye'. All he sees, at first, is darkness with a surrounding brightness – for all three 'black patches' merge into one, as do all three patches of light. He is not looking down on the diagram as we are, but

[1] The city under judgment: 1:8; 3:1, 8, 16; 4:3–4; 10:12, 24–25, 32; 22:1–14; 64:10; 66:6. The city preserved: 1:8–9; 26:1; 29:1–8; 31:5–9; 36:15; 37:10, 32–35; 38:6. The city restored: 40:2, 9; 52:1; 57:13; 61:3; 66:8. Davidic restoration: 1:21, 26–27; 24:23; 33:20. Universal city: 2:2–4; 11:9; 27:13; 60:14; 62:12; 65:25. Redeemed city: 51:17; 52:1–2, 7–8; 59:20; 62:11. Cyrus and the city: 45:13. Divine dwelling: 4:3–5; 12:6.

looking along the dotted middle line into the diagram. He identifies the brightness with the Perfect King, who will be the solution where Ahaz failed.

But then Isaiah lived on into the days of Hezekiah, in which the 'dark' problem was posed in a new way: the failure of king

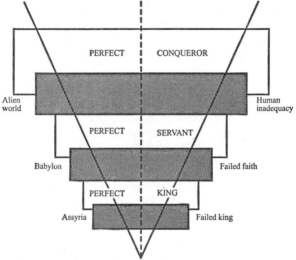

and people to trust the Lord's promises and walk the way of faith, preferring rather the way of 'works', a rebellious alliance with Merodach-Baladan. The darkness of Babylonian captivity lay ahead – but now the brightness is that of a Perfect Servant, who will succeed where they failed, and in succeeding will make atonement for their sins.

Then, envisaging the people returning from Babylon, Isaiah sees the darkness of their inability to live for God in a threatening world and a hostile society. They need a deliverer, and the light ahead now reveals a coming Conqueror-Deliverer. As is always the case in the Bible, the truth is cumulative.

ii. God, holiness, sin and salvation. Isaiah is strictly traditional and orthodox in his theology, moving in a non-innovative way among the basic principles of Old Testament thought. His innovation resides in his application and outworking of established and familiar truth.

The Holy One of Israel. In Isaiah, as throughout the Old Testament, the basic idea of 'holiness' is 'otherness' – not 'otherness' defined by contrast (other than what?), but 'otherness' as distinctiveness (other because what?). In this sense all the gods were holy because they possessed their own distinctive nature, sphere and activity, and those who devoted their lives to the gods were 'holy' as belonging to that distinctive sphere – like the 'shrine-girl', literally 'holy woman' ($q^e\underline{d}\bar{e}š\hat{a}$) of Genesis 38:20. Isaiah inherited and furthered the Old Testament understanding that the distinctive of the Lord was his ethical, moral character: to this he gave definitive statement in the 'thrice-Holy' of 6:3 (see Commentary, p. 71), a super-superlative, all-embracing holiness that made the Lord the uttermost threat to all sinfulness. Indeed, Isaiah is the pre-eminent prophet of divine holiness. He uses, for example, the adjective 'holy' ($q\bar{a}\underline{d}\hat{o}š$) of the Lord more often than all the rest of the Old Testament taken together, and focuses it in a title which he could well have coined, characteristic of the Isaianic literature: The Holy One of Israel. The title is used throughout Isaiah twenty-five times as compared with seven in the rest of the Old Testament.[1] Isaiah 6 stands as a microcosm of the whole book: the Holy One as King (6:1, 5) becomes the theme specially of chapters 56 – 66; the Holy One as the ground of condemnation of moral condemnation (6:3, 5) is the theme of chapters 1 – 37; and the revelation of the Holy One as the Saviour (6:6–7) finds its fulfilment in the Servant in chapters 38 – 55.

The Servant of the Lord. Isaiah likewise breaks no new ground in his use of the vocabulary of sin and redemption but, once again, it is in vision and application that he becomes distinctive, referring to the Servant of the Lord in chapters 38 – 55. The search for an understanding of the Servant has produced a century and more of controversy.[2] There is ground within Isaiah for thinking of the Servant as the nation, Israel: for example, the nation is called 'my servant' in 41:8 and the Servant is named 'Israel' in 49:3. But as soon as details of any such corporate identification (whether with the nation as a whole or with some 'remnant' within the nation) are probed, the theory collapses. In what sense could either nation or group claim the obedience evidenced by the Servant in 50:4–9? Did the nation ever possess the sinlessness required in one who bears another's sin (53:9; *cf.*

---

[1] 'The Holy One of Israel' occurs twelve times in 1 – 37, eleven times in 38 – 55 and twice in 56 – 66. This should be compared with the seven times elsewhere in the OT: 2 Ki. 19:22; Pss. 71:22; 78:41; 89:18; Je. 50:29; 51:5; Ezk. 39:7.

[2] H. H. Rowley, *The Servant of the Lord* (Lutterworth, 1952); C. R. North, *The Suffering Servant in Deutero-Isaiah* (OUP, 1956).

Ex. 12:5)? In what sense could the nation bring the nation back to
God (49:5–6)? Likewise, the autobiographical presentation of
49:1–6 and 50:4–9 gives substance to the question in Acts 8:34.
But again the scope and demands of the Servant's role run
beyond the character and abilities of any known individual of the
past, whether Isaiah or another – not to mention that such an
identification would mean that the Servant came, lived and died
in the past without leaving any record or ripple in history. As the
Commentary shows, if we refuse the fragmentarist approach
which began with Duhm and insist in understanding the Songs
within an integrated development, the Servant is distinguished in
turn from the errant and spiritually numb nation (42:18–25) and
from the spiritually committed and expectant remnant (51:1 –
52:12), leaving a majestic Individual to occupy our gaze (52:13)
as he dies bearing the sins of others (53:4–9) and lives to
administer the salvation he has won for them (53:10–12).

In portraying the Servant's death, Isaiah lays under tribute the
established vocabulary of Levitical/Mosaic theology and practice: substitution and peace with God through punishment laid,
by the will of God, on another (53:5–6, 8), a sinless sufferer
(53:9) who provides righteousness for others (53:11) by bearing
their sin (53:12). The towering genius of Isaiah was displayed in
that he saw so clearly that in its truest sense substitution needs a
person to take the place of people. Animal sacrifice can illustrate
the principle, but only one who voluntarily accepts the role (53:7)
and voluntarily pours out himself (53:12) – that is to say,
provides a will to take the place of the sinful will (*cf.* Heb. 10:5–
9) – can achieve by a true substitution the full, indeed final,
salvation of those for whom he dies.

ISAIAH'S BOOK

(a) Recovery of unity
No apology is needed for calling the Isaianic literature 'Isaiah's
book', for it has never been anything else. There is no manuscript
evidence other than for the literature as it stands: indeed, in the
oldest manuscript available, dating back to 100 BC, the first two
lines of chapter 40 (which is where many scholars say the book
should be divided) come without any break in the text at the
bottom of the column on which chapter 39 ends.

Furthermore, the course of present-day study is prepon-
derantly concerned with the unity of this great corpus: 'Today
scholars are beginning to move from analysis to synthesis [in
order to try to] understand the overall unity and the theological

dynamic of the Isaiah tradition',[1] and, within this, few dispute that Isaiah of Jerusalem was the initiator of the tradition and the beating heart that kept it alive through (as they would hold) the centuries that it took to bring it into its present and final shape.[2] Many are following the lead of B. S. Childs,[3] who maintains that our concern must be with the 'canonical' form of Isaiah, not because of dogmatic views of 'inspiration' but on the ground that this is the form, as P. R. Ackroyd puts it, which is 'stamped with the hallmark of experiential testing in the life of the community'.[4] Specialists differ in the extent to which they think it is important to isolate sections large and small and relate them to the different periods in history in which they are supposed to have originated. Some make this crucially significant,[5] but others take the literature as it now stands and mine the richness of its inter-relations.[6]

(b) Models of growth

Within this general approach, some view the Isaianic literature as growing by addition with three authors strung along a time-line. Isaiah of Jerusalem (c. 700 BC) was broadly responsible for chapters 1 – 39; the author of chapters 40 – 55 is 'Second (or Deutero-) Isaiah', who lived in the Babylonian captivity (586–539 BC) and worked probably about 540 BC; and the 'Third (or Trito-) Isaiah' ministered to the returned community, 539 BC onwards.[7] Another model is that of accretion: *i.e.* the growth of the literature around an original core so that what we have is the final form of what has been, at all stages, a single 'book', constantly receiving editorial adjustments to meet new situations along with additions reflecting and extending the spirit of the original (Isaianic) core.[8]

---

[1] B. W. Anderson, 'The Apocalyptic Rendering of the Isaiah Tradition', in *The Social World of Formative Christianity and Judaism* (Fortress, 1988).

[2] For contrasting approaches to the Isaianic literature see, *e.g.*, the two vols. of the New Century Bible (Eerdmans/Marshall): R. E. Clements, *Isaiah 1 – 39* (1980) and R. N. Whybray, *Isaiah 40 – 66* (1975), as compared with J. D. W. Watts, *Isaiah*, 2 vols. (Word, 1985).

[3] *Introduction to the Old Testament as Scripture*, pp. 311ff.

[4] P. R. Ackroyd, *Studies in the Religious Tradition of the Old Testament* (SCM, 1987), pp. 79ff.

[5] B. S. Childs, *Isaiah and the Assyrian Crisis* (SCM, 1967).

[6] P. D. Miscall, *Isaiah* (JSOT Press, 1993).

[7] An easy (and helpful) commentary following this approach is J. Skinner, *Isaiah,* 2 vols. (CUP, 1902, 1905) or, on a massive and less accessible scale, H. Wilderberger, *Jesaja*, 3 vols. (Neukirchner Verlag, 1972, 1978, 1982).

[8] See O. H. Steck, quoted in Rendtorff, *The Book of Isaiah.*

(c) Arguments and evaluations

This modern search for ways to express the unity of the Isaianic literature arises from the fragmentation which is the product of the last one hundred years of specialist study – whether three 'authors' working at separated intervals or an anthology collected by a supposed Isaianic 'school'. Previously, the assumption of one single author had provided the ground for considering the work a unity, but at least since the mid-nineteenth century a number of factors were taken to make a single author an impossibility.

i. Prophecy. O. T. Allis is correct in rooting the fragmentation of Isaiah in a nineteenth-century rationalism which denied predictive prophecy[1] – for if prediction is impossible, the movement of the Isaianic literature progressively into the future can be explained only by the supposition of new authors working in those later times. But today, when a modest element of prediction has been readmitted as a possibility, another problem arises: not whether Isaiah could predict the exile and return, but would he do so.[2] After all, what comfort is it to learn that in a century's time all will be well! How could Isaiah's contemporaries get their minds around the thought of a Babylonian captivity when their world was dominated by Assyria, not Babylon, and what would they make of the name of an unknown king from an as-yet-unknown kingdom? How, come to that, could Isaiah know, all those years in ahead, the name of Cyrus (45:1)?

Putting ourselves back, however, into Isaiah's situation, these difficulties begin to evaporate. First of all Isaiah says nothing about a gap of a hundred years between prediction and fulfilment. It is a caricature to claim he said, 'Don't worry! In a hundred years all will be well!'; he did not say so! G. E. Wright asserts that 'a prophecy is earlier than what it predicts but contemporary with or later than what it presupposes'.[3] His intention is to root prophetic ministry in the prophet's own situation, to insist that every message is meaningful to the prophet's contemporaries. This suits Isaiah perfectly – and in particular the Babylonian prophecy of 39:3–6. The name 'Babylon' was spoken to Isaiah

---

[1] O. T. Allis, *The Unity of Isaiah* (Tyndale, 1951).

[2] J. McKenzie, *Second Isaiah,* Anchor Bible (Doubleday, 1968), p. xvi; see also the excellent introductions to Isaiah in LaSor *et al., Old Testament Survey,* and Dillard and Longman, *An Introduction to the Old Testament.*

[3] G. E. Wright, *The Book of Isaiah* (John Knox, 1964).

by Hezekiah and thereby became a subject on which the prophet must comment: indeed, so contemporary and relevant was the message of captivity that Hezekiah had no right to assume that it would not happen in his days (39:8)! The advent of Merodach-Baladan's agents reminded him that the balance of power in Mesopotamia was a fragile thing and that Babylon was, even then, a candidate for empire.[1] Besides, how can we who have seen the sudden disappearance of the Communist empire say that quick change is impossible? Furthermore, as 14:24–27 and 29:1–8 indicate, Isaiah was aware that it would not be Assyria before whom Jerusalem would fall: 39:3–6 was a defining moment in which the dark power behind 6:11–12 was named publicly.

Regarding Cyrus (who is predicted by name in 44:28), 1 Kings 13:2 (*cf.* 2 Ki. 23:15–17) and Acts 9:12 show that name-prediction is not unknown in the Bible. The fact is that, if prediction is admitted at all, we cannot set limits to its exercise. Nothing of the 'mechanism' of revelation, inspiration or prediction is revealed to us, and the Lord of the prophets can sovereignly declare the exceptional just as much as the usual. In the case of Cyrus, we can, however, see that the name was germane to the message of comfort. We only have to picture ourselves as an ethnic minority under a dictatorship to imagine the sense of foreboding with which the news of an even mightier dictator would be greeted. In mercy, therefore, would not the Lord want to assure his people that the greater despot will be their deliverer? On the one hand, the naming of Cyrus is a relevant message of comfort to Isaiah's contemporaries, but, on the other hand, to refuse to allow that it was Isaiah who named Cyrus creates two problems: first, it is untrue to 41:25ff. with its claim that the rise of Cyrus also was a matter of prediction and, secondly, it negates the force of 45:1–6 that Cyrus would be in a position to recognize the Lord as the author of all his success. A later prophet, speaking after Cyrus became news, would be no better than the priests of Marduk, who were only wise after the event when they claimed the conqueror's success in the name of their god. Only a prophecy with a veritable claim to have anticipated the event could be presented as proof of the sole deity of Yahweh.

ii. Literary style. The difference in the style of chapters 40 – 55 was an early argument for separating them from chapters 1 –

---

[1] S. Erlandsson, *The Burden of Babylon* (CWK Gleerup, 1970).

39,[1] and it is still used[2] as a means of distinguishing authors, even though widely discredited.[3] It is and always has been a nonsense. *The Lord of the Rings*, for example, evidences a narrative style, a dialogue style and a poetic style. Must it have had three authors? Could not Milton have written in the jolly rhythms of *L'Allegro*, in the sonorous tones of *Paradise Lost* and also in the measured prose of *Areopagitica*? When Isaiah of Jerusalem is presumed to be the author, a scenario for the two main styles of the book is simplicity itself. Most of chapters 1 – 35 are a sort of rhythmic prose, Isaiah's 'record of preaching' style. The messages of the prophets as they stand could not have been preached: they are too brief, too quickly come and gone; they do not have the repetitions and elaborations essential to allow hearers to fix their minds on what is being said. Like all the prophets, Isaiah filed for the future carefully crafted encapsulations of his preaching. But the days of Hezekiah were followed by the 'police state' days of Manasseh (2 Ki. 21:1–18), and maybe in such a time the now elderly prophet would turn exclusively to writing: this is the real contrast between the two styles, the one primarily a record of sermons, the other a solely literary product.

iii. Background. It is plain to see that the envisaged background to the three sections of Isaiah is different: the earlier chapters are at home in eighth-century Jerusalem; chapters 40 – 55 envisage a Babylonian exile; and chapters 56 – 66 are once more in Palestine. On examination, however, a claim that 40 – 55 must have been written in Babylon tends to evaporate. Certainly they are Babylonian in orientation, but not so in setting. Apart from the four references to Babylon (43:14; 47:1; 48:14, 20), there is little that is exclusively or typically Babylonian about the chapters: 'When we search for evidence of the prophet's residence in Babylon, we are surprised how hard it is to find any that is convincing.'[4] Rather, Babylon receives broad-brush

---

[1] S. R. Driver, *Introduction to the Literature of the Old Testament* (T. & T. Clark, 1909), pp. 204ff.

[2] Note how McKenzie, in *Second Isaiah*, includes chs. 34 – 35 in his commentary on 40 – 66. This is typical of ongoing stylistic judgments.

[3] R. Margoliouth, *The Indivisible Isaiah* (Yeshiva University, New York, 1964), presents the most thoroughly researched and searching enquiry into the vocabulary, idioms and phrasing of the Isaianic literature and demonstrates linguistic unity. But see the different results of Reinken's linguistic researches as reported by McKenzie (*Second Isaiah*, p. xvi). Radday (see Dillard and Longman, *Introduction to the Old Testament*) used computer technology to demonstrate diversity. None of these studies has escaped searching criticism.

[4] J. D. Smart, *History and Theology in Second Isaiah* (Epworth, 1965), p. 20.

treatment; it is predicted rather than presupposed. The sort of detail which betrays an eye-witness is simply not there – what the city was like, its life, structures, the 'feel and smell' of the place – nor any indication of the organization of the society of the exiles. In the same way, when these chapters speak of the experience of being exiled (42:22; 51:14), they bear no relation to the homesick (Ps. 137:1–6) but generally pleasant (Je. 29; Ezk. *passim*) conditions of life (from which, when the time came, so few were willing to detach themselves, Ezr. 1 – 2!). In his allusions to the 'sufferings' of exile, as, indeed, in his poetic, impressionistic depiction of the fall of Babylon (47:1–15), the prophet offers not reportage but poetic use of conventional stereotypes.

Topological background is also important. While the Babylonian scene has not become clear, the Palestinian background has not grown faint. The idolater goes out into the woods to cut a tree for carving (46:14), not possible in Babylonia! The trees are those a Palestinian knows; the oils are those of West Asia (41:19; 55:13); the landscapes and climate are those of the west – mountains, forests, sea, snow and land refreshed by rain, not by irrigation.[1] The claim that in chapters 40 – 55 we move into a Mesopotamian milieu is not borne out by the evidence.

iv. Theology. Even as late as 1950, H. H. Rowley could record that in chapters 40 – 55 'the whole tenor of the message ... the ideas that lie behind it ... the thought of God ... are different'[2] from chapters 1 – 39, but this is simply not the case: expression and presentation vary but the theology is the same. First, the whole is bound together by the title 'the Holy One of Israel' (see above, p. 25–26), and when we consider the enhanced universalism of chapters 40 – 55 it is hard to see why any prophet other than Isaiah would use a title that so emphasized a particular, national God. Secondly, the six main theological foci of chapters 1 – 39 continue in 40 – 55: the Lord as Lord of history (10:5–15), his supremacy over idols (2:12–20), the remnant (8:11–20), God and sinner reconciled through atonement (6:7), Zion restored

---

Smart's research led him to place 'Second Isaiah' in Palestine 'squarely in the midst of the international upheavals generated by the exploits of King Cyrus' (p. 32).

[1] See A. Lods, *The Prophets of Israel* (Kegan Paul, 1937), p. 238. Lods was unable to accept prediction, and therefore made the author of chs. 40 – 55 a West Palestinian working in the post-exile.

[2] H. H. Rowley, *The Growth of the Old Testament* (Hutchinson, 1950), p. 95; *cf.* Driver, *Introduction to the Literature of the Old Testament*.

(1:26–27) and the Davidic Messiah (9:1–7). Chapters 40 – 48 are a set of variations on the first three of the above; 53:1–12 is the 'fulfilment' of 6:6–7; Jerusalem is as central throughout the rest of the book as in 1 – 37; and 55:3–4 anchors the revelation of the Servant in the Davidic covenant.

(d) An 'Isaiah' scenario

Apart from the special exercise of forecasting the name of Cyrus, there is an easy simplicity in relating everything else to Isaiah of Jerusalem. The prophet of a glorious future (*e.g.* 1:26–27; 2:2–4; 4:4–6; 9:1–7; 11:1–16) is also the prophet of disaster and total loss (*e.g.* 5:24–30; 6:11–12; 7:17–25). Isaiah gathered what we would call a 'home-group' around him (8:16), and these disciples would have been uncommonly restrained if they did not press the prophet to say how these strands would intertwine, especially after he had said to the king that all was consigned to Babylon (39:6–7). Surely after the events of 39:3–7 Isaiah must either tear up his earlier promises, or he must now at last answer the insistent question: how does hope fit in?

Thus circumstances compelled him on – and, since chapters 40 – 55 so admirably fulfil the required role, we must at least start by assuming that in them Isaiah answered the question. As we have seen, he builds in no time factors and he says nothing about Babylon or the exiles that knowledge and common sense would not suggest. In terms of Wright's dictum (see p. 29), Isaiah is speaking wholly within the presuppositions of his time – and, of course, a prophet's own earlier predictions are part of the presuppositional frame within which he ministers.

The basic thrust of his message is going and coming back, the certainty that doom does not have the last word. But in his developing vision of the future it is the work of Cyrus, not that of the Servant, that brings them home to their land. Their redemption (48:20–21) is political, not spiritual, and thereby hangs Isaiah's understanding of the returned community. They return as the people who went, the 'wicked' without peace with God (48:22). For this reason Isaiah's portrayal of the returned community in chapters 56 – 66 is in pre-exilic terms: their sins, temptations, failings and apostasies are all those of the pre-exile, likewise the quality of leadership they endure and their political subjugation. Isaiah's pre-exilic messages suffice to be the word of God to his envisaged post-exilic community. Is there anything in all this unavailable to the eye and inspiration of Isaiah of Jerusalem?

TEXT

The Hebrew Text (MT) of Isaiah has come to us in fine preservation without any real doubt what the text means or a serious necessity of emendation. The Targum of Isaiah (an early Aramaic paraphrase finalized in the fifth century AD)[1] witnesses to a text very close to if not identical with the MT. The Greek translation of Isaiah, says Ottley,[2] is 'by common consent one of the worst translated parts of the LXX'. Ottley, of course, assumed that the LXX translators were working from the MT as we know it (and it is true that their worst efforts coincide with places where the Hebrew is unusual in idiom or vocabulary), but it may be that LXX was in fact following a different Hebrew original[3] which we now have no chance of recovering. The Dead Sea Scrolls have yielded Isaiah material with the manuscript Q^a being our oldest witness to Isaiah. It is at least a thousand years older than the Ben Asher text (MT) of AD 1009. The overwhelming identity between these two (notwithstanding the time gap) is an astonishing tribute to careful copying. Such differences as seem to be important are noted in the Commentary, but 'our mandate', says Oswalt, 'is to interpret the text as it is before us unless there is manuscript evidence to correct that text. To do anything else would be to build our interpretations on air.'[4]

ISAIAH AND THE NEW TESTAMENT

The New Testament quotes Isaiah more than all the other prophets together, and does so in such a way as to leave no room for doubt that the New Testament writers, and the Lord Jesus, took Isaiah to be the author of the whole book that bears his name. It is true that in some references 'Isaiah' need mean no more than the book where the quotation is found. Mark 1:2, for example, seems to use 'Isaiah' (as Lk. 24:44 uses 'the psalms') to name that section of the Old Testament Canon of which, respectively, they are the first books. But when John 12:41 notes 'Isaiah' as the one who 'saw Jesus' glory and spoke about him', referring to 6:1–10, or when Luke 3:4 quotes from 'the book of the words of Isaiah', there can be no doubt that the individual

[1] See D. F. Payne, 'Targums', in *NBD*; J. Stenning, *The Targum of Isaiah* (Clarendon, 1949).
[2] R. L. Ottley, *Isaiah according to the Septuagint,* 2 vols. (CUP, 1906, 1909), pp. 8–9.
[3] Oswalt, *The Book of Isaiah*, p. 30.
[4] Oswalt, p. 31.

prophet is intended, and this is, of course, the natural and logical interpretation of the main bulk of the quotations. The New Testament quotations cover all sections of the Isaianic literature, ascribing all alike to the same prophet. The authority of the New Testament with, at its centre, the authority of Jesus, is decisive.

ANALYSIS

THE BOOK OF THE KING (1 – 37)

I. BACKDROP TO THE MINISTRY OF ISAIAH: THE AUTHOR'S
   PREFACE (1 – 5)
   a. Heading (1:1)
   b. A comprehensive failure (1:2–31)
      i. The national situation (1:2–9)
      ii. The religious situation (1:10–20)
      iii. The social situation and its consequences (1:21–31)
   c. The ideal, lost and found (2:1 – 4:6)
      i. Heading (2:1)
      ii. The great 'might have been' (2:2–4)
      iii. The actual Jerusalem – part one (2:5–21)
      iv. The actual Jerusalem – part two (2:22 – 4:1)
      v. The greatness that is 'yet to be' (4:2–6)
   d. Grace exhausted (5:1–30)
      i. A total work and a total loss (5:1–7)
      ii. The stink-fruit harvest and its consequence
         (5:8–30)
II. LIGHT BEYOND THE DARKNESS: THE COMING KING (6 – 12)
   a. The individual, atonement and commission (6:1–13)
   b. Darkness and light in Judah (7:1 – 9:7)
      i. The moment of decision (7:1–17)
      ii. Divine judgment (7:18 – 8:8)
      iii. The believing, obeying remnant (8:9–22)
      iv. The royal hope (9:1–7)
   c. Darkness and light in Israel (9:8 – 11:16)
      i. The moment of decision (9:8 – 10:4)
      ii. Divine judgment (10:5–15)
      iii. The believing, obeying remnant (10:16–34)
      iv. The royal hope (11:1–16)
   d. The individual in the community: salvation, singing
      and proclamation (12:1–6)

III. THE KINGDOM PANORAMA: THE WHOLE WORLD IN HIS
     HAND (13 – 27)
  a. The first series of oracles: sure promises
     (13:1 – 20:6)
       i. Babylon: a look behind the scenes (13:1 – 14:27)
       ii. Philistia: the Lord's sure promises to David
           (14:28–32)
       iii. Moab: salvation refused by pride (15:1 – 16:14)
       iv. Damascus/Ephraim: the way of death and the
           promise of life (17:1 – 18:7)
       v. Egypt: one world, one people, one God
          (19:1 – 20:6)
  b. The second series of oracles: the long night and the
     dawn (21 – 23)
       i. The desert by the sea: the Babylon principle
          (21:1–10)
       ii. Silence: days of darkness (21:11–12)
       iii. Desert evening: Gentile needs unsolved
            (21:13–17)
       iv. The Valley of Vision: the unforgivable sin
           (22:1–25)
       v. Tyre: holiness to the Lord (23:1–18)
  c. The third series: the world city and the city of God
     (24:1 – 27:13)
       i. The city of meaninglessness (24:1–20)
       ii. Ultimately … the King! (24:21–23)
       iii. Salvation and provision: the world on Mount Zion
            (25:1–12)
       iv. The strong city (26:1–21)
       v. The universal Israel (27:1–13)
IV. THE LORD OF HISTORY (28 – 37)
  a. The six woes (28:1 – 35:10)
       i. The first woe: the word of God and the purposes
          of God (28:1–29)
       ii. The second woe: is anything too hard for the Lord?
           (29:1–14)
       iii. The third woe: spiritual transformation (29:15–24)
       iv. The fourth woe: faithlessness and faithfulness
           (30:1–33)
       v. The fifth woe: all things new (31:1 – 32:20)
       vi. The sixth woe: home at last (33:1 – 35:10)
  b. Epilogue: the rock of history (36:1 – 37:38)
       i. The first Assyrian embassy: the helpless king
          (36:1 – 37:7)

COMMENTARY

THE BOOK OF THE KING (1 – 37)

I. BACKDROP TO THE MINISTRY OF ISAIAH: THE AUTHOR'S PREFACE (1 – 5)

As the book of Isaiah has come to us, chapters 1 – 5 form a distinct section – like a 'preface' to Isaiah's collected prophecies. This is apparent for four reasons. (a) The precise dating of chapter 6 contrasts with the undated oracles in 1:2 – 5:30. Specific events must, of course, have prompted these oracles, but Isaiah did not find it necessary to state them. (b) What we call 'chapter 6', the prophet's call, is well suited to form chapter 1 of the book, following the 'author's preface' (*cf.* Je. 1:4–19; Ezk. 1:1 – 3:27; although, since the call of Amos is not noted until Amos 7:10–17, this is not a decisive factor. (c) Apart from the illustrative reference to the Philistines in 2:6, no foreign nations are named – not even the threatened super-conqueror of 5:25–30 – and this increases the sense that these chapters offer general truths designed to form a backdrop to the 'main' content of the book. (d) Chapters 1 – 5 are coherently structured with a progressive message. The unexpected heading at 2:1 indicates a fresh beginning, and the matching passages 2:2–4 and 4:2–6 form a bracket or *inclusio* (see p. 12) making them a distinct section. In this way 1:2–31 and 5:1–30 are also marked off as separate divisions of the prefatory chapters.

Thus, the 'preface' can be summarized as follows. First is the heading (1:1). Then 1:2–31 is roundly condemnatory of what the Lord's sons have become: rebellious (2), corrupt (4), chastened (5–6), shattered (7–8), religiously unacceptable (10–15) and degenerate (21–23). This is not, however, the whole story: for the Lord has not abandoned (9) and will not abandon (25–28) his people. Nevertheless, the beginning of the preface is effectively a declaration that 'You are not what you ought to have been'.

Isaiah 2:2 – 4:6 opens with a thrilling vision of what Zion was meant to be: a rallying-point for the whole world, the city of universal truth and peace. But of course, to the prophet's eye, it simply was not so. Far from conforming the world to itself, the Lord's people had conformed to the nations (2:6–7) and would, with the world, come under ultimate divine judgment (2:12–21) and, nationally, under imminent destabilization (3:1–7). Yet this, too, is not the whole story, for where Jerusalem's sin is most in evidence, in the actions and attitudes of the daughters of Zion (3:16 – 4:1), the Lord would some day apply cleansing (4:4) and bring in his new creation (4:5–6). Yet the sad accusation has been substantiated that 'You are not what you were meant to be'.

Isaiah 5:1–30 can be reviewed as parable (1–7), application (8–12, 18–23) and consequence (13–17, 24–30), with six 'woes' spelling out the bitter fruit (2, 4, 7) produced by the Lord's vineyard. Yet the Lord had so spent himself for the good of his vineyard that there was nothing more he could have done (4). This is the heart-stopping truth on which Isaiah ends his preface, the conclusion out of which his prophecy emerges. Note how chapter 5 begins with song (1) and ends with darkness (30), and that between those two points, unlike 1:2–31 and 2:2 – 4:6, there is no message of hope. For if all has already been done, what more can the Lord do? The theme of chapter 5, therefore, is that 'You are not what you might have been, for a total divine work of grace was your inheritance and you squandered it'. As far as chapter 5 is concerned, darkness has the last word. The shutters have come down on the Lord's people.

a. Heading (1:1)

On the kings mentioned here, see Introduction, pp. 19–23. *Vision ... saw* (Heb. $h^a z\hat{o}n$ ... $h\bar{a}z\hat{a}$): these words can refer to 'visionary experience' (29:7; 33:20), but both more usually express the heightened 'perception' of truth which the Lord granted by special revelation to the prophets (*e.g.* 2 Ch. 32:32; Am. 1:1; Mi. 1:1). The Isaianic literature, then, is 'the perception of truth which came to Isaiah by divine revelation'.

b. A comprehensive failure (1:2–31)

In setting the scene for his ministry, Isaiah starts with what must have been obvious – even if the people will not accept his diagnosis, they cannot quarrel with his facts! Nationally (2–9), foreign invasions (7–8) have left a trail of desolation so that the 'body politic' (5c–6) is like the victim of a savage mugging. Religiously (10–20), there has been punctilious devotion – sacrifices in abundance (11), temple attendance (12), monthly and weekly observances (13–14), prayers (15) – but it has not got through to God and has done nothing to rectify the national plight. And socially (21–26), the city life is degenerate and dangerous (21), its leaders corrupt and self-seeking (23a–d) and its needy uncared-for (23ef).

Isaiah sets this three-part analysis of the contemporary scene as if in a court of law. In verse 2ab the witnesses are called, in verses 2c–23 the charges are laid and in verses 24–30 sentence is pronounced. Behind the observable facts Isaiah discerns the hidden causes: rebellion against the Lord (2d) as the root of national calamity (5); personal guilt vitiating religious practice (15); social degeneration through abandonment of revealed norms of *justice* and *righteousness* (21). All this gives colour to a comparison with Sodom (9–10) and builds a case for divine punitive action (5, 20, 24, 28, 29–31), but, typically of Isaiah, there is also a surprise: hope is affirmed. The Lord has not left his people (9); when he acts it will also be to purge and restore (25–26), and the very *justice* and *righteousness* they abandoned (21) will be affirmed in a divine work of redemption (27).

i. The national situation (1:2–9). 2a. Isaiah does not explain why the *heavens* and *earth* are summoned to *hear*. The parallel address (10) to the accused suggests that creation is called to court as the perpetual witness of what happens on earth (Ps. 50:4–6) and is therefore able to affirm the truth of the divine accusations. But it may simply be to affirm the dignity of the One who can convene such a court (*cf.* 1 Ch. 16:31; Ps. 69:34–35) and the awesomeness of the occasion.

2b. But even greater awesomeness is contained in the reason given why creation must pay attention: *for the LORD himself has spoken*. Here is One whom all creation must obey; it is to him that his people must render account; and in the unique marvel of revelation and inspiration the words of the prophet are 'verbally inspired', the very words of the Lord.

3. Israel's (our) sin is simply unnatural. Look at the instinctive actions of the beasts! The locus of our disloyalty is the mind (*know ... understand*) just as the mind is the focal point of all spirituality (*cf.* Ps. 119:33–34, 104, 130; Lk. 24:27, 32; Rom. 1:28; Eph. 4:17–18, 20–22). While *know* can extend to include both personal intimacy (Gn. 4:1, NIV 'lay with') and lifestyle (1 Sa. 2:12), it retains its base-meaning of knowing the truth.

4. Four nouns of privilege: the unique *nation*; the redeemed *people*; the 'seed' or *brood* (the word used for the line of descent from Abraham in 41:8); and *children* (or the Lord's 'sons'). Four descriptions of the lost ideal: *sinful*, from the participle 'going on sinning', or missing God's target; *loaded with* (possibly 'heavy with', hinting that the Lord who carried them felt the burden; *cf.* 46:3–4; Ex. 19:4) *guilt, i.e.* 'iniquity' ('*āwôn*), meaning sin as corruption of character and nature; of *evildoers, i.e.* the chosen seed has become those who commit evil; and, lastly, *given to corruption*, 'acting corruptly', from Heb. *šāḥaṯ*, to spoil, ruin. *They have forsaken ... spurned ... turned their backs*: here is the basic principle of spiritual decline, a sustained rejection of the Lord. Maybe we should translate 'turned themselves back into aliens', *i.e.* reverting to what they were prior to their redemption. On *the Holy One of Israel* see Introduction, pp. 25–26. The height of their privilege, to know the Lord in the fullness of his holy nature, became the benchmark of the depth of their fall.

5–8. What is important in these verses is not which historical invasion they reflect. The choice probably lies between the Aram-Ephraim incursion, *c.* 735 BC (2 Ki. 15:37 – 16:6; 2 Ch. 28; see Introduction, p. 20; *cf.* on 7:1–2) or the Assyrian attack in 701 BC (chs. 36 – 37; 2 Ch. 32; see Introduction, p. 21). The important thing is Isaiah's view of history as the arena of divine moral judgment. The enemy depredations (7–8) which have left the nation crippled (5–6) from top (*head*) to toe (*foot*), inwardly (*heart*) and outwardly (*head ... foot*), and without remedy (*not cleansed ... bandaged*), were a divine chastisement, with more to come if they persist in *rebellion*. None of Isaiah's kings (1:1) was inept. They managed a sound economy and followed clever policies, yet the land was devastated (5c–7), fragile internally (8bc) and threatened externally (8d). The key to national well-being is righteousness, *i.e.* what is right with God (Pr. 14:34), and in this the prophet records dismal failure.

9. But for the Lord's people there is another factor, the surprising element of hope. Merit says one thing; mercy says another. As far as desert is concerned the Lord must either apologize to *Sodom* or visit judgment on Israel! But he is the Lord Almighty, literally 'the LORD of [who is] hosts' – where the plural indicates that in himself he is and has every potentiality and power. Consequently he is sovereign to act in whatever way accords with his nature. The same Lord (2) who judges also acts in forbearing preservation (9). Because of the Lord's love, we are not terminated, for his compassions do not fail (La. 3:22). Thus Isaiah rounds off the section.

ii. The religious situation (1:10–20). Isaiah turns now to the religious life of the nation. The placing of this topic between his review of national fortunes (2–9) and social conditions (21–23) is significant. The kernel of every national problem is how people relate to God. They cannot be right anywhere if they are wrong here. Religion determines everything.

But the people were extremely religious: they expended time on monthly, weekly and other observances (13); the financial cost of sacrifices and offerings (11) was considerable. It would be strange if they did not ask why, since they did so much for him, the Lord seemed to be doing nothing for them. But that is just the point: their religion was 'what we do for God' and not 'how we enter into the grace he offers to us'.

These verses have been the centre of a difference of opinion. Some note how in verse 11 the Lord denies the significance of sacrifices, in verse 12 their divine authorization, and in verse 13 issues commands to end them. On this view, Isaiah is calling for 'morality without religion', an ethically focused walk with God devoid of ritual observance.[1] But it can be questioned whether this understanding is true to Isaiah. Is it likely that he was so revolutionary as to repudiate the tradition in which he had been nurtured and which he would have traced back to Moses? Such a conclusion would require more than the 'say so' of a brief passage like this! Furthermore, if the passage repudiates temple rites, then it repudiates equally the Sabbath (13) and prayer (15)! Rather, Isaiah invites us to recall that in the Mosaic system redeeming grace (Ex. 6:6–7; 12:13), the gift of the law (Ex. 20) and the forms of religious observance (Ex. 25 – Lv. 27) followed one another in that order as parts of a single whole. The law was given so that those who had already been redeemed by the blood of the lamb would know how their Redeemer (Ex. 20:2) wished them to live. The sacrifices were provided to cover lapses in obedience (*cf.* 1 Jn. 1:7). But as Isaiah looked around he saw people long on religion and short on morality. They were as morally negligent as Sodom (10), their offerings were *meaningless* (13; lit. 'a gift of nothing') because the Lord *cannot bear* wickedness coupled with religious punctiliousness. The hands they raised in prayer were blood-stained from wrongdoing (15). Like all the prophets Isaiah operated squarely within the Mosaic revelation, and his charge in this passage is that his contemporaries had put asunder what the Lord, through Moses,

---

[1] This same interpretation is offered by some for Je. 7:21–22; Ho. 6:6; Am. 5:24–25; Mi. 6:6–8. See the excellent overview in H. H. Rowley, *The Unity of the Bible* (Carey Kingsgate, 1953), pp. 38ff., and J. A. Motyer, 'Prophecy, Prophets', in *NBD*.

had joined together, namely, the means of grace (the sacrifices) and the obedient life which they were intended to sustain. The act – the ritual, divorced from its source in a heart grateful for redemption, and from its function in the obedient life – was meaningless and abhorrent to the Lord (13).

10. Like all the prophets Isaiah held that he was the mouthpiece of the Lord, the channel of the divine word. *Law* means 'teaching', the imparting of truth, within which, of course, there is a place for authoritative direction, command and prohibition. But the Lord's *law* first of all is the loving instruction that a caring father gives a loved child (*cf.* Pr. 4:1–2). Apart from mercy they would have been judged like *Sodom* and *Gomorrah* (9), but it surely is mercy, for they are like *Sodom* and *Gomorrah* in fact.

11. The standing error of the ritualist is that if all depends on performing the ceremonial act, then the more you do it the better. *Says* is a continuous tense: 'keeps saying' – as something he presses home upon us. Apart from Psalm 12:6 only Isaiah (1:18; 33:10; 40:1, 25; 41:21; 66:9) uses this verbal form referring to divine speech. To the Lord the ritual act means nothing (11ab), adds nothing (11cd) and does nothing (11ef). *No pleasure*: 53:10 uses the same verb ('it was the LORD's will') of a mighty sacrifice which delighted him.

12. *Appear before me* (or 'meet with me') may also be translated 'see my face', depending what vowels we supply to the consonants of the Hebrew text. The two ideas taken together express the reality and wonder of true worship (*cf.*, *e.g.*, Ex. 23:15, 17). *Trampling*: a religion of ritual is only the noise of feet on a pavement.

13–15. The denunciation continues. *Become a burden* (14): *i.e.* the rituals are not themselves a burden, for the Lord commanded them to start with. It is not the use but the abuse of divine ordinances that vexes him. This is true even of *prayer* (15), for we can 'pray on Sunday and prey on our neighbours for the rest of the week'. *Hide my eyes*: the opposite of the shining face of approval and blessing (Nu. 6:25; Ps. 4:6). What makes prayer unavailing is unrepented personal wrongdoing (*hands ... full of blood*). Not only the Lord's *eyes* but his ears too are alienated from such praying: literally 'I am not even listening'.

16–20. But there is a way back and through to God: actions they can take (16–17, nine commands), a promise they can experience (18), a blessing they can find (19) or lose (20). In verses 16–17 the nine commands fall into three groups of three. First, 'make yourselves clean before God by the cleansing ordinances he has provided' and this will *take your evil deeds* (lit. 'the evil of your deeds') *out of my sight*. The cleansing offered is effective before God. Now follow three commands to reorder personal life; *stop*, a decisive abandonment of sin; *learn*, the cultivation of a new mind; and s*eek*, set different objectives. *Justice* (*mišpāṭ* from √*šāpaṭ*), 'to determine authoritatively/judicially what is right', is often used, as here, to express the sum total of what the Lord judges right, the will of God for his people's conduct (*cf.* 42:1, 3–4). The third triad of commands calls for the reformation of society: *encourage the oppressed* translates an altered Hebrew text:[1] literally 'reform/set straight the oppressor'. Society must be transformed both at the point of the one inflicting – the oppressor – and at the point of the one suffering hurt – *the fatherless ... the widow*.

In verse 16 the Lord called his people to resort to his cleansing ordinances. In verse 18 he pledges their effectiveness. *Scarlet* is the colour of guiltiness (*cf.* 15). *Reason* (Heb. √*yākaḥ*, sometimes used of arguing a case in court, *e.g.* 2:4): the Lord calls his people to the bar of his justice where, of course, they can only be found guilty. But it is there that they hear words of free pardon based on the substitutionary death of a divinely appointed sacrifice. The Lord's pardon, like all his actions, accords perfectly with his justice. See below on 49:24–26. *Snow ... wool*: both naturally white, not made so by bleaching. The promise, therefore, is of a new, holy nature, not just the cleansing away of the past.[2]

Obedience is a serious matter (19–20). It is a 'means of grace' bringing *the best*. They must 'obey willingly' (be *willing and obedient*), not just offer conformism. The commands of verses 16–18 are backed by serious divine sanctions: obedience is the key virtue of God's people and disobedience their worst calamity. *Sword*: the forces at work in history are at the Lord's command in the interest of his just punishments, see on 10:5–15. *For the mouth ...*: a very emphatic attribution of Isaiah's words to the Lord himself.

iii. The social situation and its consequences (1:21–31).
From the literary point of view these verses contain three

---

[1] NIV (*oppressed*) alters the MT from *ḥāmôṣ* ('oppressor') to *ḥāmûṣ* ('oppressed'). The change is as unnecessary as it is minimal. 'Put right the oppressor' (lit.) deals with the cause of social breakdown, the wrongdoer, not just the consequence (the person hurt). This is what Isaiah sought.

[2] To treat v. 18 as a question ('Since your sins are ... can they be ...?') casts doubt on the promissory nature of the passage. Verse 18 is as realistic as a promise as v. 16 is as a command.

components. (a) Verses 21–26 comprise a self-contained poem with the thought of the faithful city as a bracket, or *inclusio*. The opening word *how* ('*êkâ, cf.* La. 1:1), and the prevailing 'metre', make it formally a lament. The poem sets out the social situation confronting Isaiah (21–23) and the divine reaction in judgment (24) and restoration (25–26). (b) Verses 27–28 note the alternatives: penitence or perishing. Finally, (c) verses 29–31 enlarge (29, 30) on the thought of the penitent people (27), with their deep shame for the past and its blighting consequences, and (31) on the judgment (28) on the impenitent: the self-sufficient are the cause of their own destruction. Thus three originally distinct pieces of literature are brought together into a new formation: verses 21–23 continue the explorations begun in verses 2–9 and 10–20 by sketching the state of society; verses 24–26 open the future as the arena of judgment and hope; and verses 27–28 and 29–31 reflect on this twofold prospect.

21. *Faithful city ... harlot*: only here and in 23:15–18 does Isaiah use the metaphor of sexual infidelity. Everything else followed in a downward spiral from this basic failure to live as a *faithful* wife with the Lord. Isaiah notes, first, the breakdown of moral ideals: *justice* and *righteousness*. Rooted in the divine holiness (5:16), *righteousness* embodies holiness in sound principles and *justice* expresses righteousness in sound precepts. Secondly, he observes the breakdown of moral relationships: *murderers*. When commitment to the Lord goes, breaching the 'first table' of the law (harlotry), the breach of the 'second table' follows (murder). Social values cannot be created and maintained without spiritual commitment.

22–23. Illustration (22) leads into reality (23). *Silver* which has *become dross* is totally degenerate; once *wine* is touched by *water*, no particle remains undiluted. Thus sin degrades the nature it enters and leaves no part untainted. The *rulers* provide a window into society: Godward they are *rebels* (*cf.* 2) and break his law by consorting with *thieves*; they abuse their position for self-advantage in *bribes* and *gifts*; and have no concern for other people.

24. So much for the *rulers* (23), but what does the real Sovereign think – he who is *Lord ... Almighty ... Mighty One*? He is *the Lord* (Heb. *hā*'*ādôn*), omnipotent in power, *the LORD Almighty* (*cf.* 9), and absolute ruler of his people, *the Mighty One of Israel* ('*ᵃbîr yiśrā*'*ēl*, as in 49:26; 60:16; *cf.* Gn. 49:24; Ps. 132:2, 5). Terrifyingly, this vast power is directed to a just vengeance. The sin of his people hurts the Lord, the divine nature is offended and he must *get relief*. The platitude that 'God hates the sin but loves the sinner' needs to be countered by the description of those who have hurt him as *my foes ... my enemies*. Sin sets God at variance with the sinner. But sin also invites divine retribution. The verb *avenge* (*nāqam*) makes its only appearance in Isaiah here, but *cf.* the noun (*e.g.* 35:4; 47:3; 61:2).

25 continues the thought of personal divine action against sinners, for the *hand* is the symbol of personal agency, *e.g.* verse 15; 10:13. To *turn* ('bring back') the hand is always a picture of hostile action (*e.g.* Ps. 81:14), but here, surprisingly, it leads into a work of purging (25bc) and restoration (26). The punitive and the restorative acts of God are bound into one. Truly, in wrath he remembers mercy (Hab. 3:2). Isaiah's message of hope is thus essential to the way he thinks: (a) a poem (21–26, see above) about sin and vengeance (21–25a) imperceptibly makes the transition into a poem about purging and restoration (25b–26); and (b) a menacing act (to turn the hand) becomes a work of mercy. *Purge*: 'refine as with detergent', as if to say, 'You have your means of cleansing and so have I'. *Dross*: as in verse 22. The Lord will deal with the degenerate nature as well as with the *impurities* of life.

26. It was David who *in days of old ... at the beginning* made Jerusalem the capital of the united kingdom (2 Sa. 5:6–9), and Isaiah now looks forward to David's return and the fulfilment of the promises (*cf.* 2 Sa. 7; Ps. 89). In this quiet way he introduces a theme which will become increasingly dominant in his book. *Righteousness ... Faithful*: 'right with God' in the principles and practice of holiness, *Faithful* to him as a true wife, see verse 21.

27. But how will the Lord *purge* (25) and *restore* (26)? He will do so (a) objectively, by the divine work of redemption: *redeemed* (*pādâ*), 'to pay a ransom price' (*cf.* Ex. 13:13; Lv. 27:27); and (b) subjectively, by the human act of repentance (*her penitent ones*). Thus Isaiah can insist that the Lord's mercies are moral mercies achieved in accordance with *justice* and *righteousness,* for they rest upon a price paid to meet the demands of his law and upon the moral factor of penitence and a return to God.

28. Those, however, who refuse the way of penitence remain under the claims of justice and *perish*. The Hebrew is terse: 'But shattering for those continuing to rebel and for the sinful – all at once!' Those who perish do so because of their unruly will (*rebels*), their falling short of the ideal (*sinners*) and their rejection (*forsake*) of the Lord.

29. The Hebrew opens this verse with 'For', justifying the charge of forsaking the Lord (28). Outwardly they observed the worship of the Lord (10–15), but their hearts (*delighted*) and wills (*chosen*) followed the nature and fertility cults of the day (*oaks ... gardens*), *cf.* 27:9; 57:3–6; 66:17. Isaiah did not believe that one religion was as good as another! True religion shows itself in moral commitment (10–20), has a surer basis (*i.e.* revelation) than mere human preference (29; *cf.* Am. 4:5) and plugs into a source of life not subject to earth's withering (30).

30. Evergreens were suitable symbols of undying life and became the focus of nature religion and the fertility of land, animals and humans, so important in an agricultural society. The equivalent today is a sound economy and a growing gross national product. These have ever been the chosen gods of the natural man. But earthbound religion is subject to earth's *fading* and earth's uncertain resources (*without water*).

31. *Mighty*: people who fancy themselves strong through their chosen gods; *work*: the idol gods they fashion and the gardens they have planted as the focus of their religion. Self-sufficiency and man-made gods are a dangerous combination like *tinder* and *a spark*!

c. The ideal, lost and found (2:1 – 4:6)

In the second 'movement' of his preface (see pp. 41–42 above), Isaiah's review of the contemporary scene (2:5 – 4:1) covers much of the ground surveyed in 1:2–31. Isaiah 2:5–21 concentrates on the religious situation and the failure of the false gods; 3:1 – 4:1 reviews the collapse of ordered society because of underlying moral failure. The bracket or inclusio around this is formed by two beautiful poems, beginning with what Zion was meant to be (2:2–4) and ending with what Zion will yet be (4:2–6). Chapters 2 – 4 match chapter 1 not only in content but also in underlying philosophy. The work of man is always unto destruction, with an apparent inevitability: objectives like making money (2:7ab), or security through armaments (2:7cd), contribute as much to the coming day of judgment as do making and worshipping false gods (2:8); humankind's best endeavours to construct a secure society come under divine 'deconstruction' (3:1–7) because of the unrecognized seriousness of sins of speech (3:8), and what might be thought of as the harmless luxury of a well-furnished wardrobe (3:16–23) in fact reflects frivolous and worldly vain-gloriousness. But the Lord is never nonplussed. Zion comes under inescapable wrath but Zion will be redeemed. The Lord will yet realize the ideal which his people corrupted.

i. Heading (2:1). The easiest explanation of this unexpected 'heading' is that what we call chapters 2 – 4 once 'circulated' as a separate 'book' or even as a 'wall-newspaper' (see on 8:1; 30:6). *Saw*: see on 1:1.

ii. The great 'might have been' (2:2–4). The use of this poem in Micah 4:1–4 raises the question which prophet 'copied' from the other or whether both quoted an existing hymn. The passage is equally 'at home' in each context, but possibly the variations in wording suggest that Micah's version is a free quotation. The poetic quality is worthy of Isaiah[1] and the topic more suited to him than to any other, with his enthusiastic love of Zion and its traditions. The poem is rooted in the universalism of the Abrahamic promise (Gn. 12:2–3; 22:16–18) but in its present context Isaiah makes it a challenge to his contemporaries: if the world is ever to say *Come, let us go up* (3), the Lord's people must heed the call *Come … let us walk* (5): the first requirement in evangelism is to have a church that is worth joining!

2. The (lit.) 'end/culmination of the days' is neither necessarily distant nor certainly near, but always imminent. It expresses the certainty of what God will do and the urgency of present readiness. Mythologically, mountains were the homes of the gods; historically, the Lord chose Mount Zion (Pss. 78:68; 87:1–2); eschatologically, the whole earth will be the Lord's mountain home (11:9). This is why Isaiah speaks here of the Lord's 'house' (not *temple*). A 'temple' is primarily a place for worship; a 'house' is primarily where the Lord has come to live among his people (*cf.* Ex. 29:42–46). *Raised … stream*: the supreme exaltation of his mountain home expresses the Lord's triumph over all the so-called gods on their mountains. See Psalm 48:2, where Zaphon is the mountain of Baal (*cf.* Ps. 95:3–4). The natural impossibility of a *stream* flowing upwards is intentional. A supernatural magnetism is at work.

3. The result is universal recognition. Though drawn supernaturally (2), they come voluntarily. Their unanimity (*Come, let us*) in seeking *the LORD* nullifies nationalism. Something makes them willing to seek *the God of Jacob*, namely a hunger for revealed truth. They come to learn (*he will teach*), to obey (*we may walk*), to receive what cannot be had elsewhere (lit. 'because the law/teaching will go out'), and this 'teaching' is nothing less than the actual *word of the LORD*. *Teach … walk*: this is real

---

[1] J. Gray holds that both prophets quote from a current liturgy ('The Kingship of God', *Vetus Testamentum* 11 [1961], p. 15); G. Von Rad argues that 'it cannot be doubted that the text is Isaianic' ('The City on the Hill', in *The Problem of the Hexateuch* [Oliver and Boyd, 1966], pp. 232ff.).

knowledge, a grasp of truth issuing in a changed life, the head warming the heart and redirecting the feet (Lk. 24:32–33). *Law*: see on 1:10.

4. The world will be transformed. Submission to the Lord brings the world under his rule whereby he will *judge* ('decide issues') and *settle disputes* ('arbitrate'). Where the Lord thus reigns, nationalisms are gone and weapons of war are made into garden tools: Eden has returned. The means of war (*swords ... spears*), the practice of war (*take up*) and the mentality of war (*train for*) are gone.

iii. The actual Jerusalem – part one (2:5–21). By contrast with this exciting ideal (2–4) Isaiah now faces the harrowing actual! The exhortation (5) itself implies that the Lord's people are not walking in his light, and verses 6–21 justify the implication in two poems: the first (6–9) asserting that blessing is impossible. The brackets/inclusio *you have abandoned* (6) ... *do not forgive* (9) speak of the alienation of the Lord and of his mercies because of three offences: conformity to the world (6), seeking worldly resources and securities (7) and worshipping man-made gods (8). The second poem (10–21) asserts that judgment is inevitable. Closely related to verses 6–9 by the themes of human self-sufficiency (11, 17; *cf.* 6–7) and idolatry (20; *cf.* 8), this intricate poem shows how the Lord has only to reveal his glory (10) and human arrogance falls (11), the world as it reflects human pride is flattened (12–17), idols are exposed as useless (18–19) and people defenceless (20–21). There is no exceptional exercise of divine power: only the Lord displaying what he always is!

5 offers **The first exhortation: walk with the Lord** (matched by a second exhortation in 2:22). *In the light* means in the light of the Lord's favour (Nu. 6:25), his presence and care (Ps. 27), his truth (Ps. 43:3) and his revealed word (Ps. 119:105).

The following section (6–21) can be entitled **The first exposure: the pride that makes its own gods** (matched likewise by a 'second exposure' in 3:1 – 4:1).

6. The initial 'For' (omitted in NIV) introduces an explanation of the surprising need (5) to recall the Lord's people to the Lord, but it springs from a dire cause. He has *abandoned* them, because, first, 'they are full from the East' (lit.). In contrast to the 'light of the LORD' (5), they look eastward to the sun rising, for all the light they need. Secondly, 'they are fortune-tellers like the Philistines'. They guide their lives by human ingenuity. The *Philistines*, not especially known in the Bible for *divination*, are selected as typical of the uncircumcised Gentiles (Jdg. 14:3), those untouched by special grace and revelation, the dregs (so to speak) of the world. Thirdly, they *clasp hands with pagans*: most likely 'make agreements with', *i.e.* alliances for trade or security; or, maybe, 'engage in worship with' (*cf.* Ps. 47:1, using a different verb); or 'abound in' (verb found in Jb. 36:18) what pagans have on offer. In turn, then, they were earthbound in their expectations ('full from'), their models (*like the Philistines*) and their associations (*with pagans*).

7–8. The worldliness of verse 6 is applied in three directions: values (*silver ... gold*), security (*horses ... chariots*) and religion (*idols*). In each category the adjective 'earthbound' describes their philosophy of life. *Idols* ('^{e}*lîlîm*): literally 'nonentities'. The word is a pun on '^{e}*lōhîm*, 'God'. They may seem to be the real thing but they are not!

9. *Do not forgive.* The Hebrew imperative not only commands but also can be used to express an inevitable outcome, here 'the conviction that something cannot or should not happen',[1] *i.e.* 'and there is no way you can forgive them'.

In verses **10–21**, the two main sections of this poem fall into four sub-sections. The first two (10–11, 12–17) share the theme of arrogance humbled. Note the matching endings of verses 11 and 17. The second two, each concluding with *shake the earth* (18–19, 20–21) share the theme of powerlessness exposed: people flee in terror (19) and throw away their useless idols (20). How does all this come about? Simply that *the LORD will be exalted* (11) and *he rises* (21). The Lord does not need to exert his power; he merely reveals his presence!

10–11. *Ground*: earthbound in the wisdoms they cherished (6), the values and securities they sought (7) and the gods they worshipped (8), now in their extremity they have only the earth to turn to. The terms of verses 10–11 stand in sharp contrast: *splendour ... majesty* as opposed to *humbled ... low*. It is the simple unveiling of the majesty of the Lord which brings humankind to the dust. *Splendour* is glory visibly displayed; *majesty*, from a verb 'to be high', is 'exaltedness', superiority of status and being. *The eyes*: the eye represents the direction in which one is looking and therefore stands for the aims and interests of life. Hence it is the organ of desire (Ps. 123:2), the expression of humility (Ps. 131:1) or, here, of arrogance.[2]

---

[1] GKC 190e (Pss. 34:5; 41:2).
[2] A. R. Johnson, *The Vitality of the Individual in Ancient Israel* (University of Wales Press, 1949), pp. 49–50.

12–17. *A day*: *i.e.* the day of the Lord. To the Hebrew mind, time was a moving line with the future moving into the present and away into the past. Every day was individually placed on this conveyor belt by divine faithfulness (Gn. 8:22; Ps. 74:16; Je. 33:20, 25), and sooner or later the Lord would include the *day* which he has *in store* (12). In verses 12–16 *for* means 'against'.

Cedars ... oaks ... mountains ... hills (13–14): as God's world, creation is always on his side (*cf.* 1:2); but, as our world, it is infected by our sinfulness and God's curse on sin (Gn. 3:17). The thorns of Genesis 3:18 are at one and the same time creation's reflection of divine hostility to sin and evidence of creation's corruption by sin (*cf.* Rom. 8:20–23). *Tower* and *wall* (15) represent both human achievement and human attempts to achieve community and security (Gn. 11:1–9). *Trading ship* (16): literally 'ships of Tarshish', the largest known ships, capable of the greatest voyages. Such ships demonstrated human triumph over environmental forces and human enterprise creating commercial empires (Ezk. 28:2–5). *Vessel* (16): a word found only here (*śᵉ<u>k</u>îyyô<u>t</u>*) and of uncertain meaning. If it is related to *maśkî<u>t</u>* ('figure, visual representation'; Nu. 33:52) possibly it means 'figurines', human artistic achievement as another dimension in which pride can raise its head (RSV, 'craft').

Arrogance ... pride (17): both words come from verbs expressing 'height' and are ways in which we can think of ourselves 'more highly' than we ought to think (Rom. 12:3), the opposite of the humble mind (Eph. 4:2).

18–19. The day of the Lord, when it comes, will be a world-wide event leaving the whole earth 'shaken'. The word Isaiah uses means more strictly 'to terrify' (*'ᵃrōṣ*), expressing dread before superior power (*e.g.* 29:23). The adjective (*'ārîṣ*) is used of despotic, irresistible power (13:11; 23:3–5). The Lord will reveal himself, then, in daunting, immobilizing power with a double result: in the spiritual realm, the end of the 'no-gods' (18; *'ᵉlîlîm*, see on verse 8); in the human realm, the exposure of the helplessness of humankind (19). Once more those who made human resources their security (6–8, 10) will find that now they have nowhere else to turn.

20–21. Verse 18 recorded the end of the 'no-gods' before the splendour of the exalted Lord. Now, however, their uselessness is recognized by their erstwhile adherents. The day of the Lord is the ultimate test. Nothing will avail when *the LORD ... rises*.

iv. The actual Jerusalem – part two (2:22 – 4:1).

Just as 2:5 formed a bridge between the ideal Zion of 2:2–4 and Isaiah's first exposure of the actual state of the city (2:6–21), so another exhortation (2:22) acts as a bridge to his second exposure (3:1 – 4:1), in which he concentrates on the collapse of Jerusalemite society. We saw in chapter 1 how central is a people's relationship with the Lord. Once again the point is made: he began his delineation of Zion's fall from its ideal by focusing on man the god-maker (2:8, 18, 20). Now he proceeds to show that because of this basic reality of pride – the replacement of the true God by the false gods – society must inevitably collapse. Has not the time come, then, to prepare for the day of the Lord by renouncing all merely human reliance? Isaiah 3:1 – 4:1 (note that 3:1 should begin with the explanatory word 'For') adds a further reason to cease relying on human strength. The section falls into two parts. The first (3:1–15) is marked off by the inclusio *the Lord, the LORD Almighty* (1, 15) and deals with Jerusalem's leaders under divine judgment (1–7, 12–15). Between these two passages, verses 8–11 explain the deep cause of Jerusalem's collapse (8) and the judgment that will fall (9–11). In 3:16 – 4:1 Isaiah turns from the leading men of the city to its leading women, and finds incarnate in them the spirit of arrogant self-satisfaction which is the death warrant of the city itself.

The second exhortation: renounce human reliance (2:22). Human reliance has been the story-line of Isaiah's first exposure. It has no currency in the day when the Lord in person must be faced. *Breath*: a reminder that human life is not independent or self-sustaining, but given (42:5; Gn. 2:7), and not a secure thing to rely on. *Of what account*: this does not question the value of humankind. It explains the foregoing: humankind has no value as a basis for security. The gift of breath implies a Giver and points to the wisdom of trusting.

The second exposure: social collapse and its cause (3:1 – 4:1). The great ideal (2:2–4) has suffered a second set-back: Jerusalemite society is collapsing. Far from moving towards becoming the strong focus of a stable and peaceful world, it is itself falling apart and under divine judgment. 3:1–7 makes evident the disintegration: everything that makes for a content and stable society will soon be removed by divine action; 3:8-15 speaks of the root cause and its consequences; 3:16 – 4:1 is a separate oracle focusing on the women of Zion, which balances the accusation and judgment of the leading men in 3:2-4.

1. When rulers fall or rise it is *the Lord, the LORD Almighty* who removes and appoints (4). (On his titles, see 1:9.) *Supply* ... *support* are the masculine and feminine forms of the same word, a Hebrew idiom for 'every support of every kind'. *Cf.* verse 7 for the 'other end' of this inclusio.

2–3 contains a sweeping survey of supposed social stabilizers who will be removed. All these will go: leaders in law and order (2a); national figures (2b); people of influence (2c–3), both illegitimate (*soothsayer*, *i.e.* fortune-teller; *clever enchanter*, lit. those 'instructed in whispering', *i.e.* in whispering to the dead, 'spiritists'; *cf.* 8:19; Dt. 18:9–13), and legitimate (*counsellor*; *elder*, *i.e.* local government officer, *cf.* Ex. 3:16; Dt. 19:12; *captain* or 'prince', *i.e.* civil servant); and supporting agencies (*skilled craftsmen*).

4. *Boys* (those without experience or maturity, as Je. 1:6) and *children* (*ta'ªlûlîm*, only elsewhere at 66:4, possibly 'capriciousness' or 'ruthlessness'): leaders behaving with the unpredictability and thoughtless cruelty of children.

5. At the grassroots there will be a developing 'rat race' of divisive and ruthless self-seeking (5ab), an intolerant age gap (5c) and advancement without regard to worth (5d).

6–7. Leadership is no longer treated seriously, and the most frivolous qualifications are taken as adequate (6), but, coupled with this, there is a loss of public spirit whereby people are unwilling to take responsibility (7).

8–9c are an explanation, though NIV omits the explanatory conjunction 'For' in each of its two occurrences. Why is there all this evidence of disintegration? 'Because Jerusalem has stumbled … fallen'. And why has this happened? 'Because their tongue and their deeds are against the LORD'. Thus we are led to the root cause of social breakdown. It is both spiritual (*against the LORD*), evidenced verbally (*their words*), and practical (*their ... deeds*). Jerusalem's guilt is compounded by the fact that it is not regarded by the people as their guilty secret and they have no sense of guilt. Sin is no longer sin, it is the new morality. Thus it is that societies collapse.

9d–11. In a form typical of Wisdom writers (*cf.* 28:23–29; 32:3–8) Isaiah affirms the principle of due and just reward both for *the righteous* (10) and *the wicked* (11). The *righteous* are not promised immunity to earth's troubles. Doubtless many of them would be named in the casualty lists of 3:25 – 4:1 but nevertheless *it will be well*.

In verses **12–15**, the self-contained poem of 9d–11, expressing the principle of exact retribution, is followed by this vignette of a courtroom. Together the passages are an excellent example of how Isaiah brings together into a new 'mosaic' pieces of his ministry that were originally separate or belonged in other contexts. *My people* (12, 15) forms an inclusio within which verse 12 is the situation to be remedied at law, in verses 13–14b the Judge takes his seat, and in verses 14c–15 himself brings the charge against the accused.

12 consists of an outraged exclamation, *My people!* followed by an address, *O my people*, as outrage becomes concern and we sense the Lord's heart of compassion for his mistreated ones. *Youths oppress*: the verb *oppress* is a plural participle, 'his oppressors/slave drivers', as in Exodus 3:7. Is this a 'plural of greatness', 'their chief slaver' – a reference to, say, King Ahaz (1:1)? *Youths* is a singular noun of uncertain meaning, possibly related to a verb 'to nurse' (√'ûl) and to a noun ('ōlēl), 'an infant', with overtones here of irresponsibility and wantonness. Possibly, therefore, 'Your big slave-driver is an irresponsible wanton/a spoiled brat.' *Women* could then be a reference to such a king's harem as being the powers behind the throne, but possibly, like Amos 4:1, Isaiah is commenting more widely on the influence of demanding women throughout Jerusalemite society (*cf.* 16–21). *Your guides*: ironically Isaiah uses a word meaning 'those who set you right', which is the true task of a leader; but here 'those who set you right set you wrong!' *They turn you from the path*: literally 'and the road of your paths they swallow up', 'road' here being the 'direction' that a 'path' is taking. The old established signposts of right living and sound society are gone as totally as if someone had swallowed them!

13–14. But however passionately the Lord feels (12) he does not rush to act. Everything must be done with legality and justice (Gn. 18:25). *Vineyard* (14) is symbolic of the Lord's care in choosing, delivering and settling his people and his delight in his people. But these leaders not only stripped the vineyard, they *plundered* it.

15. *Crushing* (dāḵā') is always metaphorical and always used of the severest maltreatment (53:5, 10). *Grinding* (√ṭāḥan): as in a mill (Nu. 11:8). They were not only cruel (*crushing*) but they treated those they ruled as a crop to be reaped for self-enrichment.

The section **3:16 – 4:1** is the expected sequel to the court scene of verses 13–15: the pronouncing of the sentence. Isaiah supplies it by introducing a separate oracle focusing on *the women* (lit. 'daughters') *of Zion*. In this way he (a) makes his accusation include all alike: the leading men in 3:2–4 are matched here by the prominent women. (b) He amplifies the charge: the outward offences of verses 14–15 are matched by an arrogant, self-indulgent spirit most plainly exhibited by Zion's daughters; the way in which he moves from the 'daughters' (16–24) to Zion herself (25) indicates that the womenfolk encapsulate the spirit of the city. (c) He affirms the exactitude of divine judgment: in verses 16–17 the Lord describes pride and threatens judgment; his judgment takes the form of removal (18–23), replacement (24) and destitution (25 – 4:1). Five times the knell of *instead of* sounds (24) as the manifestations of haughtiness give way to dire equivalents. (d) He creates a bridge over to what he wishes to say next (4:4), for he has in mind that, where sin abounded, grace will much more abound.

16–17. *Haughty* as they were, they used every art of manner (16cde) and ornament (16f) to be sexually attractive. Their pampered bodies will yet attract attention in a different way: *sores*, related to the word that Leviticus 13:2 uses of leprous tissue, but here maybe referring to evidences of malnutrition in siege conditions. *Scalps bald* is an uncertain translation. The verb (√*'ārâ*) is never used of 'stripping' off hair, and *scalps* is no more than an interpretative guess. The phrase could equally be interpreted 'expose their private parts', the dreadful fate awaiting them when the city falls.

18–23. *Crescent necklaces* (18): possibly 'lucky charms' related to a moon god. *Perfume bottles* (20), literally 'houses of soul/throat', are more likely 'high collars'.

24–26. Of the stated replacements, only *branding* is not associated with mourning. In verse 25 *your ... your* is feminine singular. Isaiah has moved from the daughters to the mother, Zion herself, watching her sons fall in battle. This continues into verse 26. *Gates*: the gate was the centre of the life of the city. The lamenting 'gate' is the city's broken heart, overwhelmed by the mounting casualty lists.

4:1. In 3:6 the men 'take hold of' (√*tāpaś*) a man, seeking a ruler; in 4:1 the women *take hold of* (√*ḥāzaq*) a man, seeking a husband.

v. The greatness that is 'yet to be' (4:2–6). Notice the sequence formed by the three *in that day* statements (3:18; 4:1 and 2). The day of the Lord will see sin end in blighting and death, but that is neither the only nor the last word: the 'daughters of Zion' merited judgment on their pride (3:16) but will experience cleansing from the same Lord acting in the same *spirit of judgment and ... fire* (4:4). Since 2:5, Isaiah has emphasized the social and religious side of Zion's failure. Now, in this wonderful poem, he indicates a true society with a true religion brought about by a cleansing (4:4) and creative (5) act of

God. In their humiliation the 'daughters' were willing to settle for a travesty of marriage (4:1) but the Lord designs for them a bridal *canopy* of unimaginable splendour (4:5). 'In [Christ] the sons of Adam boast/More blessings than their father lost'.[1] The poem is built on three pairs of matching themes: it begins with the Lord's Branch (2) and ends with the Lord's booth (6), two distinct provisions made for Zion's people; next it designates the Lord's people as holy (3) and bridal (5); and at its centre there is the double divine act of cleansing (4) and creation (5).

2. Many interpreters understand *Branch ... fruit* as looking forward to the earth's abundant fertility in the messianic Day[2] (*cf.*, *e.g.*, Je. 31:12; Joel 3:18; Am. 9:13). This is one aspect of the Old Testament's view of creation: just as sin brought a curse on the earth whereby it would henceforth yield its goodness only grudgingly (Gn. 3:17–19), so the day will come when the curse will be no more (Rev. 21:3–5) and the new creation will explode in bounty. This richness, therefore, is not 'pie in the sky by and by' but a messianic expectation based on the removal of sin and its curse by the Messiah. Zechariah 3:8–10 links the removal of iniquity and the enjoyment of peace and plenty with the 'bringing forth' of 'My servant, the Branch'. In other words, 'Branch' is a messianic title (Je. 23:5; 33:15; Zc. 3:8; 6:12), and the view taken here is that Isaiah 4:2 marks its · earliest occurrence. The references show that the title 'Branch' (*semah*)[3] is used to point to the Messiah's kingly and priestly offices, but in itself 'branch' is a 'family tree' motif indicating the Messiah's ancestry. To Jeremiah, he is David's Branch, tracing his human ancestry back to the great king (*cf.* Is. 11:1, using different words but the same idea). Isaiah sees him as 'The Lord's Branch', *i.e.* in some unexplained way he has a divine ancestry also. *The fruit of the land* could, of course, refer to the messianic abundance, but we ought to notice that here it is associated directly with *the Branch of the LORD* as jointly providing (lit.) 'adornment and glory ... pride and beauty for the escaped company of Israel'. It is suitable, therefore, to understand *fruit of the land* as indicating the human origin of the Messiah, in the same way as 'a root out of dry ground' in 53:2. His gifts to his people are 'adornment' (*beautiful*) and 'beauty' (*glory*), *i.e.* personal distinctiveness and attractiveness, in contrast to the false, deceptive beauty of 3:18;

---

[1] From Isaac Watts, 'Jesus shall reign where'er the sun'·

[2] See J. A. Motyer, *The Message of Amos* (IVP, 1974), pp. 205–206.

[3] J. Baldwin, '*semah* as a Technical Term in the Prophets', *Vetus Testamentum* 14 (1964), pp. 93ff.

'glory' (*glorious*) and *pride* point to a great change. 'Glory' had been their condemnation (3:8) and 'pride' their ruin (2:11–12), but now the divine glory will dwell among them (see on 5) and they will rightly pride themselves in him. *Survivors*: 'escapees', those who (by whatever means) have escaped from a calamity which has taken others.

3. The 'escapees' of verse 2 are described as *those who are left* and *remain*. They are not, however, what they were; they are *holy*, altered in status and transformed in character (see on 6:3), and this by the will of God, for they are *recorded among the living* or better 'written unto life', destined for life, registered in the Lord's book (*e.g.* Ex. 32:32–33; Lk. 10:20; Phil. 4:3; Rev. 3:5; 21:27).

4. Their transformation into holiness is now explained. *Filth ... bloodstains*: the former word means 'vomit', *i.e.* inner uncleanness; the latter, the outward marks of a wrong life (1:15). The Agent, applying this cleansing, is *the Spirit* (NIV mg.; *cf.* esp. 63:10–14), acting with *judgment* and *fire*. The Lord so acts by his Spirit as to meet the objective requirements of his absolute justice and the subjective requirements of his own holy nature, for burning and fire are symbols of divine holiness (Ex. 3:5; 19:10–25).

5. The Lord also provides the perfect environment for those whom (4) he has cleansed: a new act of creation. *Create* ($\sqrt{b\bar{a}r\bar{a}}$') is used in the Old Testament only of acts of God, things which by their greatness or newness or both absolutely require a divine agent. This supreme new reality is the Lord's own presence, signalled by the ancient symbols of *cloud ... by day ... fire by night* (Ex. 13:21–22; 19:18). His presence is of the most intimate nature, for *over all the glory will be a canopy. Canopy* (*huppâ*) is the 'marriage chamber' in Psalm 19:6 and Joel 2:16, the canopy providing privacy as bridegroom and bride come together in love and union. *Glory* is either the Messiah united in love with his bride-people, or the holy people of Zion joined in consummated love with the Lord under the overshadowing tokens of his presence.

6. In the old Tabernacle days, the Lord was present with his people (Ex. 29:43–46) but his Tent was closed to them (Ex. 40:34–35). Not so any longer! The overshadowing fiery cloud of the divine presence, the bridal canopy, will be *shelter ... shade ... refuge ... hiding-place*. The doubling of words is deliberate, conveying the idea of 'every possible protection'. Likewise the contrast of *heat* with *storm* and *night* with *day* implies 'in every circumstance and threat' and 'at all times'.

d. Grace exhausted (5:1–30)

The third movement of Isaiah's preface (see p. 42 above) is continuous with the previous two but raises a wholly new prospect: it sounds no note of hope. We saw how, in 1:25–26, against all deserving and indeed against the customary use of the expression *turn my hand*, the Lord forecast his work of royal restoration; likewise in 3:16 – 4:1 the pride of the daughters of Zion certainly receives its due but judgment does not have the last word: where sin abounded, grace superabounded (4:4). It is not unfitting to use the word 'grace', expressing as it does a total mercy to the totally undeserving. But picture the situation should even divine grace be exhausted!

Isaiah reaches this point in the Song of the Vineyard (1–7). In 1:8 the vineyard reference was associated with the Lord's preservation of a remnant of Zion; in 3:15, when the vineyard was under threat from self-seeking rulers, the Lord as Judge intervened on behalf of his vineyard-people. But in 5:4 the vineyard is the place where the Lord asks if there is anything more he could have done. A total grace has been expended but only with the result of inedible grapes. If the Lord has nothing more that he can do, what price hope? Chapter 5 therefore calls in question the bright expectations sketched in the first two sections of the preface and foresees only *darkness ... distress ... light ... darkened* (30).

Between the song (1–7) and the darkness (30), Isaiah spells out the grim reality of the inedible grapes (8–25) in six 'woes'. It is not the Lord's way to pass and execute judgment without enquiring into the facts, nor to spring judgment on those who deserve it without alerting them to its cause.

i. A total work and a total loss (5:1–7). 1ab. The recurrence of the vineyard-motif in these chapters and elsewhere (27:2–6; Je. 12:7–10; *cf.* Ps. 80:8; Je. 2:21) suggests that it was a familiar usage. When Isaiah announced, then, that he was about to 'sing about my loved One, my Beloved's song about his vineyard' (1), listeners would gather expectantly – and for a while their happy expectations were realized.

1c–2d. The various actions of the owner are not allegories of specific aspects of the Lord's care for his people; they are the typical acts of viticulture designed to make the single point that nothing was left undone to guarantee a sound crop. Isaiah's Beloved had great expectations of his vineyard. He built a *watchtower*, not a temporary hut (1:8); *winepress* should be 'wine-vat', for storage of the crop – and cut in the rock for permanency.

2ef. All this caring work issued in hope: *he looked for a crop*. But instead of *grapes* all it yielded was *bad fruit* (lit. 'stink-fruit'). Every care had been lavished, but yet the vine retained its natural wildness – as if grace had never touched it.

3–4. In true prophetic fashion Isaiah speaks in the person of his Beloved and, as Jesus will do in his vineyard parable (Mk. 12:9), by making his hearers both judge and jury in the matter, begins to manoeuvre them toward self-condemnation. *What more could have been done …?*: this is the sobering question central to this section of Isaiah's preface: if divine power, wisdom and obligation have exhausted themselves, what hope can remain?

5–6. Failure to fulfil the owner's intention brought the fourfold danger of divine antagonism (*I will*), dominant external foes (*destroyed … trampled*), rampant alien growth (*briers … thorns*) and deprivation of the means of life and fertility (no *rain*).

7. The Lord's joy and sorrow in his 'vineyard-people', plain throughout the song, comes to a climax. *Delight* (*ša*ᵃ*šûʿîm*): only here in Isaiah, an intensive formation, 'his intense pleasure'. Fruitlessness does not merely violate the Lord's formal intention, it contradicts his heart. *Justice* is *mišpāṭ*, *bloodshed* is *miśpāḥ*. The meaning is uncertain but these two words look and sound almost identical! Kidner suggests 'he looked for right but, behold, riot' – in the sense of moral and social anarchy. Likewise *righteousness* is *ṣᵉdāqâ* and *cries of distress* is *ṣᵉʿāqâ*. The façade was in place, but they were violating the Lord's norms in both practice and principle (*justice … righteousness*, see 1:21), and this was particularly evident in relationships (*bloodshed … cries*).

ii. The stink-fruit harvest and its consequence (5:8–30). Isaiah spells out the ill fruit of the vineyard in six 'woes' (8, 11, 18, 20, 21, 22). The first two (8–12) deal with abuse of the material benefits of life, and the consequences are drawn out in two *therefore* sections (13, 14–17). The second series of four woes (18–23) deals with violation of the moral and spiritual obligations of life, and it too is followed by two *therefore* sections (24, 25–30). As we will see, the first *therefore* in each case (13, 24) is short and specifies how the coming judgment matches the foregoing sin; the second *therefore* is longer and forecasts total judgment, death (13) and destruction (25–30). This is a good place to note how measured and reasoned Isaiah was in his ministry – and this applies to all the prophets. Any tendency to think of them as condemnatory demagogues, ranting and rebuking, fails to observe how they ministered on the basis of indisputable evidence (the 'woes') and then carefully drew out logical, inescapable conclusions (the 'therefores').

8. It may help us to see the balanced coherence of Isaiah's exposure of sin if we number this first 'woe' A1, and note how it is balanced by the sixth (22–23; A2). Isaiah starts with property acquisition and ends with money acquisition. In Israel land was a sacred entity. It belonged to the Lord, and his people were his 'resident aliens and settlers' (Lv. 25:23). The intention was that each family's holding would remain within the family (Lv. 25; Nu. 27:1–11). But land speculation was rife in Isaiah's day (*cf.* Mi. 2:2; Am. 2:6–8) and he gives us a picture of the wealthy creating large estates, centred on the 'big house' without a smallholder in sight. The squire, living *alone in the land*, is monarch of all he surveys. *Add house to house*: building on to an originally smaller house to create a mansion.

9–10. The NIV has smoothed out a very exclamatory piece of Hebrew with the help of 22:14 but, of itself, verse 9a reads 'In my ears! Yahweh of hosts!' The exclamation affirms direct, verbal revelation. But beyond even this vital truth there is the manifestation of heaven's outrage in the explosive quality of the exclamation. A *bath*, about six gallons, was a meagre yield for *ten acres* – 'ten yokes', usually understood as the area ten oxen could plough in a day. A *homer* was equivalent to ten ephahs, so that the yield envisaged here is one tenth of the seed sown. An *ephah* was equal to a *bath* in dry measure. Isaiah saw that the character and conduct of the owners would cause a retrenchment in what the created world is prepared to do for them.

11–12. The second 'woe' (B1), self-indulgence, is matched by the fifth (21; B2) which deals with self-importance. Their whole regard is for partying (11–12b), they have no regard for what the Lord is doing (12cd).

13. The short *therefore* takes up the preceding themes: land-grabbing (8) replaced by *exile*; alcoholic indulgence (11) by *thirst*. Those who blinded themselves to spiritual perception (12) go into exile *for lack of understanding*. How exact and even-handed the Lord is! *Will go* is a Hebrew 'perfect' tense and could express 'have gone' (*i.e.* their captivity has already taken place; they are slaves to greed and appetite), or 'are doomed to go'. Isaiah lived in times of great powers on the march (see Introduction, pp. 19–23), and it was a real contemporary possibility that little Judah would be swallowed up. *Exile* is too precise a translation, suggesting a prediction of the Babylonian exile yet to come. All Isaiah forecasts here is 'captivity', loss of their land and liberty to superior force.

14. *The grave* should be 'Sheol' (NIV mg.), the 'place name' of the abode of the dead (*cf.* 14:9–15) pictured here as an insatiable monster into which all descend. The additional description *brawlers* and *revellers* is neither an irrelevance nor a mere poetic elaboration. This was the character of those Isaiah saw around him (11–12). They go down into death unchanged; they enter Sheol in the character they forged on earth, still spiritually insensitive and all-unready to meet God.

15–16. *Holy* (*qāḏoš*) is the adjective describing the divine nature itself. In Genesis 38:21, a woman considered to belong wholly to the god she served is described as 'holy' (*qᵉḏēšâ*), part of the divine order of things. The word itself probably means 'separate' (see 6:3), but in the case of the God of the Bible what constitutes his distinctiveness and makes him separate is his moral reality. His exaltation is simply the manifestation of what has always been true of him, his holiness exerting itself in *righteousness* and in *justice*. *God* is here the noun *'ēl*, mostly used of God in his divine transcendence.

17. *The rich*, literally 'well-fed' (*cf.* 11), created their vast and very private estates (8). These have now passed into new ownership, *sheep … in their own pasture*. All the expenditure and effort now lies in *ruins*, a grim inclusio to the designer-emptiness of verse 8! Verse 17 may look like an idyllic pastoral scene; it is actually the empty achievement of human vanity; the net profit of pride. *Lambs* translates a needlessly altered Hebrew text which reads '(passing) strangers'. If we translated it 'tramps' it would give the right feeling here.

Verses **18–23** contain the second series of 'woes' (see p. 62), which exposes Isaiah's people as morally and spiritually indifferent (18–19), reversing moral values (20), recognizing no authority but themselves (21), no glittering prizes but those awarded for indulgence (22), and no obligations save to work the system for self-advantage (23). This frightening list poses the five questions by which the graph of collapsing human character can be traced: is sin abhorred or relished (18)? Is God reverenced or flouted (19)? Are moral values seen as objective absolutes or as subjective preferences (20)? Where is the authority which governs life thought to reside (21)? What excites admiration in human achievement (22)? Does the social system guarantee the punishment of guilt and the vindication of innocence (23)?

18–19. The two 'woes' in verses 18–19 and 20 can be classed as C1 and C2, united in their respective themes of sin pursued and sin justified. They form the heart of Isaiah's description of the crop of 'stink-fruit', the place that people give to morality and God (C1), and how they define moral authority (C2). Isaiah pictures people harnessed to sin, like animals harnessed to carts. Thus they are the voluntary practitioners of a sinful lifestyle but, as such, they are living an animal existence beneath their true dignity as humans and, as victims of sin's *deceit* (*cf.* Eph. 4:23; Heb. 3:13), they are involved in an increasing bondage as the movement from *cords* to *ropes* indicates. *Sin ... wickedness*: the former ('*āwôn*) stresses the inward reality of sin in human nature; the latter (*ḥaṭṭā'â*) the specific ways in which sin is actually committed (see on 6:7). By a natural progression (*cf.* 12), devotion to sinfulness (18) leads to the spiritual arrogance that refuses trust (19a–c) and demands proof (19d–f). Unable to grasp what the Lord is doing, they refuse the way of patient faith, awaiting his time; so they say, *Let God hurry ... hasten* and, until God acts visibly to their satisfaction, they suspend belief. They are determined only to *know* when they *see*. This is, of course, a plain challenge to Isaiah's whole affirmation of the divine promises and his call to a position of trust, patiently waiting until the Lord prove as good as his word.

20. The moral code has been rewritten. People no longer feel guilty when they depart from what was once considered right. Just as 'one man's meat is another man's poison', so personal taste now rules supreme; if a course of behaviour seems *bitter* or *sweet* to someone, then that's what it is.

21 (B2; *cf.* 11–12). Everything is reduced to individual reaction and opinion.

22–23 (A2; *cf.* 8–10). Once more Isaiah insists that bodily indiscipline (22) has its counterpart in moral obtuseness (22). *Champions* is (lit.) 'men of substance', meaning here 'worthwhile people'. But what a standard by which to measure worth! Can he hold his drink (22a)? Is he a good hand with a cocktail shaker (22b)? And yet these are the nation's judges (23)!

24. The punishment will fit the crime (*cf.* 13). They invited the Lord to hurry (19); their downfall will be like *fire* racing through *straw*.

Verses **25–30** raise various literary questions (see on p. 91). Earthquake (25) and storm (30), those two manifestations of divine presence and power (*e.g.* Ex. 19:18–19; Ps. 18:7–15), provide the brackets within which divine rage is expressed by means of another force that the Lord commands (26–29), the irresistible invader. Here is total judgment, matching the long 'therefore' of verses 14–17.

25. The created world, with all the immense forces contained in it, is a controlled tool in the hands of the Creator to serve his righteous purposes. The verbs could be understood as past tenses – maybe the earthquake of Amos 1:1 and Zechariah 14:5, possibly within Isaiah's memory.

26–28. In verse 25 'natural' powers expose how vulnerable we are; now Isaiah proceeds to uncover the inner workings of history (*cf.* 10:5–15). The Lord's merest gesture (*banner ... whistles*) guarantees that, without delay (26cd), even those strongest in person (27) and most potent in military equipment (28) come to do his will. The cynical request that the Lord hurry up (19) finds its nemesis in the swift onset (28cd) of the invader.

29–30. Pictures of the irresistible predator (29) and the inescapable storm (30) complete Isaiah's forecast of doom. *Lion ... young lions*: the double description (*cf.* 3:1) expresses comprehensiveness – every possible predator. The second word means lions in their prime strength. *Growl* (√*nāham*) is the satisfied growl of the lion munching its prey. In Isaiah's ear this becomes (30) the 'growl ... growling' (NIV *roar ... roaring*) of a storm, as he moves to his second picture in which *day* becomes *darkness* and the storm-bound sailor, looking hopefully *at the land* as a place of escape, finds that, even should he reach shore, only *distress* and *clouds* await him. Thus the passage ends with the same relentless hopelessness that has characterized it throughout! Hope has vanished. In other words the third movement of Isaiah's preface works according to its own logic. If there is nothing left for God and grace to do (4), then the light has indeed gone out. It looks as if the sad tale of the failure of the people of God (see 1:2–24; 2:6 – 4:1) has reached its appropriate terminus, and as if the flashes of hope which marked the first two movements of the preface (1:25–27; 4:2–6) were no more than 'might have beens'. But can it be really so?

II. LIGHT BEYOND THE DARKNESS: THE COMING KING (6 – 12)

Isaiah has now established the backdrop against which he worked as a prophet. The people to whom he was sent were the heirs of great promises but appear to have forfeited them. By the end of his prefatory chapters, darkness has closed in upon them. Grace has been exhausted; nothing but judgment lies ahead.

As we shall see, this is the position which Isaiah sketches in a very dramatic way in 6:1, but by the end of this section, darkness (6:1) has been replaced by singing (12:2, 5) and salvation (12:2–

3), and the Lord in all his holiness (6:1–3) is dwelling in Zion in the midst of his people (12:6). Darkness and judgment, then, do not, after all, have the last word. Far from it, for the very promises that appeared to have been forfeited – the David-promises of 1:25–27 and the Zion-promises of 4:2–6 – are the very things that come to pass (9:1–7; 11:1–9; 12:1–6). The exhausting of grace (5:4) has been superseded by the triumph of grace.

How then does Isaiah present this surprising hope, the dawning of the great light beyond the darkness, the coming King? The section falls into three parts. It opens with Isaiah's account of his experience of the forgiveness of sins at the hands of the holy God (6:1–7), his call to be a prophet (6:8), and the strange commission the Lord gave him (6:9–13). This opening is matched by the song (12:1–6) in which individual (12:1–2) and community (12:3) enter into salvation through the turning away of divine anger (12:1), are commissioned to worldwide prophecy (12:4–5), and have the Holy God dwelling among them (12:6). This is a very full inclusio, with sin, salvation, commissioning and divine holiness bracketing the whole section.

Within these brackets, Isaiah first addresses the situation in Judah (7:1 – 9:7), when King Ahaz faces the crisis of fresh invasions from the north (see Introduction, pp. 19–20) and decisively rejects the word of God calling him to faith (9:7). In parallel with this, Isaiah turns to the northern kingdom of Israel (9:8) where the same tragedy has occurred: the word of God was sent but was rejected. Isaiah's addresses to Judah and Israel follow parallel courses dealing with judgment on disobedience (7:18 – 8:8; 10:5–15), divine preservation of a believing remnant (8:9–22; 10:16–34) and the hope of a coming King (9:1–7). Between the brackets of chapters 6 and 12, the internal chapters 7 – 11 have their own inclusio: 7:1–17, the king who failed and destroyed the dynasty of David; 11:1–16 the true Davidic King who will rule over the whole perfected creation.

In this section we find a principle and a problem. The principle is the place Isaiah accords to hope in the life of the people of God. He always sees hope for divine action against all the odds of human merit and deserving (*cf.* 1:25–27; 4:2–6). The bright future is not brought about by a gradual improvement or by clever human planning: it is a work of God; it comes as the outworking of the logic of his faithfulness; it dawns because he is as true to himself in mercy as he is in judgment. We have seen in the brief outline above that Isaiah presents two topics in sequence: the preservation of a believing remnant of the people, and the bursting-in of the great hope. This is a deliberate juxtaposition because, on the one hand, the remnant is caught up, inevitably, in the darkness that comes upon the disobedient people – faith is never a certificate of immunity – but, on the other hand, in the darkness they have the cordial of hope, the durability to hold on because of the light which God's promise holds before them (*cf.* 2 Cor. 3:12; Col. 1:5; 1 Thes. 1:3; 5:8; 2 Thes. 2:15–16). It is for this reason that Isaiah presents the great hope as if it were about to dawn immediately beyond the Assyrian darkness (*e.g.* 8:21 – 9:2; 10:28 – 11:3) – in order that they might be buoyed up in hope just as Christians are by the scriptural truth of the imminence of the return of the Lord Jesus.

The problem raised by chapters 6 – 12 is that the message which the people actually needed to hear is not brought to them. The whole upshot of the preface (chs. 1 – 5) is that through sin they are not what they ought to have been (ch. 1), nor what they were meant to be (chs. 2 – 4), nor what they might have been (ch. 5). It is precisely the answer to this problem that Isaiah discovers in the Lord's dealings with him personally (6:1–8). Furthermore, the inclusio provided by 12:1–6 focuses on this very truth – people who have found comfort in place of divine anger and rejoice in a God of salvation. So why are chapters 7 – 11 lacking any message about atonement and forgiveness? The answer is that Isaiah met people where they were and brought them a message that they could see as relevant. They were not yet ready to face their sinfulness and hear a gospel of pardon, but in the circumstances of the time (see on 7:1ff.) they could not fail to see the inadequacies of existing royal leadership and their need for a different, perfect son of David. True prophet that he was, Isaiah plunged pragmatically into the situation that faced him and provided both an exact diagnosis of the present and a confident vision of the future. Yet, returning as he did in chapter 12 to the 'salvation' theme of chapter 6, he implies that somehow, within the promise of the royal Messiah, there lurks the Lord's answer to the problem of sin and judgment. In this way Isaiah lays the foundation on which he will presently build the theology and prediction of atonement which we find in chapters 40 – 55, centred on the Servant (53:13) who is also David (55:3).

a. The individual, atonement and commission (6:1–13)

The topic of this chapter is the call of Isaiah, and for this reason alone it would be a fitting 'chapter 1' following the 'author's preface'. But like all the prophets who recorded their experience of a call (*cf.* Paul, Gal. 1 – 2), personal facts are told not for their own sake but because they illustrate a vital theme. We come nearer to the heart of this chapter by noting that it is pervaded by the thought of death: the dying king (1), the prophet under sentence of death (5), the sacrificial animal dead on the altar (6) and the felled tree (13). Twice over, death seems to spell the end but is found not to be so. The king lies dead (1) but it turns out to be only the felling of a tree, and life remains in the root (13); the prophet lies dead, struck down by sin under divine holiness (5) but when the seraph approaches, apparently bearing the fire of judgment, it is to apply the efficacy of a sacrifice for sin and to speak the word 'atoned' (7). Death does not have the last word.

1a. Uzziah reigned for fifty-two prosperous and secure years (2 Ki. 15:1–7; 2 Ch. 26). By the end of his reign, however, clouds were gathering: Tiglath-Pileser III of Assyria, who acceded in 745 BC, was an imperialist, and already the small Palestinian states were feeling the threat. It is tempting to think of Isaiah, pondering the old king's death, anxious for the future, being comforted by the vision of a King who cannot die (*cf. the King*, 5). But if he was thus reassured by his vision he does not say so. According to 1:1 Isaiah began his prophetic career 'during the reign of' (lit. 'in the days of') *Uzziah, i.e.* before Uzziah died. Why, then, does he not date his call, as would be customary, 'in the fifty-second year of the reign of Uzziah'? Why does he date the event by a death? Uzziah had committed a dreadful sin of trespass (2 Ki. 15:5; 2 Ch. 26:16–21), intruding into the house of the Lord where, as a layman, he had no right to go. For this he fell under divine judgment and for the rest of his reign was alienated from the worshipping community, under divine displeasure. When death came, this situation was unresolved. The king died as he had lived, estranged and unclean. Following on the darkness with which chapter 5 ended, can we doubt that Isaiah saw the king as a symbol of the nation? It too had overstepped the bounds of grace (5:4) and was moving towards its demise under divine displeasure (5:13–17) and at the hands of an invincible foe (5:24–30). So has the Lord really come to the end as far as his people are concerned? In this way chapter 6 takes up the story where chapter 5 left off.

In verses **1b–13a**, the symbolism of the dying king (1a) leads into a tripartite vision of God. First, the Lord's holiness with its consequence in Isaiah's (and his people's) doom (1b–5); secondly (6–8), the Lord's atonement, bringing Isaiah's cleansing and restoration; and thirdly, the Lord's programme (9–13a) and Isaiah's ministry within it.

1b. *I saw*: John 1:18 correctly observes that 'No-one has ever seen God', for God is spirit (31:3; Jn. 4:24). Yet, in condescension, he sometimes clothes himself with visibility for the good of his people, showing now this side and now that side of his character (*e.g.* Jos. 5:13–15). For Isaiah the Lord became visible in exalted kingliness, with a throne, robes and attendants, all speaking of sovereign majesty and dominion. *High and exalted*: see 52:13; 57:15, where the same words refer respectively to the Lord's Servant and the Lord. The reference here also is best taken as (not to the *throne* but) to the Lord, *high* in his own nature, and *exalted* or 'lifted up' by the acknowledgment of his supremacy. *Train ... temple*: the flowing robes point to the place where the transcendent Lord touches the earth; the Lord is present in all his majesty at the centre of his people's life. The *temple* is no 'mere' symbol. It is where the Lord is (1 Ki. 8:10–13), the indwelling God (1 Cor. 3:16; 6:19; Eph. 2:19–22). (*Cf.* the 'footstool' motif, 1 Ch. 28:2; Ps. 132:7; La. 2:1; Is. 60:13.)

2. *Above him*: the position of a servant waiting 'upon' a master. The same preposition, 'over, upon', occurs in Genesis 18:8 (NIV 'near'). *Seraphs*, literally 'Burning Ones', are mentioned only here. Fire is the chief symbol of the holiness of God (Ex. 3:2–5; 19:18). Suitably, therefore, in this context Isaiah gives the heavenly attendants a title that matches their situation: with their down-folded and up-stretched wings they look like huge flames surrounding the throne of the Holy One.[1] *Covered ... covered*, like *were flying*, are verbs of continuous action. The wings covered their eyes (for even they must not pry into the divine, *cf.* Ex. 19:21) but not their ears (for their role is to wait for the divine word and obey it, Ps. 103:20). The *feet* are the organs of activity, of directing life towards goals (Ps. 18:33; Pr. 1:15–16; 4:27). It is impossible to be sure, but perhaps they covered their feet[2] to disavow choosing their own path.

3. The continuous song had a single theme: the Lord's holiness, concerning which we learn two truths. First, Hebrew

---

[1] The verb *śārap* means 'to burn', but a word of the same spelling is used of 'snakes' in 30:6. This has misled some (O. Kaiser, *Isaiah 1 – 12* [SCM, 1963], *ad loc.*) to think of serpent-guardians of the divine presence – very odd serpents, of course, with hands and feet. In Isaiah's Hebrew the word *śʳrāpîm* ('seraphim') has no definite article: it is a description, not a title. They were 'burning ones' who exercised a 'burning' ministry towards the prophet (6).

[2] Why did they cover their feet? There is nothing particularly 'creaturely' about the foot whereby they should reverently hide their 'creatureliness' in the presence of the Creator; 'feet' are used as a euphemism for the sexual parts (7:20), but the attribution of sexuality to heavenly beings would be inappropriate. Verses like 52:7 and Pr. 1:15–16 suggest the feet as metaphorical of the direction life takes.

uses repetition to express either a superlative, as when 'pure gold' in 2 Kings 25:15 translates 'gold gold', or a totality, as when 'full of tar pits' in Genesis 14:10 translates 'pits pits'. But here for the only time in the Hebrew Bible a quality is 'raised to the power of three', as if to say that the divine holiness is so far beyond anything the human mind can grasp that a 'super-superlative' has to be invented to express it and, furthermore, that this transcendent holiness is the total truth about God. The holiness word-group ($\sqrt{q\bar{a}da\check{s}}$) may mean 'brightness', the unapproachable God (1 Tim. 6:16; Ps. 104:2) or 'separatedness', *i.e.* the quality which marks off the divine nature, setting God apart from all else, making him the Being that he is. His holiness is, therefore, his unapproachable and unique moral majesty before which sinful humankind instinctively quakes (Jdg. 6:22; 13:22). Secondly, just as holiness is the 'whole truth' about God himself, so it is the 'whole truth' about his immanence in creation: *the whole earth is full of his glory.* Holiness is the Lord's hidden glory; glory is the Lord's omnipresent holiness.

4–5. *Shook*: the customary reaction of the created order to the presence of the divine (*e.g.* Ex. 19:18; Ps. 18:7–9). *Doorposts ... thresholds ... smoke*: the mere declaration of the Lord's holiness is enough to bar entrance and to forbid sight. Isaiah finds himself totally excluded and recognizes its consequence (*I am ruined*) and its cause (*unclean lips*). *Ruined*: from $\sqrt{d\bar{a}m\hat{a}}$, 'to be silent', used of the silence brought about by loss (Je. 47:5) or death (Ps. 49:12). To translate 'silenced' would be telling in this context: excluded from the heavenly choir – even from the possibility of participating in praise from afar. This judgment came about through the linking of what some might think of as the 'merest' sin (*unclean lips*) with the remotest contact (*eyes have seen*), but the mixture is fatal. *People of unclean lips*: why does Isaiah extend the admission of sin in this way? Possibly it is a further confession on his part: he so failed to recognize the seriousness of sins of speech that he failed to separate himself (*live among*) from such a society; but possibly he is laying down a marker for the future: if my sin can be forgiven, so can theirs. Maybe, in retrospect, in his own experience of atonement (6–7) he already saw the solution to the national darkness of 5:30 and the dawning of the light of 53:11. *The King, the LORD Almighty*: literally 'of hosts'. It was not a novel revelation of God that proved Isaiah's undoing, just a realization of what had always been true, a holy King, an omnipotent Yahweh, 'the Holy One of Israel', to use Isaiah's special title for him (see 1:4).

6–7. The Lord has taken the initiative throughout: revealing

(2–3), excluding (4–5). Now one of the seraphs, who flew only by divine command, is sent as the messenger of salvation. Though all else is shrouded from gaze by the excluding cloud, the means of salvation is left on view – the fire and the altar. *Live coal ... tongs ... altar*: the use of tongs shows that this was no 'pretend' fire but the real thing. In the Old Testament, however, fire is not a cleansing agent[1] but the expression of the active, even hostile, holiness of God (Gn. 3:24; Nu. 11:1–3; Dt. 4:12, 33, 36). This, however, was fire from the *altar, the place where holiness accepted, and was satisfied by, the death of a substitutionary sacrifice* (Lv. 17:11). The *live coal* thus encapsulates the ideas of atonement, propitiation, satisfaction, forgiveness, cleansing and reconciliation, and of these spiritual realities Isaiah, the erstwhile doomed sinner, is left in no doubt when the seraph explains: 'Behold, as soon as this touched your lips your iniquity went, and, as for your sin – paid by ransom!' The Lord ministers to us at the point of felt need (*lips*); the effect is instantaneous (the verbs *touched ... taken* are co-ordinate perfect tenses); he deals not just with sin as we are aware of it, but as he sees it in us: *guilt* or 'iniquity' (1:4; 5:18), the inner corruption, *sin* (1:4, 18; 3:9), the specific wrong; the basis of atonement is a 'covering price'. *Atoned* (*kippēr*): 'to cover'. *Cf.* the literal sense in Genesis 6:14 ('coat it'); the developed meaning of the verb used in atonement theology (*kippēr*) has retained this basic idea, but in the sense that we speak of the correct sum of money 'covering' a debt, *i.e.* cancelling by a satisfactory payment (Ex. 21:30; 30:12–16; Nu. 5:8; 31:50).

8. The immediate effect of atonement is reconciliation. Isaiah first saw the Lord afar off (1), but now he is near enough to overhear the divine musing; he had once been 'silenced' by sin (5) but as the redeemed sinner he is free to speak. The God who shut him out (4) has brought him home. But he finds that being joined to God means joining a missionary society: he has been brought in in order to be sent out. *Us*: a plural of consultation (1 Ki. 22:19–23), but the New Testament relates these verses to both the Lord Jesus (Jn. 12:24) and the Holy Spirit (Acts 28:25), thus finding here what will yet accommodate the full revelation of the Holy Trinity.

---

[1] The only possible reference to cleansing by fire is Nu. 31:21–24, but the insistence of v. 23 on 'the water of cleansing' suggests that here also fire symbolizes the active wrath of the holy God. Even on inanimate objects contaminated by Midianite life, that wrath must vent itself before they can pass to Israelite use.

Verses **9–13a** contain the message Isaiah is to convey (9), the task given him to do (10) and the programme in which he is now involved (11–13a).

9–10. The use of these verses in the New Testament (Mt. 13:14–15; Mk. 4:12; Lk. 8:10; Jn. 12:39–41; Acts 28:26–27) makes them especially important to understand, but at first sight what an odd commission they are: to tell people not to understand (9), yet to make sure that they will not (10)! This is its plain meaning. It specifies (9) the 'outer' (*hearing, seeing*) and the 'inner' faculties (*understanding, i.e.* 'discerning', and *perceiving, i.e.* 'knowing') and arranges them (10) into a rounded structure (*heart ... ears ... eyes ... eyes ... ears ... heart*) thus emphasizing total inability to comprehend. The most helpful approach is to ask how, in the light of his subsequent ministry, Isaiah understood what he was commanded. The answer lies in 28:9–10, where we learn that Isaiah presented the truth with such simplicity that the 'men of the world' of his day would pack him off to teach kindergarten! And the whole Isaianic literature bears the same mark of a plain, systematic, reasoned approach. In other words, verses 9–10 are a very stark statement of the preacher's dilemma: those who resist the truth can be changed only by telling them the truth, but to do this exposes them to the danger of rejecting the truth yet once again – and maybe this further rejection will push them beyond the point of no return and they will become irretrievably hardened in mind and heart (Heb. 6:4–8). The human eye cannot see this 'point of no return' in advance – nor necessarily recognize it when it is past, but the all-sovereign God both knows it and indeed appoints it as he presides, with perfect righteousness and justice, over the human psychological processes which he created. It was at just such a time that Isaiah was called to the prophetic-preaching office and understood what his terms of commission meant: he was to bring God's word with fresh, even unparalleled clarity – for only the truth could win and change them; but in their negative response his hearers would pass the point of no return. The opportunity which could spell their salvation would spell their judgment.

11–13a. The envisaged programme is one of mounting tragedy: destruction of *cities ... houses ... fields* (11), deportation (12) and yet further loss (13a). Assyria is the power threatening the nation at present, but Isaiah will soon learn that Assyria is not to be the agent of complete loss. Nevertheless, his prediction was 'at home' in its own times. Assyria introduced a policy of deportation (2 Ki. 17) and Babylon continued it (2 Ki. 24–25). In this way the verses are a prospectus for Isaiah's book: how the

Assyrian threat will come and go (chs. 7 – 37) and how, beyond
that, a darker threat, Babylon, will arise from a profounder cause
(chs. 38 – 48).

13b. Will divine judgment, then, have the last word for the
people with whom Isaiah identified himself (5)? In Isaiah's case
the 'Burning One' approached carrying fire (6) and it must have
seemed to Isaiah that his end had come; but the voice said
'*atoned*' (7). So here the tree lies *cut down*; but the divine voice
says '*the holy seed*' (lit. 'the seed of holiness its stump'). Noting
how this half-verse forms an inclusio with 1a (the dying king ...
the fallen tree), the implication is that the people who carry the
promise of the Messiah carry thereby the guarantee of continuing
until he comes. This is the plainest understanding of the words,
but Isaiah does use 'seed' of the people who will yet enjoy the
promises (41:8; 43:5; 45:25; 53:10; 59:21; 65:9, 23; 66:22), and
the 'holy seed' could therefore be the remnant, called holy and
'written unto life' (4:3) in the Zion that was yet to be (*cf.* Heb.
12:22).[1]

b. Darkness and light in Judah (7:1 – 9:7)

The matching fourfold addresses to Judah and Israel which begin
here (see outline, pp. 66–68) work out the position Isaiah has
now reached. Chapter 5 brought into question the possibility of
future hope, but Isaiah found that question answered both for
himself (6:4–8) and his people (6:13b). Thus a parallel was
established: Isaiah is the model for the future. The word of God is
about to come to king and people (7:1–17) and rejection of it will
bring disaster (7:18 – 8:8), but within a disbelieving people there
will be those who have personally embraced the way of faith and
base their lives on the Lord's word (8:9–22), and for them there is
light beyond the present enfolding darkness (8:23 – 9:7). Thus
the doctrine of the believing remnant flowers and, alongside it,
the dying Uzziah (6:1) is a foil for the hope with which the sub-
section ends: the birth of the child with four names (9:6), the
'holy seed' (6:13) sprouting from the stump of the felled tree.

i. The moment of decision (7:1–17).
The abiding truth of this
passage is that faith in the Lord and in his promises is a practical
approach to life however great the crisis. To this message Isaiah
received as cold a reply from the politicians and people of his day

[1] Qᵃ supports MT, save that it includes a definite article in the expression 'seed
of holiness'. LXX contains no reference to 'the holy seed' but would be an unsafe
guide, since it diverges from MT throughout this verse (and passage).

as would be the case today. Practical people, they would say, have to live in the real world where political astuteness and military muscle are what counts. But to Isaiah this was not a choice between viable alternatives. It was a life and death decision.

1–2. Threatened by the expansionist/imperialist policies of the Mesopotamian power, Assyria, the two major states of northern Palestine, *Aram* and *Israel*, had entered into a defensive alliance and, considering that an all-Palestine alliance would give greater collective security, pressed Judah to join. When diplomacy failed to entice Judah, the northern powers invaded to force Ahaz' hand (2 Ch. 28:5–8), but *they could not overpower* Jerusalem. A second invasion followed (2 Ch. 28:17–18), purposing now to replace Ahaz by a puppet king (6). For this reason Ahaz is described as *the house of David*, for it is a time of dynastic threat. What he now does will determine the future of David's line. *Has allied itself with*: the by now ten-year-old alliance could not be the cause of this fresh panic. The verb (*nāhâ*) always (sixty-three times in the Old Testament) has the meaning given in verse 19, *settle* or 'swarm'. This is indeed frightening news as spies slip back home to say 'the place is swarming with them'. Another invasion is impending, causing king and people to 'flap' *as the trees of the forest are shaken*! Contrast 28:16, 'the one who trusts will not panic' (lit.).

3. *Shear-Jashub* means 'a remnant will return'. It is an ambivalent name: the noun comes first for emphasis, but does it mean '(only) a remnant …' or 'a (guaranteed) remnant …'? Is it a threat of decimation or a promise of survival? Isaiah was so sure on both counts – that unbelief would destroy and faith would save (see 9) – that he made the word of God 'become flesh' in the person of his son. Ahaz, a man of his time, should have felt the force of this, but he was otherwise engaged at *the aqueduct of the Upper Pool*, trying to secure his water-supply against the coming siege. For until the time of Hezekiah (22:1–14), water came to the city overground and was therefore vulnerable.

4. *Be careful, keep calm* are two verbs for the price of one: 'Be careful to keep quiet/do nothing', the second verb being auxiliary to the first (as Gn. 24:6; Dt. 4:9). Ahaz, however, had it in mind to do plenty. He intended to play the clever politician by securing Assyria itself as his security against the northern powers (2 Ki. 16:7–9). Isaiah saw it differently. The aggressor kings might display 'flaming anger' but actually they were only *smouldering stubs*, fag-ends! If only Ahaz could be persuaded to disengage himself from politics, Assyria would in any case squash the northern kingdoms and the Lord would preserve Judah – as indeed he ultimately did (37:36–37). But if Ahaz links himself to Assyria he will indeed have taken a tiger by the tail! In all this the issue is clear-cut: is salvation by faith or by works? Will Ahaz be saved by trust or by astute political gambles?

5–7 describe the plans of men (5–6) and the word of God (7). Isaiah, feigning not to be able to remember the name of Israel's king – 'His father was Remaliah but for the life of me I can't place him!' – achieves a classical 'put-down' and provides a perfect foil for the word of *the Sovereign LORD*. It is the greatness of the Lord that makes faith a practical policy in even the hardest realities of life (see Pr. 16:1, 33). It also leaves unbelief without excuse.

8–9. These verses are a six-line poem. In lines 1 and 2 (8ab), 4 and 5 (9ab) the northern kingdoms are analysed: the country (*Aram ... Ephraim*) is traced to its capital (*Damascus ... Samaria*) and up to its king (*Rezin ... Remaliah's son*). In lines 3 (8cd) and 6 (9cd) conclusions are drawn: Ephraim is doomed (*shattered*); if Ahaz refuses to trust he has no future. As in much poetry, meaning is expressed allusively rather than directly. First, there is common sense. You are in a flap because seemingly powerful nations threaten. Trace them back to source and what do they amount to? Only Rezin and Remaliah's son! Secondly, there is implication. If Ephraim and Aram can be traced back to source, what of Judah? Its capital is Jerusalem and its king the Davidic King: the city the Lord chose to dwell in (1 Ki. 11:13), and the Lord's king on the Lord's throne (1 Ch. 29:23), backed by the all-commanding power of verse 7. Thirdly, there is warning. Ephraim chose the security of military alliance but time would demonstrate its folly. The reference is to 671 BC when Esarhaddon of Assyria, by importing foreign settlers (2 Ki. 17:24; 2 Ch. 33:11; Ezr. 4:2), put an end to all hope of reviving the old northern kingdom. Suppose, then, Judah goes the way of alliance? This leads to a stark choice: *Stand firm in your faith ... not stand at all* (9)! NIV reflects the telling rhyme by which Isaiah links these two lines (*ta'*^{a}*mînû ... tē'āmēnû*). Crudely, 'Trust or bust' – a paraphrastic rendering as shocking as the original is blunt. Ahaz stands at the point of no return (see on 6:9–11).

Verses **10–17** do not indicate whether this second message to Ahaz took place at the same time and place as the first or not (1). Verses 10–12 relate the attempt to move Ahaz to a position of faith; verses 13–16 denunciate Ahaz as the betrayer of his dynasty's most treasured hope; and verses 16–17 foretell the consequent calamity: a disaster greater than 1 Kings 12:16.

10. The human messenger is forgotten. The prophet's word is the Lord's word; the Lord's word is the prophet's word (see 13). This is the uniqueness of verbal inspiration and the marvel of Holy Scripture.

11–12. The sin of putting *the LORD to the test* is refusing to trust him and his past faithfulnesses unless he prove himself trustworthy all over again. The situation is transformed when the Lord proffers a sign. On his side nothing is more important than that his promises are met by trust. Therefore he is ready to go to *deepest depths ... highest heights* to help, even to make Ahaz take up a position of faith as the solution to the crisis. Pious though his words sound, Ahaz is doing the devil's work of quoting Scripture for his own purposes and thereby displaying himself as the dogmatic unbeliever. This was his moment of decision, his point of no return.

13. *House of David*: the dynasty is at stake. *Try the patience*: the verb is plural. From the start David's house has not fulfilled its divine remit, producing neither the perfect king nor the golden age. It has failed both *men* and *God*, but now this whole history of inadequacy has come to a head. The royal refusal of trust is the end of the line. For this reason the prophet can speak of *my God* but he cannot repeat the *your God* of verse 10.

14. Against the background of divine exasperation (13) and the change from 'your God', *therefore* draws a conclusion: the *sign* he proposes is no longer a movement of grace opening a door of faith to the king (10) but a movement of displeasure spelling out the dire result of his faithlessness. But can the sign itself be of less magnitude than the promise to 'move heaven and earth' (11), especially since its giver is *the LORD himself* ('*ᵃdōnāy*, 'the Sovereign One')? *The virgin* (*hā'almâ*): it is widely urged that, had Isaiah intended *virgo intacta* (as Mt. 1:23, 25 understood him to mean), he would not have used '*almâ* but *bᵉtûlâ* and that, by using '*almâ*, he meant no more than a 'young woman' who, since she was to become pregnant, must charitably be assumed to be married. But it is argued here that Isaiah did indeed intend *virgo intacta* (see Additional Note, pp. 78–79).

Be with child ... give birth: cf. Genesis 16:11; Judges 13:5. The expression is 'timeless', with the context deciding in each case. *Immanuel*: 'God with us' (NIV mg.). The case for expecting a divine Messiah is strong in the Old Testament and was, in fact, Jesus' understanding (Mt. 22:41–45). It is clear that at some point the expectations originating in 2 Samuel 7 developed into the hope of a perfect King who would reign universally for ever (9:7) and who would be both son of David and Son of God (see on 4:2;

Pss. 2:7; 45:6; *cf.* Acts 13:33; Rom. 1:4; Heb. 1:5; 5:5). The view that the '*almâ* means, collectively, the young marrieds of Judah, who in the coming troubles would either express faith by naming their sons 'God is with us' or voice prayer by naming them 'God be with us', must surely be doubted. The *you* (pl.) to whom the Sovereign One gives this *sign* is the 'house of David', represented by Ahaz. In what sense would a rash of little Immanuels, which Ahaz would dismiss as women's hysteria, constitute a heaven-sent sign, matching the momentousness of this passage, or prepare for the developing Immanuel-theme through 8:8 into 9:6?

15–17. Isaiah now allows Ahaz to believe that the birth of Immanuel is imminent and does so for a reason that hindsight justifies. *Wrong ... right*: at most this means reaching the 'years of discretion' when moral choices are understood; but it could simply mean knowing the difference between nice and nasty tastes – a very early experience. The vagueness is deliberate, but three things are affirmed: (1) the child will grow up in poverty (15), for *curds and honey*, as verse 22 shows, are the diet of those left in a devastated land; (2) the northern threat from Aram and Israel will be ended (16) – and indeed Damascus fell to Assyria three years and Samaria thirteen years later; and (3) huge disaster would fall on the house of David (17). The separation of Ephraim (1 Ki. 12:20) reduced David's kingdom to a tiny remainder. The coming of *the king of Assyria* would take even this from David: the semblance of monarchy would survive for another century but the reality would never be restored. This was indeed the case: from the time when Ahaz disbelieved, he and David's descendants reigned as puppet kings, by courtesy first of Assyria and then of Babylon, until the fall of Jerusalem in 586 BC extinguished kingdom and monarchy altogether so that (with Christian hindsight), when Immanuel was born, the heir to David's throne was an unknown carpenter in Nazareth (Mt. 1:16)! Thus Isaiah concertinas the centuries, for when Immanuel was born he inherited only the memory of a kingdom and a non-existent crown – and it was Ahaz' fault. As we shall see, in the course of this section Isaiah adjusts the historical perspective (*e.g.* 9:1), but he uttered no lie when he made Immanuel the immediate heir of the Ahaz-débâcle.

Additional Note on the term 'virgin' in Isaiah 7:14

On the assumption that the Bible is the best evidence for the meaning of its words, we note that *b^etûlâ* occurs fifty times. Of these, twelve are metaphorical (*e.g.* 37:22) and fourteen are general, where (*e.g.* Ps. 148:12) 'young men and maidens' is equivalent to 'young people' and there is no more ground for demanding that the 'maidens' are unmarried than that the men in question (*bāḥûrîm*) must be bachelors. There are twenty-one cases (such as Ex. 22:16; Dt. 22:19) where the *bᵉṯûlâ* in question would be, or be assumed to be, a virgin, but the requirement is in the context, not in the word itself. The idea is 'of marriageable age/ready for marriage'.

By contrast '*almâ* is found only eight other times. Of these, 1 Chronicles 15:20 and Psalm 46 (title) use the word in a musical direction that is no longer surely understood. Three further references are indeterminate. It is hard to see that the tambourine-girls (Ps. 68:25) would have to be specified as unmarried; in Proverbs 30:19 many commentators hold that the reference is to the mysteries of procreation, though it more reasonably suggests the often much less explicable matter of sexual attraction! Song 1:3 is more likely to mean 'unmarried girls' looking for a good match than the longing gaze of 'young married women'! But Genesis 24:43, Exodus 2:8 and Song 6:8 refer unquestionably to unmarried girls. Genesis 24 is particularly important as bringing '*almâ* and *bᵉṯûlâ* together. Abraham's servant prays (24:14) for a 'girl' (*naʿᵃrâ*) to marry Isaac; the approaching Rebekah (24:16) is described as female (*naʿᵃrâ*), of marriageable age (*bᵉṯûlâ*) and single ('no man had ever lain with her'). It is important to note that *bᵉṯûlâ* is not sufficient by itself to denote virginity but needs the explanatory qualification ('no man …'). Finally (24:43), in the light of the knowledge of Rebekah that he has thus accumulated, the servant describes her as '*almâ* – *i.e.* female, marriageable and unmarried.

In the light of this there is no ground for saying that '*almâ* must mean 'young woman' and that *bᵉṯûlâ* is the technical word for 'virgin'. Rather, to the contrary: Isaiah used the word which, among those available to him, came nearest to expressing 'virgin birth' and which, in the event, with linguistic propriety, accommodated that meaning. It is also worth noting that outside the Bible, 'so far as may be ascertained', '*almâ* is 'never used of a married woman'.[1]

---

[1] E. J. Young, *Studies in Isaiah* (Tyndale Press, 1954), pp. 171ff. See also G. J. Wenham, 'A Girl of Marriageable Age', *Vetus Testamentum* 22 (1972), pp. 325ff. Wenham concludes that *bᵉṯûlâ* has no more reference to virginity than the English word 'girl', and he cannot find evidence for it as a technical term for 'virgin' before the Christian era.

ii. Divine judgment (7:18 – 8:8). Those who hate wisdom love death (Pr. 8:36). With open eyes Ahaz rejected the way of faith. What follows is full of biblical logic. The programme has been fixed in verses 15–17: the decay of the countryside, the elimination of the northern powers and the Assyrian domination of Judah. Ahaz did not act 'unwisely' – he used every political skill, the garnered astuteness of years of diplomacy and worldly *savoir-faire* – it was just the wrong wisdom. The very things he trusted guaranteed calamity. Assyria dominates this section (7:18, 20; 8:4, 7). This is what Ahaz trusted and it will be his ruin.

The section is made up of four *in that day* oracles (18–19, 20, 21–22, 23–25) and two *The LORD said/spoke* oracles (8:1–4, 5–8).

18–20. The conquest will be complete: the land occupied (18–19), the people humiliated (20). *Whistle*: even superpowers are at the Lord's beck and call, *Egypt* to the south and *Assyria* from the north. *Flies ... bees*: the Nile inundation annually brought swarms of flies; Assyria was well known for apiculture. *Streams* (*yᵉ'ōrîm*): a technical word for Egypt's irrigation canals. In verse 20 the blight on the land (18) is matched by the humbling of the people. *Hired*: Ahaz paid tribute to Assyria in return for the promise of protection (2 Ki. 16:7–8; 2 Ch. 28:21). *Shave* is indicative of the indignities heaped on a subject people. *Legs*: literally 'feet', a euphemism for private parts (1 Sa. 23:3). The contrast between *head* and 'feet', the visible and hidden body hair, expresses totality. No part of the land (18) and no part of the person (19) will escape the hand of the enemy. And the Lord would have saved Ahaz for nothing! But, instead, worldly wisdom made him buy salvation – only to find he was paying barber's charges!

21–25 take the same two topics in reverse order. The people will be left in poverty (21–22) and the land in decay (23–25). Not enough labour will be left for arable farming and people will have to live off animal husbandry (21–22). *Abundance* (22) is surely ironic!

In **8:1–8**, Isaiah turns to the course the conquest will take, first the time-scale (1–3), then the progress of the Assyrian invasion (6–7) through the northern territories of Aram (*Rezin*) and Israel (*the son of Remaliah*), and then flooding into Judah to its virtual destruction (8).

1. *Scroll*: the word is translated in 3:23 as 'mirrors'. The meaning here must be some 'plain surface' for writing. In 30:8 the parallel idea suggests something like 'placard' or 'hoarding-space'. *Ordinary pen*: *i.e.* in ordinary writing, such as anyone can read. Publicity is 'the name of the game'. The name *Maher-Shalal-Hash-Baz* is impressionistic rather than grammatical: 'Speed-Spoil-Haste-Booty'. It is intended to provoke interest, leaving unanswered questions, but 'spoil' and 'booty' would suggest the invading foe, while 'speed' and 'haste' suggest unhindered advance: no thought of a fight ahead, only of the spoil awaiting.

2. *Uriah ... Zechariah* (see 2 Ki. 16:10–16; 18:2): contemporary notables who would subsequently vouch for the date the placard was posted.

3–4. Once more the word is about to become flesh (*cf.* 7:3) in the birth of Isaiah's second son. *The LORD said*: not until the boy was born did Isaiah himself understand the significance of what he had done. He simply walked in obedience, a model for the people of God. Now he knows that, in recording the incident, he must entitle his wife *the prophetess*, because she has been literally the bearer of the word of the Lord. The opening 'For' of verse 4 should be restored. This is the explanation: the boy is a time-indicator of what his name foreshadows. Derek Kidner explains the significance of Maher-Shalal-Hash-Baz to perfection: 'The sign of Immanuel ... although it concerned ultimate events, did imply a pledge for the immediate future, in that however soon Immanuel were born, the present threat would have passed before he could be even aware of it. But the time of his birth was undisclosed; hence the new sign is given, to deal only with the contemporary scene.'[1] *Before the boy knows* is identical with 7:16 and links this little boy with Immanuel, from whom he took over the task of being an immediate time-indicator. Like Immanuel (9:6) he has four names, but he presages doom while the former focuses hope. Thus Isaiah is able, presently (9:1), to date Immanuel's coming 'in the afterwards'. *My father*: in nine months to a year. In 734 BC Tiglath-Pileser marched down the Israelite sea coast as far as the Egyptian border. Egyptian aid was thus cut off. In 733 BC Israel lost Galilee, Transjordan (2 Ki. 15:29), Megiddo and other cities, and only the prompt submission of Hoshea gave the kingdom a few years more. Damascus fell in 732 BC.

Verses **5–8** elaborate 7:17, just as verses 1–4 'adjusted' 7:16: the Assyrian domination of Israel (6–7) is a prelude to its domination of Judah (8).

6. *This people* as an expression is used of Judah, *e.g.* in 28:14, but it refers to a foreign power in 23:13 and to Israel in 9:16.

[1] D. Kidner, 'Isaiah', in *NBC*, p. 639.

Context must decide, and here the natural sequence from verse 4 makes it refer to Samaria.[1] *Shiloah* was Jerusalem's water-supply, coming into the city from the Gihon Spring. Gihon was the site of Davidic coronations (1 Ki. 1:33–34, 45) and the stream could here stand symbolically for the Davidic monarchy. But it certainly pointed to Jerusalem as the city of faith for, though its position made it virtually impregnable, its overland water-supply made it highly vulnerable (7:3). To live in Jerusalem called for faith that the Lord knew what he was doing when he chose this city, that he would stand by the promises he had made concerning it and its king. All this the northern tribes abandoned when they defected from David (1 Ki. 12), and now they rejoice in *Rezin* and *the son of Remaliah* (on whom see 7:8–9).

7–8. *Therefore* draws out the consequences. The nemesis of choosing the world is to get the world in full and plenty. They rejected the 'gently flowing waters' (6) and chose an earthly king (Rezin); they will get *the mighty floodwaters of the River* (Euphrates) and *the king of Assyria with all his pomp*. The imperialist mind is itself a sinful thing (10:5–15) but this does not mean that it is outside the holy rule of God. The over-running waters only go where he directs them (8a) and to the extent that he allows them (8b). Thus Assyria would indeed not stop its advance when it fulfilled promises made to Ahaz to end the northern threat (2 Ki. 16:7–9) but proceeded against Judah also. This, and later behaviour (2 Ki. 18:13ff.), gave Assyria a deserved reputation for treachery which Isaiah would not forget (33:1). *Outspread wings* could refer to the extending floodwaters, but is more vivid as a change of metaphor from flood to a huge bird of prey overshadowing the land. Yet the waters do not cover the head and drown the victim, the bird of prey looms but does not kill. The Lord has said, 'Thus far and no further.' The final blow against Judah (6:11–13) lies beyond the Assyrian times and power. Nevertheless it is all part of the tragedy of *Immanuel*, for it is his land that is despoiled. The seriousness of Ahaz' decision is pressed home. *Your land, O Immanuel*: 'land' with a possessive pronoun and a following vocative is not found elsewhere. Furthermore, the singular possessive is linked with land as a political unit only in the case of kings (Dt. 2:31; 2 Sa. 24:13), Israel or some other personification (Je. 2:15; Ho. 10:1) or the Lord (1 Ki. 8:36; Ezk. 36:5). Immanuel cannot be any ordinary

---

[1] Since it is impossible to think of Judah 'rejoicing' over Remaliah's son, those who interpret 'this people' as Judah resort to a simple emendation (see RSV), making 'rejoices' into 'melts (with fear)'.

child. But as a royal heir he is now doomed to inherit only suffering and loss.

iii. The believing, obeying remnant (8:9–22). The fact that Assyria will not prove to be the end for Judah prompts Isaiah to ponder the idea of a surviving remnant. In this way this new section integrates with what the prophet has already said, but it is of immense importance in its own right. Isaiah's confrontation with Ahaz (7:3–9) hinged on the issue of personal faith, and Isaiah now sees clearly that the only future that matters for Judah is the survival of individual believers within, and in contrast to, the professing but merely formal people of God. This is the theme worked out in this key passage. Isaiah's son (see 18) Shear-Jashub, who had been involved by divine command in the crucial confrontation in 7:3ff., has a name meaning 'a remnant shall return', but is this a prediction of mere survival or does it go deeper?

9–10. Throughout Isaiah's ministry Judah was threatened by superior powers, and in these verses he meditates on the fact that where the Lord is there is security. We are reminded of Psalm 46 with its refrain 'The LORD Almighty is with us'. Indeed this psalm (with Pss. 47; 48) could well derive from Isaiah's circle at the time of Sennacherib.[1] Some, however, think that the opposition of the world to the people of God and their king was a theme in temple worship (*e.g.* Ps. 2), even an annual ritual drama[2] in which the king played a central role, was assaulted and humbled before the forces of the world, and gloriously delivered by divine intervention – the joy that comes with morning in Psalm 30:5. At all events, says Isaiah, there is a vital distinction between this single people on the one hand and even the massed forces of *nations* and *distant lands* on the other: *God is with us* (Heb. 'Immanuel'). Isaiah could not have used this way of expressing the divine presence if he had not intended a reference to the virgin's son of 7:14 and the royal possessor of Judah of 8:8. Immanuel is thus also the ruler of the nations (Pss. 2:7–9; 72:8; 89:27; Dn. 7:13–14) and his presence with one particular people is the guarantee of their continuance. *Be shattered*: in Hebrew a second imperative often expresses the inevitable consequence of the first – an outcome so unavoidable that it can

---

[1] On Ps. 46, see A. F. Kirkpatrick, *Psalms* (CUP, 1910), pp. 253ff.; J. A. Motyer, 'Psalms', in *NBC*, p. 515.

[2] A. R. Johnson, *Sacral Kingship in Ancient Israel* (University of Wales Press, 1967).

be commanded to happen. Nothing therefore is more certain than that the world, choosing to assault Immanuel's people, is choosing its own destruction (54:15–17), no matter how great the collective strength (9) or how brilliant the planning (10)! (*Cf.* Jn. 16:33.) The themes of international collapse (9) and fruitless consultation (10) reappear in the fruitless consultation of verses 19–20 and the national collapse of verses 21–22, forming an inclusio.

11–12. But there is another contrast besides that between God's people and the world. The personal word of verse 11 is followed by plural imperatives in verse 12. Isaiah and those associated with him are marked off from *these people* (12). First, they are to live under the word of the Lord (11). *Hand* symbolizes personal agency and power. To say that *the* LORD *spoke* 'with strength of hand' (lit.) means with a compelling sense of a divine word to obey. The separation of prophet and group is not a self-appointed exclusivism but (as is all true separation) obedience to the Lord's word. It is obedience that is to distinguish them from *the way* (lifestyle, or characteristic modes of thought and conduct) *of this people*. The second difference (12ab) is their unwillingness to follow popular thinking regarding some *conspiracy*. It is possible that Isaiah's action in opposing the king's policy of alliance with Assyria was considered treason by the royal court and that a rumour was spread to this effect in order to bring him into popular disrepute. If this were the case, then *do not call conspiracy everything that these people call conspiracy* is a command to keep a clear conscience (1 Pet. 3:15–16). The word, however, could be translated 'alliance', in which case the reference is to the alliance Ahaz thought he was negotiating with Assyria. To Isaiah this was no 'alliance' but submission, trading sovereignty and independence for spurious promises of safety. But Isaiah must rather continue in fidelity to the Lord's word as it called to faith rather than to worldly armed strength. Thirdly, the distinctiveness of the group is seen in their 'unanxious' facing of life. All around them there was *fear* (see 7:2), but in their hearts and in their fellowship there was to be an oasis of calm.

13–14a. Where does this distinctive life find its strength and security? In a life with God (13) and in a life in God (14a). Surrounded by fearful people, Isaiah and his group are not without fear, but their *fear* and *dread* (the same words as in 12) are differently directed – towards *the* LORD (Yahweh, the God of the exodus) *Almighty* to save his people and to overthrow his enemies (Ex. 14:30–31), awesome in holiness (Ex. 3:5; 19:20–

22; 20:18–21). Isaiah is to discover the fear of the Lord not in some new manifestation of his power and holiness but in the basic, once-for-all exodus revelation that the Lord had given of himself when he redeemed his people (1 Pet. 1:17–21). *Regard as holy*: to act towards him as his holiness warrants. *Sanctuary* is not a place of asylum but (*miqdāš*) a place where God dwells in his holiness, the word used of the Tabernacle (Ex. 25:8; *cf.* 29:43–46) and the Temple (1 Ch. 22:19), where the Lord himself came to live among his people and which, in consideration of their holy Occupant, were houses of sacrifice, offering sinners access to God and safety in his presence through shed blood. But the promise now is of a purely spiritual presence: the Immanuel-presence with the true, believing remnant.

14b–15. To others the Immanuel-presence spells doom. *Stone ... stumble ... rock ... fall* are literally 'stone of tripping ... rock of stumbling', *i.e.* careless of God, people 'trip' over him to destruction; *trap ... snare* express the watchfulness of the Holy God whereby each receives the destruction due. The rope stretched across the path, and the rock barring the way, should have warned them to proceed with caution but, ignoring and careless, they stumbled and fell. The same God in his unchanging nature is both *sanctuary* and *snare*. It depends on how people react to his holiness.

Verses **16–22** review again the contrasting groups described in verses 12–14a and 14b–15. Isaiah and his group are guardians of the Lord's *law*, deposited among them (16) for them to consult (19–20), practitioners of patient faith (17) and *signs* in Israel pointing to the right way (18). By contrast, those who refuse the word (20) forfeit the possibility of a fulfilled life (21a), alienate themselves from *God* (21b) and find nothing but darkness (22). The heart of the contrast is *I will wait for the LORD* (17), *they ... will curse ... their God* (21).

16–18. In the structure of the passage these verses match verse 11, the believing remnant under the word of the Lord (11), gathered round the word of the Lord (16). *Bind up* (16) means to 'wrap up' so as to safeguard from tampering; *seal* means to attest as final and therefore to guard from addition. *Testimony*: what God has 'testified to' as his truth. *Law*: see 1:10. *My disciples*: 'my instructed ones', *i.e.* instructed in the word the Lord speaks (50:4; 54:13). *My* can refer to either Isaiah or the Lord, but better the latter as the Lord claims the believing, trusting remnant as his own. The pronoun *I* (17) reflects the voice of each individual disciple, not just of Isaiah. Just as learning from the word (16) is a disciple's hallmark, so is patient faith. *Wait* (*qāwâ,* 40:31) combines patient waiting with confident expecting. *Hiding*: faith is made for the dark day. To 'hide the face' is a sign of disfavour (contrast, to make the face shine, see Nu. 6:25). Ahaz alienated the favour of the Lord, and Isaiah and his group were not immune from the ensuing darkness, but within that darkness they had the light of 'waiting for the Lord' (Rom. 8:25; 1 Thes. 1:3b). *Here am I*: literally 'Behold', commanding attention. Isaiah now speaks for himself. He has had personal dealings with the Lord and they are part of his confidence as the darkness gathers. *Signs* (*'ōṯôṯ*) direct attention (Ex. 3:12); *symbols*, literally 'portents' (*mōpᵉṯîm*), arrest attention (Ex. 3:3). The coincidence of the birth of Maher-Shalal-Hash-Baz with the 'great tablet' (1–4) was a portent; the names of Maher-Shalal-Hash-Baz and his brother were signs. Isaiah's own name ('Yahweh saves') was also a sign. *Who dwells on Mount Zion*: the Lord never goes back on his promises. He chose Zion for his dwelling, and this gives Isaiah an objective assurance of faith, just as his and his sons' names offer a subjective assurance.

19. Warned against popular fears (12), the group is now warned against popular superstitions. They will be under pressure to conform (19a), but there is an issue of loyalty to be considered (*their God*) as well as the sheer absurdity of much that people will do and rely on (*dead ... living*). *Mediums* (*'ōḇôṯ*): like the witch at Endor (1 Sa. 28), who had an *'ōḇ* by which she consulted the dead. *Spiritists* (*yiddᵉ'ōnîm* from √*yāda'*, 'to know'): people who claimed 'insider knowledge', especially of the future (Lv. 19:31; 20:2; Dt. 18:11). *Whisper* (√*ṣāpap*): to squeak (with alarm) (10:14; 29:4; 38:14). *Mutter*: √*hāḡâ*, here, as 38:14, 'to moan'. Both verbs mock the antics of the mediums and expose the absurdity of turning from the plain word of the Lord to mumbo-jumbo. The sad declension from 'my people' (3:12) to 'this people' (6:9; 8:12) is brought to a point here in their enthusiasm for fortune-tellers and messages from the dead. *Why consult ...?* is just a biting exclamation, 'On behalf of the living, to the dead!' It is commonly claimed that the dead are in possession of greater powers and superior knowledge to the living. In the Bible it is not so. The Old Testament knows that, leaving their bodies behind, the dead can be only shadows of what they were (Is. 14:10); the dead Samuel knows no more after death than he proclaimed when alive (1 Sa. 28:16ff.). See on 19:9.

20. Another telling exclamation. The *law* and *testimony* (see 16) are all a disciple needs. *Not ... according to this word ... no ... dawn*: NIV catches the gist of a difficult piece of Hebrew. There is no hope outside of what the Lord has spoken; every utterance, however spirit-authorized, which fails to accord with his word is darkness without light.

21–22. Enduring privation they go into exile (*roam through ...*), exasperated with their lot politically (*king*) and spiritually (*God*). They are left without hope from *God*, from *earth* or from the future (*utter darkness*). All these verbs are singular. Judgment, like salvation, is individual and personal.

iv. The royal hope (9:1–7). Isaiah now reaches the fourth and final section of his prophecies about Judah. It follows in sequence from what has gone before. Waiting in faith and hope (8:17), the remnant is sustained by the forecast of the great light that shines beyond the darkness. It is a sure hope – so sure that, according to Hebrew idiom, it is even written in past tenses as though it had happened already. Because of this confidence Isaiah can place the light of 9:1ff. in immediate proximity to the darkness of 8:22, not because it will immediately happen, but because it is immediately evident to the eye of faith. Believers walking in darkness can already see the great light and are sustained by hope. The passage includes a prose introduction (9:1), which acts as a bridge between the darkness of 8:21–22 and the dawning of the great light in the poem of 9:2–7, but this has been done so skilfully that prose and poetry are now thematically one statement in two parts: the hope described (1–3) and the hope explained (4–7). Each part covers the same three internal topics in the same order.

1. What the Lord does: a new situation by act of God. He who *humbled* will yet *honour*. The northern lands of *Zebulun* and *Naphtali*, covering the area west and south-west of the Sea of Galilee (Jos. 19:10–16, 32–39), were the first part of the promised land to fall to Assyria (733 BC). *Gloom* (*mûʿāp̄*) matches 'gloom' (*māʿûp*) in 8:22, and *distress* (*mûṣāq*) reflects the word translated 'fearful' (*ṣûqâ*). Isaiah, therefore, saw his prediction of darkness begin to be fulfilled but, as always, we have to decide what reading of our experiences we are going to live by. The darkness and distress are real but they are neither the only reality nor the fundamental reality. In any given situation we can either sink into despair or rise to faith and hope. Isaiah insists that hope is part of the constitution of the here and now. *Galilee of the Gentiles* or 'nations' (*cf.* Jos. 20:7; 21:32; 1 Ki. 9:11; 2 Ki. 15:29; 1 Ch. 6:76) was the northward extension of Naphtali. No-one else but Isaiah ever called this area 'Galilee of the Gentiles'. Undoubtedly there was a continuing Gentile component in this area (see Jdg. 1:30, 33; Ki. 9:11) and maybe this prompted Isaiah to broaden the vision. It would seem that he could not embark on his first major statement of the hope of the coming King without the worldwide dimension hinted here and developed further in verse 7 and 11:1–16.

2. What the Lord's people enjoy: darkness become light. *Walking*: living out their lives. *Darkness*: the hiding of the Lord's face, during which they persevered in believing expectancy (8:17). *Shadow of death*: the noun ṣalmût ('darkness') developed the extended poetic form used here, ṣalmāweṯ ('death-shadow'). It means such trouble as casts a death-like shadow. The idea of death is in the background in an illustrative way; nevertheless it is a very strong word for life's calamities. *Seen ... light ... light has dawned*: the motif of darkness becoming light points to a creative act of God. Those who have waited through the darkness will come to the objective reality of dawn and the subjective experience of seeing the light.

3. What follows: the Lord increases joy and his people rejoice before him. Like the New Testament, Isaiah holds in tension the forecast of a (mere) remnant and the multitude of the redeemed: 1:9; 3:25 – 4:1; 7:3 with 10:20–22; 26:15; 49:19–21; 54:1–3; 66:8–9; Mt. 7:13–14; Lk. 13:23–30; Heb. 2:10; Rev. 7:9.[1] *Before you*: 'in your presence'. There is a spiritual dimension of restoration and reconciliation, acceptance before God. The old feasts were in this regard anticipations of the messianic day (Dt. 12:5–7). *Harvest ... plunder*: both harvest and victory are divine gifts (Dt. 28:2–8). Harvest belongs in the sphere of creation; plunder in the sphere of history. The contrasting spheres express 'every sort of joy ever known'.

4. What the Lord does: his act of deliverance. This is the first explanation of the hope just described. Isaiah looks back to Egypt and the exodus: *yoke* (Lv. 26:13), *burdens* (Ex. 1:11; 2:11; 5:4–5; 6:6–7), *shoulders* (Ps. 81:6) and *oppressor* (Ex. 3:7; 5:6, 10–14). This was the foundational act of God in redemption, the fulfilment of the covenant promise to 'take you as my people and be your God' (Ex. 6:6–7). He couples this with Gideon and the defeat of Midian (Jdg. 6 – 8), a victory wrought through an insignificant agent (Jdg. 6:15) and in such a way that it could only be a work of God (Jdg. 7:2–14) but involving and benefiting Naphtali and Zebulun (Jdg. 6:35). The *yoke* is suffering endured;

---

[1] This is one of fifteen occasions where MT notes that the negative particle lō' stands for the preposition 'to him', lô. Hence the difference between AV and subsequent Eng. versions. There seems no way to make sense of a negative in this verse, and the MT is plainly right to offer 'You have multiplied the nation; to it you have magnified the joy'.

the *rod* is suffering inflicted. The contrast expresses totality: all suffering is now at an end in this expected work of God.

5. What the Lord's people enjoy: the fruits of victory. This is the second explanation (the word 'For' must be reinstated at the beginning of this verse). The burning of the military hardware recalls 2:2–4. The people enter into the fruits of a victory they did not win: it was the Lord (4) who acted.

6–7. What follows: the King and his rule. Each preceding explanation leads into this third and fundamental explanation. How does the victorious, covenant-fulfilling work of God (4) come about? By what way do the Lord's people (5) enter a non-contributory salvation? By the mere fact of the King's birth. The emphasis rests not on *to us* but on *a child is born*. *Child*: his human descent. *Son*: his maleness and dignity in the royal line. *Born* of human parentage but also *given* by the Lord. His people's *shoulders* (4) are delivered when his *shoulders* accept the burden of rule. *He will be called*: literally 'one will call his name'. In its highest use, 'name' sums up character; it declares the person. The perfection of this King is seen in his qualification for ruling (*Wonderful Counsellor*),[1] his person and power (*Mighty God*), his relationship to his subjects (*Everlasting Father*) and the society his rule creates (*Prince of Peace*). *Wonderful*: literally 'a Wonder of a Counsellor'. The vast majority of the eighty times the verb *pālā'*, its noun (as here, *pele'*) and adjective (*pilᵉ'î*) occur, they refer to the Lord, himself and his works. It is the nearest word Hebrew has to the idea of 'supernatural', here bringing a wisdom far above the human: the fulfilment of 1:26, contrasting with Ahaz whose decisions ruined his people; like, but transcending, Solomon whose wisdom remained earthly (1 Ki. 4:29–34). *Mighty God*: the repetition of this title in 10:21, referring to the Lord himself, establishes its meaning here. Translations like 'Godlike Hero' are linguistically improbable, side-stepping the implication that the Old Testament looked forward to a divine Messiah (see on 4:2; 53:1). *Everlasting* is both general (26:4) and specific (57:15). When people requested a king (1 Sa. 8) they wished to replace the episodic rule of the Judges with the permanency of monarchy. The King to come is the ultimate fulfilment of this longing. *Father*: used of the Lord,

[1] The older preference (see AV) of according the coming King a fivefold name is linguistically possible. The Heb. word 'wonderful' (*pele'*) does not admit of a special form to indicate that it is linked with the following genitive. Therefore it could stand on its own: 'Wonderful, Counsellor … ' The remaining nouns, however, are linked pairs, and this suggests that we should understand the first component to be 'a Wonder of a Counsellor'.

'father' speaks of his concern (Ps. 65:5), care and discipline (Ps. 103:13; Pr. 3:12; Is. 63:16; 64:8); *cf.* Ps. 72:4, 12–14; Is. 11:4. *Peace* is personal fulfilment (2 Ki. 22:20), well-being (Gn. 29:6), harmony (Ex. 4:18), peace with God (Nu. 6:26; 25:12; Is. 53:5). The verb, *šālēm*, means 'to be whole, complete'. *Prince* corresponds to our idea of 'administrator'. This Prince, then, himself a whole personality, at one with God and with his people, administers the benefits of peace/wholeness in his benign rule. This rule, however, will be unchanging in its character (*and peace*), without *end* in space and time (*for ever*), the fulfilment of the Davidic ideal (*David's*, Pss. 2:8; 72:8–11), reflecting the holiness of God in its devotion to *justice* in practice and *righteousness* in principle (*cf.* 5:16), and guaranteed by the commitment (*zeal*) and activity (*accomplish*) of *the* LORD. *Zeal*: as passionate commitment (37:32; 42:13; 59:17; 63:15); *cf.* the love that tolerates no disloyalty and brooks no rival (Nu. 15:11; Ps. 79:5). It is the Lord who plans the future (1), shatters the foe (5) and keeps his promises (7).

c. Darkness and light in Israel (9:8 – 11:16)

The doublet – saying broadly the same thing twice over, from different viewpoints – is one of the characteristics of Isaiah's book (*cf., e.g.*, 28 – 29 with 30 – 35; 42:18 – 43:21 with 43:22 – 44:23). In this case, 9:8 – 11:16 runs in parallel with 7:1 – 9:7 (see pp. 66–68). The prophets recognized the sad fact of the divided kingdoms of Judah and Israel (1 Ki. 12) but never accepted it. Elijah, for example, in his counterattack on the apostasy of the northern kingdom under Ahab and Jezebel, took pains to build his altar on Carmel of twelve stones, naming each stone for one of the 'tribes descended from Jacob, to whom the word of the LORD had come' (1 Ki. 18:31). Likewise Amos, a prophet to the northern kingdom, spoke in the name of the Lord who 'roars from Zion' (1:2), included Judah in his condemnation of the nations (2:4–5), and held out the great hope of a Davidic restoration (9:11–15). It is the same with Isaiah, the southerner. He accepts the fact of separate kingdoms, he knows that Judah will survive after Israel has been swallowed up by the great powers, but he sees their histories as running along parallel courses – their rejection of the Lord's word, inevitable judgment and the preserved remnant – culminating in the universal and endless reign of the same glorious King. The divided kingdoms of human sinfulness will become the one kingdom of our God and of his Messiah and he will reign for ever. He has traced out this course for Judah in 7:1 – 9:7. Now it is Israel's turn. The

Lord's people sinfully corrupt his purposes but he never alters course or allows his promises to be rewritten (Nu. 23:19); all who are 'written unto life' (lit., 4:3) will be brought home to Zion through the same divine management of history and the same promised King.

Isaiah's doublets, however, are never mere reiterations. The second element in the doublet always develops the first. In the coming section we learn that Assyria will suffer an incurable wound (10:12, 16–19, 27–34); the coming King, dated broadly 'in the future' (9:1), now lies beyond the deportation of Judah foreseen in 6:9–13, but there will be a regathering of the two halves of the sundered kingdom under him, with the old rivalry gone (11:12ff.). The thought inherent in the mysterious 'Galilee of the Gentiles' (9:1) becomes the messianic banner of 11:10.

i. The moment of decision (9:8 – 10:4). For the Lord's people everything depends on their reaction to his word. The obedience–blessing–disobedience–cursing syndrome is inherent in the covenant (Lv. 26:3–13, 14–41). When the word came to Jacob (9:8) and they chose rather the way of self-sufficiency (9:9–10), everything else followed as night follows day. In a four-stanza poem of classic biblical social analysis, Isaiah traces out the terrifying consequences of abandoning revealed truth. The four stanzas are marked off by a refrain (9:12, 17, 21; 10:4), and the occurrence of the same words in 5:25 is rightly interpreted as indicating that some of the material in chapter 5 began life as part of this poem but, with that proper freedom with which he builds pre-existing material into a new mosaic, Isaiah used part of the poem as a climax to chapter 5 and provided 10:5–15 as a new climax for the remainder. There are many suggestions regarding the original shape of the poem, none of which can claim certainty, but a very coherent piece of literature is achieved by making 5:22–25 the fifth stanza of the poem, with 5:27–30 as its original conclusion. What we must not do, of course, is reassemble the poem, for this would upset the careful structuring Isaiah has achieved by using it in two different places, each part fitting perfectly into its new context.

Stanza 1: National disaster (9:8–12). The Lord's word has been rejected in favour of a do-it-yourself reconstruction, but the internal collapse of Israel (10) will be followed by external attack (11). When the vineyard produces stink-fruit, the wild beasts come in (5:4–5). No society can recover save by returning to the word of the Lord and, as the Bible insists, large-scale consequences follow from spiritual causes.

8. The *message* came through the ministries of Amos and Hosea from 760 BC onwards. *Message* ('a word') is emphatic: this is the issue, God had spoken: will his people live by revelation or not? *It will fall, i.e.* what the word foretold will happen.

9–10. *Ephraim*, the most prominent tribal constituent of the Northern Kingdom, is used as a name for the whole. As Genesis 48:5, 13–20 records, the primacy of Ephraim was not by birth but by grace. The use of the name here, therefore, is deliberate: those who owed their status to grace were turning to works and self-salvation. *Pride* (√*gā'â*, 'to be high'), a sense of personal superiority to all challenges; *arrogance* (√*gāḏēl*, 'to be great'), sufficiency for all needs.

11–12. Jeroboam II (782–753 BC) gave the nation prosperity, restoring the kingdom to Solomonic boundaries (2 Ki. 14:25), but what went up like a rocket came down like a stick and in no time Israel reeled under blow after blow. Its internal collapse (2 Ki. 15, 17) was seen in that six kings reigned during the final twenty years, four reigns ended in assassination and only one king passed the throne to his son. So much for replacing fig-trees with cedars! Externally, *Rezin* was king of Aram and his *foes* were the Assyrians who, from the accession of Tiglath-Pileser in 745 BC, bent their imperialist ambitions westward. Threatened by Assyria, Rezin sought a defensive alliance with Israel (see 7:1ff.; Introduction, pp. 19–20) and Israel complied, but thus choosing to be like any other worldly power they paid the price by becoming what they chose, a nation caught up in the world's power struggle. But behind it all was the empowering (*strengthened*) and directing (*spurred*) sovereign purpose of the Lord (see 10:5–15). *Arameans ... devoured* is an ironic comment on the alliance: Israel saw itself as cleverly securing an ally; Isaiah saw it being devoured! *Philistines*: Amos 1:6 hints at such attacks but we do not know details. *Upraised* ('stretched out'): used often (*e.g.* Ex. 6:6; Dt. 4:34) of the Lord's power as Redeemer. But when his word is refused the Redeemer becomes the Judge.

Stanza 2: Political collapse (9:13–17). Inexorably the consequences of rejecting the Lord's word unfold. Refusal of revealed truth leads to reliance on human wisdom for national guidance, but their leaders are 'misleaders' (16) and moral decay is evident throughout society (17).

13. *The people*: virtually a title for Judah and Israel, 'the people *par excellence*', the Lord's people. They alone should have been able to see beyond the human agents of their trouble to *him who struck them*. This would have led to repentance (*returned*, Am. 4:6–11) and 'seeking' (*sought*) of the Lord – not as looking for something lost but as deliberately making for the place where he is to be found (Dt. 12:5, 11). *The LORD*, Yahweh, the God of the exodus, the God who redeems his people and overthrows his (and their) foes in his *Almighty* ('of hosts', 1:9) power would soon have delivered!

Within **14–17** the metaphor of verse 14 is explained in 15–17: verses 15–16, the downfall of leadership and the reason for it; 17, the ruin of the people and the reason for it.

14. *So the LORD*: divine sovereignty in executive management of history, visiting appropriate judgment on sin. *Head and tail … branch and reed* are contrasts expressing totality: *head and tail*, *i.e.* from one end to the other; *branch and reed*, tall growth and low growth, *i.e.* from top to bottom. *Single day*: possibly the fall of Samaria in 722 BC or the death of Jeroboam II which marked the end of stable government; in any case, that decisive moment when the Lord decreed that his people had reached the point of no return in their refusal of his word.

15. It is characteristic of Isaiah to explain his metaphors (*e.g.* 8:7). *Prominent*: 'uplifted of face', people who are important without holding official position. *Tail*: a sly 'dig' from Isaiah! The prophets considered themselves spiritual leaders but in fact they were like tails wagging at popular demand (30:9–11; 1 Ki. 22:6; Mi. 2:11).

16–17. *Therefore*: both leaders and led (16) are blameworthy and will reap their reward. The former need not have misled for the word of the Lord was available; the latter need not have followed for God's truth was openly declared to them (Am. 7:10). *Young men … widows*: in military overthrow it is the young adults who pay the price and orphans and widows are left desolate. The Lord who could be expected to delight in (lit.) 'his young men', and who is famously concerned for the defenceless (Ps. 68:5), is also the holy God who cannot abide ungodliness, wickedness and vileness. The Lord is not capricious; behind his fury lies his just appraisal of what the situation demands (Gn. 18:20–21). *Ungodly* (*hānēp̄*): apostasy alienating God, defilement by disobedience (Je. 3:1), religious terror (Ps. 106:38). *Wicked*: 'evil-doing', violation of God's moral law. *Vileness* (*n'b̄ālā*): insensitivity to moral and spiritual realities and obligations (1 Sa. 25:25; 2 Sa. 13:12–13). The three words together express that practical atheism which believes life can be lived without God, that he and his word are irrelevancies in the 'real' world.

Stanza 3: Social anarchy (9:18–21). The failure of leadership (13–17) leads to unchecked self-seeking, sweeping like forest fire through the land (18). Each is now out solely for himself (19cd) yet without satisfaction (20a–d). Relationships, whether of the nuclear (20ef) or the extended (21) family, no longer signify. 'Postmodern' individualism is as old as Isaiah: its opportunity lies in a day of social collapse; its root in rejection of the word of the Lord.

18. Life astray from God is inherently destructive (*burns*), carries all before it – both the expendable (*briers*) and the useful (*forest*) – and pollutes the very air we breathe (*smoke*). Everything 'goes up in smoke'.

19–21. It does so by the will of God expressing itself in *wrath*. The same fire of wrath produces unrestrained individual self-assertion: neither general brotherliness (19d), nor parental feeling (20e), nor tribal relationship within the same nation (21ab) raises barriers to dominant self-assertion. The only thing that unites is common enmity against another brother within the same family (21c). How perceptive the prophet is: with all this evident domestic and social need crying out for remedy, there is still energy and resource to go to war! And yet no-one is *satisfied* (20a–d). The 'grab-all' society is a hungry place to live.

Stanza 4: Blatant misrule (10:1–4). In this, the final stanza of the poem as it now stands, the social unruliness and self-seeking of verses 13–21 issues in the dominance of an unscrupulous clique making laws for their own ends. If people refuse the rule of the word of God, they end up under unprincipled human rule.

1–2. *Unjust* (*'āwen*) is basically 'trouble, mischief' and then the trouble which idolatry or sin brings. *Oppressive* translates *'āmāl*, which never means 'oppression' but 'grievousness' (*e.g.* Gn. 41:51; Jdg. 10:16). Such is this government that each next enactment means only more grief for the ruled. Their particular targets are *the poor* and *the oppressed* and their object is *prey* and *robbing*, self-enrichment. All this is the very contradiction of the Lord's ways and concerns: he identified with the poor and the oppressed in his exodus deliverance; he cares for the fatherless and the widow (Dt. 10:18; 26:5–7; Pss. 10:14; 68:5; 146:9; *cf.* Ex. 22:22); but when his people reject his word and its values, his *wrath* (9:19) consigns them to the opposite, to the values prompted by fallen human nature.

3. *Reckoning*: from √*pāqaḍ*, 'to review, make reckoning', specifically of the Lord's day of reckoning. *From afar*: *cf.* 5:26, a concealed reference to Assyrian invasion. The now all-commanding rulers will then have neither future (*To whom ... run?*) nor past (*where ... leave?*). *Riches* (or 'glory'): *i.e.* not just cash but also self-importance, pride of person and position.

4. How very far from the future that the leaders had in mind! *Fall* is the last word of the line and recalls the same verb in 9:8. To refuse the revealed word may well seem an irrelevance in the 'real world' of construction programmes (9:10), political manoeuvrings and superpower posturings (9:10), of prominent civil and church leaders (9:15), or average human wickedness (9:18) and governmental mismanagement, but in the long run it is the word which 'falls' (9:8) and those who have rejected it *fall among the slain*.

ii. Divine judgment (10:5–15). This brief passage, dealing though it does with a single historical event (the Assyrian invasions from 734 to 701 BC), is one of the Bible's profoundest statements on the nature of earthly history, the relation between the King and the kings. It corresponds to the Assyrian passage in 7:18 – 8:8. The passages coincide in affirming divine control over history (7:18; 10:6) but, while the former concentrates on the fact and effects of the Assyrian incursion, this passage asserts a philosophy of history, how the historical facts arise from hidden supernatural causes, and how the human actors who are the hinges on which history outwardly turns are themselves personal and responsible agents within a sovereignly ordered and exactly tuned moral system. From the literary point of view these eleven verses are a carefully crafted poem and a good place to appreciate Isaiah's skill as a wordsmith.

5 (A1; corresponding to A2 in 15). Two inanimate objects, *rod* and *club*, teach that the Assyrian – the then superpower – has no ability except what the Lord gives (Jn. 19:11). He is an instrument in the Lord's hands. *Anger ... wrath* are respectively felt anger and expressed anger and these are the driving forces behind the Assyrian. *Woe*: better (here) 'Ho!', a word of summons (*cf.* 7:18) rather than condemnation.

6 (B1) describes the Lord's motive. *Send ... dispatch* continue the note of divine initiative and authority behind the Assyrian incursion and contribute to the insistence on the executive, directive sovereignty of God in world affairs, which is central to the whole passage. The first verb is intensive in form and denotes the directive of a superior to an underling; the second (lit.) 'give him a command', *i.e.* 'brief him for the task'. Behind the mission is a divine moral purpose: *godless* (*ḥānēp̄*), see 9:17; *who anger me*, justly meriting my (overflowing) anger. *Seize ... plunder*: these words contain the components of Maher-Shalal-Hash-Baz, 8:1–4, and indicate the fulfilment of the word that was 'made flesh' in Isaiah's second son (*cf.* 55:11).

Verses **7–11** (C1) describe Assyria's motive.

7. The Lord intends a morally punitive expedition, but the Assyrian intends an extension of his own imperialism and the end of the national sovereignty of others.

8–9. The Assyrian has confidence based on his resources (8) and accomplishments (9). Already nations have become his vassals and their *kings* his *commanders*. In the paired towns, the first in each pair is further south than the second. Thus, from Carchemish on the Euphrates in the far north of Palestine to Calno, and from Arpad fifty miles to the south to Hamath a hundred miles north of Damascus, and on to Damascus itself and then to Samaria, his armies have proved invincible. Isaiah is a master of this sort of impressionistic picture of events (*cf.* 28–32), making us feel the surge and sweep of the advancing march: *cf.* the 'tide' picture in 8:6–8.

10–11. What price *Jerusalem* then? With heavy irony, Isaiah 'overhears' the king of Assyria envisaging Samaria and then Jerusalem as even more helpless before him because, after all, they are not quite so proficient in their idolatry! But the reality is there in the balanced words *idols ... images ... images ... idols*: it was not armaments that rendered them helpless before Assyria but spiritual falsity. *Idols* ('*e lîlîm*): the 'no-gods' of 2:8, the worthless nonentities.

12 (B2). It is probably right that NIV prints this verse as prose. We should look upon it as showing the careful way Isaiah edited his material so as to adapt it from whatever was its original shape to fit its new situation in the total presentation of his message. The way that B2 matches B1 indicates this. The Lord, who had a purpose in mind in making Assyria the rod of his anger (5), now assesses if the Assyrian has matched this purpose and finds him wanting. All the arrogant power of verses 7–11 is wholly subject to a supreme power. *Finished*: a tailoring or weaving term, to 'snip off' a thread when the sewing is finished. *Wilful pride ... haughty look*: literally 'the fruit of the arrogance of heart and the vainglory of the haughtiness of his eyes'. The 'heart' is what he is inwardly, the 'eye' is the organ of ambition, desire and objective – what he 'has an eye to'/'has his eye on'. What he did conformed to the will of God; why he did it had nothing to do with that will but only with his own vaingloriousness.

13–14 (C2) is Assyria's assessment of the situation. The king boasts of his abilities (13ab), achievements (13cde) and irresistible power (14), changing structures (*boundaries*), disregarding rights (*plundered their treasures*) and deposing rulers (*kings*). *Strength* (*kōaḥ*): not 'resources' but 'ability'. *Hand*, the organ of personal action; *wisdom*, the organizing mind behind it. Together they register the claim 'all my own work'. *Understanding* (*bîn*): discernment to see to the heart of a matter. *Mighty one* (*'abbîr*) is used of the Lord in 1:24, and here is certainly a quasi-divine claim: 'God-like, I subdued' – and it was all as easy as bird-nesting!

We can now look back briefly over the ground covered so far: the Lord had a work to do at Jerusalem and he chose to use the Assyrian to do it. Furthermore, the work was done as exactly as when a master-tailor snips off his final thread. But there the identity between Sovereign and agent ended. The Lord had a holy purpose to fulfil, expressing his moral outrage – anger and wrath against godlessness (5–6); the Assyrian had a sinful purpose to fulfil: to manifest invincible military power, to assert an immoral right to rule the world, to give free rein to vainglory, arrogance and self-importance. The deed was just, the doing was morally outrageous.

15 (A2). The same two tools, *rod ... club*, and in the same order as verse 5, form a perfect inclusio, but now the message is driven home by two further inanimate objects, *axe ... saw*. The verse matches the 'hand and mind' claim of the king (13). In the relation between man and tool, where is the organizing mind (15a)? Where is the strength of hand (15b)? *Raise itself ... boast* are related respectively to the *wilful pride ... haughty heart* of verse 12. The king is a hollow man! He would have no power except it had been given him from above (Jn. 19:11). Isaiah offers a comment on his view of history and the relation between earthly power and sovereign power in the implied illustration of horse and rider in 37:29. In that relationship all the brute energy resides in the horse; all the direction, control and management is in the rider. They are one in enterprise but distinct in function. The powers of earth fashion their policies, priorities and activities; the divine Rider appoints holy objectives, accomplishes holy judgments and visits holy retributions.

iii. The believing, obeying remnant (10:16–34). As in the parallel 8:9–22, within the Lord's just judgments there is a preservative at work, for the Lord never deserts his people nor allows them to come to an end, no matter how great the odds are against them. As so often in Isaiah, the message is in the structure as well as in the content. In verses 16–19 (a1) divine judgment on Assyria leaves only a pathetic shadow of the once mighty nation, but judgment on Israel leaves a truly believing remnant (20–23; b1); thus through the Lord there is security for Zion's people

(24–26; b2) but destruction for Assyria (27–34; a2). The two b-sections are wrapped around by the a-sections, just as the tiny Israel is surrounded by the opposing world. Sin never goes unpunished, but neither does the world manage a final triumph (Mt. 16:18; Jn. 16:33; 1 Jn. 4:4). The whole section is one of extraordinary vividness, with a telling illustration within each sub-section: wasting sickness forms an inclusio in 16 and 18, the irrecoverable decline of Assyria; the innumerable sand reduced to a remnant (22) conveys the grimly sad failure of Israel to capitalize on the Lord's promises; the historical incidents of Gideon (26ab; Jdg. 6 – 9) and the exodus (26cd; Ex. 14) illustrate, respectively, the Lord's power on behalf of the tiny few and the helpless many; and the felling of the forest (33–34) describes the decisive divine victory over Assyria.

Verses **16–19** pronounce judgment on Assyria. The metaphors of sickness (16b, 18c) and fire (16c–17) blend internal and external factors in the downfall of Assyria, the slow maturing of terminal illness, the totality of destruction by fire.

16. *Therefore*: a conclusion is drawn from the nature of earthly history as revealed in verses 5–15. Behind every historical movement is the Sovereign Lord. For holy purposes he appointed the rise of Assyria (5–6); in holy judgment he, *the Lord, the* LORD *Almighty* – 'the Sovereign One ($'^a d\bar{o}n\bar{a}y$), Yahweh the Omnipotent (of hosts)' – now appoints its decline (*disease*) and end (*fire*).

17. *Cf.* 30:27–33. The Assyrians, marching on Jerusalem, are walking straight into the fire! Israel is under judgment (6) but its *Light* has not gone out; they have offended his holiness but he is still *their Holy One*, ever on his people's side. *Single day*: see 37:36.

18–19. *Forests*, uncultivated growth, and *fertile fields*, planned tillage, form a contrast expressing totality. *Trees*: yet another metaphor (*cf.* 33–34). Following the débâcle at Zion (37:36), Assyria entered a period of slow decline – so diminished that even a child could conduct a census!

Verses **20–23** pronounce judgment on Israel. Though it is the Lord who leaps to his people's defence (17), yet it is as the *Holy One* that he belongs to Israel (17, 20). The fire that burns for them also burns within them. They cannot escape his searching judgment (*cf.* Am. 3:1–2).

20. Contrasting objects of trust: Israel had sought security in the Aram-Ephraimite alliance against the rising threat of Assyria (see 7:1ff.; Introduction, pp. 19–20), but one they trusted, Aram, had been their national foe throughout the previous century (*e.g.*

9:12; 2 Ki. 6:8:1, 24–25; 13:3), striking them over and over again. But the *day* will come when such folly will be renounced and there will be a true reliance *on the LORD.* Isaiah's experience had shown him that the God whose holiness condemns (6:3–5) is the God who forgives and reconciles (6:6–8). He sees that this will yet work on a national scale. *Rely*: 'lean', a lovely synonym for trusting.

21–23. There are two sides to the Shear-Jashub theme introduced in 7:4. On the one hand, there is the certain hope of a preserved remnant (21); on the other hand, the sad contrast (22) between 'the few that be saved' and the innumerable company of the divine promise (Gn. 22:17). NIV, however, does not offer the only understanding of verse 22. First, *only* is an interpretative addition, assuming that *remnant* here has a threatening sense. Secondly, *though* is not the most obvious translation of the preposition *kî 'im.* It is usually a strong adversative, 'But (contrary to what you might have thought)'. By itself, *remnant* in verse 21 would suggest a small number, 'but, to the contrary', *your people* will be *like the sand by the sea*: this is the *remnant* that *will return.* In a word, the Lord will stand by his promises to Abraham and they will be fulfilled. In the light of this, *destruction* (and the related word in 23) could be translated 'consummation': *i.e.* the Lord will unfailingly bring his promises to their intended conclusion. The interests of the passage are, however, best served by preserving NIV (except for restoring the 'For' which should introduce 23). The Holy One who will keep his promises must do so in a way that is true to his holiness. Therefore, the destruction due to sin cannot be withheld, and it will come upon the *whole land* (23).

Mighty God (21) plainly refers to the Lord himself, and there is no way it could be reduced to 'Godlike Hero', as some suggest, for its earlier appearance (see on 9:6). The reference here to 'a transcendent God (*'ēl*) of warrior prowess' – like the God of Joshua 5:13 – 6:27, and as Isaiah will see him in 59:15b–20 – suits this context where his people have been under the conqueror's heel.

In verses **24–34,** Isaiah focuses on Jerusalem and how it will fare against the Assyrian threat. The topic is dealt with in an orderly fashion: verses 24–26, the security of Zion notwithstanding the severity of the threat; verses 27–34, the destruction of the Assyrian invader. But in all this, however, northern Israel is not forgotten. Isaiah can offer Israel assurance about the promises of verses 21–22 only by showing what is going to happen to the nation which seemed to have killed off the promises once and for all, for it was at Zion that Assyria received its death-blow. But if Judah panicked (7:1–3) at the thought of a threat from Aram and Ephraim, with what trepidation they must have watched Assyria 'sweep on into Judah, swirling over it' (8:8). Thus verses 24–26 show how the Lord will lift that burden from them but not, however, before they have suffered under the conqueror's heel (28–31) and the ultimate disaster has threatened even the city itself (32). Notice how this passage resonates with the vocabulary of verses 5–15: *rod* and *club* (24; 5, 15), *anger* and *wrath* (25; 5), and *axe* (34; 15). Words that earlier suggested that the Lord sided with Assyria are cleverly turned around to express the opposite view as history's Sovereign visits merited punishment on the aggressor. Verses 24–26 also assert Zion's security. For northern Israel, hope was deferred. The Judge of all the earth, who always does right (Gn. 18:25), works by a logic which leaves us baffled, and we have here a good example of its operation. Israel ceased to exist following the fall of Samaria to the Assyrian in 722 BC, but Judah, notwithstanding the decisive unbelief of Ahaz (7:9), would survive the Assyrian onslaught.

24. This is the astonishing force of *therefore*. If we were to draw a conclusion from the destruction theme of verses 22–23, we would proceed to declare Judah's fall too. But the Lord's 'therefores' are not the same as ours (55:8), and it is his logic which decrees that Judah will suffer but not be finished when the same enemy attacks whose power proved terminal for Israel. Three grounds of assurance are offered to bolster the command *do not be afraid*. First, there is the nature of their God. He is *the Lord* (*'ᵃdōnāy*) the Sovereign (6:1); *the LORD* (Yahweh, the God of the exodus who delivers his people and overthrows their foes) *Almighty* ('of hosts'; see 1:9), the God who is in himself every potentiality and power. Secondly, there is their standing with him. They are still *my people*, still those *who live in Zion*, the people of the Davidic covenant with its promises. This latter element is emphatic: *in Zion* would have sufficed to make the point; *who live in Zion* underlines it. The Lord is on their side (*my*), his promises still stand. Thirdly, they have the comfort of history. Assyrian domination is only *as Egypt did* – and please remember how the Lord dealt with that!

25. The 'For' with which this verse should begin introduces it as a further explanation of the command not to fear. The problem is not Assyrian displeasure but *my anger ... wrath* (see 10:5). The *anger* he feels is passing; the *wrath* he expresses will lead to Assyrian *destruction* – and all this *very soon*. True faith is imminent expectation.

26. Two historical illustrations confirm the two sides of the message of verse 25. The Gideon incident (Jdg. 7:25) recalls the Lord's destruction of his people's foes, raising *his staff* (Ex. 14:16) recalls his deliverance of his people. *Whip* occurs in Isaiah only at 28:15, 18, where Assyria is the 'scourge' of Judah. Ironically, those who take the whip perish by the whip!

In verses **27–34**, the picture of the yoked beast (Judah, 27) and the contrasting picture of the felled forest (Assyria, 33–34) provide brackets around the triumphalist progress of self-assured invaders towards their objective (Jerusalem, 28–32). With the removal of the *yoke* (27) Judah is free; with the felling of the forest (33–34) Assyria is destroyed.

27. The *burden* implies 'under obligation', the *yoke* implies 'under orders'; with both gone, total liberation has been accomplished. *Because you have grown so fat* interprets the enigmatic expression 'because of oil' and (presumably) would mean that, since this overweight and unfit beast is no longer serviceable, its services are dispensed with. This is an odd view of why Judah was liberated and why Assyria gave up overlordship! 'Oil' symbolizes inherent richness or strength. If it alludes to an inherent, secret strength in Judah, it points to the Davidic promises (24; *cf.* 28:16). Assyria's 'sturdy warriors' (16), literally 'fat, vigorous, strong ones', uses a related word. They, however, waste away, while Judah enjoys a preservative 'fatness, oil'.[1]

28–32. Isaiah imaginatively sketches the advance of the Assyrian armies. These verses could, of course, be a description of a foreseen reality, with the prophet taking up the description at *Aiath*, probably Ai (Jos. 7:2), fifteen miles north of Jerusalem, moving south to Migron, possibly an area rather than the place mentioned in 1 Samuel 14:2 (which is south of Michmash), 300 feet down from *the pass* (29) at Michmash, where they decide not to halt but to push on to *Geba* 500 feet up the other side. At this point the foe has entered Judah. Jerusalem is but six miles off and the fortress towns of *Ramah* and *Gibeah* (29) fail to stay their progress. *Anathoth*, five miles north, with its neighbouring *Gallim* and *Laishah*, fall (30), as do the unknown *Madmenah* and

[1] The end of v. 27 is highly enigmatic. Lit. 'because of oil'. NIV, *because you have grown so fat*, paraphrases the Heb. at the expense of making no sense. The various emendations suggested by scholars are more numerous than persuasive. This is the second time the idea of 'oil/fatness' has occurred in this context. In v. 16 'wasting disease' destroys Assyria's 'fat ones' (*mišmannāw*). Their inner resources are not equal to the challenge, but Israel has a secret 'fatness' of which they know nothing. Poetry is inherently allusive, and it is probably along this line that the truest understanding of this allusion lies.

Gebim (31), and with the Assyrian arrival at *Nob* (32) – doubtfully identified as a mile off – Jerusalem is itself under threat.

The verbs *enter ... pass* (28) are past tenses, probably representing reports brought back to headquarters from the front. *Store*: better 'examine, review weapons', *i.e.* preparatory to the final assault. The introduction of quasi-direct speech, *We will camp* (29), adds vividness and also reveals the self-confidence of the enemy.

Cry out (30) is literally 'Scream at the top of your voice'; *Daughter ... Poor* ('afflicted'): words are heaped up to conjure the picture of the arrival of the pitiless Assyrian soldiery, with females, as ever, the chief sufferers of male wars.

33–34. It may be that these verses were originally the opening of the poem of the messianic King in 11:1–16 and described how the Lord would make every preparation for the emergence and growth of Jesse's shoot (11:1) – and, of course it still fulfils this function: since the coming King is pictured in a forestry motif, the preparation for his coming is a ground-clearing operation. But Isaiah has now related it chiefly to its foregoing context, as the outline above shows. The felling of the *trees* is the destruction of Assyria right at the very gates of Zion, as it were. A falling of a great tree is always dramatic; this one all the more so, following five verses of Assyrian vaingloriousness! Assyria, who was 'the axe' in the Lord's hand (10:15), now feels *an axe* (*cf.* 10:12). The view of history expressed in 10:5–15 is not wishful thinking but the sober reality of things, for *before the Mighty One* is (lit.) simply 'by a Mighty One'. The Lord is himself the Agent. Isaiah reserves to chapters 36 – 37 the narration of the actual event itself.

iv. The royal hope (11:1–16). For the outline of Isaiah 7 – 11, see pp. 66–68 above. When the prophet brought the message of royal hope to Judah, the dawning light of the birth of the King was seen against the background of the darkness of sin and death engulfing the people (8:20–22; 9:1–7; *cf.* Lk. 21:25–27); here the perfect King and his reign over a restored world are consequent on the destruction of the kings of the earth (*cf.* Ps. 2; Rev. 17:12–14; 20:7–15). Like the hope expressed in Isaiah 9:1ff., this hope also is undated, and therefore an ever-present and living hope not only for those to whom Isaiah ministered but continuingly for the church 'until he comes' (1 Cor. 11:26).

The King in Eden (11:1–10). Bracketed by references to *Jesse* and *roots/Root* in verses 1 and 10 (*cf. rest* in 2, 10), this

102

passage has four sections: 1–2, the ancestry and endowment of the King; 3–5, his rule; 6–9, his world; 10, his worldwide significance.

1. *Jesse*: the expectation is not simply of a coming king but of a coming David for, though successive kings were assessed by comparison with 'their father David' (*e.g.* 2 Ki. 18:3), only David is 'the son of Jesse' (*e.g.* 1 Ki. 12:16). When Jesse produces a *shoot* it must be David (*cf.* Je. 30:9; Ezk. 34:23–24; Ho. 3:5). The golden king of the past foreshadows the true gold to come. *Shoot* (*ḥōṭer*): 'young growth'; *Branch* (*nēṣer*): 'sapling'. Neither is the word used in 4:2, but the metaphorical significance is the same, here the human 'family tree' of the Messiah. Isaiah takes seriously his prediction in 6:13 – the time will come when all signs of life in the Davidic monarchy will have disappeared, like a tree cut to the *stump*, but there remains a secret vitality. He knew that the monarchy could not survive the unbelief of Ahaz (7:9); he foresaw too the ensuing calamity (6:9–12). It would have been odd indeed if he had not felt the tension between this vision of termination and his other predictions of future Davidic glory (1:25–27). Will the Lord then revoke his promises or will he keep them? Passages like 9:1–7 and 11:1–16 arise out of this tension in Isaiah's message and affirm the faithfulness of God to his purposes and promises.

2. This sevenfold elaboration of the divine endowment of the messianic King[1] begins with *the Spirit of the LORD.* This denotes the Spirit as himself divine, and also as the one whose 'resting' (*cf.* Nu. 11:25–26) effects the indwelling of the Lord himself in his King (Jn. 14:16–17, 23). The further six elaborations develop this in three pairs: the king's ruling attributes, *wisdom* and *understanding* (*cf.* Dt. 1:13; 1 Ki. 3:9, 12; in 3:9 'distinguish' belongs to the 'understanding' group of words; in 3:12 the adjectives 'wise' and 'discerning' match Isaiah's nouns); his practical abilities, *counsel* and *power*; and his spiritual qualities, *knowledge* and *fear*. All these characterize the true ruler: *wisdom*, the general capacity to 'have a right judgment in all things';[2] *understanding*, the ability to see to the heart of an issue (contrast the king of Assyria, 10:13); *counsel*, the ability to devise a right course of action, here coupled with *power* to see it through.

---

[1] The OT has the same general revelation of the Spirit of God as the New: personal qualities (Is. 63:10; Eph. 4:30), distinctness (Is. 63:11; Mk. 1:9–11), divine presence (Ps. 139:7; Jn. 14:16–17, 23), indwelling (Is. 63:11; Hg. 2:5; 1 Cor. 3:16; 6:19), *etc.* See J. A. Motyer, *NBCR*, pp. 28–29.

[2] From the Collect for Whitsunday, *The Book of Common Prayer*.

Knowledge goes beyond 'knowing about'. According to 1 Samuel 3:7, the young Samuel, for all his religious involvement and the 'knowledge' it must have brought (1 Sa. 2:11, 18, 21, 26), 'did not yet know the LORD', for *knowledge* is enjoying a personal, intimate relationship with a person (Gn. 4:1, RV, RSV). When that person is the Lord, the relationship demands and prompts the *fear* which shows itself in moral concern (Gn. 20:11), obedience (Ex. 20:20), sensitive conduct (Ne. 5:9, 15), loyalty (Ps. 2:11) and worship (Ps. 5:7). (*Cf.* 2 Cor. 7:1; 1 Pet. 1:17–18; 3:15.)

Verses **3–5** reveal the king responding to the Lord (3a, 5) and exercising his royal office as judge (3b, 4).

3. *He will delight*: literally 'his delighting', *i.e.* his whole capacity for delight will be absorbed in the Lord. In judgment he can go beyond the apparent (*sees … hears*) to the truth of the matter (like David, 2 Sa. 14:20).

4. *Righteousness … judge*: see on 1:21; 5:16. The king knows the divine principles of right and can apply them in correct judgments. But, on the other hand, he is also equally sensitive to the deservings of people; *justice* is here *mîšôr*, 'uprightness, straightness, fairness'. Consequently, both *the poor* and *the wicked* are dealt with even-handedly. Neither improper favour to the needy nor disfavour to the wicked subverts the exact balance of justice. *Lips … mouth*: the king needs no other weapon than his word (Rev. 19:15, 21), because his word is annexed to his *breath*, literally 'spirit' (as Ps. 33:6).

5. The motif of 'clothing' expresses both the inherent qualities of the wearer and the purposes to which the wearer is committed (59:16–17; 61:10; Jos. 5:13; Ps. 132:9, 16, 18). Here *belt* symbolizes ability and readiness for action. *Righteousness* is whatever matches and expresses what the Lord thinks is right; *faithfulness* is what is unshakeably committed to what the Lord directs. Respectively they are spiritual integrity and loyalty.

In verses **6–9** the Edenic element in Isaiah's thought appears again (*cf.* 2:4). The dawning light of a new world was explained by the birth of the King in 9:1–7; here the rule of the King produces a new order.

6. Old hostilities and fears are reconciled and allayed. Predators and prey live together: a mere *child* is safe among them, and also human dominion (Gn. 1:28) no longer takes the form of our often inhumane exploitation of animals, but wears instead this gentle and unthreatening face.

7. Natures are transformed. The point made here is not simply 'togetherness' – the message of verse 6 – but identity of nature.

They all eat the same food: carnivores have becomes herbivores. The reference to *their young* shows that the transformation is a permanent heredity.

8. The sequence in verse 6 moved from the beasts to the child; similarly verse 7 moves to 8, but now the relationship of humankind to reptiles is in focus: not the restoration of true 'dominion' as in verse 6, but the lifting of the curse of Genesis 3:15. *Infant* is the child at the breast (*yônēq*), utterly helpless in itself; *young child* (*gāmûl*) is the toddler, capable of running thoughtlessly into danger. But now there is neither a danger that strikes nor a danger that lurks. The 'enmity' has gone. All that can be said of *cobra* (Dt. 32:33; Jb. 20:14) and *viper* (59:5; Je. 8:17) is that some sort of dangerous reptile is meant.[1]

9. A summary (9a) and an explanation (9b) of verses 6–8. *Cf.* the joy in Psalms 96:11–13 and 98:7–9 when the Lord comes to judge (to make those royal decisions which will set everything to rights); *cf.* 34:13–17; 65:25. *Harm ... destroy*: literally 'act wrongly ... act corruptly', neither do what is bad nor mar what is good. *My holy mountain*: in 2:2, the Lord's mountain was the gathering-point for all the earth; now all the earth is the Lord's mountain, wholly conformed to his holiness. The key to this transformed, renewed creation is *the knowledge of the* LORD. As the holy God dwells with them, ungrieved by sin, welcoming them to his holy place, they on their part enter into personal, intimate union with him, knowing the Lord (*cf.* verse 2d). Everywhere the Lord is present in his holiness; everywhere the knowledge of him is enjoyed, knowing both the truth and the Lord of truth.

10. See on verse 1 above. The *peoples* and *nations* have a mode of access in that they *rally* to *the Root of Jesse*. The mountain is his *rest* or 'home' (*mᵉnûḥâ*; *cf.* Ru. 1:9) which he opens to them. But how can one and the same person be both the *shoot* coming from *Jesse* (1) and the *Root* from which *Jesse* comes? This is an enigma unexplained until Luke 1:32. *Glorious*: literally 'glory'. The Messiah is at home in the divine glory and to this he welcomes all who *rally*, literally 'seek'. This does not mean groping after what is lost, hoping to find it, but coming with joyous and zealous commitment to where it is known he will be found (see on 9:13).

The world's King (11:11–16). The inclusio of this section is provided by references to the Lord's *hand*, *Assyria* and *Egypt* in verses 11 and 15–16. The *hand* is divine personal action,

---

[1] The word *mᵉ'ûrâ* occurs only here and its meaning is uncertain.

matching the divine *zeal* of 9:7, an exodus-motif (Ex. 3:19–20; 13:3; Dt. 6:21). In verses 3–5, the King was seen ruling; now the Lord gathers and transforms the people over whom he will rule (12–13); the worldwide kingdom to which the Root of Jesse was the key (6–9, 10) is now realized (14). In this beautifully structured section, two pairs of verses of divine action (11–12, 15–16) enclose two verses of transformed people (13–14).

11. *In that day*, here as in verse 10, indicates the eschatological nature of the vision. *A second time*: the 'first time' was the exodus. Note how the poem ends on this theme in 16d. But now there is a wider exodus of a worldwide people. *Assyria ... Egypt* are the contemporary and ancient great oppressing powers. No force can hinder the Lord's purpose. South and further south lay *Upper Egypt* (lit. Pathros) and *Cush*, with *Elam* and *Babylonia* to the east, *Hamath* in the far north, and *the islands of the sea* are the outlying lands to the west (see 40:15)[1] – no distance or remoteness around the whole world can prevent this great exodus. *Babylonia* is literally Shinar. There is no reason why Isaiah should have avoided mentioning Babylon. It was a prominent power of his day. Did he therefore choose to use the ancient name Shinar, the place of human self-sufficiency (Gn. 11:1–9) and inherent wickedness (Zc. 5:5–11), to indicate that not even pride and sin can hinder the gathering?

12. *Exiles* is simply 'dispersed ones' (√*nādaḥ*; a synonym of *scattered*, √*pûṣ*); the translation *exiles* is too suggestive of simply the Babylonian exile. A wider dispersion is indicated by *the four quarters of the earth*. Matthew 24:31 is the fulfilment. The Lord's threats (*scattered*, 6:11–12) are as seriously meant as are his promises (*gather*).

13. Under David, the twelve tribes enjoyed a real if fragile unity. It was never so before him nor after him. This vision of reconciliation is part of Isaiah's forecast of David's return and the kingdom that will yet be (Lk. 1:32–33). This verse can be understood as a balanced statement: the *jealousy* Ephraim suffers (13a) and the jealousy Ephraim feels (13c); the enmity Judah suffers (13b) and the enmity Judah expresses (13d). Emotions (*jealousy*) and actions (enmity) of hostility are alike banished from this truly united people.

---

[1] The word translated *islands* (*iyyîm*) occurs 38 times in the OT of which 17 are in Isaiah. In chs. 40 – 55 (9 times) it is virtually a technical term for the 'Gentile world' (*cf.* Pss. 72:10; 97:1). As a word, it first means 'island' in the strict sense; then land lying along the sea coast, hence, places accessible only by water; and, finally, land masses, far-flung parts of the earth.

14. The theme of the Davidic kingdom continues. It was David who conquered Philistia (2 Sa. 5:17–25), the *east* (probably the mercenaries mentioned in 2 Sa. 10:6), *Edom* (2 Sa. 8:14), *Moab* (2 Sa. 8:2–13) and *the Ammonites* (2 Sa. 10–12). This picture of warlike conquest by the united people jars against the vision of the *Prince of Peace* and the extending kingdom of peace in 9:6–7, but in fact what we have here is a consistent use of metaphor, not a forecast of events. It is exactly the same as the metaphor of the Christian armour (Eph. 6:10ff.). Kings customarily extend their kingdoms by armed conquest. Within the picture of the coming King, therefore, Isaiah envisages the spreading royal dominion: but the force to which the nations fall is that of the Prince of Peace, the gospel (Acts 15:14ff.). The reconstituted people of God are the agents in kingdom extension.

15. The prophet now reaches back beyond David to the exodus. Then the drying up of the sea facilitated the exit of the people from bondage; here it facilitates entrance, but it is the same divine *wind* (Ex. 14:21).[1] The inclusion of *the Euphrates* not only affirms that no obstacle can stand in the Lord's path but reintroduces the Assyria-Egypt theme of a universal exodus begun in verse 11 and concluded in verse 16. The word *streams* ($n^e\bar{h}\bar{a}l\hat{i}m$) means a river bed which is only intermittently filled with water. Consequently it can be a dry river valley (2 Ki. 3:17), and that is its most suitable meaning here. The mighty Euphrates becoming a *naḥal*! What power must be at work! *Seven*: the number reflecting the perfect, complete work of God.

16. The work of new creation has been done and the world is ready for the one people. This coming exodus is as it was *for Israel.* We could translate *the remnant of his people* as 'his remnant people' (see 24:16), the gathering of his elect from the four corners of the earth (Mk. 13:27). What the New Testament will yet call 'the Israel of God' is thus envisaged by Isaiah as he foresees the one people brought together by divine action.

---

[1] NIV *dry up* makes a slight alteration to MT and loses its vigour. Lit. 'utterly destroy'. √*ḥāram* occurs 29 times in Exodus–Joshua. Typically used in Jos. 2:7; 6:17, it refers to things so vile that they must forthwith be 'separated' from human contact, and so wicked that they must immediately be dismissed to the Lord for his judgment. In the present case it refers to man-made barriers which the exclusivist and separatist tendencies of human sinfulness have erected. These are abhorrent to the Lord as contrary to his creative design. In the 'day' which Isaiah foresees here, these (and all other evidences) of sin and curse will disappear. The word translated *scorching* is of uncertain meaning.

d. The individual in the community – salvation, singing and the proclamation (12:1–6)

This song forms the concluding bracket/inclusio to chapters 6 – 12, to which 6:1–13 is the opening bracket. Isaiah began with his own story: an individual who, though he shared in the deadly sins of the whole community, yet experienced salvation, a divine provision of cleansing leading to reconciliation and commission (see pp. 68–69). His address to Judah (7:1 – 9:7) and Israel (9:8 – 11:16) concluded with the same hope, the King whose coming would put all things to rights. In 12:1–6 we see the fruits of this royal work, a community in which each knows God's saving work (1–2), all drink the saving waters (3) and share a testimony to the world (4–6). We notice therefore the first person singular (*I, me, my*) of verses 1–2; and the second person plural (*you*, coupled with plural imperatives) of 3–6. There cannot be a transformed community without saved individuals; nor can there be a saved individual who is not incorporated into the community.

1–2. An unnamed voice (1a) affirms what the also unnamed individual (1b–2) will say by way of personal testimony. Possibly we are to think of Isaiah as the speaker: in 6:8 he spoke of himself; now he foresees others along with him, unanimous in testimony. *In that day*, i.e. the *day* alluded to in 11:10–11, the day when the Lord will have constituted a worldwide people as his own and when his King reigns. *You* in verse 1a is second person singular. This individual's *praise* comes as a result of an important sequence: divine *anger* (1c); its removal (1d); divine comfort (1e); personal experience of a divine Saviour (*God is my salvation*, 2a); faith issuing in fearlessness (2b); the Lord becoming the source of personal strength and joy (*strength ... song*, 2c); assurance of salvation in and through the Lord (*become my salvation*, 2d). The basic problem of the sinner is the wrath of God. Were he not the Holy One there would be no need for salvation (Rom. 1:16–18), and until his wrath is propitiated there can be no salvation. *Your anger has* (1c) is more probably 'Oh let your anger ...' – a mere plea is the only and sufficient course for the sinner to take.

Verse 2 opens and closes with the affirmation that God himself is the source and the effecting of salvation: he *is* so (2a) because he wills to *become* so (2d). Between these two affirmations are four characteristics of the saved: the exercise of faith, the removal of fear, the infusion of strength, and the joy of song. *Trust*: in 7:9 trust was expressed by √'*āmēn*, pointing to the reliability of the one trusted, whereas here √*bāṭaḥ* points to the security into which the one who trusts enters. Hence it is followed by *not be afraid*. And this confidence is soundly based, 'for' (omitted in NIV) 'my strength and song is Yahweh' (*cf.* Ex. 15:2).[1] The objective mark of salvation is *strength*, durability in the face of life; and its subjective counterpart is *song*, the inner welling up of joy (1 Thes. 1:6).

3. To enter salvation is an individual experience (2) but to enjoy it is communal (3). *You* is here plural, and *salvation* which (2) is indeed an outreaching of God to the individual is also (3) an unfailing resource (*wells*) to which the saved community resorts with *joy*. Isaiah is following the community in its journey from Egypt, where individually they took shelter beneath the blood of the lamb, to the provision of water at Marah, and on to the wells at Elim (Ex. 15:25, 27).

4. The same voice speaks again as in verses 1 and 3, now envisaging that the whole community will react as the prophet himself did in 6:8, responding to the Lord and engaging in proclamation. The responses are gratitude (for what the Lord has done), worshipping him for what he is, and worldwide testimony to his deeds and his person. *Call on his name*: of all the shades of meaning of *call on* (*qārā' b^e, e.g.* Ex. 34:5–6; 35:30; Is. 43:1), the most suitable here is 'to invoke the Lord in worship by using his name' (Gn. 12:8). His *name* is shorthand for all that he has revealed about himself. Those to whom he has thus made himself known enter into a worshipping intimacy with him. But their secrets must be shared openly. They alone know what he has done for them in salvation and they ceaselessly thank him; they alone know the name of the Lord and they enter the privacy of worship. They also have a duty: they must tell others what he has done, share with others the revelation of the *name* which they have received.

5. Just as their personal gratitude and worship must, if they are genuine, become public in testimony (4), so must their songs of joy. *Sing*: Isaiah makes two important points. First, song is called for not as an expression of inner elation but as a response to the works of the Lord. It arises not from a stirring up of emotion but from bending the mind to recall, ponder and understand his

---

[1] Isaiah seems to be trying deliberately to recapture the joy of the exodus in this song of salvation. Thus, for example, he uses the archaic form of the word *song* (*zimrat*; Ex. 15:2) and the affectionate diminutive of the divine name, Yah, which first appears in Ex. 15:2 and thereafter sporadically in the OT (*e.g.* Ps. 118:14). It is, of course, the final component in Hallelujah, 'Praise Yah'.

majestic deeds (Lk. 24:32). Secondly, true joy in what the Lord has done overflows to *the world* in sharing this good news.

6. For the last time the voice of verses 1, 3 and 4 speaks in feminine singular imperatives to a feminine singular (not *people* but) 'inhabitant' of Zion. The thought is drawn from Exodus 15:20–21, where Miriam led the songstresses in proclaiming what the Lord had done at the Red Sea (*cf.* 1 Sa. 18:6; Ps. 68:11). The masculine singular of verse 1 is matched by the feminine singular of verse 6. Thus this lovely song of joy in salvation is bracketed by a stress on the individualism inherent in the experience, but the contrasting male and female individuals embrace the rejoicing community (3–5): neither is valid without the other. *Zion*: Isaiah once saw a different Zion with different 'daughters' (3:16 – 4:1), but now the promised cleansing (4:4) has happened and the *Holy One*, once estranged (6:3–4), has come home (*cf.* 4:5–6) to live among his people.

III. THE KINGDOM PANORAMA: THE WHOLE WORLD IN HIS HAND (13 – 27)

Throughout his vision of the coming King (chs. 7 – 11), Isaiah has alluded to the worldwide dimension of the kingdom and its unending rule (9:7) and to a time when the whole earth will be the Lord's holy mountain (11:9). He notes how the Lord's remnant people, the coming worldwide Israel, who will be gathered from Assyria and Egypt, and Philistia, Edom, Moab and Ammon (11:14), will be part of the re-established kingdom of David.

These sidelong glances at the world dimension of what the zeal of the Lord will do (9:7) now become the main theme of the book. The 'great' powers of Babylon (13:1; 21:9), Assyria (14:25) and Egypt (19:1) are reviewed along with the smaller states of Philistia (14:29), Moab (15:1), Aram (17:1), Edom (21:11), Arabia (21:13) and Tyre (23:1). Over all of them the Lord rules in serene sovereignty, determining their experiences, appointing their destinies, purposing to bring the whole world together as one people (19:24–25) gathered (27:12–13) to himself. In the thick of this world scene the professing people of the Lord live out their histories, condemned for their failures (17:1–8; 22:1–14) and yet central to the glory of the day when the Lord reigns in Zion (24:23), the city of peace whose walls are salvation and whose people are believing and righteous (26:1–4).

The structure of this long and wonderful part of Isaiah is important. There are three sections: chapters 13 – 20, 21 – 23 and 24 – 27. Of these the first two are each subdivided into five by the keyword 'oracle' (13:1; 14:28; 15:1; 17:1; 19:1; 21:1, 11, 13; 22:1; 23:1) and, as we shall see, the third main section also is in five subdivisions, though without individual headings (24:1–20, 21–23; 25:1–12; 26:1–19; 27:1–13).

The oracle headings in the first section (chs. 13 – 20) are straightforward, but in the second section (chs. 21 – 23) they are (all except one) enigmatic, and it is only on reading the contents of each oracle that the nature of its subject becomes obvious. In section three only the changing topics indicate subdivisions. Thus we move with Isaiah from the definite present, the world around him (the precise headings) into the hazier future (the enigmatic headings) and on to the remoteness of the eschaton, the Last Day where, from Isaiah's perspective, everything seems to merge into one.

These three series of five address one question as central to living in this world: where is security to be found? A number of solutions are considered: first, 'The Superpower Solution'. The question was first asked in Shinar (or Babel) (Gn. 11:1–9) and, very properly, Isaiah considers the 'Babylon' solution first. Babylon is the 'superpower', it represents the 'imperialist syndrome', the world ordered by the imposition of centralized government. But Babylon's political domination will be broken – it is as unacceptable to other nations as it is to the Lord (13:17–19; 14:5); its man-made gods give it no protection (21:9) and it will end as the ruined city (24:10), its gates broken (24:12) because it broke the (divine) laws (24:5). In a word, human efforts to unify the world as one 'city' are insufficient.

Second, 'Hope Deferred, Hope Assured': Philistia (the second oracle in the first series, 14:28–32) may rejoice when the Davidic monarchy seems to fail, but neither the monarchy (14:29) nor the Lord's purposes for Zion (14:32) are finished. It will take time and long darknesses for his purposes to mature (21:11–12; oracle two in the second series), but ultimately the Lord will reign gloriously in Zion over the kings of the earth (24:21–23).

Third, 'Pride and Collective Security': in the third position in each series Isaiah reviews the Gentile nations and reveals a world doomed through proud refusal of the good news (Moab) and determination to prove itself sufficient (Dedan). Moab (15:1 – 16:14), in dire straits, could find security in Zion (16:1–4), but it is too proud to accept this solution (16:5–6). By contrast, in 21:13–17, Gentiles turn to collective security in a time of need but live to see its failure (21:16–17). Nevertheless, the day will come when all nations (except Moab, excluded by pride) will enjoy the Lord's banquet on Mount Zion (25:6–10).

Fourth, 'The False Trails of the People of God': in the fourth place in each list Isaiah observes how Israel and Judah respond to the threatening world around them. Israel (17:1–6) seeks security in an alliance with Damascus (Aram, see on 7:1–9). But by contrast Jerusalem chooses self-sufficiency (22: 9–11) – in each case the Lord is the forgotten factor (17:10; 22:11). But worldly strength is no security (17:4, 9) and self-sufficiency is the unforgivable sin (22:14). Yet, one day, the Lord's people will enjoy the peace of salvation in the strong city (26:1–21).

Fifth, 'The Triumphant End': the Lord does not give up; his purposes will prevail. The fifth passage in the threefold series takes us right to the End when there will be one world, one people, one God (19:24, 25), when even the irretrievably materialistic Tyre will be (lit.) 'holiness to the Lord' (23:18) and when, in the day of the Lord's Jubilee, a worldwide community will be gathered to his 'holy mountain' (27:12–13).

a. The first series of oracles: sure promises (13:1 – 20:6)

In chapters 6 – 12, Isaiah painted a Zion-centred picture of the divine management of the world. This received a particular focus in 10:5–15. The five oracles in this first series blend the contemporary, the impending and the eschatological so as to show that the Lord is in executive charge of his world for the purpose of keeping his word and fulfilling his promises.

i. Babylon: a look behind the scenes (13:1 – 14:27). This Babylon oracle is typical of the whole first series. Babylon was a contemporary power but Isaiah begins by relating it to the Day of the Lord (13:6–8) and to a universal and cosmic work of God (13:9–13). Then, in case the remote should seem the unreal, he provides an interim fulfilment in the attached Assyrian prediction (14:24–27), for if the Lord cannot demonstrate his governance of history in what people see before their very eyes, why should they trust him for what they cannot see? Equally, if they actually see him running the world, with even a superpower subject to his word, they are without excuse if they fail to trust his remoter promises.

We have here the two contesting superpowers of Isaiah's day, Babylon and Assyria. Who could doubt that world history would be shaped by them? Who but a prophet of the Lord?! Isaiah takes us behind the scenes: it is the Lord who is in command (13:3), who gathers his forces (13:4) and exacts moral retribution (13:9–11). When earthly forces arise against existing powers, it is the Lord's initiative (13:17); when dominant powers fall, it is the

Lord who has cast them down (14:5–6); arrogance (14:13–14) meets with his judgment (14:22). He has planned and he will act (14:24).

This is a general view of what the section teaches but the structure of the whole displays another and very special truth. The beckoning hand (13:2; 'beckon' is lit. 'wave the hand') at the beginning is matched by the outstretched hand at the end (14:26). Thus 13:2–16 (A1) declares a universal purpose and 14:24–27 (A2) exemplifies it (see 26); next, 13:17–22 (B1), the overthrow of Babylon, is matched by 14:3–23 (B2), the overthrow of the king of Babylon; and at the very centre of it all is 14:1–2 (C), a contrasting universal purpose, the Lord's compassionate purpose for his people. This is what the course of history is all about: the Lord giving central concern and loving attention to the fulfilment of his declared purpose for his chosen.

1. *Babylon.* Why did Isaiah begin his panorama of history with Babylon as the representative superpower rather than the more obvious candidate Assyria? First, as we saw in the Introduction (pp. 21–23), Babylon was far from being a negligible power in Isaiah's time. Twice, under Merodach-Baladan, it established its independence in the face of Assyrian dominance, and it would have taken very astute political judgment to say which would come out best in the Mesopotamian power stakes. Secondly, Isaiah knew that Judah would one day be overthrown and scattered (6:9–13) and he came to know that this destroying power would not be Assyria (*cf.* 8:8; 36 − 37). There was a dark power in the shadows, biding its time. In due course (39:1–8) it was revealed to him that that power was Babylon. In the ultimate, therefore, Babylon is a more significant candidate for superpower status than Assyria. But, thirdly, humanity's bid to organize life and create security and stability by its own resources and without reference to God began at Shinar/Babel (Gn. 11:1–9). More than any other name, therefore, 'Babylon' typifies humankind's will to be its own saviour.

The Day of the Lord (13:2–16). 'The Day' is the culmination and termination of history. Step by step Isaiah depicts its seven aspects: it is the Day when the Lord implements his wrath (2–3), marked by worldwide mutual destruction (4–5) from which there is no defence (6–8); it is cosmic in its effect (9–10), moral in its motivation (11); it reverses the work of creation (12–13); there is no escape, only horrific suffering (14–16).

2–5. 'The gathering armies'. *Gates* (2) are the symbol of defence. When the enemy enters the gates, the city has fallen (see on 28:6). *Nobles*: the existing rulers of the world whom the Day will overthrow. *My holy ones*: not *holy* in themselves but consecrated to, or set apart for, the holy task of the Lord's warfare. *Who rejoice*: literally 'my exulting ones of arrogance'. These warriors exult in their own self-confident arrogance but (unknown to themselves) they have been claimed by the Lord for his purposes. The Lord is not on either side in this warfare (4–5). Humanity's armed strength comes together in an orgy of mutual destruction (*cf.* Ezk. 38 – 39; Rev. 20:8). *Mountains*: historically, Jerusalem often heard the sound of gathering forces on the hills around. This is the picture here: it will be pre-eminently the case on the Last Day (Ezk. 38:14–23; Rev. 20:9). *Weapons of his wrath*: the note of divine sovereign management of this final battle continues.

6–8. 'Helplessness'. The thought is of the immense forces gathered to the Last Battle: such power as breathes *destruction* (6), leaves people helpless and demoralized (7), strikes terror (8). *Near*: at any moment the Day is already there, awaiting the Lord's command to dawn.[1] *Hands ... heart*: the organs respectively of personal action and reflection. The terror of the Day brings total personal paralysis. *Woman in labour*: not here a picture of fruitful pain but of a process reaching its inescapable outcome (1 Thes. 5:2–3). *Aghast* (√*tāmah*): *i.e.* not aghast with fear but bereft of all certainty, in a state of confused indecision. *Aflame*: in an agony of fear; maybe also in acute embarrassment as the Day reveals that they have made all the wrong choices, trusted wrong resources.

9–13. 'Judgment on sin'. The notes of moral retribution (9) and cosmic disaster (10) are sounded as marks of the Day. *Cruel*: 'savage' (see Je. 6:23). As verses 4–5 implied, on the human level the Day is the climax of mutual hatred expressing itself in mutual destruction. It is not, therefore, that the Lord acts savagely but that sin is a savage thing in its outworking. On the divine level, however, this savage outworking is the wrath of God visiting on humankind its due. In verse 3, *wrath* (*'ap̄*) is anger expressed (*cf.* 10:5); in verse 5, *wrath* (*za'am*) is indignation felt; here it is *'eḇrâ*, anger overflowing, bursting out. For the first time

---

[1] *Destruction from the Almighty* (6) exemplifies Isaiah's skill with assonance (*šōḏ miššadday*). *Almighty* is an excellent contextual translation of *šadday*, a word of uncertain meaning. It occurs as a divine title chiefly in Gn. 12 – 50, where the context requires 'one who is almighty (in keeping his promises)'. His power does not flag like human power; he is at his most potent when people are at their most impotent. In the present context it refers to the God who is almighty to do whatever he wills. See J. A. Motyer, *The Revelation of the Divine Name* (Tyndale Press, 1959), pp. 28–30.

in the poem the moral motivation of the Day is mentioned. *Sinners* (√*hata'*, 9) points to acts astray from the norm; *sins* ('*āwon*, 11) are the inner warp in fallen human nature; *haughty ... pride* (11) is unwarranted, conceited self-esteem, expressing itself (*arrogance ... ruthless*, 11) in superiority and unfeeling domination of others. This compressed summary of characteristics and conduct which we tend to accept as commonplace brackets verse 10: the reversal of the whole of creation. Truly the wages of sin is death. Hence the awesome allusion to extermination in verse 12! *Ophir*: unknown in location but famed for its gold (1 Ki. 9:28; Jb. 28:16). *Tremble ... shake*: see Jeremiah 4:22–26. The ordered movement of the heavens, the stability of the earth – all that was achieved by creation – is undone in judgment. *Wrath ... anger* as in verse 9, acting as an inclusio, rounding off this section.

14–16. 'No escape'. The picture of gathering with which the poem began (2–5) is balanced at the end by this picture of scattering. In turn the verses reveal three facets of the Day: no protection (14), no escape (15), no mercy (16). They gathered in arrogant triumphalism (3–5), now they have everything to flee from (14) and nowhere to flee to (15). Humankind without God is without safety and without home. *All who are caught*: literally 'all who are swept away', *i.e.* into flight from the ferocity of the battle. But they might as well have stayed, for *the sword* will still find them and, should any reach their home (16), it is to find that the enemy got there first. In all this, of course, the Lord is no puppet master making automata jump to his bidding (*cf.* 10:5–15). People are simply being themselves (Tit. 3:3). 14:26 notes that the guiding power in history is the 'stretching out of his hand'. Yet in so many ways the Day is the withdrawing of his hand as he judgmentally leaves sinners, unrestrained, to implement all the savagery of the fallen nature. The more people turn their backs on God, determined to 'be themselves', to be masters of 'their own world', the less human they become, therefore the less humane. When the Day comes, sin will take centre stage as the total and savage destroyer it has always been, and those who did not want God will get what they wanted: they will be given up (Rom. 1:24, 26, 28) to be themselves.

The end of Babylon's kingdom (13:17–22). Having announced and described the Day of the Lord, Isaiah turns to the foreseen fall of Babylon. It is typical of the Old Testament to see coming calamity against the backdrop of ultimate calamity. Just as every next king was eyed with the keen hope that he might be the promised king, so envisaged turmoil raised the question whether it might be the Last Battle; in any case, many of the same issues are involved.

17–18. This case involves divine direction (*I will stir*) and human energies (*the Medes*). Not just at the (last) Day but in all its interim foreshadowings, the Lord is in executive management of history. The choice of *the Medes* as the destroyers of Babylon is unexpected. We are accustomed to think of Babylon falling to the Persians but, on the other hand, often the Medes take priority over the Persians, as in 'the law of the Medes and Persians' (Dn. 6:8, 12) and the description of Babylon's conqueror as 'Darius the Mede' (Dn. 5:30).[1] We must leave it to Isaiah to have had his own reasons for singling them out here. *Silver ... gold*: they cannot be 'bought off'; their sole motivation is conquest and in this they are merciless (18; *cf.* 14–16). *Strike down*: 'dash in pieces'. The verb is an unusual one in relation to death by arrow, but is probably chosen to make a link with its use in verse 16. The picture is of such a torrent of arrows striking home that bodies are left 'mangled/shot to pieces'. They have no concern for life (*young men*), no restraint of pity (*infants*), no thought for the future (*children*) – nothing but the fulfilment of their own imperialism!

19–22. Next Isaiah reviews the moral ground of the overthrow (19), its permanence (20), completeness (21–22a) and proximity (22b). *Sodom and Gomorrah* (19; Gn. 19) are the classic instances of divine overthrow (*cf.* 1:7). The allusion underlines the ultimate divine energy behind the 'front-line' activity of the Medes. The absence of human inhabitant (20) and the replacement of humankind by beasts (21–22) emphasize the finality of the overthrow. And why has all this happened? Because of *the Babylonians' pride* (*cf.* 11). It is not only at the Last Day but also in every interim experience of divine anger that pride is a killer, leaving utter ruination and emptiness in its wake. Not even a passing *Arab* nomad nor a *shepherd* taking an afternoon siesta will be there, but only that which replaces (*jackals, owls, hyenas*) and repels human settlement. *Desert creatures* should probably be 'desert wraiths' and *wild goats*, 'goat-demons' (Lv. 17:7). The Bible can use folk superstitions simply for effect, without extending credence to them. *Her time*, ('*ēt*): not a calendar date but a season appropriate to an event. Assyria destroyed Babylon in 689 BC (see ch. 21) but it

---

[1] See D. J. Wiseman, 'Some Historical Problems in the Book of Daniel', in Wiseman *et al.* (eds.), *Notes on Some Problems in the Book of Daniel* (Tyndale Press, 1965), pp. 9–16.

recovered; likewise it was intact after Cyrus captured it (539 BC) but its continued nuisance-value provoked Darius Hystapes to desolate it in 518 BC, and so it has remained.

The heart of history: the Lord's people (14:1–2). Here is a vision of a new world in which co-operation has replaced animosity. It is the new Day of the Lord in which the insensate passion for mutual destruction has been replaced by unity (1de), and hostility by helpfulness (2ab). But behind this display of a new humanity there is divine initiative (*compassion*), choice and settlement (1abc). What actually happened at the return from Babylon (539 BC) in no way fulfilled this: Cyrus, like many a soldier turned politician, replaced the sword in his hand by the tongue in his cheek (Ezra 1:2–4) and did what was to his own advantage under guise of piety. There was no international acclaim or will to help, no reversal of the captor–captive roles (2c–f). In a word, just as the fall of Babylon was an interim fulfilment of one side of the Day of the Lord, so the return was a pale mini-reflection of the other – each an 'earnest' that the total threat/promise would yet be fulfilled.

1. The verse opens with a vitally important 'For', not translated by NIV: it is an explanation why history works the way it does, whether on the grand scale of the Day or on the awesome but smaller scale of interim 'days'. *Compassion* (*raham*) is the highly charged emotional devotion of a mother (1 Ki. 3:26). *Choose*: *i.e.* implement the choice long since made (Dt. 7:7). *Settle*: 'give rest', a traditional expression for peaceful security (Dt. 12:10; 2 Sa. 7:1). *Aliens*: temporary residents who came seeking asylum (Dt. 14:21, 29; *cf.* Dt. 10:18–19; Lv. 25:23). In the envisaged day of settlement they will be so enamoured with the life of the Lord's people that they too will want to settle. *Join ... unite*: the idea is doubled for emphasis. This will be a real and true union.

2. For this reversal of roles, see 45:14–25; 49:22–26; 60; 66:19–24. Isaiah is still using the royal metaphor, possibly looking back to 1 Samuel 17:8–9 when the erstwhile dominant Philistines became servants. But it is still the voluntary and glad relationship of verse 1. Jacob (1) and *Israel* will enjoy the wealth of the nations (Ex. 12:33–36; Rev. 21:24–26) and be dominant domestically (*menservants*), militarily (*captives*) and politically (*rule*): but the reality, of course, is the spreading kingdom of peace (9:7), of which the convert becomes a glad member (1de) and takes a servant's place within the community of compassion.

The end of Babylon's king (14:3–23). See pp. 296–297 and the parallel section, 13:17–22 above. An introduction (3–4a) blending this section with the theme of restoration (1–2) is followed by the 'song' over the fallen king of Babylon (4b–21) and a conclusion (22, 23) which turns the final thought of the song into a divine affirmation.

3–4a. David (2 Sa. 7:1) and Solomon (1 Ki. 8:56) mistakenly thought the Lord's purposes had been fulfilled in their day, but all they experienced was an interim day of rest. The fullness still awaits the Day. *Suffering* (*'ōṣeb*) is related to the 'painful toil' (*'iṣṣābôn*) of Genesis 3:16. Its ending here signifies the removal of the curse. *Turmoil* (*rōḡez*) is restless insecurity. *Cruel bondage* is the exact expression found in Exodus 1:14. There will be no more oppression or oppressor but full redemption with all its fruits. *Taunt*: the notion of 'jeering' is not suitable to the song or to the word used here; *māšāl* is a proverb or parable, a saying or way of putting something so that its inner meaning comes to light. This is the intention here: to express the inner realities involved in the fall of Babylon's king.

In verses **4b–21**, the song about the king of Babylon,[1] the earth reacts to the end of oppression (a1; 4b–8) and Sheol reacts to the arrival of the king (b1; 9–10); the king's arrival in Sheol (b2; 11–15) contrasts dramatically with his ambition to reach the apex of heaven, and his reputation on earth (a2; 16–21) contrasts with his lot after death.

4b–6. The single *oppressor* (4) contrasts with the plural *wicked ... rulers* (5). The king against whom the Lord finally acts is the culmination of a long line of culpability: biblically this does not excuse him but rather (Lk. 11:50–51) makes him the inheritor as well as the perpetrator of wickedness. There is no point asking which king of Babylon Isaiah has in mind. If it had been essential to know, he would have told us. The description is standard for the arbitrary and totalitarian rulers of the ancient empires. The point is not to show how the Lord dealt with this or that ruler but to draw out principles of the divine government of history. The power of earthly rulers is real (*rod ... sceptre*; *cf.* on 10:5–15), and they are answerable to God for their malevolence (*anger ... fury*),[2] their reign of terror (*unceasing blows*), and their

---

[1] The authorship of this song is disputed, but needlessly. Erlandsson, *The Burden of Babylon*, p. 128, notes that 83% of the words occurring here are found in the agreed work of Isaiah. Of the remaining 23 words, 17 are pre-exilic and the six words alleged to be 'late' are found on examination not to be so.

[2] In v. 4 *fury* represents the unknown Heb. word *maḏhebâ*. Qᵃ reads *marhebâ*, which, though it does not occur elsewhere, is traceable to the verb 'to be arrogant', found in 30:7. LXX could well have invented the Gk. word *epispoudastēs*, meaning 'one who presses on'.

belligerent refusal to tolerate any point of view but their own (*relentless aggression*). Oppression (4, 6) on earth is noted in heaven and the *wicked* will be punished.

7–8. Not only people but trees rejoice at the end of the oppressor. The levelling of the New Forest to supply Nelson's fleet, the poor shattered trees on World War 1 battlefields, and the criminal defoliation of Vietnamese forests, all tell the tale of creation's suffering in human wars. But there is more in the reference to *Lebanon*, for it typifies God's, not human, ordering and beautifying of creation (Ps. 104:16). To cut down Lebanon is to seek to be like God. But note how the king himself (19) is a rotten branch: the arrogant woodman has indeed 'had the chop'.

In verses **9–15**, Isaiah takes us on an imaginative trip to Sheol, the abode of the dead. We hear how Sheol reacts to the arrival of the king (9–10) and what a contrast this is (11–15) to his ambitions and self-estimation. Imaginative though this is, great Old Testament truths are accurately expressed. First, the dead are alive. In the Bible 'death' is never 'termination' but always change of place (from earth to Sheol), change of state (from body-soul unity to the separate life of the soul) and continuity of person. Thus, in Sheol, there is personal recognition: the king is recognized as he arrives (10); the existing residents rise from their thrones – not because there are thrones in Sheol but because they are the same people as once they were on earth. But the dead are 'shades/shadowy ones' (9), *weak* (10) because death has sundered body and soul; the soul by itself is but a half-life. The Old Testament awaits the Lord Jesus to meet its implied need of the resurrection of the body. This is an illustration of the progressive, cumulative revelation which runs throughout the Bible.

9–10. *The grave* (NIV mg. 'Sheol'): the place name of the abode of the dead. See further on verse 11. *The spirits of the departed*: the single Hebrew word, $r^e\bar{p}\bar{a}'\hat{\imath}m$, is of uncertain meaning. It is probably related to $\sqrt{r\bar{a}\bar{p}\hat{a}}$, 'to sink down, droop', hence some such translation as 'shadowy ones'.[1] *Leaders*: literally 'he-goats', leaders of the herd, boundless in assertive virility. The word is ironical: 'shadowy, flabby he-goats!' *Weak* from $\sqrt{h\bar{a}l\hat{a}}$, to be sick, ineffectual.

11–15. The second part of the visit to Sheol opens with *pomp ... brought down to the grave* (11) and ends with *you ... brought*

---

[1] 'Rephaim' was the name given to some pre-Israelite inhabitants of Canaan (Dt. 2:11, 20: 3:11), noted for their fearsome power. For this reason the identity of spelling with 'the shadowy ones' can only be coincidence. Contrast Jb. 26:5; Ps. 88:18; Pr. 2:18.

down to the grave (15). *Grave* should, of course, be Sheol. It is not the cemetery where the body lies but the 'place' where the soul continues in life. Yet they are not unrelated, for the cemetery too has a testimony to bear. What a bed for a king! What a bedspread! The grave exposes the fragility of our humanity, for the body too is spoken of as *you;* it, as much as the soul, is the person. The dissolution of the one in the grave matches the weakness of the other in Sheol. In the light of all this, how 2 Corinthians 4:16 – 5:5 comes into its own!

Morning star (*hêlēl*, 12) alludes to the Canaanite myth of Helal/Ishtar who attempted a heavenly coup that failed. The Old Testament uses allusions like this without attributing reality to the characters concerned. The king had, mentally at least, made his own bid for the heights – but look at him!

In verses 13–15 we look into the king's heart, at his secret ambitions in contrast to (12) his public achievements. Note the progressively upward movement of his soaring self-esteem: *stars*, the highest visible realities; *mount of assembly* refers to the mythological belief that the gods lived on mountains (as in Greece on Olympus). The king thus envisaged his deification. But more, he aspired to the chief place among the gods, *utmost heights ... sacred mountain*, literally 'the apex of Zaphon'. Mount Zaphon, in north Palestine, was the seat of the Canaanite gods. It is mentioned in Psalm 48:2. But the king plans to go higher, *above the tops of the clouds* to be *like the Most High*. The Bible has no animus against godly ambition (Phil. 3:13–14; 1 Thes. 4:11 with Rom. 15:20; 2 Cor. 5:9), but equally it insists that, where human arrogance reaches after the stars, it grasps the pit. Tellingly here *depths* (15) is the same Hebrew word as *utmost heights* (13). *Grave* is Sheol again. *Pit* is used as a synonym for Sheol in its more threatening aspects (*e.g.* Pss. 28:1; 143:7; Is. 38:18).

In verses **16–21** the poem returns to the earthly scene, to contrast what the king might have expected with what actually happened: not a state funeral (18) but a trampled corpse (19, 20a–c); not an honoured succession but slaughtered sons (20d–21).

16–17 dwell on the king's power – over the work of God (16c, 17a), the work of human beings (16d, 17b) and people (17c).

18–20c point out the contrast. *Tomb*: 'house', used here of the ornate mausoleums in which the great ones of earth seek to perpetuate their superiority. *Branch* (*nēṣer*): as in 11:1. He is a 'shoot' of kings but is reckoned fit only for the compost heap! Once he wore royal robes; now he is (lit.) 'clothed with the slain', his body covered only by the foot-soldiers whom his arrogance directed into his battles and to their death. *The stones of the pit* is the rock-bottom of Sheol. *Join them*: *i.e.* the *kings* mentioned in verse 18. He was, of course, no worse than they (*cf.* the plurals of 5–6) – and the question has to be asked, 'Why he?' Because the world is run by a just God, who allows people time for repentance (2 Pet. 3:9, 15) and lets iniquity work until it is full (Gn. 15:16). Providence waits, probation works out, judgment falls.

20d–21. The Old Testament forbids human judicial processes to punish children for parental sins (Dt. 24:16) but, by the providential ordering of God the Creator, there is a price to be paid for being human and, for good or ill, there is a moral entail (Ex. 20:5–6; Pr. 20:7) working out under his just rule. *Wicked* ($m^e r\bar{e}\hat{i}m$, 'evil-doers') is not the same word but is the same idea as in verse 5, and forms a judgmental inclusio for the section. This brilliant, surging poem is a horrific description of devastation, carnage, disappointed hopes, dead sons, a shattered environment. The wages of sin is death.

22–23 portray 'the Lord of history'. The downfall of Babylon took a long time to happen. In spite of falling to the Assyrians in 689 BC and to Cyrus in 539, it was Darius in 516 who pushed it past the point of no return. The Bible, however, makes us look beyond second causes (here superior empires, greater rulers, stronger armies) and beyond the prolonged processes of history to the First Cause and the sole determinative factor: *I will rise ... cut off ... turn ... sweep.* World government (22a), the termination of imperial tenure (22cd), transformation (23a) and obliteration (23b) are traced to the fourfold *I* of divine initiative and action. It is not because the Bible is ignorant of second causes or denies their effectiveness that it so constantly traces all directly to the hand of God; it is because it would have us live by faith. Preoccupation with second causes encourages people to 'work the system', pull strings; focusing on the First Cause calls us to trust and to live in the obedience of faith. *Declares ... declares* ($n^e um$): see 1:24. Notice its use three times, like a triple seal of authenticity. *Almighty*: 'of hosts', see 1:9.

Assyria: a test case, an interim assurance (14:24–27). Just as, when the Day of the Lord comes, his hand will beckon to earth's forces to gather to the Last Battle (13:2–3), so in every movement of history, every foreshadowing of that Day, it is the Lord's outstretched hand (26) that rules earth's experiences. Through his prophet the Lord has allowed his people to look forward – to the eschaton itself (13:2–16), to the coming fall of a contemporary power (13:17–22) and its king (14:3–21). He has revealed to them that they are at the heart of his historical providences (14:1–2) and that it is he who is the executive of world affairs (14:22–23). Can they believe all this? Has he got them at the heart of his plans? Is he really the world ruler? Can he master earth's superpowers? In answer to these questions Isaiah in effect replies, 'Watch this space', for in 701 BC, within the experience of those he addresses, they will see the hand of their God in their own deliverance and the overthrow of great Assyria. Faith is not credulity, wishful thinking or a leap in the dark. Rather, it is a leap into the light, for faith is conviction and action based on evidence. When they see what happens to Assyria they can believe about Babylon, and, beyond Babylon, about the Day of the Lord. Isaiah could not have chosen a more persuasive example. In his day Babylon was a great power (see ch. 39), a real challenge to Assyrian domination and to the balance of power in Mesopotamia, but only intermittently so. The real superpower, dominant, savage, irresistible, was Assyria. The Lord commits himself in advance to deal with Assyria (24–25) and then asserts that this is the model for the divine universal purpose (26–27).

24–25. As in verses 22–23, there are four first-person verbs. *I have planned* ... By this neat literary move, Isaiah sets the specific case of Assyria in the context of the Lord's universal action. It is a case in point. *Planned* (√*dāmâ*) ... *purposed* (√*yā‘aṣ*): the former is the plan in the mind, the latter its formulation as a scheme of action. *In my land*: this was also the locus of the Last Battle (5, 9). The Lord will bring the Assyrian forces right into his own land (8:6–8; 10:5–15; 36–37) and overthrow them there. *Yoke ... burden*: the wording is as in 10:27.

26–27. On the universal scale there is need only for an outstretched hand, universal in its coverage (26b), irresistible in its power (27cd). *Plan, determined* and *purposed* are all *yā‘aṣ* (see 24).

ii. Philistia: the Lord's sure promises to David (14:28–32).
28. For the second time (see 6:1), Isaiah dates an oracle by a death. *Ahaz* was a significant king to Isaiah for, as we have seen, the prophet understood Ahaz' refusal to walk by faith and his commitment to political salvation by an alliance with Assyria (see 7:1ff.; Introduction, pp. 19–20) as being the death knell of the dynasty of David. Would that happen with his death? Throughout the Assyrian period Philistia was a ceaseless agitator for rebellion. In 734 BC Gath refused tribute and was sacked; in 720 Philistia connived with Egypt to rebel, and Sargon II

defeated Egypt at Gath and took Askelon and Gaza; in 711 Ashdod was somehow central to an unsuccessful west Palestinian revolt; in 705 Ashkelon rebelled and fell to Sennacherib in his campaign of 701. The death of Ahaz in 715 could well have been the occasion of a Philistine approach to Hezekiah with a view to joint anti-Assyrian action. At any rate such an embassy, maybe under cover of a mission of condolence on the death of his father, is a scenario which fits this oracle like a glove. We can start by asking what question would prompt the answer proposed in verse 32 with its emphasis 'It is the LORD who has founded Zion and it is in it that his downtrodden people will find refuge'. Was another foundation – an alliance with Philistia and Egypt – being proposed? Another refuge for a small, beleaguered people? To Isaiah all this was pernicious. The times might well be menacing and the prospect of recovering independent sovereignty enticing, but all the security Zion and its people needed was in the Lord. Typically of Isaiah this oracle is a balanced statement.

29–30, *The first contrast: ultimate destinies.* The house of David has a strong future (29cd) but not Philistia (30cd). When Ahaz decisively refused the way of faith (7:9) the doom of the monarchy was sealed, yet Isaiah at once affirmed the hope of Immanuel (7:14). So here, on the death of the unbeliever, Isaiah reasserts the promises. David was *the rod that struck you*, for no other king of Judah was so completely victorious over Philistia (1 Sa. 17:50; 18:25–30; 19:8; 23:1–5; 2 Sa. 5:17–25; 8:1). But with Ahaz *the rod ... is broken*, for up to that time the sovereign independence of David's house had remained intact but from Ahaz onwards the Davidic king was a vassal until the dynasty disappeared altogether. Thus the Philistines, even though they hoped to win Hezekiah's support for an anti-Assyrian alliance, could *rejoice* that they had nothing further to fear from that quarter. *Rod ... snake*: see Exodus 4:2–3; 7:10–12. The house of David may be broken but the Lord can make even the broken rod into a *venomous serpent*. For the inner meaning of victory over Philistia, see on 11:14.

Poorest of the poor (30): literally 'the firstborn of the poor', but it is unclear what the expression means. There may be a clue in seeing 'firstborn' as an exodus motif (Ex. 4:22). In Egypt, Israel seemed doomed and helpless but, as the Lord's 'firstborn', proved triumphant. On *poor*, see 10:2; *needy*, from √'*ābâ*, to be willing – in the good sense, to be pliant to the will of God, and in the bad sense, to be subject to the will of stronger forces, exploited. Yet, in Egypt, resourceless and defenceless though they were, they became victorious. Maybe the expression here could be translated, 'the firstborn, poor though they be'. *Find pasture*: another exodus motif (Ps. 77:20).

In other words, though David is gone and his house a poor broken thing, there are secret vitalities at work guaranteeing triumph; though David's people endure a new Egypt experience, there will also be a new exodus and a people provided for by shepherding care. But it is otherwise for Philistia. Whatever holds promise for the future (*root*) or exists in the present (*survivors*) is doomed.

31–32, *The second contrast: immediate fortunes.* The Philistines are helpless before the threat from the north (31); but Zion is secure in the Lord (32). The *gate* is the key target in an attack. Once the gate is breached the *city* falls. *Melt*: the verb (*mûg*) is used of being 'demoralized, no heart for resistance' (Jos. 2:9, 24). *Smoke* is the dust cloud raised here by the advancing armies (*cf.* Song 3:6). *North*: the Mesopotamian powers were always seen as 'northerners' because from the east they marched round the Fertile Crescent and came against the Palestinian states from the north. The reference here is to the Assyrian attack in 701.[1] But the future for *Zion* is different. In the face of the same threat it is secure. Verse 32 begins with 'and', *i.e.* in the light of the foregoing exposure of Philistine helplessness what sort of reply should be offered to their suggestion of an anti-Assyrian alliance? *Answer shall be given* is a perfectly idiomatic translation, treating the third-person singular verb as an indefinite (*i.e.* 'should one give' = 'should be given') but it might also be translated 'should he give', that is, Hezekiah, when approached by *the envoys*. This, then, would be Isaiah's reply, the reply of a stout and steady faith. First, the prior reality of the Lord himself: literally 'It is the LORD who ...'. Secondly, the status already enjoyed by Zion's people: they live in the city the Lord chose and where his promises have their home (*e.g.* 28:16): Thirdly, human weakness is not a factor in the situation: *afflicted* (*i.e.* downtrodden, at the bottom of life's heap) they may be, in their own and others' estimation, but they are *his* and are *in her*, in Zion, his chosen city (Heb. 12:22–24). Fourthly, *refuge* is open to them to flee to, for in Zion the Lord lives among his people.

iii. Moab: salvation refused by pride (15:1 – 16:14). The Babylon oracle (13:1 – 14:23) focused on the centrality of the

---

[1] *Straggler* (31) is uncertain. Lit. '... none by himself/standing alone at his appointed times/in his appointed company'. Some suggest the word (*bôḏēḏ*) may mean 'deserter'. Qᵃ offers no help.

people of God (14:1–2) in his executive control of world history; the Philistia oracle (14:28–32) confirmed this by affirming the Davidic promises and the certainty that the Lord would honour them. The Moab oracle follows in sequence, by correcting any impression that the promises are exclusivist: the promises which will be fulfilled in Zion embrace all who take refuge there – even Moab! As regards date, it is certain that Moab, like all the Palestinian states, suffered in the Assyrian crisis – Sargon II in 715 and 711 BC, Sennacherib in 701 – but beyond that neither the past tenses of 15:1 nor the future tenses of 16:13 offer enough evidence to relate the events described to specific defeats. Indeed, it is possible that the tenses of 15:1 express future certainty rather than past fact, in which case 15:1 and 16:13 refer to the same overthrow and would presumably find fulfilment in Sennacherib's attack on the west (Introduction, pp. 20–21). Certainly in any invasion by the pitiless Assyrians all that 15:1–9 describes would be true but, as so often, Isaiah's concern is with the principles central to a situation, not with dates, times and personalities. Even the foe remains vague as *the rulers of the nations* (16:8). In this way Isaiah lifts a certain tract of history on to a new level: a Gentile people is in dire straits (15:1–9) and turns to Zion for help (16:1–4a); it hears the reply that the time of aggression is temporary but the throne of David is permanent (16:4b–5), an implicit invitation to find security by coming under the governance of Zion and the shadow of the Davidic king; Moab, however, cannot bear to lose face in this way; pride inhibits responding even to such good news (16:6), and in consequence Moab's sorrows continue (16:7–11); there is no other refuge (16:12) and only destruction awaits (16:13). Isaiah's purpose is not to mark out a situation with dates and names but to use history to depict truth: the needy can find salvation by identifying with the people of God and coming within the embrace of his promises, but pride is a killer.

1, Moab's crisis. *Ar* was a border town (Dt. 2:18); *Kir*, probably Kir Hareseth (16:7, 11), was in central Moab (2 Ki. 3:25). The picture is of an invasion which has broken the border defences and penetrated to the heartland. *Ruined*: as 6:5, 'silenced', the silence of the dead; the silence of a city which flight has emptied of people. *In a night*: an attack of such speed, power and ferocity that it took only a single night.

2–4, Moab's grief. People turn to religion in their grief (2); despair spreads from town to town (3–4ab); the military are as overwhelmed as the civilians (4cd). *Dibon*, north of the Arnon; *Nebo* and *Medeba* further north still. The heaping up of names creates the impression of widespread disaster and helplessness. *Shaved*: the cutting of the hair was a sign of mourning (22:12; Mi. 1:16). *Streets ... roofs*: the mourning becomes local and domestic. The sorrows of war are not abstract; they come right into the home. *Heshbon* (Nu. 21:26), *Elealeh* (Nu. 32:3, 37) and *Jahaz* (Nu. 21:23) are all in the plains of Moab and the furthest north of the cities named. Moab has become one single weeping entity. The tragedy is so overwhelming that the soldiers are immobilized by grief.

5–9, *The Lord's grief over Moab*. *My heart* (5) leads on to *I will bring* (9), identifying the speaker as the Lord grieving over the fugitives (5), the environment (6), the pathetic efforts to salvage something from the disaster (7–8) and the further suffering ahead (9). This is all joined together in the Hebrew by the explanatory word 'for' seven times: before *they go* and *on the road* in verse 5; before *the waters* and instead of *and* (*the grass*) in 6; also at the beginning of 8 and 9, and instead of *but* in 9. In this way the verses are a long catalogue of what agonizes the Lord, who weeps even as he smites. Just as this Moab oracle corrects a possible misapprehension in the Philistia oracle (14:28ff.) by showing that the Davidic promises embrace the Gentiles, so it adjusts the Babylon oracle (13:1ff.). There the divine nature expressed itself in holy wrath; but there is another side to the Lord, a heart of astonishing sympathy and empathy, compassion and identification with human suffering.

5. In contrast to verses 2–4, the list of towns here runs southwest. The enemy comes from the north and Moab flees southwards. *Zoar* (Gn. 19:21–22) is in the southern Dead Sea area. *Eglath Shelishiyah* is unknown; *Lulith* and *Hornaim* (Je. 48:5) must have been in the same area.

6. *Nimrim* (Nu. 32:3, 36; Jos. 13:27) is probably Wadi Numeirah in southern Moab.

7–8. One of the most pathetic sights of war is the plight of civilians caught up in a disaster not of their making, and left to salvage what they can from the misfortune. Imperial glory comes at the expense of those at the bottom, not those at the top. *The Ravine of the Poplars* may be Wadi Zered on the southern border of Moab (Nu. 21:12; Dt. 2:13). *Eglaim* and *Beer Elim* are unknown. Maybe they are the 'Dan and Beersheba' of Moab, expressing the whole length of the land.

9. *Dimon* may be an alternative name for *Dibon* (2), forming an inclusio. Isaiah could well have chosen this form of the name for assonance sake: *mê-dîmôn māl^e'û ḏām*, 'the waters of Dimon are full of blood', which would have appealed to his poetic sense.[1] There is an allusion to 2 Kings 3:22–23, where Moab once saw a mirage of blood, but now it is all too real – and their own! But even rivers running with blood do not satisfy the holy justice of God, 'for' *I will bring still more.* Tears (5) and just inflictions (9) are at one in the divine nature. *Lion* is used here as a metaphor for an implacable assailant who will destroy alike those who seek to escape and those who opt to stay, that is, all without exception. 2 Samuel 23:20 and 1 Chronicles 11:22 mention 'ariels' of Moab, apparently élite warriors of some sort. The title means 'lion of God'. It is a subtlety worthy of Isaiah to threaten *a lion* (*'aryēh*) on the land of ariels. Did they boast of lions? Lions they shall have!

16:1–4b, *Moab's plea.* The scene changes. Isaiah writes as though overhearing Moab's 'Cabinet' discussing what to do. They are meeting at Sela in the far south whither, presumably, the government has fled and now pleas for help. In panting, breathless Hebrew the prophet reflects their panic.

1. *Lambs* were the traditional Moabite tribute (2 Ki. 3:4), implying a request for vassal status. *Desert*: the desert of southern Judah, which emissaries from Sela would have to cross. *Ruler* is intentionally vague. They feel themselves compelled to become tributary to the Davidic king but cannot bring themselves to say so.

2. Even though they have acted for their own safety in fleeing to Sela, the government are not without thought for their people, and what drives them to seek Judah's protection is news coming from sixty miles to the north – and near the bloodied waters of Dibon (15:9) – where terrorized Moabite girls are desperate to cross the Arnon to gain some small protection from the enemy.

3–4b records the message the envoys would take to Zion.[2] First, they appeal for immediate advice (*counsel*) and *decision* (3ab); next, they present their problem figuratively: they are like people exposed to the blinding glare of the noonday sun and needing the relief of *shadow* (3c); thirdly, they ask that *fugitives* ('those driven out') be admitted to Judah (3d) and that all demands for extradition be refused (*do not betray*, 3e); and, finally, they request that those 'driven out' from Moab be

[1] Qᵃ reads 'Dibon' instead of 'Dimon' in each case.
[2] The verbs in v. 3 are difficult. There is a textual variation whereby the first verb may be either 2nd person plural or 2nd person singular feminine; the second verb is 2nd person plural and the third and fourth verbs are 2nd person singular feminine. It would be easy to make them all 2nd person singular feminine, as an address of Zion (see *BHS*). If the first two verbs can be treated as 2nd plural, they represent discussion among the Moabite leaders.

accepted as resident aliens (4ab). *Stay* is √*gûr*, used technically for the right of temporary residence or political asylum.

4c–5, *Isaiah's answer.* As in 14:32, Isaiah proposes what his own answer would be to such an appeal from Moab. Outside this passage we have no knowledge of a Moabite approach during the Assyrian crisis – though the circumstances of the time make it far from unlikely – and no record of any reply. But Isaiah's reply here is thoroughly consistent with his thinking. In his eyes Zion's strength is not in military resources. Zion's strength is in the Lord and in the Davidic monarchy on which the divine promises were concentrated. He therefore replies that present crises pass (4cde) but the throne of David will endure (5). The implication plainly is that, if Moab is serious about wanting a secure future, they must come in on a faith basis within the protected enclave of the Lord's promises to David.

There is a great difference in style between 4cde and 5. In speaking of the crisis (4) Isaiah imitates the excited speech of the envoys, but changes to a majestic calmness when he speaks of the Davidic security. This is in effect what he has on offer: an escape from pressures and uncertainties into the calm certainties of faith and hope. First, he offers them an unchanging God. *Love* is *ḥeseḏ*, the Lord's covenanted (therefore unchanging) commitment to his people, his steadfastness, unmoved by changing times or experiences, undeviating even when they proved faithless. Secondly, there is a perpetual kingdom. The *throne ... established* contrasts with what Moab was experiencing, the fickleness of human political fortunes. Thirdly, there is an undoubted king. In *the house* (lit. 'tent') *of David*: not a usurper, but one with a true lineage and right to rule, and, most of all, the inheritor of the promises made to David. 'Tent' is a more personal word than even *house*, with the nuance of 'home' rather than merely an address. A discreditable example like 2 Samuel 16:22 shows this, as does the idiomatic expression for 'going home' in 2 Samuel 20:1, 22. The king is a genuine descendant of David, living by right in David's personal home. And, fourthly, the king will rule in *faithfulness* (the opposite of fickleness, unreliability), *justice* and *righteousness* (see on 1:21). This is the promised Davidic restoration. In a word, what Isaiah would offer the Gentiles is Zion's messianic best. His faith was consciously universal: all who appeal to Zion are welcome under the banner of the house of David.

6–8, *Moab's grief explained.* The return of Moab to tears implies that the terms on which security could be found in Zion were not acceptable – and the reason given is Moab's *pride*, *conceit* and *insolence*. Had they been asked for a higher tribute price, their pride would have been intact, but the simple price of submitting to Zion's king was too high.

6. The four nouns *pride ... pride ... conceit ... pride* all spring from √*gā'â*, 'to be high'. Its good sense is 'majesty' (2:10; 4:2); its bad sense 'haughtiness', an inflated sense of self-worth. *Insolence* ('*ebrâ*) often means '(overflowing) anger' (10:5), but here 'effrontery', a self-esteem that overflows in every direction. On all this Isaiah comments that *her boasts* (inventions, living in a world of unreality) *are empty*. It is the way of faith, trusting the Lord's promises, that is the way of reality.

7. *Therefore* (7) introduces the consequences of refusing security in Zion: wailing (7) and withering (8). *Wail ... lament ... grieve:* the first is the vocal expression of grief, the second is the 'groan' of grief inwardly felt and the third is the prostration of grief, what we mean by 'grief-stricken'. *Kir Hareseth*: see 15:1. *Men*: 'raisin cakes' (see NIV mg.). Other occurrences of this phrase (2 Sa. 6:19; 1 Ch. 16:3; Song 2:5; Ho. 3:1) do not help to explain the significance here, except perhaps that such cakes may have been considered a delicacy. Possibly, therefore, as spreading vines (8) symbolize influence extending abroad, 'raisin cakes' represent the joys and prosperity known at home.

8. *Heshbon* and *Sibmah* are unknown. *Jazer* (Nu. 21:32; Jos. 13:25) was on the extreme northern border of Moab. *The desert* lay east and *the sea* to the west. The picture is of a country extending its influence in all directions.

9–12, *The Lord's grief over Moab*. Isaiah is still drawing out the consequences of Moab's pride: verses 7–8, the consequences for Moab; 9–12, the consequences for the Lord – who mourns over the past, what Moab has lost (9–10), and over the future (11–12), the fact that Moab now has nowhere to turn for help.

9–10. *So*: 'therefore' (*cf.* 7). *I weep* (9a): the subject is identified by *I have put an end* (10d). The thought is the same as 15:5–9. What the Lord visits in holy justice he laments with holy sorrow. It is we who find tension between his justice and love; but the divine nature is one, and all the Lord's attributes are in perfect harmony (Ps. 145). In 15:5 he wept over Moab; now he weeps *as Jazer weeps*, literally 'in the weeping of Jazer'. His tears and theirs are mingled as one; he is no onlooker on the world's sorrows (even though self-inflicted) but a participant (even though the suffering is his just visitation). Attention has shifted from the withering of the vines (8) to the joy that formerly marked the vineyards and the vintage. Moab's choice of the way of pride has proved to be a joyless experience, and it grieves the

Lord when even Moab no longer finds happiness in his creation
and its fruits.

11-12 should be introduced by 'therefore' as in 9 (*cf.* 7). This
is the third consequence of Moab's pride, and again it focuses on
the Lord's grief, now over the helpless position into which pride
has led Moab. They rejected salvation in Zion and there is no
alternative salvation, no matter what effort is expended (*wears
herself out*) or what religious exercises are practised (*pray*).

13-14, *Moab's imminent ruin.* Isaiah introduces a second
'interim fulfilment' (see 14:24-27). What is predicted and fulfilled *within three years* gives ground for confident faith in the
remoter and greater promises of God. Probably this prediction
was elicited by a Moabite enquiry (*cf.* 21:11-12). The prophets
were sought out by Gentile enquirers (*e.g.* 2 Ki. 8:7ff.). The Assyrian crisis provoked intense diplomatic activity between the
Palestinian states. If Isaiah published 15:1 – 16:12 to coincide
with a Moabite embassy, seeking to press on them his sense of
their critical plight and the solution he had to offer, one or more
Moabites could well have come to him for clarification. On the
other hand, the prophets used the technique of addressing absent
audiences (Moab) in order to teach present hearers (Judah), here
enforcing the lessons of forsaking pride and resorting to faith. In
this case the time-factor not only provides an interim fulfilment
and therefore ground for faith but also a proper stress on the
urgency to respond. *As a servant*: a hired hand is a clock-watcher.
Hence, *three years* here means 'three years exactly'. Moab's pay-
day has been fixed. *Splendour ... many people*: no status or
resources can fend off the calamity. Humanly speaking, downfall
might be 'against the odds', but if the Lord has decreed it the
matter is settled, and if the Lord's salvation has been refused
nothing can save.

**iv. Damascus/Ephraim: the way of death and the promise
of life (17:1 – 18:7).** In each of the three sets of oracles that make
up this part of Isaiah, the Lord's people occupy the fourth
position (*cf.* 22:1-25; 26:1-21), here the northern people,
Ephraim (17:3, 4-6). But why does Isaiah conceal Ephraim
behind an apparent address to Damascus, the capital city of the
kingdom of Aram? This is precisely the point: the people of the
Lord live out their histories within world history. They are part of
the fivefold roll-call of the nations which makes up the series.
They are not immune from the demands, pressures, questions and
temptations of life in this world. In Isaiah's time, they too were a
small kingdom among the kingdoms and therefore faced the same

problem: where is security to be found? Ephraim's answer, when up against the Assyrian threat, was to turn to Aram (see on 7:1ff.; Introduction, pp. 19–20), to sink its national identity in that of its more forceful erstwhile enemy, coming together in an Aram-Ephraim defensive alliance. Ephraim's hard experience taught that to identify with the world for salvation was to be caught up in the world's destruction.

We must not be unrealistic about Ephraim's problem. Think of any small state in our own time threatened with absorption into a superpower! Collective security must have seemed an obvious, even wise way forward. But they could adopt it only at the expense of forgetting their saving God, their strong Rock (17:10). In the scheme of these oracles, the Lord has affirmed (14:1–2) that he sovereignly governs world history to make and keep his people secure; he never revokes his promises (14:32); and the way of salvation for Gentiles is to submit to Zion and its king (16:4–5; *cf.* Ps. 2:10–12). But Ephraim is here found seeking security in Damascus, not in the Lord, failing to trust his promises and reversing his intended procedures by finding salvation in a Gentile power instead of opening a way of salvation to the Gentiles.

The two nations (17:1–11). The first half of the Damascus/Ephraim oracle, 17:1–11, is a microcosm of history, how Damascus and Ephraim fare. They think they can be masters of their own destiny through collective security, but who is the real Ruler? Corresponding to this, 17:12 – 18:7 is a macrocosm of history, the worldwide scale of things. The same question is posed: who is the real Ruler?

1–3, *Failed security.* Damascus, the capital of Aram, comes first as the prime mover in the 'treaty organization'; *Ephraim,* the northern kingdom of the people of God, is subsumed under Damascus as having sunk itself in the alliance – in more senses than one! (See 7:1–3; 2 Ki. 16:1–9.) The only known *Aroer* (Nu. 32:34) is in Gad, one of the constituent tribes of Ephraim. Thus Isaiah allows his spotlight to swing back and forth three times in these verses: once again the structure is the message. These powers have inextricably bound themselves together – and together they will fall. Ephraim could have found security in the Lord and, on the pattern of 16:5, could have sought to bring Aram into the same security, but opted for the reverse course. Unbelieving Ephraim cannot be helped by Damascus, nor Damascus by unbelieving Ephraim. *Flocks*: not a picture of pastoral bliss but of a landscape emptied of humans and left to the beasts. *Like the glory* is possibly ironic: the glory Ephraim might have enjoyed is doomed and Damascus with it. But more likely the words are to be taken in their plain meaning: there is something imperishable in Ephraim, a glory that guarantees a future, but likewise there is a hope even for Aram. This unexpectedness of hope would be typically Isaianic and would, incidentally, form an inclusio with the Gentile hope expressed in 18:7.

4–11, *Explanations: destruction and survival.* The material in these verses has been brought together as three *In that day* oracles (4, 7, 9). The *day* in question is the time of the destruction outlined in verses 1–3.

4–6. Three pictures of the extent of the destruction: a disease which wastes the flesh away (4), reaping (5a) and gleaning (5b). The first picture touches the internal state of a patient: departure from the way of faith means personal debilitation. The second and third pictures bring external forces into play: reapers and gleaners, between them, leave nothing behind. To depart from the way of faith makes the people of God defenceless against external forces of destruction, and leaves them with nothing to show that they had ever been there. The survival of a few ungleaned fruits (6) is humanly speaking against the odds – but they are there, affirming a hope against hope that there will be some survival. Just as the destruction threatened against the allied powers (1–3) is underwritten by the divine title *the LORD Almighty* (3), so the survival (6), against all probability, of some is guaranteed by the title *the God of Israel*, the One who has pledged himself to them.

Verses 7–8 describe the beneficial outcome of the divine visitation. A spiritual purification will result: eyes will be fixed on the Lord (7) and every human contrivance for salvation will be abandoned (8).

7. *Men* (*hā'āḏām*): 'humankind'. Isaiah seems to be thinking wider than Israel, looking also to the 'remnant of Aram' (3). Divine chastening brings spiritual benefit. *Look* is a fixed gaze (*šā'â*; 31:1; Ps. 119:117), making the Lord the sole object of confidence; the *eyes* are the organ of desire and expectation (Ps. 123:2), seeking all they need from his supply. *Maker*: a deliberate contrast to the hand-made gods of verse 8 (*cf.* Ps. 96:5). *To the Holy One of Israel*: it is costly to pride to turn to the true God. Gentiles coming in have to forswear national pride by acknowledging Israel's God; Ephraim must repent of rebellion and schism and return to the Holy One who lives in Jerusalem (6:3).

8. *Look ... regard* are the same Hebrew verbs used in verse 7, and the two negative statements reinforce the message that

turning to Holy One involves sole loyalty to him, the abandonment of every other god. *Hands* ... *fingers* implies that false
religion has this identifying mark: it is an exercise in human self-
reliance. Along with the man-made gods goes their whole
religious support system: *altars* for sacrificial approach, *Asherah
poles*, *i.e.* symbolic representations of evergreens, standing for
the life and life-giving power of the goddess, and Baalistic
incense altars (Lv. 26:30; 2 Ch. 14:5), the means of communion
with the god.

Verses **9–11** contain the explanation of the downfall. This is a
perfect example of the reasoned ministry the prophets offered.
They were not demagogues winning arguments by shouting
loudest; they offered description (9), diagnosis (10ab) and
prognosis (10b–11). Faith is ever the real test of the Lord's
people: is it to be (lit.) 'the cities of their stronghold' (9) or 'the
Rock of your stronghold'(10)?

9. The Hebrew, taken in order, reads 'their strong cities will be
like the forsaken thing of forest and height which they left
because of the sons of Israel'. Doubtless the ruins of the long-
deserted, overgrown fortresses of the pre-Israelite inhabitants of
Canaan were still visible. In Joshua's time, trusting the Lord
proved stronger than 'cities ... with walls up to the sky' (Dt.
1:28), but when faith lapsed the people themselves built strong-
holds and trusted what they had once seen their God destroy.

10. Reinstate the initial 'For'. In verses 10–11 the verbs are
second-person singular feminine, indicating that they did not
originally belong with verse 9. Most likely, the words were
originally addressed to a city as representing its people. But the
words are in place in their present context as an explanation of
the devastation: cities will fall (9); what could be more appropriate than an explanation addressed to a city? *Forgotten* ... *not
remembered*: the fixed gaze and longing eyes of verse 7 speak of
a God constantly in the forefront of mind and memory. Failure in
memory is the cause of spiritual disaster (Ps. 78:9–11, 40–42).
God your Saviour: literally 'God of your salvation'. In this idiom
'salvation' is not an occasional act but a constant attribute: he is a
'saving God', and the possessive 'your saving God' means that
this attribute is ever available and active for his people. *Rock* is
more than a (static) symbol of changelessness. The use of the
metaphor in the Old Testament includes Exodus 17, the provident
rock from which the saving waters flowed. *Fortress*: specifically
a 'strong place', as also in verse 9 ('strong'). It must have seemed
realism to build cities as 'strong places' in a threatening world; it
is 'real realism' to trust the Saving-Rock-God who is our 'strong

133

place'. Instead of this stability and security of faith, what did they do? In their own estimation they built for security (9), but Isaiah depicts them fiddling around with plants! What a futile thing is human fortified security! What a silly thing is false religion! The gardening metaphor (*cf.* 1:29–31) is a reference to alien fertility cults seen as a way to secure prosperity and living strength. *Imported*: brought in from outside, like the alliance with Damascus.

11. *You* comes four times. False religion is always a reflection of human initiative (*set them out* ...) and has no vitality except what the human devotee imparts (*make them grow* ...).

Many nations (17:12 – 18:7). The enlarged topic of this second half of the oracle is announced at once: *many nations*. No names are mentioned, for, as usual, Isaiah is not so much interested in pinning events to dates as in seeing principles of truth embodied in events. Yet it is not hard to read between the lines and see the times of the Assyrian crisis: many nations in turmoil (17:12), intense diplomatic activity (18:1), apparent divine inactivity (18:4), the sudden end of the crisis (17:14). Isaiah allows his vivid imagination and brilliant pen to go to work on this scenario, and the result is a poem of immense power embodying Isaiah's distinctive view of the divine mastery of history.

12–14, *World rule in principle.* The surging and roaring of the nations (12) at the beginning stands in contrast to the dramatic *gone* (14) at the end. Between these two points there is the single Hebrew word *he rebukes them* (13).

12. *Raging ... sea*: the restless sea is an apt image of the flux of world history seen through the human eye. In particular (Ps. 93) it is the world constituting a threat to the Lord's throne and people (*cf.* 8:9–10; Ps. 2). As the kings of Assyria extended their empire they created great conglomerate, multi-national armies; on the other hand, the remaining nations, small and large, felt the wind of the imperialist threat blowing. The Assyrian crisis brought a particular time of surging, raging and threat. It will be so on a global scale at the time of the Last Battle (13:1–5).

13. A single word of command rules the world (Pss. 2:4–6; 46:6; Ezk. 1:25); *cf.* the same voice in relation to the 'forces' of creation (Ps. 104:7). In the context of this whole oracle, especially 17:1–11, what emerges is not only the sheer greatness of such a God but the folly of not trusting him. *Chaff* is both a picture of speedy and total dispersal and of swift judgment, before which its victims are helpless. The strength of the incoming tide (12), when he *rebukes* it (13), is nothing more than *chaff* and *tumble-weed*: seemingly irresistible in its coming, but helpless in its going!

14. *Evening ... morning*: *cf.* 37:36. Psalm 30:5 makes the evening/morning theme speak about the characteristic way the Lord works; Psalm 46:5, along with the present oracle, could well be rooted in the Sennacherib incident. *Sudden terror*: Sennacherib mesmerized Judah and Jerusalem with terror yet, come morning, was *gone*, literally 'nothingness of him'/'not a sign of him!' *Us*: whether on the 'small' scale of the single incident of Sennacherib or on the implied macrocosm of *nations ... peoples* (12), it is all in the interests of *us,* the Lord's people (*cf.* 14:1–2). Again, how foolish not to trust him in every emergency. There is not only his irresistible power in world rule but his unfailing central concern for his people.

18:1–7, *A signal to the world.* In 715 BC the Ethiopian Piankhi mastered Egypt and founded the twenty-fifth (Ethiopian) Dynasty. He immediately sought to be a world statesman and began sending envoys to create an anti-Assyrian conglomerate. In 17:1–3 Isaiah examined the smaller exercise in the collective security of Aram and Ephraim. Here is a larger experiment on the same lines, which Isaiah depicts in universal terms so as to test out its validity as a possible answer to world needs. It failed in the microcosm of 17:1ff. How will it fare on the macrocosm of the world stage?

1. *Woe* is the same word as 'Oh' in 17:12, and should have the same translation in order to bring out the balance between the two sections: 17:12–14 asserts a principle of world government; 18:1ff. tests it out in a world situation. *Land of whirring wings*: Egypt with its profusion of flying insects. Isaiah does not name Egypt but allows the *whirring* to suggest a busy, restless world. *Cush* is the upper Nile region, Ethiopia. The whole impression therefore is of the known world (Egypt) stretching out along its great waterways to the remote and the unknown.

2. *Envoys* go out. *Tall and smooth* is usually interpreted as referring to Ethiopians, a proverbially tall people in the ancient world. But √*māšak*, 'to draw out, prolong', is never found meaning 'tall'. 'Drawn out' could mean 'long-standing' (Je. 31:3), *i.e.* having a long record in history, and therefore well-established. *Smooth* (*môrāṭ*) means polished, as of a sword sharpened and gleaming, ready for action (Ezk. 21:9); maybe, therefore, 'in battle trim', well-armed. This understanding makes the people in question exactly the sort to seek out for an alliance.

3. We have already noticed (14:32; 16:4–5) how Isaiah can step into diplomatic situations and give his own, perhaps unpopular, answer. This is what he does here. The mandate given to Piankhi's envoys would have been to win foreign courts to an anti-Assyrian alliance, but their mission (2) now leads into Isaiah's worldwide message (3). We can picture the scene: the envoys reach Jerusalem and Isaiah takes the opportunity to publicize what he would say to the whole world in the name of the Lord. He would, in fact, send them on their way as his envoys. He addresses the *world* (3ab); he calls for universal expectancy. *A banner* (also 11:10) will be raised; a *trumpet* (also 27:13) sounded – the combination of the visible and the audible suggesting that there will be every opportunity to be aware. Thirdly, he appeals for a response: 'Oh, do see … hear!' is more suitable than the equally accurate *you will see* …

4–7. An opening 'For' (omitted, NIV) introduces an explanation of Isaiah's worldwide message. He has received a word from the Lord (4a): the Lord waits (4b), chooses his moment (5) when his harvest is ripe, the warring forces will be completely destroyed (6) and there will be a worldwide pilgrimage to Zion (7).

The Lord is the *quiet* (4) watcher in world affairs, present as naturally as there is heat with light or dew in harvest. Yet he remains the transcendent God, watching from *my dwelling-place*. But as *heat* and *dew* arc not just incidental to harvest but contributory factors, so the Lord moves the whole process of history toward its maturing.

Before the harvest (5): the harvest is ready, as the rest of the verse indicates, but it has not yet been reaped. There is a precision about the Lord's timing. The crops are ripe for harvest but the sickle will not be put in before his moment comes (Rev. 14:15). For the picture of the feasting *birds* (6), see Ezekiel 39:17–29; Revelation 19:17–18.

Verse 7 speaks of the worldwide consummation. *Time* ('ēṭ) is the 'season' appropriate for an event to happen. This picks up the idea of the quietly watching, waiting Lord (4) and the striking of his hour (5). Just as on the one hand (6) it will be the exactly right moment for universal judgment, the final collapse of human efforts to organize the world without God, so it will be exactly the right moment for the other sort of harvest: the Lord's gathering in of a worldwide people. *Gifts*: specifically 'homage gifts' (Pss. 68:29; 76:11). *Far and wide*: see verse 2. There will be those from earth's remotest bounds who have been alerted and waiting for the banner to be raised (3) and now they become pilgrims to Zion. The promise of a Gentile remnant was authenticated by *the LORD Almighty* (17:3). The same promise, seen here in its visionary fulfilment, is authenticated by the same title.

v. Egypt: one world, one people, one God (Isaiah 19:1 – 20:6). This final oracle in the first series of five fits into the sequence in two main ways. First, it follows logically from its immediate predecessor. According to chapters 17 – 18, even though Ephraim had sunk its identity in the world, it still retained its glory (17:3) and therefore its hope (17:6), but, possibly even more wonderfully, the Gentiles with whom they had identified to their loss would, 'in that day', share the glory with them (17:4). Isaiah then broadened this vision beyond Damascus to a people coming to Zion from 'far and wide' (18:7). But on what terms do they come? Isaiah replies in 19:24–25: one world, one people, one God. He proclaims the vision which Paul saw fulfilled (Eph. 3:6).

Secondly, the series began with Babylon (13:1 – 14:27) linked with Assyria as an interim fulfilment, and now it ends with Egypt. Thus the contemporary superpower threat to the continuance of the kingdoms of the people of the Lord is linked with the first superpower threat: the Lord is sovereign over the 'powers' of earth and it is, in the end, his kingdom and not theirs that triumphs. In the first oracle, the Mesopotamian powers of Babylon and Assyria were associated as a major prediction (13:1 – 14:23) and its interim fulfilment; in this final oracle, the major prediction focuses on Egypt (19:1–25) and it is followed by an interim fulfilment (20:1–6), in which the two southern powers, Egypt and Cush, are linked. The chapters fit equally snugly into the history of the times. When the northern treaty powers, Aram and Ephraim, were swallowed up by Assyria, the political centre of gravity moved south. At least from 715 BC onwards Egypt was ceaselessly active in fomenting anti-Assyrian feeling in the remaining Palestinian states, and the possibility of recovering national sovereign independence from Assyria by means of an Egyptian alliance was a constant temptation to the politically ambitious leaders of Judah (see chs. 28ff.). Isaiah resolutely opposed this – holding to the truth he enunciated in the Ephraim oracle (17:1–11) that worldly alliance was a death warrant (*cf.* 28:15). Consequently, the burden of 19:1–15 is to dissuade his people from having anything to do with a people itself destined to collapse. It would have been strange indeed, in the light of Egypt's intriguing and Judah's willingness to go along with it, if Isaiah had not turned his formidable powers of diagnosis and forecast on Egypt's present and future. In 19:1–15 the smiting of

Egypt is predicted, but this is followed by a vision of the healing
of Egypt and the bringing of even the threatening superpowers,
Egypt and Assyria, into a spiritual union and unity with Israel
(19:16–25). Then, by way of interim fulfilment – the imminent
experience guaranteeing the undated – the smiting of Egypt is
exemplified (20:1–6) in a particular historical event.

The smiting of Egypt predicted (19:1–15). This passage is
full of statements of the Lord's active opposition to Egypt, yet no
sins are specified to warrant such a divine onslaught. A clue is
found in Isaiah's emphasis on the Nile-based economy of Egypt
(5–10), the claimed wisdom of Egypt's rulers (11) and the use of
the verb *give senseless advice* (11, see below). Egypt is an
enlarged version of the Babel of Genesis 11:1–9: human determination to meet human needs, self-confident wisdom to solve
every problem without need of God.

1. Egypt is helpless *before* the Lord. *Rides on a swift cloud*:
the only other place where the divine Rider and the clouds appear
is Psalm 18:10–15, where the Lord swooped to rescue David
from Saul and set him on his throne. Now it is Egypt that is a
deadly threat to David's kingdom (see on 28:14–15) and the Lord
is *swift* to react. Before him Egypt is demoralized. *Idols* (*'ᵉlîlîm*):
the 'no-gods', non-entities, of 2:8. *Tremble* (*nûaʿ*): 'to wander',
i.e. they are disorientated by the mere advent of the Lord. *Melt*:
see 10:18.

2–4 speak of social collapse. The review covers relationships
(2), enterprise (3ab), religion (3cd) and government (4). The
general description of a divided society, *Egyptian against
Egyptian* (2), is spelled out in terms of family (2b), neigh-
bourhood (2c), city (2d) and the reappearance of the old division
of Egypt into the two kingdoms of Upper and Lower Egypt, north
against south. Divine action frustrates every effort Egyptians
make: nothing seems to work any longer (3ab) and (as ever) in
such a time religious cults flourish (3cd). Government decays
into dictatorship (4), the authoritarian solution to social collapse.
The fulfilment of this prediction could have been the rule of
Piankhi himself (715 BC), Sargon's conquest (*cf.* 20:1–6), or
Sennacherib, or the invasion of Egypt by Esarhaddon (680),
Ashurbanipal (668) or Artaxerxes III Ochus (343). But much
more important is the recognition that social problems arise from
a spiritual root: the coming of the Lord in judgment (1) and his
direct action in human affairs (2–4). Divisiveness (2) and
ineffectiveness (3ab) are symptoms, not maladies. Those who
flocked to the cults at least saw that a spiritual solution was
needed even though their solution was in fact another symptom

of the real problem. Faced with all this disintegration, why not try force where appeal has failed (4)? If people will not do what they ought to do, they will do what they are made to do! But this also is a symptom, not the malady: the malady (1) is that they are not right with God.

5–10 describe economic collapse. *The Nile*, here mentioned five times by name and four by synonym, was the basis of Egypt's economy. The drying up of the Nile (5–6) figures the breakdown of the national economy. *The riverbed* (5): literally 'a river', indefiniteness for the sake of emphasis, 'the very River itself'. *Canals ... streams* (6): the irrigation system which carried Nile waters throughout the farmland of Egypt. *River* (7) should be 'Nile': the name is sounded three times in one verse to underline the enormity of the calamity. With the failure of the water comes the failure of agriculture (*sown field*) and then erosion (*blow away*). The fishing methods used here, *hooks ... nets* (8), are depicted on Egyptian monuments. As the Nile dries up, the fishing industry collapses. The rot extends to the manufacturing sector (9). The production of flax and the techniques of weaving were well advanced in Egypt. The translation *workers in cloth* (10) is an emendation of the Hebrew text, *šᵉtîteyhā* instead of *šatōteyhā*, which means 'pillars, foundations'. The word is not used metaphorically elsewhere, but if such a meaning is allowable here then the 'pillars' of the economy are intended, the merchant venturers, the entrepreneurs, the employers. When they fail, *the wage earners* might well indeed become *sick at heart*. Once more, these problems might be tackled as if they were the malady and not merely the symptoms. But the symptom is not the malady. The Bible insists that behind sound economy lies proper spirituality (Dt. 8:17–19; *cf.* Haggai on inflation, 1:2–6).

11–13 move on to political collapse. In these verses *wise* occurs three times, 'princes' (the civil service arm of government) appears twice as *officials* and once as *leaders*, and the idea of 'counsel', noun and verb, three times. In a word, Isaiah turns to the 'Cabinet' and the executive. Here folly reigns (13), bewilderment (*dizziness*, 14), uncertainty (14cd) and helplessness (15). For all their claims the leaders are unenlightened (11), undiscerning (12) and misleading (13). So what should they do? Change the government? But once more this is to deal with symptom, not malady. Why are the leaders so foolish, undiscerning, *etc.*? Because the Lord has acted against them (14). Once more the problem is spiritual.

Zoan (11) was situated in the north-eastern delta, and was effectively the capital of Egypt at the time of the Ethiopian Dynasty. *Fools* (*ᵉwîlîm*) are downright stupid people, unable even to see the danger of their own actions (Ps. 107:17; Pr. 1:7; 10:21). *Give senseless advice*: the word √*bāʿar* means to live on the level of animal thoughtlessness, unguided by true or higher wisdom (Pss. 49:20; 73:22). In particular it means 'to be without spiritual discernment', therefore it is linked here with their inability to see what the Lord is doing, that is, to discern a spiritual cause behind national, social and economic problems. In the time of Sennacherib's invasion (701 BC) Egypt made its one and only attempt to make good all its promises of aid. The Egyptian army was routed by the Assyrians at El Tekeh, north of Ashdod. But almost immediately, without human hand or aid, Sennacherib's power was broken (37:36–37). Egypt has the same chance as had Isaiah's contemporaries to discern the spiritual behind the historical.

14–15. The poem began with the Lord approaching Egypt; now he is at work within the leaders. *Dizziness*: the word *ʿiwʿîm* occurs only here and means bewilderment or dithering. *Stagger* (√*ʿāwâ*): to deviate, *i.e.* now go this way, now that. All this is one aspect of the holy judgment of the Lord (1 Ki. 22:21–23; 2 Thes. 2:11). *Head ... or tail, palm branch or reed*: see 9:14–15.

The healing of Egypt (19:16–25). Divine hostility is not the last word. Alongside the world's problem (1–15), Isaiah places the Lord's solution. He sets out a series of five *in that day* statements. In his actions given in verses 1–15 the Lord has not finished with Egypt. The Day will reveal other aspects of what he proposes to do.

16–17. First, he will instil the fear of the Lord. Isaiah foresees an *uplifted hand*, some unmistakable action of the Lord begetting *fear* and *terror* as to what this awesome God *is planning*. They do not yet know what his plan is, nor do they know that their fear is the beginning of wisdom (Pr. 1:7). *The LORD Almighty* runs like a link through this series (16, 18, 20, 25; *cf.* 4, 12).

18 speaks of 'one language and one Lord'. The details of this second aspect of the Day are difficult to understand. What are the *five cities*? Why is *one* (or perhaps 'each') *called the City of Destruction*?[1] Yet amid all the obscurity the central truth is plain:

---

[1] Is 'five' meant to be five specific cities or does it simply mean 'a few' (17:6; 30:17)? Is Isaiah recalling the five cities taken in Joshua's campaign (Jos. 10:22–43), symbolic of total conquest? Isaiah is, of course, very capable of such an allusion, but it seems a trifle obscure. And is only *one* called the *City of Destruction*, or is *one* used here in its idiomatic sense of 'each' (*e.g.* Ex. 36:30)? Furthermore, *destruction* (MT *heres*), is not found elsewhere. Qᵃ reads *heres*, 'the

140

following on the fear of the Lord (16) there will be a turning to the Lord, marked by the adoption of *the language of Canaan*. It would be typical of Isaiah to make speech the first mark of true religion (6:5, 7; *cf.* Jas. 1:26; 3:2). *Language*: literally 'lip', looking back through Isaiah 6:5 to Genesis 11:1, where 'the whole earth was one lip'. *Swear allegiance*: their transformation showed outwardly in speech, but inwardly it was also true.

19–22. What began in the five cities now embraces the whole land from *heart* to *border* (19). There are five marks of true religion: first an *altar* (19). The *monument to the LORD at its border* signifies the place where the Lord dwells (*cf.* Gn. 28:16–19) and marks his sphere of influence (Gn. 31:51–52) and the land he claims as his own (1 Sa. 15:12, different word, same idea). But at its centre would be *an altar*, a place of reconciliation (6:6–7), and also a *sign and witness* (20), like the altar of Joshua 22:10, 23–27, that those who live where it is are truly part of the people of the Lord.

Secondly, there is prayer (20). The people have a speaking relationship with the Lord. Isaiah moves in thought from Joshua 22 to Judges 3:9: (*cf.* 1 Sa. 12:10–11). Dangers are met and problems solved because they pray and the Lord responds. Thirdly, there is revelation (21a). The Lord will *make himself known*. True religion is not people searching after God but people responding to revealed truth. Fourthly, there is worship (21b). This expresses itself publicly in *sacrifices and ... offerings* and privately in *vows*. True worship has two aspects: first there is our approach to God through the means of grace he has provided: the sacrificial system (*cf.* Heb. 10:12–22); then there is our response to him in the vowed dedication of ourselves (*cf.* Rom. 12:1–2) and the implementing of those vows in persistency of obedience. Fifthly, there is providential discipline (22). Whom the Lord loves he chastens (Pr. 3:12; Heb. 12:1–11); tribulation is a necessary aspect of kingdom membership and final entrance (Acts 14:22); every reception of the word of God is tested to prove its genuineness (Lk. 8:10–15; 1 Thes. 1:6). The purposeful discipline of the Lord is part, then, of their life under his care, designed to make them *turn to the LORD*, come back as penitents (*cf.* 1:26), look trustfully to him in prayer and receive his remedial care.

---

sun'. LXX, 'the city of Asedeq', may simply transliterate a Heb. (or supposed Heb.) text *haṣṣedek*, 'of righteousness'. But why should such a well-known word be transliterated rather than translated? The only thing that is certain in all this (to us) obscurity is *will be called* (*cf.* 4:3; 61:6) – a new name indicating a new, divinely implemented state.

23 describes harmony in worship. First it was five cities (18), then the whole land (19–22), and now the whole world. The period of the Assyrian crisis was typical of world history. The would-be imperialists, *Assyria* and *Egypt*, created a world of tension, division, uncertainty and suffering. But where worldly power divides, true religion based on revelation (*cf.* 2:2–4) unites. The emphasis in this fourth *in that day* oracle is the harmony people feel with each other and the free expression they give to it. *Highway*: what we would call a 'causeway', a raised road, and therefore unmissable. *The Egyptians and Assyrians will worship together*: this is the ground of their unity and what draws them together. They accept each other because they have each been accepted by the Lord (Rom. 14:1–3).

24–25 emphasizes again 'one people, one world, one Lord'. In the first *in that day* (16), Judah was part of the fear Egypt felt. This is proper, for true acknowledgment of the Lord involves acknowledgment of and submission to those who are already his people (1 Cor. 14:24–25). But the convert at once enjoys perfect acceptance by the Lord (*my ... my ... my ...*) and co-equal membership in and with all who are his. The titles *people, handiwork* and *inheritance* always belonged to Israel (2 Sa. 3:18; Is. 29:22–23; Ps. 28:9). In Egypt, at the exodus time, the Lord drew a distinction when he said, 'Let my people go' (Ex. 5:1), but now *Egypt* is *my people*!

The smiting of Egypt exemplified: an interim fulfilment (20:1–6). For four years Egypt had been busy fomenting anti-Assyrian rebellion in the Palestinian states, promising Egyptian aid once the flag of rebellion was raised. In 713 BC Ashdod obliged, and in 711 Assyria struck back. The king of Ashdod was replaced by a puppet. The rebellion, however, continued. The new king was driven out and, with Egypt still in the background, envoys were sent to Judah, Edom and Moab to rally them to the cause. Since Hezekiah suffered no Assyrian reprisals, it is probable that he held aloof. But Ashdod did not escape. Sargon king of Assyria sent his *supreme commander* (1) and Ashdod became an Assyrian province. True to form, Egypt then reneged on its promises.

At some time in all this, Isaiah performed an acted oracle by going about *stripped and barefoot* (2). His intention was to mime the fate of those taken captive by Assyria and thus to expose the folly of trusting Egypt. He committed himself visibly to the veracity of the word he had received from the Lord. The narrative is included here as an interim fulfilment. Isaiah has outlined a world hope (19:24–25), in which three nations of his own day figured: his own people, the imperial Assyria and the would-be imperial Egypt. His vision was that these three would become one people under one God. If this sounded incredible, then his contemporaries observe how the word of the Lord is fulfilled in the outworking of world events, even when superpowers are involved.

1. *In the year*: i.e. 711 BC. *Supreme commander* (*tartān*): the second in command to the king (2 Ki. 18:17), in this case Sargon II (722–705), one of the greatest of the kings of Assyria.

2. *At that time* ('*ēt*) is not a precise dating but refers to whatever moment was opportune for such a message. *Sackcloth* was apparently Isaiah's normal wear, whether it signifies the sackcloth of mourning (15:3) or the rough clothing adopted by prophets (2 Ki. 1:8). *Stripped*: '*ārôm* means 'naked'. Maybe NIV is correct in seeking to safeguard the proprieties by an interpretative translation, but it is not the general use of the word. Captives were often stripped (4; 47:2–3). Isaiah paid the price of obedient identification with the word of the Lord. The prophets frequently accompanied their spoken word with visible demonstrations of the truth (*e.g.* Je. 13:1ff.; 19:1–13; Ezk. 5, 12). The purpose included that of a 'visual aid' but went further, for the word of God was expressed in a double way: by speech and by act. Its fulfilment was thus doubly secured (see 2 Ki. 13:14–19).

3. For *three years* the people had watched Isaiah, wondering what his behaviour portended. Was he just telling them that rebels against Assyria would not succeed? But, as we might say, any fool could have forecast that Ashdod would not stand a chance! Perhaps the wiseacres were mocking, saying, 'Tell us something we don't know!' In fact that is precisely what he was doing. The message was not what they expected to hear, nor what the sophisticated politicians of Jerusalem wanted to hear, enamoured as they were with Egypt and its promises. The captives in question would be *Egyptian* and *Cushite* (the two linked together because the Ethiopian dynasty was in power).

4. Isaiah did not say Egypt/Cush would be conquered but only that Judahites would see sad strings of captives being deported. This would have happened certainly after the battle of El Tekeh (701 BC), Egypt's one – and failed – attempt to honour its promises. Since this took place in that year before Sennacherib's assault on Judah, it could well have contributed to Hezekiah's bleak despondency (37:1–4), just as Isaiah said it would. *Egypt's shame* is (lit.) 'Egypt's nakedness', the state of the captives exposing the bankrupt state of the nation itself.

5–6. *Put to shame*: the embarrassment of having laid plans that fell through, trusted promises that were not kept, entertained hopes which were reversed. *On this coast*: the captives would be led back to Assyria along the coast roads. Those who lived there would be the first to see before their very eyes what folly it is to trust Egypt, and the first, therefore, to conclude that some other object of trust must be sought against Assyria.

b. The second series of oracles: the long night and the dawn (21 – 23)

See the introduction to chapters 13 – 27, pp. 110–112. The first series of oracles (13 – 20) was marked by buoyant optimism. Even the world's superpowers are subject to the word of the Lord and his word is full of glorious promise. This second series is very different. Even though the content of each oracle makes its subject plain, the oracles have enigmatic titles, giving an air of mystery, even of foreboding, to the whole. There is, in fact, a pervasive sense of doom and darkness.

The series begins with a vision of such horror that Isaiah recoils from it (21:1–10); this is followed by a voice calling out of darkness and being promised more darkness (21:11–12); then come Arabian tribes in the desert without necessary supplies (21:13–17), followed by Jerusalem committing the unforgivable sin (22:14). The light at the end of the tunnel is the oracle on Tyre (23:18) where age-long materialism becomes sharing and outright worldliness becomes holiness to the Lord. It was suggested above (p. 111) that the enigmatic titles are Isaiah's way of showing that he has left the sharp clarity of his contemporary scene and is looking into the future. If so, history is not a tale of everything getting better and better. Rather, divine judgments become starker, problems remain unsolved and the people of God live below their dignity. Yet even so, darkness is streaked by the light of dawn.

i. The desert by the sea: the Babylon principle (21:1–10). According to verse 9, this first oracle predicts the fall of Babylon. But which fall? The one which most readily matches the terms of Isaiah's vision is the overthrow of the city by Sennacherib in 689 BC. This certainly matched the vision's ferocity, for Sennacherib records that he filled the city with corpses and, as for 'the gods dwelling therein, the hands of my people took them and smashed them'. Buildings were razed and, as a final gesture, 'huge volumes of water (were) released over the ruins'.[1]

---

[1] See Erlandsson, *The Burden of Babylon*, p. 91, for full discussion and cogent

Such violence has a logic to it, even if it is horrific. Babylon had been the most unruly element in Assyria's empire. Twice (in the years 722–710 BC and then 705–702) Merodach-Baladan had led Babylon into independence from Assyria and was even a threat to Assyrian dominance in Mesopotamia. As we shall see in chapter 38, he included Judah in his attempt to foment unrest. The present oracle could be Isaiah's attempt to dissuade Judah from joining Babylon in an anti-Assyrian alliance. It plays the same role in relation to Merodach-Baladan and Babylon as 19:1–15 does in relation to an Egyptian alliance. Who would want to turn for strength to the doomed?

The poetry is as highly charged as anything Isaiah ever wrote, but, because it is poetry, 'reading between the lines' is necessary. The prophet sees a picture of whirlwind after whirlwind sweeping the Negeb by the Dead Sea (1) and it speaks to him of incoming danger (1); he overhears, as it were, what Merodach-Baladan's envoys say to Hezekiah: Assyria is as deceitful as ever (2b), but Elam and Media are ready to take up arms and put a stop to all the suffering Assyria has caused (2cd). Isaiah returns to his own sense of foreboding (3, 4). He had naturally longed to see the *twilight* of Assyrian power (4c), but the vision is so dire that it becomes pain and grief to him (3). Then he hears other voices (5), evidently coming from the palace where they are laying on a banquet to celebrate their treaty with Babylon (5a–c) and confidently calling the military to take up the struggle (5de). But why is Isaiah so stricken? He now lets us into the secret revealed to him (6a): were he to set a lookout he would in due time report the fall of Babylon and the collapse of its gods in ruin (6b–9). And this is the message he must bring to the Lord's people: crushed as Judah is under Assyria (10a), what solution is it to link itself with the doomed Babylon? – and this is a word from the Lord (10bcd).

But if the oracle can be seen as addressed to the circumstances that prevailed in or around 705 BC, why does not Isaiah entitle it with reference to Merodach-Baladan? Why the cryptic *concerning the Desert by the Sea* (1)? Because, though he originally spoke the oracle with reference to the embassy recorded in 39:1ff., his purpose here is broader: he 'seems to draw upon these events in order to portray the imminent fall of the world city, the onset of the woes of the final age which precedes salvation.'[1] In

---

argument for seeing this as the Assyrian destruction of Babylon in 689 BC, not the Persian capture in 539 BC.

[1] See O. Kaiser, *Isaiah 13 – 39* (SCM, 1974), p. 128. Kaiser, however, relates

the scheme of these oracles, the actual Babylon (13:1) becomes the city behind the cryptic title (21:1) and finally the 'ruined city' of 24:10, the horror resulting from the human attempt to organize the world without God. As Isaiah probes forward he sees that there will always be a Babylon principle operating in world history: humankind's attempt (as in Gn. 11:1–9) to impose order and unity on the world and to create its own security. World order without God is a doomed endeavour.

The oracle has an A1-B1-C-B2-A2 structure.

1–2a. Isaiah receives a vision (A1). The most likely first explanation of the enigmatic title *concerning the Desert by the Sea*[1] is that this was where Isaiah received it. Would it be too 'ordinary' to think that he had taken his family on holiday and came back reporting that the weather had been dreadful, one storm after another? But as he recalled these successive *whirlwinds*, they spoke to him of 'something coming from the desert'. NIV interpretatively adds *an invader*, but Isaiah wrote only 'it comes' – all the more ominous for being left unnamed and because it came 'from the desert ... a land of terror' (Dt. 8:15).

2b–d (B1). *The traitor* ...: 'The betrayer betrays and the destroyer destroys' was originally a reference to Assyria (see on 33:1) and therefore a suitable ploy to be used by Merodach-Baladan's emissaries: Assyria will never change; we have to do something about it. In its present context, loosened from its original setting, it refers to the breakdown of values in the world: people are not be trusted, property is not respected. *Elam*: if the oracle is interpreted as referring to the fall of Babylon to the Medes and Persians in 539 BC, this reference to Elam is inexplicable, for Elam ceased to be a significant power in the latter years of the seventh century. But at the time of Merodach-Baladan, a call to *Elam* and *Media* to take up arms would create a strong pawn in the diplomatic game. Behind the imperatives we can hear the boast of the ambassadors that all they have to do is say the word and Elam and Media will take up arms. *I will bring*: Merodach-Baladan saw himself as the answer to the Assyrian oppression in his day; now the words represent the imagined

---

vv. 1–10 to the fall of Babylon in 539 BC. We need to ask how the bloodless capture of Babylon by Cyrus could be represented as this 'dire vision' and why it should be a grim, joyless duty for Isaiah to convey such news to his people.

[1] Erlandsson suggests that *the Desert by the Sea* could be the Hebrew equivalent to *māt tamtim* ('the land of the sea'), the area round the Persian Gulf, *i.e.* Merodach-Baladan's habitat. This would be a link between the oracle and its point of origin.

voice of a long line of would-be deliverers. Just as there will always be dominant powers in world history, so there will be those confident of overthrowing them.

3–5 (C). *At this* (3): *i.e.* 'Therefore'. Isaiah's reaction is one of horror, physically (3) and emotionally (4ab). There is a twilight he longed for but, seeing it in its full awfulness, it has become a horror. By contrast (5), there are those who see it all as an opportunity for a party (5a–c) and think nothing of initiating military action (5de). First, then, in the context of Merodach-Baladan's embassy (705 BC; 39:1), the twilight is the longed-for eclipsing of Assyrian power, but Isaiah knows the frightful consequences of Babylon enduring such a savage overthrow but even more for the Lord's people if they seek to bring it about by joining a worldly alliance. But Hezekiah fell easily for the ambassadors' blandishments (39:1–2), welcoming them and laying on a banquet to celebrate, with after-dinner speakers braying confidently about the rightness of their cause. *Oil the shields*: *i.e.* anoint them as for a holy war. To Isaiah all this was agonizing. Would it mean deliverance for Judah? No, because Babylon itself was doomed (9). But in the meantime they would have to endure the savage onslaught of Sennacherib. The price of an Assyrian eclipse would be far too high!

Secondly, however, as we have noted, the enigmatic titles of this second series of oracles show Isaiah looking forward beyond his own day. There will always be some superpower seeking to dominate the world; always, too, confident deliverers looking for allies; always a professing people of the Lord gratuitously throwing themselves into the conflict to their own suffering and loss; and then, at the Day itself, the ultimate horror of the Lord's final dealing with sin and sinners, and with the world system which embodies human pride, the spiritual Babylon of Revelation 18 – 19.

6–9 (B2). In order to bring home the certainty of Babylonian downfall, Isaiah pictures a *lookout* told what to watch for (7), faithful in his duty (8), seeing the predicted event fulfilled (9ab) and sharing the news which has thus been brought to him (9c–f).

Chariots … horses … donkeys …camels (7ab): literally 'a mounted troop, pairs of horses, a mounted troop on donkeys, a mounted troop on camels'. M. S. Seale notes that 'Arabian nomads, preparing to go into battle, rode one mount … and trailed another.' *Cf.* 2 Kings 9:25, which Seale translates 'You and I were riding pairs'.[1] Seale says the second beast was held in

---

[1] M. S. Seale, *The Desert Bible* (Weidenfeld and Nicolson, 1974), p. 97.

reserve as a fresh mount should flight become necessary. The watchman, therefore, is to look out for troops going into battle. *The lookout shouted* (8): literally 'A lion shouted', *i.e.* 'And lion that he is, he shouted', that is, a man of resolute strength, reliable in discharging the task given to him. The watchman is, of course, the prophet, and the verses give an insight into the demands of the prophetic office: resolute to declare only what he saw (6), intrinsic reliability of character (7), disciplined to wait until he has a sure message to declare (8). *Look, here comes* ... (9): 'And, oh look! – Here comes a mounted troop of men, pairs of horses.' Since they are still riding one horse and trailing another, they return as victors. Indeed so, for *Babylon* has failed and its ideology (*all its gods*) with it.

10 (A2). Picking up the verb *tell* from verse 2a ('shown'), Isaiah rounds the poem off. He saw a 'dire vision' and now he has reported it as a message *from the* LORD. Therefore, in the oracle's original setting, let Hezekiah be warned: Babylon may be plausible, but to identify his future with it is to share its doom. It is to go the way of the original Babylon, Shinar (Gn. 11:1–9): the epitome of the spirit of human self-sufficiency. And, of course, as history moves beyond what Isaiah sees around him, the same is repeated, the same principles operate and the same temptations beset the people of God. It is not easy to maintain a position of faith, especially in times of stress and suffering, *crushed on the threshing floor.* It is so easy to opt for anything that offers promise of release. But faith sees differently. We are still *my people*; we are (lit.) 'my crushed one, son of my threshing floor'; the crushing pressures of life come from the Lord; the blows are his blows, purposely designed to bring the crop safely into the granary. The *Almighty* power that lies behind all history is that of *the* LORD, Yahweh, who is not only the Judge of those who disobey but the redeemer, *the God of Israel* – not the God we chose but who chose us and who will never go back on his choice.

ii. Silence: days of darkness (21:11–12). Passages like 2 Kings 8:7ff. show that prophets were approached by people of other nations. It could well be that in the frenzied diplomatic activity prompted by the Assyrian threat Edomites came to Jerusalem and one sought out Isaiah for counsel. We cannot know whether this was so or whether Isaiah was privately meditating on the agony Edom too was suffering under Assyria. Sargon campaigned there in 715 BC. But we feel the poignancy of a lone voice in the darkness and of the exchange with the prophet: 'What can you tell me? I can tell you nothing. Will things change? No, they will not. Even if morning comes, night comes fast behind it.' In its setting in the matching pentad of oracles, this corresponds to the Philistine oracle in 14:28–32. The Philistines mistook the signs of the times and thought David's dynasty was defunct. They needed to be made aware of a coming, mightier fruit from David's root. But, in response to the Edomite cry, Isaiah warns that the true dawn is in the undated future and in the meantime darkness predominates. The watchman of verse 6 is still watching; the crushing of verse 10 is still unhealed. Things go on as they have always done (2 Pet. 3:4), yet it is always worthwhile to ask how much of the night is left, for darkness will not have the last word (Rom. 13:11–12). Thus a solitary Gentile mirrors world history: the end will come; the end is not yet. Hope lies in the future (12ab) and though it is deferred it is sure (12cd).

11–12. *Dumah* (11a) means 'silence' (Pss. 94:17; 115:17), and, since the questioner came from *Seir*, doubtless Isaiah meant *Dumah* both to hint at Edom and also to reflect the silence of his reply regarding the future. The Lord's programme is carried forward not only in great, dramatic events (9) but also in the regular forward moving of time (12), in huge periods when nothing seems to be happening at all. Isaiah imposed on his enquirer the hardest discipline of all, the discipline of sticking it out. *Is coming* is a Hebrew perfect of certainty: 'is sure to come, has been ordained to come'. *Come back*: though the process is protracted, the end is certain.

iii. Desert evening: Gentile needs unsolved (21:13–17). This third oracle corresponds to the crisis in which the Gentile Moab found itself (15–16). Moab could have turned to Zion for safety but was held back by pride. The Arabian tribes of the desert are in straits: can they solve their problem by mutual succour? No, their need remains unmet.

Once more the historical background is the Assyrian crisis. In 715 BC Sargon campaigned against tribes living between Tema (an oasis city far south of Elath and east of the Red Sea) and the Gulf of Aqaba; in 703 Arabs joined Merodach-Baladan in rebellion and were crushed by Sennacherib. Isaiah depicts the Arabian tribe of the Dedanites fleeing from the war and Tema is urged to succour them. The Gentile world in its need seeks to be self-sufficient in mutual aid. The interim fulfilment (16–17) puts paid to any hope that collective security will save it.

13–15. *An oracle concerning Arabia*: uniquely in this series of oracles, the preposition (*concerning*) is b^e, meaning 'in, against'; *Arabia* is literally 'Arabs'. The whole is as allusive as the previous two titles (1, 11). The consonants $b^c rb$ could just as easily mean 'in the evening' as 'in / against Arabs' – both in the title and in 13c. 'Evening' could prompt the same foreboding as 'twilight' (4c). This cannot be called a sure interpretation but it suits the cryptic titles characteristic of this series and the place of this oracle in context, Gentiles in a darkening world. *Dedanites*: NIV understands the Dedanites as receiving a command to *bring water* (14), but in order to justify this understanding it must change the Hebrew indicative tense ('they bring') to an imperative. According to the Hebrew, however, the Dedanites are obliged to camp in the *thickets*, the scrub, off the beaten track. *Of Arabia* is $b^c rb$ as above: dare we combine the two possible meanings of these consonants as 'in Arab-eventide'?

The people of *Tema* (14) bring supplies to the fugitives, literally 'To meet the thirsty, they bring water; those who live in the land of Tema with his bread (the bread he needed) were there to meet the fugitive.' The same word for *fugitives* occurs in 16:2–3 of Moabites fleeing from danger. They could have fled to Zion but the Arabian tribes seek to be self-sufficient.

The explanation of all this (15 begins with 'For') is that the fugitives had been caught up in the actuality of war: 'swords' (lit., plural) suggests being caught between two opposing forces – the grim situation of those whose land becomes the battle-arena for others. The restless world has caught them in its grip: where can they find assistance? Will the aid offered by Tema solve the problem?

16–17. This concluding statement begins with a sovereign word (16, *what the* LORD [here '$^a d\bar{o}n\bar{a}y$] *says* ['has said'] *to me*) telling of an imminent end (*within one year*), shattering Kedar's power (17, *few*). This is assured because *the* LORD, *the God of Israel, has spoken.* The distressed Dedanites and their helpers of Tema sought to master their world by their own resources. But the thing which brackets the world is the word of the Sovereign, the God of Israel (16a, 17b). It is he who will not allow humankind to be self-sufficient and to make their world their own.

The parallel oracle on Moab contained, like this one, an interim fulfilment (16:14), and both contain the words *as a servant bound by contract* (16), 'glory' (here *pomp*; in 16:14, 'splendour') and 'remnant' (16:14 and here, *survivors*). This identity of wording as well as themes bind the oracles together: the Gentile world is in straits, the good news of salvation in Zion is refused, and the sovereign Lord will not allow them to achieve their own security. *Kedar*: a general title for the Arabian area with its nomadic tribes.

iv. The Valley of Vision: the unforgivable sin (22:1–25). Once more the people of God occupy the fourth place in the series of oracles (*cf.* pp. 110–112, 130; 17:1 – 18:7), but now the actual Jerusalem, which provides the content of verses 1–14 and the setting for 15–25, is shrouded under the enigmatic title *the Valley of Vision*. We are thus alerted to the fact that this oracle too operates on two levels: the factual level of reasonably datable events, and the visionary level of principles which those events exemplified and which will continue to operate in the undated future.

At first sight the oracle is a strange mixture of the national (1–14) and the personal (15–25), the city (1–14) and the individual (15–19, 20–25), and it would be easy to question the appropriateness here of addresses about Shebna (15–19) and Eliakim (20–25), not least because no other oracles in chapters 13 – 27 concern themselves with named individuals.[1] Closer examination is illuminating. The charge laid at the door of Jerusalem is the choice of self-sufficiency. The key verses (8b–11) tell how in their crisis the Jerusalem people relied on their arsenal (8b), cannibalized the city to strengthen the walls (10) and secured a safe water-supply (9b, 11). *Shebna* is revealed as an important official in whom the spirit of self-reliance is incarnate: he is a man who can take care of his present repute (18d) and provide for his continuing glory (16). In a different way *Eliakim* (20–25) would be caught in the same trap if he should come to see himself and allow himself to be seen as the chief support of others, the indispensable man (see below on 23–25). In a word, the 'story-line' of the whole oracle is the question, Where is security found? In Isaiah's teaching, when city (1–14), individual (15–19) and family (20–25) become self-sufficient, they have committed the unforgivable sin.

---

[1] The switch from 3rd person (16–18) to 1st person (19–23a) can be accounted for by thinking in terms of Isaiah's 'mosaic' method, taking *tesserae* from different points in his ministry and fitting them together into a fresh integration. Verse 19 can be viewed as an editorial bridge, summarizing what has preceded and making the switch to 1st person in preparation for vv. 20–23. Internally vv. 15–25 are bracketed by *what the Lord, the LORD Almighty says* (15) and *declares the LORD Almighty ... The LORD has spoken* (25). The word to Shebna, *you disgrace to your master's house* (18), is balanced by Eliakim possibly becoming *honour for the house of his father* (23). See D. Stacey, *Isaiah 1 – 39* (Epworth, 1993) and Miscall, *Isaiah, ad loc.*

The self-sufficient city (22:1–14). A number of historical occasions are suggested for this passage. The roof-top joy (1–2) is possibly popular reaction to the end of the Assyrian threat as recorded in 2 Kings 19:35–36.[1] This has a nice simplicity about it but it does not wholly fit the oracle: first, Isaiah would hardly have been offended by an outburst of joy occasioned by a divine act of deliverance – even if he thought it hollow – and why, on such an occasion, would the Lord have summoned his people to lamentation (12)? In addition, there is no record of leaders deserting (3a) under Sennacherib's pressures. Another view[2] is that Isaiah is addressing the moment when Sennacherib accepted Hezekiah's gold (2 Ki. 18:16) and lifted the threat. Jollity over such a deliverance would not have met with the prophet's approval, glorying as it did in human resources and diplomacy. But once more, though the suggestion is broadly suitable, the details do not fit. It is unlikely that Jerusalem was under a sufficiently long threat at this time for the rigour of siege conditions to have bitten (2b); again, there is no record of leadership defection (3); and, furthermore, how could the Assyrian forces be represented by *Elam* (6) since throughout this period Elam was Babylon's ally against Assyria? It is simplest to note that the facts of verses 2c–3 are linked to the fall of Jerusalem to Babylon in 586 BC by the flight of the leaders (2 Ki. 25:4). In light of this the verbs in verses 2–3 must be understood as 'perfects of certainty' (see below). The passage begins with a contrast between present joy (1–2a) and coming calamity (2b–4), a 'day of the Lord' (5–7). There was a crucial moment when, sensing their vulnerability (8a), choices were made regarding security (8b–11) and, feeling that they had made themselves invulnerable in armaments (8bc), fortifications (9ab, 10ab) and water-supply (9cd, 11), they resorted to joy in defiance of a divine call to penitence (12–13). This cannot be forgiven (14).

1a. *The Valley of Vision*: Isaiah does not explain why he chose this enigmatic title. Jerusalem itself was not a valley. He could, of course, have been walking through some valley when the vision was borne in upon him but, whether this was so or not, the grimness of the vision and the intensity of his awareness of the

---

[1] Clements, *Isaiah 1 – 39*, pp. 182ff.; O. Kaiser, *Isaiah 13 – 39*, pp. 136ff. Both these commentators suggest highly complex reconstructions which, we need to remember, are not based on manuscriptal or other objective evidence, but are an interpretative exercise attempting to solve problems which they find inherent in the text.

[2] Skinner, *Isaiah 1 – 39*, pp. 162f.; A. S. Herbert, *Isaiah 1 – 39* (CUP, 1973), *ad loc.*

divine word (14a) suggest a dark valley of the soul (Ps. 23:4). Jerusalem/Zion was more than the locus of Isaiah's ministry; it was the focal point of his expectations (*e.g.* 2:2–4; 25:6–9; 26:1–4; 33:20–24; 40:9; 54:1ff.; 62:1ff.; 66:10–13). It would have brought the profoundest 'dark night of the soul' to him to foresee its coming desolation.

1b–2b. *What troubles you* is a strange translation for an address to jubilant, carefree (2ab) people! The literal 'What to you?' is a formula of repudiation (Je. 2:18; Ho. 14:8), 'What business have you …?' or 'What do you mean by …?' It implies that this course of action cannot be justified (*cf.* 52:5). Just as roof tops were places of communal lament (15:3), so also of communal festivity. *Commotion* (*t^{e}šu'ôt*): literally 'hubbub' (Jb. 39:7), the noise (Zc. 4:7) of an excited crowd. *Tumult* (√*hāmâ*): of happy excitement (as in 1 Ki. 1:40–41).

2c–4. Isaiah now explains why he has questioned their joy. He sees a different scene (2c–3), meriting inconsolable sorrow (4). Regarding the verbs in verse 3 we need to bear in mind that, in Hebrew, 'tenses' represent types rather than times of action. The 'perfect tense' (used here) stands for certainty or completedness and can therefore refer to the past (an action already completed), or the present (action 'this day', done decisively) or the future (an action so settled that its certainty can be assumed). Thus the prophet foresees as certain that there will be people dead without a fight (2cd), *without using the bow* (3), as in siege conditions, and leaders deserting the doomed city (3; 2 Ki. 25:4). *Having fled* … : NIV interpretatively adds *while the enemy was*. The Hebrew is simply 'they fled far away', the deserting leaders putting as much distance between themselves and danger as possible. *Therefore* arises from the contrast between the cheery complacency of the people and the dark vision of the prophet. He wants nothing of their curiosity (*Turn away*) nor of their sympathy (*console*). *Of my people*: literally 'of the daughter of my people'. This synonym for Jerusalem is found only here in Isaiah (*cf.* Je. 8:19). It is full of feeling for the city, as for a beloved daughter at the mercy of the merciless.

5–7. Having explained his isolation in sorrow (4), Isaiah now explains the dark vision: verse 5 begins with 'For' and looks back to 2c–3. Behind the catastrophe lies the purpose of a just and holy God. What looms is *a day* of the Lord (5a), expressed in destruction of the city (5), implemented by *Elam* (6) and inescapable (7). On the dovetailing agencies of the Lord (5a) and Elam (6a) see 10:5–15.

In verse 5, *the Lord* ('^{a}dōnāy*, the Sovereign One), *the LORD*

(*Yahweh*) is the God who made himself uniquely known to Israel and who will exact much from those to whom much was given (Am. 3:1–2). *Almighty* ('of hosts') is the One who is and has every potentiality and power. *Has a day*: *cf.* 2:12. The day is already fully prepared, awaiting his moment to insert it on the time-line of Israel's experience. This is the Old Testament view of time and history as part of the Lord's covenantal arrangements (Je. 33:20). *Tumult* (√*hāmâ*, see 2) is the uproar of the day; *trampling*, the violence and cruelty of it; *terror* (Mi. 7:4; *cf.* Ex. 14:3; Joel 1:18; Est. 3:15), the consequent disorientation of those under attack. And finally, the desperate human suffering inseparable from the sack of the city: *crying* (from √*šāwa'*, 'to cry out for help'), their screams resounding out to the encircling *mountains*.

Elam (6), to the west of Babylon, was, throughout Isaiah's period, allied with Babylon against Assyria. *Kir*: of unknown location (Am. 1:5; 9:7; not the Moabite city of 15:1). *Takes ... uncovers* are perfects of certainty (see 3). The *quiver* is part of the armour of attack; the *shield*, of defence. In between come the mobile forces, *charioteers ... horses*. The intention is to build up a picture of military prowess from which there can be no escape: the *valleys* (7) which might offer concealment for flight are occupied, and the *gates* under constant observation. To face the horrible reality of all this as *a day* (5) of *the Lord* raises questions for every sensitive spirit. Can this be true of the Lord? Would he so do? These questions are logical and unavoidable – but a negative answer would not be truly biblical. The men of Bethshemish (1 Sa. 6) faced the loss of life consequent on the temerity of 'looking at' the ark of the Lord, but they did not query the propriety of divine righteous judgment – even so condign a judgment on so seemingly small a fault. They did not ask 'Why?' They trembled before the Holy One: 'Who can stand in the presence of the LORD, this Holy God?' (1 Sa. 6:20). Our doubts are the products of an inadequate sense of what holiness is and a limited understanding of the fact that the wages of sin is death, a truth indeed, but one whose application makes us look for get-out clauses.

Verses **8–14** fall into two contrasting parts, marked by *in that day* (8b, 12), referring back to 8a. Sensing itself to be defenceless (8a) the nation focused on armaments (8bc), fortifications and water-supply (9–11ab). Note how Isaiah moves from walls (9ab) to water (9cd) and then back again (10–11), emphasizing not only where they considered their security lay but their busy determination to see the work done. Verses 8 and 11 balance each

other: *you looked ... you did not look.* In verses 12–14 Isaiah
turns from popular reaction to the Lord's reaction. He saw the
solution to the danger (8a) in spiritual terms, lamentation and
penitence (12), but so delighted were they in their do-it-yourself
security that a public holiday was declared (13). But to ignore the
Lord, refuse the way of penitence and faith, and embark on the
road to self-salvation, constitute the unforgivable sin (14).

8. *The defences ... are stripped* is an acceptable translation but
the literal is better: 'He removed Judah's protective cover.' The
onset of Sennacherib exposed Judah's vulnerability – in spite of
all the alliances and preparations that had preceded it. Hezekiah
summed it all up in two words, 'no strength' (37:1–3). But behind
the event was the Lord's purpose to test whether, under
Hezekiah's leadership, they would go the way of faith or the way
of the world (Dt. 8.2–5). 2 Chronicles 32:1–8 is a very apt
comment on this point: military solutions before prayer and trust.

9–11. The details of Jerusalem's water-supply are obscure.
The source was the Gihon Spring to the east. At an early stage
this was linked to a shaft inside the city (2 Sa. 5:6–8); at a later
date there was an overground conduit (7:3) supplying what Isaiah
calls *the Old Pool*. It was the exposed nature of this channel that
made Ahaz panic, for it meant that a city virtually impregnable
by virtue of its position could be 'dried out' by cutting off the
Gihon waters. Hezekiah, however, showed remarkable initiative
and extraordinary engineering skill by driving his tunnel from the
spring into the city (2 Ki. 20:20; 2 Ch. 32:2–4). The *reservoir*
was probably fed by the tunnel and could be the same as *the
Lower Pool* (9). The king also built walls. *The two walls* (11)
might be an area created by a new wall running outside the
existing wall of David's city. But this colossal achievement – the
tunnel – and the sacrifices made to secure the walls (10) simply
add up to the unforgivable sin (14), manifesting as they do
humankind's determined omnicompetence and self-sufficiency.
After all, why bother with faith when we have walls and water!
Why look (11) to the Lord when we can look to ourselves! But
made it ... planned it long ago tell a different story. Jerusalem
was the Lord's chosen city (Dt. 12:5; 1 Ki. 8:29). Psalm 132:13–
18 begins with the Lord's choice and then traces its consequences
in provision, the ordinances of religion and monarchy and the
overthrow of enemies. The Lord knew all about Jerusalem's
threatened water-supply, yet he *made* and *planned* ('moulded' as
a potter would) this city. He did not leave it short of water but
arranged the supply in such a way that living in Jerusalem was a
recurring challenge to faith. Hezekiah's tunnel contradicted the

principle of faith on which the Lord planned and fashioned his city.

12. *The Lord, the* LORD *Almighty*: see verse 5. This title spells out the real resource and strength of the Lord's people. Compared with him, what are walls and water-courses? Consequently, the priority in every crisis is to fly to God in penitence and contrition (Joel 2:12ff.). Tearing the *hair* and *sackcloth* were outward displays of the inner reality of sorrow.

13. Isaiah returns to the theme of verse 2 and reveals why he found their jollity so offensive: they were applauding human works (8–11) and contradicting the mind of God (12). *For tomorrow we die*: it is most unlikely that they said these words for, with their walls and water, this was the very thing they thought they had secured themselves against. The prophet is not reporting their words but verbalizing their attitudes (see on 28:14–15). In their denial of the significance of the spiritual dimension of life, they were in fact affirming that if what they had done did not save them, nothing could.

14. This is an exceedingly solemn verse in both wording and content. *Revealed this in my hearing* is (lit.) 'has unveiled himself in my ear'. Isaiah stresses objectivity, the coming of revelation from outside; authenticity, a revelation of the Lord himself; and receptivity, the genuine action of the human ear. *Sin* ('*āwôn*): iniquity, the inner reality of sin in the fallen nature, see 6:7. *Atoned* (√*kāpar*): covered by an exact payment (6:7). Where (as 12 shows) there is no 'Woe is me!' (6:5), there is no sending of the seraph on a mercy-flight to the sinner. The sin of unbelief – no looking to the Lord (11), no penitence (12), total reliance on human saving works (8–11) – is the unforgivable sin. This whole passage is a set piece on the contrast between salvation by faith and salvation by works.

Cases in point (22:15–25). See p. 151. The decision whether to live by faith or by self-reliant works is individual as well as national. In this way Isaiah's presentation of two case studies constitutes a call to his contemporaries to examine themselves. In addition, on the assumption that Shebna and Eliakim are those mentioned in 36:3, 11, 22 and 37:2, they also provide one of Isaiah's interim fulfilments in which observers could see the word of the Lord at work before their very eyes.

Verses **15–19** focus on Shebna, 'the self-reliant'. These verses fall into two parts: 15–16, the Lord's opposition to Shebna; 17–19, the Lord's intentions for Shebna.

15. *The Lord* … : see verse 5. The Lord operates worldwide (5) and also individually. *Steward* (*sōkēn*): used only once elsewhere, for David's nurse-concubine (1 Ki. 1:2–4). It is designedly derogatory here, suggesting a fawning, ready-to-please attitude. 'Lackey' might be a good rendering. *In charge of*: as 1 Kings 4:6; 2 Chronicles 26:21. It was plainly a very important office.

16. *What are you doing ...?* is virtually identical with the initial question in verse 1b. It remains dismissive, literally 'What have you here and who have you here?' The idiomatic use of the interrogatives suggest that Shebna has no personal ('what') or inherited ('who') claim to the importance he is giving himself as seen in his considerable burial arrangements.[1]

17–18. In his own estimation he is a 'big' man (*mighty man*), a person of consequence, but to the Lord, a ball to be hurled into the distance. It can be assumed that one such as Shebna could have been removed off to Assyria in any one of Sennacherib's forays. Just as, try as he will, he cannot perpetuate his glory into the future and beyond the grave (16), so also his present pomp – literally 'the chariots of your glory' – is equally vulnerable. Such a self-important, self-seeking servant is a *disgrace* to the royal house.

19. The change here to first person is continued in the Eliakim narrative (20–25). This verse, therefore, acts, as a bridge between the two.

Verses **20–25** mirror the Shebna oracle: 20–23a, the Lord's intentions for *Eliakim*; 23b–25, the Lord's warning to Eliakim. When given a position of authority (20–23) he could easily fall into salvation by works: the future of his family could be seen to depend on him. They might come to trust Eliakim, his position and his power for their security.

21–23a. *Robe ... sash* are the insignia of office; *authority* is the status and actual power the insignia indicate; *father* is the mode of exercise of that power; *key* is the power to make and enforce binding decisions; *peg* is a 'tent-peg' (unless the context indicates otherwise, *e.g.* Jdg. 16:14), which, securely driven into a *firm place*, holds the tent of the state secure no matter how the wind blows.

23b–25. Eliakim is, therefore, inevitably a person on whom much depends. He has authority and responsibility for its proper exercise; people need his fatherly care, and the whole structure of the state needs him to hold it in place. Everything then depends on how he sees himself and how he allows others to see him. It is not just that leadership position can become pride of position,

[1] See D. J. Wiseman, 'Shebna', in *IBD*, vol. 3, p. 1431.

national welfare be replaced by family interest, public good by nourishing a crowd of 'hangers-on', but that the Lord as the object of trust can be replaced by a human object of trust. Just as the individual is not sufficient for himself (Shebna) neither is he sufficient for others (Eliakim). NIV makes these verses a prediction. It is rather more telling to make them hypothetical: 'Should he, however, become ... and they hang upon him ... in that day the peg will give way ...' Corrupting power may tempt Eliakim to self-importance and to yield to adulation. *Give way ... be sheared off*: the collapse will come about by internal insufficiency (*give way*) and external force (*be sheared*), for only the Lord is sufficient and he will allow that position to no other. He alone is *the LORD Almighty* and he is committed – 'for the LORD has spoken'– to the principle that he alone must be trusted.

v. Tyre: holiness to the Lord (23:1–18). Both elements in the title (p. 144) of this second pentad of oracles have proved to be true. 'Night' was reflected in the Babylonian twilight of 21:1–10, the lone voice from the darkness (21:11–12), the uncomforted trouble of the Arabian tribes (21:13–17) and Jerusalem's unforgivable sin (22:14). But there have also been flashes of 'dawn': the message of comfort to the Lord's crushed people (21:10), the invitation to enquire again because day comes (21:12), and now – surprisingly – Tyre's merchandise becomes holiness to the Lord (23:18).

Hiram of Tyre 'always loved David' and continued his covenant and co-operation with Solomon (1 Ki. 5:1–12). But there was another side to it: Solomon was corrupted by Phoenician wives (1 Ki. 11:1–5), and the religious error he introduced remained until Isaiah's time (2 Ki. 23:13). In the northern kingdom, Tyrian Baalism made a bid to replace Yahwism in the time of Jezebel (1 Ki. 16–18). Hostility to Tyre is evident throughout the Prophets (Je. 47:4; Am. 1:9–11; Joel 3:4; Zc. 9:2–4); only of Tyre does Ezekiel fail to say that they will yet know the Lord (Ezk 25:7, 11; 30:26). Isaiah, however, makes Tyre the beacon of hope at the end of this second series of oracles, and fittingly so. Throughout the first series (13 – 20) the emphasis lay on the political upheavals of the world and the downfall of nations and states; throughout the second series (21 – 23) the emphasis rested on fallen gods (21:9) and unforgivable sin (22:14). Therefore, just as Egypt the political oppressor (Ex. 1:22) became the bearer of hope in the first series (19:24–25), so Tyre the religious corrupter becomes the hope-symbol in the second. The care that a Phoenician widow once gave to a prophet (1 Ki. 17:8–16) will be the norm of a coming relationship of holiness (23:18). The oracle is in two parts: 1–14, the fall of Tyre; 15–18, , the return and renewal of Tyre.

Lament over the fall of Tyre (23:1–14). The lament begins (1) and ends (14) with Tyre's famous shipping lines; downfall is reported in verses 2–7, dealing in turn with Tyre (2–3), Sidon (4–5) and Tyre again (6–7); the agencies, divine and human, behind the fall, are revealed in verses 8–13 with the same order of Tyre (8–9), Sidon (10–12b) and Tyre (12c–13). Egypt is referred to three times (3, 5, 10), further establishing a link between the two oracles as above.

1. *Tyre* is the only non-enigmatic title in this series (see pp. 111, 144 above). Isaiah offers no explanation, and we can only guess that he wished to 'earth' his predictions: eschatology happens to real people. The strength and durability of Tyre, along with its crass materialism and idolatry, made it in any case a good proving ground for the sovereignty of the Lord. *Tarshish*: the shipping is called to *wail* because if Tyre fell their trade would fall with it. Most references to Tarshish are satisfied by the traditional identification with Tartessus, a mining area in Spain, though its exact location is unknown.[1] What is clear is that a 'ship of Tarshish' (2:16, NIV mg.) came to mean a ship capable of the longest voyages. *From the land*: the fleet is 'off Cyprus' making for Tyre, only to be met with the news that *house* and *harbour*, *i.e.* city and port, are gone.

2–3. *Silent*, like our word 'quiet', can also express stillness. This opening word contrasts with recollections of the port of Tyre (*the island*) bustling with businessmen and sailors (2bc), importing and exporting (3). *Shihor*: a synonym for the Nile (Jos. 13:3)

4–5. In verse 3 the merchants of Sidon were busy, but now they are *ashamed*, a word with the sense of reaping shame through disappointment. *The sea has spoken*: the sea mourns its loss. Tyre had provided it with its children, the sailors who spent their lives at sea, but with the fall of Tyre the sea is as if it never had those devoted to it. But *Egypt* too will be distraught, looking to Tyrian merchants and sailors as she did to oversee her vast export trade in grain. The fall of Tyre was a disaster with worldwide implications.

6–7. Now comes the evacuation of refugees. In a fine image of the reversal of their fortunes they travel in their loss, as once they

---

[1] See J. A. Thompson, 'Tarshish', in *NBD*, p. 1153.

had to make profit, to *Tarshish*. *To settle*: to become a temporary resident. Tyre had no imperialist aims; she set out to make money, not conquests. This has been the central thrust of the review of Tyre (2–3), Sidon (4–5) and Tyre again (6–7): businessmen, trade, Egypt's concern for her export market. In the matching oracle (19) Egypt represented the *power* of the world pressing upon the people of God; Tyre stands for the *ways* of the world in economic planning, commercial cupidity, and so on.

Verses **8–13** begin with an opening question that sets the scene. What agencies have brought Tyre to dust? The enquiry follows the same pattern of Tyre (8–9), Sidon (10, 12b) and Tyre (12c–13).

8–9. Tyre achieved such dominance by its trade that it could influence appointments (*bestower of crowns*) and insist on virtually royal respect (*princes*) being shown to its representatives. But the time came when the *bestower of crowns* came face to face with the 'Disposer Supreme and Judge of the earth', *the* LORD *Almighty*, and Tyre's *pride* was no more to be tolerated. Like the Day of the Lord itself (2:12–17), so every interim day has this characteristic, the overthrow of all that embodies godless pride.

10–12b. *Harbour* is *mēzaḥ*, which, if it has anything to do with shipping, means 'ship-building', not 'anchorage'; but in Job 12:21 and Psalm 109:19 it means 'belt' and is used here metaphorically of Tyre's grip on Tarshish. Now that Tyre's power is broken, Tarshish can move at will. This has not required an extensive exercise of divine power, nothing but an outstretched hand (11a; *cf.* Ex. 14:16; 15:4–6, 12), a word of command (11c) and a voice that *said* (12a).

12c–13. The first two consequences of the outstretched hand were (12ab) loss of joy (*revelling*) and of power (*crushed*). Now (12cd) follow loss of tenure (*up*, *cross over*) and loss of *rest*. In verses 11–12 the Lord gave the *order*. Who received it? Assyria began its imperial expansion in 745 BC under Tiglath Pileser. In 738 he was able to impose a military governor on Tyre, but Tyre was a restive vassal. Shalmaneser (727–722) besieged Tyre unsuccessfully and at the end of the century Tyre was still rebelling. In 701 Sennacherib devastated the mainland and did vast damage to Tyre's trade and it was not until about 630, with the decline of Assyria, that Tyre began to revive. Yet it remained restless within the great empires, and in 586 Nebuchadnezzar opened a thirteen-year siege but without ultimate success. The rock citadel withstood all attempts to take it until it fell to Alexander the Great in 332. In the light of all this there is no problem that Isaiah should be concerned with Tyre. It constituted such a power in his day it would have been strange if he had nothing to say about it. If his oracle forecasts the fall of Tyre, then this did not happen till the time of Alexander. The thrust of the oracle, however, is that Tyre's trade has been brought to a standstill, with loss of life and people taking flight. In the light of this a reference to Assyria in verse 13 has the merit of simplicity. The devastations Sargon caused in south Mesopotamia were notorious. Seven kings from Cyprus were present at his coronation and Sargon records that when they heard what he was doing in Chaldea 'their hearts were rent, fear fell on them'. Isaiah could, therefore, well say *Look at the land of the Babylonians* (*i.e.* 'Chaldeans') as a warning. If the refugees wonder why they will not be received and allowed to *rest* anywhere – who would risk provoking Assyria by identifying with its foes? For thanks to Assyria's savage attentions its people became *of no account* – maybe, even, 'this non-existent people', its land become *a place for desert creatures* – the motif of the incoming beasts pointing to the end of human occupation, and its buildings *a ruin*.

14 is an inclusio with verse 1, rounding off the lament with only one difference. Tarshish may indeed have acquired liberty of movement with the fall of Tyre (10) but it has also lost its *fortress:* Tyre's trade was its financial bulwark, and with that gone Tarshish too is exposed. Verse 1 says they have no place to go to; 14 says they have no secure place to stay.

The postscript: Tyre's renewal (23:15–18). Isaiah offers another interim fulfilment, the recovery of Tyre after a period of *seventy years*, but beyond that again lies a different renewal of Tyre as 'holiness to the Lord'.

15–17. The *seventy years* extended from the campaigns of Sennacherib (701) until the terminal decline of Assyria (say about 630) which allowed Tyre to spread its wings again. *The span of*: literally 'as the days of one king'. The expression does not occur elsewhere but presumably means 'exactly reckoned and recorded' (*cf.* 16:14; 21:16). Kings kept daily records of their reigns (1 Ki. 14:29, where 'annals' is 'the words of the days'). Thus each day of the seventy years was recorded as it passed until the precise period was completed. *Prostitute*: an apt symbol of Tyre, where everything was done for money. *Cf.* Amos' charge (1:9) that in Tyre nothing was allowed to interfere with profit-making. *Deal with* is too punitive. The verb *pāqad*, 'to visit', must always be shaped to its context. Here, since Tyre reappears unchanged on the world's scene, we might translate it 'restore'.

18. But there is a new Tyre in the divine mind. Tyre would be there to provide materials for temple-building at the time of the return (Ezr. 3:7) but, like the return itself, this was only a token of a fulfilment yet to come (Rev. 21:24–26; *cf.* Is. 60:5). *Earnings* (*'etnān*): Deuteronomy 23:18, using the same word, forbade such earnings as an offering to the Lord, but now all is transformed and all that the old life had meant and gained can be consecrated. Isaiah foresees a new, priestly status for Tyre: *set apart for* is (lit.) 'holiness to', the very word that adorned the high priest (Ex. 28:36); a new spirit replacing the old mercenary, acquisitive spirit: not *stored ... hoarded* but given; a new harmony, linking Tyre with *those who live before the* LORD. For this incorporation of Tyre in Zion, see Psalm 87:4.

c. The third series: The world city and the city of God (24:1 – 27:13)

These chapters are often called 'the Isaiah Apocalypse'. Apocalyptic writing, as exemplified in Daniel in the Old Testament and Revelation in the New, is a special branch of eschatology with its own characteristics. For example, it relies heavily on symbolism (using animals to represent nations and their horns to represent kings), mysterious numbers and veiled references to periods of time, and angelic figures as the mediators of revelation. In the light of this it is hard to see why Isaiah 24 – 27 should be thought to be apocalyptic. To look forward to the End-time is, of course, another characteristic of the apocalyptists, but it is equally typical of the prophets: they too saw history as governed by the divine purpose, serving as an arena of conflict between the Lord and the forces of evil, and reaching a climax of both human wickedness and divine power in the Day of the Lord. Isaiah 24 – 27 is far nearer to Matthew 24 than it is to Daniel 7 – 12. In a word, it is heavily eschatological and this is the only (and insufficient) ground for claiming it as apocalyptic.

In these chapters, then, Isaiah is looking on to the End. He abandons the oracle structure which has served him in chapters 13 – 20 and 21 – 23 and adopts a form which is a mixture of poems and songs, rather like a cantata. Nevertheless, even though the sharp edges of his presentation in 13 – 20 and the hazier outlines of 21 – 23 are gone, changes of subject and structural markers divide the eschatological cantata into five sections. Thus in 24:1, 19–20, the 'broken earth' theme forms an inclusio. The unheralded outburst of song in 25:1–12 leaves 24:21–23 as a distinct unit. 26:1–20 is a unitary statement about the Lord's people, secure amid the turmoil of the world and the coming judgment of God, and 27:1 (the great sword) and 13 (the great trumpet) enclose the final section of the cantata. These five sections tally with the five sections of the two preceding series: the actual Babylon (13 – 14) and the continuing Babylon principle (21:1–10) reach their awesome conclusion in the downfall of the city where nothing means anything (24:1–20, see esp. 10); the promised Davidic shoot (14:28–32) and the extended prolongation of days and nights (21:11–12) climax in the Lord's reign in Zion 'after many days' (24:21–23); the sad refusal of Moab to find security in Zion (15–16) and the failure of Gentile mutual security (21:13–18) resolve themselves into full provision for all nations (except Moab, 25:10–11) in the great banquet; the people of God, compromising (17–18) and self-sufficient (22), are now perfected as the people of faith enjoying peace within the strong city (26); and the theme of 'one world, one people and one God', forecast through Egypt and Assyria in chapter 19 and through Tyre in 23, is fulfilled in 27, with its return to the Egypt-Assyria motif (27:12–13).

i. The city of meaninglessness (24:1–20). We can discover the meaning of this passage through its structure. It begins and ends on the theme of the devastated earth (1–3, 18e–20); the withering of the world in verses 4–6 is balanced by the wasting individual in 16c–18d; and at the centre the song that is stilled (7–12) matches the song that is heard (13–16b). The background to the whole passage is found in the flood narrative in Genesis 6 – 9. Both passages refer to the 'windows' of heaven (*floodgates*, 18c; Gn. 7:11) and to the *everlasting covenant* (5; Gn. 9:16); the *curse* (6) in the context of the 'vine' theme (7) looks back to Noah the vinedresser and to the post-diluvian curse (Gn. 9:20ff.). Isaiah is forecasting a divine visitation on the same world scale, obliterating an old order because of its sin. In a broader but deeply significant way the contraction from the devastation of the world (1) to the downfall of the city (10) reflects the movement from the universalism of Genesis 9:19 to the particularism of the city-building of Genesis 11:1–9, linked by the motif-word 'scattering'. The sin at Shinar was humankind turning to humankind for security and community. The new technology of bricks and mortar put into people's hands the means of their own salvation: they could create community and safety, and curb their perceived tendency to scatter by living within a wall of their own making. The city, therefore, is the human attempt to impose order and create security without reference to God. As Isaiah sees the End, this fever of self-salvation will be worldwide, and the whole earth (1) will be as it were a global city (10). As at Shinar in the beginning, and throughout human history, this is the point at which the Lord says a decisive 'No' and comes in judgment. There is another link also with the flood background: at the time of that judgment, grace isolated Noah and his family (Gn. 6:8); so also, at the End, the truly deathly silence of the fallen city (8–10) is broken by song (13–16b), the song of the remnant (13). Thus this opening element in the five-part cantata matches its opening predecessors in the earlier series, not only in the Babylon-city theme (13:1 – 14:27; 21:1–10), but also in the great truth that the Lord in wrath remembers mercy, so organizing the world, its history and its destiny as to save and secure his own people (14:1–2; 21:10).

1–3, *The earth devastated.* These verses are bracketed by what *the LORD* is proposing to do (1) and how *the LORD* has spoken (3c), and also by the action which the Lord will perform, *lay waste ... laid waste* (1a, 3a). The emphasis is on totality: place and people (1cd), people without exception (2) and every place (3ab). Human sin infects the human environment (2:12ff.), and is the ultimate environmental threat.

Every aspect of life – religious (2b), domestic (2cd), and commercial (2eg) – as well as every individual is under judgmental scrutiny. The active (*lay waste*, 3) of 1 is now the passive, *laid waste*. What the Lord plans will happen.

4–6, *The withering of the world.* The imagery changes from earthquake and plunder (1cd, 3b) – things which come upon the world – to withering, something that arises from within. It affects place (4ab) and people (4c).

4–5. *Earth ... world*: the former (*'ereṣ*) is the physical earth as such; the latter (*tēḇēl*), the world as inhabited. The expression *the exalted of the earth*, literally 'the height of the people of the earth', is unparalleled. It can hardly single out the 'upper classes', but we note a gradual rise from the earth as 'thing' to the world as inhabited, then, possibly, to 'that exalted reality, the people ...', *i.e.* humankind as the crown of creation: the withering disease runs throughout. But the blame runs in the reverse direction, for *the earth is defiled by its people* (5) (*cf.* Nu. 35:33; Ps. 106:38; Je. 3:1–2, 9). The 'thorns and thistles' of Genesis 3:18 show both that the earth as the repository of the life of God in the soil fights back against the sinner, and also that human sin has infected the earth and corrupted its goodness. *By its people*: literally 'under', under human dominion, the influence of their misbehaviour. First, they have transgressed revealed truth (5b). *Disobeyed* (√*'āḇar*) is to cross over a boundary. *The laws*: the plural denotes 'law of every sort' and 'law covering every aspect of life'. But the basic idea of law (*tōrâ*) is not so much authoritative imposition as authoritative instruction. God spoke but they did not submit. Secondly, they changed the unchangeable (5c). *Violated* (√*hālap*) is used of one thing replacing another. *Statutes*: from √*hāqaq*, to carve, engrave, hence to make a permanent mark. They rejected divine moral absolutes and invented an innovative morality. Thirdly, they discarded a given relationship with God (5d). *Everlasting covenant* is used of the Noahic covenant (Gn. 9:16), the Abrahamic covenant (Ps. 105: 10), the Sabbath (Lv. 24:8) and the Davidic covenant (2 Sa. 23:5) with its future messianic fulfilment (55:3; 61:8). But the world has not wished to live faithfully under the promise of the rainbow (Gn. 9:12–17), nor has it seen itself in need of the blessing that comes only through Abraham's seed (Gn. 12:3; 22:18; Gal. 3:8), nor has it ordered its timetable so as to remember the Sabbath (Ex. 20:8–11; Dt. 5:12–15), nor has it wanted this Man to reign over it (Lk. 19:14) nor loved his appearing (2 Tim. 4:8).

6. *Therefore*: it is no accident but a holy, moral consequence that earth and people perish. It is the Lord's *curse*, 'the curse of the covenant' (Lv. 26:25–45; Dt. 11:26–28; 28:15ff.; Dn. 9:11; Zc. 5:5), not the Lord breaking off covenantal relationships but enforcing covenant sanctions.

7–12, *The stilled song: the fallen city.* The Hebrew of these verses can be set out in fifteen lines, mostly of three words a line. The effect is as of fifteen successive hammer blows demolishing a city. Joy has gone (7a), and satisfaction (7b–9): the city lies desolated (10). Satisfaction is gone (11) and so has security (12).

7–9. Their lifestyle was one of self-gratification. There is a colossal irony behind it all: on the one hand they look to the productivity of the earth to service their wants, but (5–6) it is their character and conduct which blight and curse the earth! They are subject to a savage law of diminishing returns, and in the end (7a) both product (*wine*) and source (*vine*) are alike gone. But even before this point is reached, they have found themselves seeking satisfaction in that which no longer satisfies (9).

10. In the End, the whole this-worldly fabric of life built by human resources without calling upon God or acknowledging him will suffer collapse. This is the world city. Isaiah calls it 'the city of *tōhû*'. The word is translated 'formless' in Genesis 1:2, where it is used of the primary state of the earth. The divine Potter had, so to speak, brought into being the pliable clay but it was as yet without the impress of his hands. In itself it did not contain any meaning, it showed no tendency towards a purpose; it was shrouded in darkness and covered with all the instability of water. It was *tōhû*. Jeremiah (4:23–26) had a vision of the world returned to *tōhû*, deprived of all that made it habitable, without purposeful activity. It was without what only God can give. The 'city of *tōhû*' opts for that life: life without God, therefore without order, purpose or those things which sustain and gratify life. The 'city of *tōhû*' is the city where anything goes and nothing matters. The moral absolutes of verse 5 have been rejected, and the end of that choice is total relativism of values, uncontrolled individualism. Thus Isaiah started with the Babylon he knew (13:1ff.), foresaw the ongoing spirit of Babylon ever-present in world history (21:1ff.) and finally came to the ultimate Babel, Shinar resurrected, where at length humankind's self-sufficiency would bring their whole world down about their ears.

11. This verse corresponds to verse 9 but brings an additional poignancy. In 9 the supposed stimulants failed to stimulate but, having left God out of their reckoning, people have nothing left to do but cry out for failed remedies.

12. The opening lines of this section (7) noted that life in the meaningless city was unsatisfying; the concluding lines note that it is impossible.

13–16b, A song in the silence. Isaiah is a master of unexpected hope – and of drama in its introduction. Here the 'battering' of the gate (12) merges into a different sound of 'beating' (13c), the blows which harvest the crop. The 'few' survivors of verse 6 turns out to be a worldwide ingathering; the song of the city fades to be replaced by another song, acclaiming *the Righteous One*. The section consists of an explanation (13 begins with 'For'), a description (14), a command (15) and a comment (16ab).

13. 'For' looks back over all that has preceded, where statements of destruction (1–3, 7–12) bracket the note of a few surviving (4–6). This is how it will be and what it means. *Beaten*: this is the correct way to harvest olives and, reading through from verse 12, the assumption is that the 'grim reaper' is still at work, but suddenly harvesting becomes gleaning, the careful gathering of what remains *after* (lit.) 'the grape-harvest is finished'.

14–16b. The prophet hears the songs arising in the *west* and calls for the song to begin in the *east*. So the song spreads until it is coming *from the ends of the earth. Islands*, see 11:11; 40:15. The song of the ultimate worldwide gathering is focused on the Lord in his exaltedness (*majesty*), in his essential worth (*give glory*), in his self-revelation (*name*), in his exclusivity as *the God of Israel*, in his loveliness (*Glory, ṣᵉbî*, 16; see 4:2) and in his character as *the Righteous One*. There is no sense that the nations have found Yahweh incognito in whatever national gods they formerly cherished; rather, these have been jettisoned in favour of the God of another nation, *Israel*. His *name* includes his work as Saviour and Redeemer and this would undoubtedly resound in their praises, but the note of climax is his righteousness, for his saving mercies are grounded in, and must satisfy, his justice (45:21; Rom. 3:26).

16c–18d, *A personal reaction and warning.* In 21:4 Isaiah discovered an ambivalence in himself: longing for the fall of Babylon but finding its reality too grim to bear. It is even more so as he contemplates the End: his vital energies ebb away under the shock of what is to come. *Woe to me* (16c): as 6:5. Isaiah now feels the hopelessness of others as keenly as once he felt his own. On the one hand, the world goes carelessly on in its moral indifference, literally 'for betrayers betray; with betrayal, betrayers betray' (16d). None but Isaiah could multiply the same word like this and achieve such literary effect. It is a powerful statement of moral perversity. *Cf.* 21:2, where the words may have originally been used (*cf.* 33:1) to define the wickedness of Assyria, but now they encompass a whole decadent world. How the Bible picks as the really damning sins things which mean little in popular thought! – the unclean speech of 6:5; unreliability and deceitfulness here. But on the other hand, there is the doom which awaits: *terror ... pit ... snare.* The Hebrew is assonantal, *pahad wāpahaṭ wāpah*, suggesting that they all belong to the same system of inescapable doom. *O people* is (lit.) 'O inhabitant'. The judgment is universal but the experience is individual.

18e–20, *The earth broken.* This concluding section acts as an inclusio with verses 1–3. In the opening section the spotlight fell on the divine Agent; here it falls on the moral cause that provoked him. As at the great flood, the whole created order is shattered. Isaiah multiplies verbs of breakdown (19) and then embroiders the scene with two similes: the drunkard falls through internal loss of co-ordination; the hut is shattered by the external storm. The external factor is the hostile agency of the wrath of God (1–3); the internal factor is the heaviness of its rebellion (*pešaʿ*; see 1:2), the stark, single cause of all the woe: the human will deliberately flouting the will of God. God is against such (1–3); the created order too is its foe (18ef), but also it is the heaviness of its own weight upon it (20c) that brings the system crashing down never to rise again.

ii. Ultimately ... the King! (24:21–23). This is the first of six elaborations of 24:1–20. The phrase 'in that day' occurs once in each of the first five and twice in the sixth. In Isaiah's careful editing they present a coherent picture:

24:21	The Lord's victory	27:1	The Lord's victory
25:9	The saved and the excluded	27:2	The Lord's people and his foes
26:1	The strong city with open gates	27:12-13	The world in Zion

The present poem sums up the series which began with 14:28–32. Against premature Philistine rejoicing, Isaiah warned of a great Davidic king to come; to the enquiring Edomite (21:11–12) he spoke of prolonged waiting; but the climax still comes only *after many days* (22d); the king deadly as a serpent (14:29) will *punish* (21); the darkness (21:11–12) will be swallowed in brightness (23a); the long progression of day and night (21:11–12) will end as *moon* and *sun* are transcended (23a); and the promised king (14:30) will be the Lord (23b).

21–22. The first part of chapter 24 gave the same sort of undiversified overview of worldwide calamity as did its model, the flood narrative, but in the first *in that day* elaboration Isaiah particularizes: the rulers of celestial and terrestrial realms will be tackled and imprisoned. *Punish* ($\sqrt{p\bar{a}qad}$): *cf.* 23:17. The base meaning is 'to pay attention to' and, arising from this, to weigh the issues and take appropriate action. Hence the verb must always be judged contextually: here, a 'visitation of judgment'. The Lord, then, will 'visit' (lit.) 'the host of the height in the height and the kings of the earth upon the earth'. Each will be dealt with in their own sphere, where they are at their most potent but where the writ of the Lord's sovereignty has never ceased to run – as will be manifested *in that day*. Isaiah does not link the heavenly and earthly powers in the manner of Daniel 8:3ff.; 10:13, 20–21. He simply notes that there are guilty celestial powers who will be included with terrestrial powers in a comprehensive settlement extending over the whole 'field' of divine creation. *Prisoners ... prison*: deprived of power and subjected to due punishment. *Punished* ($\sqrt{p\bar{a}qad}$) *after many days*: just as *punished* forms an inclusio with the same verb in verse 21a, so *after many days* qualifies *in that day*. The singular *day* denotes that the time is fixed, the event precisely settled in the divine programme; the *many days* remove the date from human reckoning and impose the discipline of patience and the exercise of expectancy.

23. The 'Day' is often linked with brightness (30:26; 60:19–20). Isaiah picks poetic words for *moon* and *sun*, calling attention to their natural brightness: the moon is 'the white one' (*l^{e}bānâ*, 30:26; Song 6:10); the sun is 'the hot one' (*ḥammâ*, 30:26; Jb. 30:28; Ps. 19:6; Song 6:10). But bright as they are, they will (so to say) hang their heads in shame at being such poor things by comparison. *For* introduces the explanation of this wondrous brightness: it is caused by the mere fact of the divine reign! *Mount Zion* and *Jerusalem*: this reign is the climax and consummation of the Davidic monarchy. *Before ... elders* recalls Exodus 24:9–11, when the Sinai covenant was consummated with the Lord among the elders of Israel. There they saw but his feet; then they will live in the light of his full glory. When the Lord comes to reign he will bring to their intended fulfilment all the ways of blessing – Mosaic as well as Davidic – in which he has shepherded his people.

iii. Salvation and provision: the world on Mount Zion (25:1–12). This passage is made up of two sections of testimony (1–5, 9–10a) and two descriptive statements (6–8, 10b–12). As so often, Isaiah has taken pieces which originated on differing occasions in his ministry but has brought them into a telling 'mosaic' that perfectly fits its present context. The fallen city of 24:10 reappears (25:2–4) but with the fresh thought that it was central to an oppressive system. There were those, here described as *poor* and *needy* (4), who, in that city, found themselves under the heel of *the strong* and *ruthless* (3), dominated by *foreigners* (5). They lived as underdogs and aliens, but this is now past. In 24:21–23 the Lord's reign on Mount Zion was viewed in its victorious and scintillating glory; now Mount Zion is the place where *all peoples* and *nations* find abundant provision (6) and deliverance from death and sorrow (7–8). They describe this as *salvation* (9), and the *refuge* of which they sang (4) is his gently overshadowing hand (10a).

All this reveals also how the passage meshes into the wider panorama of chapters 13 – 27. The third oracle in the first two series focused on Gentile need. In chapters 15 – 16 the chronic plight of Moab could have been met through the throne of David established in Zion (16:5), but Moab's pride (16:6) could not swallow this loss of face and Moab resolved to go it alone. In 21:13–17, the tribes of Arabia huddle together for mutual aid, sharing the food and water that in fact solve nothing. But now (25:6) *all peoples* enjoy *the best of meats and the finest of wines* on Mount Zion. They have at last come home to where the king reigns – all of them, that is, except Moab (25:10b–12), still trying in *pride* to go it alone.

1–5, *Individual testimony to deliverance.* In 24:14–16, with dramatic imagination, Isaiah heard singing in the midst of overthrow. The world city was silent in its ruins but worldwide there were songs. This is the theme of verses 1–5, praise (1) in the midst of overthrow (2) and of silence (5). The Lord has acted as he long since decided to do (1); those who considered themselves strong now have to acknowledge a greater strength than theirs (2–3); in all this time he has been a stronghold for his downtrodden people (4) until the time came to still the song of the ruthless (5).

1. *My God, I: cf.* 8:9ff. The believing remnant possesses a personal knowledge of God. *Praise*, (√*yāḏâ*): 'to give thanks', a meaning essential here in a passage which dwells on benefits conferred. *Perfect faithfulness* is expressed in the Hebrew by two related nouns ('*ᵉmûnâ* and '*ōmen*) both from √*'āmēn*, 'to be reliable'. The idiom of the two nouns together means 'every imaginable faithfulness, perfect, quintessential faithfulness'. This matches the backward look of *you have been* (4). All through the years of alien domination the Lord's downtrodden ones experienced an impeccably faithful God. *Marvellous* (*pele'*): things that bear the mark of the supernatural, beyond human doing, finding their origin in another realm (*cf.* 9:6). *Planned* is a noun ('*ēṣôṯ*, 'plans'), related to Counsellor (9:6). It is all part of the royal messianic vision, the gathering of the world remnant round the Davidic king (*cf.* also 11:10).

2–3. The people of God have been dominated by *foreigners*, *strong* and *ruthless* power groups. The background of Egypt and the exodus is prominent in this passage. *Peoples ... cities* are both singular and this must be restored. Isaiah is speaking of the city of 24:10, the world structured without reference to God. The citizens of this world city are one people though composed of many *nations*, for they are one in ideology: the 'I can cope' syndrome that marks a fallen race, coupled with the 'Who needs God?' of the self-sufficient. *Honour ... revere*: this is not a saving acknowledgment of the Lord. It is the grudging testimony of Pharaoh and his officers in Exodus 10:7, 16–17; 12:33, and the cry of those overwhelmed by the glory of the Lord Jesus in Philippians 2:9–11.

4–5. The Lord is with his people in their trouble (4ab); the trouble itself can be savage (4c–f) but the deliverance is to him of the utmost simplicity (5). *Refuge* (*mā'ôz*): 'place of inherent strength'. On *poor* (*dal*), see 10:2; on *needy* ('*eḇyôn*), see 14:30.

Shelter (*maḥ'seh* is from √*ḥāsâ*, 'to seek/take refuge'): it affirms available shelter, a place to turn to. *Storm ... heat*: the contrasting threats are a Hebrew way of saying 'every sort of threat'. But the reality so illustrated was *the breath of the ruthless*. Breath is *rûaḥ*, 'spirit/wind', and here the more forceful translation 'blast' would be suitable. *Ruthless* (see 3), people of inherent strength who are prepared to use it without consideration or mercy. In the mysterious providence of God his people are often in the situation of 4c–e, yet also, in his perfect faithfulness, in that of 4ab. But when his time comes, all this hostile power is as nothing to him. The first and third lines of verse 5 deal respectively with oppressive, killing heat (5a) and how easily it is relieved by the shadow of a cloud (5c); the second and fourth lines deal with the triumphant enemy roaring in power (5b) and the silencing of his song (5d).

6–8, *The messianic banquet.* If the reference to the *elders* in 24:23 looks back to Exodus 24:11 when the Mosaic covenant was celebrated in a meal with the elders, this was all that could happen within the circumstances of the occasion even though the 'ideal' expressed (Ex. 19:13) was that the trumpet would invite all the people. But in the envisaged messianic banquet, every restriction is lifted and universality is stressed: *all peoples ... peoples* are ethnic groups, *nations* are political entities and *faces* individuals, and all are *his people.*

6. The first act of the Lord: provision. The *rich food* and *finest of wines* contrast with the bread and water of 21:14. *Aged wine* can mean the sediment that forms in the process of fermentation (Zp. 1:12), but here it means the wine itself, purified and matured by being allowed to stand. *Finest of wines* is (lit.) 'lees thoroughly filtered'; *best of meats* (lit.) 'rich food, filled with marrow', a picture of nourishment.

7–8. The second act of the Lord: destruction. *Destroy* (√*bala'*) is to 'swallow up', *i.e.* to make to disappear utterly. *Shroud* is a contextual translation, anticipating the reference to *death*, but the Hebrew says 'the veil'. *Sheet* is simply 'covering'. Until that Day dawns, the whole world is in the shadows. We are born into it and therefore we do not recognize that what we call light is but twilight. Paul expressed it by saying 'the night is nearly over; the day is almost here' (Rom. 13:12), and the same thought lies behind the emphasis on the brightness (24:23) that is to come. In banishing everything that darkens life, the Lord will in particular *swallow up death for ever.* Death is not used just in the sense that every life is to some extent blighted by transience, but principally as the primary evidence of the curse imposed in consequence of sin (Gn. 2:17; Rom. 3:23; Heb. 2:15; Rev. 21:4; 22:3).[1] In all his power (*Sovereign*) and in the fullness of his revealed nature as LORD ('Yahweh'), God will dry the *tears* of his people. *From all faces*, *i.e.* he passes from one to another, individually, until every tear is dried. *The disgrace*: see Joshua 5:9 ('reproach'). The disgrace of living in bondage and misery under alien rule in Egypt were gone, the days of living under the cloud of the disobedience of the golden calf were over: full covenant relationships were restored. So long as we live in this world, there are innumerable ways in which we are under reproach and hindered (by circumstances as well as by sin) from living up to our true dignity as his covenant people. But, on that Day, covenant promise will be covenant reality.

9–10a, *Testimony acknowledging God. In that day*: this is the second elaboration (see pp. 167–168 above). *They will say* is singular in the Hebrew: it is the individual voice fully participating in a communal testimony to *our God*, affirming the blessed outcome of trustful hope (*we trusted*, 'hoped'), found in the very presence of *the LORD*, enjoying *his salvation*. Subjective experience (*we trusted*) is matched by objective reality (*This is the LORD*). The saving work was wholly his, without human contribution. It was *his salvation* for which we simply waited in hope and trust. *Saved* (√*yāša‛*, along with its noun, *y^ešû‛â*) is the work of God whereby he rescued his people (Ex. 14:13; 15:2; Ps. 68:19), made them his own (Dt. 32:15: Ps. 98:2–3), restored them to his favour (Pss. 13:5; 106:4), and brought them under his rule (Is. 51:6) and care (Ps. 119:123, 155). Verse 10a begins with 'For', explanatory of the blessings recounted in 6–9. *Rest* is √*nûaḥ*, which in its simple active mode as here never expresses violent action (contrast the hiphil, in 28:2). The down-resting hand is a token of care, shelter and blessing. *On this mountain* forms an inclusio with the opening of verse 6 and rounds off the poem. The Lord lays his hand on his mountain and on his gathered, worldwide, saved people: they are his, he accepts them, he purposes their blessing.

10b–12, *The midden.* But there is another side. The Lord's hand rests on his people, his foot on Moab (*trampled*). *Moab* is mentioned by name (as Tyre in 23:1) to remind that eschatology,

[1] It is often urged that the idea of the conquest of death is a late arrival in Heb. thought. This is a curious conclusion. Many specialists hold that it was only the trauma of the collapse of the Davidic monarchy that produced OT messianic hope. If in this way hope arises out of the ashes of disaster, what price the constant reality of death? Surely the conclusion that a living God would triumph over death would be one of the earliest conclusions of OT faith.

both in blessing and bane, happens to real people. *Pride* excluded Moab in 16:6 and so it remains to the End. This is the ultimate tyranny of a false choice.

10b–11. Isaiah adds two illustrations. The first disgusts us (10bc) but its implication is inescapable: the alternative to the banquet is the midden. *Under him* expresses the thought of direct, divine, punitive action. The word could equally mean 'in his place': Moab chose what he received. The second illustration is the *swimmer* (11a), a perfect simile for a do-it-yourself, go-it-alone policy. He can master his circumstances, choose and reach his goal all by his own resources.

12. In verse 11b the Lord brings down the internal factor of *pride*, the attempt to be one's own salvation. Now he brings down every external edifice of security with which pride surrounds itself. Three nouns of height are matched by three verbs of bringing down. *Your high fortified walls* is 'the fortified place of the top security of your walls' – and not even ruins will be left, not even rubble, just level ground, *the very dust*. Pride before a fall indeed!

iv. The strong city (26:1–21). The sin of the people of God throughout history, in Isaiah's view, was leaving the way of faith. Ephraim (17:1ff.) replaced trusting the Lord with trusting Aram in an alliance; Judah preferred self-reliance (22:1–14). But our true reality is to be the people of faith, and in this fourth section of his eschatological cantata Isaiah allows (1–4) righteousness, faith, peace and salvation to form a cluster of characteristics of the citizens of the strong city. This, he infers, is true security amid all the threats and challenges of this world, right through to final divine judgment. Ephraim experienced only forsaken and deserted cities (17:2, 9); Jerusalem became a broken, cannibalized city (22:9–10); believers live in the strong city (26:1–2).

1–4, Secure in peace (A1; *cf.* A2, 20–21). Isaiah begins with the city's strength (1b–d), states the entrance qualifications (2), notes its perfect peace and the ground on which it is enjoyed (3) and calls for maintained trust (4).

1. *In that day*: see pp. 167–168. This is the third elaboration of the Day of the Lord as presented in 24:1–20. The first (24:21) focused on the Lord's glorious and victorious reign; the second (25:9) noted the salvation enjoyed by the universal company gathered to the great banquet. Now we enter the inner consciousness of those who are the Lord's people. When that *day* comes they will already be by faith in the strong city of salvation.

Strong ... salvation: only the Lord can be the author of salvation; he does not need to be named. His saving power surrounds the city like *walls and ramparts*.

2. *Open*: cf. Psalm 24:7–10. This call to the gate-keepers is a vivid way of highlighting the entrance qualifications into the city. *Righteous* can only mean 'right with God', for much in the rest of this chapter shows that they are not in the city in virtue of their own merits. They are, however, those of *the nation that keeps faith*. The noun (*'emunîm*) is here plural, expressing amplitude: faith in its fullness, faith in every circumstance of life.

3. *Perfect peace* is (lit.) 'peace, peace', the idiom of reduplication (6:3) meaning all-embracing peace. *Mind* (*yēṣer*) is the tendency of the mind (Gn. 6:5), its formulated purposes (Dt. 31:21); it is our mind-set, our way of looking at life. *Steadfast* is a passive participle, meaning 'maintained' or 'made/resolved to be undeviating'. This is the element within the person which is the key to the divine peace. *Because he trusts*, 'because it is trusted/trust is exercised'. There can, of course, be no belief without a believer, but what matters is not who is exercising faith but that faith is being exercised.

4. Faith is not a flash in the pan but a lifelong commitment, and it is a well-founded approach to life, not because of what it is (for it may be weak and wobbly) but because of the one in whom it reposes, *for the LORD ... is the Rock eternal. The LORD, the LORD* is 'Yah Yahweh'. The diminutive 'Yah' is a name of endearment (12:2; Ex. 15:2; Ps. 118:14) which most frequently appears in 'Hallelujah'. The idiom (lit.) 'in Yahweh is an everlasting rock' means 'Yahweh is the very essence of what an everlasting rock should be' (cf. 17:2), durable, changeless and of saving efficacy (as in Ex. 17).

5–6, *Down to the dust* (B1; cf. B2, 16–19). The 'For' with which verse 5 begins introduces an explanation. Part of the security offered by the 'strong city' (1) is the destruction of the *lofty city* (5), their oppressor. This victory is the Lord's; his people's part in it is only to trample the dust left by the victory.

5. According to 24:22, this victory will be 'after many days'. We should therefore treat the first verb in verse 5 as a perfect of certainty: 'he has determined to'; the remaining verbs (imperfects) express the future acts of the Lord. The 'strong city' is not only the security of the life to come but security here and now for those who have already come to Mount Zion (Heb. 12:22) and still await the final victory (Heb. 10:13). *On high* is either the pride of those who live there, or the secure height they think they have made for themselves, or the supernatural dimensions of the Lord's victory (24:21). If Isaiah had some particular city in mind when he first composed this poem it no longer matters. Just as 25:6 looks to the ideal – what actual Jerusalem could accommodate all nations to a banquet? – so the *lofty city* is a figure for the world organized without God.

6. All the *oppressed ... poor* can do is enter into the Lord's victory.

7–9, *The divinely smoothed path* (C1; *cf.* C2, 12–15). Though they are already in the 'strong city' (1–3), the righteous are at the same time waiting for the Lord to act (8), desiring him (9) and living in a world where his judgments are abroad (9). But faith and obedience mark their lives. They accept their allotted *path* as God-ordained (7), hold firm in expectation (8–9) and steadfastly keep his laws (8a).

7. The *righteous* are those who are right with God (on the ground of faith, 2). The voice of faith says that the *path* they walk *is level*, heading 'straight' for the target, and *smooth*, easy to negotiate. They are like the pilgrim of Psalm 84:6 who treats the valley of Baca as if full of springs! *Upright* (*yāšār*) is related to *level* (*mēšārîm*), that is to say the *upright One* (Pss. 25:8; 82:15) appoints a path for us which matches his nature. It runs in a 'straight' line from conversion to glory and places rough in prospect are *smooth* in retrospect.

8–9. *Yes:* 'What's more!' The righteous, who accept the ordering of life as from the hand of the Lord, commit themselves to it in a spirit of obedience. *Laws* (*mišpāṭîm*) is 'judgments', the authoritative decisions – and sometimes the authoritative sentences – that a judge pronounces. Either meaning suits here: the Lord's people walk in obedience to what he has decided is right, and also amid his earthly discipline (Heb. 12:1–10). So they *wait for* him, in patient faith, until he strikes his enemies to the ground (5–6). They do not seek altered circumstances, but within their God-appointed pathway they desire and yearn for him. *Name* is shorthand for what the Lord has made known about himself; *renown*, literally 'remembrance' (Ex. 3:15), is the cultivated memory of what he has revealed about himself and his deeds. The longings of the righteous are controlled by revealed truth – and that constantly (*night ... morning*). One of the things (9c should begin with 'For') that hold the people of God in their obedience is the fact that the *judgments* of the Lord on earth enable its people to *learn righteousness*. *Judgments* (see 8a) are either the law of God as obeyed by his people or the moral disciplines of God as accepted and endured. Obedience is a telling testimony (Dt. 4:5–6), as is also a demeanour of peace amid the frequently inexplicable providences and chastisements of God.

10–11, *Impenetrable blindness* (D). God has three 'ways' of showing himself to the world at large. First, there is his providing *grace* (10a; Acts 14:17); secondly, there is the granting of favourable circumstances: *a land of uprightness* or 'straight-forwardness', when life is all 'plain sailing'; thirdly, there are signal acts of God, in blessing or bane, when his *hand is lifted high* for all to see. But no matter what God does, it is met with incomprehension (*do not learn*), stubbornness (*go on doing evil*), and blindness of spirit (*do not see*). Sometimes there seems to be a dawning spiritual awareness, but it fades because *the majesty of the LORD* has not been acknowledged. *Let them see* is a fair translation but not so suited to context as 'they shall see'. It is a fact – and not one that any would desire – that, some day, those who now refuse to learn will see (11cd) and will come under judgment (11ef). The contrast between *your people* and *your enemies* gives point to Isaiah's teaching. The world continued in ignorance when it might have learned. They not only failed to acknowledge God in his majesty but failed to see what their position and choice involved, a relationship of present enmity with eternal consequences. *Fire*: the symbol of the active, consuming holiness of God (Ex. 3:2; *cf.* Is. 6:6; 30:27; 33:14; 66:24).

12–15, *The divinely ordained peace* (C2; *cf.* C1, 7–9). If, then, the people of the world, the unconverted, are of such impenetrable obstinacy and blindness as verses 10–11 insist, how does such an entity as the Lord's people come to exist at all? The answer is that the same Lord who (7–9) ordains their life's experiences has ordained their entrance into his peace and has done everything that is necessary to bring them there.

12. First, *you establish peace*. *Establish* (*šāpaṭ*) means 'to put something in place' (2 Ki. 4:38), 'to appoint someone to some experience' (Ps. 2:15), hence 'you make peace our portion'. *All that we …* is (lit.) 'For indeed all our works you have done for us'. An identical piece of Hebrew in 2 Chronicles 4:6 allows us to translate 'all our works' as 'whatever concerns us'. It is only if the Lord undertakes 'everything that concerns us' that our incomprehension, perversity and blindness of spirit can be overcome. Salvation has to be all of God.

13. Secondly, the Lord not only does all to bring his people into a relationship of peace with himself (12) but also it is he who keeps them there. *Your name alone*: this unqualified assertion of loyalty is at variance with the recorded history of the Lord's people – then as now – and the literal translation must be restored: 'only by you do we keep your name in remembrance'. The *other lords* included Pharaoh in Egypt, the alien rulers during the time of the Judges, the Philistines, and in Isaiah's day the Assyrians, but throughout all this there was one faithful God preserving a people to keep his *name*, the truth of his self-revelation, in remembrance. Fidelity to him is his gift.

14–15. The work of God remains; the other lords have evaporated. *Departed spirits*: 'shadowy ones' (see 14:9). *Punished:* 'visited' (see 24:21). Such complete oblivion must be an act of God. But, thirdly, while the other lords vanished even from *memory*, the *nation* increased. This also is the Lord's doing. *Glory for yourself*: it was not for their worthiness that he increased his people, but *for* himself, 'for his own name's sake'.

16–19, *Out of the dust* (B2; *cf.* B1, 5–6). In B1 the Lord will bring his foes down into the dust, but, fourthly, he has the opposite in mind for people he proposes to gather to himself. What the Lord has done for them already (12–15) stands in contrast with what they have achieved for him (16–18) but this does not divert him. As he has done all for them (12), so he will by-pass their failures and (19) bring people out of the dust into a fresh, new morning.

16. The book of Judges is a good commentary with its recurring bouts of apostasy followed by penitence (Jdg. 2:11–19). *Came to you* is 'visited', never elsewhere used of people coming to God; they 'paid you attention'. *Barely* ... : the Hebrew is as well translated by 'barely whisper a prayer' as we can manage in the present state of knowledge. The Hebrew relates this (not as NIV to 'discipline' but) to their *distress*: it was a sorrowing, desperate return to him. And, crushed as they were, he did not reject them.

17. *They* (16) becomes *we.* The story becomes contemporary, and *were we* should be 'we have been'. Isaiah is thinking of the Assyrian crisis and all the suffering it brought, the enslavement of northern Israel and the trauma in Judah. It has all been agony like childbirth. *In your presence*: 'because of you', *i.e.* because of the just divine ordering of life as the arena of his chastisements (10:5–15).

18. Travail in birth brings a positive result, but in this case the pain produced nothing. They knew the world needed to learn righteousness (9) and should do so through them (9), but, looking around, they have brought no *birth* into *salvation.*

19. The meaning of this verse is disputed, some seeing here nothing more than the resurrection of the community,[1] but, first, the (mere) continuance of the community as such does not meet the problems that the poem describes. The world has not come to new birth. The continuance of the community does nothing to solve this. Secondly, relating this passage to its parallel in verses 5–6, it is the inhabitants of the 'lofty city' who *dwell in the dust*. The Lord's people already inhabit the city of salvation (1). It is others who need to be drawn in. In this connection *your dead* is more likely to mean 'the dead you are concerned about' and this is then capped by the Lord's claim upon them as (lit.) 'my corpses' (not as NIV), *i.e.* 'the dead I am concerned with'. It is, then, a promise of life for the world: the counterpart of the vision of 25:6–10a. But 25:7–8 looked forward specifically to the abolition of death itself. If we view 26:19 in its context in this way (as indeed we must), then its terms go beyond any figurative significance to the literal sense of a full resurrection.[2] The call to *wake up* to *joy* is illustrated by the two figures of *dew* and *morning* or 'full light'. *Dew* is symbolic of heaven's contribution to earthly well-being (Gn. 27:28, 39; Dt. 33:13, 28), royal favour (Pr. 19:12) and divine blessing (Ho. 14:5). It is linked with the manna in Exodus 16:13–14 (*cf.* Nu. 11:19), the divine gift which cancelled the threat of death (Ex. 16:3). *Morning*: literally 'lights', a plural of amplitude, 'full light'. Death is darkness; light is life (Jb. 3:16; Pss. 49:19; 56:13) and salvation (Ps. 27:1; *cf.* 2 Sa. 23:4; Ps. 104:2; Is. 9:2; 59:9; 60:1, 3). In the parallel oracle (18:4), the Lord's presence is dew and light. As the dew descends, so he will come to the dead he is concerned with, bringing vitality, salvation. *Her dead*: 'its shadowy ones' (see 14).

20–21, *Secure from wrath* (A2; *cf.* A1, 1–4). The poem began with 'open the gates' (2); it ends with *shut the doors*. This looks

[1] E. J. Kissane, *The Book of Isaiah* (Browne and Nolan, 1960), finds here only a reference to 'national resurrection'. H. H. Rowley, *The Faith of Israel* (SCM, 1956), p. 1160, says the passage represents a stage *en route* to individual resurrection. Skinner, *Isaiah*, and Herbert, *Isaiah 1 – 39*, find the promise of individual resurrection.

[2] *Cf.* Dn. 12:2. The evolutionary supposition that OT thought progressed from poor beginnings to brilliant endings has led to the conclusion that this doctrine of death and resurrection must be late. How insubstantial is all this! The Egyptians had an intricate theology of life after death centuries before Isaiah. Even Canaanite religion, for all its brutishness, depended on the annual triumph of Baal over death. In the name of all logic, how could Israel, with its foundational belief in the living God, lack, within revealed religion, what others arrived at by wishful thinking and natural religion? See especially J. Mauchline, *Isaiah 1 – 39* (SCM, 1962), p. 193.

back to the shutting of the door of the ark (Gn. 7:1, 16) and entering indoors at the Passover (Ex. 12:22–23). In times of his just judgment, the Lord makes provision for his people. In verses 1–4 their security in the strong city was in the context (5–6) of the doom of the world city. In that day they will be as safe as in the ark or inside the blood-marked homes (Ex. 12–13). *Passed by* is the 'pass over' verb of Exodus 12:12, 23. This sheltering security is necessary, 'For' (the opening word of 21) the Lord is emerging to *punish* ('visit', 24:21). *Sins* ('*āwôn*): see 1:4; 6:7, the internal reality of sin in the fallen nature. *Blood shed*: the most flagrant outward violation of God's law. *Disclose*: even long-hidden sin – which the perpetrators thought was forgotten – will be exposed. *The earth* itself takes action, co-operating with the Creator: this is its 'moral vitality'. It has been infected by human sin but has never ceased to identify with the holiness of its God (1:2–3; 24:5; *cf.* Gn. 4:10–12).

v. The universal Israel (27:1–13). With this passage we reach the conclusion of Isaiah's panorama of history. Its companion passages (see pp. 110–111) are 19:1–25 and 23:1–18 with the shared theme of the worldwide people (19:24–25; 23:18; 27:12–13). Within the Isaiah Cantata (chs. 24 – 27) this is the denouement: in 26:20–21 the believing people, though within the city of salvation, were waiting for the final coming of the Lord in judgment. This is now envisaged. 27:1–13 consists of a central passage (7–11), dealing with past forbearance (7–8), coming atonement (9) and ultimate overthrow (10–11). On each side of it there are two 'in that day' sections (1 and 2–6; 12 and 13). These match each other: the Lord's victory in the heavenlies (1) and the Lord's jubilee on earth (13); the vineyard people (2–6) and the harvested people (12). Thus (exactly as 14:1–2 is central to 13:1 – 14:27 in the opening oracle of the series) the Lord's plans for his people lie at the centre of his cosmic, eschatological work.

1, *The Lord's victory in the heavenlies: the great sword.* Isaiah not infrequently used pagan mythological concepts illustratively (see 51:9) without subscribing to their truth. In this fourth *in that day* elaboration (see pp. 167–168), *Leviathan* is a water-beast, real or imagined (Jb. 41:1; Ps. 104:26); in Psalm 74:14 it is figurative of Egypt; and in Job 3:8 to 'awaken Leviathan' is to bring into operation disruptive supernatural forces. Leviathan stands for immense power, including supernatural power(s) ranged against the Creator God. Here, however, the mystery-name Leviathan modulates into the factual *serpent* and points to these forces as created. *Monster* (*tannîn*) can be a sea creature (Gn. 1:21), a serpent or crocodile (Ex. 7:9; Ps. 91:13), or figurative of what possesses overwhelming power (Je. 51:34). *Coiling* may be factual (twisting) or moral (twisted) or both. *Serpent* is *nāḥāš*, as in Genesis 3:1, and is doubtless used here for that reason. The threefold description *Leviathan ... serpent ... monster* is matched by the threefold description of the Lord's *sword*: *fierce* (hard, unrelenting), *great* (equal to any task) and *powerful* (dominating). Hostile supernatural forces infest the whole creation, *coiling* on land, monstrous *in the sea*. Thus has sin corrupted the 'very good' work of God (Gn. 1:31), but, however great and wherever concealed, the *sword* of the Lord will find and slay them *in that day*.

2–6, *The vineyard people.* This final song in the cantata of chapters 24 – 27 matches the vineyard song in 5:1–7. There the emphasis was on what the Lord's people made of his vineyard; here it is on what the Lord will make of them.

2. They are the Lord's delight. *In that day*: the fifth elaboration (see pp.167–168). *Fruitful vineyard* is either 'vineyard of delight' or, in some MSS, 'vineyard of foaming wine'. The former contrasts with the hostility of 5:5–6; the latter with the undrinkable wine of 5:2, 4.

3. They are under the Lord's care. Here is a total divine work: conserving (*watch over*, 'preserve') its excellence, nourishing (*water*), and protecting (*guard* is the same verb as *watch over* but here looking outward against intruders). All this care is *continually ... day and night*.

4. The Lord is at peace. *I am not* is (lit.) 'I have no anger'; *ḥēmâ* is angry feeling. Isaiah 5:5–6 and 26:3, 12, spoke of peace enjoyed by believers; here, peace is in the heart of God. *If only*: the Lord longs for a chance to show his zeal for his vineyard; just let a weed appear!

5. The Lord invites the hypothetical weeds of verse 4 to *come to me for refuge*. Vineyard membership is open to all, as once to Moab (see 16:5).

6. The Lord promises that the divinely nurtured vineyard will *fill* the earth (Ps. 80). *In days to come* may be a correct interpretation of 'the coming ones'. But as an exclamation, 'They are coming!', it might refer to those responding to the invitation of verse 5. *Fill all the world* [*i.e.* 'fill the face of the earth'] *with fruit*: the wording is exactly the same as 'cover the earth [*i.e.* "fill the face of the earth"] with their cities' (14:21). Babylon's plan was to organize the whole world without reference to God. But the Lord has a different intention and one that will be fulfilled (11:9).

7–11, *The work of the Lord*. How will all this happen? First, the Lord has never been as harsh with Israel as with Israel's foes (7–8), and this same mercy will display itself in atonement (9a), issuing in a religiously purged people (9b–f); secondly, the Lord will destroy the *fortified city* (10–11; 25:1–5; 26:5–6).

7–8. The Hebrew in verse 7 is rhythmic and beautiful but at the expense of clarity! 'Like the smiting of the one who smote him did he smite him?', *i.e.* did the Lord smite Israel to the same extent as he smote Israel's smiters? The second question is much the same: 'or like the slaughter of his slaughtered ones was he slaughtered?', *i.e.* did Israel ever suffer such casualties as the Lord inflicted on those he defeated (as, *e.g.*, 37:36)? *By warfare*: *śa'ssâ'* is otherwise unknown (NIV has followed the surmise of LXX), but cognate languages suggest a verb 'to cry sa-sa', 'to scare off by shouting' – as we say, 'to shoo away'. This matches *exile*, which means 'by sending off' – not a reference to the Babylonian exile only but to all occasions when an enemy invaded and took prisoners. On all such occasions, divine wrath could have exacted a full penalty from Israel but forbearance intervened – and even when the major exile came, it was cushioned with a promise of return. Chastisement was truly *his fierce blast*, never negligible, for divine wrath is real and divine standards non-negotiable.

9. *By this* looks back to the point just made: the Lord has ever acted with restraint, preserving his people when they merited death. *Then*: 'therefore'; the same principle of divine action will apply in atonement. *Guilt* ('*āwōn*): see 5:18; 6:7; 26:21; 53:5. *Atoned* (√*kāp̄ar*): see 6:7. The Lord will pay the atonement (covering) price for the sinful nature (*guilt*) and for *the removal of his sin* (*ḥaṭṭā't*), his actual wrongdoing (5:18; 6:7; 53:12), and this will be seen in its *full fruitage* when those atoned for destroy *the altar* and remove the *poles*. The *altar* represents all expressions of religion authorized by the Lord, and *poles* and *incense altars* stand for illegitimate and imported religious usages. First, then, there will no longer be need for an *altar* for sacrifice (Heb. 10:12, 18) and *Jacob* will acknowledge this by even grinding its *stones* to *pieces* like so much *chalk*. Secondly, the atonement will purge out erroneous religious practice. *Asherah poles*: see 17:8. *Incense altars* is probably a correct translation of *ḥammānîm* (Ezk. 6:4ff.). It is not the word for the authorized incense altar (Ex. 39:38) but is linked with Baal (2 Ch. 14:5) and 'high places' (Lv. 26:30).

10–11. Isaiah, then (9), has not forgotten the atonement-base on which this whole division (chs. 6 – 37) of his book rests (6:7), but, just as he went on in chapters 7ff. to the 'royal' theme of conquest, so he does here. The reference to the *city* links this oracle in particular to the world city and its fall (25:1–5; 26:5–6). Isaiah does not explain how it will be, but the coming atonement (9) will be the occasion for the fall of the *fortified city*, with the motif of incoming animals (10), as ever, speaking of the end of human occupation. The browsing animals leave bare *twigs*, but (11) even they disappear as firewood. *For* introduces the cause of such a total judgment: lack of *understanding* (*cf.* 26:10) has led to forfeiture of divine *compassion* and *favour* (Rom. 1:28; Eph. 4:18–19). *Understanding* is a plural of amplitude (*bînôt*, 1:3), 'true discernment'. *Compassion* (√*rāḥam*, 13:18; 14:1) is typically the love of a mother for her child. *Favour* (√*ḥānan*) is 'grace', the undeserved kindness of God (Gn. 6:8; Ps. 51:1). *Creator* is 'Potter', 'he who moulded them' (Gn. 2:7). This richness of maternal love is forfeited by sin – specifically, that of the mind failing to exercise its power to perceive, grasp and hold the truth.

12–13, *The jubilee harvest: the great trumpet.* Two *in that day* oracles form the sixth elaboration (see pp. 167–168), and they conclude just as they began. The first (12) is (like 2–6) a picture of sowing and reaping; the second (13) with its *great trumpet* of gathering matches the 'great sword' (1) of victory.

12. The Lord gathers his harvest *one by one. In that day*: see p. 168. *Thresh*: √*ḥābaṭ* does mean this (Jdg. 6:11), but is also used of gathering olives by beating (Dt. 24:20), which suits the *one by one* emphasis. *The flowing Euphrates* and *the Wadi of Egypt* were the traditional boundaries of the promised land (Gn. 15:18; Ex. 23:31) and here represent the gathering up by the Lord of every true member of his people, 'the sons of Israel'.

13. The fiftieth (Jubilee) year (Lv. 25:8ff.) followed the forty-ninth (sabbatical) year and was, therefore, a year for which there was no harvest in preparation. Thus it was a year of total dependence on the Lord. As in 25:6–10a, *in that day* the Lord will supply everything (55:1–2; Lk. 14:17). The Jubilee *trumpet* was sounded on the Day of Atonement (Lv. 25:9), linking with the atonement in verse 9. *Great trumpet*: *cf.* Zechariah 9:14; Matthew 24:31; 1 Corinthians 15:52; 1 Thessalonians 4:16. *Assyria ... Egypt*: the reference is to those living within Gentile boundaries, the ingathering of the world. *Exiled* (√*nāḏâ*) is used of Israelites driven from their land (8:22), but it is used also in the general sense of 'straying' (Dt. 22:1), people homeless before the enemy (16:3–4). The thought is not of 'exile' from the land of Israel but of being harassed and distraught in a spiritually alien environment (Ps. 120). But all such will at last experience the wonder of 19:24–25. *Egypt ... Assyria*: just as eschatological judgments fall on real people (*e.g.* Moab, 25:10), so do eschatological blessings. Isaiah relates the eschaton to the world map he knows, and even from the supreme oppressors' grasp (Egypt the first, Assyria the contemporary) there will be those whom the trumpet calls to liberty and home to Zion. All together will *worship the LORD on the holy mountain*, full participants in the holy community, and *in Jerusalem*, citizens of the strong city (Eph. 3:6).

IV. THE LORD OF HISTORY (28 – 37)

These chapters form the greatest of Isaiah's 'interim fulfilments' (see, *e.g.*, 14:24–27; 20:1–6; 23:17–18). Having listened to his teaching in chapters 13 – 27 that 'in that day' the whole world will be one people, acknowledging one God and worshipping him alone, Isaiah's discipleship group (8:16) must surely have asked the question that springs to our lips: is this wishful thinking or a serious reality? In any event, this is the question Isaiah answers in chapters 28 – 37.

The reference to Israel, Egypt and Assyria in 27:12–13 forms the bridge into this new section, which reflects a period of history in which these three powers tangled with each other – a period, that is to say, which offered a test case of the Lord's rule in history and specifically over the three powers Isaiah has used as eschatological symbols. The occasion was the 'Egyptian Alliance' (Introduction, pp. 18–19) in the days of Hezekiah. Assyria was the overlord; Hezekiah a puppet 'king' under Assyria; Merodach-Baladan, the ever-restless king and would-be king of Babylon, was canvassing an alliance with the western Palestinian states; and Egypt was covenanting intervention once the flag of rebellion was raised. In chapters 38 – 39 Isaiah will diagnose this as an issue of faith, and he does not ignore that great question here, for it was his task to oppose Hezekiah's lunatic fascination with militarist solutions by asserting the alternative course of trusting God's promises. But in the main in these chapters, the issue of faith is in the background, and he takes us through the events in order to reveal where power really lies, that is to say, in the sovereign Lord.

The section falls into two parts: first, there is a series of six 'woe' passages (28 – 35; see 28:1; 29:1, 15; 30:1; 31:1; 33:1); and, secondly, chapters 36 – 37 recount the history of Sennacherib and Jerusalem in 701 BC. The arrangement of the six 'woes' is important. We shall note as we work through them that they match each other in pairs (the first and the fourth, second and fifth, third and sixth) but there is also, so to speak, a 'story-line'. In chapters 28 – 29 no names of outside nations are mentioned, even though the intrigues leading up to the Egyptian Alliance can be read between the lines. The purpose of these chapters (like 1 – 5) is to elucidate principles of divine working in history. Chapters 30 – 32 come to grips with events. We meet Egypt and Assyria by name, and yet the more Isaiah involves himself in the realities of historical events the more easily he moves off into eschatology (as in chs. 7 – 11), so that we view the fall of Assyria side by side with the messianic kingdom. Finally, chapters 33 – 35 are wholly eschatological (like 24 – 27): the coming of the king (33); cosmic victory (34); and the pilgrimage of the redeemed to Zion (35).

a. The six woes (28:1 – 35:10)

i. The first woe: the word of God and the purposes of God (28:1–29). There are three sections woven together here into a unity of presentation. Isaiah starts with a message he prepared regarding Samaria (1–6) before the city fell in 722 BC. This is made the basis of a comparison with Jerusalem (7–22) at the time the Egyptian Alliance was being negotiated. Then Isaiah adopts the style of a 'wisdom' writer and meditates on the discerning ways of the Lord (23–29).

Samaria: a surprising hope (28:1–6). The hill of Samaria (1 Ki. 16:24), crowned by the city, is pictured as a garlanded reveller whose time is up (1). As forcefully as a storm (2–3), as instantaneously as swallowing a ripe fig (4), the Lord will destroy Samaria. But the crown of the reveller will be replaced by a true crown (5), and the city that fell so easily will become wise (6ab), strong (6c) and impregnable (6d).

1. *Woe* (*hôy*) can be a summons (55:1), an expression of anger (1:24) or of sympathy (1 Ki. 13:33). The idea throughout this series is of a summons to the bar of judgment. Samaria is charged directly not with dissoluteness (*cf.* Am. 4:1; 6:6), but with the *pride* which led them into complacent revelry. But the *flower* is *fading;* the party is almost over.

2–4. Two illustrations from nature depict the total destruction of the city. The first is the storm, with *hail*, *wind* and (lit.) 'downpour of water, mighty flooding'. *The Lord* (*'ᵃdōnāy*) stresses the divine sovereignty. *One who is* veils the name (Assyria) of the coming conqueror, for Isaiah is concerned here with principles behind events, not the events themselves. Thus, wherever pride leads people into moral indifference and a life of mere this-worldly indulgence, the Sovereign *has* at his disposal the means of overthrow. The second illustration is of a walker who sees an early fig ready for eating and with one unthinking movement it is picked and eaten. *Swallows*, used literally in the illustration, is often figurative of total disappearance (3:12; 25:7–8). The first illustration, then, is the power with which Samaria will be destroyed; the second is the ease and totality of its destruction. Behind it all on the one hand is a truly sovereign God, whose total mastery of the most potent forces of nature is but an illustration of his mastery of the forces of history; behind it on the other hand is the single sin of pride.

5–6. Often in Isaiah hope comes as a surprise. No sooner has Samaria disappeared, been submerged (2) and swallowed (4) by judgment, than a *day* is envisaged when it will be transformed. Here, then, is another principle at work: the Lord brings just judgments (1–4) but never rewrites his promises (5–6). The words *crown, glorious, beautiful* are the same as in verse 1 but here linked with the Lord. He will, in and through himself, undo all that sin has done. *Remnant*: see 8:9–22; 10:20–23. Verse 6 takes up the picture of military overthrow in verses 2–4. Where they were once weak and vulnerable there will be transformation: first, a true king. *Justice* and *judgment* are the same word, meaning 'a right judgment in all things', the ability to 'set things to rights', the truly kingly quality predicted for the coming Zion in 1:26. The implication is the reversal of the schism (1 Ki. 12) between the two kingdoms and the restoration of the throne of David. Secondly, there will be security. *Strength* is 'warrior strength', power against the enemy. *Gate*: the decisive element in city defence. If the gate yielded the city fell. This is the 'strong city' motif of 26:1.

Jerusalem: the inescapable word (28:7–22). There is a sinister parallel between Jerusalem (*these also*, 7) and Samaria. In Samaria, dissoluteness arose from pride; in Jerusalem gross sensual indulgence (7–8) issues in the dismissal of the word of the Lord. This is an acute diagnosis of the human condition: self-satisfaction becomes self-indulgence and issues in self-sufficiency.

7–8. The verses read as if Isaiah were watching an actual scene – and the Hebrew he writes itself captures the lurching, staggering – and vomiting – of the revellers. Had the ambassadors of 30:1ff. returned, waving their piece of paper, gleeful over the Egyptian Alliance (see 18), and is this the celebratory state banquet? Even the official organs of the word of God have succumbed. *Prophets* were the immediate mediators of divine revelation (*visions*); *priests* applied this truth to people's lives in their *decisions* (Mal. 2:5–7), but what they are in private (7cde) they are in ministry (7fg). Bodily indulgence saps spiritual perception. *Befuddled* is 'swallowed up' (see 4). They thought they were doing the swallowing!

In verses **9–13**, again it seems as if an actual scene is being recorded: the revellers round on the watching prophet. They mock his ministry as childish (9–10), and he replies (11–13) that what they despise as childish is but the childlike clarity of the inescapable word of God.

9–10. *Weaned ... taken*: children of pre-school or play-school age! To the sophisticated politicians, living in what they would have called 'the real world', what relevance has Isaiah's call to rest in God (12) and to stand by faith on his promises (16)? The 'wisdom' which counts strength in battalions cannot find room for prayer and faith. *Do ... rule* are respectively *ṣāw* and *qāw*. The former could be a noun from √*ṣāwâ*, 'to command'; the latter means 'line' (1 Ki. 7:23). The mockers could therefore be picturing Isaiah as a patient teacher of children, building truth upon truth, one bit at a time, *a little here, a little there*.

11–13. It is possible, however, that the words *do ... rule* (10) are intentionally meaningless, the reassuring noises made to a baby. This fits with Isaiah's reply (11). Do they think his ministry is a meaningless jumble of noises? That is exactly what they will hear – in the mouths of foreign invaders! For, come what may, *God will speak*, but when the simple intelligibility of the word of God is refused, his judgment falls on his professing people in the shape of the unintelligible (1 Cor. 14:20ff.).

Rest and *repose* (12), which 30:15 spells out as returning to and resting in the Lord, is the childlike simplicity which they called childish irrelevance. Isaiah insists that faith is the solution to even the harshest problems and severest threats. *They would not listen*: the Hebrew goes beyond the thought of merely refusing to listen to some particular message; it implies 'listening was something they were unwilling to do'. Theirs was a basic unreadiness to bow before the voice of God. The refused simplicity (10) becomes the unintelligible babble of violent and dominant conquerors (13). To reject the word of God is not to escape it.

Verses **14–19** draw conclusions from 9–13. Since the word of God must and will have its way, *therefore* (14) no human arrangements for security can succeed (14–15); the Lord has made true safety available (16) and he will allow no rival possibilities (17). Even now the invitation to *hear the word* (14) and to adopt a position of trust (16) remains, but outside that invitation there is no salvation.

14–15. *Scoffers* (√*lîṣ*): people far gone in cynical dismissal of spiritual truth (Ps. 1:1; Pr. 14:9), self-assured (Pr. 1:22), beyond correction (Pr. 13:1), arrogant (Pr. 21:24). Isaiah puts words into their mouths (15) which spell out the implications of what they actually said. *Covenant* and *agreement* point to the alliance with Egypt, supposedly guaranteeing success in rebellion against Assyria. They would have spoken of a covenant with Pharaoh, an agreement with Egypt, but to Isaiah it was signing their own death warrant! *The overwhelming scourge*, a mixed metaphor of flogging and drowning, refers to Assyrian invasion (see 8:6–8). Did they say, 'Should Assyria invade …'? Isaiah rephrased their words: you won't escape the whip, you can't escape the flood! *Lie … falsehood*: the former (*kāzāḇ*, 58:11) is the deceitful contrasted with the reliable; the latter (*šeqer*, 2 Ki. 9:12) is untruth contrasted with the truth. So much, said Isaiah, for Egypt's promises!

16. *So* recapitulates the *therefore* of verse 14. The affirmation there of what the Lord said is amplified here by what he has done (*cf.* 1 Pet. 2:4–8a). *A stone in Zion*: the *stone* could be the Lord himself, who chose and came to dwell in Zion (8:14); or it could be the Davidic throne as the focus of the promises (Pss. 2:6; 118:22); or we could translate 'a stone, namely Zion': the chosen city as the repository of the presence and promises of God. But the essential idea remains the same: promises have been made and the Lord's people are invited to build their lives on them. *Tested* (lit. 'a stone of testing') is either a stone which has undergone tests – and is therefore reliable – or one which tests whether they will take it as their foundation or turn elsewhere. *Dismayed* (√*ḥûš*) occurs twenty times in Isaiah, always with the sense of 'hurrying'. Here it means 'all haste and no speed', being in a 'flap' – in contrast to the repose of the way of faith (12; 7:4; 30:15).

17–19. *Measuring line* and *plumb-line* are respectively the tests of horizontal and vertical exactitude. When the Lord acts he will do so with precision, enforcing the principles of his holiness (*righteousness*) and applying them correctly (*justice*; *cf.* 1:21). Storm (*hail*) and flood (*water … overflow*) may seem indiscriminate, but not so. The judgment falls with exact justice. *Refuge … hiding-place … covenant … agreement*: the Lord will not tolerate human alternatives to his way of salvation. *Overwhelming scourge … beaten down*: Isaiah mixes the metaphor a little more; *beaten down* is 'a place for trampling' – the flood, the whip and the marauding beast! This is the inescapable doom on human expedience in the place of divine promises.

20–22. The section ends with two explanations (20 and 21 both begin with 'For') why terror awaits them, and a final appeal (22). First, they refused the Lord's proffered rest (12). They have made their own bed and they must lie on it – but they will discover that human provisions are inadequate. *The bed is too short to stretch out on* ...: the whole arrangement is without comfort or adequacy. Secondly, all the conquering power the Lord once used on their behalf will be turned against them: the Lord's coming is *strange*, an *alien task. Perazim* and *Gibeon* look back to 2 Samuel 5:17–25 and 1 Chronicles 14:8–17. The Lord secured David on the throne by signal defeats of the Philistines. This was the stepping-stone to national security and the establishment of Zion. But the deepest result of turning from the word of God is to excite divine enmity. Those who rejected the divine promises located in Zion (16) would find that their portion is wrath on the same scale. Thirdly, there is a final appeal. *Mocking* looks back to scoffers (14), both deriving from √*lîṣ*. *Chains* ... *heavier*: choices form character, for good or ill. If they continue in cynical disregard of the Lord, they will come to the point beyond which reformation is impossible. Sinners become the architects of their own doom by continuing thoughtlessly in wrong choices. Reformation is also always urgent, because the Lord will not endlessly delay *the destruction decreed.* The only way to flee from God is to flee to him.

The discriminating Lord (28:23–29). How then are we to understand the future for Jerusalem? This first woe hinges on the comparison between Samaria (1–6) and Jerusalem (7ff.). In the case of Samaria, judgment (1–4) suddenly became unexpected hope (5–6). Is there hope for Jerusalem too? Or is the decreed destruction (22) the Lord's last word? Isaiah answers with two agricultural parables (an inclusio with the two natural illustrations in 2, 4): 23–26 is a parable of sowing; 27–29, a parable of reaping.

23–26. The harsh *breaking up* activity of ploughing and harrowing is purposeful: it is an essential preliminary to *planting* and sowing. The verbs *sow, scatter, plant* indicate discriminating action; each seed is dealt with appropriately and also put *in its place* (or, maybe, 'in rows'), in its *plot* and *field*, that is, given an environment good for growth. All this is God's instruction and teaching (26).

27–29. Isaiah draws no conclusion from his observation that the purposeful ways of the farmer have been taught him by God, but the 'For' with which verse 27 should begin indicates that the point made in his parable of sowing is explained in the parable of reaping. The *sledge, cartwheel, rod* and *stick* were methods of gathering different crops. The *sledge* was a heavy wooden platform, studded underneath with sharp stones or metal and weighted on top, dragged to and fro to break up corn ready for winnowing. *Grain*, of course, *must be ground.* That is unavoidable, brutal though it seems, for otherwise there is no harvest, but the process is not *for ever.* Done to excess it would destroy the grain. *This also comes from the LORD*, but it goes beyond merely showing how agriculturists work. It reveals that the Lord is *wonderful in counsel and magnificent in wisdom. Wonderful* (6:6) means what is beyond the human, supernatural. *Wisdom* (*tûšiyyâ*; Jb. 5:12; 6:13; Pr. 8:14; Mi. 6:9) is foresight to plan ahead, therefore the wisdom that achieves results.

It is with this thought, then, that we move from the first woe (28:1–29) to the second (29:1–14). Jerusalem (like Samaria) will be ploughed and crushed. The Lord's wheels and horses will go over it. But it is all purposeful; the crushing will be restricted within the limits essential to the crop the Lord envisages.

ii. The second woe: is anything too hard for the Lord? (29:1–14). Since this 'woe' is a double message of hope – eleventh-hour deliverance (1–8) and coming spiritual transformation (9–14) – *woe* is not the most suitable translation. It is a summons to *Ariel* (1, 2, 7) to grasp two great truths: no problem is so far gone as to be insoluble to the Lord (1–8), and this applies spiritually as well as circumstantially (9–14). The same Lord who acts in judgment acts in transformation. He brings *Ariel* into the dust (1–4) and visits with spiritual coma those who have chosen blindness (9–12), but he also disperses the foe in his moment of triumph (5–8) and acts supernaturally to reverse wrongful understandings (13–14). Can it be, then, that Samaria faces both calamity and hope (28:1–6) and that the destruction decreed against Jerusalem is controlled by the purposeful, fruitful work of God (28:7–22, 23–29)? Yes indeed, for the Lord is never defeated by any foe (1–8): he controls even the most threatening catastrophes. Nor is he baffled by the intransigence of the human heart: he is the Lord of transformation (9–14).

Chastening and deliverance (29:1–8). Behind these verses we discern the events of chapters 36 – 37, the triumphalist advance of Sennacherib and his 'last-minute' destruction. Yet

Assyria is not named, and Zion is veiled behind *Ariel* – though its identity is no secret (1, 8). For Isaiah's purpose is to use events to elucidate principles: the Lord is sovereign in history; he has the last word and it is the word of deliverance. His people may be humbled by the foe but they are never forsaken or destroyed (2 Cor. 4:8–10).

1–3. *Ariel* means 'altar-hearth' (Ezk. 43:15), the place of the ever-burning fire (Lv. 6:12–13). It was both the privilege (Ps. 84:3–4) and the peril (Is. 33:14) of Zion to live with this fire, alike a danger to sinners (6:4) and the means of their salvation (6:6–7). It was the sign of the Lord's indwelling presence. Isaiah could hardly have chosen a more suitable cryptic title: Zion, the place of holy wrath and divine preservation. *David*: this, then, is the 'strange' and 'alien task' of 28:21. To think that sin has brought them to the point where the Lord will assail *David's* city! *Add year to year* ... is designedly ambiguous. It can mean 'add another year to this one; let the feasts come round once more' or 'let the years roll on, the circling festivals come and go'. Isaiah is not dating the calamity but affirming its certainty. *Like an altar hearth*: 'a veritable Ariel', a place where holy wrath is centred. *Encamp* ... *towers* ... *siegeworks*: the military terms imply human attackers, but Isaiah looks past them to divine agency.

4–8. What a scene of transformation! First, Ariel is reduced to nothing in status (4ab) and strength (4cd), but suddenly its enemies are as swiftly gone as blown *chaff* (5; 5:24; 17:13), as insubstantial as a dream (7) and as disappointed of their hopes as a sleeper on awakening (8). All this is because (6a, lit.) 'from Yahweh of hosts it will be visited'. As 'Yahweh' he is the God of the exodus, delivering his people, destroying his enemies; as 'Yahweh of hosts' he is and has every potentiality and power: his mastery of the 'forces' of nature (6bc) is the standing illustration of his total sovereign power and rule.

Blindness and sight (29:9–14). Spiritual blindness is both self-chosen (9b) and also a judgment of God upon the choice made (10). It is a needless, wilful and careless refusal of truth that lies to hand (11–12), and the Lord sees its hypocrisy and false-heartedness (13). In response he pledges further wonders, bringing human wisdom to an end (14). The parallel with verses 1–8 within one 'woe' suggests that the coming wonder will be a spiritual transformation, sudden, dramatic, matching the historical deliverance.

9. Did Isaiah still have Sennacherib in mind? To hesitate in the face of such a divine deliverance would surely be the point of no return in spiritual blindness! Yet it is by no means certain that all

Jerusalem would see it so. Politicians could have seen Sennacherib's retreat as the vindication of their Egyptian policy (37:8–9); others no doubt shrugged their shoulders and took it as a happy chance. While we may well see this oracle in relation to 37:36–37, Isaiah is still concerned with principles rather than events. Wilful blindness to the things of God (9ab) decreases the chances of ever thinking clearly or finding the right way (9cd). *Stunned*: √*māhâ* means 'to delay, hesitate, be indecisive' (Gn. 19:16; 43:10). *Amazed*: √*tāmâ* can mean 'to marvel' (Ps. 48:5) or 'be bewildered' (Gn. 43:33). If we are indecisive spiritually we condemn ourselves to bewilderment. Wilful refusal to see (*blind yourselves*) induces blindness (*be sightless*). In 28:7–8, intoxication promoted refusal of God's word; here refusal of the word promotes a mental and spiritual intoxication, befuddling the mind (*drunk*), confusing the life (*stagger*).

10–12. In 1 Kings 22:22, when Ahab determined to embrace falsehood, divine judgment visited him with false prophets: by the will and act of God, he got what he chose (*cf.* 2 Thes. 2:9–12). Determined spiritual insensitivity becomes judicial spiritual deprivation: first, the mind loses its clarity: *deep sleep*, 'a spirit/Spirit of coma/torpor', the mental equivalent of 1 Samuel 26:12; secondly, the means of spiritual enlightenment are removed: *prophets* and *seers* are synonyms for those whom God has raised up to receive and communicate his word. The lesson is driven home illustratively in verses 11–12: the person who can read cannot be bothered to open the book; the person who cannot read is unconcerned to find someone who can.

13. In verse 10 it was 'the LORD' who reacted: Yahweh loves his people but he is not mocked (Gal. 6:7–8). Here it is *the Lord* (*i.e.* '*ᵃḏōnāy*, the Sovereign One) who notes that religious reality has gone (13bcd) even though observance continues (13de). *Come near*: cf. Exodus 28:43. *Worship*: 'their fear of me', the sense of awe and reverence proper to those who approach God (*cf.* 23). As the Sovereign reviews their worship, all he sees is conformity to human rules. It is not that the Lord belittles the use of words; but words without the heart are meaningless; and *worship* is not worship (Mk. 7:6–8) unless it is based on and responds to what God has revealed.

14. What the Lord's new act will be we are not told. Like the parables in 28:23–29, this verse is a bridge to the next 'woe' (15–24). It is, however, something supernatural (*wonder*, 9:6; 28:19) which will result in the negation of human *wisdom* and *intelligence*. The former (*ḥokmâ*) covers the whole mind, acquiring knowledge, appraising, setting objectives; the latter (*bînâ*) is the ability to see to the heart of a matter, to 'discern'.

iii. The third woe: spiritual transformation (29:15–24). The second woe ended with an unanswered question: what *wonder* does the Lord purpose in response to the culpable spiritual blindness of his people? The third woe replies not with how he will act but with what he will achieve. Isaiah starts with the situation needing to be remedied (15–16), the folly of the human mind without God; he next affirms the coming transformation (17–21): revived spiritual perception (18), and social reformation (19–21); and he ends (22–24) by applying all this specifically to the Lord's people.

15–16. The background to this accusation of merely human planning which excludes God from their councils is indicated in 30:1–2, the Egyptian Alliance. But once more, Isaiah is concerned here not with the events in which they participated but with the principles which motivated them. To exalt the human and exclude the divine is the reversal (16a) of all that is right and proper. It is equivalent to saying (16b) that he is no more than we are – the spirit of self-sufficiency – and that he has nothing to do with what we are (16cd) – the spirit of arrogance and usurpation. It is even like saying that he is less than we are (16ef) – the spirit of thoughtless stupidity – as if that which manifests thought, craft and purpose should deny these attributes to their originator. It is a denial of the Lord's distinctiveness (*like the clay*), sovereignty (*did not make*) and wisdom (*knows nothing*).

17. Note the abruptness with which this promise of transformation is introduced. People can deny God his proper place, but he is still the Lord. He does what he will in heaven and earth (Ps. 135:6). He needs no permission. *In a very short time*, as the Lord reckons time (2 Pet. 3:8), even creation itself will be transformed. *Lebanon* typifies what is not the product of human cultivation (Ps. 104:16); the *fertile field* is 'garden-land', the product of human cultivation. But since the whole creation is infected by human sin, nothing is as it should be. It all needs turning upside down! What appeared as wildness will exhibit its true nature as the Creator's perfect design; what we thought to be an ordered garden will, in retrospect, seem like wild *forest*!

18. The metaphors of deafness and blindness look back to 29:11, where the closed eyes and book contrast with open ears and an open book here. Isaiah speaks of new faculties and new appetites (*deaf ... hear ... blind ... see*), a new condition (*out of*

... *darkness*) and new satisfaction in God's book (*scroll*) (Eph. 5:8; 1 Thes. 5:4).

19–21. Isaiah focuses on three aspects of society to sketch the coming transformation. First, there is unfettered practice of true religion. The *humble* are the underdogs, crushed by vested interests; the *needy* are those whose lack of resource makes them necessarily pliable to the will of others, but often both words describe those who seek to live devotedly for the Lord in a secular society. In the coming new society, such will be free of constraint and liberated to *rejoice in the Holy One*. Secondly, society will be free of destructive, negative elements: the unscrupulous (*ruthless*; 13:11; 25:3–5), the denigrators (*mockers*; 28:14, 22), and the trouble-makers (*an eye for evil*). Thirdly, there will be a sound legal and judicial system with no false testimony (21a) or 'nobbling' of witnesses (21b), nor the denial of the protection of the courts to the innocent.

22–24. The forecast of the coming great society is now made wider in that it is traced back to the original purposes of God, and narrower in that it is focused exclusively on the chosen people, *Jacob*. *Redeemed* (√*pāḏâ*, 1:27) is not elsewhere used of Abraham, but Genesis 48:16 uses the parallel √*gā'al* (NIV 'delivered') of the Lord's 'guardian care' of Jacob throughout his chequered life. Both verbs are essentially 'price-paying' in their meaning but can have a general sense of 'looking after', like our expression 'to bail someone out'. The reference to Abraham is emphatic in the Hebrew, with the implication 'Would the Lord have made such a caring start with Abraham if he did not intend to complete what he began?' *Jacob* is pictured as an anxious spectator of all that has happened to his descendants, but the day will come when (lit.) 'not now will Jacob be ashamed; not now will his face pale'. Verse 23 begins with 'For' as an explanation of Jacob's release from anxiety. Their downward course has been halted. Jacob's *children* are also *the work of my hands* and that guarantees, first, that they will assent to all that the Lord has revealed about himself (23c): his *name* is, in general, what he is in himself, but, more specifically, we do not know what it means unless he tells us (Ex. 3:13–16) by his self-revelation. Secondly (23d), they will live at peace with the holy God in their midst: this is the force of the added words *of Jacob*. The Lord is holy in himself (23c) and, in all his holiness, he comes to be among his people (23d). Thirdly, their knowledge and acceptance of revelation (23c), their recognition of God in their midst (23d), will issue in a life of the deepest awe (23e). *Stand in awe* is √*'āraṣ*, the parent verb of the adjective 'ruthless' (20a). It speaks of acknowledging the awe-inspiring absoluteness of divine majesty and power, a trembling reverence (1 Pet. 1:17–20). Fourthly (24), individual life will be changed. *Spirit* is the energy or 'gusto' with which life is lived. Instead of fickleness (*wayward*) there will be true discernment (*understanding*, see 14), and instead of resentful grumbling there will be a teachable spirit. *Complain* (Dt. 1:27; Ps. 106:25) means bitter refusal of the Lord's word, self-pitying determination to put the worst construction on things, paranoia in facing life. *Instruction*: from √*lāqaḥ*, 'to take', hence a 'grasp' of truth (Dt. 32:2; Jb. 11:4; Pr. 4:2; 7:21).

iv. The fourth woe: faithlessness and faithfulness (30:1– 33). The advent of the names *Egypt* (2) and *Assyria* (31), bracketing the fourth woe, herald the fact that Isaiah is starting to apply the principles of the first three woes to the events of the time. In the first woe (28:1–29) he established that the Lord works purposefully (28:23–29), even when the pathway lies through disaster (28:1–4, 5–6), for his judgments do not revise his promises; and that he calls his people to accept and trust his word (28:12, 16). All this is now demonstrated in the actuality of history. In verses 1–7 Isaiah condemns the Egyptian Alliance, affirming that Egypt will be no help (5–7). Matching this, at the end of the chapter (27–33) he insists that Assyria will be no threat. In between this inclusio, verses 8–17 and 18–26 are a balanced statement: the word of the Lord rejected (8–17) and (18–26) the word of promise kept.

Contemporary events: Egypt no help (30:1–7). This is the second time Isaiah has alluded to an embassy sent to Egypt to secure the alliance. In the parallel woe, he mocked the ambassadors coming back with their piece of signed paper (28:14–15); now (1–5, 6–7) he watches them go on their profitless exercise (5, 6, 7).

1. *Obstinate children*: 'rebellious sons' (*cf.* 1:2, 5, 23). *Declares* (*nᵉum*): see 1:24. *Alliance*: *massēḵâ* was translated 'blanket' in 28:20; the idea is of a protective covering. *My Spirit*: see on 31:3. The preposition *by* is not expressed in the Hebrew, but may be introduced legitimately, as in NIV. In this case (*by*) *my Spirit* is parallel to *mine* ('from me'), emphasizing the lack of divine authorization. On the other hand, 'not my Spirit' would parallel *alliance*, the covering they might have had if they had not chosen otherwise. *Sin upon sin*: the first sin was acting without divine prompting, the second, seeking a 'covering' other than the divine Spirit. The first recourse of the Lord's people, whether for wisdom or provision, is the Lord himself; any other course is *sin* (*haṭṭā't*), a falling short of their true dignity.

2. *Egypt* is the place of death (Ex. 1:22) – and they went there seeking life (*cf.* 28:15)! *Without consulting me*: 'and my mouth they have not asked', exactly as Joshua 9:14. The 'mouth' is the organ of expressed, personal opinion. If they had asked he would have spoken. But their eyes (*look*) were elsewhere.

3–5. The synonyms *shame* and *disgrace* do not exclude 'feeling embarrassed' but they emphasize 'reaping shame', objective disappointment of hope. *Zoan* was in the northern Delta and *Hanes* south of Memphis. The *officials* may be those of Pharaoh, indicating that the 'Ethiopian Dynasty' of Shabako had extended its power all over lower Egypt. In this case Isaiah is alluding to the supposition that such a ruler would be worth cultivating. Alternatively, the reference may be to Judah's *officials* and *envoys*, trailing from one centre of influence to another in the hope of securing Pharaoh's aid. Either way, it is all *useless*, bringing *neither help nor advantage*. 'Well, of course!' Isaiah might have said, for from the feared killer (Assyria) they were seeking help from the proved killer (Egypt)!

6–7. The separate heading in verse 6 indicates a separate poem – of beautifully crafted, sharp, compulsive Hebrew – which Isaiah publicized (see 8) to drive the message home. The cryptic title would excite interest and provoke questions (*cf.* 8:1). In verses 1–5 Isaiah emphasized the merely human planning that lay behind the Egyptian embassy; here, the sacrificial human cost. But no matter what wisdom we exercise or labour we expend, we cannot be the authors of our own security. *The animals*: what irony! The question in every mouth was, 'How will our ambassadors fare?' Isaiah said, 'Never mind them. Think about the poor beasts!' *Hardship ... distress*: the ordinary route to Egypt lay through Philistia. It would seem, however, that (in the interests of secrecy?) they went through the Negeb. In Exodus 13:17 the Lord would not let his people journey through Philistia lest opposition turn them back to Egypt. Did the ambassadors realize they were exactly reversing the exodus? *Rahab* seems to have had currency as a nickname for Egypt (Ps. 87:4; *cf.* 51:9). It means 'turbulence, boastfulness'. Perhaps 'Big Mouth' would catch Isaiah's sense! *Egypt*: overflowing with promises, but in the event *the Do-nothing*.

The word refused (30:8–17). Isaiah reinforces the message of coming judgment.

8. Isaiah is commanded to make a public record (*tablet*) and a private one (*scroll*) of his ministry. What was he commanded to write down? Verses 9 and 15 begin with the Hebrew word *kî*, which often means 'that'. If this is the case here, then verses 9–17 are what he was commanded to write – 'that' they have rebelled against revealed truth (9–14) and specifically against the call to repent (15–17). But if *kî* has its meaning 'for/because', then these verses explain why he was commanded to make a record, and we can only guess what was recorded. The public tablet would presumably be a succinct statement of Isaiah's ministry at this time: poems like verses 1–5 and 6–8 would be easy to write up in a public place (*cf.* 8:1) as a sort of 'wall-newspaper'; and as for the private, written record, it would most reasonably be the full record of Isaiah's ministry at the time of the alliance, all that we now have in chapters 28 – 37. The *tablet* is to be *for them* (lit. 'among them') where they have access to it; the *scroll* or 'book' is to *be an everlasting witness*. It is the imperishable word of God; its immediate relevance did not exhaust its endless significance.

Verses **9–14** give the first explanation of the people's situation: they have played false to the Lord (9), not by silencing the prophets but by demanding a prophetic message to suit their own tastes (10–11; 2 Tim. 4:3–4). The consequence will be the collapse of the whole social fabric (12–14).

9. On the initial 'For' see above. *Rebellious*: see 1:20. *Deceitful*: false, disappointing, failing to be what they ought. *Children*: 'sons', see 1:2. *Unwilling to listen*: as in 28:12. *Instruction* (*tôrâ*): see on 1:10.

10–11. Isaiah explains what he meant by accusing them (9) of unwillingness to listen. People, of course, do not openly ask to be told what is illusory, but their actions can make their meaning plain. As in 28:14–15, Isaiah spells out the meaning behind their words. *Pleasant* means 'smooth'; *illusions* comes from √*tālal*, to mock, trifle with. Instead, therefore, of what is *right*, they want things which will leave the surface of life unruffled, a ministry of trifles; they did not want the direction or style of life (*way ... path*) altered, and in particular they did not want to hear of a *holy* God living among them and exerting pressure on them (*of Israel*; see on 1:4). They did not ask that preaching cease; only that it be innocuous, and without the absolutes of truth and morality which derive from the character of God.

12. *Therefore ... the Holy One*: they cannot rid themselves of the Holy God (11) by wishing it to be so! Their refusal of him issues in a consequence: his holy opposition to them. To reject the word of the Lord is to make an enemy of the Lord of the word. *Message ... oppression*: they chose a new morality of 'freedom' and did not want to be held to the Lord's 'way' (11). But all who make this false choice find that they have opted for bondage to a cruel *oppression*.

13–14. We need to reintroduce the 'Therefore' at the beginning of verse 13. Consequences follow when the Lord's word is spurned. *This sin is, first, self-destructive* (13), like a wall collapsing under its own weight; secondly, it provokes divine judgment (14). *It will break*: better, 'he will break'. *Taking ... scooping* must refer to familiar practices: using a bit of pottery to carry a glowing ember to light another fire, or a bit of an old cup to dip water from a tank.

Verses **15–17** give a second explanation of the people's situation: they have refused repentance and faith.

15. Once more the rejected *Holy One* (11) imposes his unchanged character upon them, this time backed by his sovereign (*'dōnāy*) power. Note that this verse (*cf.* 9) begins with 'For' (see 8 above). The rejection of the Lord's word is now specific, whereas in verses 9–14 it was general. *Repentance and rest*: the word called them back to him. *Repentance* means 'returning', not a feigned return but one that would really bring them back to *rest* upon him. *Quietness* is the absence of panic and restlessness. It is the product not of refusal to face life but of insistence upon taking God into account in *trust*. This is *strength* (*gᵉbûrâ*), specifically strength for (life's) battle. Sadly, just as 'they were not willing for hearing' (9), so they *would have none of* (lit. 'they were not willing for') repenting, believing and finding rest and strength.

16–17. Just as they proposed an alternative morality (10–11), so they had a militarist alternative to repentance and faith, but they would experience the truth of Matthew 26:52. *Flee ... flee ... swift ... swift*: when we refuse the way of faith, whatever we choose as an alternative brings its own retribution on us. We choose to flee, we will flee; we want swiftness, we get swift enemies! *Thousand ... one*: the promise of Leviticus 26:8 is reversed; the threat of Deuteronomy 32:30 is realized. *Flagstaff ... banner* prove there were once people around to put them there. The evidence is left, the people are gone (6:11–12). This is the third picture of the total destructiveness of the one 'sin' (13) of rejecting the Lord's word (*cf.* 13–14).

The promise kept (30:18–26). The topic of this woe so far has been human faithlessness: the faithless 'wisdom' which sought Egypt's aid (1–7), and the unbelieving spurning of the word of the Lord (8–17). The remainder of the woe turns to the faithfulness of God: his faithfulness to what he has promised

(18–26) and his faithfulness to his undeserving people in their moment of crisis (27–33). First, then, though they spurn his word (8–17) he keeps his word: grace and compassion lie in readiness (18); he will respond to prayer (19); beyond affliction lies a readiness to hear his word of guidance (20–21) and a disgusted rejection of false religion (22). There will be every earthly abundance (24–25) and the renewal of creation in the day of healing (26).

18. *Yet* (*lāḵēn*) is 'Therefore', which occurs twice in this verse (matching the double 'therefore' of judgment in 12–13 and 16): 'Therefore the Lord waits … Therefore he will rise …' The faithfulness with which he punishes his people for spurning his word is the faithfulness with which he commits himself to the word he has spoken. His necessary chastisements do not nullify his grace; they only impose a waiting (*longs*) until the right moment comes, for (as 28:26, 29 have indicated) *the LORD is a God of justice*, better, here, 'judgment': judging the exact moment at which to be *gracious* (√*hānan*), to act in unmerited favour (Gn. 6:8), and to show *compassion* (√*rāḥam*), his passionate, surging love for his people (14:1).

19. The emphasis *Zion … Jerusalem* is intentional: the promises will be kept not only at the right time (18) but in the appointed place (28:16). *Weep no more*: literally 'not weep at all'. There will be unalloyed joy when grace and compassion manifest themselves in the immediate attention of the Lord to the prayers of his people (*cf.* Jn. 16:23–24, 26–27).

20–21. Isaiah makes no secret of the reality of the time of duress (40:1–2). The *bread of adversity and the water of affliction*: these are nouns in apposition and the sense is 'bread, that is, adversity', 'adversity as your bread, affliction as your drink'. This period of divine concealment (8:17) will lead to a time of unclouded relationship. *Teachers*: the plural is permissible but difficult to explain, for Judah's teachers were never hidden. The problem was not the concealment of teachers but the unwillingness of hearers (28:9–10; 30:10–11). The form *môreyḵā* could equally well be singular, 'your Teacher'. This makes sense: in the coming time of bliss, divine self-revelation of 'your Teacher' will be received and responded to. Rejection of the word of the Lord will be a thing of the past (*eyes … ears*). *You turn … voice*: the Lord's people are still potential sinners but they are preserved in righteousness. The Teacher who is before their eyes is also watchfully behind them.

22. This is the necessary negative side of their positive relationship with the Lord. Separation to the Lord must show itself in separation from what is false and wrong. The care they lavished on their idols (*silver ... gold*) will be replaced by disrespect (*defile*), revulsion (*menstrual cloth*) and rejection (*Away with you*).

23–24. In contrast to the poverty of bread and water (20), there is a coming abundance. This is not a materialistic vision as such, but a vision of creation restored. Sin brought a restraint on the in-built processes of creation (Gn. 3:17–19), but the coming glory will see the curse removed (11:6–9; Am. 9:13). The Lord will play his part in this new earth (23a), and earth will respond richly (23b; Ho. 2:21–22). In contrast to the afflictive labour to which human wisdom put them (6–7), the beasts will share the bounty of the new creation (24). *Broad meadows*: they will have wide, totally safe ranges. *Fork and shovel*: means of sieving earth. Their fodder will be doubly purified for them.

25–26. Isaiah continues his upwards movement in describing the new creation: first the soil (23a), then the beasts (23b– 24), now up to the hills and on to the heavenly bodies. He does not elaborate on the *great slaughter* and the *fall* of *the towers*, but passages like 2:12; 13:1–12; 25:1–5 show that his vision of the Day of the Lord includes the overthrow of his foes and of their systems of self-security. But the other side of the Day is transformation (arid hill-tops flowing with water), hitherto unexperienced light as creation is restored to its true powers (*seven times*; 24:23; Rom. 8:21), and healing for those whom both their own sinfulness and divine chastisements have wounded.

Contemporary events: Assyria no threat (30:27–33). This final section of the woe matches the first (1–7). The Lord's people turn from him to Egypt, but he does not turn from them when Assyria threatens. This accords with the heart of the matter (8–26), that though they spurn his word (8–17) he keeps his word (18–26). What then will happen when Assyria attacks? Why, the king of Assyria coming to Jerusalem is climbing on to his own funeral pyre! Isaiah starts with the 'real' day of the Lord (27–28). He is Lord over all the nations. (By implication, what is Assyria, compared with such a God!) The Lord's people will be safe in his Day (29–30): their part will be to sing amid the judgments of God (24:14–16). So then, regarding Assyria in the here and now (31–33), they will be shattered (31), Judah will sing (32), the funeral pyre is ready and so is the fire (33). Once more the structure of the verses proclaims their message: the great surrounding bracket is the Lord. In the Hebrew, *the Name of the LORD* is the first line and *the breath of the LORD* is the last. The next bracket is his lordship over the nations as a whole (27–28) and over Assyria in particular (30–33), and at the heart of the poem is the singing people (29). Both on the large scale (27–28) and in the actual events of history (30–33), the Lord's people are central to his concerns.

27. *The Name of the LORD* means 'the Lord in the fullness of his revealed character'. *From afar*: Isaiah uses the storm motif for the action of the Lord in wrath. He sees the storm rising in the distance and gradually approaching (Ezk. 1:4). *Smoke ... fire*: these were the exodus symbols of God's presence (Ex. 13:21) in holiness (Ex. 19:18). *Lips ... tongue*: the references to the organs of speech show that the Lord acts in accordance with the word he has spoken (Rev. 19:11–13, 15, 21).

28. *Breath*, 'Spirit', accords with the storm metaphor, but also indicates the agency through whom the Lord acts. *Sieve of destruction*: literally 'of falsehood', a sieve designed to sieve out and expose all that is false and at the same time to discriminate (Am. 9:9). The judgment of God is exact (Gn. 18:25). Along with the *sieve* to discriminate there is the *bit* to control and direct (37:29). The sovereign Lord guides all to their just and appointed destiny.

29–30. Theirs is the song (29), his the victory (30). Song, as always, typifies entering joyfully into a benefit to which we have made no contribution. The primary *night* festival was the Passover, which suits this context with its exodus references to cloud and fire (27, 30) and to the Lord as *Rock* (Ex. 17; see on 17:10). The song looks back to Exodus 15:1ff., 20–21. The Psalms give abundant evidence of music and singing in the festivals and religious life of Israel, even though we do not know what form those celebrations took. But this is no formal religious act; *hearts* are rejoicing. *Voice*: the Lord is acting according to his word. *Arm* is the organ of personal strength in action and is an exodus symbol (*e.g.* Ex. 6:6; Dt. 4:34; 5:15; 7:19). The strange mixture of *fire* and *hail* is found in Exodus 9:23. The Lord does not change: the exodus-Passover revelation is a declaration of his Name for ever (Ex. 3:15).

31–33. As once in Egypt, so also in his own land (14:24–27) he will strike. The Lord is revealed in the past and alive in the present. *Voice*: see on verse 27. It only needs the Lord to speak to *shatter* the mightiest of earth's powers. *With his sceptre ...* is better, 'who, as (the/his) rod, was smiting' (see 10:5). The Assyrian came on a divine mission of chastisement but also on an equally divine mission of self-destruction (10:12–15). *Tambourines* and (lit.) 'battles of shaking/sieving' reiterate the balance (29–30) between the song and the noise of conflict and the discriminating judgments of God. *Topheth*: see 2 Kings 23:10; Jeremiah 7:31–32; 19:6, 11, 14. The name possibly arose from taking the consonants of the word *t͟epat*, 'fire-place', and giving them the vowels of *bōšet*, 'shame, disgrace'. The result would be 'the shameful burning place'. For a reason unknown, Isaiah uses here another form of the name, *topteh*, but with the same significance. How ironic that, all unknowingly, Assyria's imperial progress to Jerusalem (10:8–11) was a funeral procession to a pyre long since prepared – and that by the Lord himself, who would also ignite it when the time came! 'So may all your enemies perish, O LORD' (Jdg. 5:31).

v. The fifth woe: all things new (31:1 – 32:20). The second woe was in two parts, for it covered both circumstantial and spiritual problems in the Lord's people. On the one hand there are the often overwhelming odds which threaten us in this world (29:1–8), and on the other the spiritual blindness which is part of our fallen nature (29:9–14). Over all this the Lord is competent to deliver (even at the eleventh hour) and transform. This matching fifth woe first (31:1–9) sees Judah, Egypt and Assyria embroiled at Jerusalem but observes a fourth 'component' enter the scene: the Lord, who will not allow Egypt to help or Assyria to hurt and who carries off Jerusalem as his personal prey (31:4–5; *cf.* 29:4–6). Isaiah then goes on to a transformation scene matching 29:9–14, the coming King and his renewed people (32:1–20). In slightly closer detail, we start with a 'prologue' (29:1–5), which deals with coming disaster and deliverance. This is balanced by an 'epilogue' (32:19–20), forecasting disaster and blessedness. The two internal sections are respectively a call to return/repent (31:6 – 32:8), looking forward to a coming king reigning over a new society, and a call to hear (32:9–18), looking forward to the outpouring of the Spirit and a new society.

Disaster and deliverance (31:1–5). Jerusalem's leaders knew that when, backed by Egypt's promises, they raised the flag of rebellion, they would incur Assyrian reprisals. On what basis did they make their choice – or, to put the matter from Isaiah's perspective: what constitutes a wrong choice? First, they abandoned faith (1); secondly, they overlooked revealed truth (2); and thirdly, they ignored common sense (3).

1. They did not, of course, abandon faith *per se*. Everybody lives by faith. It is part of the human condition. Financiers trust market forces, militarists trust bombs, scientists trust nature's regularities. Jerusalem's leaders trusted Egypt. *Go down* is a participle. They were in the very act, and the prophet would stop them because they went to *Egypt* (1a) and did not *seek ... the LORD* (1f), relied *on horses* (1b) and did not *look to the Holy One* (1e), and their *trust* was in numbers (*multitude*) and *strength* (1cd). Note how Isaiah reserves *trust* to form the centrepiece of his analysis. Around this focal point the verse presents a stark choice: the Lord, or ...? They faced the most critical of tests – the Assyrians – but the real crisis was: 'Where is your faith placed?'

2. They ignored the truth about the Lord. Life must be faced theologically, that is to say, in the light of what we know about God. *Can bring ... does ... rise up* are all perfect tenses in the Hebrew. They represent what never varies. In every situation the Lord is wise (2a); if disaster threatens, he, the one who 'brings' it (10:5–15), is the real force to be reckoned with (2a); he never contradicts, revises or reneges on what he has said (2b): in both his threats and promises he is unchangeable; the world under his rule is morally accountable, and the wicked and evildoers will find him their opponent (2cd). In making a choice, has the Lord's wisdom been consulted? Is he revered as the sovereign disposer and director? Is his word known and obeyed? Is sin being forsaken and holiness cultivated?

3. When his people seek help other than from himself, the Lord will not allow it. The helpers who step in as a substitute for the Lord come under condemnation as much as those who sought them (*cf.* 2cd). So here helper and helped alike *stumble* and *fall*. But there is something else: every other source of help possesses only derived life; it does not have life in itself. *Men* is *'aḏām*, humankind, the creature which has life only because God in-breathed it (Gn. 2:7). *God* is *'ēl*, the most transcendent of the God words, God exalted in majesty and in all the attributes of the Most High. The contrast between *flesh* and *spirit* is between that which needs life and that which possesses life (*cf.* Jn. 4:24). *The Lord stretches ... helps*: he is sovereign, not just positionally (as *'ēl*), not just distinctively (as the One who possesses life in himself), but actually and practically. A mere hand-movement suffices! A true choice brings life itself to our aid.

4–5. The 'For' with which verse 4 opens offers two similes in explanation of verse 3: *as a lion* (4) and *like birds* (5). The Lord is the unabashed lion who will not yield its prey to another. Ironically Egypt is represented as shepherds (Gn. 43:32; 46:34; Ex. 8:26)! *To do battle on* (*ṣāḇā' 'al*) is the same as in 29:8, where it was correctly translated 'to fight against'. So here, in the three-handed fight, with Assyria attacking, Judah defending and Egypt supposedly helping, the Lord comes with the Assyrian forces to exact his due chastisement (10:5–11). What Egyptian shepherds could rescue his prey? But with an abruptness copying 29:5, the picture changes: Jerusalem's leaders had despised the Lord. Would they have said, 'About as much use as a sparrow!'? But the weakness of God is stronger than men (1 Cor. 1:25). Gentle towards his erring people as a hovering bird, his is the fourfold strength to *shield, deliver, pass over* and *rescue.* The numeral four symbolizes 'on every side'. The hovering God is sufficient.

The first summons: repentance (31:6–9). Isaiah urges three reasons for repentance: rebellion (6); preparation for the Day of the Lord (7); and the coming deliverance from Assyria (8–9).

6–7. *Return:* repentance starts in the mind but shows its reality by changing the direction of the life (1:27). *Revolted:* see 1:5. It is typically biblical to keep ultimate matters in view. The *day* referred to here is the ultimate Day of the Lord (*cf.* 2:20). Biblical faith is always at the ready, not simply to surmount the next crisis but to stand before God (Lk. 21:36). Since that day will expose *idols* as the 'no-gods' they are (2:8) and as mere human expedients (*hands ... made*), the time to reject them is now, not then when it will be too late.

8–9. Historical threats as well as eschatological ones must be faced with repentance. *Not of man* ('*îš*) ... *not of mortals* ('*ādām*): the deliverance will not come about by any individual, nor any human agency. *Sword* is the Lord's sword, which has destroyed them (37:36). *Forced labour:* following the débâcle of 701 BC, the Assyrian Empire entered its long terminal illness. *Stronghold* is 'Rock', most likely a reference to the king of Assyria in contrast to the Rock of Israel (30:29) and in contrast to the righteous king who will reign (32:1). *Fall* (√'*ābar*) is 'pass away'. It is the same as the Passover verb in verse 5. The Lord 'passes over' in deliverance, the king 'passes away' off the stage of history. *At the sight* ...: the Hebrew here is extremely compressed. The NIV rendering means that when the Lord lifts his banner there will be complete collapse of power to resist. It might, however, be translated 'and his princes will be shattered far from the banner', *i.e.* having deserted the colours. *Declares* (*neʾum*): see 1:24. *Fire ... furnace* reflects the Ariel imagery of 29:1. Zion cannot escape the threat constituted by its unique privileges. It lives where the fire of the holy God burns. But all who attack the Lord's people bring themselves within range of that same holy fire too.

Righteous King, new society (32:1–8). In 29:9–14 Isaiah foresaw a coming wonder from the Lord in terms of new wisdom. Having called his people to repent not only in the light of the coming Assyrian deliverance (31:8–9) but also (and as a priority) in the light of the Day of the Lord (31:6–7), he now explores the glories of that day and the wonderful works of the Lord. In addition, it is typical of this major section of the book of Isaiah to move from Assyrian darkness to the brightness of the coming King (*cf.* 8:20 – 9:2ff.; 10:33 – 11:1ff.). In this way the light of hope shines behind the clouds of adversity and sustains the Lord's suffering people. Isaiah foresees a royal administration which secures true values (1) and affords proper protection (2). The people of this king are also themselves transformed (3–4), and false values come to an end (5–8). It is a vision of a true king and a new society.

1. *A king*: the indefinite is the idiom of indefiniteness for the sake of emphasis, as if to say 'A king – you know who I mean!' It is the messianic king of chapters 9 and 11. In 9:7 righteousness marks his throne, in 11:5 his character, and here, as in 11:4, his administration, where sound moral principles (*righteousness*) issue in sound moral practice (*justice*). The king himself embodies *righteousness*; his executives (*rulers*) apply his principles in correct decisions (*justice*, see 28:26).

2. The translation *each* is perfectly sound: true ideals of rule animate every member of the administration. But it is more telling to find here again the idiom of indefiniteness, 'a man (that unique, special man)'. In 9:6–7 we read of the king's deity, in 11:1ff. his full endowment with the divine Spirit in the context of his human ancestry, and here his personal, true humanity. In four illustrations the perfection of his rule is pictured: the contrasting dangers of wind and water (*storm* is 'inundation'; or 'driving rain', 28:2) point to protection from every threat; the supply of *water* and *shadow* in burning heat point to provision for every need.

3–4. Four transformations mark the people (*cf.* 29:11–12, 18), in perception (*eyes*), reception (*ears*), grasp (*mind*) and communication (*tongue*) of truth. *Closed*: the verb here is most likely that used in 6:10 of judicially imposed blindness and in 29:9 of wilfully chosen blindness. All this is reversed. Accompanying these transformations in abilities there is transformation of character: the *rash*, 'hasty', all too prone to act precipitately, learn to stop and think; the stammerer's hesitancy will become *fluent and clear.*

5. An imperfect society accords honour imperfectly. Isaiah foresees a true aristocracy of character. *Fool* is *nābāl*, a person who is morally obtuse, lacking a sense of moral and spiritual obligation (2 Sa. 13:13; Jb. 2:10; Ps. 14:1). *Scoundrel*: *kîlay* and the related word *kēlay* (7) are found only here. They may be derived from √*nākal* with the thought of deception, deviousness in seeking self-advantage to the hurt of others (Gn. 37:18; Nu. 25:18; Ps. 105:25). The one is a *fool* by what he lacks – moral sensitivity; the other a *scoundrel* by what he has – a drive for self-advantage at all costs. The *fool* is amoral, the *scoundrel* unscrupulous.

6–8 are a separate and, in literary form, a very clever poem, amplifying the themes of the *fool* (6) and the *scoundrel* (7), and ending (8) with a crisp statement about true nobility. *Fool*: see verse 5. *Speaks*: an imperfect tense expressing characteristic behaviour. The emphasis here and in verse 7 rests on sins of speech. *Evil* ('*āwen*) is rather 'trouble, mischief' (10:1; Gn. 35:18), often what troubles the Lord and attracts his displeasure (31:2; Ps. 92:9). Here it is the thought-life and lifestyle of one who sits loose to moral and spiritual obligation. The *fool* is against the Lord (6cd) and uncaring about the needy (6ef). *Error* (*tô'â*) is found only in Nehemiah 4:8 and means turning people off course, distracting them, leaving them without sure direction. *Scoundrel*: see verse 5. He is 'on the make', a mixture of spiv and social climber. *Evil schemes* (*zimmâ*), apart from Job 17:11, has a uniformly bad meaning. It occurs nineteen times of sexual misconduct (*e.g.* Lv. 18:17). It is planning for one's own advantage at whatever cost to others. This includes cynical manipulation of the legal system (*plea ... just*). *Noble*: liberally outgoing to God (Ex. 35:5, 22) and to others (Pr. 19:6). It can be used of 'noble' rank (13:2), but here it is nobility of character. In the envisaged society it is this nobleness which brings stability and security (*stands*).

The second summons: hearing (32:9–14). Isaiah addresses the *women*, presumably because, as in 3:16 – 4:1, he found them to be the embodiment of characteristics he felt obliged to condemn in the whole society of Jerusalem: complacency and false security. These could nullify his first call (31:6) to repentance. Therefore there is need for Jerusalem to face facts. There is going to be a loss of harvests (10), and then further loss involving land, houses, palaces and city (13–14). The call to repent (31:6) was enforced by the thought of the blessings to come; this is balanced by this second call to 'face the facts' of the disasters on their way.

9–10. *Complacent* (*ša'anān*) has a good sense, 'undisturbed' (18), but here the circumstances of ease which it expresses are assumed as a personal and perpetual right. *Secure* or 'trusting' is another great word put to a reprehensible use: a bland assumption

ISAIAH 32:11-15

that nothing disturbing can happen. The lost *harvest*: behind this is the Assyrian invasion and the inability to work the land (37:30).

11–14. The call to the women is renewed[1] and with greater intensity, because an even greater threat is coming. In verse 10 the vintage was lost; now it is the vines, the land (12–13) and the city (14). The unfettered life of the animals (14d) bespeaks the absence of people (5:17). This was foretold in 6:11–13, implied in 11:11 and predicted again in 30:8–17. *Strip*: the verb is not used as a sign of mourning. It here describes captivity and enslavement. (20:2–13), a fate indeed for the women of Jerusalem (3:16ff.)! *Thorns ... briers*: the former can grow anywhere, the latter is a plant of the wasteland. Together (the Hebrew has no *and*) they express the thought that what was formerly cultivated has now become one with the *wasteland*. *Fortress* is 'palace/ large house'; maybe here the royal palace is meant. *Citadel* could be the place-name Ophel (Ne. 3:26), a southern projection of the temple mount. *Watchtower* could refer to 'the tower of the flock' (Mi. 4:8), though the word *baḥan* is found only here.

Outpoured Spirit, new society (32:15–18). But though disasters are coming, they do not have the last word – as Isaiah discovered in 29:1–14. The Lord has a way both of reversing disaster at the last minute and of looking beyond the disaster to what he, in his undeflected will, determines to do. The coming of the King (32:1) and the consequent new society are amplified here in a new way. There will be an effusion of new divine life (15a), transforming the world (15bc), establishing true moral and spiritual values (16) and a peaceful, secure society (17–18).

15. *The Spirit*: the Spirit of God was the divine power at work in creation (Gn. 1:2; Ps. 33:6). He is the life-giver (40:7; 42:5; Ps. 104:30). He raises people to new heights of ability (Ex. 35:30–31) and empowers for mighty deeds (Jdg. 14:6; 15:4; 1 Sa. 10:6). He indwells the great line of messianic figures (Nu. 11:17; 27:18; 1 Sa. 16:3; Is. 11:2; 42:1; 61:1) and is the Agent in the regeneration which will mark the messianic future (Ezk. 36:27).

[1] The verbs in vv. 11–12 are difficult. *Tremble* is masculine but addressed to women; the following four imperatives (11) are unusual in form: possibly aramaized 2nd plurals feminine, or masculine singular in the emphatic form (GKC 48i). In v. 12, 'beating the breasts' is a masculine plural participle (GKC 48). Gender switches are not uncommon in Hebrew (23:1 offers a masculine singular imperative with a feminine plural noun). There may be nothing more here than Isaiah failing to maintain the fiction of addressing the women when his words apply to all. Emendation, if thought necessary, would be simple: see *BHS*, *ad loc.*

Poured: the Spirit originates in God who 'pours out' his own life for purposes of renewal (44:3; Ezk. 39:29; Joel 2:28). The first result of this future outpouring is a transformed creation (15). What now appears as *desert* will be changed into 'garden land' (*fertile field*), with all the beauty the ordering hand of God will impart; what is now reckoned as 'garden land', ordered and purposeful, will, by comparison with the true order and beauty of that day, seem as haphazard as scrubland (*forest*).

16–18. The second result is that the new environment will be animated by true moral and spiritual principles (*righteousness*), expressed in sound moral regulations and practices (*justice*; *cf.* 1:21, 27; 9:7; 11:4) over the whole area of the new creation, *desert* and *fertile field* alike. Thirdly, there will be a human society marked by *peace*, in its full realization as peace with God, harmonious relationships and personal fulfilment; *quietness*, that is, 'rest' and 'restfulness' (28:12, 16); and *confidence*, meaning both 'trust' and 'security'. And fourthly (18), there will be security of tenure. *Undisturbed* (*šaʾᵃnān*) and *secure* form an inclusio with verse 9, but it is more than a literary device. In verse 9 the words expressed the hollowness of mere human wishful thinking and confidence. In the new creation, all that lacked substance in life will be replaced by solid reality.

Epilogue: Blessedness beyond disaster (32:19–20). This matches the prologue (31:1–5), with its poetic expression of disaster and deliverance. We now look forward to what Isaiah describes as the fall of *forest* and *city* (19) and, beyond it, the peace and spaciousness of a new world (20). Both judgment and glory lie ahead, and now (31:6; 32:9) is the time to decide.

19. *Hail*: the verb occurs only here, but the noun occurred at 28:2, 17. The 'forces' of nature depict the advent of God, as a good example. *Cf.* Psalm 18:7–16, where what 1 Samuel 16 – 2 Samuel 1 depicts as a patient, unspectacular work of God in delivering David and bringing him to the throne is described in dramatic storm metaphors. The falling *forest* (*cf.* 6:13; 10:33–34) is the toppling of earth's powers. The levelling of the *city* (*cf.* 24:10; 25:1–5) is the termination of human organization of the world without God.

20. But there is blessedness for those who repent and hear God's voice (31:6; 32:9). This pastoral scene recalls the messianic picture of 30:23–26. *Blessed* (*ašrê*) has three shades of meaning: under divine blessing (Ps. 32:1), enjoying fulfilment of life (Ps. 112:1) and doing the right thing at the right time (Ps. 2:12; 137:8–9). All three meet in the messianic future: divine favour, personal fulfilment and total rectitude. *Sowing ... letting* is the life of those who enjoy home and tenure in such a place. *Every ... free*: there is no danger in this land. Crops can be sown anywhere without fear of marauders (Jdg. 6:3–6), and animals left to roam.

vi. The sixth woe: home at last (33:1 – 35:10). The balanced presentation of the six woes continues into this final one. First, the matching third woe (29:15–24) was wholly visionary and eschatological, as is also this one. Historical events can be read between the lines, but our eyes are held all the time by the undated future. Amongst many similarities between these two passages we may note the Lebanon theme (29:17; 33:9; 35:2), the blind and deaf (29:18; 35:5), redemption (29:22; 35:9–10) and spiritual transformation (29:24; 33:24; 35:8). The main thrust of the third woe was the transformation of the world and of 'Jacob', and both these lines are now further developed in typical Old Testament ways. Secondly, this sixth woe continues from the fifth. In brief, the royal theme (32:1) is developed in chapter 33; the allusion to disaster preceding the great dawn of light (32:19) is the 'text' for chapter 34, and the blessings in environment and life awaiting the Lord's people (32:15–18) are beautifully expressed in chapter 35. As a simple outline of the contents of these chapters we can consider 33:1–12 as a prologue, sketching the salvation of Zion (1–6) and the judgment of the peoples (7–12). Then there are two universal proclamations (33:13; 34:1), the first dealing with Zion and its king (33:13–24), and the second with the final overthrow (34:1–17); lastly, there is an epilogue: the pilgrimage of the redeemed through a renewed world to Zion (35:1–10).

Ultimate realities: salvation and wrath (33:1–12). In 30:27–33 Isaiah used the Lord's overthrow of Assyria as a preview of ultimate divine worldwide action (30:28). In the present passage Assyria is veiled behind the reference to *destroyer* and *traitor* (1), and judgment reaches out to *the peoples* (3, 12). But there is the same feeling of eleventh-hour rescue. The people of God struggle through one day at a time (2); there is a sense of despair within a dying world (7–9) followed by the dramatic threefold *now* (10).

1–6, *The salvation of Zion.* Salvation, eventually, will come to Zion.

1. *Destroyer ... traitor*: the background is Assyria's duplicity in seeming to accept Hezekiah's ransom-money (2 Ki. 18:13–18) and then continuing to attack Jerusalem as if no agreement had ever been reached. As in 21:2; 24:16, Isaiah sees this two-faced approach to moral issues as characteristic of the ongoing world to the End. *Not been destroyed*: Assyria in its own day, and all Assyria's successors in worldly power, have 'got away with it'. *Not been betrayed*: it was not the treacherous action of others which provoked a response of treachery; it was simply a matter of lack of moral scruple. *When you stop*: *i.e.* when your career of treachery has run its appointed course. *Be betrayed*: under divine rule the world is a system of exact moral retribution. The punishment will be what the crime merits.

2. *O LORD*: within a morally perverse world (1), the people of God live by heavenly resources sought through prayer. *Gracious*: see 30:18. *Long*, as in 30:18, should be 'wait' (√*qāwâ*) which combines the patience of waiting with the confidence of hope. It is the mark of the remnant (8:17; *cf.* 40:31). *Our strength*: lit. 'their arm'. The 'arm' is the organ of personal strength in action (52:10). Probably here we have a snatch from a liturgy actually used in Isaiah's time, in which the leader prayed, 'Be their arm every morning', and the assembly replied, 'Be our salvation in time of distress'. Instead of saying prosaically that every day (*morning*), and in response to trouble (*distress*), the Lord's people resort to prayer, Isaiah slipped in a little cameo of prayer actually happening (Acts 4:24ff.; 12:5).

3–4. The spotlight returns to the world. The praying people (2) express their confidence that the whole world is helpless before divine power (3ab) and will be utterly plundered (3cd). *Flee ... scatter* are perfects of certainty: 'sure to/doomed to'. *Rise up*: the seated Lord awaits his appointed moment (Heb. 10:12–13), and when it comes all he needs to do in the face of the massed powers of the world is to stand up. The battle (*plunder*) is over before it started (Rev. 19:19–20). *Men pounce*: the verb is a singular participle without any subject expressed – 'there is one pouncing'. If it refers to human activity it is an enthusiastic entering upon the victory the Lord has wrought, but it is more likely to refer to divine action bringing the victory to a total conclusion by taking the spoil (53:12).

5–6. Isaiah moves from the defeated world (3–4) to the coming *Zion*. The Lord rose up to battle (3). How will Zion fare when he is exalted? – for he does not change, *he dwells on high*, and it is the same transcendent God, who demolished the power (3) and stripped the spoil (4) of the nations, with whom they have to do. First (5b), he will act to make Zion what he promised it would be (1:26–27), just in practice, righteous in principle. Secondly (6a), he will himself be Zion's stability. In contrast to all the times ('*ēṭ*) of distress they had known (2), they will enter upon their true times ('*ēṭ*) of security. Thirdly (6b), the Lord will be his people's resource. *Store* (from √*ḥāsan*, 'to be strong') is practical resource for life. *Salvation* is here a plural of amplitude, hence NIV *rich*, a divine sufficiency for every emergent need. *Wisdom* caters for the practical understanding and management of life. *Knowledge* is knowledge of the truth as such, the result of 29:18. *The fear* …: literally 'the fear of the Lord, that is his treasure'. To whom does 'his' refer? Zion is feminine and Judah is not mentioned in the passage. It must, therefore, be the Lord. In 29:23 one of the blessings predicted was 'awe' before the Lord. To fear him with a true fear is not a human emotion worked up but a gift he gives to those whom he delights to bless.

7–12, World judgment. The moment for the Lord to rise up (3) has come (10).

7–9. The Assyrian crisis provides the backdrop to what is now a vision of world collapse before the Lord rising to judge. *Brave*: the military who gathered their forces to rebel against Assyria came belatedly to realize they had no hope (37:3), and where human strength failed, human wisdom was equally at a loss: *envoys* were sent (2 Ki. 18:14), but lived to weep over the duplicity which broke *the treaty*. But what thus happened in connection with Assyria is no more than a reflection of the End. Humankind's effort by strength and wisdom to organize the world without God will end in collapse, strength exhausted (7a), wisdom baffled (7b), the busy world hushed (8ab), moral values rubbished (8c). *Witnesses* (see NIV mg.) is 'cities'. In pursuit of world dominion Assyria left a trail of destruction. At the End, the determination to create world order, a world city (24:10) on human principles, will crash, and human life itself be discounted (8d). Finally (9) what started with the thorns of Genesis 3:18 will end with the withering of all nature. *Lebanon* typifies the permanent, what has always been; *Sharon*, the beautiful; *Bashan*, the fertile; and *Carmel*, the 'garden land', planned and ordered. *Withers* occurs only here and in a similar context in 19:6. It may mean 'to be infested (with lice)' – but here a pest so virulent that even Lebanon falls to it. This is what human sin does initially, progressively and permanently to the environment.

10–12. *Arise*: the Lord's arising (*cf.* 3) has two simultaneous consequences, the self-destructiveness of sin (11) and divine judgmental action in fire (12). *Conceive … give birth*: past decisions have inevitable outcomes; acts produce results (Gal. 6:7). Life without God is *chaff* producing *straw*, and the destructive agent is part of the same mechanism: *your breath*. Sinners are both the ultimate (*conceive*) and immediate (*fire*) cause of their own ruin. But the passive *be burned … set ablaze* points to another agent. *To lime* stresses the intensity of the blaze. *As if* should be omitted and 'in fire' added. 'Fire' is the holiness of God in its active hostility to sin and sinner. The tragedy of sin is that it turns life to straw; its danger is that it excites the wrath of God.

The first universal proclamation: the new Zion (33:13-24). Isaiah now brings us within the expected Zion. He has already dealt with the city in broad principle (5-6); now he describes its people and its king. The central verse of this section is 20, the city of peace; this is flanked by the presence of the King (17-19, 21-23); and the picture is completed by Zion's people (14-16, 24).

13, *The summons.* The opposites *far* and *near* express totality. In its worship Israel was often conscious of a worldwide dimension (Pss. 47:1; 96:3, 10; 98:4). This implied that what the Lord revealed of himself and what he had done, savingly, for his people, were also for the world (*cf.* 2:2-4). The world must hear *what I have done* (Acts 2:11). *Power* (*gᵉḇurâ*) is warrior power, power of accomplishment. But *hear* and *acknowledge* (lit. 'know') show that the world is not going to be won by a display of overwhelming force but by the persuasion of the truth.

14-16, *Zion's people (part 1).* First (14), the people are gripped by the seriousness of sin and the impossibility of sinners dwelling with the holy God. *Sinners* (*ḥaṭṭā'im*): see 1:28; 30:1. Sin is a falling short (Rom. 3:23). *Godless* means 'profane' (9:17; 10:6; 24:5; 32:6). It implies defaming the divine nature and dismissing God as negligible. *Burning* is translated 'altar hearth' in Leviticus 6:9 and therefore has the same significance as Ariel (29:1). There is always *fire* burning on the Lord's altar to proclaim the presence of the Holy One. This fire is a threat (*consuming*) and a changeless reality (*everlasting*). Dwell is the verb for temporary residence, as of a person who has no natural right to be there.

There are, however, entrance qualifications (15). This verse is what is called an 'entrance liturgy' (like Pss. 15; 24:3-6), *i.e.* a formal examination of someone desiring to enter the Lord's courts, in order to establish his right to do so. The sequence in Isaiah's poem is thoroughly biblical: before people can hear the word of forgiveness (24) they must face the rigour of God's law, for only those who meet the law's demands can enter the new Zion. The verbs throughout are singular: the demand is individual and, first, comprehensive: *walks* covers a person's whole outward lifestyle, characteristic behaviour; *righteously* (lit. 'in righteousnesses') is a plural of amplitude, righteousness in all its aspects and in all life. Secondly, there is straightforward truth in speech: *right* means 'straight'. Thirdly comes finance, with particular reference to how money is gained: *extortion*, refusal to subordinate people to profit; *bribes*, refusal to subordinate truth to profit. Fourthly, there is the mind: the *ears* receive what others say, the *eyes* look where the observer directs. They are both channels into the thought-life. *Plots of murder* is literally 'hearing of blood-guilt', which is listening either to what will bring guilt before God on the hearer, or to that which tells of guilt incurred by others. For the one who is thus righteous immense privileges open up (16): fellowship with the Lord, *i.e. dwell on the heights* (of Zion); security: *refuge* is 'top security', to be set on an inaccessible height; and provision (*bread* and *water*).

17–19, *Zion's King (part 1)*. Isaiah shows the King in his personal attractiveness (17a), his wide domain (17b) and the absence of the once dominant enemy (18) and of all evidence of foreign occupation (19). *Your eyes will see*: *i.e.* you will see for yourself. Alongside the exclusion of sinners (14) and the impossible demands of the law (15), how can there be any in the presence of the King to see his personal excellence (*beauty*; Ps. 45:2)? This is a question awaiting an answer. *The king* lacks the definite article in the Hebrew and, as in 32:1, exemplifies indefiniteness for the sake of emphasis. As the presence of the King is enjoyed, so also is the absence of former foes. The description of the officials is vague. *Chief officer* is 'one writing', *took the revenue* is 'one weighing', and *in charge* is again 'one writing'. Perhaps the first listed prisoners for deportation, the second registered the spoil, and the third made an inventory of buildings for demolition. But now they and their troops and all their unintelligible talk are in the past (*no more*). There is nothing to distract from the presence and contemplation of 'a king – you know who I mean!'

20, *The city of peace*. This is the beating heart of the poem. *Look* ($\sqrt{}$*ḥāzâ*) is the same verb as *see* in verse 17. In itself it is simply a verb of 'seeing' but here used of a fixed examination of the city, such as the beauty of the King himself would command. *Our festivals*: Zion is first a city of religious privilege and joyous fellowship with the Lord. The main festivals of the past were recollections of the exodus and of redemption (Dt. 16:1–17, note esp. 3, 12; Lv. 23:42–43). Thus the Zion to come is a redemption-centred city. *Peaceful*: 'untroubled' (32:9, 18). *Not be moved ... pulled up ... broken*: from its redemption centre Isaiah moves to the security of Zion: unthreatened from outside, with no need ever to move, and unthreatened by any weakness in itself (*ropes*, *stakes*). *Tent* looks back to the wilderness days, so often thought of as an ideal of walking with God (Je. 2:1–3), but here the tent pegs are never moved again, so pilgrimage is over and the travellers are home at last.

21–23, *Zion's King (part 2)*. Two thoughts alternate: the Lord in power (21a); much water, no shipping (21bcd); the Lord as king (22); helpless shipping, abundance of spoil (23). In the parallel verses (17–18) Isaiah introduced the King and his wide lands; here is the King and his wide seas. He is thus in principle the King of all. He is also the *Lord*, the divine King (9:6). *Mighty* (*'addîr*; Ps. 93:3) signifies absolute or dominant power. *Our* means 'belonging to us' or 'on our side'. *Streams* are 'Nile-canals', suggesting, as in Egypt, an endless water supply. *Galley ... mighty ship*: the passage might require that these are men-of-war, and that for all the abundance of water there is no sea-borne attack. But the wording is not explicit. *Mighty* is *'addîr*, as above, but it could intend 'able to dominate the seas'. In this case the thought is absence of commercial enterprise, pointing to the self-sufficiency of Zion. This suits the explanation offered in verse 22: we have the Lord; what more do we need! He is *judge*, sufficient in leadership, victory and government as were the judges of old; *lawgiver*, sufficient in day-to-day guidance; but, unlike the episodic judges of old, he is *king*, permanent in office and able to *save*. This last function is now explained in a telling picture of a crippled ship which nevertheless carries off an abundance of spoil (23). As a 'ship of state', Zion is helpless, yet this limping hulk takes the spoil! *Spoils ... plunder*: the battle is over and the victory has been won – surely by the Saviour King!

24, *Zion's people (part 2)*. In verses 13–16 Zion's people faced the impossible and helpless condition of sinners before the holy God and the demands of his law; yet in verse 17 there were those enjoying the personal sight of the king. This second view of Zion's people is an explanation without an explanation: the people in Zion are forgiven sinners, but we are not told here how their forgiveness came about or how the demands of the law were satisfied in their case. Yet where the former passage was 'the law's loud thunder', that thunder has now been hushed and the gospel takes over. In Zion there is neither sickness (*ill*) nor sin (*forgiven*). We can understand this as physical well-being along with spiritual well-being; or we can understand *ill* as figurative (like the lameness of 23; *cf.* 53:4; Ps. 107:17–20), *i.e.* the malady of sin is gone as is also its guilt. *Forgiven* (*nāśa'*): 'to lift up, bear, carry'. This usage derives from the sin-bearing 'scapegoat' (Lv. 16:21) on which were placed all Israel's iniquities, so that it might carry them off, never to be seen again. So here Isaiah simply says 'and as regards the people living in it, iniquity will be carried off'. *Iniquity* ('*āwôn*): see 1:4; 6:7.

The second universal proclamation: final judgment (34:1–17). This theme is exactly what one would expect at this point in the sixth woe. The prologue (33:1–12) introduced the topics of salvation (1–6) and judgment (7–12). The former was elaborated in the first universal proclamation (33:13–24); the latter is developed now.

1–10b, *The judgment is the Lord's.* Following the call to nations and peoples to listen (1), Isaiah announces the Lord's anger against earth and heaven (2–4), the Lord's sword falling on Edom (5–6d), the Lord's sacrifice in Edom (6e–7), and the Lord's vengeance on behalf of Zion (8–10b). In the Hebrew each of these divisions opens with 'For' and each announces its topic in matching words: the Lord 'has indignation' (2), 'has a sword' (6), 'has a sacrifice' (6e), 'has a day' (8).

1. Typically of the Bible, the summons to hear of coming judgment is not the Lord's first word to the world. The first summons was to hear of sin (33:14), the standard of the law of God (33:15) and the message of forgiveness (33:24). The world must hear what the Lord has done for Zion because the same salvation reaches out to the ends of the earth (Ps. 96 – 98). But should the 'gospel call' remain unheeded, the sanction of divine judgment remains and the world must hear that too.

In verses **2–4**, judgment proceeds from the nature of God (*angry*). If the Lord were not a holy God, and if his holiness were not a positive force against sin and sinners, there would be no need for salvation (Rom. 1:16–18). Earth (2–3) and heaven (4) alike are caught up in this final judgment: nations (2), individuals (3ab), the environment (3c), the cosmos (4).

2. Reintroduce the initial 'For'. This is the first explanation of the summons to the world. *Angry* (*qeṣep̄*): for the noun, *cf.* 54:8; 60:10; for the verb, 8:21; 47:6; 54:9; 57:16–17; *etc.* This is the sharp outbursting of anger. *Wrath* (*ḥēmâ*), 'heat', is its abiding animosity. *Totally destroy* is √*ḥāram*, which provides the noun 'harem', the place of segregation. In judgmental contexts this is the removal from further human contact of that which is so appalling that it must at once be consigned to God for his decision. The noun *ḥerem* occurs in verse 5 (*cf.* 11:15; Nu. 21:2; Jos. 2:10; 6:17–18). Finally, *slaughter* is the death due to sin and sinners.

3. *Their dead bodies*: God does certainly hate the sin and love the sinner, but if the sinners refuse the 'gospel call' they suffer the penalty of their sin and the distinction between sin and sinner breaks down. *Soaked*: literally 'melted' by a new and dreadful soil erosion through the torrential blood of the slain.

4. Here only the 'fabric' of the heavens (not the heavenly 'host', 24:21; 27:1) is mentioned. The whole cosmos has been infected with human sin. *Dissolved*: 'decayed', 'rotted', an internal corruption working destruction. *Rolled up*: the Lord determines when the story is finished and closes the book. The internal rotting is matched by the external decision to write 'Finished'. *Fall* ('fade') ... *withered* ... *shrivelled*: the inner forces of life are gone; also harvest-time has come and the harvest has been reaped.

5–6d. *Edom* is presented as a case in point. Even though Esau himself had no capacity for sustained animosity (Gn. 33:4–16), it was with him that relations with Jacob were soured (Gn. 27:41) and by the time of Numbers 20:14–21 hostility had become an established pattern. Saul made war on Edom (2 Sa. 14:47). David became the only king to subdue and annex Edom (2 Sa. 8:14; *cf.* 1 Ki. 11:15–16). Edom rebelled against Solomon (1 Ki. 11:1–17, 23–25) and was still rebelling a century later (2 Ki. 8:20). Fifty years further on, there was still fighting (2 Ki. 14:7, 10), and at the fall of Jerusalem the bitter hostility of Edom became notorious (Ps. 137:7; Ob. 10–14). Consequently Amos' accusation (1:11) of perpetual hatred is well founded. Jeremiah 49:7–22 shows that, even prior to Edom's behaviour at Jerusalem's fall, the idea of judgment on Edom was part of the prophetic worldview. Obadiah saw Edom as both a place and a symbol: meriting judgment in its own right but also picturing the judgment which would mark the Day of the Lord. He was not innovating: in Psalms 60:8; 83:6, Edom had already a symbolic place in the theme of hostility to Zion. Two factors make Edom specially fit to stand as a motif for the whole world in the final judgment: first, its ceaseless hostility to the Lord's people, and secondly the fact that it was only to David that it ever really succumbed. Thus Ezekiel, foreseeing the coming David (34:23), moves immediately to the conquest of Edom (35:1–15). Isaiah stands in this same tradition by following his forecast of the King (ch. 33) with the rout of Edom in the final judgment (*cf.* 11:14; 63:1–6). Recollecting 29:22 and the establishing of the family of Jacob, the overthrow of Edom/Esau makes the End the exact fulfilment of the beginning (Gn. 25:23). The purposes of God according to election stand. *Totally destroyed*: literally 'the people of my *ḥerem*' (see 2). *Fat ... blood* were the parts of the slaughtered beast that belonged only to God (Lv. 3:16–17; 7:23–

27). In judgment the Lord seeks what is peculiarly his, that to which he alone has a right.

6e–7. The hint of a sacrificial rite in 6a–c is now explicitly developed. *Bozrah*, twenty-seven miles south of the Dead Sea, was Edom's capital. *Sacrifice* was the appointed way in which the demands of the divine holiness had to be met. *Wild oxen* were not used in the sacrifices. Possibly therefore Isaiah is using animal metaphors for the important people and leaders of Edom.

8. *Vengeance*: the sacrifice required by divine holiness (6e–7) is also the exact requital human sin merits. *Zion's cause* adds a third divine motive to sacrifice and vengeance. Zion has a just cause against Edom, and it can be left to him to whom vengeance belongs.

9–10b round off this whole picture of judgment by noting, first, the blighted environment, substantiating the Bible's view that the greatest environmental threat is human sin, and, secondly, the perpetual result, *night and day … forever.* This thought forms a bridge into the second half of the section.

10c–17, *The judgment is in perpetuity.* Isaiah continues his development of God's judgment of the world.

10c–15. The opening words *from generation to generation* not only form a link with the preceding half of the poem (1–10b) but announce the theme of this second half. That this great judgment of God is for perpetuity is shown by the disappearance of humankind (10d–13) and the incoming of the beasts (14–15). The ordinary events of life (10d, *pass through*), and the special duties of life (12, *nobles*, *princes*) are things of the past, and in their place come wild creatures (11ab, 13cd) and weeds (13ab). All this happens by divine action (*God will stretch*). The *measuring line* is a picture of dividing up a land for new ownership, and the *plumb-line* depicts how what happens accords with what ought to be. *Chaos … desolation* are respectively *tōhû* and *bōhû*, the 'formless and empty' of Genesis 1:2; see 24:10. Before the ordering hand of God imposed beauty, purposefulness and design upon it, the created physical substrate of the world was meaningless, dark, uninhabitable, shapeless, empty (*cf.* Je. 4:23). It is this to which sin brings everything at the End. The End is a world without people or purpose, shape or meaning. The Lord imposes on a world of sinners that which they chose and achieved. The permanency affirmed in verse 10 is depicted in 14–15. The verses are bracketed by references to the animals and their mates, and the intermediate lines speak of *rest* and raising broods. It is all a cosy scene of settled and undisturbed domestic security. *Wild goats* may hint at the supposed 'goat-demon'

(13:21), and *night creatures* suggest *lîlît*, the 'night hag', but it is more probable that Isaiah gives the beasts emotive names to increase the sense of frightful change.

16–17. These verses are a final summons, with plural imperatives matching verse 1 and rounding off the presentation. We read of horrific coming judgment and, with our blurred understanding of holiness and diminished capacity for moral outrage, we incline to say, 'Surely not!' Just as much as Isaiah's hearers, we need this word of stern reminder that it will indeed be so. *Mate* recalls the same word in verse 15. *By measure* mirrors the metaphor of verse 11. It will be as stated! The sequence *mouth ... Spirit ... hand* guarantees that the event will correspond to the Lord's word, be implemented by his power, and come about through his direct personal touch. *In the scroll*: there is no other passage of Scripture to which appeal may be made. Are we, however, right to understand Isaiah to mean 'and read that ...', *i.e.* there are passages in Scripture supportive of what is asserted? Maybe we should translate the connective *kî* (overlooked in NIV) as 'and read, because ...' In this case, Isaiah is calling us to a searching acquaintance with God's written word, on the grounds that every smallest detail – down to the birds and beasts – comes from his mouth, will be implemented by his Spirit and applied by his hand.

Ultimate realities: pilgrims to Zion (35:1–10). In the matching third woe there was an understated reference to redemption (29:22). It is now the climax to the whole series, expressed in one of the most beautiful poems ever written. It is an exodus-based poem. Pilgrims through a desert land (1–2) find that their bleak environment changes for them – and exults to do so (2b)! The pilgrims themselves, however (3–4), are under oppression, just as the exodus people were, but they are summoned to fortitude in full confidence of divine salvation. In verses 5–7, they are once again in the desert but, this time, not only is it being transformed for their benefit (6c–7) but there is another transformation also: the pilgrims are renewed for their journey (5–6ab). Their salvation has been accomplished. Now a clear highway lies before them (8a), a raised causeway. It is only for the holy (8bc); it is unmistakably clear (8e) and free of danger (9). Thus, at length, the Lord's redeemed arrive with joy in Zion (10).

1–2, *New world, a promise to the pilgrims.* The exodus background to these verses is plain. When Israel set out from Egypt, the most unpromising places supported them (Ex. 15 – 17) and it was in the wilderness that they saw the glory of the Lord

(Ex. 16:10). To *be glad* we must add 'for/of them' as the Hebrew does.[1] These unnamed people reappear in verse 2e as *they*, in 8d as *those* (lit. 'them') and, finally, in 10b they are identified as the *redeemed* who come to Zion. Either their presence brings new life to the world ('glad of them'), or the world hastens to put on new beauty 'for them'. The former accords with Romans 8:19–21; the latter implies the removal of the curse and the restoration of that free bounty with which the Garden greeted the man and woman before the fall. Doubtless, in Exodus 17, the water which flowed for the Lord's people made the desert blossom momentarily, but Isaiah foresees the final pilgrims making their way through a glorified environment, in which 'Heaven above is softer blue,/Earth around is sweeter green;/Something lives in every hue,/Christless eyes have never seen.'[2] *Lebanon* represents the work of God, and not of man (Ps. 104:16); *Carmel* actually means 'garden-land', ordered cultivation; and *Sharon* (Song 2:1) provides a standard of beauty. All this transforms the former *desert ... wilderness*, but those who walk through it see more than the beauty of creation: they see the *glory* and *splendour* of the Creator. Nothing now hinders the full display of the glory of the Lord in the works of the Lord. His *glory* is his inherent worth; his *splendour* is his majesty and dignity seen outwardly.

3–7, *New life, salvation for the pilgrims.* The exodus pilgrims, looking ahead, did not see the blossoming, only the barrenness (Ex. 15:21). The blossoming came as they walked the pilgrim path.

3–4. It is for this reason that Isaiah now calls his pilgrims to *strengthen* their *hands. Hands* means strength for personal action (as we speak of 'putting our hands to the task'); *knees* suggests stability and persistence, the durability to stick with the pilgrimage; *hearts* need nourishing in those convictions that keep us going with mental, emotional and spiritual commitment. In this last matter especially we must minister encouragement to each other (*say ... 'Be strong, do not fear ...'; cf.* Heb. 10:24–25). But the great ground of encouragement is *your God.* Again, we may think of the darkest days in Egypt when one and another would recall the promise of God to Jacob, 'I myself will go down

---

[1] The verb 'will be glad' includes the suffix of the 3rd person plural masculine pronoun. Hebrew does, however, exemplify direct objects with transitive verbs (GKC 117x, e.g. 27:4; 35:9; Zc. 7:5), therefore 'be glad over them' is linguistically accurate. Theologically it links, as in Rom. 8:22, the liberation of creation with the revelation of the children of God.

[2] From G. W. Robinson, 'Loved with everlasting love'.

to Egypt with you, and I myself will surely bring you up again'
(Gn. 46:4, lit.), or the words of Joseph, 'God will surely visit you
and bring you up out of this land' (Gn. 50:24, lit.). *Vengeance*
(*nāqām*, 34:8) takes account of the wrong suffered by his people;
retribution (*g^{e}mûl*) repays the wrong done to his people.
Vengeance and *retribution* are what he will do to his adversaries;
but for his people he will work salvation.

5–7. Verses 5 and 6 both begin with an emphatic *Then.* They
refer to the work of divine salvation (4f). God's work of salvation
will make his people new (5–6ab). The weaknesses of the present
(3–4ab) will be transformed into new abilities. The contrast
between two faculties of reception (*eyes, ears*) and two of action
(*leap, shout for joy*) is meant to express totality. On *eyes* and
ears, see 29:11–12, 18; 30:20–21; 32:3. *Water* is preceded by
'For'. The renewal of life in nature explains as well as illustrates
what has happened to the saved. Only God can bring about such
transformation (*water … in the wilderness*), such reversals
(*burning* and *thirsty … pool* and *springs*; *i.e.* places that absorbed
moisture now retain and provide it), and such restorations
(*jackals* – the inhabitants of inhospitable areas – go and their
former haunts become *grass, reeds* and *papyrus*): this is the
opposite of the incoming beasts as the sign that human habitation
is over (34:14–15).

8–10, *New highway, homecoming for pilgrims.* **8–9c.** *Highway* is exactly what it says: a causeway raised above the
surrounding countryside so that it is unmistakable. *The Way of
Holiness*: this is obviously a seriously-meant requirement, for *the
unclean* cannot travel it. This is the equivalent of the 'law of
God' passage in 33:14–16. The Lord never reduces his standards
to match the weaknesses of his people; he raises his people to the
height of his standards. How this will happen Isaiah does not say;
he simply leaves us to assume that such meeting of the
requirements of the law is achieved for the Lord's people by his
work of salvation (4f) and redemption (9d, 10a), for *the redeemed
will walk there*! *Unclean* (*ṭāmē'*) refers to impurities catered for
by the sacrifices. Those disqualified from walking *the Way of
Holiness* are therefore self-disqualified through failure to use the
means of grace available to them. *Those* is 'them', see on verse 1.
Fools ('^{e}wîlîm) are the 'gormless', those who will inevitably get
it wrong even if not given half a chance, those who lack steady,
guiding principles. The intention here is to emphasize that
certainty of arriving at the destination is not dependent on human
ability or 'nous'. The assurance of final salvation is inherent
in the initial work of salvation (4f) with its consequence of

radically overcoming human frailties (5–6ab). This thought is continued in the reference (*no lion*) to the absence of any external threat such as would stop the pilgrim from reaching the end of the road.

9d–10. *Redeemed ... ransomed*: the verb 'to redeem' makes its first appearance in Isaiah here.[1] √*gā'al* stresses the person of the redeemer, his relationship to the redeemed, and his intervention on their behalf. The participle, *gō'ēl*, is the technical term for the next-of-kin who has the right to take his helpless relative's needs as if they were his own (Lv. 25:25; Nu. 5:8); *gō'ēl* is often translated 'avenger', the one whose right it is to pursue the murderer of his next-of-kin. This dramatically indicates the essentially substitutionary nature of the relationship – the one being dead, the other acting in his place (Nu. 35:12; Dt. 19:6). The place of the *gō'ēl* was something no other dare usurp (Ru. 3:12; 4:1–6). It was, however, a right rather than an inalienable duty. It speaks here, therefore, of the Lord as the only one who can redeem his people; it is his inalienable right; it is he who identifies with them as their Next-of-Kin, taking their needs as if his own, the Mighty in the place of the helpless, paying their price (Lv. 27:13, 19, 31). On *pādâ* ('to ransom'), see 1:27. *They will enter*: travelling (8–9) gives way to arriving (10b). *Gladness ... will overtake them* (10c) or 'they will overtake gladness ...', as if all their lives they were reaching after a true happiness which they never quite reached. Either way, at last the people of the Lord and the joy of the Lord are united. *Sorrow and sighing* are the negative counterparts of *gladness and joy*. Their exit leaves *joy* in sole possession of the city and its happy band of pilgrims.

b. Epilogue: the rock of history (36:1 – 37:38)

These chapters are a historical narrative matching 2 Kings 18 – 19.[2] Isaiah cuts into the story at 2 Kings 18:13–16. The Assyrian

---

[1] *Cf.* 35:9; 41:14; 43:1, 14; 44:6, 22–24; 47:4; 48:17, 20; 49:7, 26; 51:10; 52:3, 9; 54:5, 8; 59:20; 60:16; 62:12; 63:4, 9, 16.

[2] Did Isaiah take this passage from an original in 2 Ki. 18:13 – 20:21 (as the majority of specialists seem to hold), or did the Kings historian take it from Isaiah (Oswalt, *The Book of Isaiah 1 – 39*; Young, *Studies in Isaiah*), or did both adapt it for their purposes from an original (J. Wilderberger, *Jesaja*, Neukirchner Verlag, 1982)? (a) If the Kings historian composed it, why is it unique in his book? Apart from 2 Ki. 14:25 it would be the only reference to a writing prophet by name and the only extended quotation of a prophetic oracle. Such an innovation would require explanation. It is most comparable to the Elijah-Elisha cycle, and most would agree that Kings derived this from an independent source. (b) If the material is original to Kings, why are the two incidents (36 – 37, 38 – 39) out of

king had apparently accepted Hezekiah's submission and a monetary satisfaction, but immediately renewed his pressure on Jerusalem. This is the 'treachery' referred to in 21:2; 24:16; 33:1. In Isaiah's narrative the scene is thus set for a straight clash between two kings: the 'great' king of the earth (36:4) and the beleaguered Davidic King in the city of promise (28:16). There is important background in Isaiah which makes this single incident of crucial significance. (a) In 14:24–27, the first 'interim fulfilment' within chapters 13 – 27, Isaiah alerted his hearers to watch out for the crushing of 'the Assyrian in my land' (14:25). This is what the Lord has 'planned' and 'it will stand' (14:24), but it is also part of the Lord's purpose for 'the whole world' (14:26), that is to say, a case in point of his universal sovereign sway. The emphases 'it will stand' (14:24) and 'who can thwart him?' (14:27) make this a point at which (if we may say so) the Lord cannot afford to fail. (b) The purpose of the cosmic panorama of chapters 13 – 27 was to display the dimensions of the kingdom of the coming King of David's line (9:6, 7; 11:1–16). Isaiah used the world map of his day and – as in 19:24–25 and 27:13 – made Egypt and Assyria symbols of the Lord's determination and power to make all nations his empire. (c) The series of six 'woes' in chapters 28 – 35 were historically concentrated on a situation in the last years of the eighth century BC, in which these very nations, the Davidic kingdom, Egypt and Assyria, were embroiled with one another. Now is the time, if ever, for the Lord to demonstrate his mastery of history! In this way, the present chapters put the rock of history under the fabric of eschatology.

---

chronological order? There would be no justification for this in the Kings narrative. (c) The two accounts are far from identical and, in their differences, there is no consistency of practice. The major Isaianic addition (Hezekiah's prayer) is consistent with the claim (2 Ch. 32:32) that Isaiah wrote an account of Hezekiah's reign. (d) It is best to think of Isaiah and Kings as both having access to court records. This would explain, for example, why Kings (18:14–16) includes and Isaiah omits Hezekiah's submission – the former aiming at completeness of detail, the latter at history wedded to a theological purpose. Or again, the abbreviated account of Hezekiah's illness and the addition of Is. 38:9–20 reflects the prophet's unwillingness to call attention to himself when his purpose is to stir faith in the Lord, and also reflects his privileged access to Hezekiah's private papers. (e) Only Isaiah would have an interest in, and a justification for, the reversed chronology, using the Sennacherib narrative as the crown to chs. 12 – 39 and the Merodach-Baladan fiasco as the perfect introduction to chs. 40ff. Though for the most part the evidence of Kings and Isaiah suggests independent access to existing records, the reversed chronology indicates that the Isaiah account was well established by the time of the Kings historian.

i. The first Assyrian embassy: the helpless king (36:1 – 37:7). Sennacherib acceded as Assyrian king in 705 BC and was greeted by uprisings throughout his conglomerate empire. The most serious was that of Merodach-Baladan in Babylon, and it took two years to quell his revolt. Then the king turned on his western rebels, among whom was Hezekiah (2 Ki. 18:7; *cf.* Is. 38:1). According to Sennacherib forty-six Judean cities fell and their people were deported. In the light of this collapse of his armed rebellion, Hezekiah sought terms (2 Ki. 18:13–16). Isaiah does not bother to record all this: he wants to bring us straight to the point where he can demonstrate the effectiveness of faith, not the results of faithlessness.

The first Assyrian speech: no salvation in faith (36:1–10). **1.** Since Sennacherib's attack took place in 701 BC, *the fourteenth year* would date Hezekiah's accession in 715. This conflicts with 2 Kings 18:1, 9, which dates his accession in 729/8. Some would therefore make a slight emendation in the Hebrew text here to read 'twenty-fourth'. But both 2 Kings 18:13 and Isaiah 36:1 seem quite clear that the *fourteenth year* was the date of Sennacherib's arrival in Judah. Others appeal to a theory of co-regency. Davidic kingship did not operate on the principle of primogeniture. David, for example, was expected to nominate his successor (1 Ki. 1:5–30). Supposing therefore that Ahaz, Hezekiah and Manasseh all had periods of co-regency with their predecessors as well as periods of sole reign, then perhaps Hezekiah was co-regent with his father in 729–715 and sole king in 715–696, when he took Manasseh into a co-regency lasting till 687. With a modicum of speculation this would harmonize the dates as we have received them.[1]

2–3. *Field commander* is the Rab-shakeh, an Assyrian title, possibly originally 'chief cup-bearer' but by this time some high officer of state. *Lachish*: thirty miles south-west of Jerusalem. A pit has been unearthed with remains of about fifteen hundred casualties of Sennacherib's attack. By this time Sennacherib had defeated the Tyrian and Philistine rebels, and the Egyptian army (on its one intervention) at El Tekeh, north of Lachish. Hezekiah was now isolated. Politically there was no reason why Sennacherib should return home without dealing with the last rebel state. To this extent his cynical acceptance of Hezekiah's gold was typical of the amoral element in politics: it lessened Hezekiah's capacity to buy allies and therefore further exposed him to

[1] See H. H. Rowley, *Men of God* (Nelson, 1963), pp. 98ff.; K. A. Kitchen and T. C. Mitchell, 'Old Testament Chronology', in *NBD*.

Assyrian might. *The aqueduct* where the various officials met the Rab-shakeh was the very place (7:3) where Ahaz had refused the way of faith; Hezekiah is about to reap the harvest of unbelief.

In verses **4–10** the Rab-shakeh's speech has four themes: Egypt is no hope (4–7); trusting the Lord is no longer an option, for he has been alienated (7; 2 Ki. 18:4); Hezekiah has no man power (8–9); and Assyria is backed by divine authorization (10).

4–5. *The great king* was a title the Assyrian kings commonly used. *This confidence* refers to Hezekiah's boldness in raising a rebellion. *You say* follows the reading in Q^a and 2 Kings 18:20. The Isaiah text has 'I say', namely the Rab-shakeh's own opinion that Hezekiah's rebellion is based neither on wise planning (*strategy*) nor on military capacity (*$g^e\underline{b}ûrâ$*, see 30:15). Isaiah had said (28:9 11) that if they refused his plain message they would hear the same words from foreigners. Here are his very words: confidence, rely, trust and power.

6. *Egypt* had made its one attempt to redeem its promises (28:14) and its army had been beaten at El Tekeh. The Rab-shakeh had himself seen this, but his words are more far-reaching and damaging, exposing the criminal stupidity of Judah's leaders: surely, he said, they knew that anyone who ever trusted Egypt suffered for it, confirming Isaiah's assessment that to ally with Egypt is to sign one's own death warrant (28:15).

7–9. Hezekiah had centralized religious observance (2 Ki. 18:1–7; 2 Ch. 29 – 31). The closure of country sanctuaries (however correct) would not have passed without opposition and criticism. The Rab-shakeh knew how to play on the nerve-ends of any who were less than convinced by what the king was doing. He then tries to bargain with *horses* (8), which were always in short supply in Israel.

10. It would seem that behind this statement there must lie some knowledge of what Isaiah had been saying (*e.g.* 10:5–6). Spies are not a modern invention. *This land*: the account in 2 Kings 18:25 reads 'this place'. This difference is inexplicable if the Isaiah-account is dependent on Kings. Isaiah's deep Zion-centred theology would never have permitted 'place' to become *land*.

The second Assyrian speech: a popular appeal for peace (36:11–21). The Rab-shakeh ignores the politicians and goes straight to the people, reminding them (12) that rulers declare war but citizens suffer it. It is an understandable ploy to advise against trusting Hezekiah or the Lord (14–15); it is a plausible move to offer a new home instead of the horrors of a siege (16–17), but the Rab-shakeh made his cardinal error in equating the

Lord with other gods and in scorning his power to save (18–20).

11–12. *Aramaic* was the language of the diplomatic service, but the Rab-shakeh sweeps it aside and addresses the ordinary people, *the men sitting on the wall*, literally 'the inhabitants on the wall'. *Like you* should be 'with you', implying 'as long as they maintain their insane attachment to you and your policies'. In one sentence he would scare the citizens and alienate them from their leadership.

13–17. He was well informed, seemingly, about Isaiah's ministry and the emphasis on the way of faith, for why else should denial of the viability of trust figure so prominently in his argument. *Trust* is the vocabulary of Isaiah (30:15); *deliver* is the promise made to Hezekiah (38:6ff.). The Rab-shakeh was pressing for a quick solution. 37:9 shows that Sennacherib did not want a long war in western Palestine – maybe his position at home was not as yet totally secure. He makes his offer sound as attractive as possible: an unmolested present (16) and an agreeable future (17). He cannot hide the well-known Assyrian policy of deportation, but he does his best to sweeten the pill.

18–21. Here comes the fatal error, the word of blasphemy which the Lord heard (37:7). *Hamath* ... *Arpad*, see 10:9; *Sepharvaim* is of unknown location.

The king's reaction: faith at last! (36:22 – 37:7). The king reacts at once with penitence and turning to the Lord (1). A deputation is sent to Isaiah (2) eating humble pie (3), noting the element of blasphemy and asking prayer (4). Isaiah, however, does not pray nor make any new approach to the Lord: the word of the Lord, once given, stands (5–6): the Lord will remove both threat and threatener (7).

1. We are not told what transpired between Hezekiah and the Lord on this occasion. We are told only *how* he went – with the torn clothes and *sackcloth* of penitence, and *that* he went to the 'house' of the Lord, the place where the Lord lived among his people and is always to be found.

2–4. The implication is that what the deputation was to say to the prophet expressed the essence of what Hezekiah would say to the Lord. First, there was admission of failure (3). *Distress* is the fact of adversity; *rebuke* acknowledges that the trouble was merited; *disgrace* notes the public shame which followed; and *children* ... *deliver* is the frustration of all that was planned, helplessness to accomplish. Hezekiah's sackcloth (1) was not an unreal show! Furthermore, when Hezekiah goes on to plead for help he bases nothing on his own needs. It is as though he is so ashamed and so aware of failure and helplessness that he rules himself out of the picture, for, secondly, there is the Lord's honour (4). *The living God* is a striking example of the idiom of indefiniteness for the sake of emphasis: 'a living God'. The indefinite article throws all emphasis forward on to the adjective. The Rab-shakeh has enumerated the idol-gods of the heathen and of Samaria (36:18–20), but here is a God belonging to a different category of being, 'a *living* God'. Will not the Lord now stand by his own dignity (*cf.* Nu. 14:11–16; Dt. 9:28; Jos. 7:8–9)? Thirdly, Hezekiah mentions the needs of the Lord's people (4), *the remnant that still survives*, or 'that happens to be here'. City after city has fallen to Sennacherib and long lines of deportees are already snaking their bitter way into exile – and it is all Hezekiah's fault! He followed the lunatic policy of rebellion and was bewitched by Egyptian promises. He might as well have sold his people himself. But even when a matter is our own fault we can still pray about it. And the Lord can always be trusted to pity his people (*cf.* Nu. 14:17–20).

5–7. Hezekiah's officials came to ask Isaiah to pray (4), ever one of the functions of a prophet (Gn. 20:7; 1 Sa. 7:5; Je. 11:14; 14:11), but he neither prayed nor sought the Lord. He took for granted that what the Lord had already said he meant (Nu. 23:19). Therefore he can respond at once with a word of assurance (6) and a promise of action (7). *Underlings*: a deliberately belittling expression, 'the king of Assyria's lads/flunkies'. How Isaiah must have delighted to cut the Rab-shakeh and the king of Assyria's other officials (2 Ki. 18:17) down to size! What pomposity of title and verbiage – and what were they but boys at the beck and call of Sennacherib! *I am going to put ... cut down ...* : here is real sovereignty – and over the mightiest powers on earth at the time. *Spirit*: *cf.* 19:14; 29:10 (1 Ki. 22:21–23; 2 Thes. 2:11; Rev. 17:17). Those who merit delusion are visited with error. *Report*: see verse 9 below. The Lord is sovereign in Egypt as well.

i. The second Assyrian embassy: the godly king (37:8–35). We learn here of the withdrawal of the Rab-shakeh from Jerusalem and Sennacherib's letter to Hezekiah (8–9), the letter itself (10–13), Hezekiah's reaction (14–20) and Isaiah's reaction (21–35). The crisis continued, but was resolved, on the human level, by prayer and the word of God.

8–9. Did Hezekiah reply to the Rab-shakeh's speech? Maybe we can find the germs of a reply between the lines of verses 10–13. But however this may be, the Rab-shakeh heard of the royal move from *Lachish* to *Libnah*, ten miles north. This was itself occasioned by a *report* the king heard that Egypt was again on the march, and the northward move must surely indicate that, in the face of a lengthening Palestine campaign, Sennacherib thought it best to begin to withdraw homewards. *Tirhakah*, here called 'king of Cush', was the sixth Pharaoh in the twenty-fifth, 'Ethiopian', Dynasty in Egypt.[1] In 701 BC he would have been twenty years of age, and he acceded to the Egyptian throne in 690. If NIV is correct in introducing a reference to *King of Egypt* here, it will be a proleptic attribution of the title by which Tirhakah was later and better known. The likelihood of an Egyptian intervention after the battle of El Tekeh was small, though obviously, from Sennacherib's reaction, not impossible, but in any event the rumour was divinely inspired. The Lord of history knows when a whispered word is enough for (as the old prayer says) 'the hearts of kings are in his rule and governance'.

Hezekiah, man of faith (37:10–13). Hezekiah is a different man. As recounted by the Rab-shakeh in 36:6–7, he had been keeping his powder dry and trusting the Lord (in that order), but here there is no reference to Egypt, only to (lit.) 'your god on whom you are trusting' (10). Whether or not we can therefore say that Hezekiah had replied to the Rab-shakeh in terms of simple trust, that is where he is now seen to stand: a man with a personal and unequivocal faith. Sennacherib addressed Hezekiah both verbally (9b, lit. 'messengers to say') and in a letter (14). He attacked his faith (10), asserted the invincibility of Assyria before nations (11) and gods (12), and hinted at a particular risk to kings in opposing him (13). It seems clear that Hezekiah was at last taking seriously the divine promise of deliverance from Assyria (38:6) and had staked his all on this promise by saying to Assyria, '*Jerusalem will not be handed over* ...'(10).

11–13. *Destroying ... completely* (√*hāram*): see 34:2, 5. The word is used of removing something from human contact and consigning it to God's possession – or, in Sennacherib's case, to the possession of his god. This is the spiritual contest now in hand: can the city of God be consigned to a god? *Gozan* ...: all these places are in the Upper Euphrates area, the far north of Palestine. Sennacherib tries to play on Hezekiah's nerves as *king* but actually, without knowing it, he is testing the man of faith in another direction. Hezekiah is heir of the Davidic promises. Will he trust the promises that guarantee him as king against the

---

[1] K. A. Kitchen, *The Third Intermediate Period in Egypt* (Warminster, 1973), pp. 154ff., 387ff., and *Ancient Orient and Old Testament* (Tyndale Press, 1966), pp. 82ff.

threats made to him as king? *Hamath* ... , see 36:19; *Hena and Ivvah* are unknown.

Hezekiah, man of prayer (37:14–20). In verses 1–4 Hezekiah tore his clothes and asked Isaiah to pray. Now there is no tearing of clothes and he does his own praying! He knows his way about in the country of faith. First he commits all to God (14), and then turns to petition (15–20).

14. It would seem that Hezekiah simply read the letter, presumably said 'thank you and goodbye' to the messengers, and went off to the Lord's house. 'What did he say?', Sennacherib will ask them and they will reply, 'Well ... er ... nothing.' Isaiah said truly that he who believes will not panic (28:16; *cf.* 7:9).

Verses **15–20** contain Hezekiah's prayer and, as with all Bible prayers (*e.g.* Ne. 9; Dn. 9; Acts 4:24–31), this prayer is preoccupied with God: who he is (16), his honour (17), his uniqueness (18–19) and the revelation of his glory in the world (20).

16–17. The substance of the prayer is not its petitionary content but its acknowledgment of God. He is omnipotent in his own person as LORD *Almighty* ('Lord of hosts') and omnipotent in creation as Maker of *heaven and earth;* he is *God of Israel* and *God over all the kingdoms*; and, at the centre of verse 16, he is *enthroned between the cherubim.* These heavenly creatures were set at each end of the mercy-seat (Ex. 37:6–9). They formed the pedestal of the invisible throne of the Lord (Ezk. 1:22–28). The feet of the enthroned Lord rested on the mercy-seat (Pss. 99:1–5; 132:7). As Ezekiel saw them, the cherubim represented all creaturely excellence: the lion chief among wild beasts, the ox among domestic beasts, the eagle among the birds and man as excellent above all. But this Lord of all is actually present at the heart of his people's life, enthroned and yet touching them at the point of mercy. *Living God* (17) conveys indefiniteness for the sake of emphasis, see verse 4.

18–20. *Only wood*: pagan worshippers would, of course, have looked beyond the material representation of their gods to the spiritual force they considered it to represent, but the Old Testament always coolly identifies god and idol. Its monotheism was so rigorous that it refused to acknowledge any reality beyond the material (*cf.* 41:5–7). *You alone, O LORD, are God*: NIV adapts the Isaiah text to that of 2 Kings 19:19. In Isaiah, however, Hezekiah simply says, 'You alone are Yahweh.' Just as he identifies the heathen god with its idol, so in reverse he makes the name of his God, Yahweh, equivalent to the noun 'God': to say 'Yahweh' is to say 'God'. It both declares Yahweh alone to be God, and also identifies this only God with Yahweh who saves his people and overthrows their foes (as once he did, definitively, in Egypt).

Isaiah's message: Hezekiah, the man of the word of God (37:21–35). In 36:5 Hezekiah received a word of the Lord in response to his request for Isaiah's prayer; here he receives a word without asking. His commitment to the way of faith opens the door for him to speak to God (14–20) and for God to speak to him (21–35). These two things belong together: *Because you have prayed ... this is the word the* LORD *has spoken* (21–22). The oracle that follows tells that the whole problem is solved. Thus the way of believing prayer is the truly practical way of dealing with the harsh realities of life in this world. What neither armaments (36:9) nor diplomacy (30:1–2) nor money (2 Ki. 18:13–14) could do, prayer has done. But what the Lord is about to do he had already planned of old (26–29). Here is a mystery of prayer: it is a way the Lord brings his eternal counsels to pass. He performs foreordained purposes in answer to the prayers of his people (*cf.* Mal. 3:1 with Lk. 1:13, 17). Isaiah's oracle begins with the fact that prayer was answered by the departure of the Assyrians (22) and ends (33–35) with the explanation of this fact, the Lord's defence of his city. Within these brackets, verses 23–25 show two 'sovereigns' in conflict; 26–29 assert the sovereignty of the God who directs history; and 30–32 testify to the faithfulness of that sovereign God to his promises.

21–22, *The prayer-answering God. Virgin* is used here in the sense of being untouched by the marauder. The Assyrian came intent on rape but his victim remains unharmed *because you have prayed.*

23–25, *The holy Sovereign.* The king of Assyria has exalted himself as lord of heaven (23, 24ab) and of earth (24c–25).

Raised ... lifted are the verbs of divine exaltation in 6:1 and doubtless deliberately used here for that reason. The king has been a preview of 'the man of sin' (2 Thes. 2:4). In particular he has challenged, first, the holiness of the Lord, that is, his distinctiveness as God; secondly, his particular commitment to be Israel's God (23d); and, thirdly, his actual sovereignty as *Lord* ('*ᵃdōnāy*, 24b). Alongside this he has registered a personal claim to earthly power (24d) and to dominion over the earth in its *heights* (24e–h), its remote recesses (24ij), its resources (25ab) and its peoples (25cd). *I have dried* may be a sidelong glance at the victory at El Tekeh or it may be a perfect of certainty: 'I am determined to'. *With the soles*: the Egyptian farmer ran water from the Nile through small irrigation channels into his fields. He could block the flow simply by making a little heap of soil with his foot. The king's foot is equal to blocking the Nile itself!

26–29, *The executive Sovereign.* Divine sovereignty is absolute over the course of history (26a–d), over fortified strength (26ef), over people (27) and over kings (28–29).

26. *Ordained*: literally 'did', a perfect of certainty: so settled was the plan that it could be spoken of as already accomplished. *Planned* is the potter's verb √*yāṣar*, 'to mould, shape'. *Brought it to pass*: the plan as conceived in the divine mind (26ab) and moulded by his hands on the wheel of historical events (26c) is precisely what happened at the end (26d). The facts of human history are the plan of God (45:7; Am. 3:4–7; 4:6–11). *Cities* symbolize humankind's attempt to achieve security and community, to organize the world without recourse to God (*cf.* 24:10; Gn. 11:1–9), but, as in Genesis 3, not even supreme efforts to throw off the 'yoke' of God alter his sovereignty one whit. The *you* who did it is the Assyrian king; but the plan (26ab), the procedure (26c) and the agency (26d) are the Lord's.

27. To the Assyrian king people were only *plants in the field*, not persons but a crop to be reaped for self-advantage; *tender ... shoots*, helpless under the Assyrian boot; *grass sprouting*, of no more ultimate significance than weeds. The world of power-politics is a sad place for people to live in. Imperial glory is always at the expense of the rank and file. But even here the eye of faith is taught to acknowledge that a sovereign God is at work, achieving pre-planned purposes, holy, moral and just in all his ways (10:5–15).

28–29. Not even Sennacherib is outside divine sovereign management! His life (28ab) and thoughts (28c) are known, and it is these inner factors that in particular invite and excite divine punitive reaction (29ab). *Rage* (√*rāḡaz*): to be in agitation (*cf.* Ps. 2:1). *Insolence*: 'complacency' (as in 32:9, 18), here the king's bland assumption of omni-competence. *My hook* is cruelly apt for, according to the monuments, this is the way Assyria led its captives away. As they did, so it shall be done to them: that is the way the world is under God. *My bit* is Isaiah's very apt illustration of the relation between the sovereignty of God and the real power of sinful emperors: all the energy, brute strength, even violence, belong to the horse; all the wisdom, direction, purposefulness, the guiding touch, belong to the rider (*cf.* 10:5–15). *Return by the way you came*: this is the absoluteness of divine sovereign direction. The king came on the Lord's errand and he is limited to that; he cannot take a step out of that way. Divine sovereign rule is not just the broad sweep and general thrust of things; it is the detail, the fine print of history.

30–32, *The faithful sovereign.* In case anyone should think that the Assyrian destruction and withdrawal were just happy chance, Isaiah adds a *sign*, a visible token that it was the Lord at work. For two years, owing to the Assyrian invasion, agriculture was impossible, yet the land would, of itself, produce enough until in the *third year* normal tillage could be resumed.

30. *Grows by itself* (*sāpîah*): see Leviticus 25:5, 11. *What springs* (*šāhîs*) is found only here and in 2 Kings 19:29, and seems to mean self-set seed (*e.g.* just as in a garden potato crop some small potatoes remain undug and 'set themselves' to grow the following year). The invasion prevented sowing in 702 BC, but when the threat lifted in 701 they would find sufficient growth to preserve life; in 701 the withdrawing Assyrians still inhibited agriculture, yet in 700 there would still be enough through 'chance growth'. Thus the Lord would confirm retrospectively that it was his hand that dispersed the threat. *Vineyards*: viticulture needed years of patient care (5:2; 7:25; Lv. 19:23–25; Dt. 20:6). Zechariah 8:12 calls the vine 'the seed of peace', because it required conditions of peace to come to fruitage.

31. This vitality in nature pictures the vitality of the people who will enter a time of security (*take root*) and prosperity (*bear fruit*). How gracious is the moral sovereignty of the Lord! Isaiah knew the nation was doomed even before Assyria attacked (22:14; 31:6) yet, belatedly, Hezekiah repented (36:1) and believed (37:10), and the Lord would not let this go unrewarded (*cf.* 1 Ki. 21:27ff.).

32. *Remnant*: the word always looks beyond immediate experiences to the fact that the Lord will always preserve a people for himself. His *zeal* – his wholehearted commitment – will see to this, and his sovereign power as *the LORD Almighty*, Yahweh of hosts, will guarantee it.

33–35, ***The preserving God.*** Sennacherib will neither approach (*enter* is 'come to'), nor threaten either from a distance (*arrow*) or at close quarters (*shield, ramp*). He is hemmed in to the divinely imposed path and will *return* as he *came*. He is under the Lord's control; the city is under the Lord's care. Thus what 38:6 offers as a promise and 37:21–22 sees as an answer to prayer is here a divine decision based on motives interior to the divine nature (*for my sake*) and on long-standing covenantal undertakings (*for ... David*).

iii. The finale: Assyrian overthrow (37:36–38). Isaiah foretold the breaking of Assyrian power in Judah (14:24–27) and this is how it happened. Light on the event from outside the Bible is sparse, for it was not the Assyrian way to record disasters. All we know is that a divine act of massive proportions, performed with consummate ease, settled the issue and provided a crowning proof of Isaiah's contention that the Lord is master of history and that the way of faith is effective in the affairs of this life.

36. *The angel of the LORD*: it would better reflect the rest of the Old Testament if this were printed 'the Angel of the LORD', for among many angels there is one special personage. He is the Lord, and yet he is distinct from the Lord (Gn. 16:7, 11; Jdg. 13:21–22); and he combines in himself divine holiness and divine condescension (Ex. 23:20–23). (*Cf.* Gn. 22:11ff.; Ex. 3:2ff.; Jdg. 2:1ff.; 13:2ff.; Is. 63:8–9; Ezk. 44:2; Ho. 12:4 [*cf.* Gn. 32:24ff.]; Zc. 1 – 6 [*cf.* 1:12–13 with 3:6–10]; Mal. 3:1.) Isaiah, then, brings together five major divine manifestations: the word (31:2), the Spirit (30:1; 31:3; 37:7), the hand (31:3), the arm (30:30) and the angel. The Lord is 'the Lord of hosts'.

37–38. *Sennacherib ... returned*: although he reigned for another twenty years, he never again campaigned in Palestine: that road was closed to him. He was assassinated in 681 – and maybe Isaiah lived to see this final stroke and to note the distinction between 'a living God' who hears prayer and in whose house king Hezekiah began to find his true security, and a god of wood and stone in whose house king Sennacherib met his death (38). *Addrammelech* is mentioned outside the Bible as Ardamulissi. The Babylonian Chronicle records the assassination of Sennacherib and the accession of Esarhaddon.

THE BOOK OF THE SERVANT (38 – 55)

V. HEZEKIAH AND THE WAY OF FAITH:
THE DECISIVE SIN (38 – 39)

We are never allowed to know in advance the full significance of our decisions, and sometimes the simplest acts are discovered by hindsight to have had, for good or ill, the most far-reaching consequences. In 1 Samuel 14 Jonathan's individual assault on a Philistine outpost (1) issued in a local victory (14), spreading panic among the Philistines (15), the break-up of the invading armies (16), the restoration of compromisers (21), the return of exiles (22) and a resounding feat of arms (31) which (30) could have been even more decisive. Of this Jonathan knew nothing in advance. Or again, David lightly committed adultery with Bathsheba (2 Sa. 11:3–4) and in a chilling 'Mr Fixit' spirit set about covering his tracks (6–24). Did he know in advance that this one act would lead to rape and murder within his family (13:14, 28), the exile and subsequent rebellion of Absalom (13:38; 15:1ff.), disruption in the kingdom (20:1ff.) and, in the end, David's own last days as a toothless tiger (1 Ki. 1) who left to Solomon a horrifying testament (1 Ki. 2:1–10, esp. 5–6)?

We must read Isaiah 38 – 39 (*cf.* 2 Ki. 20) with this in mind. The tale is simply told: in his terminal illness (38:1) Hezekiah prayed for healing and the Lord replied with a double promise (5–6): first, that Hezekiah would recover and live a further fifteen years; secondly – a divine promise added in sheer grace – that king and city would be delivered from Assyria. So serious were these promises in the Lord's mind that he confirmed them with a most remarkable sign (7–8). Indeed, in 2 Kings the divine promises are attested by a double sign: not only the sign in the sun as in verses 7–8 (2 Ki. 20:8–11), but also the notable sign that, coming out of a terminal illness, the king would go to the Lord's house 'on the third day' (2 Ki. 20:6), *i.e.* the day after tomorrow.

It is hard to think that promises could have received greater confirmation, both objective and subjective, or could, at that moment, have struck home to Hezekiah with more confidence. He would be personally healed and politically delivered!

But Scripture is very plain that our grip upon the promises of God does not go untested (Lk. 8:12–14; 1 Thes. 1:5–6; 2:13–14; 3:5), and so it was with Hezekiah. The testing came in the form of messengers from Merodach-Baladan (39:1). To the Assyrians Merodach-Baladan was a terrorist; to himself he was a freedom-fighter with his life devoted to the liberation of his beloved Babylon from Assyrian tyranny. He was remarkably successful. For twelve years from 722 BC he secured Babylonian independence and reigned as king, and the loss of his kingdom at the hands of Sargon did not cool his ardour in his great cause. The conglomerate empires of the ancient world held together only while the emperor himself kept a firm grip on government. In consequence, the death of the emperor signalled a relaxing of central control and an opportunity to break free. Just as Merodach-Baladan had capitalized on the death of Shalmaneser in 722 BC, so he was ready for the death of Sargon, which happened in 705.[1] Thanks to Merodach-Baladan's careful planning, both east and west of the Assyrian empire rebelled.

Hezekiah was part of this great scheme. Taking opportunity from the king's recovery, Merodach-Baladan sent 'sick visitors' with a gift – and a letter (39:1). We are not told what the letter contained, but we do know how Hezekiah reacted, giving the

[1] For further information on Meroch-Baladan, see D. J. Wiseman, *NBD*, pp. 751f.

envoys a conducted tour of his store-rooms, money and arsenals (2). The letter was manifestly an invitation to become a partner in a rebellion, and Hezekiah fell for it.

Isaiah 36 – 37 has already recounted the historical consequences: the tragic suffering of Judah and the eleventh-hour triumph of grace. Isaiah 39:3–7 explores the spiritual significance of Hezekiah's act, the far-reaching consequences of a single decision. For we must ask, 'What should Hezekiah have said to the envoys?' The answer is plain: 'Thank you for coming and thank Merodach for his gift and invitation, but the fact is I have a divine promise to lean on; it has been confirmed personally in my return to health and cosmically in the sign of the sun. I cannot turn from faith in the promises of God.' But he did turn – and Isaiah responded with impeccable logic: you want to commit all you have to Babylon, therefore all you have will go to Babylon (3–7; Rom. 6:16).

The 'shape' of the section helps us to see its meaning:

> A^1 (38:1a) Hezekiah faces death
> > B^1 (38:1b) *Isaiah ... went ... said ... the LORD says ...*
> > > C^1 (38:8–22) Hezekiah's dedication
> > > C^2 (39:1–2) Hezekiah's defection
> > B^2 (39:3–7) *Isaiah ... went ... said ... the word of the LORD ...*
> A^2 (39:8) Hezekiah faces life

There is nothing in all this to warrant any scepticism about the historicity of the events.[1] Merodach-Baladan figures precisely in the character revealed outside the Bible; Isaiah acts and reacts exactly as the rest of his book would lead us to expect and as a prophet, in the most up-to-date understanding of a prophet's role, should; and Hezekiah is still the good-hearted, human person trying to handle a job that is above his ability.

a. One prayer, two answers (38:1–8)[2]

1–3. Did Isaiah's bedside manner leave much to be desired?

---

[1] Contrast Clements, *Isaiah 1 – 39*, pp. 288–289.

[2] Mauchline proposes 710 BC as the date for Hezekiah's illness but does not explain how this harmonizes with the 15 extra years promised to Hezekiah. Hezekiah's death, dated about 687, would provide a date in the region of 702 BC when Meroch-Baladan was in his second period of rule in Babylon. Maybe, if this were the case, he was trying to foster a western rebellion to relieve the pressure he was under.

Surely he spoke sensitively as well as seriously to the king, with tears as much as with candour, and his frankness brought benefits that medical equivocation would not have done. Hezekiah was displeased (*face to the wall*; *cf.* 1 Ki. 21:4), yet he turned to prayer and shed tears. When the Lord replied (5), he only alluded to the fact of prayer and the evidence of tears; he did not comment on Hezekiah's mistaken reliance on his claim to steadfastness in action (*walked ... faithfully*) and inner integrity (*wholehearted devotion*). It is a measure of the Lord's mercy that he hears prayer even when it rests on a false assumption like the bargaining power of good works.

4–6. 2 Kings 20:4 explains the need for *Go and tell*. The ground of answered *prayer* is not human faithfulness but divine faithfulness. The Lord had made promises (2 Sa. 7:16) to *David* and his house and he would not go back on them, yet he also says, *I have heard your prayer*. It is in answer to the prayers of his people that the Lord performs his faithful mercies and keeps his promises (Lk. 1:13). But the answer exceeds the implied request (Eph. 3:20): the Lord addresses the specific need in the promise of *fifteen years*, but then he runs beyond it to meet needs that Hezekiah had not mentioned, *i.e.* the deliverance of both king and city from Assyrian power, that is to say, the restoration of Davidic sovereignty, the end of puppet status, and Judah as a nation once again. Significantly at this point 2 Kings 20:6 adds 'for my sake and for the sake of my servant David' – an implicit rebuke to Hezekiah's appeal to self-righteousness. The Lord's mercies rest on the surer foundation of his purposes and promises.

7–8. Textual uncertainties[1] in verse 8 do not imperil the reality of the sign. The *stairway of Ahaz* may have led to his 'upper room' (2 Ki. 23:12). By accident or design its steps were a sun-clock. The *sign* confirming the double promise was that the shadow would recede. It would be as improper to suggest how this was done as to deny what is recorded. The Creator is master of his creation and even time is his created servant (Jos. 9:12–14). *Aḥaz* was the king who was invited to ask for a sign moving

---

[1] Lit. 'Look, I am going to bring back the shadow [masc.] on the stairs which it [fem.] has gone down on the stairs of Ahaz by the sun [fem.] back ten stairs. So the sun returned ten stairs on the stairs which it had gone down.' It is simple to change *baššemeš* (by the sun) to *haššemeš*, the sun, providing a subject for the following verb. The curious 'ten stairs on the stairs' may be an accidental repetition, which then required the adjustment of an original definite article to a preposition, 'on'. But, as so often, uncertainty of detail does nothing to obscure what the text means.

heaven and earth (7:11) to vouch for the Lord's commitment to the house of David (7:12). It was fitting that the Lord should provide just such a sign of his faithfulness to David's house and city. The least requirement of the verse is that the *shadow* moved – and did it then resume its former position? But in any case, a miracle of God was performed in confirmation of the double promise. The deliberate linking of Hezekiah and Ahaz at this juncture is itself a warning to Hezekiah that he stands where his father stood, at that perilous crossroads where the way of faith and the way of works, trusting God and self-reliance, meet. And, like Ahaz, if he will not believe, he will not continue (7:9).

b. Death and life (38:9–22)

Isaiah had access to Hezekiah's 'papers' (2 Ch. 32:32) and therefore to this 'writing' (9). This would not, of course, by itself have made him include it here. The fact is rather that the psalm has a part to play in the plot of these two chapters by providing essential background to chapter 39 and the decision Hezekiah made there. The psalm's title (9) is (lit.) 'when he was sick and lived/returned to life from his sickness'. It is the writing of a man who knew he had been under sentence of death – who felt he was about to die under divine wrath (13), without hope (17), with sin unforgiven (17); who knew prayer had been heard (14), by an act of God (15); and who in response to his healing had made his commitment for the future (15). It was to this man, with this experience of the Lord and with this personal commitment, that Merodach-Baladan's offer came. When, then, he made the wrong decision, it flew in the face of the proved promises of God (38:7–8) and of Hezekiah's own assessment and response to his experience.

10–11. *Death* (NIV mg. 'Sheol'): the place of the departed (5:14; 14:9). Sorrow over 'untimely' death is not peculiar to the Old Testament (see Phil. 2:27). Throughout the Bible this life has its unique preciousness which not even the illumination of immortality in Christ (2 Tim. 1:10) takes away. Hezekiah does not write that he will never see God or humankind again, but that the relationships formed *in the land of the living* are terminated by death. *The LORD* is the affectionate diminutive 'Yah' (as 12:2, *etc*.). *Living* involves an alteration of MT to read *ḥeled*, 'world', instead of *ḥedel*, which is a noun derived from the verb 'to cease', hence 'cessation', but which appears nowhere else. If *ḥedel* is retained, then beyond this life Hezekiah sees himself as 'with those who dwell in cessation' – still alive but this life has ceased.

In verses **12–14**, four pictures set the scene: how fragile is life (12a), how decisive is death (12b), how hostile the Lord has proved (13), and what a feeble thing prayer seems to be (14). These represent Hezekiah's feelings as he waits at 'the gates of Sheol' (10).

12. *House*: literally 'encampment'. This life has no more fixity or solidity than a tent (2 Cor. 5:1). *Taken*: literally 'taken captive'. Death has come in like a conqueror. *Weaver ... loom*: once the full pattern has been woven, the thread is snipped off and the tapestry rolled up. Notice, however, *I ... he*: the individual weaves the pattern of his life; the Lord determines the time allowed for the weaving. *Day and night*: 'from day to night', an idiom of imminent action implying 'before the day is out'. *Made* is either 'make' or 'will make'. Either way, it acknowledges that the moment of death, ever imminent, is God's decision.

13–14. *I waited patiently*: better 'I composed myself'. The sick man came through another day and settled himself as best he could for the night but found no cessation of divine hostility. Hezekiah is not teaching that sickness itself is a divine hostility, but that, in his case, he knew it to be such. As death approached apace he sensed himself to be under the wrath of God, but *cf.* verse 17. *I cried* is 'I keep chattering on ...' The only way to flee from God is to flee to him. Hezekiah kept up an endless stream of intercession, but, apart from sounding as ineffective as birds chattering, he *grew weak* because of the effort. It says much for Hezekiah, then, that the cry continued, *Lord, come to my aid*, literally 'go bail for me' – the one who stands by me when my resources fail. Prayer seems unavailing (14ab) but is not; weakness, far from excusing prayerlessness, is a call to prayer (14c); our need is a ground of appeal for divine aid (14d).

15–17. The difficulties presented by the highly allusive wording of verses 15–16 do not obscure the general movement of thought. Hezekiah has been 'at death's door' (10–11), despairing of life but persevering in a simple prayer (12–14). So what can he now say (15a)? In his recovery he discerns the voice (*he has spoken*) and act (*he has done*) of God (15b). The *lion* (13b) heard the coo of the *dove* (14b), spoke the healing word (Ps. 107:20) and performed the healing act (15b). Hezekiah cannot explain answered prayer (*What can I say?*) but he can see the point of it all: *because of this anguish* his life will now be different – *I will walk humbly*, not as a superficial reaction, but a lasting commitment *all my years*. Interestingly the phrase *all my years* only occurs here in the Bible, the customary phrase being 'all my days'. But it was to Hezekiah that the Lord said (in the memorable, if unintended, rhyme of the Authorized Version), 'I have heard thy prayer; I have seen thy tears; behold, I will add unto thy days fifteen years' (5). It is these *years* that he now responsively consecrates. But (16) there is a lesson here for everyone: *by such things*, *i.e.* by suffering faced in prayer, by the Lord's answer to prayer, and by responsive commitment. Here is a way of life all should practise, and (16b) Hezekiah can vouch for it in his own experience: his *spirit* has found life and vigour along this line. *Let me live* is too weak: 'You gave me health and made me live' – that is, when, in suffering, I called out of weakness for your strength. Thus (17) suffering is purposeful. For Hezekiah it brought, first of all, personal benefit (17ab). The suffering was intense (*such anguish*) but *it was for my benefit*, literally for wholeness, well-being, peace (Heb. *šālôm*). Secondly, it brought a special awareness of the Lord's love (17cd). The Lord has been his deadly foe, as menacing as a *lion* (13); what then brought him back from the edge of that awful pit? What else but *your love*! The word √*hāšaq* is the love of passionate delight and longing (Gn. 34:8; 1 Ki. 9:19; *cf.* Dt. 7:7; 10:15) – 'You have loved my soul out of the pit' (lit.). Thirdly, he knew the forgiveness of sins (17ef). How can the hostility of divine wrath (13) change to the yearning of divine love (17cd)? The first word of 17e is the explanatory 'For' (translated 'Surely' by NIV). The great change takes place when sin has been dealt with. (*Cf.* 12:1–2, where 'salvation' is the middle term between anger and comfort.) Hezekiah does not explain how this has happened, he knows only that it has: his *sins* (see 1:4) no longer stand between him and God because God has himself (lit.) 'hurled' them behind his *back* (Mi. 7:18–19).

In verses **18–20**, in a beautifully rounded way, Hezekiah brings his 'writing' to a conclusion. Verses 18–19, with their theme of returning to life from the brink of death, match 11 with its theme of sinking from the land of the living into the 'land of cessation'; verse 20 finds Hezekiah in the 'house of the Lord', matching 10 where he was about to go through 'the gates of death'. These contrasts bring into focus the whole movement of the psalm from death to life.

18–19. When Hezekiah says that *the grave* [*Sheol*, NIV mg.] *cannot praise you*, he is not, of course, making a comment on death as such but on the sort of death he would himself have experienced, death under divine wrath with sin unforgiven.[1] In

---

[1] Pss. 6:5; 30:9; 88:10–12 are often understood to teach that the OT lacked hope after death. In each case, however, the context (like Hezekiah's 'writing') is

such a death there is no hope, no continuing, joyful relationship with God (18ab), no future to look forward to, bringing experience of divine *faithfulness* (18cd). The initial *For* makes this the explanation of the Lord's saving mercies to Hezekiah. The Lord finds no pleasure in such a death; rather it is 'to the praise of his glorious grace' (Eph. 1:6) that he has devised and bestowed his saving mercies, the *love* which *kept me from the pit* (17). *Praise* (19), therefore, is the mark of the saved. They are the truly *living* (note the repetition, designed to emphasize that this is the life that is life indeed, Jn. 10:10; 20:31; Rom. 5:17). *Fathers ... children*: *cf.* Deuteronomy 6:4–9; 11:18–19; Proverbs 4:1; Ephesians 6:4. Hezekiah is true to the Bible when, having pledged personal devotion (19ab), he goes on to pledge parental devotion (19cd).

20. *Will save*: literally 'was for saving'. The idiom expresses 'direction, tendency or aim'.[1] We might say 'the Lord was all out to save me'. Salvation is rooted in the mind and will of God (Eph. 2:4) and accomplished by the work of God (Tit. 3:4–6). *We will sing*: the saved individual (17) at once finds that he belongs to a whole company of joy. Yet individuality is not lost in the group, for (lit.) 'with my music we will make music'. *In the temple*: rather 'house', for that is what the temple was – the Lord's house. When the Lord's people were a camping people, the Lord commanded them to pitch a tent for him (Ex. 25:8–9). He is the indwelling God (Ex. 29:42–46). In the same way, when the Lord's people became a settled people, the Lord commanded that they build him a house (2 Sa. 7:13) with the same purpose, that he might dwell among them (1 Ki. 8:13). When we call our church 'the Lord's house', we mean that it is a place we go to be with him; when the Old Testament calls the temple 'the Lord's house', it means the place where he has come to be with us. The Lord's house was a place of atoning sacrifice, because sinners cannot draw near to the Holy One without the efficacy and shelter of shed blood. All this lies in the background of Hezekiah's statement that we spend 'all the days of our lives in the house of the Lord': salvation is an individual matter (20a); it creates the joyful company of the saved (20b); and initiates a permanent access into the presence and fellowship of the Lord (20cd).

21–22. As one would expect, 2 Kings includes this record of Isaiah's 'prescription' and Hezekiah's asking for a sign within the

---

the prospect of death without divine favour. See J. A. Motyer, *After Death* (Christian Focus, 1996), pp. 18–26.

[1] Lit. 'the Lord to save me', where the Heb. infinitive expresses direction, tendency or aim. See GKC, pp. 114–115.

flow of the narrative at the appropriate point (20:7–8). (See Additional Note, below, regarding the abrupt intrusion of the same material here when, to all intents and purposes, the narrative has been concluded.) *Poultice of figs ... boil* (21): whether Hezekiah's health problem was a septic ulcer or some internal poisoning we are not told. Neither do we know whether figs were in current medical use, or if Isaiah was simply using the (lit.) 'lump of figs' as a visible symbol of the healing power of God, an 'acted oracle'. His actual command was to 'rub it on the boil'. There is, of course, no contradiction between healing in answer to prayer (2–5) and healing by means of medicine. There is no healing apart from the Lord (Ex. 15:27), who retains his sovereign authority to use or to dispense with 'means'.[1] The figs, coupled with the prophetic word, would have been a visible assurance to the king that healing was in progress. Coupled with the visible assurance of the figs, Hezekiah asked for (22) and received (2 Ki. 20:7–8) the cosmic sign of the movement of the shadow on the stairs. We move on, therefore, into chapter 39 in the light of promises made and vouched for in both ordinary and spectacular ways. Surely the king was fully equipped to stay in the pathway of faith ...?

Additional Note on the 'intrusive' narrative at Isaiah 38:21–22

Prayer had been made and answered, and Hezekiah had responded with joyful recognition of the work of God and personal commitment. The narrative has, therefore, apparently concluded. Have we here, then, the thoughtless work of some later editor, taking a bit from 2 Kings, apparently forgotten by his editorial predecessors, and patching it in regardless of suitability? But, surely, any such editor would have been skilful enough to make the insertion at the same point as he found it in Kings; it is never a satisfactory solution of a problem to ascribe literary idiocy to the long-dead guardians of the text! But the question then remains why this double statement (lit. 'And Isaiah said ... and Hezekiah said ...') stands where it does.

Of course, it is reasonable that Isaiah would wish to play down his part in the healing of the king, slipping it in at the end; and this might suffice as an explanation, were it not so carefully balanced with a parallel quotation of the king's words. The two 'sayings' together give the impression of a deliberate pause in the flow of the narrative: as if to say, 'Before we go on to what

[1] B. Webb, *The Message of Isaiah* (IVP, 1996), p. 156.

happened next, stop and recall the heart of what has happened already: this is what the prophet said ... this is what the king said.' Taken in this way, the double saying slots into the balance of the whole narrative of chapters 38 – 39. In 38:1 Hezekiah is sick and Isaiah came to him, and in 39:1 Hezekiah is well and Merodach-Baladan's men came to him; 38:2–3 records the king's reaction, and so does 39:2a; in 38:4–8 the Lord promises deliverance, but in 39:2b Hezekiah embraces a human promise of deliverance; 38:9–20 is Hezekiah's affirmation of what the Lord has done for him and how he responded, and 39:3–4 is Hezekiah's record of a human approach and how he responded; 38:20–21 is a double statement, 'And Isaiah said ... and Hezekiah said', and this is paralleled in 39:5, 'And Isaiah said', and 39:8, 'And Hezekiah said'.[1] Each element in this series of contrasts, therefore, contributes to the sad message of the whole, but none more than the final contrast in which, in 38:21–22, Hezekiah receives proved tokens of grace; but, in 39:5–8, he is revealed as the architect of disaster, shallowly content with his own immunity.

c. The moment of decision (39:1–8)

1–2. That Hezekiah should have received the envoys *gladly* is understandable. It was a proper courtesy responding to a kindly gesture. But beyond the gesture lay the *letters*, the hidden agenda. Their contents are not divulged but are plain from the king's reaction. What must the letters have said if they provoked the response of displaying the resources and armed strength of the kingdom? From such a source as Merodach-Baladan, only one thing: 'Join me in rebellion' – and Hezekiah fell for it. It was a clear choice: the promises of God (38:4–8) or the power of man (39:2), and Hezekiah forgot the promises.

3–4. But alongside forgetfulness there was pride. Notice the emphasis in verse 4. The king's reply to Isaiah's question begins *From a distant land* and ends *from Babylon*. These are the two points of emphasis: 'Imagine them coming all that way to see me! Imagine Merodach-Baladan wanting me as an ally!' Forgetfulness of the word of God is the prime enemy of faith; pride in one's own importance runs it a close second.

5–7. Isaiah's response could not be more bleak: defeat, captivity, exile. But it could not be more just, a perfect *quid pro quo*. 'Everything in my palace', said Hezekiah (4); *everything in*

---

[1] These renderings are literal. NIV accommodates Heb. narrative style to English usage.

your palace, responded Isaiah (6). 'Babylon', said the king (3); *Babylon,* responded the prophet. Commentators dispute if Isaiah could and would have predicted a Babylonian captivity.[1] It is not greatly questioned nowadays that Old Testament includes prediction, but what is rightly queried is bare prediction – a mere forecast of the future designed to satisfy our curiosity about 'what is going to happen'. The forecast must (a) emerge from the current situation and (b) speak relevantly to that situation. John the Baptist's cry, 'Repent, for the kingdom of heaven is near' (Mt. 3:2), is a perfect example: he addressed his contemporaries; he told them of the future; he made the future bear on the present. Plainly Isaiah's word to Hezekiah fits this framework. First, Isaiah did not snatch the name *Babylon* out of the air. The king spoke it to him before he spoke it back to the king. Isaiah has no option but to comment on it. Secondly, his message about Babylon has a direct bearing on the present: to depart from the way of faith is to walk in the way of destruction (7:9). Babylon will be his destruction. Thirdly, Babylon was part of the current map of the world. It was where already a viable alternative to Assyrian dominance had been established. Merodach-Baladan had credentials as a world-beater. If Hezekiah interpreted the prediction as a fairly prompt future Babylonian captivity, there was nothing in the current political scene to contradict the possibility.[2] But this brings us, fourthly, to the fact that we are actually requiring Isaiah to predict something which lay in the remote future, over a century off, and this point would appear to have even greater force if we count the 'Comfort' of 40:1ff. as the actual words of Isaiah. Where is the 'comfort' in saying that everything will be fine in 170 years' time? But just ask another question: where does Isaiah say anything about 'over a century' or 'in 170 years' time'? We know by hindsight of the passage of the years; the prophet says nothing of it, maybe even was ignorant of it! Right from the time of his call he knew there was a dark power in the offing which would destroy Zion and carry off its people (6:11–13); he came to know that Assyria would not be this power (10:5–15; 14:24–21; 29:1–8; 30:31–33); maybe it was at this very moment that the name of the 'dark power' was revealed, when Hezekiah said 'Babylon'! Isaiah probes no further: that is where they are going and from where (48:20–21) they will in due course come back. The message of the future, both in

[1] See A. S. Herbert, *The Book of the Prophet Isaiah* (CUP, 1973); Kaiser, *Isaiah 13 – 39*; and compare Oswalt's telling rejoinder.
[2] Erlandssen, *The Burden of Babylon.*

judgment and mercy, is inevitable as the prophet faces the king.

8. The prediction in 39:6 is every bit as categorical as the prediction in 38:1, which was met by prayer, and divine mercy turned it into blessing. But, in the course of this chapter, works have replaced faith, man has replaced God, and pride has replaced humility. When smug self-importance replaces tears and prayer, the word of God proves its obduracy and accomplishes its grim purposes.

VI. UNIVERSAL CONSOLATION (40:1 – 42:17)

The division of the Bible into chapters and verses is a practical help, but it is not original to the text, and to fail to 'read straight through' is often to miss important meanings. It is worth remembering that in Qᵃ, the Dead Sea Scroll of Isaiah, what we call Isaiah 40:1 begins two lines from the bottom of the column where 39:8 ends, without any suggestion of a break or a new beginning.

It is remarkable that the word of doom (39:5–7) and the word of comfort (40:1) lie side by side. No sooner is just judgment pronounced than (an equally) just comfort is heralded. Indeed, while one voice speaks the word of doom (39:5ff.), the plural imperatives of 40:1 summon a company of comforters out of which three voices are heard speaking (40:3, 6, 9) so that the comfort is more abundant than the condemnation. And not only so, but while judgment comes on one sinful nation (39:5ff.), the consolation, as we shall see, spreads out to embrace the whole world.

a. Consolation for the Lord's people (40:1 – 41:20)

The message of comfort begins where the need for it is sharpest. The situation fits with what we know of Isaiah, who, following his word to the king regarding exile to Babylon, would inevitably find himself at the sharp end of questioning by his discipleship group (8:16): if the days of the monarchy are numbered – all deported to Babylon and the males of the royal family eunuchs – what about the great royal promises which have been the substance of the prophet's ministry to date (*e.g.* 9:1–6; 11:1–16)? Plainly Isaiah must either tear up his earlier prophecies or else seek further truth regarding the future.

Further truth indeed he did seek, and he sets it out in a beautifully balanced statement: three voices proclaim promises of comfort (40:1–11); the promises are then guaranteed by the nature of the Lord who, as Creator (40:12–31), rules the whole creation and cannot forget his people (40:25–31) and, as Lord of history (41:1–7), directs the whole historical process, raising up the world's rulers (41:1–4), and exposing the world's idolatries (41:5–7); finally, matching the three voices (40:3–11), there are three pictures of consolation (41:8–20).

i. The message of comfort (40:1–11)

Introduction: the heralds of comfort (40:1–2). 1. *Comfort, comfort*: the verbs are plural imperatives commanding an unnamed band to bring comfort to those whom the Lord still calls *my people*. They have abandoned him but he has not rejected them. Like tiny children they have stumbled in the uncertain paths of the world and will be bruised by their fall, but they have a God rushing to pick them up in his arms (11).

2. *Speak tenderly*: 'speak to the heart', like a young man wooing his girl (Gn. 34:3), someone bringing reassurance (Ru. 2:13), a deserted husband seeking to win his wife back (Ho. 2:14). *Hard service*: the word *ṣābā'* means 'army/host' (Jdg. 8:6), but extends its meaning to cover a fixed period of service (Nu. 4:3) or the fixed duration of life (Jb. 47:1), and, here, an appointed period of hardship. *Sin ... paid for*: here is the element of justice that lies behind the word of comfort. How can the God of judgment (39:5ff.) become the God of pardon? Not just by saying so – for that would be to treat his holiness as negotiable and sin as negligible. The verb *paid for* (√*raza*, 'to be favourable') is used of the Lord's 'pleasure' (1 Ch. 28:4) and particularly of the acceptance the Lord accords to atoning sacrifices (Lv. 1:4; 22:27). It stresses, therefore, not so much that the sacrifice offered is sufficient to cover the sin committed (though that has to be true also), but that it satisfies the requirements of the holy God. *Sin* (*'awōn*): the inner reality of the warped, sinful nature (1:4; 6:7). The word is mainly the fact of 'iniquity' but also, as here, 'punishment of iniquity' (Lv. 26:41), the price paid to deal with sin. *Received ... the LORD's hand*: to the sinner it is a free gift, offered to be 'taken'; the donor and agent is the Lord. *Hand* symbolizes personal agency. The provision for sin is not a human expedient, hoping for the best that it will work, but a divine provision (Lv. 17:11; Is. 53:6, 10) and action. *Double* (√*kāpal*) means 'to fold over, fold in half' (Ex. 26:9); the noun, as here (*kiplayim*), occurs only in Job 11:6, where divine wisdom is 'two-sided' in the sense that it always includes hidden realities beyond the reach of the human mind. So here, the thought is not of an excessive punishment running beyond what the case required, but of a dealing with sin that includes realities beyond our comprehension. On the other hand, when something is folded over, each half corresponds exactly with the other half, and this would yield the thought of exact correspondence between sin and payment.[1] *For*: *i.e.* 'in payment for'. As we will see, it is the task of the coming chapters progressively to unfold what this payment will turn out to be. *Sins* (*ḥaṭṭa'ṭ*): see 6:7.

The message of comfort (40:3–11). Three unnamed voices obey the call to *comfort my people* (1). The first voice (3–5) says that *our God* is coming to reveal his glory worldwide; the third voice (9–11) brings this message to bear on Zion: the coming Lord is the shepherd who will gather his people and lead them home; the second voice affirms the enduring quality of God's word: he has promised universal revelation (5) and good news for Zion (9) and his word will not fail. These truths summarize the whole message of chapters 40 – 55. The Lord has an interim plan for the consolation of his exiles in Babylon (43:14; 44:24 – 45:7; 48:20–21), but he also has a second plan, bringing his word and salvation to them and to the whole world (42:1–4; 49:1–6; 55:1–13).

3–5. *A voice*, or the exclamatory use of the noun (13:4; 66:6): 'Listen! Someone is calling out.' *Way* is not an exodus-type picture of the Lord's people journeying home from captivity (see 48:20–21), but the old picture of the Lord's desert journey to his people's aid (Dt. 33:2; Jdg. 5:4; Ps. 68:4, 7); and there is also a reference elsewhere suited to this context. A Babylonian hymn says, 'Make [Nabu's] way good, renew his road. Make straight his path', referring to the creation of special processional routes along which the images of the gods were carried on festivals. The creation of a road that is *straight* (3d), unmistakable (*highway*, or causeway, 3e), level (4ab) and smooth (4cd) pictures a journey made without difficulty and therefore with certainty of arrival. *The glory of the* LORD (5) means 'the Lord in all his glory', not necessarily with awesome manifestations but in the fullness of his personal presence. *For the mouth*: a typically Isaianic affirmation (1:20; 58:14; also 21:17; 22:25; 25:8), stressing both the origin of the word in the Lord (*mouth*) and the identity of what the prophet said with what the Lord said.

6ab. *A voice*: or, as above, 'Listen, someone is saying.' *And I said* adopts the reading of Q[a] and LXX and is widely interpreted

---

[1] The idea that a tradesman pinned the folded account to the door of the customer once it was paid and that this was called 'the double' is more likely to derive from Is. 40:2 than to be an explanation of it. Nevertheless, as a picture it is helpful.

as hinting at the 'call' of 'second Isaiah', the supposed author of chapters 40 – 55. This is a classical example of making the 'facts' fit the theory. It is better to follow MT, which reads 'and he said' or 'and someone said'. This matches well the anonymity of the 'voices' in verses 3 and 9. It is the message, not the messenger, that is important.

6c–8. The message is the contrast between human transience and divine permanence, designed to affirm that what the Lord promises he will most surely keep and perform. If, therefore, he promises universal self-revelation (5) and shepherding care (11), nothing can stop these things happening. *Men*: literally 'flesh', humankind in its vulnerability. *Glory* (*ḥesed*): the word used (*e.g.* 54:8, 10) of the 'ever-unchanging' faithful love of the Lord for his people. It occurs also of the love that humans owe back to the Lord but, by comparison, what a fickle and transient thing that turns out to be (Ho. 6:4)! The reference is not to our fading physical 'glory' or anything like that but to our moral and spiritual unreliability. *Because the breath*: literally 'spirit'. This could be a reference to the Holy Spirit. Certainly he is the 'Lord, and Giver of life' (Ps. 104:30), but equally 'the Lord, and Giver of death'. Just as the flower fades under adverse conditions, so the moral and spiritual constitution comes under testing (Mk. 4:16–19). Furthermore, what Isaiah says about 'all flesh' (6cd) he notes to be equally true of those from whom more would be expected: *Surely* (lit. 'Why, even') *the people* – the Lord's people! – show the same moral instability (*are grass*). *But*, by marvellous contrast, there is a changeless factor at work in the world: *the word of our God* (Nu. 23:19; Ps. 119:89).

Verses **9–11** reveal that the promised coming of the Lord (3–4) will not be in vain. Exile is not the last word for the Lord's people – whether the exile in Babylon of old or the continuing 'exile' of his scattered people (Jas. 1:1; 1 Pet. 1:1). The homecoming is certain.

9a–f. *You who bring*: a feminine verb – drawing on the occasion when Miriam took her tambourine and sang of the victory the Lord had won (Ex. 15:20; *cf.* 1 Sa. 18:6–7; Ps. 68:11) – pictures the celebratory company of singing women being led out of Zion to meet the returning victor-Shepherd. *High mountain*, so that all may hear; *with a shout*, 'with strength', because there is no doubt about the message, nothing to merit hesitancy.

9g–11. *Here is ... See ... See*: the same word on all three occasions, 'Behold/Look!' It is all happening before their very eyes: the divine coming of One who is *God*, the mighty coming of One who is *with power* (lit. 'as a strong One') and the successful coming of One who brings with him what he has achieved. The synonyms *reward ... recompense* describe what he has 'earned' by his victory (*cf.* the victorious David in 1 Sa. 31:20). But, mighty though he is, there is nothing ruthless in his power. Towards his people it is a power working by love: the care that *tends*, the gentleness that makes provision for the weak (*the lambs*) and that caters for particular needs (*those that have young*). Note the contrast between the 'ruling arm' of 10b and the gathering (lit.) 'arm' of 11b.

ii. God the Creator, guarantor of his promises (40:12–31). This wonderful poem moves to a climax in verses 27–31, the security of *Jacob/Israel* under such a God: this sovereignly wise Creator-God (12–14) blends all things exactly together (12); in his greatness (15–17) he dominates creation and its peoples (17); he alone is God (18–20); he rules (21–24) all earthly 'powers' (23), and controls (25–26) creation down to the last detail (26). So how then can *Jacob/Israel*, his very own people, be forgotten (27) or be left without strength (31)? This is one of the central Old Testament passages on the doctrine of creation. It teaches that the physical fabric of creation is a direct artefact of the Creator: *dust* and *waters* (12) have been weighed and measured out in his *hand*. The presence of organized human strength (*nations*, 15, 17) makes no difference to the Creator's absolute sovereignty over his creation. The Creator God is the sole God (18–20), compared to whom all claimants to deity are but the product of human skill (19–20). The Creator presides over the inhabited world (22) and rules earth's rulers (23–24). With attention to detail he decrees the movements of the cosmos (26). In one way or another the fourfold Old Testament doctrine of God the Creator is represented here: he originates everything, maintains everything in existence, controls everything in operation, and directs everything to the end he appoints.

The Creator in his wisdom (40:12–14). 12. The contrast between *waters* and *dust*, *heavens* and *earth* exemplifies the Hebrew idiom of 'totality expressed by contrast'. This Creator God is the creator of all. *Measured ... marked out ... held ... weighed*: the whole creation is precision work with every component present to the exact amount. *Marked off* is the verb we would use to express 'fine tuning'. *Hollow ... breadth ... basket ... scales ... balance*: in human terms these are the measures we use for small-scale working, here they underline the immensity of the Creator in comparison to his creation.

13–14. Just as verse 12 was full of words in the tool-vocabulary, here is the vocabulary of wisdom: *understood ... instructed ... counsellor ... consult ... enlighten ... taught ... knowledge ... understanding*. There are, of course, shades of meaning in all these words, but their force lies in their total impact: the unbounded, unsurpassed, underived wisdom of the Creator. *Understood* is the verb translated *marked off* in verse 12. The Creator did not need anyone to 'fine tune' him! *Enlighten ... right way ... understanding* all share the idea of discernment, seeing to the heart of a matter. In sum, therefore, whether we view the creation as a task accomplished (12) or whether (13–14) we go behind the task to the wisdom which planned it, there is only the one Creator God.

The Creator in his greatness (40:15–17). Isaiah now turns to the inhabited world. The relationship between the Creator and the creation (12–14) is 'asymmetrical' – that is to say, the Creator has total power over the creation; the creation has no power over the Creator. Does the advent of humankind alter this? No, the relationship is still 'asymmetrical'! *Nations* (15, 17) describes humankind in collective, organized strength but, in relation to the Creator, they are only *a drop ... dust ... nothing ... worthless ... less than nothing*.

15. The omission by NIV of the double 'Behold' in this verse is a loss. 'Look at this', says the prophet: a person carries a bucket of water from the well and a drop splashes out! Does he notice the loss? A chemist measures out a substance; total accuracy is important, so he wipes or blows the dust off the pan of his scales. Now 'look at this': to the Creator, total land masses (*islands*) are as easy to weigh! The double 'Behold' points first to the human, then to the 'fabric'. In each case, and equally, the dominance of the Creator is total.

16. From organized humanity, Isaiah moves to religious humanity. There is nothing we can do which would adequately match the greatness of the Creator – not even were we to make all *Lebanon* a fire and all its animals a holocaust (Ps. 50:9–13). In verse 15 we are under his power; in verse 16, he is beyond our power. Nothing we can do puts him in our debt or at our disposal. This is the death-knell to all 'do-it-yourself' systems of salvation. Over every human effort to move God, to meet his demands, satisfy his requirements, manoeuvre him to our advantage and climb into his 'good books', Isaiah simply writes, 'Not enough.'

17. Now the prophet turns to *all the nations*. Suppose the whole world became one huge 'collective', how would we compare with the Creator? *Nothing ... worthless ... less than nothing*! Do these words suggest that humanity 'means nothing' to the Creator? This would not be correct, for, far from 'meaning nothing', Scripture insists that humankind is the crown of creation, the bearer of the divine image, appointed to the dignity of vice-regent in the created world (Gn. 1:26–28; Ps. 8). This verse, then, is not assessing man's *value* to God but his comparative *stature*. Here is the ultimate statement of the 'asymmetrical' relationship. *Before him*: standing 'in front of him', humankind's collective strength is *nothing;* 'they are to be reckoned in comparison to him as non-entity'. He alone possesses life; of themselves they do not. *Less than nothing* is the 'formless' of Genesis 1:2, meaning 'lacking evident purpose and meaning': 'compared to him they are to be reckoned as pointless.'

The Creator in his sole deity (40:18–20). This topic lies at the centre of the poem. On each side of it, Isaiah examines the relationship of the Creator to organized humankind: the nations (15–17); princes and rulers (21–24). On each side again of those topics he deals with the Creator and the creation: the wisdom that planned and the power that executed (12–14); the management skill that keeps everything in place (25–26). But here, centrally, is the Lord's sole deity, the absence of anything that can be called 'God'. For apart from the God who reveals himself in Holy Scripture, people are confined to their own thoughts, imaginings and devisings, a truth most plainly seen in the making of an idol. Such merely human religion is exposed at two points. In verse 19 the beauty of an idol is that of human artistry and earthly richness, and in 20 the life of the *wood* ('a tree') comes from the soil; its durability is only that of nature (*will not rot*), its shape and 'character' are the gifts of a *skilled craftsman* (*i.e.* human imagination), and its stability something contrived (*not topple*). The emphasis throughout is on the human, earthly, origin of such a 'god' and the fact that its 'powers' cannot extend beyond that which it naturally is. Note how verse 19 begins and 20 ends with a reference to *a craftsman*. That says it all; it is a human invention.

The Creator in his role as King of kings (40:21–24). 21. The 'heaping up' of questions resembles that in verses 12–14. There the expected answers affirmed only one God who is all-wise; here the expected answers point to a wisdom humans should have – and our culpability if we ignore it. *Cf.* Psalm 19:1–6; Romans 1:20; Hebrews 11:2 – according to which passages there is a 'voice' speaking from and about the world, proclaiming that it is not self-originating. Is it to this 'voice' that Isaiah refers when he asks, *Have you not heard?* (21b).[1] What he says is appropriate enough to 'natural religion', but he is actually addressing Israel and progressively moving to the moment when (27) he can challenge their failure in faith. They have always known the all-wise, omnicompetent Creator (12–14), the unchallengeable Lord of the nations (15–17), the sole God (18–20) and now the King of all kings. They had a revelation going back to the very beginning, and always, as part of the doctrine of creation, they acknowledged a sole (Ps. 96:5) and sovereign (Je. 10:12–16; 27:5–6; 32:17–20) Creator God.

22–24. Envisaging his people as destined to be swallowed up among the nations, dominated by a totalitarian conqueror – all of which would occupy his imagination following the Babylonian prediction of 39:5–7 – Isaiah knows how important it is that they have a theological perspective on the question of earthly power. Hence he shows them in turn the transcendent supremacy of their God (22), how earth's rulers appear when compared with him (23), and the retrospective judgment of history on them (24). *Tent to live in* pictures either the inhabited earth as humankind's tent dwelling under the canvas of the sky, with the Creator exalted over all, or else the greatness of a God who needs the whole expanse of the sky to provide a tent sufficient for himself. Either way, the phrase emphasizes his dominance over the world of people. *Naught ... nothing*, as in verse 17, express a comparative judgment. *Naught* is the word 17 translates as 'nothing', and *nothing* appears there as 'less than nothing' (Gn. 1:2, *tōhû*, evidencing no meaning or purpose). In his own estimation and to those around him, a ruler is a 'somebody', but to the Lord his power and prestige mean nothing; he alone is King. *Like chaff*: a picture of that which is quickly dispersed. History is long as we live through it, brief as we look back. 'Time, like an ever-rolling stream,/Bears all its sons away;/They fly, forgotten, as a dream ...'[2]

The Creator in his direct management of the cosmos (40:25–26). Matching verses 18–20 where the Lord was incomparable in his deity, here he is incomparable in his role as 'Managing Director'.

25. *The Holy One*: His power and wisdom (12–14), greatness (15–17), deity (18–20) and dominance (21–24) put the Lord

---

[1] See W. Temple, *Nature, Man and God* (Macmillan, 1940), Lecture XX; P. Davies, *The Mind of God* (Simon and Schuster, 1992).

[2] From I. Watts, 'O God, our help in ages past'.

beyond compare, but the killing blow to any comparison is his holiness, his unique moral majesty (see 6:3). Holiness and creation often appear side by side (Ps. 104:24–25; *cf.* 93:5). It is as if the Old Testament found it impossible to meditate on the Creator and world Ruler without moving intuitively to the holiness of his rule over the earth. So it is here. Certainly the Lord's holiness lifts him out of the realm of comparison with any other, but is this also a word in season for Israel? In their earthly need, they can rest in their Creator's sovereign care, trust his sovereign wisdom and so on, but it is always the sovereignty of *the Holy One*; part of what they need to understand in their plight is that their guiltiness before such a God merits his holy wrath and requires their penitence. There is a demanding moral dimension in living in the Creator's world.

26. The ancient world was just as full as the modern world of astrologers anxious to tell us how the stars create the conditions of life. Isaiah, however, would simply have us admire the Creator's handiwork and understand the movements of the heavens (not as exerting influence but) as demonstrating the wonder and exactness of the Lord's direct management of his cosmos. His direction is individual (26c): the stars are like so many pet dogs called by name to take their place in their master's design (26d), and innumerable though they are, their number is never less than complete (26ef).

The Creator in his self-giving (40:27–31). 27. The questions expose the frailty of faith and also the absurdity of faithlessness. First, can *my way* on earth have become so tangled that the Lord has lost sight of me? And second, there is no use pleading *my cause* before him only for it to be dismissed out of hand. The particular value of the doctrine of God the Creator is, of course, that it brings all that is true about God to bear on this world. Consider, then, the absurdity of losing faith in One who, in relation to earth, is all-powerful (12), all-wise (13–14), dominant (15–17), with no god to challenge, check or rival him (18–20), King of kings (21–24), sovereignly in charge of his world down to the smallest detail so that everything is in its place, nothing overlooked, nothing lost!

28. These truths are now in principle recapitulated. He is *the everlasting God*, therefore there is no time when he is not; *the ends of the earth* are his, therefore there is no place where he is not; *not … tired or weary*, his strength does not flag, deficiency of inner resources cannot limit him, nor can lack of *understanding*.

29–31. The string of attributes of the Lord – eternity, omnipresence, untiring strength, wisdom (28) – continues in the opening Hebrew participle: he is also one who shares his strength, not as a whim or an occasional act but as part of what he is. *Weary* (29) and *tired* (30) are the same word (translated *tired* in 28). It means failure through loss of inherent strength. *Weary* (30) is a different word, pointing to exhaustion because of the hardness of life. It is part of the 'understanding' (28) of the unwearying God that he knows our frailty and provides an antidote. *Youths*, those in the prime of young life; *young men* – from the verb 'to choose' – those 'picked' out for bodily prowess. Thus native strength, whether simply natural or specially cultivated, can fail, but *those who hope in the LORD ... renew their strength. Hope* (with, of course, its biblical component of certainty) is one meaning of √*qāwâ*, which also means 'wait' (patiently) and 'rest' (trustfully). Here it is a participle, pointing to a maintained relationship. *Renew*, from a basic meaning 'to change' (√*halap*), comes to mean 'to put on afresh': here, 'keep putting on fresh strength'. It is a different strength, as if people become eagles, a strength brought about by transformation; it is divine strength, a strength like the Lord's own that does not *weary* or *faint* (28e). *Run*, the exceptional demands of life; *walk*, the ordinary daily grind.

iii. God the world ruler, guarantor of his promises (41:1–7).

Isaiah now turns to bring into sharper focus truths he has already affirmed in principle: that the Lord dominates nations (40:15–17), is the Ruler of rulers (40:21–24) and has no rival god to challenge or hinder (40:18–20). His purpose is the same: arising from the comforting promises of 40:3–11 and leading into the comforting pictures of 41:8–20, this truth of the Lord as the sole director of history serves to guarantee his pledges. The heart of the passage is the double question *Who ...?* (2–3 and 4). Even the most dramatic of earth's 'movers and shakers' owes his career to the initiatives of the only God. This core truth is bracketed by a summons to the nations to ponder this truth (1) and an exposure of the futility of their response to history's threats (5–7).

The court is convened (41:1). In this opening court scene the Lord is the Judge, summoning the world before him (1ab), but he is also one of the litigants (1cd), there to argue his case with his adversaries-at-law. Basic to the use of the courtroom imagery is the truth that the Lord can and will proceed only on the basis of absolute justice. *Silent: i.e.* in recognition of the dignity of the Judge. *Islands*: see 11:11; 40:15. Isaiah uses the word '*iyyîm* as shorthand for the far reaches of earth. *Renew their strength*: the expression is the same as in 40:31, 'put on new strength'. There it was an invitation to return to a position of undoubting faith and to experience the renewal that faith brings; here it implies that the same way of renewal is open to the whole world: they too are invited to put their trust in the God of Israel and find new strength. Thus Isaiah quietly introduces a theme he affirmed in 19:24–25; 27:13, and to which he will return in 41:21 – 42:17; 45:14–25; 55:1–13. *Judgment* is, as commonly in the Old Testament, not 'condemnation' or 'sentence' but 'decision'. The nations are invited candidly to argue out the case and then to hear the authoritative decision of the court.

The issue is: who rules the world? (41:2–4). Who is the conqueror of whom these verses speak? The oldest interpretation says it is Abraham, referring to his conquest of the kings of the earth in Genesis 14; most interpreters now think rather of the coming reference to Cyrus (44:24 – 47:15). The fact is that any and all views can be accommodated in this non-specific passage while, at the same time, Isaiah is soon going to apply the truths sketched here to the particular example of Cyrus. But it is best to let him spring that on us in his own time and to treat the present verses as mainly exploring a problem in principle: where do would-be conquerors come from (2a)? Whose purposes are they serving (2b)? How are their victories to be explained (2c–3)? In a word, who really rules the world? Is history a meaningless jumble of events or is it a plan in the hands of a master?

2–3. *Stirred*: literally 'roused' as if from sleep, 'stirred' to activity, not motivating someone already on the move but giving the initial impulse to act. *East*: the situation is Palestinian, where every serious incursion had its origin in the east (see 25) in Mesopotamia. *Righteousness*: in pursuance of a righteous purpose. *Service*: 'to his foot' (lit.), a regular idiom meaning 'to follow him'. This righteous purpose works out in domination (*hands ... over ... and subdues*), total victory (*sword ... bow*), invincible progress (*pursues ... unscathed*) and expanding empire (*not travelled*). In a word, Isaiah raises the whole problem of the *violence* of history: why did it start in the first place? Why is one person allowed to rise to such power? Why is such violence permitted to succeed? Why is it all such a mess? The prophet insists that in every movement of world affairs, the Lord initiates, purposes and achieves, and that all is in accordance with a purpose of *righteousness*. He does not say that we can ever see that it is so; he teaches that it is. *Unscathed* (3): 'in peace', contrasting the serenity and self-satisfaction of the conqueror with the havoc he creates. *Before* is an interpretative addition, literally 'the path with his feet he does not come', possibly intended to suggest travelling with such speed that his feet do not seem to touch the ground! – a picture both of expanding sway and of the easy success that often attends the conqueror's way.

4. The question of verse 2 is reiterated along with the verdict of the Judge. The two verbs *done ... carried through* are more simply 'worked ... acted': what agency lies behind world-shaking events? *Calling* (omit *forth*) means either 'announcing' (the Lord plans history's programme), or 'calling (by name)' (the Lord appoints his own agents) or 'calling on' (the Lord appoints the destiny to which history and its agents are moving). (*With*) *the first* (*of them*) *and with the last*: the brackets here indicate where NIV has made additions. MT as it stands affirms the Lord as the sole Origin ('The First') and implies his presiding presence right through the course of history until at the end he is 'with the last'. *I am he* may simply be the answer to the question *Who ...?* but more likely it expresses the changeless self-consistency of the Lord (46:4; Ps. 102:27–28) or his unqualified existence (43:10; 48:12), whereas all others live by his will and permission.

The pathetic alternative to the invitation and the verdict (41:5–7). Universally (*islands*, see 1; *ends of the earth*), the only alternative to the God who reveals himself (*I, the LORD ... I am he*, 4) is man-made gods. Isaiah introduced this topic in 40:19–20; he pursues it here and it remains one of the major emphases of chapters 40 – 48. The sequence of thought here is typical: universal nervousness (5ab) drives humankind into collective security (5c, 6ab) and a brotherhood of fear (6b). Out of this emerges the need to have a 'spiritual' power on their side (7) but the product cannot exceed its source: human skill (7abc), human approval (7d), human stability (7e). Humankind's 'gods' are only projections of humankind's weaknesses.

iv. Three pictures: guaranteed consolations (41:8–20). The common theme of these three pictures is transformed helplessness. In verses 8–13 Israel is twice addressed as *servant* (lit. 'slave'), that is to say a person without position or rights – but this slave belongs to a great master: he is *my servant* (8–9) and he has on his side *my righteous right hand* (10), therefore the powers ranged against him must fail. In verses 14–16, *Jacob* is a *worm* (14), but by the Lord's *help* (14) the worm triumphs over impossible obstacles (15). In verses 17–20, there is the exodus imagery of helplessness before the adversity of the desert: terrible life-threatening thirst. But now *the God of Israel* comes to the rescue, transforming circumstances and making creation itself

new. Thus, then, hostile forces are vanquished (8–14), impossible
barriers removed (15–16) and killing conditions transformed (17–
20). And all this through divine action: *I will strengthen* (10), *I
will make* (15), *I will ... answer* (17). In context, therefore, the
three pictures affirm that the divine life promised in 40:31 is not
wishful thinking but a practical reality, even in a world of
superior powers (8–13), colossal difficulties (14–16) and adverse
circumstances (17–20).

Victory for the lowly (41:8–13). 8–9. *My servant* (8–9): the
great keyword of chapters 40 – 55 makes its first appearance.
Logically we want to know what a *servant* does, but this passage
tells us nothing of his task. It tells us, first, that *Israel* came to be
the Lord's *servant* by divine choice (8b, 9d; Eph. 1:4); secondly,
that the relationship began with *Abraham. My friend* (2 Ch. 20:7;
Jas. 2:23) is literally 'my loving one'/'who loved me'. Thirdly, it
tells us that the extension of the covenant promise to Abraham's
descendants (lit. 'seed', Gn. 17:7) still stands (*chosen you ... not
rejected you*); and, fourthly, that in his choice and calling of
Abraham the Lord showed that his power extends to *the ends of
the earth ... its farthest corners*. In all this there is nothing of any
function the *servant* may perform; only that Israel has an
honoured status. In other words, a slave as such is a social
nonentity, but before you kick him, ask who his owner is!

10–13. It is to this Owner that Isaiah now turns. Just as the
thought of status (expressed by *servant*) bracketed verses 8–9, so
the thought of safety (*do not fear*; *my right hand ... your right
hand*; *help*) brackets 10–13. Within the bracket, the words
describing opposed forces are in each case emphatic (*who rage
... oppose ... enemies ... war against*, 11–12). Thus all opposition
is held within the embrace of pledged divine presence and help,
and consequently it will come to nothing (*disgraced ... perish ...
not find ... nothing at all*). The Lord's presence (*with you*, 10) and
commitment (*your God*) are the antidote to *fear. Dismayed* is to
dart glances this way and that, being at a loss to know what to do
for the best. The Lord, however, is no mere passive companion.
His presence brings his active strength, expressed as a mounting
tide of assistance: 'Yes, I will strengthen you; Oh indeed, I will
help you; Why, I will uphold you ... !' For *uphold*, see Exodus
17:12. *My righteous right hand*: the *hand* (40:12) is the organ of
personal action; the (lit.) 'right hand of my righteousness' is the
Lord's personal action implementing his righteous promises and
purposes.

Verses 11–12 express, first, a mounting tide of hostility,
starting with the emotion of *rage*, moving on to the formulation

of a complaint (*oppose you* means 'have a case against you'); next comes active opposition (*enemies* is 'the men of your struggle', lit. 'those who actively oppose you'), leading to open *war*. But each verse (11d, 12d) ends with the opposition coming to *nothing*. Verse 11 describes this descent to nothingness from the point of view of the opponents; 12, from the point of view of the one opposed, pictured as searching for a now non-existent foe. The Lord's promises and reassurances (10) are the ground of actual safety and deliverance (13).

Transformation for the negligible (41:14–16). Here is a remarkable picture: a *worm* faced with *mountains* and *hills*! An impossible barrier! But the *worm* is transformed into a *threshing-sledge* of such mammoth proportions that the mountains are chopped into *chaff* and carried away on the wind.

14. Contrasting with human incapacity (*worm*) in the face of daunting obstacles, there is, first, personal divine action (*I myself*), then, secondly, the affirmed word of divine promise (*declares*, lit. '[it is] the word of', see 1:4). Thirdly, *the LORD*, Yahweh, who purposes to act, has already proved both his willingness and power to do so through the exodus (Ex. 3:15). Fourthly, he himself undertakes whatever we need: *Redeemer* is *gō'ēl*, see 35:10, the Next-of-Kin who takes upon himself his people's needs as if they were his own; and, fifthly, God is on the side of his people in the fullness of the divine nature: *the Holy One of Israel* (see 1:4). The title always holds two ideas together: as *holy* he possesses the divine nature to the full; as *of Israel* he has pledged himself to his people.

15–16. Note the balance between *I will make* and *you will winnow*. The Lord's transforming power is not meant to immobilize but to enable his people. A *threshing-sledge* was a heavy wooden platform with sharp cutting edges fitted underneath. *Thresh the mountains*: *i.e.* tackle the seemingly impossible, remove the seemingly impenetrable (Zc. 4:7). *Wind ... gale*: the 'forces of nature' are often used as symbols of divine action (Pss. 18:7–15; 104:4). So, here, the Lord who transforms (15a) and mobilizes (16a) his people leaps in powerfully on their side to scatter and remove what stood in their way. *The LORD ... the Holy One of Israel* occurs here as the end 'bracket' matching verse 14. *Rejoice ... glory*: joy, here (*cf.* the singing of 54:1) symbolizes glad entrance into what the Lord has done for us; he is the Agent, we the beneficiaries; his the work, ours the joy.

Provision for the needy (41:17–20). The righteous God who upholds (8–13), the Redeemer who transforms (14–16), is now the Creator who provides. He transforms his creation for the benefit of his people in their need. The details of the picture are drawn from Exodus 13 – 17.

17. *Poor* means 'lowly' and comes to mean 'down-trodden', crushed under life's burden (10:2). *Needy* has the positive connotation of 'willing' (especially, willing to go God's way) but the negative connotation of 'pliable', bending before life's more powerful forces, resourceless (14:30). In Exodus 17, faced with lack of water, the people grumbled; Moses prayed, and prayer, not grumbling, was the solution to the crisis. When needs are faced by prayer, *I the LORD will answer ... not forsake*.

18–19. Water (18) and shade (19) are the two great needs of the desert traveller (Ex. 15:27). None of the trees mentioned are fruit trees: the point is shelter, not sustenance. The trees, also, are all Palestinian, not Mesopotamian, indicating the location of the author. The Lord's answer to prayer comes by innovation (*rivers* on *barren heights*), multiplication (*springs* where water already flowed in the *valleys*) and transformation (*desert* and *parched ground* becoming *pools and springs*). *Together*: 'all at once', a dramatic miracle of provision.

20. *People*: simply 'they', *i.e.* the 'needy' of verse 17, forming, with *the LORD* and *Israel*, a bracket around the section. On *Lord ... Holy One*, see verse 14; *created*, see 4:5.

b. Gentile hope (41:21 – 42:17)

The first two of the three voices of comfort in 40:3–11 had definite universal dimensions: *all mankind ... all men* (40:5–6). The passages on God the Creator and the Lord of history (40:12–31; 41:1–7) both flowed out into assurances for Israel (40:27–31; 41:8–20). Yet the three pictures in 41:8–20 focus completely on *Israel* (8), *Jacob* (14), the 'exodus people' under the care of *the God of Israel* (17, 20). So what has happened to the universal dimension? Isaiah has made his readers face the grim reality of belonging to the world outside Israel – in particular the spiritual plight of worshipping man-made gods (40:18–20) and the consequent defencelessness of life on earth with none to turn to but gods who are themselves products of human trembling (41:5–7). But the Creator God, who cannot forget his chosen (40:27ff.), does not forget the wide reaches of his creation, and it is to this topic that Isaiah now turns, revealing how the universal aspects of the message of comfort will be met.

i. Summoned before the court: the plight of the Gentile world (41:21–29).

This section falls into two parallel halves. In verse 21 the idol gods are summoned to court and, in parallel

(25), the Lord testifies before the court; 22–23 state the question which is to be tested at law: can the idols predict the future? Apparently not! But (26–27) the Lord can! Consequently, the Judge sums up both the uselessness of idols (24) and the plight of their devotees (28–29). As usual in Old Testament courtroom dramas we must accept that the Lord calls the court into session, appears before it as one of the witnesses, and finally pronounces the decision himself as Judge. The topic being tested at law – ability to predict – arises from what we have already been told about the Gentile world. In 41:2–7, in the face of the conqueror, the world trembles and rushes to make gods to meet a challenge which has caught them unawares. Their gods, like themselves, are wise only after the event.

The courtroom (1): idols and idolaters challenged (41:21–24). 21. *The LORD ... Jacob's King*: this emphasis on a (merely) national God is deliberate. The Lord comes before the court as one God among many – because this is the point at issue: which of all the claimants to divinity is genuine?

22–23. *Bring in your idols ...* , literally 'Bring them near and let them tell us' (22a), is best understood (with NIV) as a command to idolaters to carry in their gods. The challenge is expressed in general terms: predict the future (22ab)! This is then set out in its two aspects: first, 22cde explains the 'flow' of history, so that in the light of *former things* (what has happened already) they might deduce what the *outcome* will be. Can they foretell the future by understanding the past? Alternatively, can they say simply what will happen next (23ab)? These abilities, says Isaiah, would prove that *you are gods. Do something*: better, 'Indeed, do anything!' Isaiah gives them *carte blanche*. His contention, sensibly, is that deity will show itself in two ways: by actions (23d) demonstrating life, and by predictions demonstrating sovereign rule over the world in all its complexity. A real God will show himself by speaking his word and then watching over his word to bring it to pass (Nu. 23:19; Je. 1:9, 11).

24. To catch the effect, allow a silence between verses 23 and 24. The gods who can do nothing can say nothing either (Ps. 115:4–7). So the Judge rounds on them as one whose point has been proved. 'Behold' (omitted in NIV), or 'Just look!' *Less than nothing*, 'partakers of nonentity'; *worthless*, an otherwise unknown word, is possibly related to the verb 'to gasp', hence a 'sigh', something insubstantial and evanescent. *Chooses you*: a deliberate contrast with verse 8. *Detestable*: a technical word, 'abhorrent (to the Lord)' (Dt. 7:25–26). People become like the gods they choose (Ps. 115:8; Je. 2:5).

257

The courtroom (2): the true God in action and prediction (41:25–29). The idol gods have been exposed as ignorant of the future (22–23) and unable to act (23) but, by contrast, the Lord is the Agent behind history (25) and the Predictor of what he will do (25–27).

25–26. *Stirred*: the same verb as in verse 2 with the same meaning of 'rousing as from sleep', the initiation of the subsequent flow of events. The advocates of a 'Second Isaiah' (see pp. 28–33) place the prophet in Babylon, living and ministering within the period of Cyrus the conqueror. If we had only verse 26 this might be a feasible view. *From the beginning* could mean that the Lord was able to do the second thing he had challenged the idols to do: to discern the flow of events and judge their tendency; specifically to understand and interpret the activity of Cyrus. But the *stirred up* of verse 25 claims more. The initiative rests with the Lord; the conqueror was, so to say, asleep till the Lord woke him up. The Lord can do the first thing he asked of the idols: tell the future from scratch! This is the implication of *beforehand, i.e.* prior to something else (Jos. 11:10; 14:15). Hence, here, 'from the beginning and (even) before the beginning'. The Lord is the Originator of events. *North ... rising sun*: from his Palestinian viewpoint, Isaiah describes the coming conqueror in typical terms: in his lifetime the great threats to the western states arose from the east and invaded from the north. But, as Isaiah develops this theme, the unnamed conqueror becomes Cyrus (44:24 – 45:7), who did indeed originate in the east and descended on Babylon from the north. *Calls on my name*: the Hebrew (*qārā' bᵉšēm*) has four possible meanings: to worship (Gn. 12:8), to call by name (40:26), to bring into close relationship (43:1) and to proclaim a name (Ex. 34:5). In this context the suitable meaning is that, since the rise and career of the conqueror confirms the predictions, he will by his coming and actions proclaim the Lord as the only God. *He was right*: used in lawcourts of the one in whose favour the verdict was pronounced.

27. Marvellously staccato Hebrew betrays Isaiah's excitement: literally, it reads 'The first thing – to Zion – Watch, watch for them – a bringer of good news – I will give!' The 'first thing' is not the event but the Lord's predictive word. Those who believe it watch for its fulfilment. To a captive people another conqueror is usually bad news, but as well as predicting coming events the Lord also tells their significance: this conqueror is good news.

28–29. Matching verse 24 with its exposure of the uselessness of the idol gods, Isaiah now turns to the plight of those who live their lives without divine revelation. No-one gives them counsel or answers their questions. They are *false*, delusive, fraudulent (32:6). *Deeds* best refers here to the 'work' of making an idol. Where there is no veritable voice from heaven (28) nothing that humans can do will fill that gap – except with nonentity (*nothing*, see 40:17), insubstantiality (*wind*) and meaninglessness (*confusion, tōhû*, 24:10; 40:17).

ii. The Servant: the great solution (42:1–9). The NIV fails to bring out the dramatic link between 42:1 and what has preceded. In two parallel passages (41:21–24, 25–29) Isaiah exposed the deadness of idols. Each passage ended with a dramatic summons (Heb. *hēn*), 'Look!' or 'Behold!': verse 24, 'Look at this! – Meaningless idols!'; verse 29, 'Look at this! – Pathetic idolaters!' Now, for the third time, the same word rings out (42:1, *hēn*): 'Look at this! – My Servant!' See Introduction, pp. 26–27. The advent of the Lord's Servant is unexpected but not inappropriate: he comes as the Lord's answer to the plight of a world without divine revelation. His ministry is *justice* (verses 1d, 3c, 4b): *to the nations*, worldwide justice (1d); *in faithfulness*, genuine justice; and justice established *on earth* (4b), permanent justice. We naturally think of *justice* as implying a fair and pure society, and of course the word *mišpāṭ* – caters for this – but only derivatively. The parallel in verse 4bc between *justice* and *law* provides us with the clue that in this passage Isaiah is using the word to express one aspect of divinely revealed truth. *Law* means 'teaching' (1:10): *mišpāṭ* – to mention no other examples – occurs nearly thirty times in Psalm 119 (7, 13, 20, *etc.*) and nearly twenty times in Deuteronomy (4:1; 5:1; *etc.*) as one aspect of what we would call 'the word of God'. The verb behind the noun (√*šāpaṭ*) means 'to give judgment', the authoritative pronouncement of king or judge. Just as the Lord's *law* is his teaching, so his *justice* ('judgment') is what he has pronounced to be true, the decision he has reached. The Servant comes, then, as the bearer to the *nations* of what they have hitherto lacked: a veritable word from God, the answer to their needs as exposed in 41:24, 28–29. At this point, Isaiah does not ask who the Servant is. His task, to be the Agent of worldwide revelation, corresponds to the worldwide role of Abraham and his 'seed' (Gn. 12:3; 18:18; 22:18; 26:4). Furthermore, in 41:8, 'Israel' has been addressed as 'my servant' so that, at this point, the connection must be made: the Servant is Israel, the 'seed' of Abraham. We must wait to see how Isaiah will develop this basic truth.

1. *Uphold*: literally 'grip fast'. The idea is not so much of imparting strength as of the Lord's rights over his Servant and his determination to keep his Servant for himself. *In whom I delight*: literally 'in whom my soul delights'. 'Soul' here represents personal commitment, as we might say 'delight with all my heart'. Someone can be chosen for a task without necessarily being approved of or even liked – as every employer knows! Not so here! He is not only the Lord's man for the job, he is (like David, 1 Sa. 13:14; Acts13:22) the Lord's man for the Lord himself. *My Spirit* is the Lord's personal presence (Ps. 139:7) in action (40:7; Ps. 33:6), endowing for leadership (Nu. 11:16ff.; 1 Sa. 16:13; *cf.* 11:1–2; 61:1–2). As a consequence of this divine enduement, the Servant will perform the universal task of bringing divine truth (*justice*) *to the nations*, the Gentiles worldwide.

2–3. The keyword *justice* occurs for the second time (3c), now linked with the manner of the Servant as he brings God's revelation. He is not self-assertive (2): probably the three verbs here are cumulative, stressing his quiet, unaggressive demeanour, but *shout* ('shriek') could suggest that he is not out to startle, *cry out* ('raise his voice') not out to dominate or shout others down, *raise his voice* ('make his voice heard') not out to advertise himself. He is not dismissive of others: however useless or beyond repair (*bruised reed*), however 'past it' and near extinction (*smouldering wick*) they may seem. The negative statements imply their positive equivalents: he can mend the broken reed, fan into flame the smouldering wick. The former has been internally damaged, the latter lacks the external nourishment of oil. The Servant is competent both to cure and to supply.

4. *Falter* and *discouraged* ('burn low ... bruise [easily]') match the corresponding words in verse 3. The Servant comes right into the human situation. The things that crush and quench he will experience, but he will triumph and succeed in 'establishing' *justice*, the revelation of God, *on earth*. *Establishes* ($\sqrt{s\hat{i}m}$): used in Deuteronomy 4:44 of Moses' 'setting' the Lord's law before Israel. Through the Servant's *law* (teaching) the privilege of the one nation becomes the possession of all. *Islands*: earth's remotest bound (see 40:15). *Put their hope*: when they hear, the Gentile world will stake their future (confidently) in what he reveals.

Verses **5–9** comprise the 'tailpiece' to verses 1–4. One of the features of the key passages about the Servant – usually called 'the Servant Songs' (also in 49:1–6; 50:4–9; 52:13 – 53:12) – is that each is followed by a 'tailpiece' (49:7–13; 50:10–11; 54:1 – 55:13) confirming whatever has just been said. This particular 'tailpiece' first (5) confirms the universal task of the Servant by dwelling on the Lord of all creation, secondly (6–7) pledges the

Lord's aid to his Servant (*cf.* 1), and thirdly (8–9) confirms the Servant's success (*cf.* 4) by forecasting the overthrow of false gods and affirming the ability of the Lord of history to bring about the promised new situation.

5. *God* here is *hā'ēl*. The word *'ēl* is God transcendent (40:18). The addition of the definite article (*hā*) is for emphasis: 'he who is indeed the true transcendent God'. *LORD*, as the capital letters indicate, is 'Yahweh', the God who revealed himself to Israel (Ex. 3:15). In 40:12ff., the truth of God the Creator was turned to the exclusive comfort of Israel (40:27–31), but the Creator of all cannot forget the 'all' he has created. The saving mercies he revealed to Israel are for his whole world. The verbs *created ... stretched ... spread ... gives* are in Hebrew all participles expressing the unchanging relationship between the Lord and his world. He, who in the beginning created, continues in creative care and dominance; *heavens* and *earth* are maintained in place by his constant activity; all life comes from him. *Created*: see 4:5. *All that comes ... breath ... life* ('spirit') are respectively productivity, life itself, and vitality or personal ability. The 'life' of the natural world, just as much as the life of humans, is the constantly ministered life of God. Life is not inherent in the soil, nor is human life the product of a self-existing evolutionary surge, but the direct gift of the Creator. It is not held in perpetuity but is enjoyed by the faithfulness of his continuing 'giving'.

6–7. *You* is the Servant. *Righteousness*: both the conqueror (41:2) and the Servant are called in pursuance of the Lord's righteous purposes. The same Lord rules in history and in grace. *Take ... keep ... make* express purpose: 'in order to take', *etc.* The Lord does not call (6a) and then leave the Servant to his own devices. Included in the calling are a divine commitment to accompany (the *hand* held), to keep safe (*keep*) and to achieve his objectives (*make*). *Keep* (√*nāṣar*) is to preserve, safeguard; but the form here could derive from √*yasar*, to shape, fashion; whom the Lord calls 'shapes' for the appointed task. *Covenant*: the Servant is the covenant – not just that through him *people ... Gentiles* are brought into a covenant relationship with the Lord, but that in him covenant blessings are enjoyed. The 'covenant' is God's free decision and promise to take and keep a people for his own possession. It was Israel's unique privilege – to be drawn to the Lord in deliverance and redemption (Ex. 6:2–7), to know and obey him as redeemer (Ex. 20:1–3). It began on a universal scale with Noah (Gn. 6:17–18; 9:8–17); it became specific to Abraham (Gn. 15, 17), the man entrusted with the universal blessing; it reached its normative form in Moses (Ex. 2:24; 24:7–8); and now, in the Servant, it extends once more to the whole world. Universality is not, therefore, a violation or adjustment of the covenant; it is its fulfilment. It brings, in the Servant, the *light* of truth, the healing of disabilities (*open eyes*), liberation from oppressive restrictions (*free captives*) and transformation of circumstances (*from ... darkness*): like Eden, with perfect people, perfect society and perfect environment (61:1).

8–9. These verses repeat what has been either a main theme or a sub-theme in chapters 40 – 41: there is no God but the Lord (8) and he is in charge of the flow of events (9). We can imagine the Servant, faced with the task of bringing divine revelation to the Gentile world. It is a world full of 'gods' who, however unreal they are, nevertheless exercise unimaginable power over human minds and hearts. What an assurance, then, that in reality there is only one God, jealous for his *name* and *glory*, a God as much in control of the future as he is of the past, therefore the Guarantor of the fulfilment of his Word. *My name* is the Lord's distinct personal identity, differentiating him from *idols*. He does not exist *incognito* among them; his *glory*, his own glorious nature, is not for sharing. Even should they ape him, it is a coincidence: he is not there. Furthermore, he is their foe and will not ultimately tolerate their continuance. In the sequence of Isaiah's thought from 41:1 onwards, the *former things* are the events linked with the irresistible conqueror (41:1–4, 25–27) and the *new things* are the now-foretold work of the Servant (42:1–4). Isaiah envisages himself, for dramatic effect, as looking back on the one and forward to the other, so that the certain fulfilment of the one set of predictions gives assurance of the prospective fulfilment of the other.

iii. Singing world, saving Lord (42:10–17). Rounding off this section on the hopelessness and hope of the Gentile world which began at 41:21, *the ends of the earth*, the *islands* (10), and the Gentile towns of *Kedar* and *Sela* (11), combine in praise to the Lord who marches against his enemies (12–13). The Lord himself then (14–17) elaborates this cause for praise. His age-long silence is broken (14), he plans a world transformation (15), the world's needy are cared for (16) and idolaters exposed to their proper shame (17). This lovely song fits accurately into its context. The Servant brought hope to the islands (4) and *islands* now rejoice (10); the Lord guaranteed that the Servant would open blind eyes (7) and their *darkness* becomes *light* (16); he promised that his glory would no longer be given to idols (8) and the former devotees of the idols now give him praise (12). A world's song to a saving Lord indeed!

10–13. There is a call to sing (10–11), the subject of the song (12), and the cause of celebration (13). The viewpoint is universal: the wide perspective (10) of *earth* and *islands* contrasts with the local perspective (11) of *desert*, *Kedar* in the north (Syrian) Arabian desert and *Sela* in Moab; the remote *ends of the earth* contrast with nearby *Kedar*, *islands* with *desert*, *earth* with *sea*, and *down* to sea-level with *mountaintops*. Thus the whole world unites in a *new song* (10), that is, a song (Pss. 33:3; 96:1; 98:1) responding to a new display of the goodness of God, a *new song* prompted by the 'new things' (9) and, as always, the motif of entering with joy into a freely given benefit (54:1). The conqueror provoked universal terror (41:1–7); the Servant prompts universal song. The earth (*islands*, *desert*) joins its people (*all who live*) in praise because creation itself has been released from the bondage of corruption into the liberty of the children of God (Rom. 8:19ff.). The repeated call to praise (12) introduces the cause of all this overflowing joy (13): the triumph of the warrior Lord. *Mighty man* is specifically 'warrior', the noun *gibbor* matched by its verb *triumph over* (√*gāḇār*), 'prove himself a warrior indeed'.

In verses **14–17** Isaiah turns abruptly from the war metaphor of verse 13. In chapters 40 – 55 he makes no secret that the Lord has enemies and that the day of their defeat will come, but as a topic this belongs to chapters 56 – 66 – in exactly the same way that the Lord Jesus terminated his quotation of 61:1, 23 (Lk. 4:17–19) without mentioning *the day of vengeance*, because that belongs to his second coming, not his first.

14. The *long* silence comprises the whole history of the Gentile world. That it should have been left without a word from God is not accidental or purposeless. It was a self-imposed divine restraint but, as with pregnancy, it was a period leading step by step to a planned, dated and inevitable outcome. The Lord had never forgotten the whole world in his prior engagement with the family of Abraham. He has been gestating a great purpose, and now it has come to birth.

15–16. It will be a time when the old order is brought to an end: the fertility (*vegetation*) and water (*rivers, pools*) that sustained life will disappear, but that does not mean the end of life, only a different way of life – a life dependent on the Lord's care for whose whom he leads out. He caters for everything: their personal incapacities of blindness and ignorance (16ab),

circumstantial problems of darkness and rough terrain (16cd) –
and all with the guarantee of his personal presence and action
(*lead ... guide ... turn ... not forsake*). It would be totally
unsuitable to think that this refers to the return journey from
Babylonian exile. That was a way on which they needed no
guide. The Lord is in fact himself undertaking the task he earlier
(7) appeared to depute to his Servant. It is the Gentile world,
blind without divine revelation, being brought from darkness to
light, and from the power of Satan to God (Acts 26:15–18).

17. However, the theme of victory over foes cannot be forgotten, and verse 17 matches 13. The former verse merely notes
confrontation and victory; the latter offers explanations. Who are
the Lord's enemies? Those who stubbornly hold on in faith to
false gods. In a world of praise (10–12) it is they who will experience shame; some will be led to safety under divine care (16),
others will refuse. *Shame* always has the idea of 'reaping shame',
experiencing disappointment of hopes, suffering loss where they
reached for gain. Their *trust* was in *idols ... images* – the former
carved, the latter molten: either way mere human artefacts.
Ultimately their trust was in themselves and what they could do.
It was the way of works – not that simple trust in the Lord,
beautifully illustrated when the blind take a proffered hand (16).

VII. THE LORD'S PLAN UNFOLDED (42:18 – 44:23)

Isaiah has seen his people caught up in a double plight: *captivity*
because of *sin* – and that the deadliest of all sins, the
abandonment of the way of faith, the rejection of the Lord's
promises in favour of a do-it-yourself remedy (chs. 38 – 39). But
the double plight was matched by a double cure, the word of
comfort (40:1–2): both that the time of duress would end, and
that iniquity would be pardoned. The section that now opens
continues along this twin track – and it really is a twin track: the
parallel development of two themes. Captivity will be ended by
national liberation (42:18 – 43:21), and sin dealt with by spiritual
redemption (43:22 – 44:23). Under the former heading, Isaiah
moves through four topics: captivity (42:18–25), the meeting of
this need (43:1–7), the Lord, Saviour and sole God, in contrast
with idols (43:8–13), and redemption from Babylon (43:14–21).
He then offers four matching topics: sin (43:22–24), the meeting
of this need (43:25 – 44:5), the Lord, Redeemer and only God in
contrast with idols (44:6–20), and redemption from sin (44:21–
23). It is important to grasp this overall plan. Isaiah wrote a book
with planned development and everything in its proper place. As

an example of this, note how, with the matching passages on idols (43:8–13; 44:6–20), each suits its own context: the former focuses on the inability of other 'gods' to act in history, the latter on their inability to save spiritually.

a. Israel's bondage and liberation (42:18 – 43:21)

i. The blind servant (42:18–25). 18–19. In verse 18 *blind* (like *deaf*) is plural, in verse 19 *blind* is singular. The plural looks back to verses 7 and 16, where the *blind* are the benighted Gentile world out of which the Lord will lead, by his Servant and by his personal action, those whom he illuminates. Since verse 19 is about the Lord's servant, this is plainly a topic of vital concern to the Gentile world, for their spiritual illumination and deliverance is at stake. But when they look, it is to see a *servant* as *blind* as they are! This *servant* is the one mentioned in 41:8, the Lord's people, Israel: but now an *Israel* in 'prisons' (22), consigned to 'the plunderers' (24); and, as if this were not disappointment enough for the *blind* Gentiles, an Israel under punishment for sin (24) and without spiritual sensitivity (25). Isaiah, then, is doing two things: first, he is ruling out the possibility that the servant nation (41:8) can be the Servant revealer and rescuer (42:1–7). Can the *blind* lead the *blind*? Some other Servant must emerge if the great role is to be fulfilled. But, secondly, Isaiah is dramatically introducing the topic of this section: how deep is Israel's need! The heaping up of honorific titles, *servant ... messenger ... committed ... servant*, underlines the dignity of the calling of the people of God. *Servant* as defined in 42:1–4 confers the duty of bringing divine revelation to a bereft world; *messenger* (lit. 'my messenger whom I send') speaks of a commission given to one on whom the Lord has a personal claim ('my'); *committed* comes from √*šālēm*, 'to be at peace, enjoy wholeness/well-being'. The form of passive participle found here means 'brought into peace, reconciled', *i.e.* enjoying the benefits and blessings of salvation. But Israel, sadly, is *deaf* to his word and *blind*, or spiritually untransformed. This latter thought is the one Isaiah hammers out, *blind ... blind ... blind*,[1] underlying the need for the work of transforming grace which it is the servant's task to bring to the world.

---

[1] The double use of *blind* in vv. 19cd where parallelism would expect *deaf* in the final line has provoked adverse comment. Whybray (*Isaiah 40 – 66*) calls it 'extremely ugly'. But in Heb. poetry parallelism is a tool, not a bondage. It is the genius of Heb. poetry to make 'form' flexible to meaning, and the unexpected *blind* is exactly the right emphasis in context.

20. The blindness and deafness of the Israel-servant is now carefully diagnosed. It is not the total darkness of the Gentile world (41:7, 16). The Lord's Israel has sight, *you have seen many things*, an abundant revelation of divine truth has been granted; spiritual deafness has been remedied, *your ears are open*. The problem with the Lord's people (then and now) is not that the basic work of transformation is yet to be done, but that, transformation having taken place, *no attention* has been paid, the open ears *hear nothing*. The word of God is available but ignored.

21. The verse speaks of something that delights the Lord (*pleased*, as in 53:10), of something that expresses his righteous nature and fulfils his righteous purpose (*righteousness*) – his *law* or 'teaching', the truth of God imparted by revelation to his people – and of the purpose he envisaged in giving his *law*, literally 'that he should make the law great and mighty/splendid'. The 'he' in question may be the Lord himself: he gave his teaching to his people, purposing through their obedience that divine truth should be seen in its greatness and splendour. Alternatively the 'he' may be Israel: that they should set out, by faithful adherence to Scripture in conviction and practice, to display the wonders of divine truth to the world (*cf.* Dt. 4:5–7; Tit. 2:10).

22. But, far from winning the world, the world conquered Israel (*cf.* 2:5–9)! Through failure to 'make the law great', Israel lost its distinctive status in the world (22:a–c) and its protected status before the Lord (22d–g) – the truth taught in the Song of the Vineyard: no fruit-bearing, no protection (5:1–7). *Pits ... prisons*: no prophet living with exiled Israel in Babylon could so describe the exile. Conditions were not quite as bad as that (Je. 29). Isaiah is using conventional stereotypes of captivity to underscore the enormity of Israel's downfall from the divine intention.

23–25. Recognizing that he has an unpalatable truth to share (*Which of you will listen?*), Isaiah takes us to the theological heart of Israel's situation. First, the key question to ask is not 'Why?' but 'Who?' 'Why?' is the cry of logic looking for a way to make life's tragedies fit into a humanly satisfying pattern. To this there is no answer (55:8). 'Who?' brings us to rest on the executive sovereignty of the Lord. *Was it not the LORD*? Secondly, for the people of God the word of God is the clue to life: the tragedy came about through sin. *They would not follow ... did not obey*: *i.e.* specifically the sin of having revealed truth but not conforming to it. *Would not follow*: (lit.) 'were not willing to walk in', *i.e.* an unsubmitted will. *Obey*: 'listen to', the submission of the mind to the word of God. Thirdly, there is the reality of divine chastisement: his personal *burning anger*. On *anger*, *cf.* 5:25. *Violence of war:* the Lord of history uses the forces of history to punish his disobedient people. Fourthly, disobedience brings suffering and loss, *flames ... consumed*. But, fifthly, not even suffering on the scale of defeat, bondage and deprivation (22) produced reformation: as Isaiah viewed his people he saw in them spiritual incomprehension, they *did not understand ... take it to heart*. The Lord's people though they are, possessing his truth though they do, they are still direly in need of an inner work of transformation, first touching the mind (*understand*, lit. 'know'), and then the *heart*, the inner spring of responsiveness and direction (Pr. 4:23).

ii. Unchanged divine care (43:1–7). With great drama, Isaiah moves from the Lord's people in the Lord's fire (42:25) to the Lord who will not allow the fire to burn them (43:2).

1. *But now* makes a logical connection with what has gone before: 'Now then'. Israel has been revealed as blind (42:19), inattentive (42:20), falling short of the Lord's plan (42:21), defeated (42:2), sinfully disobedient (42:24), spiritually uncomprehending and insensitive (42:25). 'Now then' is enough to make us quake in our shoes! How will the Lord react to such a catalogue of culpability? *Created ... formed*: the verbs are used in their established sense, the former to bring into being, *de novo*, by a sole and free act of God, and the latter to fashion and mould into shape as a potter would. So the Lord determined to have a people for his very own, brought them into being and shaped them on the wheel of circumstances. This is the first ground on which the Lord will say, *you are mine* (Eph. 1:4; 2:10). The second ground is redemption. The verb is $\sqrt{g\bar{a}'al}$ (35:10). The Lord made himself the Next-of-Kin of the people he had created. They are his family and he shoulders all their needs as if his own. The third ground is the personal relationship between the Lord and his people (*summoned by name*) whereby, as we might say, they are on first-name terms.

2. The Lord will not now desert his people. They may have given up on him (42:18–25), but not he on them! Many see the hardships mentioned here as those of the exiles returning from captivity, but such extreme hardships rather suggest those of captives being dragged off by their captors (*cf.* 47:2). When Isaiah speaks of homecoming, he does so in terms of a new exodus journey, with miraculous provisions and supplies (48:20–21).

3–4. The safety they enjoy under and within such life-threatening experiences (2) is explained (*For*) in five ways. (a) By the Lord's name, *LORD*, Yahweh, the everlasting statement of his character (Ex. 3:15). Yahweh is the God defined in the exodus revelation as the One who delivers and redeems his people (Ex. 6:6–7) and overthrows his foes (Ex. 12:12). Unless he changes his name (alters his character), he is committed to his Israel. (b) By the relationship between himself and his people: notwithstanding all their failings (42:18–25), he still calls himself *your God.* (c) By his holiness: the great Isaianic title, *the Holy One of Israel* (1:4), holds together the reality of his holiness and the reality of his relationship with Israel. If his holiness and their sinfulness did not militate against forming the relationship, then it cannot militate against its continuance. (d) By his saving ability: while the verb √*yāša'* expresses salvation from sin (64:5), it majors on deliverance from afflictions (1 Sa. 9:16; 2 Sa. 22:4), suitably to this context. (e) By the evidence of the past: NIV follows many in the translation *I will give*, and, of course, the Hebrew perfect tense can well express a confidence for the future ('I have determined to give'), but this is understandable only if we take it to mean 'I have determined to give (if I have to)', for Egypt has no part to play in the Lord's future care of his people. Furthermore, to translate the perfect here as a future destroys the contrast with *I will give* at the end of the verse. Rather, the titles of the Lord in verse 3ab flow naturally into a reference back to the exodus: because he is Yahweh, Israel's God and Holy One, their Saviour, he actually did give Egypt as their ransom. Faced with Egyptian intransigent refusal to let the people go, the Lord, so to speak, weighed up whether he was prepared to shatter Egypt in order to free Israel. There was 'no contest', and it was 'at the expense of' (*ransom, kōper*, the price paid; see 6:7) Egypt that Israel was freed. *Cush* and *Seba* are respectively the extreme south of Egypt and lands still further south. They are a poetical elaboration of the picture of the price paid. *In your stead* expresses one taking the place of another (Gn. 22;13; 1 Ki. 11:43). Israel was under sentence of death (Ex. 1:16, 22), but Egypt 'died' (Ex. 14:27, 31) instead. This past flows into the present, in which the Lord treasures his people (*precious*) and has not withdrawn their *honoured* position as his people. Consequently, for the future, not even humankind (*men*) itself nor all *people* ('peoples') would be too high a price.

5–7. *I will bring*: the wide reference to 'humankind' in verse 4 is now justified. The Lord foresees a worldwide scattering and a worldwide regathering. From all the compass points (5–6), embracing *everyone* of his people (7). *My sons ... daughters*: right up to the End the Next-of-Kin relationship (1; Ex. 2:21) remains unchanged, and the initial thoughts of *created* and *formed* are enhanced by the added thought that, in so doing, the Lord purposed his own *glory*. Thus his honour is bound up with the final security of those whom he chose to be his people.

iii. No other God: sure promises (43:8–13). Whether we think of Isaiah's people as in Palestine or taken into exile or residents in Babylon, they are surrounded by other gods and their devotees. Therefore they need to get their theology straight: what sort of entities are these who seem so powerful and whom others worship with such conviction? This short passage, therefore, has an abiding relevance. Notice how it climaxes on a claim by the Lord to be the only *saviour* (11). This not only links it with verses 1–7 (see 3), but it turns the discussion to the practical question of who can effectively deliver in the thick of the world's adversities. In form, the passage is another courtroom drama (*cf.* 41:21–29). The court assembles (8–9b), the issue is stated (9c–f), the Lord's witnesses are presented (10a–d) and his claim is affirmed (10c–11), the issue is settled (12), and the verdict given (13). The point of this quasi-legal presentation is that what Isaiah asserts about the Lord (11–12) is not a fable but a truth tested at law, a verified conclusion based on evidence.

8–9. We must not miss the pathos: imagine any litigant depending on the blind to testify to what they have seen and the deaf to what they have heard! The Lord's people could have been very different: theirs is a culpable deficiency, for they have *eyes* and *ears*; they were granted faculties of spiritual perception but chose to be blind and deaf, refusing to see and hear (6:9–10; 29:9; 42:20, 24) – and the Lord's case depends on their testimony! *Which of them*: the voice is that of the Presiding Judge. *This ... the former things*: the interpretation of this turns on how we understand verse 3. We noted that many make verses 3–7 refer to the future (see p. 268). If so, then *this* could be the fact of the coming conqueror (41:1–4, 25) as in that earlier court scene, and *former* (lit. 'first') *things* would be an open request to the idols to mention any earlier prediction they may have made. If (as we hold) verse 3 refers back to the exodus, then *this* and *former* both look back to that first great act of the Lord for Israel. Do the 'gods' have any such thing to their credit (*cf.* Dt. 4:34–37; 2 Sa. 7:22–24)? *Right*: *i.e.* in the right, gaining the verdict. The case must go to the one who can demonstrate by credible evidence his sovereign capacity to determine beforehand what he is going to do, and then do it without alteration, let or hindrance. This is the mark of deity.

10–11. The pathos continues. *You are my witnesses* – as if the Lord has to prompt his witnesses to testify on his behalf! How well Isaiah knows our guilty silences! *Declares*, see 1:24; s*ervant*, as in 41:8 (see 42:1). The 'servant people' inherit the Abrahamic vocation to the world, but their privileged conscription to be the Lord's (*chosen*) was intended (*so that*) to bring them to spiritual conviction (*know ... understand*, lit. 'discern, see to the heart of') and to faith. *Believe me*: the construction *ha'ᵃmîn lᵉ* mostly means to believe what someone says (Gn. 45:26) but it also includes trusting (Dt. 9:23). *I am he* is the answer to the question *Which?* in verse 9. *Before me ...* : the attempt to prod the *witnesses* into action has failed, and the Lord speaks in his own cause about his uniqueness (10ef) and his work (11). *Formed*: the gods of the pagan world were often spoken of as coming into being, but the Lord is derived from none (*before me*) and succeeded by none (*after me*). Unique in his being, he is also unique in action (*no saviour*). Only he can enter into the circumstances of his people (Ex. 3:8) and 'save' them out of all their afflictions (Ex. 14:18, 30; 15:2; Dt. 33:29).

12–13. Thus the issue is settled (12) and the verdict pronounced (13). *Revealed* ('declared') is the verb translated 'proclaimed' in verse 9. It was only the Lord who thus proclaimed what he would do, not the idols. The sequence of the three verbs *revealed* ('declared') ... *saved* ... *proclaimed* ('made [people] hear') is important. Moses and his people were not left to look back on the exodus, surmise that it was an act of God, and fumble about to discern its meaning. Revelation comes first (Ex. 3 – 4) in clear divine speech: the actual words of God anticipating the acts of God; then the events confirm the words; and finally there is the ministry of Moses, spelling out what the Lord has done and what it means. *You are my witnesses*: again the prompting to witness, but yet again (13) the Lord must take the task on himself. In keeping with the court scene, this last divine statement takes the form of the verdict. The Lord alone is God. *From ancient days* (*miyyôm*) can mean 'since time began' or 'today' or 'from today on' – a comprehensive claim to a deity which pervades all time. *No-one can deliver*: this is no remote or ornamental deity but a sovereign over every other possible agency, human or 'divine'. The Lord is the God who has absolute rights over all people and, as *who can reverse ...?* adds, over the whole course of events as he determines they shall happen.

iv. A new exodus: the problem of bondage solved (43:14–21). This passage concludes the section which began at 42:18: the problem of national enslavement and the Lord's promise to solve it. The sequence is coherent: the problem (42:18–25), the Lord's unchanged care of his people (43:1–7), his sovereign ability to save (43:8–13) and, finally, the deliverance he will effect. The exodus which has been alluded to throughout (43:3, 9, 11) now dominates the imagery (16–17, 19–20): what the Lord has done is the model for his coming acts.

14–15. *Redeemer*: *gō'ēl* (see 1). *Babylon*: this, the first reference to Babylon in chapters 40 – 48, picks up the Babylon reference in 39:6: they will be going *to Babylon* and the Lord will send *to Babylon*. The 'Chaldeans' (NIV mg.) were a well-known component in the population of Babylon and appear here as a poetical variant for Babylon. *Ships*: Babylon is not generally linked with shipping but Jeremiah (51:13, 26) notes it as well watered. It is easy to think of the city delighting in its sea-borne trade and now to envisage the same shipping laden with refugees. This did not happen when Babylon fell (see on ch. 47). Once more (see on 42:22) Isaiah is not describing but using stereotypical images of the fall of a city. A prophet present at the event would not have spoken thus. *Holy One ... Holy One*: such emphasis on the holiness of Israel's God is unexpected. Maybe Isaiah is laying down a marker for the future by reminding Israel that political liberation is not the whole story; there remains the deeper problem of how to be right with a holy God. *Creator*: see on verse 1. *King* adds a more personal dimension to the relationship, for the king was father and shepherd of his people (9:6; Ps. 78:71).

16–21. Isaiah derives his pictures from the Red Sea event (16–17; Ex. 14) and from the wonders of that earlier wilderness journey (19c–20; Ex. 15 – 17), but he issues an important reminder: the past can teach and illustrate but it must not bind (18–19b). The Lord always has greater things in store; he is revealed in the past, but he is always more than the past revealed. *Made ... drew*: the verbs are participles in the Hebrew. What the Lord did then remains a changeless aspect of what he is: undeterred by opposing circumstances (16) or hostile people (17). *Former things* (18), *i.e.* the exodus, as in verse 9; *new thing*, *i.e.* the deliverance from Babylon, patterned on the exodus. *My people, my chosen* (20): 'people' is the relationship sealed at the exodus (Ex. 6:7); 'chosen' is the divine will behind and implementing it. *Formed*: the motif of the potter means that we can face with confidence the troubles of life – even when, as here, we are the causes of our own misfortune by disobedience. The pressures of life are loving touches of the Craftsman's hand as he perfects what he has planned.

b. Israel's sin and redemption (43:22 – 44:23)

See p. 264 above for an outline of the whole section 42:18 – 44:23 and for the place and content of this present part. The verb 'to redeem' and the title 'Redeemer' link the coming passages with the preceding (see 43:1, 14; and 44:6). The fundamental idea is that of the Next-of-Kin who has the right to come alongside his relative and take upon himself the debt, trouble or burden of the other, *whatever it may be*. It is for this reason that rescuing the exiles from Babylon (43:14) and rescuing sinners from sin (44:21–22) can both be called redemption. It is to the latter topic that Isaiah now turns.

i. Diagnosis (43:22–24). The charge apparently levelled here of failure to engage in the ritual of the sacrifices (23ab, 24ab) raises a difficulty because there is no known time in Israel's history when it would be justified. Before the exile, the complaint of the Lord through his prophets was of inordinate and over-punctilious ritual activity (1:10–15; Je. 7:21; Am. 4:4–5; 5:21–23; Mi. 6:6–7). During the exile, far from the Lord's house, sacrifice was not possible and they could hardly be blamed for failing to do what was not open to them. After the exile, their first communal act was to restore the sacrifices (Ezr. 3:3), and Haggai (2:10–14) and Malachi (1:7) both imply continuing sacrificial worship. The meaning of the present verses, therefore, must lie beneath rather than on the surface.

First, then, the emphasis in the Hebrew of verse 22a requires 'Not upon me did you call ...', an accusation matching 1:10ff., not that ritual and prayer had ceased but that they failed to reach the God to whom they were supposedly addressed. This emphasis appears only in the wording of 22a, but if we allow it to set the pattern throughout, the passage makes sense. Their religion was a failure.

Secondly, there is the verb *burdened* (23c, 24c), literally 'I did not make slaves of you with grain offerings ... you made a slave of me with your sins.' By the exodus the Lord brought his people out of slavery (Ex. 6:6) and gave them his law, both moral and cultic, as a sign that they were no longer slaves (Ex. 20:2, 3ff.) but could walk at liberty (Ps. 119:45). As we saw in 1:10–15, however, they had brought themselves into a new bondage, a religion of incessant observance. But ritual for its own sake, observance divorced from moral and spiritual commitment, neither satisfies God (1:11, 13) nor brings blessing to people (1:15). Indeed, to the contrary, for they had made ritual a technique for manipulating blessing, putting the Lord at their beck and call. Thus, enslaving themselves all over again, they sought also to make him their slave!

Thirdly, the verb *wearied* runs through these verses (22b, 23d, 24d). Verse 22b is (lit.) 'you have wearied of me'.[1] In verses 23–24 the causative active means, 'I did not make you weary ... you made me weary.' The sacrificial system was meant by the Lord to be part of the joy of possessing his law: through the sacrifices atonement was made, sins were forgiven and fellowship with God was enjoyed (Lv. 1:4; 4:31; Dt. 16:10–11). But when the sacrifices were allowed to become an end in themselves, the people remained in their sin and became a weariness upon the Holy One. Seen along these lines, verses 22–24 join the other passages of pre-exilic rebuke at misuse of the sacrificial system. There was much religious fervour, no religious reality; where they assumed they were pleasing God, they were trying his patience; where they were most confident they were right with God, they were proving only that they were still in their sin. In this searching way Isaiah establishes Israel's sin and need for divine forgiveness.

22. *Called upon*: Genesis 13:4 shows that this expression includes the cultic side of religion, but it cannot but emphasize the personal side of prayer and communion with God. *Upon me*: again, emphatic. Their religion left God out, so far was it from the divine intention (1:15; Am. 5:21–23; Mt. 15:9).

23–24. The pronouns *me ... me* here need emphasis to convey the correct interpretation. *Honoured ... sacrifices*: Malachi 1:6–7 says that the Lord is dishonoured by religion on the cheap; the dishonour here is done rather by mechanical religion, the assumption that the rite is instrumentally or medicinally effective. The moral majesty of the Lord is dishonoured by subjecting him to a form of magic. *Burdened ... wearied*: see opposite and above. *Incense* (Ex. 30:34ff.; Lv. 2:2): indicative of the Lord's delight in the sacrifices when used according to his will. *Calamus*: see Exodus 30:23; Jeremiah 6:20. *Lavished*: literally 'saturated me', *i.e.* given me superabundant satisfaction. This is central to true religion – not that we should 'find it helpful', but

---

[1] The verb is √*yāga'* with the preposition *b*ᵉ following. This means 'to work for', *i.e.* so as to gain (62:8), 'to be involved with, taken up with' (47:12), 'to be weary of' (57:10).

that God should find it delightful. 'True religion must be conformed to the will of God as its unerring standard.'[1] *Sins* (*ḥaṭṭā'ṯ*), and *offences* ('*āwôn*), see 6:7.

ii. Remedy (43:25 – 44:5). No sooner is the need diagnosed than the remedy is prescribed. Compare the same alacrity of mercy when 40:1–2 follows 39 or when 43:3–7 follows 42:18–25! The God burdened and wearied by sins is the God who *blots* them *out* (25) and brings refreshing (44:3).

25. Note that there is no connecting word between this verse and 22–24. There is no logic whereby we might connect sin with forgiveness, nor does the Lord explain himself. The logic whereby the offended God is the forgiving God is hidden in his heart. The emphasis *I, even I* catches at this truth – as though to say, 'You would not know what to do about this (22–24), you have no remedy – but I am myself all you need.' *Blots out*: 'wipes clean' (2 Ki. 21:13; Ps. 51:1). Sin leaves a mark which only the Lord can wipe away. The verbal form here is a participle, making this ability to wipe sin's stain clean a divine attribute. *Transgressions*: 'deliberate rebellions' (24:20). *Remembers ... no more* (Je. 31:34; Mi. 7:18–19): the Lord's inability to remember anything against us. *Sins*, as in verse 24.

26–28. The simplest way to understand these verses is as a brief court scene in which the accused is given the opportunity to establish *innocence* (26), the prosecution case is stated (27) and divine judgment justified (28).

Argue the matter (26) is, specifically, 'to argue a case at law'. Whether in forgiveness or in condemnation, the Lord will proceed only on the basis of justice. In this case, before adverse sentence is noted, the accused must be confronted by the hopelessness of their case and the rightness of sentence. *First father*: this tracing of sin back to remote forebears is not a departure from the accusation levelled at the present generation in verse 26. In biblical thought, each generation takes over from the last in a cumulative guilt, and each new generation 'fills up' the measure of its predecessors (Mt. 23:31–32, 35–36). The *first father* in this tragic moral entail could be Adam (the father *par excellence*), Abraham (the ultimate ancestor, 41:8), Jacob (the immediate father of the twelve-tribe nation) or Aaron (the founder of the priestly order; note how priests may be the topic in 28a).[2]

---

[1] J. Calvin, *Institutes of the Christian Religion* (SCM, 1960), 1.iv.3.
[2] I owe this suggestion to H. Blocher, *Original Sin*, New Studies in Biblical Theology (Apollos, 1997), p. 31.

Identification is immaterial: the point is the weight of demonstrable guilt in which the current generation participates. *Spokesmen*: the verb √*lîṣ* is best known in the Bible by the noun formed from it, *leṣ*, 'a scorner, scoffer, cynic' (Ps. 1:1); the participle found here does bear this meaning (Jb. 16:20), but is also used as 'interpreter' (Gn. 42:23) and 'envoy' (2 Ch. 32:31). The idea here may be 'representative', even 'your typical ones', those who best typify the present generation. This would give a suitable transition from the past (27a) to the present (28b).

Disgrace (28): the tense cannot be determined with certainty. It could be past ('disgraced'), incipient ('began to disgrace'), determinative ('determined to disgrace') or future ('will disgrace'). Unless the text is emended to fix one of these meanings, we are better to assume that the ambiguity is intentional: at every point from the earliest days there was sin and guilt; at any moment divine judgment would have been and is justified; the mind of God is made up: sin must meet its reward. *Dignitaries of your temple*: literally 'princes of holiness'. 'Holiness' often needs the translation 'sanctuary', and the 'princes of the sanctuary' would be the priests (1 Ch. 24:5). Alternatively, 'princes of holiness' more naturally means 'holy princes', those who were set over the Lord's 'holy' people. If the reference is to priests, then those who were raised up to nourish the Lord's people in holiness were themselves signally guilty; the reference to princes (though the description is unexemplified) fits in the back reference to (fore)fathers. Kings were fathers to their people and, just as earlier and actual fathers sinned and saddled their family with guilt, so those with an office of fatherly care were themselves fatally compromised. *And I will consign*: or 'so I had to consign'. *Destruction* (*ḥērem*) is not 'destruction' pure and simple but the utter 'separation' from the face of the earth of that which the Lord abhors (Jos. 6:17; 8:26). What a verdict! – not pardon (26) but the divine curse (28).

44:1. *But now*: see 43:1. What is the logical consequence of the accusation of age-old and contemporary sin and rebellion in 43:26–28? How does the decision at law reflect on 43:25 with its promise of a full (*blots out*) and final (*remembers ... no more*) dealing with sin? Was the wonder of 43:25 put first in order that we might know what we have lost by sin? No, for now in 44:2–5 a parallel promise is given: not the negative 'blot out' but the matching positive, the gift of new life – and to the same people, for note how the 'Jacob ... Israel' of 43:28 is repeated in 44:1. The Lord never deserts his mercy towards us.

2. *Made ... womb*: just as 43:26–28 traced the fact of

sinfulness back to the *first father*, so now Isaiah traces the entail of divine creative oversight back to the *womb*. Divine paternity antedated sin and is not knocked off course (*will help*) by our sin. Hence the status of the Lord's people, *servant ... chosen* (1–2), remains unchanged. The gifts and calling of God are irreversible (Rom. 11:29). *Afraid*: the fear in question is not that of life's adversities but of the consequences of sin; not fear before people but fear before God. The promise to 'blot out' and 'forget' stands; cancelled sin leaves no room for fear (Lk. 5:8–10; 1 Jn. 4:17–18). *Jeshurun*: see Deuteronomy 32:15; 33:5, 26. The ending '-un' is a diminutive of affection. The name may be related to *yasar*, 'upright'. This is what the Lord wished his people to be. Used here, it emphasizes that, though they have failed to match his ideal, this is still his will for them.

3–5. The ground of fearlessness is now positive: the gift of *my Spirit*, the Agent of ongoing *blessing* (*offspring ... descendants*), the vitality of new life (4), personal assurance of fellowship with the Lord among his people (5). In verse 3 new life is imparted; in 4–5 new life is displayed. On the Lord's *Spirit*, see 11:2; 30:1; 31:3; 40:7; 42:1. On the 'outpoured' Spirit, see 32:15. The parallel between *Spirit* and *blessing* indicates that it is by imparting himself that the Lord brings new life to his people. In verse 5, the renewing activity of the Lord's Spirit becomes evident in individual response and the creation of a people bound together by a common confession. Twice over Isaiah makes turning to the Lord (5ac) inseparable from turning to the Lord's people (5bd). The reference here is not to Gentiles coming into membership of the Israel of God (Gal. 6:16) – that would be totally against the context (contrast 45:22–25) – but to 'formal' Israelites becoming 'true, assured' Israelites. Three things combine to bring this about: sin finished (43:25), new life imparted (44:3–4) and personal response (45:5). *Hand*: the organ of personal action. To write *on his hand* symbolizes the commitment of personal, active life to the Lord (*cf.* Dt. 6:8). If we translate 'with his hand' the meaning is the same: personal commitment.

iii. No other God: sure promises (44:6–20). See 43:8–13. The purpose of this section is announced in verses 6–8: since there is only one God, nothing can stand in the way of his purposes. This truth is then underlined by an exposure of the whole idea of other or alternative 'gods' (9–20). In 40:18–20 and 41:5–7, idol gods were exposed by contrast with the glory of the God of Israel; in 43:8–13 and the present passage the argument is reversed: the glory of the God of Israel is seen by contrast with the absurdity and uselessness of the idols. The present passage has its own central focus. It is not just the nonsense that, had things turned out differently, what the idolater worships would have been used to cook his lunch (15–17), but that what he worships has no power of spiritual transformation, only the reverse (18–20) – unlike the true God (43:25; 44:3–5)! Isaiah has not forgotten the test of prediction and fulfilment (7), but he adds another: what consequences follow from worship? Transformation (44:3–5) or degeneration (18–20)?

Verses 6–8 begin and end on the note of the only God (6cd, 8cd), and this brackets his uniqueness (7). All this truth about God is related to his people's good: the only God is the *King*, *etc.*, of *Israel* (6) and their *Rock* (8), the One in charge of the whole course of their history, past and future (7). In all this he is unhindered by any challenger.

6. *King ... Redeemer*, see 43:14–15; *Almighty* ('Lord of hosts'), see 1:24. This title occurs here for the first time in chapters 38 – 55 (45:13; 47:4; 48:2; 51:15; 54:5). Unlike the idols, possessing only whatever their makers impart to them (9–17), the Lord is, within himself, every potentiality and power. *First ... last*: not, as 41:1, 'with the last' with the thought of purposive direction of history. As *first* he does not derive his being from any other, but is self-existing; as *last* he remains supreme at the End. *God* is the common plural word *^{e}lōhîm*, but since its singular form occurs in verse 8 maybe the plural should be taken here as a plural of amplitude, 'God in the fullness of the divine attributes'.

7. What makes him incomparable? (a) He alone understands the totality of history from the beginning. *Proclaim*: √*qārā'*. In 40:26 'calls' is his executive control of each item in the physical universe, and in 41:4 'calling' is his direction of the events of history. *Lay out*: √*'āru'*, to master all the details (Ex. 40:4), draw up a (battle) plan (1 Sa. 17:8–9), *i.e.* to get everything in its right place. The Lord alone masters and orders the complexity of history. (b) In particular, *since I established* demonstrates his presiding care of his people from the start. (c) *Yet to come* shows his predictive ability, the proof that it is he who purposes and then directs everything to the fulfilment of his purpose.

8. The point of this argument (7) is not so much the exposure of false gods as the demonstration of the glory of the true God and therefore the security of his people. They can be without fear (8a) on the basis of revealed truth (8b) and can attest it (8c). *God*: the singular *^{e}lôah*, the only time it is used in Isaiah. The intention must be to stress the singleness of this one and only

God (as compared with the multiplicity of the claimants implied in 7). *Rock*: a symbol of refuge (Ps. 71:3), trustworthy changelessness (26:4), 'solid' reality (Dt. 32:31), the God who gives life to his people (Ex. 17:6 with Ps. 95:1).

In verses **9–20**, the message of 6–8, that there is one incomparable God, is justified by a searching examination of idolatry. Verse 9 sets out a basic proposition: that idolatry makes no sense (9a), brings no profit (9b) and can be commended only on the basis of blind ignorance (9cd). With this latter point verses 18–20 form an *inclusio*: idolaters are ignorant and blind (18); idolatry is logically indefensible (19); but at a deeper level this dead, meaningless, profitless thing grips the idolater in a hold he cannot break (20). Between these brackets, the argument has two main thrusts: the idol cannot rise above its human origin (10–13) nor above its material basis (14–17). Isaiah both acknowledges and refuses to acknowledge any invisible spiritual reality of which the idol is the outward symbol. On the one hand there is nothing in idolatry but the artefact: 'The heathen in his blindness bows down to wood and stone' — or, as the Roman poet Horace put it, 'Once I used to be an oak tree ... A craftsman, however, preferred I should be a god.' Paul would concur: 'We know that an idol is nothing at all in the world and that there is no God but one' (1 Cor. 8:4). For the apostle, as for the prophet, an unambiguous monotheism determined the question. There is nothing behind the visible idol because there is only one God. But, on the other hand, the idol holds the idolater in an iron grip from which (20) *he cannot save himself* (lit. 'deliver his soul'); and to this Paul also would assent, in the same passage, that 'indeed there are many "gods" and many "lords"' (1 Cor. 8:5), and, at the deepest, most awful level, that 'the sacrifices of pagans are offered to demons, not to God' (1 Cor. 10:20). The meaningless and dead idol has a grim power to make its devotees like itself (Ps. 115:8).

9. The verse starts with the idol-maker (9a), moves to the idol (9b) and thence to the idolater (9cd). *Nothing* (*tōhû*): see 24:10; 29:21; 34:11; 40:17, 23; 41:29; 'meaningless', 'making no sense', would be a good translation here.

In verses **10–17**, the description of the idol factory exposes the two inadequacies of idols. First (10–13), the idol is the product of mere humans (10–11), therefore of diminishing human energy which itself needs to be sustained from outside (12), and of human skill (13a–d) and design which cannot rise above the best it knows (13e). Secondly, the idol, in itself, is a product of earth (14) and of chance (15–17). These two inadequacies are seen

278

most clearly in the idolatry of which Isaiah speaks – physical objects of worship – but, equally truly, in the idols of which John speaks (1 Jn. 5:21): whatever captures the human mind and heart as an alternative to Jesus and the way of faith, *i.e.* the subtler idols of 'market forces', shrewd management of the economy (and all such aspects of modern Baalism), or security through militarism, the reckoning of national prestige in terms of force.

10–11. *God ... idol*: the idolater plans the spiritual and achieves the material! *He and his kind ... but men*: collective enterprise makes no difference. No matter how many craftsmen are involved, they cannot break out of the restriction that they are merely human. *Stand ... terror ... infamy*: they are not guiltless in their idol-making. They know better. If only they would *stand*, that is, stop and take a candid look at what they are doing – they would all at once become afraid (*terror*), and 'ashamed' (as in 9), or 'realize what fools they have been' (*infamy*). Fear and folly would *together* come over them. They are culpably living below their true dignity.

12–13. *Might of his arm ... water ... faint*: the exposure of faulty thinking goes on – not only the folly (11) that the human can create the divine, but also that human strength can create the almighty, and that strength needing outside nourishment can produce the self-existent, self-perpetuating life of God. The prophet then turns from the workshop to the drawing-board, the conceptual side of idol-making. The end-product may be awesomely impressive in beauty or terrifyingly horrific. Either way it is only the product of a carefully drawn blueprint and a competent designer. *Form of man ... man in all his glory* (13ef): yet, of course, it is not always so. Sometimes it is astral or brutish in form, sometimes a hybrid of human and animal, sometimes gross, revolting. But taking the designer at his best, he intuits that the human is the highest he knows and designs accordingly. *Glory* is 'beauty'. *Dwell in a shrine* (lit. 'a house'): it has been made humanlike so it must do the human thing! How Isaiah hammers away at its humanness! No matter what their intent, the result of human effort cannot rise above the human.

14–17 introduce another devastatingly ironic aspect of this humanness: choice and chance. The full-grown tree, *cedar ... cypress ... oak*, is a hugely impressive thing, but trace it to its origin and what do we find? A seed or cutting, a tiny thing, *planted* in the ground, nourished by *the rain*. Its ancestry is earthly, its cultivation human, its life derived from the creation – and its 'deity' is the chance which allowed it to survive the needs of the kitchen fire! And the idolater's 'logic' suggests that what has given him the physical benefit of cooked food (*roasts*, 16) and the comfort of bodily warmth (*fire*) can also nourish his soul: '*Save me, you are my god*' (17).

18. *Know ... understand* (lit. 'have knowledge ... see to the heart of the matter'): see 29:14. *Plastered over*: who has done the 'plastering'? There is an implied external agent creating blindness. The justice of God visits people with what they choose, and this could be his judicial visitation of blindness (6:9; 2 Thes. 2:10–11); or is Isaiah implying that, dead though the idol is, it has the power to blind the minds of the unbelieving (2 Cor. 4:4)? *Cannot understand* (√*sākal*) means in general to act with the prudence that achieves success (Jos. 1:8); here, the ability to appraise the situation, to sift truth from error (and then act accordingly).

19. *Stops to think ... knowledge ... understanding*: this is a devastating analysis of the fallen mind. First, as to the processes of thought: *stops to think* (lit. 'takes to heart'), the ability to size up the plain facts; secondly, the content of *knowledge*: truth as held and entertained in mind and memory; and, thirdly, *understanding*: discernment to sift and probe, to arrive at truth. All this fallenness of the mind is illustrated by *detestable thing ... block of wood*. In respect of a doctrine of God, intuition should tell people that to give divine honours to a man-made thing is 'abominable' (*cf.* Acts 17:29); in respect of the doctrine of humankind, intuition should tell people that to prostrate the human before the material cannot be right. The fallen mind 'cannot understand' (1 Cor. 2:14).

20. The idolater is 'hooked' on idolatry. A whole area of freedom has died and he is not able to save himself. First, there is his own chosen action: *feeds on ashes*. *Ashes* looks back to verses 15, 16, 19. When wood is reduced to its substantial reality, what is it but ashes? The idol may impress, but it is in reality no more than the substrate, the dead embers. Secondly, there is the inner consequence of this choice: *deluded*. The idolater chose a delusion and became deluded (Ps. 115:8). Who is the agent behind this induced delusion? Is it the Lord acting in the providential laws he has instituted that a false choice begets a false person? Is it the idol, the delusion producing its own likeness? Thirdly, there is the ensuing state of bondage. *Cannot save ... right hand*: the idolater picks up the figurine in his hand, holding it, but in reality it holds him. He is in bondage to *a lie*.

iv. Redemption from sin (44:21–23). See p. 264 for the place of this section in the overall scheme. The first element in the divine plan for Israel was redemption from Babylon (43:14–21). The second element, redemption from sin, is now completed: first, we are invited to enter into the mind of God (21–22), and, secondly, to join in the responsive praise of the redeemed. The tenses in verses 22–23 (*return ... sing ...*) are either imperatives commanding response, perfects expressing the determination of the Lord (he has purposed redemption, therefore it is a sure fact), or imperfect, forecasting what he will yet do.

21. *Remember* looks back broadly over the whole section (43:22 – 44:20): remember your need of redemption (43:22–24), my pledge of forgiveness and new life (43:25 – 44:5), and the certainty of my promises, since I am the only God (44:6–20). To remember stresses the primary importance of mind and memory in God's plan: God's people should always first ponder the truth they know. *Made* (lit. 'formed'): unlike the idolater who forms his god (12–13), here is a God who fashions his people (43:1), shaping them for himself in all the experiences of life. *Servant ... servant*: the repetition is surely deliberate and related to the fact that a servant is a 'bondman', but, unlike the idolater in his blind and unbreakable bondage (20), here is a position of privilege – the servant of such a Lord, the 'bondage' of one who has been brought out of bondage into the law of liberty (Ex. 20:1–3, *etc.*; Rom. 6:17–22; Jas. 1:22–25). *Not forget*: in parallel to the *remember* with which the verse opens, we might expect the corresponding negative, 'do not forget', but Isaiah neatly turns it round: *I will not forget you.* In idolatry, everything depends on the devotee, but here, everything depends on the living God. Even should they forget, yet 'I will not forget you' (49:15).

22. *Swept*: 'wiped' as in 43:25. *Offences*: 'rebellions', the wilful root of sin (43:25). *Cloud ... mist*: that which can be easily obliterated as though it never was (Ho. 6:4; 13:3). *Return ... for* ... : coming back in repentance is not a good deed rewarded by redemption; the redemption has already taken place, opening the door for a return, making it both possible and effective. *Redeemed* (√*gā'al*): see 35:9–10; 43:1, 14.

23. *Sing*: the picture of those who enter, with responsive joy, into a salvation to which they have made no contribution (54:1) but which has been achieved for them – hence *for the LORD has done this. Earth ... mountains ... forests*: when the Lord accomplishes redemption for his people, the curse is lifted from the whole creation (Pss. 96:10ff.; 98:7ff., where 'to judge the earth' has the meaning 'to set everything to rights'; Rom. 8:19–21). *Trees*: the idolater cut down trees, but redemption frees them to joy in the Lord. *Displays*: an imperfect tense here; better 'will display', when the redemption he has accomplished is fully evident in his people. *Glory*: 'beauty' (Eph. 4:24; 1 Jn. 3:2).

VIII. THE GREAT DELIVERANCE:
THE WORK OF CYRUS (44:24 – 48:22)

Isaiah moves his subject forward a step. The Lord saw the needs of his people in political and spiritual terms (42:18–25). He has stated in outline that these needs will be met (42:18 – 43:21; 43:22 – 44:23). Now he turns to the question 'How?' As to the political deliverance of exiled Israel, the Lord's agent is *his anointed* ... *Cyrus* (45:1); and as to spiritual redemption, the Lord's Agent is *my servant* (49:3). In this way the two passages of promise (42:18 – 43:21; 43:22 – 44:23) are paralleled by two passages of fulfilment (44:24 – 48:22; 49:1 – 55:13).

The present section deals with three subjects: first, the work of Cyrus (44:24 – 45:8); secondly, Israel's reaction to Cyrus and the Lord's reassurances (45:9 – 46:13); and, thirdly, the fall of Babylon (47:1–15) and the release of the captives (48:1–22).

a. Cyrus: builder and conqueror (44:24 – 45:8)

Three self-affirmations by the Lord hold this passage together. The first is the broadest (44:24de; lit. 'I am the Lord who does everything'), a claim to total directive control of the universe; the second (45:7c; lit. 'I am the Lord who does all these things') claims direct responsibility for the Cyrus events, his mission to Jerusalem, Judah and the temple (44:26–28) and his whole career as conqueror (45:1–4); and the third (45:8f), *I, the LORD, have created it* is, in context, most likely a perfect of determination: 'I have determined to create it' commits divine creative power to the total enterprise, making it a direct, sole and unique act of God. All this gives enormous solemnity to the passage: the Lord is solely at work (44:24), wholly at work (45:7) and creatively at work (45:8).

i. The Lord and his word (44:24–26b). The Lord who 'does everything' (24) fulfils the word he has given to his messengers (26).

24. Very often the things that the Lord does seem threatening to his people – and, as we shall see, the Cyrus plan was something they groused about (45:9–13; 46:8–13). The solution is rather to look at what God is, *your Redeemer, who formed you in the womb*: his loving sufficiency, he is the *Redeemer*, *gō'ēl*, the Next-of-Kin, pledged to take and bear every burden as his own;

in his purposeful love, he formed his people in the womb. They are his family by his will (Jas. 1:18), and nothing will ever touch them except what fatherly love directs. *Alone stretched out ... spread ...* : his continuing work as Creator is the guarantee that he is in sole charge of everything (40:26); there is no other god (Ps. 96:5).

25–26b. *False prophets* translates *baddîm*, used in 16:6, Job 11:3 and Jeremiah 48:30 in the sense 'idle talk'; here and in Jeremiah 50:36 of the pretentious claims of fortune-tellers. *Makes fools of*: 'bewitches, drives mad'. Since they choose folly, the Lord will see to it that they become fools (44:18, 20)! *Diviners* claimed special means of telling the future; *the wise* tried to apply human wisdom to the task. Isaiah is not consigning all human wisdom to the rubbish heap: in context, alongside *diviners*, there is a 'wisdom' which tries to make sense of life, the flow of history and the trends that lead from present to future and which seeks to apply this helpfully to individual needs. But, compared with the higher wisdom which orders all things, it is no more than upside-down (*overthrows*) *nonsense* (1 Cor. 1:18–25). Yet the word of the *messengers* (26b), those who carry God's word, which can so easily be scorned by worldly sophistication (28:7–13), carries deeper and eternal truth. In this matter the Lord is jealous of his position and no word but his will come to pass. *Predictions* is simply 'advice, counsel' without any necessary reference to forecasting.

ii. The Lord and his purpose (44:26c–28). Isaiah covers in turn the restoration of Judah (26d–f), the opening of a way home for the exiles (27) – the wording is deliberately reminiscent of the crossing of the Red Sea, leaving Egypt, heading for home – and the restored city and temple (28). Notice again the strong element of reassurance. We are aided by hindsight, and we know that Cyrus was, so to speak, 'a good thing'. Israel in Babylon, however, saw only a greater conqueror on the way, and doubtless said, 'We could do without this.' They wanted liberation, not worse bondage. Hence the Lord literally wraps the reference to *Cyrus* (28ab) in references to what the exiles actually wanted: restoration (26), homecoming (27) and rebuilding (28cd). In the Lord's purposes, the good dominates and outlasts the harsh. (See Additional Note on Cyrus, p. 284.)

28. *My shepherd*: kings were called 'shepherds' as being guardians and carers of their people (56:11; 2 Sa. 24:17; 1 Ki. 22:17; Je. 2:8). The title here signifies that the coming conqueror is the Lord's appointed carer – even, as a shepherd would, to lead them into their proper pastures. *Foundations*: interestingly, as Ezra records (3:10–13; 5:16), in the days of Cyrus the rebuilding of the temple did not progress beyond the laying of the foundations.

Additional Note on the prediction of Cyrus in 44:28

Many see the detailed prediction of the personal name of Cyrus in 44:28 as a problem, and suggest a variety of solutions. Those who find difficulty with prediction place the author of the prophecy in Babylon in the thick of the Cyrus events – the so-called 'Second Isaiah' (see pp. 28–33). In this case, the prediction involved would be the prophet's discernment of Cyrus as liberator. The main difficulty with this view is that it does not accord with what these chapters claim: that the prophet did not forecast only the outcome of Cyrus' career but also its inception (41:25–27). Furthermore, if the prophet was a resident in Babylon, it is remarkable that his prophecy is totally lacking in 'local colour' – particularly that he envisaged situations for the exiles which do not accord with their actual state (see on 42:22) but resorts to conventional images; the same can be said of his poetical depiction of the fall of Babylon (47:1ff.).[1] Others would argue, though, that it is essential to insist that the Old Testament is our only source book on the subject of Old Testament prophecy. We can, of course, choose to disbelieve what it says, but we must not adjust its testimony to suit modern conventions, tastes or prejudices. The evidence of the Old Testament (as of the New) is that pre-knowledge of personal names is given when, for whatever reason, the situation warrants it (*cf.* 1 Ki. 13:2 with 2 Ki. 23:15–17; Acts 9:12). This special dimension of prediction is at home in Isaiah, who, more than any other prophet, makes prediction and fulfilment the keystone of his proof that the Lord is the only God.

---

[1] Smart (*History and Theology in Second Isaiah*) would remove all reference to Cyrus, treating it as a 'reinterpretation' of 'Deutero-Isaiah' by the fifth-century Jerusalem community. It is perhaps sufficient comment to note Smart's own rebuke to those who would remove the name 'Israel' from 49:3, as 'contrary to all good procedure in the critical handling of texts'. Sadly, R. K. Harrison (*Introduction to the Old Testament* [Tyndale Press, 1970], p. 794) concurs with Smart. If the fact of predictive prophecy is accepted, we are in no position to set limits to its exercise, and, since the OT does not let us into the secrets of the mechanisms or 'psychology' of inspiration, we do not have the clues to decide what is possible and what is impossible. Within the total biblical context, the revelation of names is perfectly at home (see, *e.g.*, Gn. 16:11; Mt. 1:21; Lk. 1:13).

iii. The Lord and his anointed (45:1–7). There is much in this passage that Isaiah's people could have accepted without comment: that when a conqueror arises, 'the authorities that exist' have been 'established by God' (1; Rom. 13:1); that the conquering power they exercise is by divine gift (2–3), that somehow the Lord's own people are always at the centre of his concern (4), and that the Lord is working out a worldwide plan (6). But to call *Cyrus* the Lord's *anointed*! That is quite a different matter! This was in particular the kingly title. It was the special dignity (1 Sa. 12:3, 5; 26:11; 2 Sa. 1:14, 16) and sacrosanctity (1 Sa. 24:6, 10; 26:9, 11, 23) of Saul as king; above all it was the divinely granted status of David (1 Sa. 16:6; Ps. 18:50; 132:10), of the Davidic king (Ps. 84:9) and of the expected 'David' of the future (Ps. 2:2). The vision of this coming Davidic king had hitherto preoccupied Isaiah's own depiction of the future (1:24; 9:1–7; 11:1–16; 14:28–32; 16:4–5; 32:1; 33:17) – but now the coming king, the Lord's anointed, is not David at all but a pagan named Cyrus! This was not at all what they wanted to hear or the way they hoped the future would shape out. As we shall see, this sense of recoil at what was proposed is essential to understanding 45:1 – 46:13 (see on 45:9). But the Lord's purposes are always on a longer scale (Lk. 1:32–33) and a wider canvas than humans can grasp, and filled with a more complex wisdom (55:8).

1–3b. The unbroken success of Cyrus' career from its early origin in the distant kingdom of Anshan to his replacement of the Babylonian empire by his own Persian empire was a matter of marvel to his contemporaries. They could see him only as 'beloved of the gods'. Isaiah takes us behind the scenes to the reality: it was the Lord who led him out on to the stage of history (*take hold of*), fashioned the purpose Cyrus was to fulfil (*to subdue*), engineered his triumphs (*open doors*), made his progress easy (*level ... break ... cut*) and enriched him with earth's *treasures* (3a). Verse 7 correctly sums up the Lord's management of history with 'I do all these things'.

3c–6. *So that you may know*: Isaiah does not say that Cyrus will come to know the Lord, but that the Lord has put all the evidence before him to make such knowledge possible. Likewise, in the Cyrus plan, the Lord has two other purposes in mind: the welfare of his chosen people (*for the sake of*, 4; see 14:1–2) and revelation to the world (6). As we shall learn (45:9–13; 46:1–13), Israel remained blind and the watching world remained uninformed. Cyrus was at the centre of the Lord's purpose but failed to fulfil that purpose. Mercifully, the Lord had another and more glorious person and plan waiting in the shadows (49:1 – 55:13)! Are we meant to ask how Cyrus could have come to know the Lord? There can be no doubt how Isaiah would have answered. When Cyrus entered Babylon, it would seem that all the resident 'gods' rushed to claim the credit for his triumph. Indeed, in the Cyrus Cylinder,[1] Cyrus acknowledges Marduk as the god behind his career in the same way that he gives the glory to the Lord in Ezra 1:2. The gods had all won and all must have prizes. Soldiering is an uncompromising occupation, but the soldier-become-politician must exchange sword-in-hand for tongue-in-cheek. Yet (Isaiah would say), among all the claimant gods, only One was wise before the event; only One predicted (not just the career and success of Cyrus but) his emergence in world affairs – and even his name! The God who can thus predict must be the only God (5–6). Cyrus had the evidence but he either did not or would not face its implications.

7. The foregoing review of the career of Cyrus is summed up in this magnificent statement of the Sole Energizer of history. *Light ... darkness* stand here either as metaphorical, the delightful as contrasted with the threatening aspects of life, or as literal, the ordered sequence of day and night. Either way is true: the Lord is executively behind all life's experiences and the sustainer of its regularities (Gn. 1:16; 8:22; Je. 31:35; 33:20).[2] *Prosperity ... disaster*: the older, literal rendering 'peace ... evil' caused unnecessary difficulties. Can the Lord 'create evil'? Out of about 640 occurrences of the word *ra'*, which range in meaning from a 'nasty' taste to full moral evil, there are about 275 cases where it refers to trouble or calamity. Each case must be judged by its context and NIV has done so correctly here. Cyrus was 'bad news' to the kings he conquered and the cities he overthrew. But Isaiah's (and the Bible's) view of divine providence is rigorous – and for that reason full of comfort. Sinful minds want the comfort of a sovereign God but jib at saying with Job (2:10), 'Shall we accept good from God, and not trouble (*ra'*)?' But when we

---

[1] For the Cyrus Cylinder, see D. W. Thomas (ed.), *Documents from Old Testament Times* (Nelson, 1958), pp. 92–94; D. J. Wiseman, 'Cyrus', in *NBD*, p. 250. It was a propagandist account, produced by the priests of Marduk to punish Nabonidus, and it therefore determined to leave no stone unturned in buttering up Cyrus as one raised by Marduk to punish Nabonidus. But, of course, Marduk kept all this to himself until after the event.

[2] Light and darkness are typical themes in Zoroastrianism and this has been used to suggest a Persian milieu for this verse. This is grossly overpressing the occurrence of two well-known biblical motifs. In any case, the texts on which Zoroaster based his light/darkness dualism go back to about 1200 BC and could not therefore be used to establish a post-Isaianic date for this passage.

make it our confession that the God who 'made all things' (44:24) does all things (45:7), we find it 'full of sweet, pleasant, and unspeakable comfort'.[1]

iv. The Lord and his creative resolve (45:8).[2] The truth which 44:24 – 45:7 has stated plainly are now repeated pictorially. Earthly events have heavenly origins. The initiation, continuation and climax of Cyrus' career are the Lord's doing: just as he is the doer of all (44:24), so his *word* lies behind all things (44:25–26) in their outcome (44:26–28), their details (45:1, 3) and their motivation (45:3cd, 4ab, 6). It is exactly like the way in which the fertilization of earth begins with the rain from heaven.

Righteousness: the Lord's absolutely right purpose for the world and for his people as executed by Cyrus. *Salvation*: the Lord's purpose of deliverance for his people (from Babylon) through Cyrus. These are the fruits on earth of the process set in motion from heaven. To this the Lord commits himself in the 'perfect of determination'. *Have created it*: as 'creation' it is something which by its newness and greatness can only be an act of God; as past, *created*, it is an established certainty in the mind and purpose of God; as yet to happen on earth it is something 'I, the Lord, have determined to create'.

b. Rebellion and resolve, quibbling and consolation (45:9 – 46:13)

The 'shape' of this section is an important element in its meaning. It is bracketed by matching passages (45:9–13; 46:1–13), each of which covers the same ground. The quarrelsome folk addressed in 45:9–10 appear again as rebels in 46:8; the reaffirmation of the Cyrus plan (45:11–13) is repeated in 46:1–7, 11–13. Each passage is full of divine comfort for troubled Israel: Jerusalem will be rebuilt and the exiles freed (45:13), the Lord continues to carry his people on his broad shoulders (46:3–4). History may not *look* as if it is shaping out for the welfare of God's people but nevertheless it *is*! Within these bracketing passages, 45:14–25 takes up the topic of the place of Israel in the Lord's purposes for the world. The Cyrus plan would not succeed in revealing the Lord on a worldwide scale; the then Israel may think that Cyrus

---

[1] Article XVII of the Thirty-nine Articles of the Church of England.

[2] In 45:8 Isaiah's Hebrew is not at all easy to translate (why should it be?), but the meaning is plain. NIV handles the Hebrew 'broadly' but offers an accurate interpretation. *Cf.* RV, NKJV, NASB.

is the negation of the universal hopes they entertained, but the Lord is not deserting his intention that one day *all* the *ends of the earth* will *turn ... and be saved* (45:22–23). To the embarrassment of those who rebelled and quibbled, there will be an Israel of God exulting in praise (45:24cd, 25).

i. The potter and the parent (45:9–13). 9–11. The Cyrus plan has been announced as the Lord's purpose bringing to Israel the blessings of restoration to home, city and temple (44:26–28). Why, then, should there be quibbling where we might expect joyful anticipation? But their problem was real, and their grousing had real substance. When they had lived in Jerusalem before the exile, it was as a subject people under a puppet king. However misconceived their successive rebellions against their overlords of Assyria and Babylon had been, they were evidence of a strong groundswell of longing to be a sovereign state under a Davidic king. Of course, far from achieving this, their rebellions had in fact only hastened the end of kingdom, king, land, city and temple. But now, to be told that the exile will end through a pagan king and their home-going will be as a still-subject people with a city and temple rebuilt by his direction – and without any reference to a Davidic restoration – why, they would be even worse off than before! The quarrelling arose, then, not from hurt pride at being under an obligation to a pagan, but from, if anything, a worse condition than had prevailed before the exile. Then at least there was a Davidic king in Jerusalem, however much on sufferance! Now they could see only a cruel blow to their hopes, the exchange of one bondage for another. To all this the prophet makes a twofold reply: it is impossible for the artefact to question the potter (9), and impermissible for the child to question the parent (10). The potter exercises an unquestionable sovereignty; the parent possesses a sole right. *Maker* (11): 'potter / fashioner'.

12–13. Our preoccupation with how the creation began does not allow us to see the significance of the claim here. In the Old Testament the Creator is not only the One who began everything, but also the One who maintains everything in existence, controls and guides everything. Hence, if he decides to *raise up Cyrus* (13), that is the end of the discussion! *Not for a price*: the Creator has not struck a bargain with Cyrus! Both his uprising (*raise up* is 'wake up / rouse up' as 41:2, 25), his ease of conquest (*ways straight*) and his function (*rebuild and set ... free*) are a sovereign dictate of the LORD *Almighty*, 'the LORD of hosts' (1:4), the One who is in himself every potentiality and power.

ii. An unchanged worldwide purpose for Israel (45:14–25).
This passage replies to the unspoken assumption behind verses
9–13 (and 46:1–13) that the Davidic promises have been lost in a
Gentile take-over. It was part of the Davidic vision that the
promised king would rule the nations (9:7; 11:12–16; Ps. 2:7–12)
and that they would submit to him (7:23; Ps. 72:8–12). Isaiah
does not relate the present passage explicitly to the Davidic hope,
but its content is inseparable from the expectation of the king
who is to come. There are two divisions, 14–17 and 18–25, each
beginning with *This is what the LORD says* (14a, 18a) and each
ending with the triumph of Israel (17, 25). In verses 14–17 the
keynote is the centrality of Israel in the Lord's worldwide plans
as Gentiles submit to Israel on the ground that the only God is
found among them (14); in 18–25 the keynote is the reality of co-
equal membership in the Israel of God as Gentiles respond to the
universal invitation to turn to the Lord and be saved. (*Cf.* the
vision of 'one world, one people, one Lord', 19:24–25; 27:12–
13.)

14–17, *The submission of the world.* On 9:1–7 we noted an
apparent clash of ideas: the victory of the child-king was by force
of arms (4–5), yet the spread of his kingdom was in reality a
spreading peace (7). In 11:1–16 the perfect Davidic King copies
his ancestor by military conquest of Philistia, Moab and Edom
(14). Isaiah was simply being faithful to the kingly motif. Kings
extend their realms by way of arms, conflict, victory and subjugation. So, here, the way to Israel's God is through submissive
union with Israel. It was the way that Moab's pride refused to
take (16:5–6) and there is no other way. The true and only God
revealed himself to one people only; he set up the way of
approach to himself in one place only, the Jerusalem temple and
its sacrifices.

14. The nations do not come out of weakness, for they bring
their wealth (*products ... merchandise*) with them; they have not
lost their natural vigour or prowess (*tall*). They come seriously
(*over to you ... yours*); they take second place (not *trudge* but
simply 'walk/come after you', following where you lead); they
come humbly (*in chains ... bow down*); they come earnestly
(*plead*); they come for God's sake, as in 2:2–4. National barriers
are transcended (*come over*), actual membership is realized
(*yours*) and a new lifestyle adopted ('walk after'). *Egypt ... Cush
... Sabeans*: see 43:3. Isaiah is using exodus symbols: the nations
then subordinated to Israel typify those who will one day seek for
themselves the blessings Israel has in the Lord. *To you ... yours
... behind you ... before you*: the pronoun is feminine singular

throughout. This may be a deliberate ploy in case a masculine pronoun might be understood to refer to Cyrus.

15–17. *Hides himself*: this allegation could be the voice of the converts from among the nations, late-comers to the revelation of the only God; it could be Israel's (or Isaiah's) comment that the Cyrus plan seems to negate the Davidic promises, but not so. The submission of Israel to the Gentiles will yet be swallowed up in the submission of the Gentiles to Israel. *God and Saviour of Israel* (lit. 'God of Israel, Saviour'): the God of Israel is the Saviour of the world. Isaiah has a universal view of salvation, but not a universalist doctrine: salvation is for all, but not all will be saved. *Go off* (16) is 'walk', the verb translated 'trudge' in verse 14. These are the alternative destinies: those who will not walk after Israel will walk into shame. *Saved ... salvation* (17): when verse 15 describes the *God of Israel* as *Saviour* it refers to worldwide salvation. Therefore, the *Israel* here *saved ... with an everlasting salvation* cannot be one nation to the exclusion of the world; it must be the whole company of the saved, what Paul will yet call 'the Israel of God' (Gal. 6:16).

18–25, *The salvation of the world.* Isaiah spells out more explicitly the gathering of a worldwide people into the salvation-community. He speaks of God in creation (18), revelation (19), salvation (20–22) and affirmation (23–25).

18. *For*: this passage is offered in explanation of the preceding passage. How are we to understand this worldwide salvation and the world Israel? First, God is the Creator who had a worldwide people in mind when he created the earth. Four verbs sum up his work: he initiated (*created*), moulded into shape (*fashioned*, as a potter would) until all was completed (*made*) and he imparted stability to the whole (*founded*). This work of creation proves that *he is God* (Ps. 96:5). It is also purposeful: *empty* is *tōhû* (24:10; 29:21; 40:17; 41:29; 44:9), see especially Jeremiah 4:23–25, a desolate, unstable, meaningless thing without light or life. When the Lord planned the world he also willed a worldwide people (*formed ... to be inhabited*). It stands to reason therefore that this Creator will have a concern for all his creatures.

19. Secondly, the world vision of verses 14–17 is to be understood in the light of revelation. In quiet rebuke of the allegation (15) that he 'hides himself', the Lord asserts that he never spoke *in secret* (lit. 'under cover'): his word was openly available; nor *in a land of darkness* where one might lose one's way: his word was intrinsically plain and straightforward; and it led them straight to himself: his word was not *in vain* (*tōhû*, 18), solid ground not shifting sand. What he said was *truth* and *right*:

the former is 'righteousness', conformity to the absolute norm of divine truth; the latter is 'plain, straightforward', without deviance or duplicity. The link with verse 15, seen in the contrast between *hides* and *not ... in secret*, makes 19 a comment on the matter of the Gentile hope: if Israel had heeded the word spoken to them, they would have known that their God, the Creator, had plans for the whole inhabited world. Such was, for example, plain in the Abrahamic promise (Gn. 12:2–3; 22:18) and in the vision of a worldwide Davidic kingdom (9:6–7).

Thirdly, verses **20–25** describe how this universal gathering will actually come about.[1] The general invitation to *gather ... from the nations* (20) is supported by drawing a contrast between gods *of wood* (20c) and the only God (21f), between gods *that cannot save* (20d) and *a righteous God and a Saviour* (21g). This distinction rests on proof: *who foretold this ...?* (21cd). Consequently, since the only God has proved his reality by prediction and fulfilment and has affirmed himself to be a Saviour, the general invitation (20a) can be particularized as an invitation to be saved (22). This invitation, in turn, rests on the *integrity* of the word of God (23ab): this one, saving God has gone on oath that all the earth will own him (23de). Not all will be saved (24cd), but the worldwide *Israel* will share the divine nature ('righteous', 25b).

20. *Fugitives* (*pālîṭ*, lit. 'escapers') implies danger, the danger of lingering where there is no salvation (20d), of choosing pretend gods and meriting shame (16, 24cd; 42:13, 17). *Carry about*: *i.e.* in processions, but Isaiah's irony sees in the 'carrying about' the helpless inertness of such gods. *Gods*: literally 'a god.' Isaiah, with further irony, uses the noun *'ēl*, the word for God the transcendent! Imagine claiming to be 'God' over all and yet being 'non-salvific' (lit.) – their inability to save is not a momentary lapse but an inherent condition.

21 describes a brief court scene. As ever in these chapters, deity is demonstrated by prediction and by the control of history that brings prediction to fulfilment. *This* is the gathering to the Lord of a worldwide people. In essence it is a prediction which goes back to Abraham (Gn. 12:1–3; 22:18); it has been a recurring feature of Isaiah (2:2–4; 9:1; 11:10; 19:23–15; 25:6–9;

---

[1] A common interpretation is that the *fugitives* (20b) are those who have survived the conquests of Cyrus and consequently appreciate what the Lord has done. *This* (21c) refers to Cyrus' career, by the foretelling of which the Lord demonstrated his unique deity. All this fits broadly with these chapters, but poorly in the immediate context and in the structure of 44:24 – 48:22.

27:13; 42:1–4). *Righteous* looks back in the first instance to verse 19 (where 'truth' is, lit., 'righteousness'). Thus it refers to the trustworthiness of the word God speaks, so that when he invites the *fugitives* to *gather*, they can rely on his invitation. But more, a righteous God is one who is eternally true to himself and can be guaranteed to act in ways that satisfy his own nature. Paul's allusion to this verse in Romans 3:26 is fully justified. *Saviour*: literally 'saving'. His work of salvation is not a momentary urge but an eternal attribute.

22. *Turn*: Numbers 21:8–9 illustrates this perfectly. *Be saved*: Hebrew often uses an imperative to express the absolute certainty with which a result will follow: 'Just turn to me and your salvation will be certain beyond all doubt.' The invitation is for everybody, *all you ends of the earth*. *God*: Isaiah uses *'ēl* (*cf.* 20d) but here with its full implication: the only, transcendent, saving God.

23a–c. *By myself ... sworn*: word for word as in the Abrahamic promise (Gn. 22:16; *cf.* Heb. 6:13). *My mouth*: just as 'to see with the eyes' (Dt. 4:3) is to see personally, so 'to speak with the mouth' is to make a personal statement. *Integrity*: 'righteousness', a word invested with the Lord's own character, expressive of his purpose, totally trustworthy. *Not revoked*: *cf.* 55:11.

23d–25. Here, then, is the 'righteous word': (a) there will be universal submission to the Lord expressed by *knee* (submission) and *tongue* (acclamation) (23de; Phil. 2:9–11); (b) though all submit, not all turn savingly to the Lord (24): some are looking to *the Lord alone* (24a), but others have rage in their hearts – the enforced submission of unreconciled foes – and go away into shame (24cd); (c) the saved company is called *the descendants of Israel* (Ps. 87). *Swear*: i.e. 'swear allegiance'. *Righteousness* is plural, signifying 'true righteousness, righteousness in all its fullness', that is to say, all that makes his people right with God, conformity to his character and requirements. This inner reality is matched by *strength* to live out this new relationship and status. *Will come to him*: it is hard to think what this might mean in relation to those who maintain their rage against the Lord, and very likely NIV's estimate of the Hebrew cannot be sustained. Certainly the lines could be translated differently: 'Each will say of me, "In the Lord alone ...". Right up to him shall each come, but ashamed shall all be who enrage themselves against him.' In other words, along with the status of *righteousness* and the enduement with *strength* comes the privilege of access. *Raged ... righteous*: like the parallel 14–17, verses 18–25 end with two statements side by side: those who reap shame (24cd, *cf.* 16), and the saved Israel (25, *cf.* 17). *Raged*: a reflexive participle, 'keep themselves incensed', a decisive commitment to their gods involving sustained animosity towards any counter-claim. *Descendants* (lit. 'seed') *of Israel*: a merely national significance of *Israel* would make nonsense of the whole argument from verse 14 onwards. The Lord has promised and predicted worldwide salvation, and here, as in 17, the honoured name of *Israel* casts its mantle over a worldwide confessing community. Within the community there are not first- and second-class citizens: the description *descendants* (lit. 'seed') indicates reality of belonging and co-equality of status. All are 'born there' (Ps. 87:4–6). In verse 24 *righteousness* (the new status before the Lord) brought with it *strength* for daily life and fellowship with the saving God; here the *righteous* respond with exultant praise.

iii. The unchanging Lord and his stubborn rebels (46:1–13). These verses are both parallel to and different from 45:9–13. Both passages expose Israel's opposition to the Cyrus plan (45:9–10; 46:8, 12) and reaffirm that, none the less, the plan will go forward: the Lord can be as stubborn as his people (45:13; 46:10–11, 13)! – but 46:1–13 majors on the Lord's care for them (3–4) and also goes beyond the earlier passage in the severity of its condemnation of rebellious Israel. In other words, while 46:1–13 fundamentally says the same thing as 45:9–13, it also takes into account the material traversed in 45:14–25, that Israel is central to the Lord's world purposes and that, in all he does, he safeguards them as special and therefore is prepared to expose unsparingly (8, 12) how exceedingly culpable is their opposition. Isaiah expresses this in a vigorous poem in five sections.

1–2, *The burdening gods.* Isaiah 44:24–28 heralded the advent of Cyrus and 45:1–8 saw him launched on his dazzling career. Now the heart of the matter as regards Israel is imminent – the fall of Babylon – and we are given privileged seats as the great 'gods' of Babylon sway down from their pedestals to lie prone on wagons to be unceremoniously carted off from the doomed city. It did not happen, of course, in this way. Isaiah is dealing with pictures and principles (see on 10:28–32); his purpose is not to describe but to expose. There is no recorded evacuation of Babylon in anticipation of Cyrus' assault, but in a strikingly visual way Isaiah presents the truth that these gods cannot save (*cf.* 2:20) and, when the crunch comes, are themselves dependent on pack-animals! *Bel* (1, the same title as Baal, 'lord') is Marduk, the patron god of Babylon; *Nebo*, Bel's son, was patron of nearby Borsippa. He was the god of wisdom, and was carried annually to Babylon to accompany his father in the New Year processions and to write on 'tables of destiny' what the coming year held for Babylon. He apparently got it wrong about Cyrus! *Burdensome*: literally 'loaded up' – like so many great parcels! In 703 BC when Sennacherib attacked Babylon, Merodach-Baladan organized just such an evacuation of the 'gods'. It is thus within his own times that Isaiah finds the components of this picture. *The burden* (2) is the 'gods' themselves, and *they* is the supposed spiritual entity behind the visible image, but there is nothing there to intervene.

3–4, *The burden-bearing God.* Just as verses 1–2 move 'chronologically' forward to the approach of Cyrus to Babylon, so Isaiah addresses the Israel of that time, those who have survived the captivity or have been born in exile. The fact of captivity and the experience of exile do not contradict the fact that their God has been carrying them and continues to do so. They have changed – the child in the womb (*conceived*), the infant growing through adolescence to adulthood (*since birth*), the onset of *grey hairs* in old age – but one thing remains unchanging: the burden-bearing God (*upheld* ... *carried* ... *sustain*), 'Who was and is the same, / And evermore shall be; / Jehovah, Father, great I AM'.[1] *Upheld*: the same verb as *burdensome* (lit. 'loaded up', 1): 'who have been loaded (on me)', been my burden. In verse 4, except for *I will rescue*, all the pronouns *I* are emphatic, *i.e.* 'I will myself' – a touching underlining of directly personal tender loving care. *I will rescue* is expressed as a co-ordinate verb with *sustain*, so as to say that rescuing is not a separate act but intrinsic to the service automatically rendered to his people by the burden-bearing God. *Sustain* (*sābal*, 'to shoulder') ... *carry* (*nāśā*'): if any difference is to be pressed, the former is 'to accept a burden', the latter 'to take up a burden' (see 53:11–12).

5–7, *The made gods, unable to save.* The contrast established in verses 1–2 and 3–4 is further emphasized. *Compare* (5) refers to a general resemblance (as of a 'family likeness'), a belonging to the same group. *Equal* means to 'be on level terms', equality of status or capacity. The Lord denies that he belongs to a category labelled 'god' in which others too are found; then he goes on to assert that, even were such the case, he cannot be equalled in his divine attributes and acts. *Liken* (√*māšal*, the verb used of making one thing a 'parable' of another) denies that there

---

[1] From T. Olivers, 'The God of Abraham praise'.

is any point of comparison. Fundamentally there cannot be any point of contact between the God who says 'it is I who have made' (4) and the 'gods' who owe their origin to earthly substances (*gold ... silver*, 6), human activity (*pour*), precision (*weigh*), expenditure (*hire*) and skill (*goldsmith*). No wonder Isaiah ends with the scornful (lit.) 'forsooth bow to it!' The disastrous exposure of idols continues with their lifelessness in themselves (7): dependence on their devotees for movement (*lift ... carry*), intrinsic immobility (*set ... stands*), and the absurdity of such a 'god' as the object of prayer and the hope of salvation.

8–11, *The living God.* This passage (with 12–13) turns out to be Isaiah's final appeal to Israel to accept the Lord's will and trust his providence.

8. *Remember*: the way through a problem is to think about God: in particular to recall who he is and what he has done. 'His love in time past/Forbids me to think/He'll leave me at last.'[1] But it is hard to cut through disappointment and bewilderment to this point of comfort. Israel wanted a Davidic restoration and they got Cyrus! What a disappointment! They were nonplussed by what their God was doing. Yet they had to heed a record of age-long divine care (3–4; Ps. 77:7–20, esp. 10). *Fix ... in mind*: the verb √'* āšaš* is found only here, and meanings like 'to be firm' have been suggested. The oldest interpretation relates it to the noun '*îš*, 'a man', and hence 'to act as a man would, take a rational account of things'. Of the suggested emendations, that to √'*āšam* ('to be guilty') is the most suitable. The form here would mean 'acknowledge yourselves guilty'. But there is no use pretending that our knowledge of Hebrew – either in vocabulary or meaning – is anything like complete, and 'prove yourselves men' could well be the prophet's intention. He has been contending against the sheer stupidity of idolatry. Israel did and could know better – if only they would take a thoughtful account of things as humans should. *Take to heart*: give serious thought to.

9. *Former things*: all the Lord has done in the period indicated in verses 3–4. *I am God* (9b) should have an initial 'For'. The recollection of all that has gone before is meaningful because it is *God* who has so acted and he cannot change. *God ... God*: the former is '*ēl*, God in his transcendent deity; the latter '*elōhîm*, God in the fullness of his divine attributes. He is the only (*no other*) and unique (*none like*) God.

10–11. *End ... beginning ... still to come*: i.e. the whole sweep of history, from its inception to the things still in process, and on

---

[1] From J. Newton, 'Begone, unbelief; my Saviour is near'.

to the end, is under his sovereign rule. He does not await the turn of events and then wonder what to do about them: they all emerge in order on the stage of history (like the stars, 40:26) at the dictate of his word (*I make known*, lit. 'declare'). *From ancient times* is just 'from beforehand'. *My purpose will stand*: in a word, the Lord is a God who is truly God. As in creation (Ps. 33:9), so in history, he cannot be thwarted or gainsaid. Even when some particular in human experience bothers his people, it is still the unalterable will of God. Here, the Lord does not conceal or alter the Cyrus plan. He comes as a rapacious victor (*bird of prey*, 11) under the compulsion of the divine will (*purpose*). God has spoken (*said*), God will act (*bring about*); it is the product of divine wisdom (*planned*) and backed by divine action (*do*).

12–13, *The saving God.* Verses 10–11 have dealt with the will of God in the abstract. Isaiah now voices reassurances about the way God's will always works out for his people. Sadly they are in this instance *stubborn-hearted*, 'mighty in heart', precisely our idea 'headstrong'; *far from righteousness. Righteousness* is (as always) 'that which is right with God'. They refuse to align themselves with his righteous purposes. Nevertheless, his will is *righteousness ... salvation ... splendour* (13). It embodies and implements all the Lord's absolutely right purposes, brings salvation/deliverance to his people and is designed for their (lit.) 'beauty', *i.e.* to make them the lovely thing he desires them to be. The idolater makes a god in his own image; the Lord intends to make his people in his.

c. Free at last (47:1 – 48:22)

Seventy long years had passed since the first exiles were deported from Jerusalem. Life in Babylon was far from oppressive (Je. 29), but there were still those who were gripped by the insatiable longing for Zion (Ps. 137). For them the day of salvation/deliverance (48:20–21) could hardly dawn quickly enough. But come it did, and, in the end, with all the lightning speed of which Cyrus was famously capable. It is on all this that Isaiah now meditates: the fall of Babylon (47:1–15) and the call to the captives to go home (48:1–22). The prophet had foreseen that Cyrus would release the captives (44:24–28) and conquer Babylon (45:1–8) – putting first what was most important to him. He now deals with these topics in chronological order.

i. Pride before a fall (47:1–15). In October 539 BC, Cyrus advanced into lower Mesopotamia and, leaving Babylon till last, conquered and occupied the surrounding territory. Seeing which way the wind was blowing, Nabonidus of Babylon deserted his city, leaving it in the charge of his son, Belshazzar. For whatever reason, the taking of Babylon was as bloodless and effortless as Daniel 6 implies. Certainly the priests of Marduk, Babylon's patron god, had their noses put out of joint by Nabonidus' religious fervour for other gods, and the Cyrus Cylinder represents Marduk as accompanying Cyrus on the march and 'made him enter his town ... sparing Babylon any calamity'. Very likely the priests of Marduk connived with Cyrus and secured his entry while Belshazzar feasted. But of all this drama Isaiah says nothing! This would be impossible to explain if indeed we are dealing with a 'Second Isaiah' resident in the city at the time. Chapter 47 looks meditatively at the situation: Babylon fell because of divine vengeance (1–7), pride (8–11) and the impotence of false religion (12–15).

1–7, *Divine vengeance applied and explained.* 1. Babylon is humbled (*dust*; *cf.* 4:1), deprived of former glory (*without a throne*) and repute (*no more ... called*). *Tender ... delicate*: what is easily hurt and what needs shielding from life's roughnesses.

2–4. Babylon has new experiences (2–3b): the cosseted girl of verse 1 works like a slave (*millstones*), goes as a naked captive into exile (*lift up*, lit. 'strip off', ... *legs ... streams*, *cf.* 43:2), and suffers sexual violation (*nakedness ... shame*). Behind all this dire suffering lies the Lord's *vengeance* (3c). The word used (*nāqām*) expresses equivalence between offence and requital. Babylon's downfall is but her just due. *Spare* (3d): the verb 'to meet' adapts its meaning to its context (*cf.* Gn. 23:8, 'intercede'; Jos. 16:7, 'touch'; 1 Sa. 10:5, 'meet'; 1 Ki. 2:32, 'attack'); here (as in 64:5) it means 'to meet with favour', or simply 'to favour'. The situation has to be one of 'no quarter'. Verse 4 adds three comments. First, in the overthrow of Babylon the Lord acted for Israel's sake (*cf.* 14:1–2). He is his people's *Redeemer*, the Next-of-Kin shouldering his kinsperson's need (41:14; 43:14; 44:6, 24). Secondly, he demonstrated his almighty power: LORD *Almighty*, 'of hosts' (1:9). Thirdly, he acted in holiness: *the Holy One of Israel* (1:4). Such is the way the world is run: by an almighty God, acting in holiness, centralizing and meeting his people's needs.

5–7. Babylon loses authority (*silence* replaces dictating the rules to others, 5), liberty (the *darkness* of the dungeon, *cf.* 42:7) and status (*queen*). As in 10:5–15, though Babylonian action against *my people ... my inheritance* (6ab) was formally within the will of God, it was nevertheless an offence to him. It was not that the situation got out of the Lord's control and Babylon inflicted more than was deserved. Their sin lay in the assumptions behind their actions and in their manner: pitilessness (*no mercy*, 6d; specifically 'compassion', tender feeling that should have restrained them), indiscriminateness (*even on the aged*, 6e), arrogance (*for ever ... eternal queen*, 7b), absence of moral thoughtfulness (*did not consider ... what might happen*, 7c; lit. 'the outcome of it'). The holy will of the holy God must be done in a way suited to that holiness – personally as well as collectively. The Old Testament does not subscribe to the view that 'war is war' – a situation where the moral and humanitarian restraints which ordinarily operate are in abeyance and where outrageous deeds can be done with impunity. It does not believe that national needs justify what would be criminal if done by a private individual (*e.g.* Am. 1:3, 6, 9, 11, 13). Babylon assumed a right to tenure (*continue*), authority (*queen*) and immunity (*what might happen*) – ever the blind spots of the imperialist and of those at the top. *Consider*: 'lay to heart', take a thoughtful view. *Reflect ... happen* should be rather stronger: 'remember ... the outcome'. It is not a matter of 'might happen' but of 'remembering' that they live in a moral world ruled by a holy God in which crime and punishment are inseparable.

8–11, *Things which merit judgment.* The single word 'pride' well expresses the accusations levelled as justifying the fall of Babylon, but in particular there was self-assurance for present and future (8), and moral complacency (10). To each is added the warning that the disasters these sins merit cannot be averted either by spiritual (9) or by financial (11) measures.

8–9. *Saying to yourself*: Babylon is overheard. *Wanton* is rather '(self-)indulgent' or 'pampered', the opposite of the *widow* in her unprotected, unprovided state, and sheltered from the blows like *loss of children*. It is not that there is anything wrong with possessing and enjoying the good things (1 Tim. 6:17); it is a matter of the spirit with which such privileges are viewed. Babylon saw them as no more than was her right (8cd). Pampering replaced by poverty (*widowhood*, 9), joy by bitter bereavement (*children*) – and *on a single day*! The future which Babylon ignored (7) brings the tragedies which Babylon dismissed (8). *Sorceries ... spells*: the word translated *spells* means 'bonds', with the idea here of entering into 'associations' with occult powers in order to 'bind' the future; *sorceries* are the incantations used to invoke these powers.

10–11. Here is the astonishing optimism of all who say there is no God and no life to come. They opt for a world without moral consequences. Such is a misleading *wisdom* (in the practical guidance of life) *and knowledge* (the conceptual background or philosophy of life). These in turn arise out of a view of oneself: self-sufficiency (*I am*) and unaccountability – *no-one besides me*; in this context, no authority outside myself to which I must render an account. *Disaster* is the word translated *wickedness* in verse 10a. They chose 'wickedness' and 'wickedness' they will get! *Conjure it away*: this translation can be justified by appeal outside Hebrew to cognate languages; the Hebrew more plainly means 'you will not know its dawn', the thought of un-expectedness matching the suddenness with which the verse ends. *Ransom* (√*kāpar*): specifically 'ransom price'. The disaster cannot be bought off. *Cannot foresee* is 'do not know', *i.e.* unprecedented.

12–15, *Religion that failed.* True religion gives strength in time of need (12) and a sufficient understanding of what the future holds (13). The time of trouble exposes false religion as unable to save (14) and its officiants as inadequate – or self-seeking (15).

12–13. *Spells ... sorceries*: see verse 9. *Keep on*: what sadness lies in this command! Those who do not know the true God have no other recourse than to continue in self-effort (*laboured*) and uncertainty (*perhaps*). *All the counsel* (13) is 'the abundance of', a reference to the conflicting ideologies and directives of poly-theism and (today as then) the conflicting *counsel* of astrology. *Astrologers* are here 'those who divide the heavens', *i.e.* into the various signs of the Zodiac. *What is coming*: *cf.* 41:5–7, the rush of business in the idol factory in the face of coming events.

14–15. In fact false religion, far from offering protection (12), only adds fuel to the fire. *Stubble*: see 5:24. Far from saving others (13), they *cannot even save themselves. No fire*: false religion may seem to offer the warmth of 'helpfulness', but it is not a *fire to sit by*, rather a *fire* which *will burn up*, a furnace of destruction. *Trafficked with* should be 'trafficked with you'. Babylon *laboured* at its religion but the religious officiants were making a trade out of it. Consequently, when the bottom dropped out of their market, *each of them goes* (lit. 'wanders off, making his exit'). *Save*: on √*yāša'* here and √*nāṣal* in verse 14, see 25:9.

ii. Home, yet not home (48:1–22). In this chapter Isaiah heralds the departure of the exiles from Babylon and their embarkation on a protected journey home – a mini-exodus (20–21). Thus Cyrus has fulfilled his vocation within the plan of God (44:26–28) in the manifesto of deliverance sketched in 42:18 –

43:21. Step by step the prophet's theme develops. Alongside the joy of deliverance and the prospect of home-coming, however, lies another, and darker, truth. With a suddenness that has led some commentators to pronounce it a later intrusion into the text, verse 22 states flatly that *there is no peace for the wicked*. But, abrupt though it is, a careful reading of the chapter shows that it is not inappropriate. Who is this people delivered from Babylon and shepherded home? They are people who have forfeited the right to the name *Israel* (1–2), *stubborn* (4), idolatrous (5), inattentive, uncomprehending, *treacherous* and *a rebel* (8). So savage and unrelenting is this tide of indictment that again commentators have wondered how it could originate in one whom they call (from 40:1) 'the prophet of comfort'. How can he be so 'uncomfortable'? But we should rather ask if, in the light of his development of his theme from 38:1 onwards, Isaiah could have spoken here in any other terms. After all, it was the dire sin of unbelief that landed the people in Babylon in the first place (39:1–8). They are obsessed by morbid self-pity (40:27); the Lord's blind servant (42:18), in bondage for failing his law; spiritually insensitive to chastisement (42:21–22, 25); culpably blind and deaf (43:8); weary of the Lord and corrupting true religion (43:22–24); stung by nationalistic pride into rejecting the Cyrus plan and impervious to warning (45:9–13), reassurance (45:14–25) and appeal (46:1–13); arguing with the Lord beyond the point of possibility and propriety (45:9ff.); rebellious (46:8), stubborn (46:12) and far from righteousness (46:12). Thus chapter 48 stands out from chapters 38 – 47, not because it is alien but because it is climactic. What is diffused throughout the earlier chapters is concentrated here into one. To return home from Babylon, then, is not to come home to God: *there is no peace for the wicked*. A change of address is not a change of heart. Great as was the deliverance from political captivity, peace with God, deliverance from sin, is another matter altogether and has yet to be accomplished. But this too is announced here in principle. Verses 3–6b and 6c–7 deal respectively with *former things* and *new things*; in the broadly parallel sections of chapter 48 (1–11, 12–22) the matching verses supply the interpretation: the *former things* are the Cyrus plan (14–15), and the *new things* begin with the advent of the Servant (16).[1] In faithfulness the

---

[1] Isaiah uses 'former things' and 'new things' flexibly. 'Former things' can be the general past (41:22), events linked with the coming conqueror (44:29), or the exodus (43:9, 18); 'new things' are the ministry of the Servant (42:9) and the return from Babylon (43:19); the context decides. Here, to class the former things

Lord has kept the Cyrus promises, but he has yet more in store for his people.

1–2, *Israel described: unreality.* An honoured name (1b), an impeccable pedigree (1c), a true religious allegiance (1de), a privileged citizenship (2a) and a mighty God (2bc) to rely on – but (1f) it is all unreal. There is no genuineness (*truth*) in it, nor does it satisfy the standards of God (*righteousness*).

1. *Jacob ... Israel ... Judah*: respectively, the people in their origin, their covenant status and their particular ancestry. *Line*: 'waters' (see Dt. 33:28; Ps. 68:26). *Take oaths*: swear allegiance. *Invoke*: engage in the whole round of religious practice by which they called on the name of the Lord.

2. *Call yourselves citizens* is 'call themselves after'. Isaiah narrows the focus down: Jacobites (1a), Israelites (1b), Judahites (1c), and now Jerusalemites. A proud claim – and all without reality. The same applies to the narrowest focus of all: *rely on the God of Israel*. This brings us into the realm of personal trust. Taken simply by themselves, these words would be the hallmark of genuineness in religion, the element that turns all other spiritual and religious activities into gold, but in context this too is marked as unreal. The Hebrew of verse 2 has an introductory word (*ki*) omitted by NIV. It requires here the translation 'though', thus exposing as hollow both of their claims, that of citizenship and that of personal faith. *The LORD Almighty is his name*: when this expression was used in 47:4 it underlined the almightiness of the Lord as world ruler, the One with power and authority to take vengeance on Babylon. In 48:2 the Lord faces a very different situation: the total failure of those who claim to be his people. But he is 'the Lord of hosts' in this situation also: he can deal with it. They have failed but he is not beaten. As 'the LORD', he revealed the meaning of his name, Yahweh, when he came to Egypt to bring his people out of the jaws of death. Their claim to be his is an unreal claim, but he affirms that he remains *the God of Israel*. Once again he will prove himself their Saviour.

3–6b, *The former things: blessing for the unworthy.* The Cyrus events (see pp. 296–297) were the subject of prediction

---

as simply the rise of Cyrus and the new things as the return (Skinner) is impermissible, for in this passage the former things must be favourable to Israel and there is nothing at all favourable in the advent of the conqueror as such. Whybray sees the new things as the fall of Babylon and the return but, on his Deutero-Isaiah hypothesis, how can this be? What would be 'new' and unheard of beforehand in something already predicted by Jeremiah and Ezekiel?

long before he made his appearance (3). The reason for this anticipatory prediction was the spiritual infidelity of a people wedded to idols. The argument Isaiah had earlier used to expose the deadness of idols is here used to expose the deadness of Israel! Distant prediction and sudden fulfilment both deprived them of a chance to give credit to their idols.

Stubborn (*qāšeh*, 4): 'brusque' (1 Sa. 20:10), 'cantankerous' (1 Sa. 25:3), temperamentally difficult. *Neck ... iron*: incapable of submission, self-confident. *Forehead ... bronze*: opinionated, the closed mind. *Admit* (6): to all the other charges he has levelled against them, Isaiah here adds an unreadiness to be convinced by the evidence.

6c–11, *The new things: the glory of God.* 6c–8. The 'former things' (3) were kept hidden until their sudden realization, lest it all be attributed to idols; the *new things* (6c) are revealed before their fulfilment, lest Israel arrogantly claim knowledge of them already. Devotion to idols (5) is matched by devotion to self (7). Spiritual disloyalty (5) is matched by the wilfulness of the rebel (8). How can the Lord possibly continue to bother his people? Ready to misinterpret (5), refusal to allow the facts to persuade (6ab), arrogancy that 'knows it all' (7), imperviousness to revealed truth – the cardinal sin of the Lord's people (Am. 2:4). *Treacherous* (8): the identical accusation levelled against Assyria (33:1). Israel, with a vocation to make the world like itself, rather allowed the world to squeeze it into its own mould (see on 2:1–4, 5ff.; Rom. 12:1–2).

9–11. What is it, then, that moves the Lord to persevere with his so desperately undeserving people? First, he acts *for my own name's sake.* His *name* is a summary statement (shorthand) for what he is in himself, and within that nature there is a divine logic at work (55:8) whereby merited *wrath* is restrained. But his *name* is also what he has revealed himself to be, and (see 2) 'Yahweh' (Ex. 3:15) is not only the holy God visiting judgment (Ex. 12:12) but also the saving and redeeming God (Ex. 6:6–7; 12:13). His people play false to revelation, but he is always true to what he has revealed through his word. Secondly, there is *my praise*, the praise due to me (see 11). This is illustrated in Exodus 32:12 and Numbers 14:13–14 – the abandonment of rebellious Israel would expose the Lord's character and power to misunderstanding. Thirdly, there is the Lord's choice (10),[1] see 41:8–9;

---

[1] MT reads *bᵉḥartîkā*, 'I chose you'; Qᵃ reads *bᵉḥantîkā*, '*I tested / refined you*'. The change is minimal as far as the text is concerned. It is a question of suitability of meaning. Since Israel's 'silver' is all 'dross' (1:22), a refining would leave

43:10; 44:1–2 (*cf.* Dt. 4:37; 7:6–8; 10:15; 1 Ki. 11:24). Why the Lord should so choose is a secret he has kept to himself, but his choice is no passing whim: it is an inalterable commitment of his will. He chose knowing exactly what his people are (8), and he will not be diverted from his choice till he has fulfilled its intention.

Refined ... *though not as silver* (10): silver endures the crucible until all dross is gone. Were the Lord to deal with his people just like that, nothing would remain (1:22). Therefore, though he brings his people through trials, there is always a limit set: they are never treated as they deserve, always for the fulfilment of his purpose (Heb. 12:10). *Furnace of affliction*: classically this refers to Egypt (Dt. 4:20; 1 Ki. 8:51), and (10b) he will never alter the choice there made. In the present context the *furnace* could be Babylon, and the verb 'to choose' could exhibit the same meaning as in 14:1 and Zechariah 1:17, 'to renew choice'. *Glory to another*: if Israel's sinfulness defeats the Lord's purposes, then sin gets glory over him; if the people remain in exile, then the gods of Babylon triumph. But neither the forces of history (Babylon) nor the power of sin will win the day.

12–16, *The all-controlling Lord.* Verse 12a repeats 1 and indicates that we are now entering the second half of the poem. The repeated calls to *listen* (12a, 14a, 16a) mark the divisions of this section: the Lord controls the whole universe (12–13), he controls history, bringing on to the scene the one he has chosen to fulfil his purpose (14–15), and he controls the advent of his Servant endowed for his task (16).

12–13. *Called*: note the same verb in verse 1, exposing Israel's gross unfaithfulness. But their unfaithfulness does not nullify the faithfulness of God: they denied their calling; he affirms his calling of them. *I am he*: he is the unchanged, unchanging God. *Summon* (13) is, again, the verb 'to call'. By his 'calling', he masters the whole universe and gives it stability and continuance. *Stand up*: 'stand in their position'. This sovereignty of the divine 'calling' proves that the calling of Israel cannot fail of its purpose either. As *first* the Lord was not under any external compulsion to do what he did (either in the creation of the world or in the calling of Israel); as *last* he stands at the end unchallenged by any force that might have tried to oppose him, bringing to triumphant conclusion (for the world and for Israel) what he started (Phil. 1:6).

---

nothing. But to say that, when this particular silver was in the 'furnace', the Lord 'chose' to set a limit to the process and 'renew his choice' is exact.

14–15. The focus then narrows from the universal (13) to the particular (14), and moves from creation to history. The Lord is different from all gods in that he predicts and fulfils (14ab); his Cyrus plan will succeed against Babylon (14cd); the calling of God is the governing factor in history (15ab); and in this the Lord is not a remote deity but one working his purpose out in the details of the historical process (15cd). Thus he is both over and in history: its movements begin in his mind (14ab), he determines the powers that arise and the purposes they will achieve (14cd), and having spoken the determinative word (15ab) he personally superintends its fulfilment (15cd). The word of God (14ab, 15) brackets the history of the world.

The argument from prediction and fulfilment has been used to challenge the idols (*e.g.* 41:21–24) and to recall Israel to true faith (48:6). It is used here in verse 14 rather to reassure the people of God in the light of the Cyrus plan about which they have such misgivings (45:9–10; 46:8, 12). The Lord himself is behind it, and all must therefore be well. *The LORD's chosen ally will* ... (14): literally 'The-Lord-loves-him will perform ...', where the hyphenated phrase becomes as it were a title. It is an interesting anticipation of what the Cyrus Cylinder says about Marduk, that 'he called Cyrus ... went at his side like a friend ...' But Marduk was wise only after the event and, even so, said nothing about Babylon and how it would fare. Isaiah predicts how a greater 'friend' planned and superintended Cyrus from inception to climax. *Called* (15): *cf.* 12–13 (*summon*). The sovereign call of God is the dominant factor within the covenant (12), over creation (13) and in world events (15).

16. Once more the word of God is the initial and initiating factor, now seen in the sending of an unnamed speaker. We are told, however, that he is sent by *the Sovereign LORD* (*'ᵃdōnāy yahweh*) and (endowed) with *his Spirit*. The only Spirit-endowed person in these chapters is the Servant (42:1), and in the immediate context the divine designation 'Lord Yahweh' occurs in the third Servant Song as endowing (50:4), directing (50:5) and helping (50:7) the Servant. In addition, when the Servant reappears in chapters 56 – 66 as the Conqueror, 61:1 opens with *the Spirit of the Sovereign LORD is upon me.*[1] We can hardly question, then, that the present verse is an interjection by the Servant of the Lord as the Agent of the 'new things' announced in the matching verses 3–6b. The balance of the passages is a

---

[1] Isaiah mentions the enduement of the Spirit nine times (11:2; 30:1; 32:15; 42:1; 44:3; 48:16; 59:21; 61:1; 63:11). Of these, five relate to the Messiah.

striking illustration of the way structure aids interpretation: former things (3–6b), new things (6c–7); Cyrus (14–15), the Servant (16). While the interjection does, of course, take us by surprise, it is far from inappropriate that the Servant should step from the shadows like this. First, it suits what has immediately preceded. The Lord is the sovereign ruler of creation (13); his rule of the flow of history is signally seen in Cyrus (14–15); but the Servant, as revealed by Isaiah, is the climax to which all history is leading. Secondly, it is appropriate to what follows: with 48:20–21 the significance of Cyrus has ended. But, for the problem raised by verse 22, the Servant is the appointed answer. As the one actor leaves the stage, the other quietly reveals his presence.

17–22, *A problem solved; a problem raised.* The thought of *peace* enfolds these verses, the peace that might have been (17–19) and the peace that cannot be (22). In between there is the great exit from Babylon (20) and the exodus-like journey home (21). The political solution – the people home from Babylon – does not recover the *peace* that might have been. It was the sin of disobedience (18) that forfeited peace, and until wickedness has been dealt with peace must remain unrealized.

17. *Redeemer* (47:4): as their Next-of-Kin the Lord has taken on himself their need of liberation. His almighty power has directed history in the rousing of Cyrus, the conqueror-liberator. *The Holy One of Israel*: in chapters 40 – 55 Isaiah calls the Lord 'Redeemer' ten times, and in six of these he links the Lord's next-of-kinship, as here, with the title *the Holy One of Israel* (41:14; 43:14; 47:4; 49:7; 54:5). That the Holy One should draw near as the Next-of-Kin is a truly overwhelming display of grace and condescension, but it raises in a crucial form the problem not only of unworthiness but of sin. Can the Next-of-Kin shoulder this problem also? Surely it is for this reason that Isaiah so insists on holding the two concepts together. Whatever help he brings to his people (41:8), whatever rescue he effects (43:14), whatever victory he wins (47:4) – whatever burden he takes from them and loads on to himself – he remains the Holy One. Sooner or later the disparity between his holiness and their unworthy sinfulness much be taken into account. In this way Isaiah prepares for the stark announcement in verse 22 and for the ensuing spiritual redemption through the Servant. *Teaches ... directs*: the Lord ministers to his people through the word he speaks. This is their distinguishing privilege: to possess the revealed word. It is, first, a divine address to the mind ('teach'), and then, secondly, through the mind to the will ('direct'), and finally, in

the life of obedience, it is *best for you*, the way of the highest
good.

18–19. These verses develop the leading thought of 17, the
word of God, the way of blessing, but they do so wistfully,
recalling what might have been. Obedience promises, first, *peace*,
all-round well-being – Godward, manward, selfward (9:6; 26:3,
12; 32:17) – and that peace is as a constant, full reality, a *river*
(66:12), not a seasonal stream; and, secondly, *righteousness*, here
a life conformed to what is right before God. *Waves* often picture
overwhelming power (Ps. 42:7; 65:7; 107:25), and that is probably the thought here: a life impervious to the threat of opposed
forces, a steady, consistent righteousness of life. Thirdly, by
obedience, the Lord's people enter into his covenant blessings:
descendants ... like the sand (Gn. 15:5; 22:17), including the
particular blessing (noted in Pr. 20:7) of the prevalence of
godliness through the generations. The fourth blessing
consequent upon obedience is perpetuity in the favour of God:
name ... never cut off. It is not, of course, that our obedience
earns the blessing of eternal security, but that the obedient life is
proof of the reality of our standing before God (Jn. 15:7–8; 1 Jn.
2:3–6).

20–21. In spite of the record of failure in verses 17–18, the
mercy of God prevails in the call to exit from Babylon into the
caring blessings of a new exodus. *Leave* (lit. 'go out') and *flee* are
both exodus verbs (*e.g.* Ex. 12:41; 13:3; 14:5). They are used
here not to express any danger from which flight is needed but to
begin to create the picture of another exodus. The fact that the
historical return (Ezr. 1 – 2) was numerically meagre does not
minimize it as a mighty, exodus-like act of God: the rousing and
bringing of Cyrus, the marvel of a conqueror turned liberator, the
blessedness of a promise fulfilled (Je. 25:12–13; 29:10; with Ezr.
1:1). The people's failure to enter worthily into the Lord's opened
door should not surprise us in the light of verses 17–18, nor
should we allow it to reduce for us the magnitude of what he did
to the poor dimensions of their response. *Announce ... shout* (20):
had they responded worthily and obediently, their liberation
could have been a witness to the world. It was, in fact, an event
of world proportions, though they did not see it as such.
Redeemed: taken upon himself the burden of their need and met
it. *Thirst ... rock* (21): this is a broad recollection of a journey
that never lacked divine provision (Dt. 8:1–4), but Exodus 17:1–7
is carefully chosen, for it was also an example of divine care for a
grumbling people – just as here they are blessed by the Lord's
Cyrus plan against which they had groused (45:9–10; 46:8ff.).

22.[1] A change of scene does not produce a change of heart. Leaving Babylon, they do not leave behind their characters and characteristics. They are the people of verses 17–18, who have left the way of *peace*. *Wicked* is a broad word, an apt summary of the charges levelled against Israel in this chapter. It writes an epitaph to the Babylonian experience. They went because of sin (42:18–25); they stayed without moral reform or even the recognition of need; they return as they went. They come back to Canaan, but they still need to be brought back to the Lord.

IX. THE GREATER DELIVERANCE:
THE WORK OF THE SERVANT (49 – 55)

The emphasis on the sinfulness of Israel (48:1–8), the unexpected interjection from the Servant (48:16), and the assertion that the people have come back from Babylon but still need to be brought back to the Lord (48:22), prepare us for chapters 49 – 55, the redeeming work of the Servant. He is given a double task relating to Israel and to the world (49:5–6), and when he has performed the great work of sin-bearing (52:13 – 53:12) the call goes out to Zion (54:1ff.) and the world (55:1ff.) to enter gladly and freely into what he has done.

a. The Servant's double task (49:1–6)

Isaiah 49:1–6, the second Servant Song, has the same relationship to 48:1–22 as the first Servant Song (42:1–4) has to what precedes it. There, the mounting awareness of Gentile need (41:21–29) was answered by the announcement that the Lord had a Servant at the ready who would bring justice – divine revelation – to the helpless and hopeless world (42:1, 3–4). Following this a new factor entered the equation. Israel, the 'official' servant of the Lord (41:8), bound, blind and sinful (42:18–25), was unfit for the task, and Isaiah's awareness of Israel's need came to dominate his presentation, reaching its climax in 48:1ff. This is the cue for the Servant once more to occupy centre stage as he testifies to his prior call to *bring Jacob back to him ... to bring back ... Israel* (49:5–6) while also bringing *salvation to the ends*

---

[1] Commentators wonder if these words are original to the text. F. Delitzsch (*Commentary on Isaiah* [T. & T. Clark, 1873]) and Young (*Studies in Isaiah*) note their meaning but do not explain their position here. Kissane (*The Book of Isaiah*) observes the same words in 57:21 where he believes them to be in place, but reckons them misplaced here. Whybray (*Isaiah 40 – 66*) wonders if both occurrences may be editorial markers dividing the text into sections, but he does not offer an analysis to support this.

of the earth (49:6). The Servant's job description has been re-written: he is still committed to the whole world as in 42:1–4, but now, conforming to the development in 42:18 – 48:22, he has a prior task in relation to Israel. His testimony falls into two parts.

i. The first testimony: Israel as it was meant to be (49:1–3). **1ab** is a summons to the world in all its extent (*islands*; 11:11; 24:15; 41:1; 42:4, 10, 12) and all its peoples (*leummîm*, a general word possibly emphasizing the human element). Thus the testimony starts as it will end (6) on a universal scale, a message (1) and a ministry (6) to all humankind. *Listen to me*: the prophets are extremely sparing in worldwide address (41;1; Je. 31:10) but neither Jeremiah (though called to a worldwide ministry, 1:5) nor any other prophet ever said, 'Listen to me', just like this. Only Isaiah uses *to me*, and then only of the Lord (46:3, 12; 48:12; 51:1, 7; 55:2; *cf.* 41:1). How then can the Servant thus address the world? His demand for a worldwide hearing, based on the qualifications listed in verses 1c–3, is as absolute as 'Listen to him' in Mark 9:7. At the very least he is no 'mere' prophet!

1c–3. The Servant justifies his call to the world by his position (1cd), his preparation (2) and his person (3). There are eight paired lines, carefully balanced: the first line in each pair (*called ... mouth ... arrow ... servant*) is about service: calling, preparation, effectiveness, status; the second line (*name ... shadow ... quiver ... Israel*) is about personal identity and secrecy. *Born ... birth*: literally 'from/in the womb ... from my mother's body'. The Servant is truly human and is not a divine afterthought. Nevertheless, as a prophet of the Lord (Je. 1:5), he is truly special. In respect of the Messiah there is often this sort of reference to his mother: 7:14; Genesis 3:15; Psalm 22:9–10; Micah 5:2 and possibly the enigmatic Jeremiah 31:22. *Called* (√*qārā'*) is not used of 'calling' a prophet but is used of the Lord making a sovereign appointment (*e.g.* 40:26 [stars]; 41:4; 44:7, NIV 'proclaim' [events in history]), specifically of Israel (41:7; 43:1), Cyrus (41:2; 45:3–4; 46:11; 48:15) and the Servant (42:6). The thought, then, is not of a 'calling' to be a prophet but of sovereign conscription to a special status and function. *Mouth* (2): the Servant has a prophetic task. The sharpness of a *sword* makes it effective. Cyrus had an effective sword (41:2), but the *sword* of the Servant is of a different nature: the imagery of war used in the interests of the gospel of peace (9:1–7; 11:11–16; *cf.* Heb. 4:12; Rev. 1:16; 19:15). *Polished arrow*: the shaft of an arrow was rubbed down to make it aerodynamic and free it from roughness which would deflect its flight. The contrast between the *sword* for close encounters and the *arrow* for distant attack implies that the Servant is equipped for every contest. *Quiver*: under the personal care of the Lord's *hand*, the Servant is also reserved for the specific target the Lord intends. *Servant, Israel*: Israel was the name of an individual before it became that of a nation, and with the name came responsibility for the Abrahamic promises of world blessing (Gn. 28:13–14; 35:9–15). The whole weight rested on the shoulders of one individual. Isaiah now brings that responsibility full circle. He has discerned that the nation-servant is unfit (42:18–25) – indeed, so unfit that it can no longer claim the name (48:1–2). So, must the Lord admit defeat? No, he has prepared a worthy Israel! – the Servant divinely shaped for the task and, as we shall soon discover (49:14 – 50:11), the only one worthy of the name.[1] *Display my splendour* (lit. 'beauty') occurs thirteen times in the Old Testament, of which nine are in Isaiah. On all other occasions the Lord shows his beauty by what he himself does (44:23; 60:21), but here it is by what is done for him. Elsewhere the plural is used of those in whom the Lord shows his beauty; here it is just the Servant. This is never said to any individual, to Israel or any group within Israel: Isaiah says a unique thing about one whom he sees as a unique person.

ii. The second testimony: the Agent, the task and the result (49:4–6). The despondent Servant (4) becomes the Servant buoyant regarding his primary task (5) and divinely assured in regard to his ultimate objective (6).

4. *Laboured ... no purpose; spent ... in vain*: no effort has been spared; no good has been achieved. If the servant is to be identified with Jesus Christ, we cannot but ask where, in him, do we find this darkness? Gethsemane does not suit, for there the darkness sprang from the impending future. But throughout the Gospels Jesus faced rejection, unbelief, prejudice and misunderstanding. He cried out, 'How long ...?' (Lk. 9:41), was grieved

---

[1] Commentators either find the attribution of the name 'Israel' to the servant so inexplicable that they excise it (Smart), or else, on the general pattern set by Skinner, try to use it to identify the Servant with the nation or with the 'true' Israel, the remnant within the nation. See Introduction, pp. 26–27. One MS (Kennicott 96) lacks the word 'Israel', but it is infamous for its variants and no importance can be attached to this omission (Rowley, *The Servant of the Lord*, p. 8). C. R. North notes that 'even if K 96 were a good MS we should hardly be justified in following it in defiance of the otherwise unanimous textual evidence' (*Second Isaiah* [OUP, 1964], p. 187).

by his disciples' failure to understand (Mk. 8:21), and foresaw the falling away of the core group (Mk. 14:27). Perhaps what is thus diffused throughout Jesus' ministry is, so to speak, compressed by Isaiah into this single utterance. *Yet* ('*ākēn*): 'But indeed', a conjunction emphatically countering what has preceded. When despair threatens, there is an antidote. *Due to me* corresponds to the despondency which says, 'I am a failure.' Literally, 'my judgment is with the Lord'. It is for the Lord to decide whether I am a failure or not. All I can do is labour and spend my strength, beyond that it is for him to judge. *My reward* corresponds to the other side of despondency: 'Nothing has been achieved.' But this too is the Lord's business; it is for him to 'give the increase' (1 Cor. 3:7–9; *cf.* AV). The answer to despondency is to look to God, acknowledge his sovereignty and rest trustfully in him to perform his perfect will. But notice that Isaiah foresaw a truly human Servant, tested, and himself testing the way of faith, but still saying *my God* when everything seems *to no purpose*, 'empty' (*in vain*; *tōhû*), without sense or meaning, and *for nothing* (*hebel*), without substance or solidity, evanescent.

5. This verse begins with the Servant's (fresh?) awareness of the way the hand of God has been upon him (5ab), and ends with his sense of his dignity before God (5e) and of new spiritual vitality (6–7). In this he admits us to another secret in relation to despondency: work to which God has called can never be a failure; the one who obeys the call has a rich dignity before God and an unfailing strength. *In the womb* is identical with verse 1c and notes that every single experience of life from conception onwards has been a sharpening of the sword and a polishing of the arrow (2). So it is with every servant of the Lord, therefore there is no room for despondency: 'The work which His goodness began / The arm of His strength will complete.'[1] *To bring Jacob back to him*: the task for which the Servant is renewed is the restoration to the Lord of *Jacob … Israel*,[2] the spiritual counterpart of the restoration from Babylon (48:20–22), the fulfilment of the pledge made in 43:22 – 44:23. *Has been my strength*, *i.e.* all along, even when obscured by the darkness of despondency.

6. This Servant Israel (3) is, first, distinct from the nation

[1] From A. Toplady, 'A debtor to mercy alone'. *Cf.* Phil. 1:6.
[2] *Gather Israel to himself* is a place where there is tension between *lō* ' ('not') and *lô* ('to him'). *Cf.* 9:3. 'And that Israel be not swept away' is possible in context, but the Masoretes (now supported by Q^a) recommended the more suitable 'to him'.

Israel, for it is his task to bring the people back: the nation cannot be its own saviour from sin. Secondly, he is the true and only Israel, for he is going to do what Israel was always meant to do (*cf.* 2:2–4) – gather from the whole world. *Those of Israel I have kept:*[1] 4:3 describes 'those who are left in Zion' as (lit.) 'written unto life', that is to say, destined in advance by the Lord for the promised cleansing (4:4). In the same sense, then, it is the Servant's task to bring to the Lord, not all who claim the name *Israel*, but those whom the Lord has 'kept' with that intention in mind. *Light ... salvation*: the Servant in his own person is the Light of the world (*cf.* 42:1–4, 5–9). We should translate 'that you may be my salvation'. Thus 'you are my servant' (3) is balanced by 'you are my salvation'. Just as the world will find him to be the light they need, so he is the salvation they need. This task runs beyond what any prophet or any mere human could fulfil.

b. Divine confirmation: worldwide success (49:7–13)

The first Servant Song (42:1–4) set a pattern which each in turn repeats – the addition of a confirmatory 'tailpiece' (see 42:5–9): here, his significance for the whole world is divinely confirmed as the Lord forecasts Gentile submission to the Servant (7), balancing this with a *covenant* for a restored Israel (8); Israel's exodus journey home (9–10) is then balanced by a worldwide ingathering (11–12) and the call to universal praise (13). What the Servant is called to do (1–6) is guaranteed by the divine word (7–13).

7. *Israel* (lines b and h) refers to the Servant. Throughout chapters 49 – 55 the nation is called *Zion* – following the contention in 48:1 and because it has lost the right to the name which has passed to the Servant (3). In the full reality of his divine nature (*Holy One*) the Lord stands as Next-of-Kin (*Redeemer*) to meet his Servant's every need and guarantee his success. Isaiah is aware that the Servant will be *despised* by his own *nation* and dominated (*servant*) by the world (*rulers ... kings*), but the *faithful* Next-of-Kin will bring his Servant through to the point where *kings will ... rise up* and *princes ... bow down*. The contrasting actions of rising and bowing indicate total respectful acknowledgment.

---

[1] There is a slight textual uncertainty here. The word in the text (*nāṣîr*) is not found elsewhere, though it would be a respectably formed passive noun, 'preserved one'. MT recommends reading *nāṣûr*, a passive participle with the same meaning.

8–9b. The reference to *people*, *land* and *inheritances* shows that the topic is now what the Servant will do for the Lord's professing people. Through prayer (8b), as covenant man (8d), he will bring a fourfold blessing: restoration (8f), possession (8g), liberation (9a) and transformation (9b). *Salvation* includes 'when you need my delivering action' – picturing the Servant as under duress – as well as the wider meaning of what the Servant will accomplish for others. *Be a covenant*: he will *be* the covenant in his own person, that is to say it is only in him, in union with him, that the covenant blessings can be enjoyed. *Reassign*: literally 'cause to inherit/to possess', *i.e.* bring into actual, secure possession. Isaiah sees the future in terms which come naturally to him. In the light of John 18:36 and Acts 15:15–18 we see that land, restoration, captives and darkness are all figurative of spiritual blessings.

9c–10. As the exodus from Egypt led to a journey under God's care, so in this journey of the heart back to the Lord there is provision (9cd), with pasturage *beside the roads*, *i.e.* readily available, and the *barren* become fertile; protection (10ab) from the inner weakness of *hunger* and *thirst* and the outward threat of *heat* and *sun* (*heat* translates *šārāḇ*, which may possibly mean 'mirage' – in context, the threat of disappointment); and *guardianship* (10cd), as the journey is under divine superintendence. The Lord has taken the people to his heart in *compassion* (√*rāḥam*, a love that is both maternal [1 Ki. 3:26] and paternal [Ps. 103:13]), under his care (*guide ... lead*), and into his bounty (*springs of water*).

11–12. Nothing is allowed to stand in the way of the world-wide ingathering: *mountains*, blocking the way, become *roads*. No-one can get lost: *highways*, *raised* above the surrounding countryside, cannot be missed. Neither distance (*afar*) nor dispersion (*north ... west*) can stop them, nor can strangeness of location: *Aswan* is only a guess at the original *sînîm*.[1] It is most likely that Isaiah was being consciously obscure. Even unmapped places are known to God, and even from them he will gather his pilgrims.

13. *Heavens* and *earth* are the contrasting realities that make up the totality. *Mountains* are perhaps singled out as places from which good tidings were shouted (40:9), or possibly as typical of

---

[1] '*Sinim*', NIV mg., is unknown to us. 'Aswan' is only a guess (*cf.* Ezk. 29:10; 30:6). Qᵃ reads *swnyym* which, again, might be Aswan, but more likely Qᵃ was just as much guessing as we are. The identification of *Sinim* with China lacks evidence.

the solid earth itself, once corrupted by human sin and now liberated in the liberation of the children of God (Rom. 8:20–21). *Shout ... rejoice ... song*: singing expresses entering responsively into what the Lord has accomplished and to which his people contribute nothing (12:1; 24:16; 25:1; 30:39; 54:1). The Lord has done it; all they do is sing! *His people*: just as in 45:17 and 25 the context required that *Israel* should cover the worldwide gathered people, so here *his people* are all those embraced by the work of the Servant (5–6, 7–12). *Afflicted*: the downtrodden, pointing in the present context to their spiritual need and helplessness. *Comforts* is what the Lord does, *compassion* (see 10) is what he feels.

c. Nation and Servant, a contrast: unresponding and responding (49:14 – 50:11)

The voice of complaint (14) is a tragic anticlimax after the exuberance of 13, but it sets the tone for the next stage in Isaiah's argument. Ruined, broken Zion, desolate after its long years of emptiness, offers an apt picture of the people themselves – just as we met them in 40:27; 45:9–11; 46:8–12, despondent, defeatist and grumbling. But, while they prefer their misery to the Lord's promises (49:14 – 50:3), the Servant again speaks in responsive, trustful obedience (50:4–9). In 42:18–25 Israel's unworthiness unfitted it to be the Lord's Servant; now the Servant's contrasting worthiness qualifies him for the office. On the one hand, Zion is offered inducements to trust (49:14–26) but will not; on the other hand the Servant is forewarned of suffering to come (50:5, 6) yet responds with commitment. The contrast between the Servant who is Israel (49:3) and Zion who used to be Israel (48:1–2) is striking. Yet the Lord does not give up on his people but seeks to win them to faith by his rich promises.

The promise of unforgetfulness (49:14–16). 14. *Forsaken ... forgotten* correspond to 'out of sight, out of mind'. *The LORD* (Yahweh) is the God who chose and redeemed his captive people in Egypt (Ex. 3:15): can he forget his captives now? *The Lord* (*ᵃdōnāy*) is the Sovereign One who can be neither compelled nor prohibited.

15–16. Mother and infant are bound by ties of dependence (*at her breast*) and life (*child she has borne*, lit. 'son of her body'), yet even this relationship can fail, but not the Lord. *I* is emphatic, 'but as for me'. The Lord's unforgetting love transcends even earth's best. *See* suggests a gesture, the hands held out for inspection, incised with self-inflicted wounds of love. *Your walls* are either the ruined walls in their mute appeal (Ps. 74:3; 102:13–14) or perhaps the Lord's blueprint of the new Jerusalem.

The promise of increase (49:17–20). The gathering family[1] is, in earthly terms, the supreme cordial for parental gloom.

17. *Laid you waste* is two verbs in the Hebrew, 'demolished you and left you waste', as if the Lord would assure poor Zion that he understands how awful was the process of demolition and the resultant desolation.

18–20. There are three aspects of promised transformation: the despondent mother given a fresh start in joy like a *bride* (18), the empty city filled and free of threat (19) and the new inhabitants positive and forward-looking (20).

The promise of world dominion (49:21–23). Zion's question is also ours: what is this ingathering and increase that the prophet promises (20)? How will it happen? It is not any natural development (21) but an act of God (23ef) on a worldwide scale, involving the subservience of the world to the interests of the Lord's people (22–23d). Behind it lies the messianic banner of 11:12, the Jubilee of 27:12–13 and the world vision of 44:14–25. The explanation of transformed barrenness will come in 54:1–17. Isaiah is using the imagery of the ruined city, the captive exile, the barren woman and the worldwide reunion but, against the background of 49:1–6, 7–13, the transformation is the fruit of the work of the servant, people and world brought back to God.

21. *Bereaved and barren*: doubly infertile, husbandless and sterile. *Exiled and rejected*: 'captive and evicted / dismissed', now belonging to others, rejected by her own.

22–23. *Beckon*: 'lift my hand'. Divine sovereignty is such that a mere gesture is enough. *Gentiles* (lit. 'nations') ... *peoples* ... *kings* ... *queens*: whether in its massed organization or in the persons of its great ones, the world is at the Lord's beck and call to serve the circumstantial (*bring* ... *carry*) or personal (*foster* ... *nursing*) needs of Zion's children and to do so with true subservience (*bow* ... *lick*). As in 45:14 the picture of servility emphasizes a spiritual truth, that those who would join the Lord's people must first submit to them (1 Cor. 14:25). The imagery is political subservience, the reality is spiritual indebtedness. *Hope* is 'wait for (with trustful expectancy)' (40:31).

The promise of deliverance (49:24–26). 24. Calling Zion's children home involves, first, breaking the powers which hold

---

[1] In verse 17, MT reads *bānayi*, 'your sons', but many prefer Qᵃ, *bônayi*, 'your builders', as offering a good contrast with 'those who laid you waste'. The true contrast, however, is between those who banished the sons and the return of the sons, marking the end of the rule of the destroyers. The theme of sons is central to the section.

them (*plunder ... from warriors*, 24), but there is something else as well: *fierce* is an emended text;[1] MT has 'righteous' – that is to say, delivering captives requires not only the strength to do so but also the legal right. Suppose they are lawfully held prisoner? If the captor has a right to his prisoners, can that right be denied?

25. Both questions in verse 24 are answered: *warriors* – even *fierce* ones – must submit to superior power; furthermore the Lord proposes to take to law those who claim a legal right to his people: *contend* is here used in its forensic meaning, 'to plead a case'. The Lord's almighty power is sufficient against any foe but he will never use that power except in accordance with the claims of law (45:21; 53:11; 54:14, 17; Rom. 3:26), violating neither his own righteous character nor the rights even of his foes (Gn. 15:16).

26. The pictures of eating *their own flesh* and drinking *their own blood* draw on the horrors of siege conditions. The reality is that those who oppose the Lord and his people experience the self-destructiveness of sin – a recurring feature of the wars of the Lord (Jdg. 7:22; 1 Sa. 14:20; 2 Ch. 20:23–24). This will constitute a worldwide revelation (*all ... will know*) of the Lord as Yahweh (*LORD*) – who, as in Egypt, delivers his people and overthrows his enemies; as *Saviour* (√*yāša'*, 25:9); as *Redeemer*, or *Next-of-Kin* (35:9–10); and as *Mighty One of Jacob. Mighty* focuses exclusively on the attribute of power, the absolute strength of the Lord wedded to the welfare of his unworthy *Jacob*.

The promise of ransom (50:1–3). 1. Isaiah pursues the question of legality, raised in 49:24–25. He offers two pictures: divorce and slavery. According to Deuteronomy 24:1–4, a divorce could initiate a series of events making reconstitution of the original marriage impossible. The absence here of a *certificate* shows that this process has not even started. As to slavery, in default of payment, a creditor was legally entitled to enslave the debtor's dependants (Ex. 21:7; 2 Ki. 4:1ff.; Ne. 5:1–5), and, as long as this situation obtained, all rights lay with the creditor, none with the debtor. In both cases there were legal requirements to be met. But are these situations applicable? Divorce accuses unfailing love of failure; slavery accuses sovereign power of weakness and sovereign resources of inadequacy. The truth, however, is very different, for it was all a matter of due reward of *sins* (*'awōn*, 1f), inner perversion of heart (6:7), and *transgressions*

---

[1] The alteration of *zaddîq* ('righteous') to *'arîs*, following Qᵃ, is commonplace, but can be made only at the expense of doctrinal fullness.

(*peša*', 1g) , 'wilful rebellion'. *Sold*: cf. Judges 2:14; 3:8; 4:2; 10:7.

2–3. *Why ... no-one?* Since neither divorce nor slavery explains the banishment of Zion, they cannot plead irretrievable breakdown or legal barriers; they cannot justify self-pitying despondency. If the Lord chooses to call them back to himself he can do so – he is the offended party, not they! So why no response? The wording is very emphatic – 'not a single individual ... no-one at all' – and provides a telling contrast with (4) the single responsive voice of the Servant. *Arm ... short* is (lit.) 'hand ... short'. The idea of the 'short hand' occurs in 59:1 (see Nu. 11:23) and is related to the use of 'hand' meaning (financial) resources (Lv. 5:7, *cannot afford* = 'hand cannot reach'; 12:8; 14:21). The verb *to ransom* involves 'paying the price' (1:27; 35:10) required to obtain freedom. The question therefore indignantly asks whether the Lord is short of the cash to buy back his wife (Ho. 3:2), to redeem his slaves or to find the due payment for their sins – in short: can the Lord satisfy the law? The next question asks if he has the power *to rescue* (lit. 'to deliver', *i.e.* from the grasp of a captor), and it is answered by an appeal to the evidence of the creation (2e–3; *cf.* Am. 4:13; 5:8–9; 9:5–6). The Lord's power over creation demonstrates his ability to do whatever he wills, promises or threatens. In particular he can effect dramatic change on earth (2ef; Ps. 106:9), among living things (2gh; Ex. 7:17–18) and in the sky above (3; Ex. 10:21–23). Isaiah chooses illustrations of divine power which also illustrate the Lord's interventions to save, power on behalf of his people against their oppressors. To fail to respond to such a God is without excuse.

Obedient Israel: the responsive Servant (50:4–9). (On this section, see further on 53:7–9.) A new voice cuts across the Lord's indignant expostulations (2–3). Contradicting the 'no-one at all' of verse 2, there is one who testifies to listening and responding (5). The speaker uses the first person but does not identify himself, and it is not until the 'tailpiece' (10–11) that we learn we have been listening to the Servant. Arising from the easily overlooked clue in 49:7 that the Servant is a sufferer ('despised and abhorred') and subordinated, deeply personal sufferings are described and traced back to their cause in resolute obedience to the Lord. Four times *the Sovereign LORD* – Yahweh, the saving God in all his absolute power – is given the emphatic position (4, 5, 7, 9) and divides the testimony into its component parts.

4. By gift of *the Sovereign LORD* he has *an instructed tongue*, (lit.) 'a tongue of those who have been / are being taught': in short 'a disciples' tongue'. The same word (*limmûdîm*) is translated 'disciples' in 8:16. And, because he has been discipled by the Lord in how to speak and what to say, he is able to exercise an effective spoken ministry: *to know the word that sustains*. The verb translated *sustains* ($\sqrt{}$'*ût*) is not found elsewhere. Suggestions include 'to incline towards = to console', 'to respond (to needs)'; emendations include 'to shepherd' and 'to care for', but the oldest suggestion is still possible, relating the verb to the noun '*ēt*, 'a timely moment, a season', hence 'to be seasonable', 'to speak a word in season'.[1] This emphasizes the 'prophetic' role of the Servant, prominent throughout (42:2; 49:2; 53:9). *Weary*: 'fainting' under life's demands. In verse 4cd we move from the word spoken to the word heard. The connection is not spelled out but is obvious: only those who hear the word can share it. He testifies of an experience (*he wakens*), a time (*morning*), a regularity (*morning by morning*), an objective (*my ear to listen*, lit. 'hear') and a characteristic (*like one*, lit. 'those', who is *being taught*, or 'like disciples'). It is the Lord who takes the initiative, rousing his Servant for the morning fellowship; the word of God is central to it; the objective is to convey truth through the ear to the mind – and this is the essence of what it means to be a disciple: the 'morning watch' is not a special provision for a unique Servant; it is the standard curriculum for all who would be disciples.

5-6. In the *morning by morning* discipleship the Servant learned the Lord's will. It was in one such session that the Lord *opened my ears* (lit. 'ear'). The following *not rebellious* indicates what was revealed: what the Lord wanted him to do and be. It was an issue of obedience, in which he was *not rebellious*. *Drawn back*: literally 'slip away backwards', take evasive action. In other words, the revelation he received was one that made demands from which there would be a natural tendency to 'back off'. Already therefore he is exhibiting the resoluteness which will reappear in verse 7, and for this reason we could well translate the following verbs as 'perfects of resolve': when the will of God was revealed 'I resolved to give my back ... not to hide ...'. There was a forewarning of hardship to come, and it was bravely faced, resolutely accepted and perseveringly carried through:

---

[1] From a linguistic point of view, $\sqrt{}$'*ût* is most reasonably related to '*ēt*, a 'season'. North (*Second Isaiah*) reports a possible meaning arising from Arabic, 'to console'. Instead of *lā*'*ût*, BHS prefers the emendation *lir*^{e}'*ôt*, 'to shepherd'. C. C. Torrey thought that *lā*'*ût* was a mistaken reduplication of the immediately preceding *lāḏa*'*at* ('to know'), but from an identically spelt verb, 'to care for' (*Second Isaiah* [T. & T. Clark, 1928]).

flogging (*back*), torture (*cheeks*) and sickening humiliation (*mocking and spitting*; see Mt. 27:26–30; Mk. 15:15–20; Jn. 19:1–3).

7–8. The same *Sovereign LORD*, who equipped and taught (4) and called to hardship consequent upon obedience (5–6), now accompanies to help. The Servant's awareness of this divine help (7a) strengthens him to believe he can do it (7b), to set himself to the task with determination (7c) and confidence (7d): right is on his side and the Lord will be his advocate (8). *Disgraced ... shame* (7): the verbs are synonyms, here meaning that, having set his hand to this particular plough, he will not be found to have made a fraudulent commitment. *Set my face*: cf. Luke 9:51, 'resolutely set out' (lit. 'set his face'), and 9:53, 'he was heading' (lit. 'his face was'). *Vindicates*: in 45:21 and 49:24–25, it was emphasized that the sanctity of the law must be preserved. Here, therefore, the conflict between the Servant and his oppressors is pictured as a court scene. Whatever he has been called to by the Lord (5), whatever it is that involves such suffering (6) and requires such resoluteness (7) must satisfy all legal requirements. *Near* (8) is parallel in use to *gō'ēl*, Redeemer, the Next-of-Kin (Lv. 21:2–3; 25:25; Nu. 27:11; Ru. 2:20; 3:12). *Charges against me*: the Servant is himself in the dock, but he is confident that whatever *charges* are made (8b) or whoever makes them (8d), they cannot be made out (Mt. 27:3–4, 19, 24; Mk. 15:3; Lk. 23:4, 10, 14–15, 41; Jn. 8:46; 19:6).

9. The law-court setting continues but the emphasis changes: just as the Servant was confident (8) of gaining the verdict, so he is confident (9) of the rout of his opponents. Since God is on his side, who can be against him? – but not as a matter of favouritism or of superior power as such, but because no condemnation can be sustained against him. *Condemn* means 'prove me guilty'. Internal factors (*wear out*) and external forces (*moths*) will expose the transience of his accusers.

The Servant, exemplary and decisive (50:10–11). The 'tailpieces' of the first two Servant Songs (42:5–9; 49:7–13) confirmed aspects of the Servant's task; the present and final 'tailpieces' (54:1 – 55:13) are appeals to respond to the Servant. The uniting idea of these verses is *light* (10d, 11c). There are two sorts of people: the one sort (10) *has no light* but *obeys the word of* the Lord's Servant by facing the darkness with *trust* and reliance. The others (11) seek to conquer the darkness by fires of their own making. The outcome for the first is not specified; the others suffer an adverse divine reaction (11e) and *lie down in torment* (11f). The perfection of the One against whom no charge can be made (8) makes him our model (10); the fate of his accusers (9) is shared by those who refuse his way (11). Just as he lived in obedience (5), trust and reliance (7, 9) so do those who model themselves on him (10).

10–11. *Fears the LORD* and *obeys ... his servant* are in parallel. The way to reverence the Lord is to obey the Servant. *Dark ... no light*: as for him, the way of obedience (5–6) brings days of darkness. Just as he is the model, so his experiences are the norm. *Rely*: 'lean'. It is not simply (11) that those who opt for a do-it-yourself approach to life's darknesses have then no other resource to turn to (*walk in the light of your fires*); but, refusing the way of trust and reliance, they incur divine opposition. The *hand* of God goes out against them. *Torment* (*maʿᵃṣēḇâ*), is only found here but its verb √ʿāṣēḇ (*e.g.* 63:10) guarantees its meaning of grief, pain and displeasure – even 'the place of pain' – specifically the pains of sin under the curse of God (Gn. 3:13–14; 5:29).

d. Salvation in prospect: the watching remnant (51:1 – 52:12)

Isaiah 50:10 is important in Isaiah's progressive delineation of the Servant. When the Servant first appeared in 42:1, it was logical to link him with the servant, Israel, of 41:8; but the exposure of Israel as blind, bound and spiritually guilty (42:18–25) ruled that identification out, and 48:1 together with 49:3 sealed the contrast between the Israel who had lost its right to the name and the Servant who alone possessed the name. The tailpiece to the Servant's testimony in 50:4–9 takes matters another step forward: the Servant is distinguished as the model for all who would live the life of trust and reliance – in other words, the identity of the Servant is not the believing remnant within the nation. In 8:9–20 Isaiah made fear of the Lord (8:13), finding refuge in him (14) and loyalty to his 'testimony', 'law' and 'word' (16, 20) the hallmarks of the remnant; but now that 'fear' and obedience are centred on the Servant, who is the point of differentiation between believers (50:10) and unbelievers (50:11). It is on this note that 51:1 launches the next section with its opening address to all who *pursue righteousness* and *seek the LORD*, *i.e.* the faithful remnant. It is a continuous and coherent presentation: the opening three calls to listen (51:1, 4, 7) are matched by the concluding three calls for alertness and action (51:17; 52:1, 11). At the centre lies a dramatic appeal to the Lord to act (51:9–11) followed by a meditative interlude (51:12–16).

i. Commands to listen: promises of salvation (51:1–8). These three appeals are in sequence: the first (1–3), addressing the remnant, promises *comfort* to *Zion* (3). The promise is, however, couched in Abrahamic (2) and Edenic (3) terms, and these worldwide implications are pursued in the second appeal (4–6) with its promises to *nations* and *islands* (5). The third appeal (7–8) is an affirmation that no opposition can survive (8ab) and that the Lord's purposes are eternal (8cd).

Abraham, Zion and Eden (51:1–3). The *me* of verse 1 is the *I* of verse 2, the Lord who called Abraham; but the last voice to say *Listen to me* (1) was the Servant (49:1). Can we say Isaiah is beginning to imply that there is more to the Servant than his human origin (49:1) – a thought he will make more explicit in 53:1?

1–2. *Pursue ... seek*: both verbs belong to the vocabulary of religious devotion. (For 'pursue', see Dt. 16:20; Pss. 34:14; 38:20; Pr. 21:21; Ho. 6:3; for 'seek', see Dt. 4:29; 2 Ch. 15:15; 20:4; Pss. 27:8; 105:4; Ho. 3:5.) Both simply express determination or commitment; just as 'pursue' does not picture something out of reach, neither does 'seek' imply something lost. The faithful ones pursue *righteousness* – that is, persevere in conforming their lives to the revealed norms of God's law – and *seek* God's presence. From the unpromising beginning of *Abraham* and *Sarah* (2), the Lord produced the sons, nations and kings he had promised (Gn. 17:3–7; Rom. 4:17–21; Heb. 11:11–12). Isaiah does not dwell on the human impossibility of what the Lord did in bringing a family out of barrenness; he focuses on the solitariness of the progenitor – he was *one* and became *many* – and he makes this the measure of what the Lord can do.

3. *Comfort ... compassion* are both from the same Hebrew verb, as in 40:1. The doubling is an idiom of certainty (Gn. 41:32). Behind the word *ruins* lies the idea of aridity, therefore barrenness. *Deserts* more generally means open countryside, land not under cultivation but *wastelands* catches the idea exactly (the Dead Sea is called 'the Sea of the Wasteland', Jos. 3:16). This picture of transformation – the unproductive becoming fertile, the wild ordered, the waste rich and abundant – is crowned by the reference to *Eden* restored, an image going beyond order, beauty and richness to the removal of the curse (Gn. 3:18) and the restoration of creation to the divine intention: the new earth.

The world, light and salvation (51:4–6). If anything, this section confirms the thought that *Listen* (lit. 'pay attention') *to me* may well be the voice of the Servant, speaking in his divine nature. The verses are full of reminiscences of the first Servant passage (42:1–4, 5–9) with references to *justice, light* and *righteousness*. The created order in 42:5 illustrates the Lord's power to do as he has planned through his Servant; here its transitoriness is a foil for his eternal salvation. Likewise the reference to *arm* (5) prepares for verse 9 and looks on to 53:1.

4. *My nation*: the word *le'ûm* is used in the plural meaning 'peoples', but the singular appears elsewhere only in Proverbs 11:26; 14:28 and in Genesis 25:23, which distinguished the Jacob-line from the Esau-line. Isaiah is possibly recalling this and making the point that, within the totality of all descendants, there is found a true people – the 'pursuers' of verse 1. In 2:2–4 it was the outgoing of law from the Lord's city that drew in the nations, and Isaiah recalls that truth here. *Justice*, as in 42:1–4, is part of the vocabulary of revealed truth, the decisive declaration of the Lord's mind.

5. On the human side, *righteousness* is conformity to the revealed character and claims of the Lord, the mark of his genuine people (1); on the divine side, it is the quality and standard of all that the Lord does – for his people (49:25), for his Servant (50:8, 'vindicates' = affirms my righteousness) or what the Servant does (53:11). In the present verse, *salvation* is what the Lord does; *righteousness* is the quality which infuses it. His saving work satisfies his righteous requirements. *My arm* (5c) is literally 'my arms'. It is possibly a plural of amplitude, the fullness of divine personal action. The only other place where the plural is used of the Lord is Deuteronomy 33:27: what was formerly exclusive to Israel is now for the world.[1] *Justice*, settled divine truth; *islands* (11:11; 40:15; 42:4), 'earth's remotest bounds'; *look to ... hope*, cf. 42:4. In what sense do they wait and hope? There are always those like Cornelius (Acts 10) who hunger for greater light, but, at the deepest level, there is an inarticulate human longing for a truly human life – the 'eager expectation' of creation itself (Rom. 8:19). Through the Servant – *my arm* (see 53:1) – life will become life indeed (Jn. 10:10).

6. The Lord's universal salvation (4–5) is also eternal. Even the most durable things in our experience – *heavens ... earth* and the continuance of humankind (*inhabitants*) – are transient, but not so that *salvation* which satisfies the Lord's *righteousness*. *Vanish*, 'be dispersed', 'fall to bits'; *wear out*, succumb to its own

[1] A. D. H. Mayes holds that Dt. 33 must have been in existence 'some considerable time before its incorporation in its present place in Deuteronomy' (*Deuteronomy* [Oliphants, 1979], p. 397). Whatever date is accepted for Deuteronomy, therefore, Isaiah could have had this reference in mind.

evanescence; *like flies* is probably simply 'in like manner'.[1] *Last ... never fail*: literally 'be ... not be shattered'. 'Be' refers to intrinsic durability, 'not shattered' to imperviousness to external forces.

Knowledge, imperturbability and confidence (51:7–8). Those who *know* need not *fear* and can rest assured that all will be well.

7. *What is right* is 'righteousness'. The righteousness which they 'pursue' (1) is no external code but the indwelling reality of minds (*know*) and *hearts* – at the centre of their personalities. But what they are excites hostility, bringing *reproach* or 'taunt' and *insults* – the noun occurs only here but has a close relative in 43:28 ('scorn'; see also Zp. 2:8). The verb (√*gādap*) is only once used of verbal hostility to people ('revile', Ps. 44:16); its seven other occurrences concern blasphemy against God. This indicates the strength of the word Isaiah chose. *Men* ('*enôš*) is man in his mortal frailty – which is all that human opponents ultimately amount to!

8. Faith recognizes that, no matter how strong and interminable life's hostilities are, forces of destruction are at work like *moth* and *worm* in garments (8). *Eat ... devour* are the same verb twice, another telling repetition (*cf.* 3). *Righteousness ... salvation*, *cf.* verse 5; *last* (lit. 'be'), *cf.* 6. *For ever* expresses intrinsic permanence; *all generations* expresses permanence within human experience.

ii. A dramatic appeal: exodus past and future (51:9–11). Like 45:8 following 45:1–7, the promises of 51:1–8 prompt an excited appeal that the Lord will act without delay. Who is the speaker? It cannot now be the Servant because (53:1) he is the Arm of the Lord to whom this appeal is made; maybe it is the prophet, excited beyond restraint by the vision he has enunciated; maybe it is the believing remnant longing for the prompt realization of all they have ever wanted. The fact is that the way to react to the Lord's promises is to pray urgently for their fulfilment (*cf.* Ps. 44:23).

9. *Awake, awake*: the doubling here is for emotional intensity of appeal. Just as the anthropomorphism of Exodus 2:24 suggests a sudden reviving of the divine memory after a long lapse, so here to the human eye it may have seemed that the Lord had gone to sleep over his promises. But it is anthropomorphism only in

---

[1] MT, *kᵉmôkēn*, naturally means 'in like manner'. As to 'like flies', the word *kinnîm* (plural), 'gnats', occurs in Ex. 8:16. It is not found in the singular.

the sense of calling on God to act with the same dispatch and urgency that would be the case with us if we suddenly recollected a long-overdue duty. *Clothe*: when the Lord dressed himself as a soldier in Joshua 5:13, his garments revealed what he is and what he intends. By 'clothing himself with power' the Lord marshals all the almighty power of the divine nature and commits himself so to act. *Arm of the LORD*, like so much else in these verses, looks back to the exodus (Ex. 6:6; Dt. 4:34; 5:15; *cf.* Ex. 15:16; 1 Ki. 8:42). Just as the 'hand' symbolizes personal agency, so the 'arm' symbolizes personal strength in action (52:10); here, the Lord himself in his intervening mightiness. Not even the greatest people of the Old Testament are described as the Lord's *arm*. Rather, 'the Arm' went with Moses (63:12) and strengthened David (Ps. 89:20–21). The metaphor calls upon the Lord himself to act. *Rahab* (meaning 'loud mouth') was Isaiah's nickname for Egypt (30:7; *cf.* Ps. 87:4) and certainly Egypt was shattered by the Lord's exodus acts, but the reference here transcends the historical. *Rahab* ('Tiamat') was also the sea *monster*, in Canaanite-Babylonian mythology the deified personification of disorder, typified by the restless, threatening sea, which the creator-god Marduk must subdue before he may pursue the work of ordered creation. The Bible, of course, knows of no such pre-creation combat of opposing forces, but it is not above using the sea and Rahab as a means of asserting the sole and sovereign power of the Lord (Jb. 26:11–12; Ps. 89:8ff.; Am. 9:3). Isaiah does not give credence to the existence of such 'gods', but signals in this way that the people of God are always challenged in their loyalty by other claimants to devotion, yet their history displays their God as the only God and One with power over all the power of the enemy. The Red Sea crossing (10) exemplified that the 'sea' for all its monstrous unruliness can do only the Lord's bidding (Ps. 93:3–4). Nothing can stand in his way, neither impenetrable physical barriers nor supernatural powers.

10–11. See on 35:9–10, where Isaiah has already used these words. *Cf.* the repetition of 48:22 in 57:21. By this interleaving of words and ideas he binds the literature together. Here *redeemed* looks back to Exodus 6:6, and *ransomed* looks forward to the coming acts of God effecting his righteous salvation (5, 7) and the renewal of Zion (3). The prayer of verse 9 modulates, under the influence of God's exodus acts (10), into the key of confident, forward-looking faith (11).[1]

---

[1] The thought that as a section of Isaiah ends at 35:10 so the matching words at 59:11 should signal the end of another section – and likewise with 48:22 and

iii. Interlude: a final briefing (51:12–16). The doubling of *I
... I* (12) responds to the double *awake, awake* (9) – 'I am every
bit as awake as you may need!' At first sight these verses excite
doubts about their textual reliability: in verse 12a *you* is masculine plural; in 12bc, feminine singular; and in 13–16 masculine
singular! In 13–14 *you* is a *cowering* captive, but in 15–16 a
prophetic figure with a universal ministry.[1] It would be the work
of seconds to harmonize all this, but it would leave the question
unanswered as to who is being addressed. It is better to ask if,
within the context, anyone matches the changes of masculine and
feminine. The masculine singular of verses 15–16 matches the
Servant, endowed with the Lord's word (16a, 42:4; 49:2; 50:4),
sheltered (16b, 49:2) and with a universal, Zion-centred task
(16c–e, 42:1; 49:5–6). The doomed prisoner of 13–14 is a picture
drawn from captivity. The accusation (13a) of forgetfulness
refocuses the complaint of 49:14. The feminine in 12bc is therefore desolate Zion, the 'mother' of her inhabitants. This leaves
the plural word of comfort (12a) as an address to all (Zion, the
captive and the Servant), and, significantly, 12b–16 follow the
same order (city, captives, Servant) that has already occurred in
49:14–21; 49:22 – 50:3; and 50:4–9, and that will be repeated in
51:17 – 52:2; 52:3–12; 52:13 – 53:12. The mosaic in verses 12–
16 is thus coherent. The Lord offers his reassurance to all the
dramatis personae of the coming events.

12. *I ... I*: a duplication of intensity (see p. 322). The Lord
offers himself as the constant comforter (the verb is a participle)
to petrified Zion. *Men* is *ᵉnôš* (*cf.* 7), but here human frailty is
underlined by three additions: *mortal* (lit. 'who die'), *sons of men*
('Adam / humankind') and *grass* (40:7–8). They suffer a threefold
frailty: death is at work, they are of (mere) human origin, and are
essentially fragile.

In verses **13–15**, Zion is encouraged (12bc) to look around in a
candid assessment of opponents; the masculine *you* addresses the

---

57:21 – has been canvassed. See p. 307 n. 1. This can only be decided pragmatically: does it 'work'? And does it work more persuasively than other ways of
analysing the literature? I cannot personally find ways of analysing Isaiah along
these lines, and therefore I look on the recapitulated words and thoughts as Isaiah
putting down markers of this continuing authorship.

[1] On vv. 12–16 North (*Second Isaiah*, p. 214) remarks that these verses are the
Achilles' heel of any theory that no subsequent additions were made to the
original work of the prophet. This, however, will hardly do, for surely it is
impermissible to solve problems by assuming these were lunatic sub-editors who
worked without thought for sequence or syntax. Our first duty is to the text we
have inherited; our second duty is to respect those through whose careful
guardianship we have come into this inheritance.

captive of verse 14, facing terror but encouraged to look up to God. All the panic-making factors (13d–g, 14) are bracketed by the Lord who is (13a–c) *your Maker*, Lord of *heavens* and *earth*, and (15) the LORD *Almighty* (lit. 'of hosts'; 1:9), sovereign over all earthly forces.

13–14. *Your*: committed to you. *Maker*: the One who has made you for himself (44:2) and will go on 'making' (the word is a participle in the Hebrew) until you are what he intends. *Stretched ... laid the foundations* are both participles. The absolute sovereignty the Lord displayed in the original act of creation continues in his direct managerial control of his created world, where he is for ever over (*heavens*) and under (*foundations*). To *forget* him – to live without consciously holding in mind and memory who he is, what he has done, what he promises – is to live in defeat (Ps. 78:9–11) and disobedience (Ps. 78:40–42). *Terror ... wrath ... oppressor ... destruction* were not the conditions of the Babylon exile (Je. 29), and a prophet actually living in the exile would not have spoken in this way. Here and in verse 14 (*cowering ... die ... dungeon ... bread*) Isaiah is using stereotypical images of captivity to underline how desperate in reality are human needs – fearful, doomed and imprisoned – from which the Lord can and will rescue. *Die in their dungeon*: (lit.) 'die into the pit', 'die as one doomed to the pit'. This may be a metaphor of the condemned criminal – to die and be flung into a common grave; but it is also a picture of death without divine favour (38:17; Ps. 49:9), the opposite of the ransomed soul (Ps. 49:7–8, 14–15).

15. *For I am* (lit. 'As for me, I am') turns the gaze from plight and fate (14) to the divine sufficiency. *Sea* pictures the turbulent forces encountered in life (Ps. 93), but the raging is itself his work (Ps. 107:25–26; Je. 31:35; Am. 4:13; 5:8; 9:5–6). If we find ourselves 'in the soup', it is he who has decreed the recipe and the temperature. *Almighty* (lit. 'of hosts'): see 1:9.

16. The Lord now assures his Servant: his equipment (16a), security (16b) and task (16c–e). The Servant's prophetic status is put first to emphasize what is of primary importance. What is true of every prophet – the divine word in the human mouth (Je. 1:9; Ezk. 2:7–3:4; Am. 1:1, 3) – will be true also of this great One. But the covering hand is placed second in order to assure that the same hand which hid him until the time came (49:2) still covers him as he goes to his task. *I who set* (lit. 'planted') is an extremely improbable translation of this, the first of three Hebrew infinitives setting out what the Lord has in mind for his Servant to do: 'that I may (*i.e.* through you)' or 'that you may (on my

325

behalf) plant ... lay ... say'. Planting is a new beginning; laying foundations represents permanence of achievement. The Servant is the origin of a new cosmic reality. Jeremiah (1:9–10) was called to 'plant kingdoms'; the Servant will plant heaven and earth, a new-creational work such as only God can do. Finally, the Servant is 'to say to Zion': at the centre of the Lord's cosmic purposes is his people. *My people*: the ultimate fulfilment of the covenant promise (49:8; Ex. 6:7).

iv. Commands to respond: what the Lord has done (51:17 – 52:12). Three double commands, balancing the three promises of 51:1–8, suggest that the promises have been fulfilled and the time has come to enter into them. Zion is called to wake up to the fact that divine wrath is over and gone (51:17–23, esp. 22), to wake up to holiness (52:1–10) and to embark on a new exodus as pure pilgrims (52:11–12). But the question remains: how have the promises been fulfilled? How has wrath been removed, holiness established and the way opened for the pilgrims? The answer comes with the final command in the series: 'See, my servant' (52:13).

Wrath removed (51:17–23). The first promise (51:1–3) was of Eden restored, the curse removed. So here the wrath of God is over. This is where salvation begins: the satisfaction of the requirements of a holy God (Rom. 1:16–18). This section is in two parts: the cup drunk (17–20 and the cup removed (21–23). Divine wrath reduced Jerusalem to helplessness, but while she slept the cup has been removed: the wrath is over.

17–18. *Cup*: the picture of the cup is of the Lord blending all life's experiences for his people (Ps. 16:5), and this includes mixing a cup of wrath for sinners (Ps. 11:6, NIV 'lot'; 75:8). So Jerusalem was paid for her unbelief by being bereaved of all her *sons* ('children') and left helpless.

19–20. Duplication is an idiom of totality, and Jerusalem's troubles came in twos: *ruin and destruction* destroying the fabric of the city, *famine and sword* destroying its population. *Who can console you?* is (lit.) 'Who I can comfort you?', meaning either 'How can I comfort you?' – presumably Isaiah admitting inability – or 'Who but I can comfort you?', *i.e.* the Lord, who commands comfort (40:1; 51:3, 12), advertises himself as the only hope. The former is possibly more usual for the idiom and suits the context: ruined and helpless, there is no comfort when the wrath of God falls. The duplication continues with the picture of the doubly helpless *sons* (20), both *fainted* and *caught*, under a double imposition of *wrath* and *rebuke*. In summary, when wrath falls, there is no help (18), no comfort (19) and no future (20a–c).

21–22. *Therefore* introduces (not human but) divine conclusions from 18–20. *Afflicted* ('downtrodden'): in this case, under divine wrath. *Drunk* resumes the metaphor of the 'cup' (17; *cf.* 29:9), the exact measuring out of wrath. The *therefore* of verse 21 – held in suspense while the prophet described the humiliated city – is now further delayed while he describes the Lord. First, he is *Sovereign*. Exceptionally, Isaiah uses the plural of the word here ("*ᵃdōnayîk*) usually reserved for human relationships – as of husband to wife (1 Ki. 1:17), parent to child (Gn. 31:35). Could it be that Isaiah chose this form here in order to stress that the divine lordship comes down into the ordinary affairs of life? Transcendent though he is, his sovereignty is not remote but practical and everyday. Secondly, he is the LORD, revealed once and for all as the God who saves his people and overthrows his foes (Ex. 3:15; 6:6–7); thirdly, *your God*, the God who has freely committed himself to you and your welfare; and, fourthly, the God of absolute justice and legality *who defends* (√*rîb*), 'pleads the cause' of his people, takes their case to the bar of his justice. Now at last the conclusion that the Lord has reached is stated: *See, I have taken* (22c). The poor drunkard is awakened to a wondrous fact: the *cup* has gone from the *hand* that so justly held it. Wrath was deserved, wrath was measured out, wrath is gone – and gone for ever (*you will never drink it again*). This is the logic of God to which *therefore* (21) was the introduction – a logic operating within the divine nature whereby the due reward of their deeds is, with perfect justice, averted and wrath satisfied.

23. At the exodus the Lord's redemption of his people coincided with his just visitation on their captors who had refused to obey his word (*cf.* 10:5–15). But it was not the execution of wrath on Egypt which redeemed Israel (else why was the Passover sacrifice needed?). The removal of wrath from the one and the infliction of wrath on the other were two sides of perfect divine justice. But the question yet to be answered here is what Passover work of God waits to be revealed as the explanation of verse 22. For his wrath does not evaporate; it demands satisfaction.

Holiness enjoyed (52:1–10). In verses 1–2, Zion is awakened to a new condition of holiness (1b–d), separation (1ef) and royalty (2); the initial *For* of verse 3 introduces an explanation: a free redemption (3), bondage (4–5) ended by divine self-revelation (6), bringing the triumphant news to Zion (7–10). There is a tension between the 'already' of verses 1–2, Zion awaking to holiness; the 'not yet' of verses 3–6, the Lord pondering the need of his people; and the 'now' of verses 7–10, the divine action accomplished. Logically and chronologically the sections should be in a different order, but drama dictates otherwise. In effect, then, Zion can awake to holiness (1–2) because (*for*, 3) the Lord contemplated her need (3–6) and took action (7–10).

1. The ideal of priestly people (Ex. 19:4–6) had never been realized (*cf.* Ex. 33:26; Nu. 8:5–22), but, on awaking (1a), Zion finds the priestly garments laid out for her (1bc) and a new reality as the *holy* (1d) and separated city (2). It was not the Lord who was asleep (51:9) after all – though in a dark day it is easier to blame him than to walk believingly in the darkness (50:10). *Clothe*: on the metaphor of clothing, see 51:9. The background to the *garments of splendour* (lit. 'beauty') is Exodus 28:2. The requirements of the Lord's holiness were met in 51:17–23; now divine holiness is shared with his people. *Uncircumcised and defiled*: in this envisaged holy Zion, each possesses a legitimated membership (one of the significances of circumcision, Ex. 12:43–44) and each displays a conformed (no longer *defiled*) character and life. When Aaron donned the garments of holiness, there was an element of unreality: a disparity between claim and character. It will be so no longer (Heb. 12:22–24 ; Rev. 21:27).

2. Babylonian bondage ended at 48:21. After that point Isaiah continues to use the images of bondage, but only as illustrative of a spiritual state to be remedied. In this present verse, what the Lord had actually done for the archetypal King David (1 Sa. 30:1; 2 Sa. 1:1; 2:1–4; Ps. 113:7–8) is now available to his people. Priests already (1), they are now kings as well. Surely not only the parallel with David but the contrast with Babylon (47:1) was in Isaiah's mind.

In verses **3–6**, in explanation of the new city (*For*, 3), the Lord looks at the past (3b) and pledges coming redemption (3c); next he looks at the present (4) and sees his name dishonoured; and finally he looks at the future and announces a coming revelation of himself (5–6).

3. *Sold*: passed into other ownership (see on 50:1); note esp. the references in Judges which show that the Lord still retained ownership which he could resume at will (2:14; 3:8; 4:2). *For nothing*: the sale did not reach the point where money changed hands and the deal was sealed. *Redeemed* ($\sqrt{g\bar{a}'al}$): see 35:10. Redemption is essentially a price-paying concept, so what does *without money* (lit. 'not for money') mean? Either without cost to you, or by some payment other than money. Someone else will pay – and the price will not be silver (1 Pet. 1:18–19).

4. Notice the change from LORD (3) to *Sovereign LORD*.

Recalling *Egypt* and considering *Assyria*, Isaiah suitably recalls a sovereignty over all earth's powers. *To live* (√*gûr*): to take up residence as a protected alien. Jacob entered Egypt by Pharaoh's invitation (Gn. 45:16ff.), but the laws of hospitality were later violated and Pharaoh's edict of ethnic cleansing was enacted (Ex. 1:10–22). *Lately, Assyria*: a prophet living in Babylon during the terminal years of the Babylonian empire could not say *lately* (lit. 'at the end', *bᵉ'epes*). How very aware the Lord is of his suffering people (Ex. 3:7)!

5–6. Two things move the Lord: the misery of his people (5bc), and the honour of his name (5de). *What do I have here?*: *cf.* 22:1, 16.[1] The expression is used either incredulously, 'What do I think I am playing at?' / 'What can I have been thinking?', or seriously, 'Does this matter to me?' *Those who rule them mock*: literally, as MT stands, 'their rulers wail'. Isaiah had lived through the day when he saw the weeping helplessness of Hezekiah before the Assyrians (37:1–4) – and if rulers are helpless, how grim is the state of the people (2 Ki. 6:26–27)! Here, the helpless tears picture their spiritual plight, helpless in their sin. *All day long ... constantly*: in 51:13, the same Hebrew words referred to the people's plight; here, to the dishonour to the Lord's name. What hurts them hurts him. *Therefore ... therefore* (6): the repetition expresses emotional intensity. First, the people will come to a new appreciation of the Lord's *name* (6a) – events will confirm all that the name means, the eternal name of Exodus 3:15, the Redeemer of Israel. Secondly, in this coming *day* the Lord will be present himself (6b–d), in word (*I who foretold*) and in person (*it is I*). At the exodus, the Lord set up a mediator to speak for him (Ex. 6:28 – 7:3; 19:9); in this coming *day* he himself will speak and he himself will be there.

In verses **7–10** the focus changes again. Dramatically Isaiah brings us to the very moment when the 'awake, awake' (1) sounds in Zion's ears as a messenger comes over the hills to announce *salvation* and proclaim a sovereign God (7). Zion's watchmen cannot contain themselves (8), and the joy spreads through the city (9ab). The Lord has himself acted to save (9c–10). The fourfold message of verse 7 and the fourfold ground of rejoicing (9c–10) bracket the swelling joy of the city (8–9b).

---

[1] The idiom *mah-lî-p̄ōh* ('What-to-me-here?') has differing shades of meaning: 'What brings you here?' (1 Ki. 19:9); 'What's the matter with you?' (Gn. 21:17); 'What do you want?' (Est. 5:3); 'What right have you?' (Is. 3:15); 'What do you think you're playing at?' (Jon. 1:6); 'What concern is it of yours?' (Ho. 14:8); 'What does it signify to you?' (Ex. 12:26).

7–8. *Those* is singular in the Hebrew, 'the one'; not a straggle
of fugitives from a defeat, but a single runner (as in 2 Sa.
18:24ff.) with shining face and a spring in his step because he
comes with *good news*. *Good tidings* repeats the same word for
emotional intensity (lit. 'good news of good'). *Peace*: the picture
is news from the battle, but the reality is the end of God's wrath
(51:17–23), the city awaking to holiness (52:1), the status of its
people as priests and kings (52:1, 2), redemption without cost
(52:3) – in a word, peace with God. *Salvation*: the divine victory
over every binding foe, the power of sin's oppression broken.
Your God reigns: the cry of the herald of good tidings comes full
circle from the third comforting voice of 40:10–11. They used to
sing 'The LORD reigns' in their temple songs (Ps. 93:1; 97:1;
99:1), living then in the same faith as Christians who sing
Ascension Day hymns of the present reign of the Lord Jesus. But
Isaiah envisages a day (still future for us, too) when faith will
pass into sight and, *when the LORD returns to Zion, they will see
it with their own eyes* (8). Hard on the heels of the herald comes
the Lord himself. *With their own eyes*: literally 'eye to eye'. This
does not mean, as with us, 'with agreement' but 'with total
clarity'.

9–10. *Ruins*: as we have seen, in so many ways 42:18–25 set
the scene for all that has followed: not only did it make a radical
distinction between the Servant of 42:1–4 and Israel the nation-
servant, but also, in setting out the reasons why the nation could
not be this Servant, it linked political facts ('plundered', 'looted',
'trapped in pits', 'prisons', 42:22) with the spiritual faults ('no
attention', 'hear nothing', 20; 'we have sinned', 'not follow', 'not
obey', 24; 'not take to heart', 25). By 48:20–21 the political
problem had been solved, and in 48:22 – 49:13 the Servant was
confirmed to solve the spiritual problem. We need constantly to
bear in mind, then, that from that point onwards the images of
captivity act, as they did in 42:18–25, as evidences of spiritual
need. *Comforted*: see 40:1; 49:13; 51:3, 12. The Lord has done
what he said: he has *redeemed*. *Arm*: the symbol of personal
strength in action; *bare*: with sleeves rolled up for work. *Sight* ...
see: the former is the public nature of the divine act; the latter,
their personal participation in the experience (Pss. 49:19; 89:48;
90:15).

The greater exodus (52:11–12). The calls to 'awake' (51:17;
52:1) invited entrance into provided blessings; *depart* (11) calls
for the entrance upon a new lifestyle, that of holy pilgrimage
involving abandonment of the old life. Once the Passover had
been offered, there could be no tarrying in Egypt! The same

offering which made peace with God (Ex. 12:13) could be eaten only by those committed to pilgrimage (Ex. 12:11), and the blood-marked door which welcomed them into salvation (Ex. 12:24) ushered them out into pilgrimage (Ex. 12:33, 37).

11. *Touch no ... be pure*: negative and positive holiness, separation from and to. *The vessels*: most commentators relate this to Ezra 1:7–11, the historical return from Babylon to Zion. This ignores the dramatic change of focus that we noted immediately above whereby, from 48:22 onwards, the motifs of captivity – or, here, release – are within the context of the Lord's work of redemption from sin. The exodus pilgrimage provides all the clues, except that now the Lord's whole people are his holy priesthood (52:1) and are called here to live according to their God-given dignity. Numbers 1:50–51 is the only other place where 'carry' and vessels of the Lord occur together; it refers to the levitical duty of porterage, to be shared with no other (Nu. 3:5ff.). Now all who go out in this greater, truer exodus are the tribe of Levi, the priests of the Lord.

12. *Haste ... flight*: contrast 48:20; Exodus 12:11. There is now no opposing power that can keep them in bondage. Indeed, to the contrary, they come under every possible divine care (*before ... rear*); cf. the caring warrior of 40:10–11. The imagery here is from Joshua 6:9, the guards marching before and behind the priests, and from Exodus 13:21; 14:19, in which the pillar that leads also guards.

e. Worldwide salvation (52:13 – 55:13)

As we would now expect, this climactic section falls into two parts: the fourth Servant Song (52:13 – 53:12) and its 'tailpiece'. The latter extends to two chapters (54:1 – 55:13) in which, first, Zion is called into a covenant of peace (54:10) and, secondly, the invitation to the free banquet goes out to all (55:1–13).

i. The triumph of the Servant (52:13 – 53:12). Isaiah starts with an enigma: how can such an exaltation (13) arise out of such suffering (14); how can such suffering (14) lead to universal benefit and acknowledgment (15)? The Lord's testimony to his Servant (13) blends into the statement of suffering and benefit (14–15). Balancing this opening there is the concluding section (53:10–12) which solves the enigma: the Servant's suffering was a bearing of sin. This time the explanation of his sufferings (10–11b) blends into the Lord's testimony to his Servant (11c–12). The three intervening stanzas follow a theme of birth (53:2) to death (53:9): how he grew up to an adult life of rejection and sorrow (1–3), the hidden explanation of his sorrow and suffering (4–6), and how such suffering reached its outcome in death and burial (7–9).

A surprising success (52:13–15). Exaltation (13) followed on from cruel suffering (14), with worldwide consequences (15).

13. The command to watch (*see*) is in effect the last of the series of commands which began in 51:1. They were glorious in their implications but lacking in explanations. After each in turn we want to say, 'Yes, but how will this happen?' The command to *see* brings us into the realm of accomplishment: watch the Servant and what he did. *Act wisely*: √*sākal* is wisdom to know exactly what to do in a given situation so as to bring the intended result. This wise and successful action will bring the Servant a threefold exaltation (*raised ... lifted up ... highly exalted*) – a trio which many link with the threefold exaltation of Jesus Christ in resurrection, ascension and heavenly enthronement.

Verses **14–15** can be understood structurally in two ways. First, the *just as* clause of 14a is taken up by the *so* clause in 15a. Corresponding to an understandable reaction of horror (14a) there is the matching outcome of sprinkling/startling (see NIV mg., 'marvel'). Just as *many were appalled*, so *many* will benefit. This perhaps involves a stress on *many* that is more than the Hebrew requires, but otherwise it is free from difficulty. Secondly, Hebrew does not always express the 'so' which completes an 'as ... so' construction. Maybe, in the present case, the initial horror (14a) is elaborated by a double explanation (*so disfigured ... marred*, 14bc) based on what they see, and the subsequent reaction (*shut their mouths*, 15b) is elaborated by a double explanation (15cd). The framework of these verses would then be, 'Just as many ... (so) kings ...' – the measure of shock-horror will be the measure of amazed response. In this case the comment *so will he sprinkle* (15a) stands at the midpoint as the pivot of the whole. In general, this second view is fuller and more exact.

14. *Many* (see 15a; 53:11c, 12ae) is a keyword in this passage for the beneficiaries of the Servant's suffering. *Appalled* (√*šāmam*): 'shocked, shattered' (49:8, 19; 54:1), a very strong word. *Man ... human likeness*: the former refers to individuality, the latter to common humanity. The Servant's sufferings brought such a disfigurement that those who saw said not only, 'Is this he?' but 'Is this human?'

15. *Sprinkle* (hiphil √*nāzâ*): this verb (occurring twenty-two times in the Old Testament) deals with hallowing persons (Ex. 29:21) and things (Lv. 8:11), cleansing (Lv. 14:7) and atonement

(Lv. 16:14–16). The meaning 'startle' is not found elsewhere. Neither meaning is wholly free of difficulty. In its well-exemplified usage as 'sprinkle', there is always a preposition ('on') governing the object sprinkled (*e.g.* 63:3), but here there is no preposition before *many nations*, which stands as a direct object. Regarding 'startle', the meaning derives from Arabic, where the verb means 'to jump up', but where it is only used literally and never in an emotional sense ('you made me jump'). Thus 'startle' imports a verb unexemplified in the Old Testament, in a meaning unexemplified anywhere, in order to solve a very minor variation from the customary usage of a well-known verb in an established meaning.[1] The priestly idea of atonement sprinkling (*e.g.* Lv. 4:6, 17; 5:9) is suitable to this context, and the element of surprise that such blessed results of cleansing and atonement should follow such tortured suffering is what makes *kings shut their mouths, i.e.* be dumbfounded. New truth has come to them, formerly untold, unheard before, but now seen and understood. The next three stanzas of the poem explain what it is.

The man who is God: suffering observed but misunderstood (53:1–3). This stanza asserts two truths about the Servant: on the one hand, he was *the arm* [or 'Arm'] *of the LORD* (1); on the other, he was truly human (2–3).

1. *Believed* (*he'*ᵉ*mîn l*ᵉ) means to believe what someone has said, but in this case statement was not enough; the truth needed also to be *revealed*. There was hearing (*message*) and seeing (*appearance*, 2) but no believing without revelation. *Revealed* (√*gālâ*): to uncover objectively (1 Sa. 9:15, uncovering truth), or subjectively (1 Sa. 20:12, lit. 'uncover your ear'). The particular truth that needs this divine uncovering concerns *the arm of the LORD*. In 51:9 the 'arm of the LORD' was the Lord himself, acting in person at the exodus; in 52:10 the arm was bared, the sleeves rolled up for action, because the Lord purposes again to act personally. We could suitably paraphrase Isaiah: 'Who could have believed that this was the Arm of the Lord?', *i.e.* the Lord himself come to act in salvation, as promised in 52:10.

2–3. The first thing that made it incredible to look at the Servant and see the Arm of the Lord was that *he grew up before*

---

[1] It is not altogether a foregone conclusion that the thing on which the sprinkling is done is never a direct object. In Lv. 4:16–17 (*cf.* 4), *'et-p*ᵉ*nê* has the sign of the definite object (*et*) and, while the translation 'before' is allowable (*e.g.* *'et-p*ᵉ*nê*, Gn. 19:13), the translation 'the face of/the surface of' cannot be dismissed out of hand. But, in respect of Is. 52:14, it is certainly more acceptable to allow a minor adjustment of an *established* verb in its *established* meaning than to import an *unknown* verb in a meaning it does *not exemplify elsewhere.*

him. He was distinct from the Lord (*before him*). He was also plainly human, with a natural growth (*tender shoot*), and a traceable human ancestry (*root out of dry ground*). Furthermore, he looked unimpressive (*no beauty ... to attract*). To such an extent was he but a man among men that the ordinary tests of *beauty* ('looks'), *majesty* ('impressiveness') and *appearance* could be applied – with negative results. He was not the Lord (*before him*), not expected (*out of dry ground*), not special (*beauty ... appearance*). Only those to whom truth was revealed could see that this was *the arm of the LORD*. Consequently he was shunned (3a–c) and misunderstood (3d). *Man of sorrows*: sorrows makes a 'domino' link between verses 3 and 4, and it is only in 4 that we discover that his sorrow and suffering arose not from a sickly constitution but because he took our sorrows as his own. *Esteemed* is an 'accounting' word, a reckoning up of value. They saw ordinariness (2), the world would call him an 'unfortunate' (3b), so they did not choose to follow him (3a) but turned from him (3c). They appraised what they saw and it added up to nothing (3d).

The substitute: suffering explained (53:4–6). These verses are central to this whole Servant passage: bracketed by verses dealing with birth and life (1–3) and trial and death (7–9), and by passages of introduction (52:13–15) and conclusion (53:10–12). They stress that what the Servant did he did alone: the emphatic pronoun *he* (4a) separates him from us in what he did; we were separate from him in what we thought (4cd); he was the agent, we the beneficiaries (5); the Lord isolated him for an awful task (6).

4. The Servant is the Agent, we are the uncomprehending onlookers. *Surely* ('*āḵēn*): a conjunction emphasizing the unexpected (*e.g.* 40:7). *He ... we*: emphatic, 'he for his part / it was he who' ... 'yet as for us, we ...' *Took up ... carried*: the imagery is drawn from Leviticus 16:22, which uses the first of these verbs. To 'take up' (√*nāśā'*) is to lift a burden; to 'carry' (√*sāḇal*) is to 'shoulder', to accept that burden as one's own. *Infirmities ... sorrows*: both words derive from verse 3, where the former is translated 'suffering'. In 3, the sufferings were thought to be personal and led to the Servant being shunned; here the sufferings are misunderstood as a divine infliction (a disfavour of God directed personally against the Servant). Just as the person of the Servant (a genuine man who was also the Arm of the Lord) could be grasped only by revelation, so also the true understanding of his sufferings: that they were deliberately 'taken' by him and that they were in reality ours. Matthew 8:17 (*cf.* Rev. 21:4) sees this verse fulfilled in the healing work of the Lord Jesus, as indeed it is: for our total redemption, body as well as soul, comes from him and from his work on the cross, and in the new heaven and new earth sickness will be as completely banished as will sin. Here, however, the main emphasis is on the damage (*infirmities*) and blight (*sorrows*) that sin brings to us.

5. The pronoun *he* is again emphatic, so as to bring the Servant sharply before us – 'He (and no other)'. *Pierced*: as in 51:9; when they called on the Arm of the Lord who dealt the monster Rahab a death blow, they did not know they were calling the Arm to his own death. *Crushed*: used of cruel agonies ending in death (La. 3:34). *For ... for*: the preposition *min* means 'from', hence it is used of one thing arising from another, a relationship of cause and effect. Our *transgressions* were the cause, his suffering to death the effect. Like verse 4, this verse cannot be understood without the idea of substitution to which, here, the adjective 'penal' must be attached. *Transgressions* (*peša'*), wilful rebellions (1:2, 28; 43:25; 44:22; 46:8; 50:1); *iniquities* (*'āwōn*), the pervertedness, 'bentness', of fallen human nature (1:4; 5:18; 6:7; 40:2; 43:24; 50:1). *Punishment* (*mûsār*): 'correction' by word or act, 'chastisement'. Just as 'covenant of peace' (54:10) means 'covenant which pledges and secures peace' so (lit.) 'punishment of our peace' means punishment which secured peace with God for us. This peace was lost (48:18) by disobedience, and, since it cannot be enjoyed by the wicked (48:22), the Servant stepped forward (49:1) to bring us back to God (49:6). This is what he achieved by his substitutionary, penal sufferings. *Upon*: the same preposition as used in Leviticus 16:21–22. *By*: the particle of price, 'at the cost of'. *Wounds* (*ḥabbûrâ*): used in 1:6 of open, untreated lacerations, hence the actuality of blows inflicted and experienced. *Healed*: (lit.) 'there is healing for us', the accomplished reality of restored wholeness.

6. What the Servant did, the Lord did. After the concentration on the Servant in verses 4–5, the change of subject here is very striking, as is also the precedence given to us and our self-will as compared with the precedence of the Servant's saving work in 4–5. Coupled with the new subject, this has the force of saying with astonishment, 'To think that he would do that for people like us!' *We all* at the beginning is matched by *us all* at the end: the perfect equivalence of remedy to need. *All ... each*: common culpability, individual responsibility. *Like sheep ... astray*: the folly and thoughtlessness of sin leading to the danger inherent in being sheep without a shepherd. *Turned*: the deliberateness of sin. *And the LORD*: with this emphatic subject Isaiah corrects the misunderstanding involved in 'stricken by God' (5) – revelation corrects incomprehension: he was indeed *stricken by God*, but with the astonishing purpose of laying our sin on him. *Iniquity*: as in 5. *Laid*: (lit.) 'caused to meet', descriptive of the divine act of gathering into one place, on to one substitutionary Victim, the sins of all the sinners whom the Lord purposed to save. The Servant is the solution of *the LORD* to the needs of sinners.

Voluntary acceptance of death (53:7–9). Matching the 'narrative' aspect of verses 1–3, Isaiah now records the procession to the place of execution (7), the execution (8) and the burial (9). Verse 7 stresses voluntary acceptance, 8 injustice, and 9 finality.

7. *Oppressed*: *e.g.* Exodus 3:7. *Afflicted* is the verb used in verse 4d, but what was imposed there is voluntarily accepted here. The verbal form here (reflexive niphal), with an emphatic pronoun, means 'but he for his part submitted himself'. *Did not open … silent … did not open*: animals go as uncomprehending to slaughter as to shearing, but the Servant who knew all things beforehand (Jn. 18:4) went to his death with a calm silence that reflected not an uncomprehending but a submitted mind and tongue. *Lamb … sheep*: the former was used in the sacrifices (Gn. 22:7–8, *etc.*), though not the latter, but this is of no significance. Verses 4–6 have already established that we are to think of the Servant's death in terms laid down in the levitical sacrifices. The point here is the contrast between the silence of ignorance and the silence of deliberate self-submission. Yet a great principle of the sacrificial system is involved. Verses 4–6 first established our sinfulness (4–5), and then revealed it as our common folly (6a) and our individual culpable choice (6b). This is to say, sin involves the will. But this is precisely the point at which animals can only picture the substitute we require and cannot actually be that substitute: they have no consciousness of what is afoot nor of any deliberate, personal, self-submissive consent to it. Ultimately only a Person can substitute for people. This is the importance of the stress in verse 7 on the Servant's voluntariness expressed in the acceptance of humiliation and the deliberately maintained silence.

8. *By oppression and judgment* can be translated in different ways. NIV points to an oppressive use of judicial procedures: 'without restraint and without right' describes victimization; 'without restraint and without justice' conveys injustice to which no limits were set; 'from arrest / prison and sentence' offers fact without comment – this is what happened. *Who can speak of his descendants?*: a very free rendering, meaning that the Servant was cut off in his prime, leaving no family – as (presumably) does 'Who will declare his generation?' (NKJV). But better is 'Who of his generation considered … ' (NIV mg.), *i.e.* to his sufferings was added the pain of total lack of sympathetic understanding from those around. *Cut off*: 'hacked off' (√*gāzar*), a violent verb (1 Ki. 3:24). *From the land of the living*: *cf.* 38:11; Psalms 27:13; 116:9; 142:5; *etc.* If the verb 'cut off' were not enough to indicate that the Servant was done to death, these additional words demand it. *For* (*min*): as in verse 5, 'because of'. *Transgression*: 'rebellion'. *He was stricken*: Isaiah is again correcting the misapprehension of verse 3. Both NIV and NIV margin (*to whom the blow was due*) are allowable. In each case the idea of substitution is fundamental, though, of course, explicit in the marginal rendering.

9. *Wicked … rich*: the former is plural and the latter singular. If Isaiah had merely intended the contrast between a shameful and a sumptuous burial he would have used two singulars. The use of a plural and a singular suggests that he is talking not about categories but about actual individuals. He offers no explanation, nor is there one until the fulfilment: Matthew alone of the Gospels specifies that Joseph of Arimathaea was 'rich' (27:37; *cf.* Mk. 15:43; Lk. 23:50); John brings out the contrast between the expected (19:31) and the actual (19:38ff.) burial of Jesus. But, as Isaiah foretold, 'His burial was appointed with wicked men but (he was) with the rich man in his death.' *Death*, literally 'deaths', is to be understood as a plural of majesty, 'his supreme, wondrous death'.[1] *Though* or 'because': the former points the contrast between what happened (7–9b) and what was merited (9cd); the latter explains the unexpected splendour of his burial. *Violence* is active hostility against people (*e.g.* Gn. 49:5; Pr. 10:6, 11); *deceit* is a state of the heart; *mouth* specifies sins of speech (Mt. 12:34). Together they affirm the sinlessness of the Servant in thought, word and deed. Thus Isaiah completes the picture of the Servant as our Substitute, for he displays all the needed characteristics: acceptable to the offended God (6), without stain of our sin (9), identified with us in our need (4–5) and voluntarily standing in our place (7–8).

[1] The plural 'deaths' occurs only in Ezk. 28:10. This throws no light on Is. 53:9. Unexpected plurals of the same order as 'deaths' here are exemplified by 'graves' (Jb. 17:1; 21:32), which GKC 124c and E. Dhorme (*A Commentary on the Book of Job* [Nelson, 1967]) class as 'plurals of extension', *i.e.* 'graveyard / place of graves'. The same plural in 2 Ki. 22:20 and 2 Ch. 1:14 must be a plural of amplification / majesty, 'his splendid / royal grave'. The idea of 'his wondrous death' would be very suitable to the present context.

The Servant triumphant (53:10–12). Isaiah does not use the word 'resurrection', but these verses display the Servant 'alive after his suffering' (Acts 1:3). Not, however, alive in the usual Old Testament sense that the dead possess the half-life of Sheol. There could not be a greater contrast than between the vain-gloriousness of the erstwhile king of 14:9–12 and this majestic One. The dead (9) is alive (10), the condemned (8) is righteous (11), the helpless (7) is the victor (12).

10. This verse begins and ends on the topic of *the LORD's will ... the will of the LORD*. The Lord accomplished his will through his Servant's suffering (10a); the Servant lives to *prosper* what the Lord has done. Or, to put it another way: the Servant's suffering achieved salvation; the Servant is now the Executor of the salvation he achieved. The Lord was the architect of his suffering; he lives to apply its achievements. *And though*: there are three main ways of translating this line. (a) 'When you make his soul a guilt offering': NIV (whose *though* is surely erroneous) adapts this by making it explicit that 'you' is the Lord. This means that the Lord was the effective Agent behind the Servant's saving work and, therefore, it is effective in both its objective fruits (*offspring*, 10c) and its subjective rewards (*prolong*). (b) 'When his soul makes a guilt-offering': the precious reality at the heart of the saving work is the person ('soul') of the Servant. Because he was so uniquely fitted to be the substitute, his saving work was successful. (c) 'When you make his soul a guilt-offering': here 'you' is the individual drawing near to the Servant to nominate him as the needed offering for guilt, thus making his personal, individual response to what the Servant has done. Each of these is legitimate as a translation and significant as a truth. If we can see more than one meaning in what he wrote, we may be sure that Isaiah did too, and that he deliberately left it like that. The *guilt offering* is found in Leviticus 5:1 – 6:7. The heart of its distinctiveness is its insistence on minute exactness between sin and remedy. It could well be called the 'satisfaction-offering'. It is used here not so much to affirm that the Servant bore and discharged the guiltiness of our sin, but that what he did is exactly equivalent to what needed to be done. *Offspring*: we strayed as sheep, we return as sons. The Servant's work is successful in 'bringing many sons to glory' (Heb. 2:10) but, because it was perfectly done according to the *will of the LORD*, it results also in his own prolongation in life – as Romans 4:25 says about the resurrection.

11. *After* is the preposition *min* (as in 5, 8) and should again be 'because of' (*cf.* Heb. 2:9). *See the light of life*: this is the only really significant difference between MT and Q^a. The former has 'he shall see ... be satisfied' and the latter 'he shall see light'. NIV expands this to 'the light of life'. If the reading 'light' is correct, it has the metaphorical meaning of 'joy', a happy outcome. But this, too, is what MT means: (lit.) 'he shall see, he shall be satisfied' is an idiomatic way of saying 'he shall be satisfied with what he sees'. The verse goes on to say what it is that delights the Servant: *by his knowledge, i.e.* because he knows exactly what is required in order to save sinners, *my righteous servant, i.e.* 'that righteous One, my Servant', an emphatic divine commendation, *will justify many* (a unique turn of Hebrew phrase), *i.e.* 'will provide righteousness for the many'. 'The many' is Isaiah's keyword for those whom the Servant designed to save: what Jesus calls 'all that the Father gives me' (Jn. 6:37). Over these he casts the robe of his own righteousness. We are not only family members (10) but wear the family likeness. *And*: used in its frequent explanatory sense, 'you see'. *Bear*: 'shoulder' (see 4). Every benefit and blessing come from the substitutionary work.

12. *Great* is actually 'many', and again refers to those whom the Servant designed to save; but *among the great ... with the strong* cannot be correct. It cannot be that this Servant who will 'prosper' with a threefold exaltation (52:13), before whom kings are stunned into silence (52:14), who is alive from the dead and the Executor of the Lord's plans (53:10) will, in the event, share the supreme place with any other. In the light of this, a closer glance at the Hebrew yields, 'Therefore I will apportion to him the many' (*cf.*, again, Jn. 6:37), 'and the strong he will apportion as spoil'. *Because*: this great victory rests on four facts. (a) *He poured out*: the Servant's voluntary self-offering even to the point of death (Phil. 2:8ff.); (b) *was numbered*: his identification with those in need of salvation (we could translate, 'He allowed himself to be numbered'); (c) *he bore the sin of many* (*i.e.* of all whom he designed to save): his effectiveness as substitute; and (d) *made intercession*, probably better as 'interposed' but, of course, it could refer to his mediatorial intercession whereby he 'saves to the uttermost' (Heb. 7:25): his work as mediator. The latter verb, however, is used in verse 6 for 'caused to meet' (NIV 'laid'). Just as the Lord placed him in the mediating position, so he personally took it as his own.

ii. The great invitation (54:1 – 55:13). Like its predecessors, the final Servant passage is followed by a 'tailpiece', which, as befits its dignity, takes up two chapters. In 54:1 the invitation to *sing* – to enter with joy into a provided benefit – goes out to a

barren woman, who turns out to be Zion (11–15). In 55:1 a
worldwide invitation to the feast goes out to all who desire to
come and eat freely, and this is seen as the fulfilment of the
promise that David will rule the world (3–4). Thus chapters 54 –
55 match 40:1 – 42:17, where the message of comfort to Zion
merged into a vision of world blessing.

Zion restored: five pictures of benefit (54:1–17). Humanity
falls into two groups: those who possess the revelation of God
(whether they live comfortably to it or not), and the rest who are
still to be brought within the circle of privilege. When the Servant has performed his great work of salvation (52:13 – 53:12),
the first invitation goes out to those already within the Lord's
sphere, so that they may enter freely (*sing*, 1) into the benefits of
what the Servant has done.

1–3, *Worldwide increase: the barren woman and the
spreading family.* The link with the Servant is provided by the
reference to *descendants* ('seed') in verse 3 (*cf.* 53:10, *offspring*
= 'seed'): his seed are the barren woman's seed, the children of
salvation. The one who is *barren* (1; *i.e.* without ability to have a
child), who *never bore* (without a child in fact), and who is
desolate (without a chance to conceive since she is without a
husband's care), will actually have more children than one who
has a husband. There is no natural explanation of this fertility.
Tent life (2) pictures an 'ideal' relationship between the Lord and
his people (Je. 2:1–3); *cf.* 16:5, where the Messiah reigns 'in the
tent of David'. *Stretch* ... *strengthen*: roominess and stability.
Spread: 'burst' – as we say 'burst at the seams', a picture of
vigorous growth. *Dispossess* (lit. 'take possession of') ... *settle*:
Genesis 22:17 says (lit.) 'your seed will possess', but only
Exodus 34:24, Deuteronomy 9:1; 11:23 and Joshua 23:9 – all
ultimately fulfilled in David – refer to 'possessing the nations'
(*cf.* Ps. 2:8). Thus, out of the Servant's work, both the Abrahamic
and Davidic promises are fulfilled.

4–8, *Security in God: the solitary wife and the everlasting
love.* The two pictures of *widowhood* (4) and *a wife deserted* (6)
could suggest, respectively, a dead and an unfaithful husband,
and thus create a wholly wrong set of impressions. Isaiah is
prepared to risk this in order to make us feel as sharply as
possible the deadly results of sin and, correspondingly, the joyful
results of salvation.

4. *Shame* ... *disgrace* ... *humiliated* represent three
synonymous Hebrew verbs sharing the fundamental idea of disappointed hopes, the embarrassment of expecting – even publicly
announcing – one thing and then reaping another. In context here

shame and *reproach* convey the same thought. *Widowhood* is such a disappointment, such a blighting of bright hopes – especially when it comes in *youth*. But fear can go for ever (4) because there is a *husband* who cannot die (5), who wants his wife *back* (6) and who pledges everlasting love (7–8).

5–8. *Maker* (5), see 44:2; LORD Almighty, 1:9; *Holy One of Israel*, 1:4; *Redeemer*, 35:9–10. As *God of all the earth* he cannot be challenged, hindered or diverted from his promises by any opposing power. *Your God* (6) is, as always, not the God you chose but the God who has freely made himself yours. Behind the pictures of widowhood (4–5) and desertion (6) lies the reality of an angry God who turned away, hiding his face. This is the reason why sin is like bereavement and desertion, because it alienates the Holy One. *Compassion* (noun in 7, verb in 8) is the emotional love which makes the heart beat faster (1 Ki. 3:26). *Kindness* (8) is love as a commitment of will. A couple 'fall in love' (*compassion*) and in marriage they pledge their love (*kindness*). *Redeemer*: the ever-present Next-of-Kin, at hand to meet every need, bear every burden, pay every price.

9–10, *The end of wrath: Noah and the covenant of peace.* This poetic meditation on the flood takes up the 'surge of anger' theme (6) from the last picture. The pledge that *the waters of Noah would never again cover the earth* (Gn. 9:12–17) was linked to the hanging up of the Lord's war-bow (the translation 'rainbow' is contextual; the word is that for a fighting bow): the war is over, the weapon has become a sign of peace, indeed a covenant sign, a visible pledge of the Lord's promise, an incitement to trust the Promise-maker. So also now there is the pledge *not to be angry ... to rebuke*. The former is the outburst of exasperation (the same word as in 8); the latter is the mental attitude lying behind such an outburst, a sense of being offended. Both in emotion and in expression – *i.e.* totally – wrath is gone. For Noah, a stable ordinance of creation became the guarantee of peace with God, but Isaiah goes further: even should creation lose its stable permanence with *mountains* (10) shaking and *hills* (lit.) 'tottering', there is a *covenant* that cannot (lit.) 'totter'. The Servant bore the punishment that made peace (53:5) and now that peace is a covenanted reality, more steadfast than the cosmic fabric and rooted in the divine *compassion* (see 7–8). The emotion of anger is gone for ever but the emotion of surging love abides.

11–14, *Untouchable security: the city of truth and righteousness.* The city theme is fundamental in Isaiah: the Davidic city (1:26–27); the world city (2:2–4); the cleansed city

(4:2–6); the joyous city (12:1–6); the 'tale of two cities' (24–26) – one destroyed (24:10), the other redeemed, universal and strong (25:1–9; 26:1–3); another 'tale of two cities' (47–52) – one fallen (47:1), the other raised (52:1); the comforted city (66:10ff.). In the first two pictures in this series (54:1–3, 4–8), desolate Zion represented the Lord's privileged people in their need of the blessings the Servant achieved. In the final two pictures (54:11–15, 16–17), the city represents beauty and security. Note how this makes the *covenant of peace* (9–10) the centre of the whole series.

11–12. *Afflicted*, 'humiliated' by stronger forces; *lashed* ... , buffeted as by a tornado, defeated by circumstances; and *not comforted*, without any external help. But now a comforter will put an end to the humiliation (*build*) and insecurity (*foundations ... battlements ... gates*) and will display his care in enrichment and beautification.

13–14. The community which it encloses enjoys a relationship with the Lord in the light of his truth (13a) and on the ground of his righteousness (14a), and a total peace: peace with God (13b) and peace from earthly disturbance (14b–e). *Taught* is *limmûdîm*, as in 50:4ad. Like the Servant they are disciples, instructed in the word of God. The gift of revealed truth has always marked off the Lord's people from all others. It was the distinguishing mark of the city of 2:2–4. Jeremiah 31:34 predicts the identical blessing, and offers no other explanation of it than that it is the fruit of a full and final dealing with sin; so also in Isaiah, the perfect work of redemption brings the redeemed into the central privilege of being taught divine truth by a divine teacher. The outward beauty, then, of *precious stones* (12) is matched by the inner possession of the truth (13); the hidden reality of *foundations* (11c) is matched by the secret ingredient of divine *righteousness* (14a), the blessing bestowed by the Servant who 'provides righteousness' (53:11) for the *many* he designed to save. *Tyranny* ('*ōšeq*), a general word for disruptive forces at work within society; *terror* (*mᵉšittâ*), assault from outside (Ps. 89:40) as well as internal alarm (Pr. 10:14). *Fear* both as an emotion and as a circumstance (*not come near*) is gone. It is a picture of total, unbroken peace.

15–17, *Protected status: the Creator and his servants.* The security of the strong city (11–14) is traced to its root in the care of a sovereign Creator God. Never again (as, *e.g.,* 10:5–15) will he move a punitive attacker against his city (15a), and not only will every hypothetical attacker be foiled of his purpose but that purpose will be reversed in his submission (15b). Why is this?

Because everything ultimately is part of creation and therefore under the Creator's executive control (16). He guarantees his people's immunity (17a) – and if we press beyond the *weapon* (16) and the attack (17a) to the formulation of a hostile plan (17b), even there too the Creator is active to secure his people's immunity. Behind all this lies what they have inherited and possess (17c), a particular dignity (*servants*, 17ac) and standing (vindication, 17d, or 'righteousness').

15–17b. *Surrender*: (lit.) 'fall (down) to you' or 'come over to your side'. Danger (*weapon*) is traced to its source in crafts-manship (*coals*) and the craftsman (*blacksmith*), and then beyond that to the Creator (*I who created*). The Creator begins all things, maintains them in being, controls them in operation and guides them to the destiny he appoints. If this great God were at work only in the 'nice' things, how grim would be our plight in this menacing world; but he is at work, and in full operational control of all things. He is God the Creator, alike in charge of the initiating agent (16a) and the ultimate agent (16d).

17c. *Heritage* (*naḥ^alâ*) does not describe how something was acquired but rather the reality of possession. Probably we should see 17cd as applying not only immediately to the blessings of 15–17b but also broadly to all the blessings arising from the Ser-vant's work as listed in this chapter. But, in particular, the word of the Servant creates *servants*, those with whom, by his saving work, he shares his dignity. Up to this point in chapters 40ff., Isaiah has used 'servant' only in the singular; from now on it will only appear in the plural. The Servant by his saving work creates servants. According to 53:11 'my righteous servant' provides righteousness for the 'many'. The Lord himself now validates this gift of 'righteousness' (not *vindication*) by affirming that it comes *from me* – an emphatic preposition suggesting 'straight from my presence'.

The whole world invited into the new world (55:1–13). In contrast to the particular command to Zion to 'sing' (54:1), the great invitation (lit.) 'O [not "Come"] all you who are thirsty' brings before us the worldwide consequences of the Servant's work, namely that he was designated to establish 'justice [re-vealed truth] on earth' (42:4) and to be 'my salvation to the ends of the earth' (49:6). What, then, does the saving work in 52:13 – 53:12 offer to the whole world?

1–2, *Free provision for every need.* The contrasting promises of *waters* to drink and *the richest of fare* (2d) to *eat* embraces every need and every necessary supply. The first invitation, *Come to the waters*, underlines a life-threatening need and an abundant supply. The second invitation, *come, buy and eat*, extended to the one who has *no money*, highlights inability and helplessness: on the one hand, how can one without money *buy*? But, on the other hand, nothing can be had without payment (*buy*). Someone – in context, by implication, the Servant in his saving efficacy – has paid the purchase price. The third invitation, *Come, buy wine and milk, without money*, stresses the richness of the provision: not just the water of bare necessity but the wine and milk of luxurious satisfaction. Isaiah has already pictured the idolater pouring out gold and silver (46:6) in order to 'feed on ashes' (44:20). The antidote to such lack of discernment (44:19; *cf.* 40:18–20, 25), mental delusion (44:20) and pointless labour (44:12) – what an exposure of religion without revelation! – is to *listen, listen* (lit. 'listen listeningly'): to give full attention to listening and do nothing else at all, to give full and undivided attention to the word of God. It is in this way that the ashes of false religion are replaced by the *richest of fare*.

3–5, *Co-equal citizenship*. The 'outside world' is not invited to a soup kitchen or mere charitable handout. *Come* (3a) picks up the illustrative invitation to the banquet (1–2) but moves on from picture to reality. What is promised to those who *hear* and *come* – that is all they need to do! – is true life (3b), the opposite of the thirst, hunger and lack of satisfaction of verses 1–2; the security of a permanent covenant with its promised benefits (3c); in fact, life under David (3d) to whom world rule was promised (4) and whose kingdom will prove magnetic (5ab) because of the attracting presence of the Holy One (5c–e).

3–4. *Come to me*: the Lord himself is the promised banquet. *Covenant with you* should be 'covenant for you'. The formula *kārat bᵉrît lᵉ* (*e.g.* Ps. 89:3) means 'to inaugurate a covenant in favour of', to bring a person into the benefits that the covenant pledges. The benefits covenanted here are (lit.) 'the trustworthy loves' promised to David. Psalm 89 is the key text explaining this expression: 89:1 announces the theme, (lit.) 'the loves of the Lord', which finds expression in 'a covenant for David' (3); 89:49 concludes the psalm by appealing for the enactment of these great 'loves'. The body of the psalm explains why the plural is used: the Lord's 'loves' for David are, first, the love (24) which pledges universal rule (22–27) and, secondly, the love (28) promising David an enduring kingship (28–37). Into this world kingdom, and under the sway of this enduring king, come all who respond to the invitation. *Witness* (4): David is not elsewhere spoken of as the Lord's witness, but the idea of worldwide Davidic testimony is rooted in the Davidic psalms (9:11; 18:49;

57:9–11; 108:3–4; 145:21). Psalm 18 affirms that 'a people I do not know will serve me'. But if David is nowhere spoken of plainly as the Lord's witness, the Servant is (42:1–4; 49:2–3; 50:4), and the function of the present passage is to bring together the presentations of the Royal Messiah (chs. 1 – 37) and the Servant Messiah (chs. 38 – 55). All the soul-renewing blessings of 55:1–3 are to be found within the rule of David because David and the Servant are the same Person.

5. *Because of the LORD* (5): the same powerful magnetism is at work here as in 2:2–4, a magnetism overcoming all nationalistic objections to embracing the God and king of another nation (contrast 16:4–6). In 49:7, the Lord so endowed his Servant that kings rose to greet him with respect and princes bowed to acknowledge his supremacy; here the same enduement adorns the appointed King, and sure mercies lie waiting in his kingdom for all who respond to the open invitation.

6–9, *The fundamental issue.* The key to entering upon sure and lasting blessing is the simple 'Come ... come ... come ... listen, listen ... Give ear and come to me' (1–3). What is involved in this simple coming? (a) A recognition of urgency while the day of opportunity lasts (6); (b) an acknowledgment and renunciation of sin (7ab) and a return to the God of compassion and pardon (7cd); and (c) a submission of whatever we think or do to what the Lord thinks and does (8–9).

6–7. The threefold 'come' (to the banquet, 1) and the 'Listen ... give ear' and 'come to me' (2–3) are now brought to their specific meaning: *Seek ... call ... forsake ... turn.* To *seek* is, as ever in religious usage (*e.g.* 8:19), not to look for something lost but to come with diligence to where the Lord is to be found. It speaks, therefore, of commitment, determination, persistence in spiritual concern and in longing for the Lord's presence and fellowship. To *call* is at one and the same time to acknowledge him in worship (Gn. 13:4; Ps. 105:1) and to appeal to him in need (Ps. 50:15). *Forsake* and *turn* are the two sides of true repentance, turning from and turning to (1 Thes. 1:9). *Wicked* (7) and *evil* are broad, non-specific words. If any difference is to be found, the former points more to character and the latter to the ill effects of sin. *Way* and *thoughts* (*cf.* 8) are respectively 'lifestyle' (as when we excuse somebody for being rude by saying, 'He doesn't mean it. It's just his way') and the 'mind' which lies behind it, entertaining ideas, fashioning plans. *Mercy* is 'compassion' (see 54:8). The penitent is embraced in a surge of divine love. *Freely* is 'abundantly', (lit.) 'he will act multiplyingly in pardon', as though it were pardon with compound interest.

Pardon (√*sālaḥ*; widely used about forty times, *e.g.* Nu. 14:20; 1 Ki. 8:30, 34) is a word of general meaning: to do whatever must be done to deal with sin, a word focused on the fact of forgiveness without reference to reason or means.

8–9. The Lord is completely different from humans (*not ... neither*) in what and how he thinks (*thoughts*) and in his characteristic *ways* of action. This is a verse of very wide application, covering every aspect of life. It cancels the useless and debilitating question 'Why?' in face of life's difficulties; it opens the door to the blessed reality of faith in a God who is truly God. In context its focus is narrower. People would give many different answers if questioned about the nature of their need and to what sort of banquet they would like free access in order to meet that need. But the Lord is thinking his own thoughts and pursuing his own road when he meets the moral and spiritual need (spelled out in 6–7). If the words *not ... neither* seem stark in expressing the distinction between our thoughts and the Lord's, this is no more than is just. How much *higher* (9) is heaven? The answer is 'immeasurably'. In relation to any who question the Lord, this comparison cultivates a due humility. In relation to the point at issue – human moral and spiritual plight – we see the wonder of repentance if it can indeed bridge and cancel such a gap, and how marvellous is the Lord's remedy.

10–11, *The sure word.* Verse 10 opens with an explanatory 'For'. It is logical to question whether the simplicity of 'Come ... Listen ... Come to me ... Seek ... call ... forsake ... turn' can really and effectively make people right with God. But it is not repentance that is effective but the word of divine truth.

Rain is a heavenly gift, *come down from heaven*, designed for effectiveness (*not return ... empty*), producing transformation (*watering ... making it bud*) and turning deadness into life (*seed*) and nourishment (*bread*). Even so, *my word* (11) is supernatural in origin (*goes out of my mouth*), effective in mission (*not return ... empty*) and instrumental in achieving what the Lord wills (*what I desire ... the purpose for which I sent it*). Here, again, is a truth of wide and important application. The Word of God – in our privileged day, the Holy Scriptures – comes from the Lord himself and is the Lord's chosen instrument to achieve his purposes. The Bible reveals his thoughts and ways, sets his targets, voices his promises and is powerful to achieve what it expresses. But immediately in this passage the focus is narrower. It speaks particularly of the divine word heard in the call to repentance, the command to come back to God, the promises of compassion and forgiveness. These are effective in achieving what they say, not because the sinner responds and uses words of penitence and faith but because God has spoken.

12–13, *The promise of a new world.* Once more (*cf.* 10) there is an initial 'For'. What the word of God is sent to achieve is a sure and certain reality, 'for' those who respond will find that they *will go out with joy* into a world unlike anything they have previously known (12c–f), a world transformed (13ab) where everything is for the Lord's glory (13c) and which is an eternal reality (13de).

12. It is typical of the Bible to represent responding to the Lord as coming to a party (1–2), and this is now expressed in the *joy* (12) in the Lord into which his people enter and the *peace* he gives (53:5; 54:10). *Go out*, as at the exodus, from bondage into liberty, from alienation back, through the Servant's work (49:5–6), to God. *Led forth, i.e.* by the Lord himself (42:16; 52:12; Ex. 13:21–22). The personal transformation – new emotions (*joy*), new relationships and expectations (*peace*), new guardianship (*led*) – are matched by a new environment. This is immediately true in that 'Heaven above is softer blue, / Earth around is sweeter green; / Something lives in every hue, / Christless eyes have never seen'.[1] But the ultimate reality is the new earth, creation released from the bondage of corruption to share the liberty of the children of God (Rom. 8:19–21). The curse has been removed and all creation explodes in fresh joy (*burst into song*) and praise (*clap*).

13. *Thornbush* (*na'ªṣûṣ*; elsewhere only in 7:19) and *briers* (*sirpāḏ*) are both of uncertain meaning. The latter seems to be related to a verb 'to wail' and Isaiah may have invented a botanical term to reflect the sorrows from which creation has been released. In any case, the situation is Genesis 3:18 put into reverse. *Pine ... myrtle* are likewise uncertain except that they are evergreens. Death and the curse have been replaced by life and ever-freshness. *For the LORD's renown*: (lit.) 'this will become a name for the Lord'. The new exodus community of joy and peace (12ab) and the exultant (12c–f), transformed (13ab) creation will themselves speak in revelation of the nature and character of the Lord: his free invitation, his call to the simplicity of repentance, his guarantee of compassion and forgiveness, the certainty of his ways, the power of his word, the move from alienation to fellowship, from death to life, from the old into the new, from the transient into the eternal, from need to fullness – such is the Lord and such what his Servant has done.

[1] From G. W. Robinson, 'Loved with everlasting love'.

THE BOOK OF THE CONQUEROR (56 – 66)

Some perspective on these chapters can be achieved through a New Testament parallel. With the birth of Jesus Christ, the promised King arrived, heir of David's throne and dominion (Lk. 1:31–33); with his death, the saving work of the Servant was completed and acknowledged in the threefold exaltation of resurrection, ascension and heavenly enthronement (Heb. 10:12). But his kingship is, at present, publicly *incognito*, and, even though redeemed, both we and the world we live in are far from ideal. Its rulers are inadequate, frequently hostile and never free from sin. There are also, still active, the world rulers of this darkness (Eph. 6:12). In brief, the King is reigning, the work of salvation has been done, but the world is in an interim, awaiting the day when foes will submit (Heb. 10:13), every knee bow (Phil. 2:9–11) and his people become like him because they see him as he is (1 Jn. 3:2).

Historically and politically, Isaiah has reached the point where, thanks to Cyrus, the people have returned from Babylon (48:20–21), and it is to this situation that he now turns his prophetic powers. He has alerted them to the fact that they will return as they went. Prior to the exile the House of David was an empty husk. Ahaz had sold his sovereignty to the Assyrians and his successors were but puppet kings. Isaiah foresaw (45:9–13; 46:8–13) that it would be a point of contention with the exiles that, on their return, they would still be beholden to a pagan emperor – no David, no Davidic throne – and therefore, in principle, under the same sort of inadequate, self-seeking local rulers as in pre-exilic Jerusalem. All the royal promises (9:1–6; 11:1–9; 32:1–8; 33:17–24) are true but await realization. Furthermore, the returning people were warned that 'there is no peace for the wicked' (48:22). Political blessing is one thing, spiritual transformation another, so that, like us, even those who 'fain would serve Thee best / Are conscious most of wrong within'.[1]

In drawing this parallel between the Christian's situation and Israel's situation in 539 BC, we have in fact offered a fair summary of the themes of Isaiah 56 – 66. In the returned community, Isaiah sees a replication of the Jerusalem society he knew – and he uses pre-exilic terms to describe it.[2] The community,

---

[1] From H. Twells, 'At even, ere the sun was set'.

[2] From the point of view of literary styles, chs. 56 – 66 are perfectly at home in the Isaianic literature, exhibiting the same *genre* of rhythmic prose (the style of

under inadequate leaders (56:9–12), will be spiritually divided (57:1–2; 59:14–15; 65:11–12) with much evidence of false religion (57:3–13; 65:3–7) on the one side and a deep sense of sin (59:1–15) and of spiritual longing (64:1–2) on the other. The prophet answers this longing by encouraging great expectations: the Lord himself will intervene (59:16–19; 66:14–16) bringing healing, peace (57:15–21) and provision (65:13–16); Zion will become glorious, the focal point of all the earth (60; 62; 66:7–13, 17–24), the centre of the New Creation (65:17–24). Central to all as the focal expectation and the sole Agent of the coming salvation and vengeance is a messianic figure, the anointed Conqueror (59:20–21; 61:1–3; 61:10 – 62:7; 63:1–6).

X. THE IDEAL AND THE ACTUAL: THE LORD'S NEEDY, UNDER-ACHIEVING PEOPLE (56:1 – 59:13)

This section falls into four parts. The vision of a worldwide, inclusive 'Sabbath-people' (56:1–8), is balanced by the actual state of the community (56:9 – 57:21), divided, hostile, a mixture of the 'righteous' and compromisers. 58:1–14 returns to the theme of the Sabbath as the ideal life of the Lord's people, and this is balanced by confessions of failure (59:1–13).

a. The waiting people (56:1–8)

The Lord announces a brilliant future: on the one hand it is the realization of his *salvation* and *righteousness* (1), on the other it is the gathering of scattered *Israel* along with *others* (8). The marks of those who set themselves to wait for this day are *justice* and *what is right* (1), perseverance (2ab), Sabbath-keeping (2c) and separation (2d). They will include the *foreigner* (3ab, 6–7) and *the eunuch* (3cd–5). The pre-exilic people of God was implicitly universal. Exodus 12:48 makes provision for the conversion of the resident alien; Ruth 2:12 records a Moabite girl taking refuge under the wings of the God of Israel; and the

---

Isaiah's recorded sermons which predominates in 1 – 37) and of high poetry (the style predominantly found in 38 – 55). Thus, for example, the rhythmic prose of 1:10–20 reappears in 48:1–19 and again in 57:3–10; the high poetry of 2:2–4 or 35:1–10 can be compared with 43:1–3 or 55:1–13 and reappears in the exquisite 61:10 – 62:7, and so on. It is the 'mixture as before'. The concepts presented in 56 – 66 are plainly pre-exilic. The religious aberrations Isaiah exposes are what he saw in pre-exilic Judah and are unknown in the post-exile. Like all visionaries, he furnishes his visions with the existing furniture of his mind, using what he knows as typifying or providing a motif of what will be – not, in this case, predicting but diagnosing.

presence of Isaiah 2:2–4 in Micah 4:1–3 (or vice versa) indicates the popularity of the thought of a universal people. Isaiah shaped this universalism into ever-clearer forms. He started with the typical pre-exilic vision of David's spreading kingdom (9:7; 11:12–16) but moved on to forecast one world, one people, one God (19:24–25; 27:12–13). Another forward move came with the extension of the name 'Israel' to this universal people (45:14–25), and the capstone was put in place in the Servant who brings revealed truth to the world (42:1–4), who is salvation to the ends of the earth (49:6) and who calls all to his banquet (55:1–13) – hence, here in 56:1–8, the vision of a worldwide, non-exclusive worshipping community.

1. *Justice ... what is right* (lit. 'righteousness'). In the typical Isaianic combination of 'judgment and righteousness' (1:21; 5:16; 9:7; 16:5; 28:17; 32:1, 16), 'righteousness' means the righteous principles of life the Lord has revealed and 'judgment' their specific application. Those who model their lives on the Servant (50:10) 'pursue righteousness' (51:1). Some urge that the concept of 'doing righteousness' is different in chapters 56ff. from 40 – 55, but examination does not bear this out. Isaiah is not inviting people to seek salvation by righteous works but calling them to live the life the Lord has revealed as 'right'. This is not offered as a means of salvation but as a characteristic of those awaiting salvation. *My salvation* looks back to 49:6; 51:5–6; 52:7, 10, and forward to 59:11, 17; 60:18 (*cf.* 26:1); 62:1. *My righteousness* is shorthand for 'the fulfilment of my righteous purposes' (as in 45:8, 23; 46:13; 51:6, 8).

2. This is all typical of biblical ethics: a summons to holiness (1ab), based on knowing what the future holds (1cd), issuing in present rewards (2ab). *Sabbath*: some scholars, referring to Nehemiah 10:31 and 13:15, would see this emphasis on the Sabbath as evidence of a post-exilic date.[1] But Isaiah 1:13 and Amos 8:5 show how punctilious was Sabbath observance in the pre-exile. Ezekiel 20:12; 22:8, 26, condemn profaning the Sabbath as a pre-exilic sin, and Jeremiah 17:19–27 makes Sabbath observance a test of obedience to the Lord. Isaiah makes the same point. Acceptance of the Sabbath involves the reorganization of the whole of life in order to accommodate the principle of one day set apart; it is also the Lord's invitation to his

---

[1] G. A. F. Knight states: 'Actually the ever recurring Sabbath day was the only institution the people possessed that was able to hold them together ... those long fifty years' (*Isaiah 56 – 66* [Eerdmans, 1985], p. 5). This, however, seems a highly dubious understanding of the life of a captive people in a captor country.

covenant people (Ex. 31:16) to enter into his rest (Ex. 23:12; 31:17). There could be no plainer testimony to belonging to the Lord's separated people.

3. *Foreigner* and *eunuch* are examples of an all-embracing inclusiveness. The Old Testament was never exclusive on a nationalistic basis. Deuteronomy 23:3ff. dealt with nations requiring special disciplines but (Ex. 12:48–49) the foreigner was always in principle welcome. Again Ezra 4:1–3 and Nehemiah 2:19–20 are not jingoism but measures to preserve the distinct people. Once distinctiveness is lost there is nothing for the outsider to join! The exclusion of the *eunuch* (Dt. 23:1) is never explained, and Isaiah leaves it there because his purpose is not to explain exclusion but to emphasize incorporation. All middle walls of partition are down.

4–5. *Covenant* includes both the pledges which the Lord makes to his people and the revealed law to which they responsively bind themselves. *Eunuchs* are as free as any other people to enter this sphere of grace. This is another way of expressing co-equal (not second-class) participation. To them the Lord grants access to his presence (*temple ... walls*), personal acceptance (*memorial ... name*), more than abundant recompense for deprivations (*better than*) and eternal security (*everlasting ... not cut off*).

6–8. Entrance is open but not unconditional. *Bind*: there must be personal decision. *Serve ... love* (*cf.* Dt. 10:12, 20) are the marks of Israelite devotion. The reduplication *serve ... worship* (lit. 'be his servants') makes the same point: no mere conformism but commitment to 'be his servant'. *These* (7), the formerly unprivileged (foreigner) and unwelcome (eunuch), are brought by the Lord to where he is (*mountain*), to a speaking relationship with him (*prayer*), to the ordinances which guarantee acceptance and atonement (*sacrifices ... altar*) – and all this not as a concession but a fulfilment of what *my house* was always intended to be, *for all nations*. The order *Israel ... others* (8) follows 49:6. *Exiles*: (lit.) 'scattered ones', alluding neither to Babylonian exile, nor geographical dispersion, but to those scattered from the Lord (Jn. 11:52). *Others*: like the foreigners and eunuchs, the previously unreached and unwelcomed. *Besides*: better 'to be'; *Israel* and the *others* all alike brought home to become the Lord's one gathered people.

b. The divided people (56:9 – 57:21)

We come down with a bump from the heights of vision to the grim realities of inadequate leaders (56:9–12) and life at the ground level (57:1–21), where there is tension and worse between 'the righteous' (1) and those who have apostasized to the cults (3–13) and forgotten the Lord (11). One group is destined for peace (2, 19), the Lord dwells with them (15) and leads them home (14); the other he abandons to what help their idols can give (13) and they know no peace (21).

i. The failure of the leaders (56:9–12). Savagery of imagery and of style reflects the prophet's loathing of a major factor in the loss of the ideal: leaders who are blind and self-seeking. There is a feast in waiting as the beasts close in to *devour* (9); there is a feast in progress, the indulgence of self-absorbed rulers (11). They lack requisite foresight and knowledge (10ab), are as useless as somnolent watchdogs (10c–f), active only for indulgence (11ab), shepherds who look after themselves and not the sheep (11).

9. *Beasts* (*cf.* Lv. 26:22; Dt. 28:26; 32:24; 2 Ki. 17:25): the advent of the beasts betokens abandonment of the Lord's law. *Come*: note the inclusio with the same word in verse 12. Isaiah's irony is almost frightening: the rulers gather to feast, ignorant that other guests have been called.

10–12. *Watchmen ... shepherds* are the twin aspects of true leadership: to guard from coming danger and care for present needs (Ezk. 3:16–21; 33:1–9; 34:2–9). Between the picture of *watchmen* with no concern for security (10a–d) and thoughtless *shepherds* (11c–e), Isaiah puts his finger on the cardinal sin of the ruler: insatiable self-concern (10e–11b). It would be laughable were it not tragic to read side by side *watchmen* and *blind* (10a), *dogs* and *mute* (10c). They are unqualified (*knowledge*), unmotivated (*lie around*), insatiable (*never enough*), undiscerning (*understanding*, the ability to see to the heart of a thing), improvident (*tomorrow ... better*). Life at public expense is a bottomless purse.

ii. The prostitute's brood and the Lord's household (57:1–21). The apparent jumble of this passage reflects the 'mix' of life at ground level in a secular society: the 'righteous' having a difficult time (1), people caught up in cults (3–5) and in politics (9–10). Some find God near (15) and live with a peace and confidence not experienced by all (19–21). Yet the verses are not really a jumble but a presentation: the peace enjoyed by the righteous (1–2) contrasts with the lack of peace of the wicked (20–21); the prostitute and her family (3–13) contrasts with the Lord and his household (14–19).

Security, come what may (57:1–2). It was a society hostile to true believers – not necessarily irreligious, for often the harshest opponent of genuine faith is formal ecclesiasticism (Am. 5:12–13; *cf.* 5:21–24; 7:10–17). But behind all the malignity a purpose is at work which *no-one ponders … understands. Devout men*: literally 'men of unfailing love', those whom the Lord loves with a never-failing love. *Taken away … taken away*: the first is plural, the second singular; the general truth followed by the particular case. It is always the same: the death of the *righteous* (those right with God) is never simply the inevitable end that comes to all, neither is it ever accidental or untimely, but always purposeful, deliberate, a 'taking away' in order to be *spared from evil* (1 Cor. 10:13; 2 Ki. 22:20) and brought into *peace* and *rest. As they lie in death*: literally 'they lie upon their beds', an entering into comfort. *Walk uprightly* is the last phrase in the MT, just as *the righteous* is the first; those who are 'right with God' display an upright life as others watch them.

The prostitute and her family (57:3–13). The terms of this passage are taken from pre-exilic cults and are written with such vigour as to suggest that the cults were in full operation when Isaiah wrote (see also p. 33). There is no evidence of corresponding post-exilic practices. A prophet in the post-exile could not have written like this. Isaiah furnishes his vision of the post-exile stereotypically with the religious clutter of his own day.

3–5, Parentage and practice. 3–4. But you: in this mixed society, alongside the 'righteous', are those who are unfaithful to the Lord. *Sorceress*: one who has opened herself to control by a spirit or supernatural entity. *Adulterers … prostitutes*: adultery, breaking the marriage covenant, is figurative of reneging on loyalty; prostitution is entering upon an illicit relationship, figurative of giving loyalty.[1] *Mocking … sneer … tongue* (4): they practised a mounting tide of rejection of the Lord, from poking fun to scornful sneer and vulgar repudiation. *Brood of rebels … offspring of liars*: 'born of rebellion … seed of falsehood'. The 'rebellion' is the *adulterer* who has repudiated a sworn obligation; the 'falsehood' is the prostitute whose whole life is a lie. To turn from the Lord, then, is wilful disobedience, departure from the truth to the lie (2 Tim. 4:3–4).

5. Isaiah selects two leading aspects of Canaanite religion: first, the fertility cult, with its evergreen *tree*, symbolic of

---

[1] Harlotry as a metaphor occurs about 43 times in the OT. *Cf.* Ezk. 16:23ff. It is most deeply diagnosed in the book of Hosea. *Cf.* Is. 1:21; 23:15–17. There is no evidence of harlotry being levelled as a charge post-exile.

undying life (1:29; Dt. 12:2; 1 Ki. 14:23; Je. 2:20), and its sexual rites, prompting the god to fertilize land, animals and humans. Today, this takes the form of reliance on whatever seems to secure economic prosperity. For the Canaanite, the 'religious' use of sexuality was a necessary factor in securing the agricultural economy; for the Bible, such practices were not hallowed by being 'religious': they were *lust*, the satisfaction of the worshipper replacing the will of God. Secondly, there was the even darker, more repulsive side to Canaanite religion: Molech and human *sacrifice* (2 Ki. 23:10; Je. 32:35), *children* burnt alive as a charm against death, propitiating the god of the underworld. Again, this acquires no sanctity by being done in the name of religion. It is (lit.) 'slaughtering, butchering', treating babies like cattle.

6–13, *The ways of the mother.* Isaiah, using second-person singular feminine verbs, moves from the family (3–5) to the mother, the prostitute herself, and offers a diagnosis of what Hosea (4:12; 5:4) calls 'the spirit of prostitution'. The Hebrew here has a manic quality reflecting a person driven by a demon, now this way, now that, frantic for security – into the valley (6), up the mountain (7), deep to Sheol (9), paying any price (7–9) for worldly safety – and all the time (13ef) it was there, without cost, in the Lord.

6. What is the significance of *smooth*? Some find in the word *ḥeleq* a link with Ugaritic, meaning 'dead gods'.[1] It is more typical of Isaiah that the word means 'slippery' so that, in one move, he exposes the stupidity (*stones*) and duplicity ('slippery') of false religion, but there is one further twist: *portion* is a word with the same spelling. What a folly then to swap the Lord (Ps. 16:5; 119:57) for *stones*!

7–8. From valley bottoms to mountaintops, the spirit of prostitution fills the whole land. The *bed* on a *hill* pictures blatant immorality. *Behind your doors ... doorposts ... pagan symbols*: this whole phrase defies certainty. 'Symbol' is *zikkārôn*, 'memorial'. It occurs with a possessive only in Job 13:12, meaning 'your memories'; but why should memories be behind the door? Or *zikkārôn* may be related to *zāḵār*, 'male', and used of some sort of sexual symbol; but again, why behind the door? NIV seems to understand *zikkārôn* as 'what reminds you', the symbols typifying the apostate paganism. Is the meaning, then, that they practised paganism 'behind the door' while publicly professing true religion? But Isaiah has been stressing the blatant

[1] Young, *Studies in Isaiah*, pp. 402–403.

publicizing of apostasy. More likely 'your reminders' has a good meaning: the writing up of the Lord's words on the doorposts (Dt. 6:9) as a public declaration of faith and a constant recall to basics. But now the sin of compromise hides the traditional profession behind the door! *Uncovered ... climbed into ... opened wide*: they publicized their immorality, paraded themselves as available and made room for all comers. *Made a pact with*: (lit.) 'made a covenant for you from them', bargained for what was most advantageous for themselves at others' expense. But the covenant lay at the heart of their relationship with the Lord (*cf.* 56:4, 6); to make another covenant violates fidelity. The *pact* emphasizes the financial motive, but there was more: *whose beds you love, i.e.* money apart, the heart was given to another. *Looked on their nakedness*: literally 'you saw a hand'. There is no evidence for 'hand' as the sexual organs. 'Hand' symbolizes personal resources, including financial. In Leviticus 25:26 'acquires sufficient means' is literally 'his hand overtakes'. Before sealing the *pact*, the prostitute prudently appraises her clients' finances! 'Hand' is also used of a memorial stone (1 Sa. 15:12; 2 Sa. 18:18), securing remembrance. 'You saw a hand' could mean 'you saw a chance of achieving lasting fame'. This suits the security theme (see 9–10) – as for example in Hezekiah's lunatic delusions of grandeur in the alliance with Merodach-Baladan (39:1–8).

9–10. The metaphor of prostitution is explained. For *Molech* read *the king* (NIV mg.). Israel 'prostituted herself' (apostasized from the Lord, gave her loyalty to others) to secure military 'clout', to have the 'great powers' on her side (*cf.* Ezk. 16, 23). The background here is chapters 7 and 28 – 31 (*cf.* 2 Ki. 16:10–20) when Judah flirted disastrously with Assyria ('the king') and Egypt (*ambassadors*; *cf.* 30:1–7). *Grave*: 'Sheol', used in 28:14–15 to expose the stupidity of the politicians who returned from Egypt crowing over their success. It does not refer, here or there, to seeking strength through supernal powers but to the fact that signing covenants with the nations is signing their own death warrant. *You went*: literally 'you descended', *i.e.* abased yourself below your dignity as the Lord's people, the dignity of faith in such a God, to the demeaning work of currying worldly favours. And somehow, when the demon of a do-it-yourself salvation grips people, though evidence mounts that it is a burden we do not have strength to bear (10a), an unachievable goal (10b), there always seems to be strength for one more try (10cd)!

In verses **11–13**, Isaiah rounds off his diagnosis of false religion – the religion of disloyalty (3–6) and frenzied pursuit of alternative salvation (7–10) – by pointing out the awesomeness of a God who is to be feared (11a–d), the people's misunderstanding of a God who is patient (11e–12), the justice of a God who gives us the consequences of our own choices (13ab), and the ultimate contrast between the impermanence of human schemes of security and the inheritance that comes through trust (13c–f).

11. Unbelief is, first, groundless: what is more to be feared than the Lord (11a)? Secondly, it is sinful (11b): *been false*, 'tell lies', in this case to affirm that the Lord is our God but, in practice, to withhold the reverence due to him and give it to others. Thirdly, it is inexcusable (11c): to forget all the former mercies, the great acts of the Lord, and to use his name – the very thing he wished to be remembered by (Ex. 3:15) – and yet to forget him! Fourthly, it is insulting (11d): *pondered this in your hearts*, (lit.) simply 'laid to heart', meaning 'gave me a thought', the practical atheism of living without the Lord. *Long been silent*: √*ḥāšâ* for the most part means inactivity rather than silence, and this must be the meaning here. The people of God were never without the voice of God through the prophets and in the law. Yet Gideon was able to ask, 'Where are all his wonders that our fathers told us about?' (Jdg. 6:13). Why is God doing nothing? Such apparent inactivity begets misunderstanding (Ps. 50:21), and leads to moral and spiritual complacency. But of what period could it be said that the Lord was inactive while his people pursued other gods and sought salvation in alliances? Certainly not in the post-exile, where these sins were absent; certainly not in the exile, since it was itself the act of God in judgment; only in the pre-exile could people look back on a long tenure of their privileges, shrug off prophetic warnings and assume divine inactivity. In no other period could this message have originated. Here, as throughout chapters 56 – 66, Isaiah is seeing post-exilic Israel with pre-exilic eyes and using his existing oracles to address a future generation. But considerations of date are far less important than what the prophet is saying: the people of God are called to live by the word of God – the record of past acts which abidingly declares what he is; the divine law, infallibly directing life's pathway, inspired messages already vouchsafed, enshrining unchanging truth. It is these things that beget and perpetuate that *fear* (11f) of the Lord which excites obedience, faith, loyalty and holiness.

12–13. People can drift very far indeed from the Lord and still assume that they are 'right' with him (*righteousness*) and that what they do (*works*) is acceptable to him. The day of the Lord's judgment – including the final judgment (Rev. 20:12) – is simply that he *will expose* all this. *Expose* is 'I will declare'. To hear the voice of God reading out the catalogue of works in which people have trusted is to see through them: *they will not benefit*. There is nothing more dreadful than that the Lord should leave us to the mercy of our own choices! *When you cry out*: literally 'shriek'. This is the first hint of the coming divine judgment, central to these chapters. That day will declare the worthlessness of every alternative object of trust (2:20; 31:7). *Idols*: with this word Isaiah brings the first part of his presentation full circle. It is no accident that he can move so easily from false religious practice (3–6) to the picture of advertising for lovers (7–8) and the reality it pictured, seeking international alliances (9–10). Turning from the Lord, where else is security to be sought than in the logical exercises of power politics? But all this is so fragile that it is threatened by *wind*, destroyed by *a mere breath*. The politicians had no time for Isaiah's remedies (28:7–13) – kindergarten stuff, they called it. They refused to shelter trustfully in him (*makes me his refuge*). But this is the faith that brings security: permanent tenure (*inherit the land*), access to the Lord's presence, certainty of his goodwill, and care and blessing (*possess my holy mountain*).

The Lord and his family (57:14–21). This passage, concerned with the Lord's gracious care of his household, picks up and develops the thoughts implicit in verse 1–2. There the righteous move out of hostility into peace; here the opening thought is the *road* (home) and the concluding thought guidance into *peace* (18–19).

14. In 40:3 the road was prepared for the Lord to come to rescue his people; here it is an uncluttered way by which they travel (35:1–10): a causeway (*build up*) and therefore unmissable; free of *obstacles* and therefore those who use it cannot but reach their destination. They are *my people*, and the *for* with which verse 15 begins heralds an explanation of the road, the travellers and the destination.

In verses **15–19** Isaiah introduces the divine Speaker (15ab) who purposes to share his home (15c-f). There are three aspects of this favoured company: the end of accusation (16), anger replaced by healing (17–18a), the bestowal of comfort and peace (18b–19).

15. The Lord speaks of himself (15ab), his home (15c), his household (15d), his purpose of renewal and the characteristics of his family (15ef). *High and lofty*: as in 6:1; 52:13, respectively what the Lord is in himself and what he is in relation to all else. *Lives for ever*: as 'father of eternity' in 9:6 means 'eternally a father', so here 'inhabiter of eternity' means 'eternally the inhabitant'. The word √*šāḳan* (Ex. 25:8; 29:45) is used of the Lord coming to dwell among his people and, just as at the exodus the Lord gathered his people to himself by redemption (Ex. 6:6–7) with the deliberate purpose of dwelling among them (Ex. 29:42–46), so now he purposes exactly the same but on an eternal scale (*cf.* 33:5, 16). *High ... holy*: again as at the exodus, the Lord purposes that his people should be gathered to him without any compromise to his transcendence and holiness; this implies some provision equivalent to that of the levitical sacrifices whereby a sinful people could come near to God, and, in the context of Isaiah's book, this can only point to the levitical/priestly work of the Servant (52:13–53:12). Whether *contrite*, literally 'crushed', *i.e.* under life's burdens, oppositions or whatever, or *lowly*, at the bottom of life's heap, whether in their own estimation (1 Tim. 1:15) or that of the world (1 Cor. 4:9–10), it is not the Lord's intention to leave his people thus but rather to *revive*, to give (new) being to, in *spirit* and *heart*. When used together like this, *spirit* is the ability to enter into life with gusto, and *heart* is the interior capacity for true thought, pure delight, accurate reflection.

16. The initial *For* (omitted, NIV) makes this verse an explanation. How will the Lord thus introduce people into the high and holy dwelling? First, by satisfying his own legal requirements (*accuse*, lit. 'engage in legal proceedings') and bringing to an end his own anger (*nor ... always be angry*). Were this not to happen, it would mean the end of all living things (*grow faint*, lit. 'faint away'). How it will happen Isaiah has no need to say, because he is speaking against the background of the Servant's work of satisfaction. But his point is not to explain *how* but to affirm *that* the Lord intends to bring people into his household, by satisfying his just law and his holy nature.

17–18. These verses respectively match Genesis 6:5–7 and 8. An unbroken human history of *sinful greed* – 'the iniquity' (perverseness, crookedness) of an unscrupulous pursuit of self-interest – roused anger (*enraged*) and provoked hostility (*punished*, 'smote') and alienation (*hid my face*) but to no good effect (*kept on*, lit. 'backsliding in the way of his heart'). A further and different work of God is needed but not obligatory, and Genesis 6:8 rightly defines it as a work of grace (NIV 'favour'): here a true diagnosis, *I have seen*; an effective remedy, *heal*; a new lifestyle, *guide*; and a different relationship with the Lord, *restore comfort*. The latter means (lit.) 'fulfil comforts to him and to his mourners': to 'fulfil comforts', 'give comfort in full and plenty', betokens a new attitude on the Lord's part, a change from anger to loving concern; 'and to his mourners' betokens the meeting of human needs, the application of the comfort where it is consciously needed.

19. The explanation of what the Lord purposes to do to achieve the vision of verse 15 continues. *Creating*: there will be a new creative act, the Lord doing what only the Lord can do (see on 4:5): in particular he will create the capacity to respond verbally. *Praise on the lips ... Israel* is not a translation but an attempted explanation. The sequence in Isaiah's Hebrew is 'give complete comfort to him and to his mourners as I create the fruit of the lips' (no reference to *Israel*). The Lord will enable the mourners to say whatever it is appropriate for these mourners to say, *i.e.* to use their newly-created gift of speech in repentance and contrition. Thus they come into *peace, peace*. The duplication (see 6:3) means peace in its full reality and nothing but peace. *Heal*: *i.e.* bring into that complete wholeness that peace implies.

20–21. In contrast to 'the righteous' (1), here are *the wicked*. This typical biblical pairing is specially relevant to this section of Isaiah which focuses on the balancing ideas of salvation and vengeance (59:17; 61:2; 63:4–6). The righteous are those who are 'right with God' and acquitted before his tribunal; the wicked are those who are pronounced guilty. *Tossing*: better 'disturbed'; subject to disordering forces from outside, but at the same time within itself ill at ease (*cannot rest*), at odds in its own nature, lacking the ability to become integrated, and a source of corruption (*mire and mud*). *No peace*: *cf.* 48:22, where those without peace were the returnees from Babylon, still needing the Servant's work to bring them home to the Lord; here, in contrast to the righteous brought into their eternal home (1–2), the wicked are, as Isaiah will show, on their way to wrath and judgment.[1]

c. The Sabbath people (58:1–14)

Isaiah now embarks on a second contrast. In chapters 56 – 57 he contrasted the inclusive unity of the Lord's Sabbath people (56:1–8) with the inadequacies and divisions of the actual community (56:9 – 57:21). Here he contrasts the true Sabbath life (58:1–14) with their actual, disconsolate awareness of themselves (59:1–13). As he shows, true Sabbath-keeping demands con-

---

[1] On the place of 57:21 in seeking to analyse the Isaianic literature, see on 51:10–11 with n.1 (pp. 323–324); also p. 320 n.1.

ISAIAH 58:1–4

secrating one's timetable to God (cf. Ex. 16:22–30; Nu. 15:32–
36), but (see esp. 13–14) the Sabbath is also a test whether the
heart delights in God. Within the Isaianic literature, chapter 58
belongs with 1:10–20, in condemnation both of the 'unholy
alliance' between religious punctiliousness and personal and
social indiscipline, and of a religion that assumes a relationship
with God while discounting a relationship with other people. In
structure, rebuke (1) is matched by promise (14); the fast without
blessing (2–5) is balanced by the feast with blessing (13–14a);
and the central verses (6–12) expound the Lord's chosen fast and
the enrichments it brings.

1. The call to acknowledge *rebellion* looks back to 57:19,
where it is the gift of repentance that marks those at peace with
God, and looks forward to 59:1–13, where we meet people
acknowledging sin and need. Thus it is the proclamation of his
word that the Lord uses to create responsiveness (Rom. 10:17).
Rebellion ... sins: in Jeremiah 17:19–27 the Sabbath is the test of
obedience; here its misuse is a cardinal sin.

In verses **2–5**, the initial *For* introduces this whole paragraph
as an explanation of the accusation of 'rebellion' and 'sins' (1).
To all outward appearance there is a committed practice of
religion (2) in which they approach God (2a) and want him to
approach them (2f). But (with correct interpretation) NIV says that
there is a *seem* and an *as if* about it all. This is spelt out as the
prophet exposes their motivations (3a–d), their behaviour (3ef)
and the outcome of their fast (4ab). It is mere outward show (5a–
d), unacceptable to the Lord (5ef).

2. Assiduous (*day after day*), committed (*seek*, 31:1; 55:6),
spiritual (*me* is emphatic), *eager* (lit. 'are delighted to') – to all
appearance a model of spiritual reality, and of ambition *to know*
and to do *my ways ... right ... commands*. *Eager for God to come
near*: literally 'for the nearness of God'. The verbs 'to come near'
and 'to bring near' are the characteristic verbs of the levitical
system in which sacrifices were 'brought near' and thereby
worshippers enjoyed the nearness of God. This is indeed model
religion: God-centred (2a), with concern for truth a priority,
together with the lifestyle that accords with the truth (2b–d),
living by the word of God (2e), and using the ordinances as true
means of grace (2f).

3–4. But there was a fatal flaw: it was all done in the pharisaic
spirit of Luke 18:12. What seemed like eager devotion was
actually aimed at earning benefit (3a–d). Not only so, but what
was a day off for the employer was a day of exploitation for the
employee (3ef). We are not told how this worked out, only that

what was doing *as you please* on the one side was pain on the other: *exploit* (√*nāḡaś*), the taskmasters' verb (Ex. 3:7); *workers*, a noun (otherwise unused) from √'*aṣaḇ*, to be in pain – toilsome work, sweated labour. Moreover, every fast day ended in a fight. Fasting was intended to win divine approval, but it brought out the worst in people – understandable if a basically unspiritual family was forced to spend a hungry day together!

5. This was the problem: nothing went beyond conformism, doing the right actions in the right way. <u>*Like a reed* exposes the total formalism of the whole day; their very act of self-abasement was as meaningless as a reed nodding in the wind</u>. This is not, of course, to say that there is not a proper use of bowing low before God and of the disciplined self-humbling of *sackcloth* (Ne. 9:1). Humans are a body-soul unity, and these things can be bodily aids to spiritual reality (just as fasting has the effect of giving a purer detachment of mind to seek God), but no 'aid' is immune from degenerating into a performance.

Verses **6–12**, describing how a fast day should be used, fall into two parts, each specifying activities (6–7, 9c–10b) and promising blessings (8–9b, 10c–12). First, a fast day is for the creation of a caring society (6), meeting needs (7a–c) and family welfare (7c), and it brings consequent personal blessings: new beginnings (8a), personal restoration (8b), security (8cd) and a free-flowing relationship with the Lord (9ab). Secondly, a true fast is for correction of inhuman conditions (9c), banishing mischief-making (9d) and meeting needs (10ab), and it results in clear guidance in life's perplexities (10cd–11a), renewal (11b), durability (11c), ever-fresh resources (11de), restoration and continuance (12). What seems like deprivation – fasting – is actually enrichment when used according to God.

6–7. *Chains ... cords*: time made free by being set apart in fasting should be used to correct every way in which social structures or wrongdoers within society destroy or diminish the proper liberty of others. *Untie ... yoke*: to eliminate every way in which social mismanagement treats people like animals. *Break ... yoke*: it is not enough to *untie*; action must be taken to see that such bondage cannot ever be repeated. Work on the structures of society (6) must be matched by personal care for the individual (7) – the hungry, the homeless and the unclad. *Provide ... with shelter* (lit. 'bring ... home'): as food is shared, so is the home opened. *When you see*: immediacy of response to known need. *Your own flesh and blood*: it is possible to be socially clear-sighted and domestically shortsighted.

8–9b. *Then*: get the fast right and the Lord will respond in blessing! He will give, first, a fresh beginning, like a new *dawn*. Secondly, personal restoration, the *healing* of wounds and disabilities from the past: *healing* ('*ᵃrûkâ*) is used of new flesh growing over a wound (Je. 30:17) and of 'repair work' (Ne. 4:12). Thirdly, he will give security with *righteousness* as a protective advance guard and *glory* as a rearguard (52:12). The Lord provides righteousness (53:11; 54:17) and the believer wears it as an armour (Rom. 13:12; 2 Cor. 6:7). *The glory of the LORD* is the personal presence of the Lord in all his glory, his presence in every place (6:3); here, his guardianship of his own. Fourthly, a free mutuality of relationship with the LORD: unfettered prayer, prompt response. *The Lord* (9a) is emphatic, 'the Lord himself', his personal attention to our cry. *And he will say*: the construction here (a co-ordinate verb) suggests 'at once he will say': *Here am I*: literally 'Behold me', the response of a waiting, obedient servant (Gn. 22:1, 11; 1 Sa. 3:4). Answered prayer is not like the sending of a food parcel; it is like a home visit by the doctor.

Verses **9c–12** specify the second series of principles with their consequent blessings (*cf.* 6–9b).

9c–10b. *Do away with the yoke* (*of oppression* is an NIV addition) recapitulates verse 6, but possibly there 'injustice' points to burdensome, enslaving social structures, whereas here the following *pointing finger* suggests personal behaviour, the way we can so easily be a bind and burden others. *Pointing finger* is not found elsewhere, but Proverbs 6:12–14 shows that 'motions with his fingers' means acting by hint and innuendo, the nod or wink in the right place, 'putting the knife in', the destructive sneer and the unattributable 'leak'. It is possible to have a very developed dutifulness (6) but to be personally malicious and mischief-making (9). *Spend yourselves on*: literally 'grant your soul to'; since 'soul' (*nepēš*) can mean 'desire, want', the words could mean 'give to the needy what you want for yourself', a determined, self-sacrificing commitment going even beyond verse 7.

10c–12. *Light*: the first blessing here is clarity in life's darknesses and perplexities. *Light* is not related to 'dawn', as in verse 8, but to *darkness*, those occasions when we do not know which way to turn, when troubles close in around us. *Guide* interprets the imagery of light in darkness. Our experience may well continue to be *darkness*, and we step falteringly into it as best we know, but the reality is divine guidance; he does not suffer our foot to slip (Ps. 121:3). The second promised blessing is of timely supply: *sun-scorched* (11b) is found only here, but is

ISAIAH 58:13–14

related to √*ṣāḥaḥ*, 'to be white' (La. 4:7); hence the adjective 'bare' (Ezk. 24:7), 'unprotected' (or 'exposed', Ne. 4:13). We are not told what satisfaction the Lord will give but when and where he will give it – when everything seems bleak, when we are vulnerable. In such a time he *will strengthen your frame*, give durability in the face of harsh demands. Thirdly, there is the blessing of fresh, incoming resource and vitality, like water brought for the *garden* (11d), but, balancing the ministry of the watering-can, there is the *spring*, an unfailing internal fountain (11e; Jn. 4:13). Fourthly come the blessings of restoration (*rebuild*, 12) and continuance (*Dwellings*), recovery from past disaster (*ancient ruins*), provision for future secure living (*Walls ... Streets*). This could, of course, refer to building and restoration work after the return from Babylon but, alongside the pictures of light (10), the traveller in the sun-scorched land (11) and the garden (11), this too is more likely to be a picture, but highly relevant to Isaiah's community which knew the devastations described in 1:6–9.

13–14. In the structure of this poem, verses 13–14a are the feast with a blessing, matching the fast without a blessing in 2–5, and verse 14b–d is a promise, matching the rebuke of 1; but the verses also form a third *If ... then* series, *i.e.* keep a true *Sabbath* and blessings will follow. The Lord is more concerned with the enjoyment of his blessings through obedience to his commands than in self-imposed deprivations. In 13a–d, Isaiah emphasizes positive recognition of the dignity of the Sabbath as *holy* and *honourable*, and in 13ef the protection of the Sabbath from improper activities. *Keep your feet from breaking*: (lit.) 'turn back your foot from', equivalent to 'watch your step', take a thoughtful approach to how you use the day. It is not a 'free-for-all', a day for *doing as you please*, yet it is an 'exquisite delight' as the lexicons translate *delight* (*ōneg*). Isaiah deals in principles, not directives: what is done on the Lord's day must recognize that it is a holy and special day; it must be conducive to finding true delight; it is not a matter of personal preference (*going your own way*) or indulgence (*doing as you please*). *Speaking idle words* is 'speaking a word, talking talk'. The expression in Deuteronomy 18:20 means a word without divine authorization, a merely human word, here 'chit-chat'. *Then*: an emphatic conjunction as in verses 8–9, of one thing assuredly following another. True Sabbath-keeping brings delight in the Lord. *Find your joy* is a reflexive form of the verb which yielded the noun *delight* in verse 13c: 'bring exquisite delight to yourselves'. In addition, we will *ride on the heights*, rise above earthly difficulties, enjoy an uplifted life (Dt. 32:13; 33:29; Hab. 3:19) and enter into the sufficiency and provision (*feast*) that the Lord has for us, including all his past promises and covenanted mercies (*your father Jacob*).

d. The guilty people (59:1–13)

Following in sequence from 58:1–14, the charges continue (59:1–8), but now they are met by an admission of guilt and helplessness (59:9–13). Within this broad division the passage consists of accusations (1–4b, couched in second-person plural verbs), descriptions (the third-person plural verbs of 5–7) and confessions (the first-person plural of 9–12). Verses 4cd, 8 and 13 are concluding summaries.

i. Accusations (59:1–4). Verses 1–2 reply to the complaint in 58:3–4 of divine inattention in spite of every effort to catch the Lord's eye. The problem is not his inattention but our sin. Verses 3–4 spell out the sins which have averted the Lord's face.

1–3. *Arm*, literally 'hand', the symbol of personal action; *ear*, ability and willingness to hear. It is not that he possessed the power but did not hear, nor that he heard but lacked the power. The problem is *iniquities* 'causing separation' and *sins* causing alienation. He certainly *can* hear but *will not*. *Face*: the Lord is personally offended and alienated; so to speak, it shows in his face. *You ... from you*: it is not only the sin but also the sinner who drives the Lord away. *Will not hear* is expressed as an absolute statement, totally ruling out a possibility of hearing . Sin alienates him personally (*face*) from us personally (*you*) on a permanent basis. *Hands* (3): not the word in verse 1 (*yaḏ*) but *kap̄*, the palm or grip of the hand; a specific accusation of involvement, gripping, holding on to. *Fingers*: direct, detailed touch (2:8; 17:8). *Stained* is 'defiled', sin leaving a mark which remains visible to God; *blood*, violence done to others (1:15). *Guilt*: 'iniquity' as in verse 2, the inner corruption and perversion from which all wrongdoing flows. *Lips ... tongue*: duplication for the sake of emphasis, every aspect of speech. The only other reference to *lips* in Isaiah is 6:5; on *tongue*, see 3:8; 32:4; 35:6; 57:14. *Lies* (*šeqer*), specific falsehoods; *wicked things* ('*āwᵉlâ*), a broader word, 'deviancy', untrustworthiness, both what is not right and what is not seemly. As in 6:5, sins of speech come first in the catalogue of importance (*cf.*, *e.g.*, Lv. 19:11; Jb. 5:21; Pr. 12:14; 22:21; Mt. 5:37; 12:36–37; 15:18).

4. The first two lines (4ab) continue the catalogue of what offends the Lord. *Calls for justice*, or 'proclaim righteousness', probably refers to taking a public stand for what is right; *cf.* Amos 5:13, where prudence dictates silence. Both prophets have the same situation in mind – a society hostile to taking a moral stand. *Pleads his case*: the reference is not to corruption on the bench but to misuse of the legal process for illegal ends. The final two lines (4cd) are differently expressed (infinitives absolute) as broad sketches of current situations: 'Reliance on emptiness and speaking valuelessness, conceiving mischief and bringing forth trouble.' *Empty arguments* is *tōhû* (24:10), what lacks stability and sense. Isaiah is not describing but diagnosing. They may think they are acting sensibly but actually it is all nonsense: to all appearance they have reached a thought-out position – trust the government, trust armed strength, trust alliances, trust the fundamental instincts of people of goodwill – but the fact is that all trust, except that reposed in the Lord, is trusting *tōhû*, the unstable. *Lie:* the word in verse 3 is specific falsehood (*šeqer*), but *šāw'* here means the spirit of unreliability, the whole ethos of disregard for the truth.

ii. Descriptions (59:5–8). This is an objective, third-person statement of the situation, made both figuratively (5–6b) and in reality (6c–7), with a summary (8).

5–6b. Who are *they*? Probably an indefinite is intended, as when we report that 'they say' or 'everybody thinks'. Taking a broad view of society and its members, then, they produce what is harmful to others (*hatch the eggs of vipers*), a thought developed in 5cd; they produce what is useless to themselves (*spin ... web*), a thought developed in 6ab. *Eats ... is broken* are the contrasting relationships of fellowship and opposition. There is something about sinful humans which is a constant potential menace to others and makes all efforts ultimately ineffective for any good purpose. *Eggs ... adder*: what starts bad always gets worse. *Cannot cover*: sinners are unable to satisfy their own true longings and needs; their best efforts leave them unsatisfied (*useless*) and unprovided for (*cannot cover*).

6c–7. Typically Isaiah now explains his metaphors: whatever they do (*hands*), wherever they go (*feet*), whatever they think (*thoughts*) they cannot escape the contagion of what they are. *Evil deeds*, 'works of trouble-making'; *violence*, disruptive behaviour (*ḥāmās*, 53:9). *Rush to sin* is 'run to wrong', prone to wrong objectives, wrong actions. *Innocent*: those who have done nothing to deserve what they received. *Thoughts*: the way we appraise things, the conclusion we reach when we add everything up, thoughts leading to formulating plans. *Evil*: as in 6b, 'trouble-making'. *Ruin* (*šōḏ*), a general word for wreaking 'havoc'; *destruction* is specifically 'breaking'. Together the words comprise everything that promotes the breakdown of standards and of society, or threatens what is ordered and stable.

8. In this general comment (like 4cd) on what has been said, *peace ... peace* is the bracketing idea. They do not *know peace* (8a) nor can their lifestyle (*walks*) lead to *peace*. This is peace in its most comprehensive sense: peace with God, peace in society, peace in a mature personality no longer at war with itself. *Justice*: at base there is no submission to God's 'judgment', what he has authoritatively decided to be right; but in the broader sense also there is no setting up of what is right and just – for themselves, for other people, for society as an entity – as the objective at which *their paths* aim. Indeed, to the contrary, *they have turned them into crooked roads*, literally 'they have twisted their paths for themselves/to their own hurt'. There has been a deliberate adoption of crooked/tangled paths, and in them they will meet sin like a boomerang coming home.

iii. Confessions (59:9–13). The change in these verses is marked by first-person plural verbs. The secret work of divine enabling (57:19) and the proclamation of God's law (58:1–14) have brought the people to the place where they acknowledge the *darkness* (9), helplessness (10), bitterness (11ab), hopelessness (11cd) and guiltiness (12) of sin. The grave problems revealed in the accusatory (1–4) and descriptive (5–8) sections are not to be laid at the door of 'society' or deprivation or whatever; they are the outward manifestation of *us* (9) in our personal sinfulness. Verse 13 has the same distinct grammatical forms (infinitives absolute) as verse 4c, and in the same way provides a concluding summary.

9–10. *Justice ... righteousness*: see 56:1, where the Lord summoned his people to a life of *justice*, or 'judgment, a life conformed to the Lord's decisions' (42:1, 3–4), and promised the coming fulfilment of his purposes of *righteousness*. But the standards of revealed truth and the life that accords with it are beyond us, and the promised righteous salvation has not yet come. Inwardly and all around we *look for* ('wait expectantly, hope for', 40:31) *light*, but *all is* (lit. 'Behold') *darkness*. The illustration Isaiah chooses shows what this *darkness* is: the darkness of personal blindness (10). We may very well live in a 'dark' world, but the darkness that first calls for rectification is within. Whatever external conditions may be like – *midday* or *twilight* – it makes no difference. The darkness is in ourselves;

we are *like the dead* (14:9–12). The world around seems to be full of *the strong*, but we *grope* as those who cannot see where they are going, *stumble* as those who cannot be relied upon for constancy and stability, and are *dead* as to the vitality we need to live the godly life.

11. This verse rounds off the first section of confession: note how *justice ... deliverance* ('salvation') matches 'justice ... righteousness' (9); and *cf.* again 56:1. *Growl* is an angry growl (5:29–30), the anger of believers at the havoc caused by sin. (*Cf.* the holy groaning of Jesus, Mk. 7:34 and Jn. 11:38; the groaning of a frustrated creation in which we share, Rom. 8:22–23.) *Moan ... like doves*: as 38:14, where Hezekiah labours under the sentence of death and longs for life. *Justice*: *cf.* 9. *Deliverance* should be 'salvation' (as 56:1), the rescuing, transforming work of God.

12. Isaiah, master of drama, has used blindness (10), bears and doves (11) illustratively. Finally, he presents a court scene, with sin as the prosecutor and the Lord (*in your sight*, lit. 'before you') as judge. We may labour under sin's disabilities (10), lament its hurts and frustrations (11), but these pale into insignificance before the reality of divine judgment and the sentence of the law. *Offences*, 'wilful rebellions', and *sins*, specific lapses, are known to God (*in your sight*), active in our condemnation (*against us*) and an ever-present reality (*with us*). *We acknowledge*: this is simply the bowing of the consciously guilty head, the 'yes' of the burdened conscience. The same word is the key to blessed repentance and cleansing in Psalm 51:3.

13. As in verse 4, infinitives are used here to pass generalizing comments; also, as in 4, sins of speech are specified and the metaphor of conception employed. The divine judge of verse 12 is not a detached outsider brought in to hear a case; he is also the offended party: *against the LORD. Rebellion*, the wilful refusal of his way, *cf.* 12; *treachery*, deceitfulness, falsity and dissimulation in our pledges of loyalty. *Backs on our God*: literally 'from (following) after'. Jeremiah 2:2 uses the picture of a new bride lovingly going along with her husband – but now this has been reversed. There is no longer the love that keeps company and the devotion that accepts leadership. *Fomenting* is 'speaking' and, along with (lit.) 'the conceiving and uttering from the heart words of a lie', it not only gives sins of speech their proper biblical importance but makes the tongue the index of the heart (Mt. 12:34). *Conceived*: the sinner cannot admit faulty conduct but plead purity of heart: it was the heart which 'conceived' all that later came to birth.

XI. THE PROMISED CONQUEROR:
VENGEANCE AND SALVATION (59:14 – 63:6)

a. Preface: situation and remedy (59:14–20)

The recapitulatory *So* looks back over all the ground covered since 56:1 and introduces a summary statement (14–15ab). This is followed by the Lord's reaction (15c, 16ab) and proposed action (16c–18), and the preface ends with a new world centred on Zion (19–20).

14–15ab. *Justice ... and righteousness* are respectively moral action arising out of moral principle (*e.g.* as in 1:21; 56:1). Society, however, repels the one (*driven back*) and marginalizes the other (*distance*). This applies, first (14cd), to public life (*in the streets*), where truth – integrity, reliability, probity – has collapsed (*stumbled*, 'tripped over') and *honesty* ('uprightness') finds no entrance. Secondly, the same is true (15ab) of individual life (*whoever*). *Truth* (as in 14c) *is nowhere to be found* – the verb *ādar* means 'to be missing': personal probity is the missing ingredient – and forces at work in society set out to ruin (*prey*) anyone who *shuns evil*. Things have gone beyond merely acting against the person who seeks to stand up for what is right (Am. 5:10). Even to avoid wrong on a personal level makes one a marked man. This is a very adequate summary indeed of society as seen in 56:1 – 59:9. So what is to be done?

15c–16ab. Typically of the Bible, the Lord is depicted as moving step by step to a decision as if he had been taken by surprise at what has happened (*cf.* 52:5)! He was immediately struck by two things: the state of people (*no justice*; *cf.* 9, 14) and their helplessness (*no-one*). This latter observation matches 59:9–13 in the same way as the former matches 59:3–8. Those to whom the Lord granted the gift of repentance (57:19) and who came under the disciplined correction of his word (58:1–14) are helpless to eradicate their own sin (12–13), much less to purge the world around. *Displeased*, he 'took it badly'; *appalled* is 'devastated, shattered'. *Intervene*, to 'interpose' (*cf.* 53:12f) so as to save people from the consequences of personal and social breakdown.

16c–18. First (16cd), the Lord possesses within himself all that is needed to solve the problem: his *arm* (51:9; 52:10; 53:1) is the Lord himself acting in all his personal power. *Worked salvation*: since the work of salvation still lies ahead, the past tense here expresses what the Lord has determined upon – personal action in *righteousness*: his determination to fulfil all his righteous purposes and to do so in full accord with the righteous demands and standards of his holy character. What the Lord is (*righteousness*) and what he can do (*arm*) are the solution to the world's needs. Secondly (17), he dresses for the task. Clothing represents what he is and what he commits himself to doing (Jos. 5:13). The military metaphor is significant. What remains to be done to fulfil the vision of the King (chs. 1 – 37) is that his enemies be overthrown worldwide; likewise, what remains from the work of the Servant is the victory mentioned, for example in 42:13. *Righteousness* (17) is the moral integrity of all the Lord will do, *salvation* is the deliverance of his people, *vengeance* is the just requital of his foes, and *zeal* the determination which will bring the work to completion. Worldwide (18) this work will be done with exact justice (*what they have done ... their due*).

19–20. First, the Lord's achievement will be worldwide: he will be made known in his eternal nature (*name*, Ex. 3:15) and receive the reverence that is his due (*glory*, 6:3). No-one will know the truth (the revealed *name*) without responding in reverence; and no-one will worship a *glory* they do not know. This will, secondly, be a work of power (19). NIV (adopting a minutely altered Hebrew text) presents this pictorially as a *pent-up flood*, released and driven by a divine wind. The change is not, however, necessary and is uncertain in detail. The words more naturally mean, 'When an adversary comes in like a stream, the Spirit of the Lord lifts a banner against him.'[1] This could well be a proverbial saying used appropriately here: the 'adversary' is all that opposes the Lord and his helpless people, but the Lord's Spirit rallies his own forces (in context, the Lord's 'arm' and 'righteousness', 16cd) to his banner (11:10) and wins the victory. Thirdly (20), this new world is Zion-centred. From his victory over their foes worldwide, the great Next-of-Kin who has taken upon himself all their needs comes as victor to *Zion* (40:9–11; 52:7–10). But in Zion too there is a sifting. Not all who claim to be of Zion will be saved in Zion: only the penitents (1:27–28; 57:18–19; Heb. 12:22–23; Rev. 21:27). The Lord is as holy in redemption as in vengeance.

---

[1] NIV reflects the understanding most favoured by commentators. The picture is suitable, and involves only one tiny change to MT along with a slightly questionable translation, 'drives along'. This form of √*nûs* occurs nowhere else; 'to cause to hurry' is possible, if not wholly certain. But the form *nōs^esâ* could derive from √*nāsas* (Zc. 9:16), 'to use or wave a banner'.

b. The Covenant Mediator and his achievement (59:21 – 60:22)

i. The Covenant Mediator (59:21). The sequence of 59:1–20 is suddenly – and mysteriously – interrupted. The three sections of accusation (1–4), description (5–8) and confession (9–13) have been followed by a section on rectification (14–20), in which the Lord himself undertakes to do what his people cannot do – achieve vengeance and salvation on a worldwide scale, with Zion at the centre of it all – and the sequence might well have ended with glorification (60:1–22): Zion, the centre of world pilgrimage. What then do we make of 59:21?

First, the idea of a *covenant with them* fits into what has preceded. 'They' are the worldwide people of verse 19 and the penitents of 20 (*cf.* 1:27; 57:19), the world Israel of 19:24–25; 27:12–13; 45:14–25; 54:1 – 55:13. To each of these components the Lord has already pledged a covenant relationship (54:10; 55:3; *cf.* 42:6; 49:8). Thus verse 21 actually brings 14–20 to a suitable conclusion. Secondly, the worldwide, Zion-centred vengeance and salvation were attributed to the Spirit of the Lord (19d, NIV *breath*). Verse 21 extends this truth: the Spirit who effected the work of rectification now indwells the world Israel. Thirdly, we have already met an Individual endowed with the Spirit for a ministry of the word, the Lord's Agent to the world and to the people (42:1–4; 49:1–6; *cf.* 50:4), the Servant of the Lord, who brings worldwide (40:3–5; 52:10), Zion-centred (40:9–11; 52:7–9) revelation and salvation. When the Lord undertakes to rectify all that is amiss (59:14–20), it is not so surprising, as it seems at first sight, that a Covenant Mediator comes into the picture at verse 21. Fourthly, like the Servant of the Lord (53:10), this Spirit-endowed One has a family extending through the generations. His covenant status reaches back to 54:10 (*cf.* 53:5), the peace secured by the death of the Servant, and to 55:3, the covenanted blessings accruing through the eternal and universal kingship of David. Along with this he is the repository and mediator of the Lord's Spirit, bringing the gift of the Lord's word. As ever, the distinguishing mark of the separated people is their possession and expression of revealed truth.

Finally, this introduction of the Covenant Mediator in 59:21, with its 'tailpiece' (60:1–22) affirming the worldwide significance of the city of Zion, is the first of four passages in which he figures as the appointed Executor (53:10) of the Lord's purposes. The second passage is 61:1–4, where the Anointed One brings in the day of favour and vengeance. Its tailpiece (61:5–9) pledges restoration and a priestly people central to the nations. In the third passage, 61:10 – 62:7, he receives the 'garments of salvation' which, in 59:17, the Lord himself donned in order to undertake for his helpless people, and to achieve (*cf.* 59:18–20) the glory of Zion at the centre of the world, a truth confirmed in the tailpiece (62:8–12). And the fourth, 63:1–6, describes how this splendidly robed figure returns, having accomplished vengeance and redemption. Formally, these four passages recall the Servant Songs: the same number, with added tailpieces; and, in each series, the first and fourth are reports, the second and third are testimonies. In each series, too, the first passage (42:1–4; 59:21) concerns status and task, the second (49:1–6; 61:1–3) ministry and objective, the third (50:4–9; 61:10 – 62:7) personal commitment, and the fourth (52:13 – 53:12; 63:1–6) completion of the work. In brief, here is a third messianic figure, completing the portrayals of King (chs. 1 – 37) and Servant (38 – 55). The King reigns, the Servant saves, and the Anointed One consummates salvation and vengeance.

ii. The universal city (60:1–22). This poem meditates on the Abrahamic theme (Gn. 12:1–3) that those who bless him will be blessed and those who curse him will be cursed. In the same way, the coming glorious Zion (*cf.* 2:2–4; 4:2–6; 25:6–10a; 26:1–6; 35:1–10) settles the destiny of the world (12). No geographical Zion could contain the gathering world with its flocks; Isaiah is foreseeing, in terms natural to him, both the present Zion of Hebrews 12:22 and the coming Zion of Revelation 21:9–25.

The Lord in Zion (60:1–3). The city is not named immediately, but the feminine imperatives from verse 1 onwards look back to Zion in 59:20 and forward to Zion in 14.

1. The *light* of the *glory of the LORD* is both an objective reality (*rises*, lit. 'flashes') a new dawn, and a subjective experience (*your light*; *cf.* 9:2). It is given as a benefit to be enjoyed ('rise up', 52:2) and a transforming experience (*shine*).

2–3. Moreover, the Lord's glory in Zion is related to a world darkness, present everywhere (*earth*), binding all (*peoples*). Light dawning in Zion is the first banishment of this darkness, and is designed to magnetize the world into blessing (3). *Nations ... kings:* the contrasting pair (ruled and rulers) is an idiom of totality; *cf.* 49:7; 52:15, and the universal call of 55:1. The Lord starts with his people in order that he may encompass the world (Ps. 67:1–2).

The world in Zion (60:4–9). The magnetism – the typical Old Testament emphasis in winning the nations (2:2–4; Dt. 4:5–8) –

works. Zion is glorified in the gathering company (4–5), and this universal people will be accepted as the Lord's worshippers (6–7) and will find their aspirations met in him (8–9). To confine or even to link this vision to the return from Babylon is to fail to listen to what Isaiah is saying. He envisages a whole world on the move, involving even sea travel (9).

4. The reference to *sons* (also 9; *cf.* 49:18) and *daughters* views the world (49:22–23) in its traditional biblical 'compartments': those who ancestrally belong to Zion but need to be brought back to the Lord (49:5–6), and those who are drawn from the 'outside' world (Jn. 11:52), the whole Abrahamic family of faith (Rom. 4:11–12). But *all* (lit. 'all of them') in the first instance refers to the nations and kings of verse 3. In other words, the whole gathered 'Israel' of 45:14–25 is on pilgrimage homewards, with no barrier of distance (*afar*) or of infirmity (*carried*) allowed to hinder.

5–7. Two factors unite to bring radiant joy to Zion: first, this great throng is coming with homage gifts *to you* (5c, which begins with 'For', and 7a), and with devotion to *serve you* (7b); secondly, they come, on their part, to (lit.) 'tell the good news of the Lord's praises' (6e), and, on the Lord's part, as full participants in his worship (*offerings ... my altar ... temple*). *Temple* should be 'house'. The thought is not primarily of a place of worship but of a 'house' where the Lord lives among his people. The gathering company is literally coming home to God. *Midian* (6; *cf.* Jdg. 6:1, which Isaiah may have had in mind; the former despoiler is the coming worshipper) was in the south; *Ephah* was to the east of the Persian gulf; *Kedar* (7) and *Nebaioth* to the northeast, in the northern Arabian desert. The names are impressionistic of a world converging on Zion.

8–9. *Clouds ... nests*: the former is a picture of speed; the latter of homecoming and safety (Ps. 84:3). *Islands*, see 11:11; 24:15; 41:1; 59:18; *look to me*, literally 'wait' (42:4). Consciously or unconsciously, the world's longings can find fulfilment only in *the Holy One of Israel*. They come contributing not insights but *silver and gold*, gifts of submission, homage and devotion *to the honour*, literally 'to the name'. There is no suggestion that their religion is even part of the truth; they come to where the truth is to be found (2:3), to the Lord whose name encapsulates what he has revealed of himself – found only in Zion, in which they discern a divinely given 'beauty'. *Tarshish* (2:16; 23:1) may be in Spain, in which case Isaiah adds west to the compass bearings in verse 7; but in any event *ships* adds sea travel to land travel to complete the picture of the gathering multitudes.

The city of destiny (60:10–14). Here is the heart of this great Zion poem. Verses 10 and 14 share the theme of international enterprise to build Zion; 11 and 13 bring us inside the restored city: its ever-open gates speak of unworried security (11; Zc. 2:4–5); the Lord's sanctuary speaks of his holy presence (13). The central verse 12 makes Zion determinative of destiny: to hold aloof from Zion is to come to destruction.

10. *Foreigners*: literally 'sons of a stranger'; *cf.* 'sons of your oppressors' as an inclusio in 14. *Rebuild ... serve* are not pointers to menial status but evidence of committed service. They are full members of the community (7) and play their part. *Though in anger ... compassion*: according to verse 3 they came magnetized by the light in Zion, and in 9 they came because of the name of the Lord; 3 is pictorial, 9 is general and 10 is specific. This is the light which drew them, the name they needed to know, the God in whom anger has turned to *compassion* (12:1–2), literally 'in my anger I struck you and in my favour / acceptance I have had compassion on you'. The anger was real: *qeṣep̄*, explosive anger (34:2; 54:8), but it has been replaced by 'surging love', *compassion* (54:7).

11. Though the open gates cannot but speak of security, the reason given here is that there is an unbroken stream of entrants. *Led in triumphant procession* is probably the right interpretation. Literally 'and their kings led along' could be a picture of captives (45:14), which would of course symbolize willing subservience; but the abbreviated expression rather means 'with their kings escorted', coming in their own right as kings with their entourage, yet as Zion's willing subjects.

12. *Nation* (*gôy*) ... *it* (lit. 'nations'; *gôyîm*): the word typically means the world outside the people of God. But it is not their alien status which condemns them but their refusal of Zion's supremacy: the Lord's light (3) is there but they will not be drawn, his 'name' (9) is there but they will not come to learn, his compassion (10) is there but they are careless of the threat of his wrath. Their self-chosen fate is to perish in ruination.

13. Isaiah is drawing on the record of Solomon's temple, where Gentile Sidonians were enrolled because they were the best (1 Ki. 5:2–9). *My sanctuary*: not, as now, a place in which the endangered seek safety but 'a place of holiness' – holy for, and because of, its holy Inhabitant (1 Ki. 8:12–19). *Feet*: *i.e.* the Lord's footstool, the point at which the transcendent God touches earth. Here, the Holy of Holies is the place (in La. 2:1 it is Zion; in 1 Ch. 28:2; Ps. 99:1–5; 132:7 it is the ark; and in Is. 66:1, earth itself).

14. In verse 10 the thought was of glad service; here the emphasis is on reversal of roles: *your oppressors*, 'those who humiliated you', now themselves come *bowing before you*. They made you take the lowest place, now they willingly take it themselves in order to enter the privileges and joys of Zion. Only a triumph of grace could achieve this, for it is not Zion that produces this ready submissiveness but the recognition that *the LORD is in his City* in all his reality as *the Holy One of Israel*.

Zion transformed (60:15–22). In verses 15–16 three items of rejection (*forsaken, hated, no-one*) are matched by three items of transformation (*pride, milk, Saviour*) – a transformation of repute and fortune only to be explained as the Lord's doing (16cd). In 17–18, Zion is transformed materially (17a–d), socially (17ef) and spiritually (18). Never-failing spiritual illumination will replace creational radiance (19, 20a–c) and with it all sorrow will vanish (20d). Zion's people will be right with God (21a), eternally secure (21b), made what they are by the Lord in order to 'embody' the Lord's beauty (21c–e) and personally transformed in power (22ab). This vision is not too good to be true but, as guaranteed by the Lord (22cd), too good not to be true.

15–16. *No-one travelling through*: *i.e.* shunned. *Everlasting ... all generations*: the former is continuance in time, the latter continuance in human experience. *Drink ... be nursed*: a picture of enjoyment of the very best of loving care, maternal self-giving. *Nations*, the erstwhile excluded, now brought in, cannot do enough for the Zion in which they have found the Lord's love (10). *Royal breasts*: even earth's greatest are ready to take a ministering place in the city of salvation (18c). *Saviour* points to the consummation of the promised salvation of 56:1. It has all come about because the Lord, as *Redeemer*, has been willing to act as Next-of-Kin and shoulder all the needs of his people.

17. The best of Jerusalem's past (1 Ki. 10:21, 27) is laid under contribution to convey the coming glory where everything is transformed upwards. *Peace*: social transformation matches material well-being. Here is the peace of a mature, harmonious society where well-being and government are synonymous – in the Hebrew here *peace* and *governor* (rather 'government') are in apposition, meaning that each is the exact definition of the other; to say 'peace' / well-being' is to say 'government', and vice versa. *Righteousness* is that which matches the Lord's own righteous character and wishes. *Ruler* is 'taskmaster' (Ex. 3:7). Even the very worst that the past exemplified in oppressive rule will become the very best the Lord would wish.

18. *Violence* is specifically anti-personal behaviour; *ruin* and *destruction* are here every force for the breakdown of good social order. *Salvation ... Praise*: see 26:1–3. The words balance each other: *salvation is what the Lord effects; praise is how we respond.* The Lord's saving work keeps Zion secure and our harmonious, appreciative relationship with him provides gates to exclude every harmful thing.

19–20. In the old order of creation, life was governed rigidly by night and day and unpredictably by the fitfulness of sun and moon. But in the new order of salvation, the ruling principle is the changeless presence of the Lord. *Light ... glory* (lit. 'beauty'): the Lord will illuminate and beautify his people; bathe them in his light and change them into his likeness. The former is explained by the promise of his unchanging illumination (20c, beginning with 'for') and the latter illustrated by the banishment for ever of *days of sorrow* (20d), whatever would cast the least blight.

In verses **21–22**, having reviewed repute (15–16), society (17–18) and circumstances (19–20), Isaiah finally turns to people: their standing before God (21a), security of tenure (21b), how they have come into being (21c–e), their prospects (22ab) and the confidence with which they can face the future (22cd).

21. *Righteous*: right with God, leading to righteousness of character and conduct. *Possess*: Isaiah uses what he knows to predict what he foresees. Did he know that these territorial predictions would (not be contradicted or modified by but) find their realization in a 'kingdom not of this world' (Jn. 18:36)? Probably he did, for he was the one who foresaw that the levitical sacrifices would (not be contradicted or modified by but) realized in the substitutionary death of the Servant (52:13 – 53:12). In any case he is using the terms and conditions of the gift of the promised land (Dt. 6:18–25; 28:63–64; 2 Sa. 7:10). When righteousness is perfected, tenure is secure (Rom. 5:1–2, 21). *Shoot ... planted ... hands*: behind their enjoyment of righteousness and security lies the careful work of the divine Gardener. Isaiah (11:1; 14:19) uses *shoot* of the messianic King and of a rejected king (only elsewhere used in Dn. 11:7). In the heavenly Zion (Heb. 12:22) all the inhabitants will be like their king, who has put them where they are (*planted*), made them what they are (*work*) and done all for his own purpose, *the display of my splendour* (lit. 'beauty'). The likeness of the king is the likeness of the Lord.

22. *Least ... thousand ... smallest ... mighty*: 51:2 recalls another *least* who became a *thousand* and a *nation*. Isaiah is envisaging the ultimate fulfilment of the Abrahamic promise (which John was yet to outline in Rev. 7:9–17). *Do this swiftly*:

i.e. without delay or hindrance within his own pre-determined timetable (2 Pet. 3:18–19). But the verb may mean 'to enjoy' (Ec. 2:25), and so express the delightful truth that the joy which the Lord lost when sin entered the world (Gn. 1:10, 12, 18, 21, 25, 31) he, too, will recover in the new Zion and its people. Since Isaiah would have been fully aware of these two meanings, we do not have to choose between them but gratefully hold both in the richness of scriptural truth.

c. The Anointed One and his transforming work (61:1–9)

i. First testimony of the Anointed One: transformation (61:1–4). The Servant Songs meshed into their context, and the same is true of the coming three passages on Isaiah's third messianic figure, the Anointed One. (See pp. 370–371.) Here, as in 59:21, he is anointed with the Lord's Spirit for the ministry of the word. In addition to this, (a) as in the second Servant Song (49:1–6), his job description is elaborated and extended. The donation of the divine Spirit to Zion's citizens (59:21) is now a ministry of comfort (1–2) and transformation (3), and moves also in another direction altogether in the executing of *vengeance* – the recipients of which are left undefined. (b) Just as the Servant does what the Lord undertook to do (*e.g.* 52:10; 53:1), so the tasks of *favour* and *vengeance* were previously the Lord's (59:17). (c) The transformation of Zion's experiences (2c, 3) was forecast in 60:17ff., and the work of planting (3) links with 60:21. Isaiah is thus taking his messianic portraiture into its next stage: the endowed Zion of 59:21 becomes the transformed Zion of 60:17–22 through the anointed ministry of 61:1–3. This is the passage which Jesus chose to read in Nazareth (Lk. 4:16–22), establishing the messianic credentials of Isaiah's presentation. It is to be noted that Jesus ended his reading at *the day of the* LORD's *favour* (2a). What Isaiah saw as one messianic work, the Lord Jesus divided into two: the salvific purpose of his first coming (Jn. 3:17), and the judgmental component of his second coming (Jn. 5:22–29; *cf.* 2 Thes. 1:7–10). The testimony is in three unequal parts: his preparation (1ab), his task (the seven infinitives of 1c–3g), and the results to follow (3h–4).

1. *The Spirit ... preach*: a link is immediately made with 59:21, but we are now allowed to learn for what purpose the Anointed One shares the Spirit and the word with his children: it is, in fact, the 'word in season to the weary' of 50:4, transforming in its effect. *Sovereign* LORD: this title links with the second Servant Song (50:5, 7, 9). LORD is 'Yahweh', the exodus God (Ex. 3:15) who saves his people and overthrows his and their foes, in fact the God of *favour* and *vengeance* (2ab). In this work he is *Sovereign*, *i.e.* able and irresistible. *To preach good news*: see 40:9; 42:1; 49:2; 50:4. *Poor*: the downtrodden and disadvantaged, helpless in themselves and at the mercy of powerful people and adverse circumstances. *Bind up*: to 'bandage', speaking of a personal ministry of soothing and healing. *Broken-hearted*: a word covering any and every human breakdown, emotional prostration, conviction of sin (57:15). *Freedom*: specifically manumission of slaves (Lv. 25:10; Je. 34:80), linking the ministry of the Anointed One and the Year of Jubilee (*cf.* 27:13), *cf. year*, 2a. *Captives* ... *prisoners*: the former are those held captive by people, the latter those imprisoned in jail; the contrast expresses 'release of every sort'. *Release*: the verb √*pāqaḥ* means 'to open the eyes'. The reduplicated form here (*pᵉqaḥ-qôaḥ*) would mean 'wide-opening (of the eyes)', the bringing of prisoners out of the dark dungeon into the light (42:7).

2. The repetition of *to proclaim* indicates that Isaiah is dealing with the same subject but from an altered point of view. In verse 1 the proclamation touched on the human side – freedom, release – but now it concerns the divine side. *Favour ... vengeance*: in 49:8 the Lord's favour guaranteed the Servant's success; in 60:7 the Lord (lit.) 'accepts with favour' the offering of the Gentiles; and in 60:10 his favour expresses itself in 'compassion'. The coming of the Anointed One marks the *year*, the prolonged period, in which the Servant's achievement can be enjoyed: Gentiles are fully accepted and compassion flows freely. But his coming also makes inevitable *the day of vengeance*. *Day* contrasts with *year*, a sharp, quickly accomplished work. *Vengeance* (*nāqām*): just requital, the apportionment of what is justly due (35:4; 47:3; 59:17; 63:4; *cf.* the verb in 1:24). *To comfort* is the other aspect of requital: exact recompense for wrong suffered (57:18).

3. *Provide ... bestow*: in verse 2c the hurt was soothed, but now every possibility of further hurt is removed by a divine replacement therapy. The first verb points to a decision of God and the second to an act of God: he wills our comfort and then gives that which brings and perpetuates comfort. Note the downward movement of the transformation: from the *crown* (lit. 'head-dress'; 3:20; *cf.* 61:10; Ex. 39:28), to the head (*oil*), to the clothing (*garment*). (*Cf.* the *running down* of Ps. 133:2–3, significant of heavenly outpouring.) Note also the inward movement of *ashes*, the visible evidence of grief (58:5; 2 Sa. 13:19), to *mourning*, grief in the heart, to the inner *spirit of despair*. The Lord thus acts to pierce progressively to the innermost need. *Oil* *of gladness*: in Psalm 45:7 the 'oil of joy' explains the distinctive character of the king. Thus the Anointed One replaces mourning with new life. *Garment*: more properly 'a wrap', over-all cover. Just as (see 59:17) donning garments symbolizes character and commitment, so the gift of an all-covering garment symbolizes the gift of a new nature leading to a new life. *Despair* (*kēhā*): used in 42:3 of the dimly burning wick, what is dull, listless, expiring. *They will be called*: the infinitives that express the aims of the Anointed One give way to a statement of achievement; literally 'It will be called to them', stressing the objective reality of the gift of a new name, *i.e.* a new nature with new potencies (Gn. 17:5–6). *Oaks*: used in 1:29 and 57:5 in connection with false religion, but here they have been recovered for the Lord and given an established place in his garden. *Righteousness*: their status and acceptance before God are entirely of his doing (as in 53:11; 54:17): they are *a planting of the LORD*. *Splendour*: see 60:21e.

4. Matching 'they will be called' (3), we read *they will rebuild*. Given a new status, a new name with new powers, they are able to enter upon new activity. The picture, of course, is of the return from Babylon to face the task of reconstruction; the reality is the new life into which the Anointed One will bring his people (healed, 1de; comforted, 2c; clothed, 3a–g; rooted, 3h–j), bringing with it powers of reconstruction to mend every past breakdown, no matter how long-standing (*ancient*, *generations*).

ii. Transformation confirmed (61:5–9). This is the tailpiece to the Song of the Anointed and, like the tailpiece to the second Servant Song, it falls into two parts: the subservience of the nations (5–6; 49:7) and the Lord's covenant with his people (7–9; 49:8). The picture of life and prosperity confirms verses 3–4, while at the same time building on the internationalism of 60:10, 14. This is a world community (5–6), transformed (7ab), settled (7c–e), joyous (7f), brought into covenant (8), under divine blessing (9).

5–6b, *Recognition by the nations, nearness to the Lord.* The picture is not of slaves or second-class citizens but of the glad commitment of those coming in from the 'outside' to serve the people of God, to take their place within a serving community (*cf.* 60:10). *Shepherd*: (lit.) 'stand and shepherd', used of the Messiah (Mi. 5:4); 'stand' indicates steady continuance. *Priests*: the hitherto unrealized ideal of Exodus 19:6, fully realized in the priesthood of all believers. *Cf.* 66:21, where incoming Gentiles are included in this priestly nearness to the Lord.

6c–7d, *Reversal, recompense and transformation. Wealth ... riches,* see 60:16 (Rom. 15:27); *riches* is 'glory' (Rev. 21:26). *Shame* goes beyond feeling embarrassment; it is reaping shame, disappointment of hope, exposure as fraudulent. *Double*: amply, more than fully. *Rejoice*: 'sing' (54:1), *i.e.* enter with joy into what has been freely provided. *Inheritance*: literally 'portion', what the Lord has allocated to them.[1]

7ef, *Possession and joy.* These two lines are the heart pivot of the poem. *Double* may, as in verse 7b, mean 'abundantly, more than enough', or it may here be the double portion given to the firstborn (*e.g.* Gn. 48:22; Dt. 21:17; 2 Ki. 2:9; *cf.* Ex. 4:22).

8, *Divine justice, recompense and covenant.* The initial *For* explains the blessings listed in verses 6–7, which are due to the Lord's *justice* (8a), his hatred (8b) and his *faithfulness* (8c). First, in bringing this world Israel into being, with all its transformed status and joys, he acts with the *justice* he loves. In 'favour' as well as in 'vengeance' (2), the Lord is impeccably just. His 'favour' is not favouritism; it is the justice required by the just nature of his saving work. Secondly, he abides by his own standards: *robbery and iniquity* is an emendation[2] from 'I hate robbery in burnt offering', an expression parallel to (lit.) 'their due in faithfulness' (8c). The burnt offering 'held nothing back' (Gn. 22:16), and anything less was robbing the Lord of his due. The Lord recalls this as he pledges that he will live up to his own standards: in his *faithfulness* he will hold nothing back when he 'gives his people their due'. Thus the 'double' (7) is the Lord's perfect *justice* (8a), his due and full requital (8c), and turns out to be (8d) his *everlasting covenant with them*, rather 'for them', to their advantage (*cf.* 55:3). The reference is to 59:21, where the Anointed One shares with his children the blessings of his anointing, but the blessings secured to them by this covenant are now also the fruits of the ministry of the Anointed One in verses 3–4.

9, *Recognition by the nations, blessed by the Lord. Descendants* (9a) and *peoples* (9d) are both 'seed', referring to 59:21 where *children ... descendants* are both 'seed'. This worldwide

---

[1] In 61:7de, the translation *inheritance... inherit* clouds the fact that the Heb. uses different words. In 7d, *ḥēleq* means 'apportionment'; in 7e, √*yāraš* is 'to come into possession'.

[2] MT reads *bᵉʻôlâ*, 'in burnt offering'. The emendation is *bᵉʻāwᵉlâ*. Watts accepts this and translates 'robbery by injustice', depriving a person of his goods by unjust social action (*Isaiah*, p. 87). This is a contrived meaning for *ʻāwᵉlâ* which, of itself, has no juridical overtones and is not so used elsewhere. The word simply means 'deviation from norm'.

recognition is the ideal intended (Dt. 4:5–8) but never hitherto realized. But it is the Lord who will be 'glorified in his holy people and ... marvelled at' (2 Thes. 1:10) – which is meant to be the case now, as we live in the interim between verse 2a and 2b.

d. The Saviour and his gathered people (61:10 – 62:12)

i. Second testimony: acceptance of the role of Saviour (61:10 – 62:7). The parallel with the four Servant Songs continues. In the third Song (50:4–9) the Servant testified to his acceptance of the Lord's will and committed himself to obedience and suffering. In the present verses someone accepts with joy (Heb. 12:2) the task of *salvation* (61:10) and commits himself to its completion (62:1). Who is this? The first-person singular continues from 61:1, which in turn looks back to the Anointed One of 59:21. This beautiful poem is in four sections, two alternating pairs. Joy in the work of salvation (61:10) is matched by joy in transformed Zion (62:4–5); note how each section has the same pictures of marriage and the productive earth. The single intercessor (62:1–3) is matched by the interceding company (62:6–7): in the former, kings see the new Zion; in the latter, Zion is the praise of the earth.

10–11. The motif of 'clothing' expresses character and commitment. To be clothed with *garments of salvation* is to be commissioned and fitted to be Saviour; to accept the clothes stands for self-commitment to the task. A decisive point has been reached in the delineation of the Anointed One: his sharing of himself with his family (59:21) and the blessings he brings (61:1–4) are now seen as a saving work. At the outset (59:14–17), the Lord's distress over his helpless people was such that he robed himself as Saviour. Now he confers this task on the Anointed One, who accepts the task with *delight* and rejoicing (10ab). *Salvation* ... *righteousness*: the former is that which meets our need; the latter what meets the Lord's holy standards. *Robe*: a 'wrap' (see 3). *Bridegroom* ... *bride*: as their garments proclaim to all that they are bridegroom and bride and announce their commitment to marriage, so with the same care the Lord has fitted his Anointed One for the saving work. This, then, is the first reason for his joy (*For*, 10c): he has been designated and equipped by the Lord. The second reason (*For*, 11a) is that the work is destined to succeed; it is as certain as the processes of germination and growth. As with *come up* ('sprout') and *seeds*, the *Sovereign LORD* will himself see to it that this will come to universal (*nations*) fruition (*spring*). *Righteousness* ... *praise*: the former is the saving work as it satisfies God (10c), the latter is the response it excites in the recipients.

62:1–3. Matching the face set like a flint (50:7) in pursuance of the Lord's will, the Anointed One determines that the work of salvation and righteousness will be consummated.

1. *For Zion's sake*: the Anointed One's delight in the Lord (61:10) is matched by his longing for Zion's well-being, *i.e.* the well-being of those whom he designs to save. *Silent*: the verb √*ḥāšâ* applies as much to action (*e.g.* Jdg. 18:9; Ps. 107:29) as to words (*e.g.* Pss. 28:1; 39:2). The parallelism of the poem (see opposite) balances this section with the posting of intercessors (6), and this suggests that what is in mind is a ministry of prayer (Heb. 7:25). *Quiet* (√*šāqaṭ*): to be inactive. The Anointed One commits himself to ceaseless action, just as to ceaseless prayer. *Righteousness ... salvation*: *cf.* 61:10cd. The Servant (lit.) 'provided righteousness for the many' (53:11). It is in this sense that *righteousness* belongs to *her*, the righteousness with which she is clothed as a result of the work of the Servant, and now of the Anointed One. *Salvation*: if the Anointed One is clothed to accomplish salvation (61:10), then salvation can only be 'hers' by his gift. *Dawn* (lit. 'brightness') and *blazing torch* both refer in the first instance to the dramatic way in which the work of righteousness and salvation was done but, secondly, to the 'dawning' of righteousness and salvation in the lives of the saved.

2. What the Lord does for Zion is for the world to see and (4ab) acknowledge. *Nations ... kings*: see 49:7; 52:15; 60:3, 10–11, 16. Before the world (2ab), Zion will display her new righteous nature in all its *glory*; personally (2cd), Zion will be aware of a new nature, signified by a *new name* (see Gn. 17:5), bringing with it new potentialities and powers; in relation to the Lord (3), Zion *will be a crown*. A *crown* is a sign of royal dignity. The surprising picture here is that the Lord holds his people as the sign to the watching world that he is king.

4–5. The Anointed One will achieve a transformation like the change from lonely desolation (4ab) to happy marriage (4c–5) – the result of the work of the Servant in 54:1–8. The emptied city and the wasted land become the objects of delight (4ce), devotion (4df) and joy (5). The new names *Hephzibah* ('*My delight is in her*', NIV mg.) and *Beulah* ('*Married*', NIV mg.) are explained in the two halves of verse 5: respectively the wedding and the honeymoon. Zion's *sons* make their marriage vow to their bride to 'love and to cherish', to give themselves in devoted service to the welfare of Zion, and the Lord goes on honeymoon with his people, rejoicing over them. With such economy of words and beauty of imagery Isaiah depicts the loving unanimity that characterizes Zion and her intimate union with the Lord – which Revelation 19:7 foresees as the marriage of the Lamb.

6–7. The Anointed One committed himself to the task of creating a people who would publicly display their saved and righteous status so that Zion might become *the praise of the earth.* The duty of those who have received the Lord's righteousness and salvation is to take their stand on Zion's walls and pray unceasingly that this might come to be. The fulfilment of the Lord's purposes for Zion comes through the prayers of Zion's people. Our prayers, as we both live in Zion (Heb. 12:22) and wait for Zion (Rev. 21:10), are our part in the guardian care of our city (*watchmen*). It is a ceaseless task (*day* ... *night* – lit. 'all the day ... all the night'), vocal (*never silent*) and vital (*give yourselves no rest* ... *give him no rest*) – as if, without our prayers, the Lord would be slack concerning his promise ('pray as if on that alone hung the issue of the day') – and also unremitting: *till he establishes Jerusalem. The praise of the earth*: that for which the earth renders praise. Why the earth should give praise for Zion this passage does not explain, but the fact is that the Lord's salvation of his people is not just for display purposes (61:11cd; 62:2ab). In saving his people, the Lord has also saved a worldwide people (*cf.* 55:1).

ii. The Lord's oath, summons and proclamation (62:8–12). This tailpiece has significant links with the foregoing testimony of the Anointed One (61:10 – 62:7). First, there is a picture of security of possession and assured enjoyment (8–9). Loss of crops was a familiar pre-exilic experience, and the denial of its recurrence would have spoken tellingly of secure tenure and enjoyment. Secondly, both Zion and the nations figured in the testimony, each looking forward to something yet to be experienced, something for which Zion prays and into which the nations will enter with praise (6–7). Now both *the people* (10a) and 'the peoples' (NIV *nations,* 10e) are summoned to take to the road as pilgrims. Thirdly, the promise was made that the desolate and forsaken would be married and cherished (4), and this is now the subject of a divine proclamation: salvation is coming (11) and the perfect Zion is in sight (12). In short, verses 8–12 confirm all that was promised or implied in 61:10 – 62:7.

8–9. *Hand* ... *arm*: the *hand* is personal intervention and the *arm* is personal power – the Lord's commitment of all that he is to the task. *Grain* ... *enemies*: a picture not just of safety but of obedience (*cf.* Lv. 26:16; Dt. 28:30–33; Jdg. 6:1–6). *The courts of* *my sanctuary*: or, 'in the courts of my holiness'. The secure plenty that the people enjoy is accompanied by an unclouded intimacy with the Holy God.

10–11. Isaiah likes double imperatives in moments of high drama (51:9; 52:1, 11; 57:14), and the pilgrimage to Zion is something that captured his imagination (24:16; 25:1–9; 27:12–13; 35:1–10). Thus the invitation is issued, the roads resurfaced (*prepare*), the way unmistakable (*highway*), hindrances gone (*stones*) and a worldwide people summoned (*banner for the nations*, lit. 'peoples'; *cf.* 11:10, 12; 49:22). In verse 11 there are three 'beholds'. The first (11ab, omitted in NIV) calls attention to the fact that the invitation goes out with the Lord's own authority. The second (11cd) alerts *Zion* to her coming 'salvation' (not *Saviour*): this does not retreat from the universal proclamation of 11ab, for Zion's salvation (54:1) is the world's salvation (55:1). It is what the Lord himself undertook (59:16) and then committed to his Anointed One (61:1f), clothing him with the *garments of salvation* (61:10) for the task. It was pledged as coming (56:1) and now is imminent. New Testament theology thinks here of the ever-imminent return of Jesus (Phil. 3:20–21; Heb. 9:28). The third 'behold' (11ef) calls attention to the completed task of the One who comes: his *reward* and *recompense* are defined in the next verse as 'they … the Holy People'. For what he has done he has received 'pay' (*reward*), the people whom he has gathered to himself from the whole world. They are also what he has accomplished (*recompense*, 'fruit of work'). In 40:10 this coming Shepherd-Warrior is the Lord himself. In the flow of the present context it is the Anointed One.

12. This gathering universal company (*they*) are *holy* (*cf.* 4:3). This is no longer an ideal prefaced by the 'if' of Exodus 19: 5–6, for *they will be called* speaks as if from the point of view of an observer: holiness is what such a one would see. They are the finally perfected people, living in the full reality of a finished salvation (Heb. 10:12–14). *Redeemed*: those to whom the Lord made himself Next-of-Kin, taking all their needs as his own (35:9–10). *Sought After*: the verb 'to seek' is often used of people assiduously coming to the Lord (56:6; 65:10), but here it is the Lord himself seeking, finding and gathering his worldwide people (Ezk. 34:11; Jn. 1:43; 9:35; 11:52). *Deserted:* as in 54:6. Every former woe is a thing of the past.

e. The consummation: the Anointed One completes his task (63:1–6)

In 62:11 we were called to watch for a coming 'salvation', which

62:12 personalized into the coming of One who had completed the saving work. Now we are invited right into that situation, and given a privileged position alongside watchmen on Zion's walls as a mysterious figure approaches majestically and proclaims the execution of *vengeance, redemption* and *salvation.* The message of the Lord's garments (59:16), given to his Anointed (61:10), is now proclaimed as completed, exactly as in the vengeance and salvation greeted with the resounding hallelujahs of Revelation 19:1–8.

1. *Cf.* 52:8: watching for the king (52:7), for the Lord making bare his arm (52:10), they actually saw 'my Servant' (52:13) ... 'the arm of the Lord' (53:1). Now, afar off, they see an unrecognized figure (*Who ...?*), noticing only that he comes from *Edom ... Bozrah* (see on 34:1ff.). *Edom* is the ceaseless foe (Am. 1:11), typical of David's victories (2 Sa. 8:13–14), the final, eschatological enemy (34:5; Ezk. 35). Just as the Servant is David (55:3), so the Anointed One comes now like David as the Victor over Edom. But *Edom* means 'red', matching the reddened garments (2), and *Bozrah,* its capital city, means 'vintage', matching the winepress motif (2). The chosen foe and the just requital match each other. But, as yet, the watchmen can see only generalities: first, his *garments* – not *stained crimson* (the word *hāmûṣ* means 'sharpened', indicating the 'sharp' colours they see in the distance), but his 'vivid garments'; secondly, his *splendour* – no bedraggled figure this, but 'majestic'; thirdly, his gait – *striding forward,* the purposeful and energetic walk of One who is confident; and, fourthly, his *strength.* There is no weakness, nor even – notwithstanding that he comes, as we will learn, from battle – tiredness. *Greatness* is more exactly 'abundance'. He is brimming with vigour.

Who is he? First, he is a speaker (*speaking*). The Anointed One was first introduced as endowed with the word (59:21); he exercised a ministry of the word in vengeance and salvation (61:1–2); when he donned his *garments* (61:10) he vowed not to keep silent (62:1; Rev. 19:13, 21). Now he speaks again, and does so as one whose *righteousness* is intact and whose self-awareness is that he is *mighty to save* – One whose saving work is effective and matches every standard of righteousness. *Mighty* (*cf. greatness*) is 'abundant'. Merely 'great' strength could rise to an occasion and then, perhaps, be spent; 'abundant' strength cannot be exhausted, and as abundant as his strength so is his salvation, inexhaustible in its efficacy.

2–3. *Why ...?* The Marcher is now close enough for the watchers to observe that the 'sharp' colour is not a colour at all but a stain, as in treading grapes. The Anointed One takes up their simile (2). There has indeed been a winepress – but of wrath; and a vintage to tread – but of people; with a consequent redness – but of blood! *No-one*: as in 59:16 (*cf.* 50:2); solitariness is stressed. *From the nations* ('peoples'): as we would say 'no-one in the whole wide world'; but also 'peoples' looks back to 62:10e. The recipients of the benefit (62:11–12) had no part in reaching their blessedness. The whole work of judgment (3), like the whole work of salvation (5), is exclusively, uniquely, individually his. The vigour of his action (*trampled ... trod*) is matched by the rage that motivated it: *anger* ('*ap̄*) is the snort of an anger personally felt; *wrath* (*hēmâ*) is the heat and intensity of anger. *Blood* (*nēṣaḥ*), only here and in verse 6, is 'spurting blood'; *stained* (√*gā'al*) equally means 'pollute'. As to the fact, his clothing was stained; as to effect, it was polluted: his task involved exposing himself to 'defilement', yet he returned with his *righteousness* intact (1).

4. Now comes the explanation (*For*). A task undertaken alone (3ab), the venting of anger rigorously applied (3cd), garments soaked in blood, defilement risked (3ef) – what is the explanation? It was like the exodus acts of God. *Vengeance* must be distanced from any thought of sinful vengefulness. It is due, exact requital – like the visitations on Egypt in return for persistent refusal of the word of God. It is *redemption*, the loving act of the Kinsman, who cannot bear that his next-of-kin should suffer any more or any longer but longs that they should be rescued.

5–6. The fact of sole action is again asserted. It is stated in verse 3, and hinted at by the reference to *heart* in 4: verse 3 is the fact of solitariness; 4, his willingness to act alone; and 5, his sense of the tragedy of things as they are – *i.e.* that *wrath* should remain uninflicted and *salvation* unaccomplished. On *arm ... salvation*, see 59:16. What the Lord undertook, the Anointed One performed. *Drunk*: *cf.* the picture of the cup of wrath (51:17, 21–22). *Blood on the ground*: *i.e.* lifeblood irretrievably shed and therefore a work of wrath decisively finished.

XII. THE NEW HEAVEN AND NEW EARTH: PRAYERS AND PROMISES (63:7 – 66:24)

The theme of these chapters is the praying people (63:7 – 64:12) and the promising God (65:1 – 66:24). The sombre passage 63:1–6 described the requital of every foe and the redemption of all the saved. What can possibly remain? Only prayer for its fulfilment, resting on the sure promises of God.

a. A 'remembrancer' at prayer (63:7 – 64:12)

In 62:6, the Anointed One, zealous for the realization of the worldwide glory of Zion, posted watchmen-intercessors to pray till all was fulfilled. They are described there as 'you who call on the LORD', literally 'you who keep the Lord in remembrance'. The same word now occurs in the singular (63:7): 'I will keep (someone) in remembrance' (*I will tell*, NIV). Here is the watchman-intercessor at his task. Typically of Bible prayers, the 'remembrancer' begins by 'telling God about God' (63:7–14) before turning to intercession (63:15 – 64:12). (*Cf.* Ne. 9:6ff.; Dn. 9:4; Acts 4:24–30.)

i. Remembering (63:7–14). God's people desire to ask according to his will. Their primary concern is to know the God to whom they speak. The 'remembrancer', then, reminds himself of the Lord's unfailing love and goodness (7), his caring commitment to his people (8–9), and, above all, how his ongoing patience with them has been secured by his foundational acts of redemption (10–14).

7. In the Hebrew this verse begins and ends with *kindnesses*. The word *ḥesed* is the Lord's pledged love for his people; here plural, to intensify and amplify, a love that never changes and that contains to the full every ingredient of true love. About this love he recalls three things. First, it has been displayed in action: *deeds ... done*; the verb √*gāmal* means 'to do completely' and underlines the rich sufficiency of the Lord's love in action. Secondly, it is bountiful and beneficent: *many good things*, literally 'abundant goodness' (*cf.* 'abundant' in 63:1). Thirdly, it is a heart-love: *compassion* (49:15; 54:7; 55:7; 63:15), emotional, passionate, personal (1 Ki. 3:26).

8–9. In love the Lord identifies with his people (8a), hopes the best of them (8b), commits himself to them in saving action (8c), feels their sorrows (9a), lives savingly among them (9b), undertakes the position of Next-of-Kin (9c) and bears the burden of them (9d) perseveringly (9e). The references to *sons* (see Ex. 4:22), *became their Saviour* (Ex. 14:30), shared *distress* (Ex. 3:7) and *my people* (Ex. 3:10) indicate that already Isaiah is recalling the exodus as the great proof of the relationship of love. Love cannot be seen to be love until it does some benefit for the loved one. The Lord loved not in heart or word only but in deed and effectiveness: he *became their Saviour ... saved them.*[1] *Angel of*

---

[1] *He too was distressed*, lit. 'adversity to him', is another occasion where a choice has to be made between *lōʿ*, 'not', and *lô*, 'to him' (here, in a possessive

his presence: literally 'of his face'. We recognize people by face; 'face' is the Lord's very own presence (Ps. 139:7), among them in the person of his angel – that unique 'Angel of the Lord' (*e.g.* Gn. 16:7ff.; 21:17; 22:11, 15; Ex. 3:2; 14:19; 23:20–23; Mal. 3:1) who speaks as the Lord and is yet distinct from him, in whom the holy God 'accommodates' himself to live among sinners, an Old Testament anticipation of Jesus. *Love*: the noun *'ahᵃḇâ* occurs here for the only time in Isaiah (*cf.* the verb √*'āhēḇ*, 43:4; 48:14; 61:8). It is the love which delights in the companionship of the loved one. *Mercy* (*ḥemlâ*) is well illustrated by its only other occurrence in Genesis 19:16 – the gentle pity that spares. *Redeemed*: see 35:9; used also in Genesis 48:16 of a Next-of-Kin's identification with all the cares of life.

Verses **10–14** meditate on the exodus experience of Israel: the hurt they inflicted by rebellion (10ab), provoking divine antagonism (10cd; *cf.* Ps. 78); the changeless divine mind (11a, lit. 'and he remembered'), expressed in fundamental acts of salvation (11–12) and providential care (13–14); the intertwining of the welfare of the people and the good name of the Lord (14).

10. *They*: emphatic, 'they of all people!' *Rebelled*: √*mārâ* (1:20; 3:8; 50:5), provocative rebellion. *His Holy Spirit*: 'the Spirit of his holiness', possessing, matching and expressing his holy nature (30:1; 31:3; 48:16; 59:19; Ps. 51:11; *cf.* Ne. 9:20, 30; Hg. 2:5). This passage is full of the person of the Spirit as a distinct divine Being: *Holy* (10b, 11f), personal (*grieved*; *cf.* Eph. 4:30), and the agent in the Lord's care of his people (14). Along with (lit.) 'the angel of his face' (9b), and his 'glorious arm' (12; 51:9; 52:10; 53:1), these references to the Holy Spirit reveal the richness of the Old Testament's understanding of the divine nature. God is 'one' (Dt. 6:4) but not a bare unit. Rather, he is 'one' as the tabernacle was 'one' (Ex. 36:18), a rich unity of many elements. The New Testament does not (so to speak) multiply the one God of the Old Testament by three but refocuses this rich diversification within the divine nature to reveal Father, Son and Holy Spirit (Mk. 1:9–11; 2 Cor. 13:14; 1 Pet. 1:2). God revealed in the Old Testament is the Holy Trinity incognito. *They rebelled ... he turned*: those who refuse his way become his enemies (1:24) – and he theirs.

11. *His people recalled*: see *may he recall* (NIV mg.), but translate 'And he remembered'. Note the sequence: 'they rebelled

sense, 'adversity was his'). Either is acceptable. The former would yield the translation 'In all their adversities no adversary he', a negative statement of the Lord's identification with his suffering people.

... he turned ... he remembered'. In the thick of their rebellion and his holy revulsion, the Lord's mind returned to basics. *Moses* would 'remind' the Lord of his purpose to save (Ex. 3:7–8); *his people* would remind him of his saving achievement (Ex. 6:6–7). *Where ...?* introduces a divine soliloquy, as if the Lord were meditating, 'Why am I different now from what I was then?' *The sea*: the Red Sea deliverance was the consummation of the saving work (Ex. 14: 13, 30–31). *Shepherd*: literally plural, either plural of majesty, referring to Moses as the 'supreme shepherd', or numerical plural, referring to Moses and Aaron (Ps. 77:19–20); but, in either case, recalling that saving deliverance was followed by providential care (13–14). *Set his Holy Spirit*: see Haggai 2:5. The reference is to the indwelling of the Lord himself in the tabernacle (Ex. 29:44–46).

12. *Glorious arm of power*: (lit.) 'his beautiful arm'. In contrast to 53:1, Moses was not the Arm of the Lord but knew the companionship of that Arm. *Divided ... waters*: at the start of the journey, the Red Sea (Ex. 14); at the end, Jordan (Jos. 4). What the Lord did in the exodus was a completed work: he brought them out in order to bring them in (Dt. 4:37–38) and the question is implied, 'Can I now give them up?' To this the motive *to gain for himself everlasting renown* (lit. 'an everlasting name') provides the answer (*cf.* Ex. 32:12; Nu. 14:13–16; Jos. 7:9; Ezk. 20:9, 14, 22). The repute of the Lord is bound up with his commitment to his people.

13–14. In those days no barrier was allowed to hinder his people. Rather, to the Lord, even uncrossable water (*depths*) was as straightforward as *a horse in open country*, and, under the superintendence of the Lord's *Spirit*, they were *given rest*, brought home into the promised land. Behind all this review lies one fundamental assumption: the Lord does not change; what he was then he still is. It is to this thought that the remembrancer finally comes (14cd). First, *guided* sums up the whole course from slavery in Egypt, through redemption, shepherding care, removal of barriers, into Canaan. Such love! Such forbearance! Such power! Was it all for nothing? Secondly, *your people* recalls that the exodus redemption set up a permanent relationship which (8, 11) has not changed. True, they have never lived up to their dignity, but are they not still loved with a never-changing love (7)? Thirdly, it was all designed to reveal the Lord's 'name of beauty', a task he will never desert.

ii. Asking (63:15 – 64:12). Now that he has considered the nature of his God, the remembrancer can turn to prayer. He has discerned that the Lord is always on the side of his people: his love never ends (7); he feels their plight even when he is grieved by their sin (8–10); though they merit wrath a door opens for mercy (10–11); and always he will act for the sake of his name (12, 14). To such a God prayer can be made confidently for such a people. The prayer is in seven sections.

Where is God's love? (63:15–16). The remembrancer's first memory (7) becomes a question: if the Lord's love never changes, where is it now? – especially (15ab) since the Lord remains the Sovereign One! As God in *heaven* he dominates the earth (40:22–24); neither his authority (*lofty throne*) nor his character (*holy ... glorious*) has altered, so why has he apparently changed in his concern (*zeal*), in his warrior *might* competent to deal with every foe, and in his tender *compassion*? *Tenderness* points to being moved by felt inward emotions. *Compassion*: see verse 7f. *Abraham ... Israel*: in 48:1–2 the charge was laid that the people could no longer validly claim to be Israel; here that charge is acknowledged as right: *cf.* Deuteronomy 33:9, where the same verbs (*know ... acknowledge*) are used in the sense of detachment from family relationships and refusal of family obligations. Yet, even if the ancestors disown their descendants, surely the Lord is still *Father ... Father ... Redeemer*. In Egypt he claimed Israel as his son (Ex. 4:22), pledged himself to redeem (Ex. 6:6–7), and declared that his *name*, thus revealed, was eternally true (Ex. 3:15).

Why does the Lord remain alienated? (63:17–19). 17. *Make us wander* is not an attempt to lay the blame on the Lord, rather a recognition that the guilt of his people is such that the Lord had no option but to drive them from him and into the far country of sin which they had chosen. Likewise *harden our hearts* does not blame the Lord for our sin. The heart choosing disobedience hardens progressively against God's way until the moment (known only to God and fixed by him) comes when the point of no return is reached, when the final, decisive choice of sin is made. When this point is passed the situation is humanly irretrievable: only God can change it[1] – if only he will *return*.

---

[1] Pharaoh's heart is the classic place to study the question of heart-hardening. Three verbs are used: √*ḥāzaq*, in the qal form, 'to become hard' (Ex. 7:13, 22; 8:19; 9:35) and in its piel form, 'to make hard' (4:21; 9:12; 10:20, 27; 11:10; 14:4, 8, 17); √*kāḇēḏ*, qal, 'to be heavy, unresponsive' (8:15, 32; 9:34; 10:1); and √*qāšâ*, hiphil, 'to make stubborn' (7:3). The human act of deliberate disobedience results in the hardening of heart, the disposing of the character and will towards that line of action, with a diminishing power to act otherwise until, in the sovereign decree of God, power of reformation is lost altogether. The three

18–19. It is usual to claim that these verses must be post-exilic, describing the return to a devastated *sanctuary* (2 Ki. 25:8), but post-exilic experience is against this view: the return was itself proof that the Lord was active in love on behalf of his people. They could not, then, say 'Where are your zeal ... might ... compassion?' when their home-coming was evidence of it. They could not cry out 'Return' since, very plainly, he had already come back to them as their Restorer. We could envisage these verses as a prayer of the exiles (somewhat like Ps. 137), looking back in misery and forward in half-hope; but, were they such, it would be impossible to explain their appearance here. Isaiah, however, could pray this prayer. Either he could imaginatively project himself forward into the situation he had predicted (6:12–13; 39:8–9) and voice this prayer for a return of divine mercy and transforming grace; or the verbs may be 'perfects of certainty': 'For a while your people have possessed ... our adversaries are sure to tread down ... we are to become ...' Either way, he adopts the role of one longing for a change in God, bringing new acts of rectification. Verse 19 is not straightforward to translate but, more literally rendered, says, 'For a long time we have been those you did not rule over, on whom your name had not been called.' The Hebrew virtually makes clauses into titles: 'We have become "You did not rule them", "Your name was not given them".' This is the essence of the 'land of wandering', entered when the Lord judicially imposes the consequences of sin: it is as though they are now beyond the pale of his kingdom and guardian care and have lost the intimacy of the shared name.

Why didn't God do something? (64:1–3). The rules of Hebrew require that verse 1 refer to the past: 'Oh that you had rent ... !' Isaiah has been reviewing a tragic past (17–19). It didn't have to be like that; the Lord's mere presence would have altered everything! The rent *heavens*, trembling *mountains* and *fire* are the traditional motifs used to express the coming of the Holy One (Pss. 18:7ff.; 46:1ff.). And just as creation is helpless before him (1b), so are *nations* (2). The problem is perennial: are not we too baffled at the way he runs the world – when he could so easily do things so differently?

Maybe it is too late to hope (64:4–5). The sad question with which this stanza ends faces the harshest reality. It is the central

---

statements that Pharaoh hardened his heart, God hardened Pharaoh's heart, and Pharaoh's heart became hard, view this procedure from different but interlocking points of view.

stanza of the poem and raises the central issue. God indeed could deal with any problem with consummate ease (1–3), but why should such a God intervene for such as we? In the Hebrew *ancient times* (4) and *continued* (5) are the same word; God has continued for ever – but so has sin! The issue of this dilemma is no foregone conclusion. There are two conditions of blessing (4d, 5ab) but they have never been met. Neither the course of history (*ancient times*) nor shared information (*ear ... heard*) nor perception (*eye ... seen*) has brought another God into the picture. But the only God has his principles and procedures. First, he *acts on behalf of those who wait*. *Wait* (√ḥāḵâ) is synonymous with (√qāwâ) (3, *cf.* 40:31); both, at their purest, refer to patient, confident, expectant faith, a faith truly 'simple' in its unwavering trust in the divine promises. Secondly, there is the moral requirement of doing *right* (5ab). On the one side, the perfect tense, *come*, expresses a set characteristic; on the other side, the participles in *gladly* (lit. 'rejoice and') *do right* express an unchanging state covering both heart and life, emotional and practical obedience. The verbs *sin* and *angry* are perfect tenses – it was your fixed mind to be angry and ours to continue in sin. What a collision course! So is salvation possible?

Sin and helplessness (64:6–7). In verses 1b and 2d, *before you* conceals a reference to the Lord's 'face'. All he need do is show his face and the nations would be helpless. But the reality is rather that *we shrivel* (6c) and *waste away* (7d) because of his hidden *face* (7c). This is both the inner and personal and the spiritual and eternal consequence of sin. We perish because he is alienated. As to sin which has these dire consequences, it is uncleanness (6a). *Unclean* is the leper's cry (Lv. 13:45), and the word speaks of unfitness for the fellowship of God and exclusion from the Lord's people. Sin is the defilement which a fallen nature imparts to all we do. *Filthy rags* is (lit.) 'a garment of menstruation'; bodily discharges were considered a defilement, because they were the 'outflow' of a sinful, fallen human nature. So, even what we might consider to be in our favour, *righteous acts*, partake of the defilement of fallenness. Sin brings decay and death *like a leaf*. There is an inherent destructiveness in sin whereby it *sweeps us away*. Sin is lack of interest in the Lord: it is of no importance to bring him into our lives and needs by calling on *his name*. *Strives* is 'rouses himself', 'wakes from sleep'. Life without a living relationship with God is the life of sleep! And because of all this, the Lord is alienated (*hidden your face*) and antagonized (*made us waste*).

The unchanged God (64:8–9). In his holy hostility to sin and sinners, the Lord is unchanged, but he is also unchanged in grace and mercy – and therein lies the ground for continuing pleading. The relationship of *Father* (8) to his children is permanent: through all the vicissitudes of family life the relationship itself cannot be erased. The potter cannot disown the pot – it is there only because he made it – nor can the artisan (*your hand*) disown the artefact (*work*). Again, this is not to shift blame on to God for our failure, but to assert a permanent relationship – the love of the father, the sovereign decision of the potter, the skill of the craftsman. The children may always ask to come home; the pot may seek refashioning in the hand of the potter. In verse 6, *all of us ... we all* uses the same Hebrew word twice as confession; here, in *we ... all*, it comes twice as plea. *Beyond measure*: (lit.) 'unto muchness', meaning 'in all its inherent energy', *i.e.* 'do not let your anger have full play'. The end of the old – a changed moral reaction (*angry*) and an erased memory (*remember*) – is matched by the onset of the new divine attitude (*look upon us*) and a revivified divine memory (*we are all your people*).

Can love still be withheld? (64:10–12). The reference to desolate *cities*, a burnt-out house and precious things *in ruins* suggests the situation to which the exiles returned from Babylon, as indeed they did; but the prayer in verse 12 is not one they could have used. Their very return was proof that the Lord had not restrained himself or remained silent. How could they pray about punishment beyond measure when their return proved that punishment was already over? Furthermore, the problem in the immediate post-exile was not divine but human inaction – the carelessness that left the house unbuilt (Hg. 1:2–3). The alternatives of interpretation here are the same as in 63:18–19: either an exilic plea, or an Isaianic meditation. As we noted in chapter 39, the Babylonian prediction was undated but was a live option within Isaiah's lifetime. Inevitably he would face – and others would make him face – the rigour of what he has predicted. A poem such as this is just the guidance needed for coming uncharted days. The verbs are best taken, then, as perfects of certainty: 'your sacred cities are to become ...,' *etc*.

12. *After* suggests sequence in time (*i.e.* after these things have happened), but the Hebrew means 'in response to such eventualities'. The verb *hold back* appeared in 63:15 in the first stanza of the poem. There the intercessors knew themselves to be the cause of the 'withholding', but in the course of the poem sin has been exposed and the Lord has been sought in penitence. The wonder of repentance is that it works – so will not the Lord now leap into action and create a new situation that will transcend the ruins of the past? It is to this topic that Isaiah turns in the remaining two chapters.

b. The Lord responding: sure promises, coming consummation (65:1 – 66:24)

These chapters provide a fitting conclusion both to The Book of the Conqueror (chs. 56 – 66) and indeed the book of Isaiah as a whole. The prayer of the remembrancer (63:7 – 64:12) ended with the Lord's people waiting and longing for the remedial work of God. The ruins in which they find themselves living are the fruits of their own failure – all that was exposed in chapters 56 – 58 and acknowledged in 59:1–13. Only the coming of the Conqueror (59:14 – 63:6) can redeem the people, relieve them of their foes, and restore their fortunes. How great that restoration will be is now revealed.

i. Pleading and provocation (65:1–10). The contrast which becomes more and more emphatic as these two final chapters proceed is established here. There are those who 'seek' the Lord (1; lit. 'I have let myself be sought', not *revealed myself*) and who meet with blessing (8–9); there are those who refuse his appeal (2) and meet with requital (6–7).

The Lord's world initiative (65:1). The Lord asserts that he has taken the initiative towards people who neither asked for him nor sought him. Who are they? Majority opinion understands them to be Israelites who have failed to respond. The actual terms of the verse are, however, against this. There was no time when Israel could be described as *a nation that did not call on my name*, for there were always those who did call; even if we understand the words to imply 'but not sincerely', the accusation is still too sweeping; and even if it were not, there is nothing in the Hebrew to warrant importing the required thought of insincerity. Furthermore, *did not call* alters MT (from *qōrā'* to *qārā'*). MT says 'a nation not called by my name', plainly excluding Israel who were so called (43:7). On the other hand, the apparent meaning – the Lord's call of grace to the Gentiles (Rom. 10:20) – forms here an inclusio with the reference to the nations who 'have not heard of my fame' and who gather to the Lord in 66:18–21. Towards these the Lord has taken an initiative: (lit.) 'let myself be sought ... let myself be found' (tolerative niphals). (*Cf.* Jn. 15:16.) He has reached out through his word (*I said*), acted in self-revelation (*Here am I*, lit. 'Behold me!') and brought them within the embrace of the revelation granted to

Israel (*name*, Ex. 3:15). Looking back to the eunuch and alien in 56:1–4, 8, and the ingathering Gentiles of 60:3, Isaiah sees here the fruit of the extension of the gospel of God to all the world.

Provocation and penalty (65:2–7). Verse 1 leads into 2ff. through the truth enunciated in Ezekiel 3:6: namely that the guilt of Israel is deepened because those who did not enjoy their privileges none the less embraced so promptly the revelation of God once it came to them (*cf.* Mt. 21:31–32). Commentators recognize that the religious corruptions mentioned (3–5) belong to the pre-exile (1:28–30; Je. 2:20, 27; 3:2, 6, 13; Ezk. 8:1–18; 16:1ff.; Mi. 5:12–14) and were not found in post-exilic Israel, yet, inexplicably, many still ascribe these verses to a post-exilic prophet.[1] They are, however, comfortable in the mouth of Isaiah, who here uses pre-exilic evidences as stereotypes in order to expose the continuance of religious apostasy into the future. (*Cf.* 65:11–12; 66:1–4, 15–17.)

2–3. Israel's apostasy is seen, first, in the refusal of a wonderfully condescending appeal. *Held* ('spread') *out my hands* is elsewhere used of prayer (1:15; 1 Ki. 8:22). So desirous is the Lord to win his people that he deigns to become a supplicant! But he is met by stubborn rebellion (*obstinate*, √*sārar*: *cf.* 1:23). Secondly, this rejection arises from self-confident adoption of an individualistic lifestyle based on personal *imaginations* ('thoughts, plans') and issuing in conduct *not good*. Divine revelation, the basic 'reality' of the people of God (Am. 2:4), has been ousted from its fundamental position and replaced by the relativism of individual preference. Isaiah traces this out (3ff.) as contradicting, one by one, the commandments of the Decalogue. In the first commandment, they were commanded to have 'no other gods before me' ('*al pānay*, Ex. 20:3), but they offered provocation *to my very face* ('*al pānay*). *Sacrifices in gardens*: the 'garden' (*cf.* 1:28ff.) symbolizes fertility, and the worship of the so-called 'fertility gods' involved the replacement of Yahweh by Baal or the addition of Baal functions to Yahweh. The second commandment dealt with outward forms of worship. *Brick* was an unauthorized material (Ex. 20:25; Dt. 27:5–6; Jos. 8:31) – what humans made or shaped became infected with their unclean sinfulness. But disobedience often begins thus, at a point where obedience would be easy (*e.g.* to build an altar of uncut stone) but is considered unimportant.

[1] The so-called 'Third Isaiah' was supposedly responsible for the material in chs. 56 – 66.

4–5. Beyond the outward trappings of religion ('gardens' and 'altars'), Isaiah now probes the deeper matter of spiritual loyalty. The third commandment specified the pledging of allegiance to the Lord's name only – the Lord as he revealed himself – but the Lord's people are found *among the graves*. For the purpose of necromancy, they *spend ... their nights keeping secret vigil*, literally 'in guarded places', *i.e.* secure from interruption, the living finding spiritual guidance among the dead! (*Cf.* 8:19–20; Dt. 18:9ff.) The fourth commandment dealt with the distinction between the ordinary and the holy, but they developed their own notions of holiness (4c–5b). What the Lord forbade (Lv. 11:7, Dt. 14:8) they practised (4cd), and cultivated a holiness of élitism, a first-class citizenship, an exclusivistic approach to spirituality. No wonder such are a constant irritant, *smoke in my nostrils* (5cd)! They cultivate other gods (3a–c), flout even his simplest worship requirements (3d), resort to other sources of revelation (4ab), neglect the obedience factor in the separated life (4cd) and adopt a spirituality of pride (5ab). The *all day* of the Lord's appeal (2) is paralleled by the *all day* of their provocation (5).

6–7. The Lord's reaction is decided upon (*written*), personal (*I will*), measured (*pay back in full*), individual (*laps*) and a final settlement of *sins*, both personal and ancestral. In Scripture, sin becomes more aggravated with each succeeding generation – not that coming generations are pre-doomed by the sins of the past (Ezk. 18), but that failure to break with the past involves bearing the entail of the past (Lk. 11:47–51). This is the price of being human. *Because* introduces a concluding summary. Worship *on the mountains* is exclusively pre-exilic – the exposed mountain-top being chosen as more likely to 'catch Baal's eye' and prompt a response. Canaanite religion was human initiative pressuring the god, as compared with the biblical religion of obedience responding to divine grace.

Blessings for the remnant (65:8–10). Not all participate in verses 2–7. The community was divided. The theory of a 'Third Isaiah' makes this party division a special mark of the post-exile, but in fact there is nothing here that goes beyond, for example, 1:26ff.; 8:11–20; 10:20–23 (*cf.* 4:3; 6:11–13; Je. 4:27; 5:10, 18; 30:11; Ezk. 11:13–20). We can find here a different doctrine of the remnant, or a different application of the doctrine of the remnant, only if we first invent post-exilic circumstances. In the dark days of Isaiah's ministry the remnant would have prized these words of comfort. Three reassuring pictures are sketched: the vintage (8) depicts delighted preservation, the land (9) depicts possession, and *Sharon and Achor* (10) depict renewal.

8. *Juice* (*tîrōš*) is wine made from the first drippings of the juice before the press was trodden.[1] *Found* suggests that the grapes were oozing as they were picked and that this was specially prized. Hence *there is some good* (lit.) 'there is a blessing'. Marvellously, then, the Lord finds his people a blessing, and he prizes and guards them. All merit the winepress of 63:3, but some are chosen and saved.

9–10. *Possess ... inherit*: the same word twice, repeated to denote certainty. The picture is of Joshua's people entering in to possess (Jos. 1:1–5). *Chosen ... servants*: the two sides of the same reality: the sovereign fact of divine choice, and the responsive reality and commitment within a new status (54:17; 57:18–19). Isaiah uses *Sharon* to typify deterioration (33:9) and renewal (35:2). *Achor* (Jos. 7:24–26) symbolizes a bright beginning marred by disobedience. But the time is coming when Sharon will be what it was meant to be and Achor transformed from curse to blessing. *Seek*: those gathered from the world (1) and those preserved from the people (10) share one characteristic – their diligence to enjoy the divine presence.

ii. Contrasting destinies (65:11–16). 11–12. The reference to *mountain* (11b) looks back to the mountain religion of verse 7. The Lord's mountain was where he built his house, made his home and indwelt his people; it was the place 'sought' by those who loved him (Dt. 12:5). Others rejected Zion and favoured the mountains of Baal. But to *forget* the *mountain* was to *forsake the* LORD. When he appoints means by which he is to be approached (Heb. 10:19), everything else leads away from him. *Spread a table ... fill bowls* exposes the silliness of false religion: gods who need to be wined and dined and are yet considered arbiters of *Fortune* and *Destiny*! *Fortune* (*gad*) was a Canaanite god (*cf.* the place-names in Jos. 11:17; 15:37), worshipped in the pre-exile. *Destiny* (*mᵉnî*), 'apportionment' (of fate),[2] is a noun derived from the verb √*mānâ*, which appears in *I will destine*. The destiny they chose was the destiny they received; the dead gods brought the sentence of death. There were two reasons for this outcome: refusal of the Lord's word (12cd), and contradiction of the Lord's way (12ef). Their response contradicted the will (*I called*), the

---

[1] See F. S. Fitzsimmonds, 'Wine', in *NBD*, p.1242.

[2] C. Westermann is typical of the post-exilic fixation of commentators on chs. 56 – 66: 'A charge of open idolatry is surprising in the post-exilic period. It might hint that both the oracle ... in verses 9f and ... in verses 11–12a were simply taken over from tradition' (*Isaiah 40 – 66* [SCM, 1966], p. 405). But why should they be 'taken over' if they were totally inapplicable and unsuited?

word (*I spoke*), the mind (*in my sight*) and the heart (*displeases*, lit. 'I did not delight') of God.

Verses **13–16** draw a conclusion (*Therefore*, 13), and the stark contrasts of the alternative destinies are worked out in verses 13–15. *My servants* looks back to 'my servants', the remnant in 8–10, and *you* (masculine plural) continues from the address to 'you' in 11–12. Verse 16 states the outcome objectively.

13–15. *Eat ... drink* (13a-d) match 25:6–9; 55:1–2. The contrasts of hunger and thirst picture the meeting of every physical need, and the use Isaiah makes of this motif transfers it to the realm of spiritual need and supply. The externality of eating and drinking is balanced by the internal contrast of *sing ... joy* and *cry out ... anguish* (14). To *sing* is to enter joyfully into a proffered benefit, and those who do so find inner fulfilment. But, by contrast, those who refused the Lord, his word and his way (12c-f) find that they have condemned themselves to *shame* (disappointment, non-fulfilment), *anguish* (pain and grief at the very *heart* of experience), and *brokenness of spirit* (the breakdown of every vital energy and purposeful activity). Even to recall those who rejected the Lord will be as bleak as dwelling on the Lord's *curse* (15), which has reached its inevitable outcome in *death*. *Put you*: the you-plural which has prevailed since verse 11 suddenly changes to you-singular. Divine judgment falls individually. But, by contrast to the name which matches the curse, there is *another name*, not revealed, indicating the gift of a new nature and the inheritance of the promises of God – as with Abram (Gn. 17:2–8).

16. The new name makes a new person with new potentialities and prospects. *Invokes a blessing* is reflexive, and this should be made explicit by adding 'on himself'. The same verb expresses the universal Abrahamic promise (Gn. 22:8; 26:4). The idea is of entering into the blessing appropriate to one's needs. *Land*: in the light of the links with Abraham, 'earth' would be better, the realization at last of a world at one with God. In parallel to (lit.) 'invokes on himself the blessing he needs', there is *takes an oath*, *i.e.* 'swears loyalty', 'makes his commitment'. The *God of truth* is both the source of blessing and the great object of devotion. *God of truth* is (lit.) 'the God of (the) Amen' (explained by 2 Cor. 1:20), the God who says 'amen' to all his promises, affirming their reality and his trustworthiness to keep them: the God who promised of old in Abraham that a worldwide people would find the blessing they needed and who will keep his word. *Forgotten ... hidden from my eyes*: what no longer has a place in the divine mind (*forgotten*) or presence (*eyes*) no longer has any ground of being. The old has passed away – behold (see 17–25 below), all things have become new (2 Cor. 5:17; Rev. 21:5).

iii. All things new (65:17–25)
The new creation (65:17–18b). The purpose of this short poem is to explain the promises in verses 13–16, so the initial 'For' of verse 17 should be restored. *Create*: see 4:5. *Heavens ... earth*: totality expressed by contrast (Gn. 1:1). Everything the Lord created at the beginning will be made new at the end. *Former* picks up 'past' (lit. 'former', 16e) but the conception is now grander: not only its sorrows but everything in the old order, dimmed and diminished as it was by the infection of human sin, will undergo this great renewal. *Remembered ... mind*: not now the divine mind (16ef) but the mind of the redeemed, renewed participants. Their awareness will be of total newness, in which nothing prompts recollection of what once was. The new creation will be observed and enjoyed by new, fresh minds. All (*I will create*) is the work of God, a work of such greatness and newness that no other agent could account for it. It will be eternal (*for ever*) and without anything to disturb its *joy*. Note how this delightful little poem begins (17a) and ends·(18b) with *I will create*, balances the new creation (17b) and those who inhabit it (18a), and centres on total newness (17cd).

The new city (65:18c–20). This second compact poem describes the joy of the Creator (18c–19b), the experience of the citizens (19c–20e) and the unchanged moral factor (20fg).

18c–19b. The new creation (17) is now *Jerusalem*, the new city. The city (Gn. 11:1–9) was humankind's earliest effort to organize the world for its own security and stability. With Isaiah we watched the same human urge move from the imperialist Babylon that he knew (chs. 13 – 14), to the Babylon principle at work in ongoing history (21:1–10) and, at its end, to the fall of the world city where meaning had ceased to exist (24:1–10). By contrast he showed us another city – of joy and provision (25:6–9), strength and salvation (26:1–3). It is in this way that the new creation becomes the new Jerusalem: the Lord's perfect organization of his new creation as a perfect setting for his new people. *Its people* are *my people*. There is no longer a spiritual schizophrenia in the community, nor is there anything to cause sorrow or blight life: *weeping* is felt pain; *crying* (lit. 'scream') is inflicted pain. The emotion and its cause are both gone.

20. Throughout this passage Isaiah uses aspects of what we know to create impressions of what is to come – *e.g.* a life totally provided for (13), happy (19cd), secure (22–23), at peace (24–

25). What we have no capacity to understand can be grasped only through what we know. In this present order, death cuts life off. Not so in the new Jerusalem: no *infant* will fail to come to maturity, nor the elderly be foiled of fulfilment. It is not meant to suggest that death will still be present. This would contradict *for ever* (18), *no more* (19) and the death of death in 25:7–8. It simply affirms that, over the whole of life, the power of death will be gone. The only exception is that (lit.) 'the sinner, a hundred years old, will be accursed' (20fg). There will, of course, be no sinners in the new Jerusalem (6–7, 12, 15c). We are again dealing with metaphor: even if, *per impossibile*, a sinner were to escape detection for a century, the curse would still search him out and destroy him. In reality, just as death will have no more power, so sin too will have no more place.

The new society (65:21–25). The society to come will know security of tenure (21–22), fulfilment in blessing (23), peace with God (24) and total harmony (25).

21–22. To build and not inhabit was the fate of the disobedient (Dt. 28:30). The opposite experience, therefore, speaks of a life that is right with God in home (*houses*) and work (*vineyards*). *As the days of a tree* pictures longevity and durability, *i.e.* a secure hold on location. *Long enjoy* is (lit.) 'wear out', *i.e.* 'use to the absolute maximum, enjoy to the limit'.

23. Within the security of verses 21–22 there will be cloudless enjoyment of that for which they laboured. *Doomed to misfortune*: literally 'for terror'. There is no darker parental cloud than to see a dear child touched with tragedy. Such will never be the case in the new society, 'for they will be a seed blessed by the Lord' (*cf.* 53:10; Gn. 17:7). *Their descendants with them*: parents will not see their children troubled, but they will see them at one with themselves in the things of God.

24–25. The common thought in these verses is oneness: first, oneness with the Lord, as he anticipates their needs (24a) and, because they are in such harmony with his will, the words they use commend themselves to him for immediate action (24b). Secondly, harmony prevails throughout creation (25), as Eden is restored (11:6–9), old enmities are gone (*wolf*), fears removed (*lamb*) and natures changed (*lion ... eat straw*). In 11:6–9 there is no reference to the great enemy of creation, *the serpent* (Gn. 3:14), but it is accurately in place here. There is a point in the new creation where nothing changes: the curse upon sin still stands. The Lord is still the Holy God. *Neither harm nor destroy*: the positives of 25ab are strengthened by the negatives of 25de, ruling out both damage (*harm*) and destruction (*destroy*). The whole is *my holy mountain* (*cf.* 11), the place where the Lord in holiness dwells among his people, and they with him.

iv. Judgment and hope (66:1–24). The broad theme of Isaiah's final chapter follows on from the vision of the new heaven and new earth. How will the wrath to come be avoided and a confidence attained of enjoyment of the glory to come?

Chapter 66 is best understood by looking first at the shape of the whole. It begins (1–4) and ends (18–24) with the theme of the house of the Lord. In the opening section, Isaiah moves quickly from the house itself (1–2) to contrasting worshippers – those who 'tremble at my word' (2), and those who, though they engage in the ritual (3), do not answer when the Lord calls (4). In the closing passage, Isaiah starts with a worldwide pilgrimage bringing a pure offering to the Lord's house (18–21), and 'all mankind' keeping Sabbath (22–23). But, by contrast, there are those upon whom the final judgment of God has fallen (24). The two internal sections of the chapter deal respectively with these two groups of people: a message of assurance and hope for 'those who tremble' at the Lord's word (5–14), and the Lord's fiery judgment on the false worshippers (15–17). The Lord's 'house' is, of course, the 'place' where he comes to live at the centre of his people's life. This is his 'tabernacle', his tent-dwelling at the heart of his people's 'encampment'. As Isaiah teaches, there is but one proper response to the presence of this 'house' and its holy Occupant: do we tremble at his word, or do we refuse him when he calls?

The house and its people (66:1–4). 1–2ab. Solomon provides us with the perspective we need for these verses. In his dedicatory prayer (1 Ki. 8:12–29) he asked the key question: 'Will God really dwell on earth?' (27) The whole context of that question demands the answer 'Yes': he affirms the house as a divine dwelling (12), the divine mandate to build the house (14–21), and the Lord's faithfulness to the Davidic promises regarding the house (22–26). Thus the answer is never in doubt: great as the Lord is, he will come and live in this house among his people. But Isaiah adds his own perspective with the question *Where ...?* – indeed, more literally, 'Wherever ...?' Yes, indeed, the house will be his *resting place* (the word *mᵉnûḥâ*, used *e.g.* in Ru. 1:9, means 'a home') where he makes his home among his people – but he is so great (*the earth is my footstool*), so transcendent (1a), earth itself is so tiny (1b) and, besides, he is himself the maker of all (1ef), that human artefacts contribute nothing to him. In a word, the house simply as a building is nothing!

2c–e. *This is the one I esteem* is a good interpretative rendering, but a more literal translation is 'But to this one I will look'. The Lord has to ask directions to find the house (1cd; *Where ...?*, *'ê-zeh*), but he has no problem spotting people (2c; 'to this one', *'el-zeh*). The Lord will graciously, condescendingly, make the miniscule house his home. The *humble* are, socially, those who are at the bottom of life's heap, dominated by stronger forces and interests; religiously, they are those who willingly take the lowest place before God. *Contrite* (*n^{e}kēh*): 'lamed' (2 Sa. 9:3), or disabled, here used with spiritual significance: one who is aware of the damage wrought by sin, of personal inability to stand upright before God. *Trembles* speaks of a sensitive, concerned longing to please. (The verb √*hārēd* and its adjective are used in 2 Ki. 4:13 of the caring and painstaking trouble to which the Shunnamite woman went to get everything ready for Elisha, but Ezr. 9:4 and 10:3 match this use in Isaiah.) This, then, is what looms large before the Lord's gaze: our lowliness before him in worship, our self-awareness and our painstaking sensitivity to his *word*.

3. Four pairs of permissible acts of worship are matched with impermissible ones. Throughout, the words *like* and *is like one who presents* (3f) are interpretative additions. Leaving them out, we find that Isaiah simply sets lawful and unlawful actions side by side without comment: one slaughters a bull, but one kills a man (*i.e.* sinful action); one sacrifices a lamb, but one strangles a dog (*i.e.* meaningless); one brings a gift of grain, but another brings pig's blood (*i.e.* unacceptable); one makes an incense memorial, someone else blesses an idol (*i.e.* apostate). According to Ezekiel 8, pre-exilic worship went hand in hand with just such deviations. Isaiah's purpose is to present the element of choice: the Lord has made his will known in his word. He is not repudiating the place and use of sacrifices (as the words *like, etc.*, suggest); he is contrasting the revealed way in the matter of worship with human ways, and his accusation is (3ij) is that some have *chosen* and ordered their worship accordingly (*ways*); this is no outward formality but involves their hearts (*delight*). But to the Lord it was *abominations* (*šiqqûṣ*) – everything he detested!

4. The divine response is exact: they 'have chosen' (3i); now he *will choose*. Harsh treatment: in 3:4 *ta'ªlûlîm* meant unpredictable capriciousness; here, probably, sudden or summary treatment, rather than *harsh*. Dread suggests that they flew to their religious practices as a protective technique (*cf.* 65:11). Far from protecting, however, false religion provokes what it would prevent. But the heart of the matter was refusal of the Lord's declared will (*I called*), plain word (*I spoke*) and practical directive (*did evil*).

The word of God and eternal security (66:5–6). Those who tremble at the Lord's word are now scorned (5–6), but they will rejoice and flourish (14) because the Lord has made promises to Zion of children (7–9) and peace (12–13), and in Zion mourning will be turned to joy and rich provision (10–11). *Tremble*: cf. verse 2; here it is the key to divine blessing, the hallmark of the true believer. *Brothers*: in the formal sense of belonging to the same religious community. Here is the same hostility as in 5:18–19 (cf. 29:9–10); the same two parties with the same contrast between seeking the cults and seeking the Lord as in 8:11–20; the same outcome of wrath (8:21–22) and glory (9:2ff.). *Because of my name*: exclusion was based both on rejection of what the 'word tremblers' understood by the *name*, and on infatuation with what the others wished the name to mean. They really thought that the name of the Lord was more truly understood and more perfectly honoured in their self-chosen theologies than by loyalty to the Lord's word. In particular, the 'word tremblers' profess a coming *joy*, but their hope is thrown back in their faces (cf. 2 Pet 3:3). Yet time will justify their eschatology, as *city* and *temple* resound with the uproar of divine requital (6).

Impossible for people, possible for God (66:7–9). Eschatology is one of the major points at which those who accept the Bible's testimony are still subject to scorn. It was evidently the same in Isaiah's day, and consequently he moves from affirming eschatological certainty (6) to affirm that what seems impossible to the human mind is yet God's simplicity. Can there be birth without labour, children without pain (7), a country and nation born instantaneously (8a-d)? But it will be so (8ef, 9)! Everything comes down to what the Lord is (9). First, he is faithful to the end: he does not advance his purposes (*bring to the moment of birth*) only to abandon them; secondly, he is sovereign: what he initiates he completes – (lit.) 'Do I beget and (then) close (the womb)?', start what I do not intend to finish? *Give delivery* and *bring to delivery* are the same word (hiphil participle, √*yālaḏ*) but the meaning *bring to delivery* (*i.e.* preside over the period of gestation up to the birth) is unexemplified. It means either 'beget' (the moment of conception) or 'cause to bring forth' (the moment of birth). The latter suits verse 9b and the former 9cd. *Says ... says*: the former is imperfect tense, 'keeps saying', a usage peculiar to Isaiah among the prophets (1:11, 18; 33:10; 40:1, 25; 41:21); the latter is perfect tense, something said and settled. Suitably to the illustrations, the Lord persists in what he has declared (imperfect tense), and what he has declared is backed by a sovereign commitment (perfect tense) to do it.

Joy and provision (66:10–11). Present attitudes to *Jerusalem* are ambivalent: joy in the city of God – the place of his house and presence, worship, fellowship, atonement – all the great spiritual verities centred in Zion, even now, for its members (Heb. 12:22–23); and yet mourning – over a divided community, opposition to true, biblical religion, the scorn of the world for the people of God, the denial of eschatological hope. But a different time is coming, in which all that Zion means will be offered and enjoyed to the full. There is a double picture of the maternal breasts of Jerusalem: the first stresses the satisfaction of the infant (11ab); the second, the more than sufficient *abundance* of the mother, (lit.) 'the nipple of her glory'.

The world city of peace (66:12–13). The Lord's promises rest on the sole guarantee of his word, *for this is what the LORD says. Peace ... like a river* was what they lost through refusal of the Lord's word (48:18), but all that was lost by sin will be recovered, and the long story of peace (48:22; 52:7; 53:5; 54:10, 13; 55:12; 57:2, 19, 21; 59:8; 60:17) will reach its conclusion: the river will flow again. *Nations ... stream*: in 2:2 the nations came 'streaming' to Zion, and this is no illusory vision. *Wealth* is 'glory', and as 'the glory of the Lord' means 'the Lord in all his glory', so in the Zion that is yet to be (Rev. 21:24–26) every nation will be present 'in all its glory', *i.e.* the glory of what it was meant to be and will be when its individuality is brought to mature perfection in the city of God. *Flooding* (√*šāṭap*) was Isaiah's typical metaphor of the Assyrian threat (8:8; 10:22; 28:2, 15, 17–18; 30:28). The measure of international threat to Zion will become the measure of international enrichment of the city. In 49:23; 60:4, the nations fostered Zion's children – a picture of their willing acceptance of servant membership. But coming into Zion, it is they who, as true, full children (Ps. 87), themselves experience Zion's maternal care – nursed and carried (12c), cuddled (12d) and comforted (13a). The real source, however, of all the comfort is the Lord (13c), found only (lit.) 'in Jerusalem', the 'Solid joys and lasting treasure/None but Zion's children know'.[1]

Settlement (66:14). *When you see* matches and cancels out the scornful 'may we see!' (lit.) of verse 5ef. To 'see' is to experience personally and directly. In the eternal Zion this is an

---

[1] From J. Newton, 'Glorious things of thee are spoken'.

experience which cannot be taken away – because (14cd) the same *hand* (personal, intervening action) which will bring perfect bliss is matched by the anger with which the Lord has dealt with his *foes*. Verse 14 thus cancels out 5. While the Lord's servants live in a spiritually divided community, joy is ever under threat, and therefore never enjoyed for long or to the full. But divine action will at one and the same time secure eternal joy and remove every threat. It is the day of vengeance and salvation of 63:1–6.

The holy and jealous God (66:15–17). The sharp tension evident in verses 5–6 between the 'word tremblers' and the compromisers sketched a situation demanding settlement one way or the other. The Lord responded by declaring his hand. He is always on the side of those who love his word, and for them there lie ahead the joy, comfort, abundance and worldwide fellowship of verses 7–14ab. That the Lord should be angry with the compromisers (14cd) is implied, but what form will his anger take? The answer is clear when the initial 'For' (removed by NIV) of verse 15 is restored. Verses 15–16 present a stylized presentation of divine visitation in anger, and 17 (*cf.* 65:3–5) makes a direct application to the compromisers.

15–16. The main components of this terrifying theophany are *fire* (15ad, 16a), *whirlwind* (15b) and *sword* (16a). The leading motif, *fire*, represents, as always the active holiness of God, roused against sin. The *whirlwind* is his sweeping, irresistible wind of judgment that leaves nothing behind – linked here with *chariots* to depict pursuit as of mobile warfare, leaving no escape. The *sword* is the application of judgment individually. In Scripture, the whole sweep of human history lies between this fire and this sword of holiness (Gn. 3:24; Is. 27:1). Thus the Lord *will execute judgment*, 'exert his judicial right'. *Judgment* is the enforcement of total righteousness – the righteousness which the Lord donned as a robe in 59:17 and then bequeathed to his Anointed (61:10), who himself returned from the winepress of wrath 'speaking in righteousness'. Every act of God is pure righteousness, and it will be so when he turns at the end to deal with *all men* (lit. 'all flesh').

17. But, in particular, the apostates of the present context are singled out, the compromisers among the professing people of God, the worshippers who follow their own pleasure and do not respond to his call, listen to his word or walk in his way (66:4). When people cease to heed revealed truth, it is not that they then believe nothing, but that they will believe anything – *gardens, pigs, rats,* whatever! On *gardens*: *cf.* 1:28–31; 65:2–5

Consecrate concerns the state of the person; *purify* is their fitness to stand before God. *Following the one in the midst* has its nearest parallel in Ezekiel 8:7–11 – the worshipping elders with 'Jaazaniah standing in the midst'. We do not know enough about ancient worship forms to pursue the matter further. It sounds like a worshipping group with a central leader, but there must be more to it than that, maybe some cultic significance which made it abhorrent to the Lord. But the total picture and its meaning are clear. The Lord is a jealous God, and worship must conform to his revealed will if it is to render to him the worth and honour that are his due. In default of this there is a roused and holy jealousy working in judgment.

The new house at the centre of the new creation (66:18–24). This final passage makes a necessary link with 66:1, the foundational thought of the whole chapter. The mark of worship is whether or not people were trembling at God's word (2c–4). Indeed, we might trace a progression from the new creation (65:17) to the new city (65:19) to the new society (65:20ff.) and, finally, to the new house (66:1). It is no surprise, therefore, that Isaiah brings his eschatological vision to its climax in a worshipping people: envisaged (18–19), enjoying equal acceptance in Jerusalem (20–22), and in constant communion with the Lord (23–24).

18. The opening sentence here is an unresolved conundrum. It seems like disconnected words: 'And I their deeds and their thoughts it has come.' Have some connecting words been lost? Is the whole context in a disorganized state, leaving these words isolated like driftwood? Or is this idiomatic or colloquial Hebrew that is beyond our reach? NIV makes what sense it can by inserting *because of* and adjusting the verb *come* to make it refer to the coming of the Lord. In so far as it helps, this has the support of LXX. Yet it creates an insuperable problem: for any coming of the Lord because of our actions cannot but be a coming in judgment, and the *glory* would then be that of the Judge. But this cannot be so: the *glory* (18) leads to a gathered people acceptable to the Lord. Since, therefore, we are obliged to make what we can of the text, a harmonizing suggestion (and only a suggestion) is to make *I* and *imaginations* (lit. 'thoughts') look back to what precedes, and *glory* to look on to what follows: 'As for me regarding their words and their thoughts, it has come. Now, to gather all nations ... they will come and see my glory.' The work of vengeance is done; here is the parallel work of salvation (59:17; 61:2; 63:4).

19. The Lord will gather the nations, not by a banner lifted

afar (1:12–13; 49:22; 62:10) but by *a sign among them*, around
which they rally. Isaiah does not say what the *sign* is, but since in
its biblical context this passage lies in the interim between the
two comings of Jesus, the *sign* can only be the cross. *I will send*
is the Old Testament's expression of the New Testament missionary mandate. Broadly, 2:2–4 summarizes the Old Testament
ideal: a community of the word of God, magnetic to the
surrounding world; Matthew 28:19–20 summarizes the New
Testament ideal: an outreaching church. Each is equally important in the total biblical view, but here the Lord sends (as once
he sent Isaiah) *those who survive*, 'the escapees'. In context,
these are the people whom the judgment of God (16) does not
touch, those for whom the work of God is not vengeance but
salvation, who have heard the cry of 'Peace, peace' and exercised
the gift of penitence (57:19). *Some* of these are now his
missionaries worldwide, as the impressionistically chosen place
names are intended to suggest. *Tarshish*: see 2:26; 23:1; 60:9.
Libyans ... Lydians: (lit.) Pul and Lud, mentioned along with
Cush in Jeremiah 46:9 and Ezekiel 30:5. The link with Cush is
thought by some to suggest a southern location, but most agree
with NIV. *Tubal* was in the far north (Ezk. 39:1) and *Greece* is
Javan. *Famous as archers*: why should this be mentioned?
Possibly just to balance the vagueness of the place-names with a
reminder that the missionaries go to real people who may
represent a real threat – organized, independent people, ready to
resist. *Islands* stand for 'earth's remotest bounds' (11:11; 40:15;
60:9). There is no suggestion that such might have a religion
'good enough for them', or have enough truth to be going on
with, or that Yahweh might perhaps be present incognito in their
theology and ritual. The fact is that they know nothing and have
seen nothing of him, and this constitutes the reason for the
missionary mandate. Neither revelation (*heard of my fame*) nor
experience (*seen my glory*) has been theirs. They need the
knowledge of the only true God.

20. *Cf.* John 11:52. It would be a nonsense to make *brothers*
refer to regathering Israelites. What an anticlimax to promise that
such would become priests (21)! No, it is erstwhile Gentiles –
now become *brothers* (19:24–25; 45:14–25), fulfilling the
promise of 56:8. *Offering* (*minḥâ*): 'gift' is the broadest word of
all the offering vocabulary. The missionaries return with a gift to
the Lord – those whom their testimony has won from the nations.
Horses ... camels: the transportation list is impressionistic. No
distance or difficulty can stand in their way of reaching
Jerusalem, because every mode of travel is put under contribution

to get them there, and all will come safely to *my holy mountain*, as acceptable to the Lord as the *grain offerings* he himself authorized Israel to offer. And not only to the *mountain*: right to the 'house' (*temple*) itself, the divine abode, the Lord's 'home' (66:1).

21. In 61:6, as a result of the work of the Anointed One, Israel became a priestly people, fulfilling Exodus 19:6. The privilege is extended. Just as in Isaiah's day only some Israelites were priests and Levites, but through them Israel was constituted as the Lord's priestly people, so now he foresees Gentiles incorporated on equal terms, into equal privileges (Eph. 3:6).

22–23. The new creation, new city and new house constitute the eternal climax of the Lord's purposes. This is what *I make*, a participle expressing the impending future: 'I am in process of making / am going to make'. This coming reality has all the eternal validity of the Lord himself (*endure before me*). It is his stated commitment (*declares*: 'is the word of', 1:24). The Lord's people are here, (lit.) 'your seed and your name', referring to the Covenant Mediator of 59:21, the people of the Anointed Conqueror, brought into their inheritance by his work of vengeance and salvation. They have the same permanence, eternal security and assurance as the new creation itself, and they are specifically the *New Moon* and *Sabbath* people. Isaiah ends with the two feasts whose corruption distressed him at the beginning of his book (1:13). They are feasts, not fasts: mourning is in the past, joy is the eternal present. The people enter into the reality of a worldwide community, acceptable in equality before the Lord (56:1–8); they are now at last able to match the Lord's requirements (58:1–14) in practical holiness. Each month as it comes and each week as it comes is met by joyful dedication of life's programme to the Lord. Contextually, the locus of all this is Jerusalem, but the thought of 'all flesh' (*all mankind*) in one place shows that the prophet is thinking in terms of the world mountain of 11:9 and the world city of chapters 25 – 26, the Zion to which believers have already come (Heb. 12:22–23) and into which they will yet enter through the gates (Rev. 22:14).

24. Remarkably there is a cemetery by the city, and when 'all flesh' comes to worship they make a point to *go out and look* at the fate from which they have been rescued. They enjoy the day of salvation, but they do not allow themselves to forget the day of vengeance. These are *dead* because the judgment of God is for real: they are those 'slain by the LORD' (16). The accusation levelled and made out against them is that they *rebelled*: they knew the word of the Lord but deliberately and wilfully went their own way (4). Consequently, the *worm* in the bud – the heart of rebellion, the corrupt, fallen nature – was the winner, and it is their endless lot to live the life of corruption (*their worm will not die*) under the endless antagonism of divine holiness, *i.e.* the unquenched *fire*. On the lips of Jesus, these words are used to express the burning 'life' of Gehenna (Mk. 9:43–48), and ultimately they become the reality of the second death, a final change of place and state with continuity of person (Rev. 20:15). The purpose of visiting the cemetery is not to gloat (it is too awful for that), nor even to pity (though who could restrain pity?), but rather to register again something *loathsome* (*dērā'ôn*, *cf.* Dn. 12:2), to be repelled and revolted; that is to say, to see again the wages of sin and the fruit of rebellion, and thereby to be newly motivated to obedience and love of the word of God. There is also another thought which we noted in verse 14: it is part of the saints' sense of the reality of their security to be assured that the Lord has dealt, finally and fully, with everything that could ever threaten or blight their eternal joy.